STANDARD LESSON COMMENTARY

1988-89

International Sunday School Lessons

published by

STANDARD PUBLISHING

Eugene H. Wigginton, *Publisher*

Richard C. McKinley, *Director of Curriculum Development*

James I. Fehl, *Editor*   Hela M. Campbell, *Office Editor*

Thirty-sixth Annual Volume

In This Volume

Cover photo by Photofile

Index of Printed Texts, 1988-89

The printed texts for 1988-89 are arranged here in the order in which they appear in the Bible. Opposite each reference is the number of the page on which it appears in this volume.

Cumulative Index

A cumulative index for the Scripture passages used in the *Standard Lesson Commentaries* for the years September, 1986—August, 1989, is set forth below.

V

Encourage One Another

by Charlotte Adelsperger

A YOUNG WAITRESS chatted with our family as she served us. She commented that she could tell we were having fun on vacation together. Her caring showed through. She was efficient and gracious. When my husband left the tip, I left a little note with it. "Carol, thanks for your excellent service today. We were impressed with your cheerfulness and your kind interest in our family. God bless you."

After Carol found the note, she hurried to catch up with us. "Oh, thank you for your note," she said. "It really meant a lot—'cause today's my very first day as a waitress!"

One of the most exciting and enjoyable ministries, for many Christians, is to encourage others. Encouragement springs from God's love alive within them. It focuses on another's assets or gifts and helps to build that person's sense of worth. When offered to Christians, it cheers them in fulfilling God's purposes.

The Bible says, "We have different gifts, according to the grace given us. . . . If it is encouraging, let him encourage" (Romans 12:6, 8). And how the world *needs* encouragers, abiding in Christ, today!

As you reach out to others, be natural; be yourself. The Holy Spirit will guide you in sincere appreciation of others—never using flattery. The same Spirit may direct you to witness about the good news of Christ.

We, like Christ's followers of centuries ago, are told, "Therefore encourage one another and build each other up, just as in fact you are doing" (1 Thessalonians 5:11).

Be An Encourager Wherever You Are

A famous movie star was asked to describe a "charming woman." That could take a whole seminar, but he gave an insight in two sentences. "When a beautiful woman enters the room, you notice her," he said. "When a charming woman enters the room, *she* notices *you*."

One Christian friend of mine is a truly charming woman. She has a sparkle to her personality, but most of all, she is a good listener—with a gentle spirit. She identifies with others and often offers an encouraging word. She is using her spiritual gifts.

In this fast-paced world, do we really take time to notice others and take interest in them? Those are first steps toward showing appreciation. Then, like managers in business are told to do, catch people doing something well. And tell them!

Remember the story of the short man Zaccheus (Luke 19:1-10), who was perched in a tree above the crowd, waiting to see Jesus? When Jesus reached the spot, even though distracted by all the people, He looked up and *noticed* Zaccheus. He called to him by name and spent time in his home. Jesus' actions brought exciting results. Zaccheus made some difficult choices in repentance and turned his life around. Salvation through Christ came to him that day!

In Christlike ways we should seek to notice others, call them by name, and share with them. What blessings can come because of this, in a world in which so many people are treated as non-persons! The apostle Paul gave a first step: "Accept one another, then, just as Christ accepted you, in order to bring praise to God" (Romans 15:7).

Show your acceptance of another person by your eye contact, facial expression, and tone of voice. Psychologists tell us that our nonverbal messages, including mannerisms, often communicate more strongly than what we say. As Christians, we want to get across the confidence, caring, and hope that is within us.

What makes a Christian an effective encourager? He loves himself as an accepted child of God and operates with a healthy level of self-esteem. He is then free to take the risk of reaching out to others. He shares out of the bounty God has given. He desires to love the Lord with all his heart, mind, soul, and strength, and to love his neighbor as himself.

Next, he looks for ways to encourage God's children! He recalls what has helped him in various situations, and uses it. He is a loving communicator, who cares about people.

One way to start becoming a steady encourager is to ask God's help. You might pray, "Lord, show me whom to encourage today. Lead me in timely ways to reach others in Your love and joy." Such a prayer will open up many possibilities in your neighborhood, when traveling, or anywhere you go.

Be an Encourager to Christians

Matthew 8 tells about a centurion who came to Jesus for help. His servant was at home paralyzed and suffering. Jesus responded right away—"I will go and heal him." But the man protested. He did not deserve to have Jesus in his house, he said, and then he affirmed his belief in what Jesus could do: "Just say the word, and my servant will be healed."

The Lord answered, "I tell you the truth, I have not found anyone in Israel with such great faith." What an encouragement!

Here Jesus modeled how to recognize a quality in someone. He did not focus on the person's worthiness, but on his gift—his active faith. Jesus compassionately healed the servant that very hour.

Unfortunately, we find churches in which only trickles of encouragement are being passed around. Some members seem to be waiting for the minister to give it all. What a drought! Incredible changes can occur when Christians look for and appreciate the fruit of the Spirit active in one another. We know the list: "But the fruit of the Spirit is love, joy, peace, patience, kindness, goodness, faithfulness, gentleness and self-control" (Galatians 5:22).

When we see any Christlike qualities growing in a believer, we can edify the person as Jesus did. We can point to a specific strength or talent. For example, "It's beautiful to see the gentleness you have in working with those in the nursing home. Your patience shows through, too. It's an inspiration to me to see how God is using you."

As we come to know our minister, leaders, and others in the church, we will witness many abilities given by the Holy Spirit. It is our calling to encourage them to use their spiritual gifts and developed talents to serve the Lord.

Most significant are the fruit of the Spirit. We should yearn to nurture such fruit in Christians' lives. When love, peace, joy, faithfulness, etc., are alive in the body of believers, they have tremendous potential to glorify God and draw people to Christ.

Ways to Encourage Christians

The apostle Paul told the early church: "And let us consider how we may spur one another on toward love and good deeds. Let us not give up meeting together, as some are in the habit of doing, but let us encourage one another" (Hebrews 10:24, 25).

Here are some ways you can spur on Christians in the church.

• Write your ministers and other staff members surprise notes at least once a year. Do it when their ministries have blessed you in specific ways.

• Meet with others in a small group like a Sunday school, Bible study, or prayer group. Get to know individuals and recognize their qualities. In a sincere way, tell them what you appreciate about them. If you are a leader, reinforce effective discipleship in members. Encourage them to share what they are learning.

Build relationships of caring and nurturing. It's important to accept others just as they are. I love what author Joyce Landorf has stressed in some of her talks. She said that it's time for Christians to stop evaluating each other, and to begin affirming each other.

• Take time to encourage those on the staff. Pick one of these people and make his or her day: church secretary, youth director, custodian, choir director, organist, Vacation Bible School teachers, etc. Leave them messages with personal notes. Give homemade, humorous gifts. Have fun with them!

• If it's easy for you to write notes and letters, use that ability to write people in your church. I know retired persons who have marvelous ministries to others through the mail. They reach the weary and the rejoicing. One woman told me, "I say a prayer for the friend when I lick the stamp. The more I pray and send, the more I dispel self-pity that's so easy to have at my age."

• Be sensitive to the needs of the lonely, the hurting, and the grieving members of your church. Develop a relationship with some of these people and call them regularly. Visit when you can. I remember one Christmas when I phoned several new widows. Our conversations were full of warmth, and I heard such precious statements of personal faith in Christ. They blessed my Christmas!

• Expect God to act in the encouragement process in Christians' lives. Your outreach in active love is just a small part. Surrender it to God, and do not seek praise from anyone. Discourage people from falling into an "I'm indebted to you" attitude. The joy is your inner satisfaction and gratitude to God for what He is doing.

I've seen results like these when Christians touch lives through steady encouragement.

(1) People take on new radiance because they know someone cares and accepts them as they are. They experience God's love in action.

(2) Individuals show new hope and motivation, because someone believes in them and recognizes their gifts and abilities.

(3) People, in turn, become encouragers.

(4) Christians who are edified and nurtured move on in rapid spiritual growth and love of God. They often choose exciting ways to reach out to others in witness and service. The results in God's purposes are truly endless!

Scripture quotations are from the *New International Version*.

This article is adapted from the book, *Effective Encouragement*, by Charlotte Adelsperger. ©1986 by The STANDARD PUBLISHING Company. Used by permission.

Autumn Quarter, 1988

Theme: Through Suffering to Hope

Special Features

Lessons

Unit 1: Job—Probing the Meaning of Suffering

Unit 2: Isaiah—Interpreting a Nation's Suffering

Unit 3: Jeremiah—Looking for a New Day

Related Resources

The following publications contain additional help for the subjects included in the Autumn Quarter's study. They may be purchased from your supplier. Prices are subject to change.

Beloved Sufferer, by Edwin V. Hayden. How one man copes with his wife's disabling illness. Order no. 3178, $5.95.

Claiming God's Promises, by Alger Fitch. Order no. 41028, $2.95.

Divided We Fall, by James E. Smith. Order no. 40087, $2.25.

Effective Encouragement, by Charlotte Adelsperger. Order no. 3197, $2.95.

God's Word B.C. (Old Testament Survey), by John W. Wade. Order no. 41020, $2.95

How to Use Your Bible, by Wanda Milner. Order no. 3200, $2.95.

Special Ministries for Caring Churches. Compiled by Robert Korth. Order no. 3183, $5.95.

Sep 4
Sep 11
Sep 18
Sep 25
Oct 2
Oct 9
Oct 16
Oct 23
Oct 30
Nov 6
Nov 13
Nov 20
Nov 27

Victory!

VICTORIOUS LIFE is an underlying theme in the International Sunday School Lessons for 1988-89. Suffering, both personal and national, holds our attention in the Autumn quarter. But victory over personal tragedy is seen in Job's example of trust in God. And though the prophets Isaiah and Jeremiah warned that Judah would suffer for rebelling against God, they also gave assurance that God's new covenant with the nation and all mankind would make possible ultimate victory over sin.

The Winter quarter allows us to examine once again the earthly ministry of our Lord Jesus Christ. Come to fulfill the will of His Heavenly Father, Jesus lived a truly victorious life. Our study shows that acts of love and compassion for those with physical and spiritual needs characterize such a life.

In the Spring quarter we study Paul's prison epistles. Imprisoned in Rome, Paul yet exhibited a positive, confident attitude. His writings showed that his thoughts turned ever upward to Christ and outward to others. Certainly the word *victorious* describes the life of this man.

The Summer quarter first takes us back to Israel's conquest of Canaan. In the period of the judges, which followed, the nation had its ups and downs; but one lesson that came through remains to this day: true victory in life comes only to those who remain faithful to God.

International Sunday School Lesson Topics
September, 1986—August, 1992

	AUTUMN QUARTER (Sept., Oct., Nov.)	WINTER QUARTER (Dec., Jan., Feb.)	SPRING QUARTER (Mar., Apr., May)	SUMMER QUARTER (June, July, Aug.)
1986-1987	Beginning of the Covenant People (Old Testament Survey)	The Arrival of a New Age (New Testament Survey)	God's Constant Love (Luke and Hosea)	The Righteousness of God (Romans)
1987-1988	Genesis: Book of Beginnings	The Call to Discipleship (The Gospel of Matthew)	Facing the Future With Confidence (Matthew, Hebrews)	Moses and His Mission (Exodus, Numbers, Deuteronomy)
1988-1989	Through Suffering to Hope (Job, Isaiah, Jeremiah)	Scenes of Love and Compassion (Luke)	Letters From Prison (Philemon, Colossians, Philippians, Ephesians)	Conquest and Challenge (Joshua, Judges, Ruth)
1989-1990	Visions of God's Rule (Ezekiel, Daniel, 1 and 2 Thessalonians, Revelation)	Lord of Life (The Gospel of John)	Lord of Life (cont'd) Abiding in Love (1, 2, 3 John)	Wisdom As a Way of Life (Ecclesiastes, Proverbs, Psalms, James)
1990-1991	Prophets, Priests, and Kings (Conflicts and Concerns)	Stories Jesus Told (Parables)	Counsel for a Church in Crisis (1 and 2 Corinthians)	After the Exile (Ezra, Nehemiah, and Prophets)
1991-1992	From the Damascus Road to Rome (Life of Paul—Acts)	Songs and Prayers of the Bible (Song of Solomon, Psalms, others)	The Strong Son of God (Mark) God's People in the World (1 and 2 Peter)	God's Judgment and Mercy (Minor Prophets) Organizing for Ministry (Pastoral Epistles)

Trouble and Triumph

by Orrin Root

YOU THINK YOU HAVE TROUBLES? Or if not, are you concerned about the troubles of your neighbors, your country, your world? If you are, these studies are for you. Through thirteen weeks we shall come face to face with problems: personal, national, and world problems.

Living in the world of today and looking at the world of long ago, we shall see how persistent its problems are. The achievements of proud science and technology have scarcely touched the most troublesome problems. It is easier to fly to the moon than to answer the question of Job or to solve the problems of Isaiah and Jeremiah.

Job, Isaiah, Jeremiah. We may search all history without finding three characters more fascinating. They intrigue us because their problems are our problems, their answers are valid still, and the questions they left unanswered are unanswerable today. Best of all, the stories of these men enrich our thoughts of the living God.

Job

When did Job live? Nobody knows. From the little we learn about his big ranch, we think he may have been running it when Abraham or Isaac or Jacob was ranching in an area not very far away—but Job may have been earlier or later. Where did Job live? Somewhere in the east, a wide area with no fixed boundaries. But though his time and place are unknown, his ranch is real, his wife and children are real, his friends are real, his problem is real, even today. Perhaps that is why his time and place are indefinite. He belongs to every time and place.

Prosperous and pleasant and placid, Job was untroubled. He may have supposed he was beyond the reach of trouble, but he was not. Then as now, the devil was prowling around looking for someone to devour. He leaped on Job. His claws and teeth sank deep, but Job was too tough to be devoured. Are we?

Isaiah

When we come to Isaiah, the time and place are not so vague. He lived in Jerusalem, on the very spot where Jerusalem can be seen today. He proclaimed God's word in the days of four kings of Judah: Uzziah, Jotham, Ahaz, and Hezekiah. This puts his time in the eighth century B.C.

The history of that time is plain in the books of Kings and Chronicles. Israel and Syria together launched an attack on Judah, where Isaiah lived, intending to overthrow King Ahaz and put a king of their own on the throne. Isaiah urged Ahaz to be calm and trust in God, but Ahaz thought it wiser to make an alliance with mighty Assyria. It proved to be a costly alliance. Later, King Hezekiah listened to Isaiah's advice, and the Lord rescued Judah from Assyria. When will nations learn that righteousness is a better defense than any alliance with unbelievers?

With God's revelation to guide him, Isaiah accurately foretold events in his own time. He even foretold events of future centuries. He is called the gospel prophet because he told so much about Jesus. It was Isaiah who said, "The Lord himself shall give you a sign; Behold, a virgin shall conceive, and bear a son, and shall call his name Immanuel" (Isaiah 7:14). It was Isaiah who penned this glorious song: "For unto us a child is born, unto us a son is given: and the government shall be upon his shoulder: and his name shall be called Wonderful, Counselor, The mighty God, The everlasting Father, The Prince of Peace" (Isaiah 9:6). In dark times the people of Judah found in that prophecy the hope of a deliverer. Unfortunately, they did not realize that the same deliverer would be led as a sheep to the slaughter (Isaiah 53:7). Of that prophecy they asked, "Of whom speaketh the prophet this?" (Acts 8:34). Guided by their own wishes more than by Isaiah's words, they failed to recognize the deliverer when He came. Are we always wise enough to put God's Word above our own wishes?

Jeremiah

Jeremiah also lived in Jerusalem, but a century later than Isaiah. He supported good King Josiah's effort to clean up the country; but after Josiah died, the prophet of God had no staunch ally on the throne. King Jehoiakim scornfully burned the book of Jeremiah, but he could not destroy the truth. The kingdom moved on toward destruction. King Zedekiah called on Jeremiah for advice, but he did not follow it. In his time Jerusalem was besieged for a year and a half and finally crushed. Jeremiah lived to see the destruction that he had foretold.

"The weeping prophet." That name has been given to Jeremiah because he mourned over the fate of Jerusalem. However, his word was not altogether a word of gloom and doom. Steadfastly he held that destruction could be averted very easily—simply by doing right. "If ye thoroughly amend your ways and your doings; if ye thoroughly execute judgment between a man and his neighbor; if ye oppress not the stranger, the fatherless, and the widow, and shed not innocent blood in this place, neither walk after other gods to your hurt; then will I cause you to dwell in this place" (Jeremiah 7:5-7). Only by willful disobedience would destruction come; and willfully Jerusalem went on disobeying.

Jeremiah's repeated prophecies of captivity are interrupted by the assurance that captivity would not be forever. "For thus saith the Lord, That after seventy years be accomplished at Babylon I will visit you, and perform my good word toward you, in causing you to return to this place. For I know the thoughts that I think toward you, saith the Lord, thoughts of peace, and not of evil, to give you an expected end. Then shall ye call upon me, and ye shall go and pray unto me, and I will hearken unto you. And ye shall seek me, and find me, when ye shall search for me with all your heart. And I will be found of you, saith the Lord: and I will turn away your captivity, and I will gather you from all the nations, and from all the places whither I have driven you, saith the Lord; and I will bring you again into the place whence I caused you to be carried away captive (Jeremiah 29:10-14).

Trust the Lord

"Though he slay me, yet will I trust in him." That was Job's cry from the depth of his misery. He could see no justice in what was happening to him, but he would not doubt that God was just. Furthermore, he was determined to do right himself; "I will maintain mine own ways before him." And he added, "He also shall be my salvation" (Job 13:15, 16).

Trust in the Lord and do right. This message comes through clear and strong in all these studies. "Behold, God is my salvation; I will trust, and not be afraid: for the Lord Jehovah is my strength and my song." Such will be the song of God's people in the day when Christ rules (Isaiah 11:1-3; 12:1, 2). Some rulers of Judah preferred to trust in Egypt with its horses and war chariots (Isaiah 30:1, 2; 31:1), but Isaiah told them, "Thus saith the Lord God, the Holy One of Israel; In returning and rest shall ye be saved; in quietness and in confidence shall be your strength" (Isaiah 30:15).

Jeremiah likewise begged his people not to put their trust in lying words, nor think they would be safe because the Lord's temple was among them. He urged them rather to amend their ways and to do right. Then they could trust God to care for them (Jeremiah 7:3-7). To illustrate his own trust, Jeremiah paid out good money for a field when the Babylonians were about to take over the whole land (Jeremiah 32:6-12). His title would be worthless while Babylon ruled; but God said His people would again possess houses and fields, and Jeremiah believed Him (Jeremiah 32:15).

It is not easy to trust in the Lord when that trust is costly, and it is not easy to do right when money can be made by doing wrong. But in the long run God's way is best.

Happy Endings

Job kept his faith through all his loss and pain, and in the end God gave him twice as much as he had had before. That was twice as much material wealth, but in his misery Job found a conviction that was even better: "I know that my Redeemer liveth, and that he shall stand at the latter day upon the earth: and though after my skin worms destroy this body, yet in my flesh shall I see God" (Job 19:25, 26). If his prosperity had been unbroken, perhaps he never would have looked for anything better; and if he had not kept his faith, he would not have found the better thing.

The Bible does not tell how Isaiah's earthly life ended. An old story says he was murdered by evil King Manasseh. It does not matter, for Isaiah knew about the happy ending: "Of the increase of his government and peace there shall be no end" (Isaiah 9:7). The Prince of Peace will rule forever, and His people will be glad eternally.

Jeremiah lived in Jerusalem till Jerusalem was no more. Nebuchadnezzar's troops drove most of the surviving people to Babylon. When a tiny remnant later fled to Egypt, Jeremiah went along to minister to them. But that was not the end. The Lord was going to make a new covenant with His people, writing His law in their hearts and forgiving their sins (Jeremiah 31:31-34).

"Through Suffering to Hope" is the title of this quarter's study. No matter how dismal the story may be, there is always a happy ending if we walk with God. "Our light affliction, which is but for a moment, worketh for us a far more exceeding and eternal weight of glory" (2 Corinthians 4:17). "Now thanks be unto God, which always causeth us to triumph in Christ" (2 Corinthians 2:14).

> Tho' clouds may gather in the sky,
> And billows round me roll,
> However dark the world may be
> I've sunlight in my soul.
> —JUDSON W. VAN DEVENTER

Responses to Suffering

by Charles P. Herndon

REVERSALS ARE ALWAYS WITH US. Nonetheless, a person anchored in Jesus enjoys resources not dependent upon favorable circumstances. Christian contentment does not depend upon favorable situations. It results from a right relationship to God through His Son. Accordingly, Paul wrote, "I have learned, in whatsoever state I am, therewith to be content. I know both how to be abased, and I know how to abound: every where and in all things I am instructed both to be full and to be hungry, both to abound and to suffer need. I can do all things through Christ which strengtheneth me" (Philippians 4:11-13). Losses did not deter this apostle to the Gentiles. He said, "I count all things but loss for the excellency of the knowledge of Christ Jesus my Lord: for whom I have suffered the loss of all things" (Philippians 3:8).

Job, a Role Model in Suffering

Within God's permissive will, Job endured Satanic attack. He lost livestock, servants, and children. In the face of such overwhelming adversity, this man who is described as perfect and upright "fell down upon the ground, and worshipped" saying, "Naked came I out of my mother's womb, and naked shall I return thither: the Lord gave, and the Lord hath taken away; blessed be the name of the Lord" (Job 1:1, 20, 21).

In addition to Job's economic loss and the emotional trauma of losing his children, he was stricken with a loathsome disease. All of this made Job an object of pity. His wife and friends attempted to bring relief. However, he reproved his wife for her advice, and rejected the counsel of his three friends, describing them as "forgers of lies" and "physicians of no value" (Job 13:4).

In hope, Job asked and answered the question of death and life beyond the grave (see Job 14:14, 15). He expressed knowledge of redemption (19:25-27). Restoration came; misfortune departed; and God "gave Job twice as much as he had before" (42:10).

Patience in Suffering

James reminds his readers "Ye have heard of the patience of Job" (James 5:11). Other Old Testament personalities are cited in the same context. "Take, my brethren, the prophets, who have spoken in the name of the Lord, for an example of suffering affliction, and of patience" (James 5:10). Isaiah and Jeremiah are two prophets who come to mind. Their faithfulness to God, despite the waywardness of Judah and Jerusalem and the ignoring of their prophecies, is an example of patient endurance.

Job, however, stands out in supplying noteworthy responses to adversity. Not only was he noted for patience, but he also rejected false remedies and refused to see suffering as a divine punishment for personal sin. Neither did he resort to cynicism nor passively accept the false thought that, for him, there was no way out.

Reversals Come to Everyone!

Many things can cause life to suffer brokenness. Among them are marital unfaithfulness, treason of friends, false philosophies of life, disaster, disease, and bereavement. All of these, or any one of them, can play a part in causing disturbing disruptions. Homes, hearts, hopes, and health can be broken. Sometimes it is necessary for stubborn wills to be broken, so that God's work of recovery can begin.

From a spiritual standpoint, some suffering comes to Christians because of their affiliation with Jesus Christ. Christians know how to deal with such afflictions, for they have learned to cast their personal anxieties upon God who cares for them (see 1 Peter 5:7). Reviewing Christ's sufferings and understanding that the trials of His disciples came about because of their service for the King help believers today accept hardship for Christ's sake as a norm of spiritual life.

Christ's Suffering—and Ours

Isaiah 53 details sufferings of the Son of God from the prophetic view. The Gospels accentuate this matter further in depicting the passion of the Savior. Jesus shared the Passover meal with His disciples with full knowledge of His suffering that would follow (Luke 22:15). At least six months before that time He had begun to show them "how that he must go unto Jerusalem, and suffer many things of the elders and chief priests and scribes, and be killed" (Matthew 16:21).

As recipients of the love and salvation of Christ, and as His witnesses in an adversary world, Christians must accept the fact that they may be called upon to suffer for their Redeemer. Adversaries shouldn't terrify the faithful, for unto the followers of Christ Paul wrote, "It is given in the behalf of Christ, not only to believe on him, but also to suffer for his sake" (Philippians 1:29). Paul aspired to know "the fellowship of his sufferings" (Philippians 3:10). He further wrote, "Yea, and all that will live godly in Christ Jesus shall suffer persecution" (2 Timothy 3:12). See also Romans 8:17 and 2 Timothy 2:12. Christ's example of suffering is to be followed by His buffeted disciples (1 Peter 2:20-24). He who died to save us (Hebrew 2:9, 10) lives to sustain us, "for in that he himself hath suffered being tempted, he is able also to succor them that are tempted" (Hebrews 2:18).

Joy Beyond Suffering

Joy arising from the Christian's trials is not to be confused with the fun and fleshly pleasures of this life. One has not matured in Christ unless and until lasting joy is valued above temporary enjoyment. Though filled with incredible pain and shame, the Calvary experience held joy in prospect for the Savior. Thus the writer of Hebrews spoke of Jesus, "who for the joy that was set before him endured the cross, despising the shame" (Hebrew 12:2). Our Lord had no fun that day of His crucifixion, but He rejoiced because He knew His suffering would open the way for our salvation.

Consider the roll call of Old Testament faithful as recounted in Hebrews 11. Moses certainly had no fun when "choosing rather to suffer affliction with the people of God, than to enjoy the pleasures of sin for a season; esteeming the reproach of Christ greater riches than the treasures in Egypt" (vv, 25, 26). No enjoyment was experienced by those faithful pilgrims who "were tortured, not accepting deliverance; that they might obtain a better resurrection" (v. 35). Those who were "stoned," "sawn asunder," and "slain with the sword" (v. 37) while awaiting the fulfillment of the promise had no physical pleasure in those experiences; but eternal joy, set before them, sustained them. Similarly, Christians under stress, whether from illness, loss of a loved one, or from persecution for their faith can have joy, despite suffering.

Rejoicing in Hope

According to Paul, we who are Christians "rejoice in hope of the glory of God. And not only so, but we glory in tribulations also; knowing that tribulation worketh patience; and patience, experience; and experience, hope: and hope maketh not ashamed; because the love of God is shed abroad in our hearts by the Holy Ghost which is given unto us" (Romans 5:2-4). Such hope defies all human estimates and limita-

tions. Abraham illustrated the power of hope, for against all hope, as men would define it, he "believed in hope, that he might become the father of many nations" (Romans 4:18). In predicaments thought to be beyond human relief, Christian sufferers cherish hope that rests in the hands of God. Hope anchored in unseen realities generates patience in awaiting fulfillment.

Even if the Christian's hope is not rewarded by relief from reversals in this life, it reaches for the ultimate deliverance "from the bondage of corruption into the glorious liberty of the children of God" (Romans 8:21). Eagerly awaiting the end of all pain and suffering of our present existence, we who are Christians groan within ourselves in anticipation of "the adoption, to wit, the redemption of our body" (v. 23). Paul continues, "For we are saved by hope: but hope that is seen is not hope: for what a man seeth, why doth he yet hope for? But if we hope for that we see not, then do we with patience wait for it" (vv. 24, 25). Christians have been begotten again "unto a lively hope by the resurrection of Jesus Christ from the dead, to an inheritance incorruptible, and undefiled, and that fadeth not away, reserved in heaven" (1 Peter 1:3, 4). Though we may be weighed down by many temptations our joy is not dispelled; for we await the second coming of Jesus Christ, believing and rejoicing "with joy unspeakable and full of glory" (vv. 6-8).

Revisiting Christian Affliction

Paul, by contrasting external and internal (eternal) values, provided support to troubled followers of Christ. He surveyed the adverse situations into which his commitment to Christ had led him, and, difficult though those situations were, his response remained positive (see 2 Corinthians 4:8-10). Expressing the certainty of ultimate resurrection, the apostle gave a triumphant analysis of affliction in Christian experience. He said, "Though our outward man perish, yet the inward man is renewed day by day. For our light affliction, which is but for a moment, worketh for us a far more exceeding and eternal weight of glory" (2 Corinthians 4:16, 17; see also Romans 8:18).

Paul is saying that the Christian's affliction, though undeniably unpleasant, is comparatively light, momentary, and eternally fruitful. While ignoring visible, transitory things, and visualizing invisible, eternal promises, the faithful servant of the Lord Jesus is assured that, after his earthly body goes the way of all flesh, there remains for him "a building of God, a house not made with hands, eternal in the heavens" (2 Corinthians 5:1).

Quarterly Quiz

The questions on this page and the next may be used in several ways: as a pretest at the beginning of the quarter; as a review at the end of the quarter; or as a review after each lesson. The questions are based on the Scripture text of each lesson (King James Version). The answers are found in italicized references.

Lesson 1

1. Job is described as being the (wisest, greatest, holiest) of all the men of the east. *Job 1:3*
2. Satan said to God, "Put forth thine hand now, and touch all that he [Job] hath, and he will _____ thee to thy face." *Job 1:11*
3. Having lost his wealth, his servants, and his children, Job tore his garment, shaved his head, and fell on the ground and (wept, wished to die, worshiped). *Job 1:20*
4. Satan confidently told God that a man will give all that he has for his life. (true/false). *Job 2:4*
5. Who urged Job to "curse God, and die"? *Job 2:9*

Lesson 2

1. The names of Job's three friends who came to comfort him were Eliphaz, Bildad, and (Zedekiah, Zophar, Zephaniah). *Job 11:1*
2. Job's three friends believed that in this life God punishes the wicked and rewards the righteous. (true/false). *Job 4:7, 8; 8:5-7*
3. One of Job's three friends told Job that God was punishing him even less than he deserved. (true/false). *Job 11:6*
4. After telling his three friends that they were "physicians of no value," Job urged them to (stop talking, go home, pray for forgiveness). *Job 13:5*

Lesson 3

1. One of Job's complaints was that he cried out to God for help, and God did not hear him. (true/false). *Job 30:20*
2. Job went so far as to charge God with being cruel to him. (true/false). *Job 30:21*
3. Even though Job was suffering intensely, he believed that God would keep him from dying from his affliction. (true/false). *Job 30:23*

Lesson 4

1. When God finally spoke to Job, God spoke to him out of a (brilliant light, whirlwind, burning bush). *Job 38:1*
2. God's comments to Job were in the form of (parables, proverbs, questions). *Job 38—41*

3. When God finished speaking to Job, Job understood why a good person may suffer bad things in this life. (true/false). *Job 42:1-6*
4. After Job's ordeal was ended, the Lord gave him (two, three, four) times as much as he had before. *Job 42:10*

Lesson 5

1. In Isaiah's song of the vineyard, the owner, who had given his vineyard the best of care, expected it to produce grapes; but instead it brought forth (leafy vines with no fruit, briars and thorns, wild grapes). *Isaiah 5:2*
2. Isaiah's song said that God "looked for judgment, but behold _____ ; for righteousness, but behold a _____ ." *Isaiah 5:7*
3. The message of the song of the vineyard was that God was going to remove His blessings and protection from His people and allow them to be overrun and destroyed by their enemies. (true/false). *Isaiah 5:5-7*

Lesson 6

1. Isaiah saw a vision of the Lord in the year that king (Hezekiah, Uzziah, Ahaz) died. *Isaiah 6:1*
2. The six-winged attendants who stood above the throne on which the Lord sat were called (cherubim, seraphim, angels). *Isaiah 6:2*
3. What did one of the six-winged attendants touch to Isaiah's lips when he announced that Isaiah's sin was purged? *Isaiah 6:6, 7*
4. When Isaiah heard the Lord ask whom He could send to speak to the people on His behalf, Isaiah volunteered without hesitation. (true/false). *Isaiah 6:8*

Lesson 7

1. In the opening verses of the fortieth chapter of Isaiah we read of the condemnation that God was going to bring upon His people. (true/false). *Isaiah 40:1-5, 9-11*
2. "Prepare ye the way of the Lord" was spoken by the voice crying in the wilderness. (true/false). *Isaiah 40:3*
3. Isaiah said that every valley shall be made low and every mountain exalted. (true/false). *Isaiah 40:4*

4. By using the figure of (a father with his son, a shepherd with his flock, a vinedresser with his vineyard) Isaiah illustrated the care and concern God would show for His people in bringing them back to their homeland following their captivity in Babylon. *Isaiah 40:11*

Lesson 8

1. Isaiah prophesied that Jesus' suffering would be regarded as being punishment from God. (true/false). *Isaiah 53:4*
2. Jesus was to be wounded for His transgressions. (true/false). *Isaiah 53:5*
3. Isaiah declared that Jesus would stoutly defend himself when oppressed and afflicted. (true/false). *Isaiah 53:7*
4. Isaiah prophesied that Jesus would make His grave with the wicked, and with the rich in His death. (true/false). *Isaiah 53:9*

Lesson 9

1. Speaking through the prophet Isaiah, God declares that He will create new heavens and a new earth. (true/false). *Isaiah 65:17*
2. Referring to the future security of His people, God said, "as the days of a (candle, tree, river) are the days of my people." *Isaiah 65:22*
3. Regarding the prayers of His people, God promised, "Before they call, I will _____ ; and while they are yet speaking, I will _____." *Isaiah 65:24*
4. In God's perfected kingdom, there will be nothing that will hurt or destroy. (true/false). *Isaiah 65:25*

Lesson 10

1. God told Jeremiah that He had ordained him to be a prophet before Jeremiah was born. (true/false). *Jeremiah 1:5*
2. Jeremiah was not to be afraid of the (threats, faces, power) of the people to whom God would send him. *Jeremiah 1:8*
3. The Lord reached out and touched Jeremiah's (mouth, eyes, hand). *Jeremiah 1:9*
4. God said He had made Jeremiah (a defensed city, an iron pillar, brazen walls, all three) against the people and their leaders. *Jeremiah 1:18*

Lesson 11

1. The Lord directed Jeremiah to stand in the (front, gate, court) of the Lord's house and deliver His message of warning to the people. *Jeremiah 7:2*
2. The people of Judah in Jeremiah's day felt they were secure in their land because the temple of the Lord was in their midst. (true/false). *Jeremiah 7:3, 4*

3. God stated that He would enable the people to dwell safely in their land only if they would thoroughly amend their ways and their doings. (true/false). *Jeremiah 7:5-7*
4. God told His people to go to (Shechem, Shiloh, Samaria) where His tabernacle first stood after Israel entered Canaan, and see how that place now lay in ruins. *Jeremiah 7:12*

Lesson 12

1. The princes of Judah wanted Jeremiah put to death, for they said he was demoralizing the military forces and everyone else who remained in Jerusalem. (true/false). *Jeremiah 38:4*
2. The princes of Judah accused Jeremiah of wanting to hurt, not help, the people of Judah. (true/false). *Jeremiah 38:4*
3. The king who said he could not stop those who wished to harm Jeremiah was (Jehoiakim, Jehoiachin, Zedekiah). *Jeremiah 38:5*
4. The man who rescued Jeremiah from the cistern in the prison court was (Hilkiah, Ebed-melech, Shaphan). *Jeremiah 38:10*

Lesson 13

1. A saying popular in Jeremiah's day was, "The fathers have eaten a _____ _____ , and the children's _____ are set on edge." *Jeremiah 31:29*
2. Jeremiah prophesied that God would make a new covenant with Judah. (true/false). *Jeremiah 31:31*
3. Israel was excluded from the blessings of the New Covenant that God was going to establish. (true/false). *Jeremiah 31:31*
4. Speaking of the New Covenant that He would make with His people, God said, "I will put my law in their _____ parts, and write it in their _____ ." *Jeremiah 31:33*

Answers

Lesson 1—1. greatest. 2. curse. 3. worshiped. 4. true. 5. his wife. *Lesson 2*—1. Zophar. 2. true. 3. true. 4. stop talking. *Lesson 3*—1. true. 2. true. 3. false. *Lesson 4*—1. whirlwind. 2. questions. 3. false. 4. two. *Lesson 5*—1. wild grapes. 2. oppression, cry. 3. true. *Lesson 6*—1. Uzziah. 2. seraphim. 3. a live coal. 4. true. *Lesson 7*—1. false. 2. true. 3. false. 4. a shepherd with his flock. *Lesson 8*—1. true. 2. false. 3. false. 4. true. *Lesson 9*—1. true. 2. tree. 3. answer, hear. 4. true. *Lesson 10*—1. true. 2. faces. 3. mouth. 4. all three. *Lesson 11*—1. gate. 2. true. 3. true. 4. Shiloh. *Lesson 12*—1. true. 2. true. 3. Zedekiah. 4. Ebed-melech. *Lesson 13*—1. sour grape, teeth. 2. true. 3. false. 4. inward, hearts.

Satan Tempts Job

September 4
Lesson 1

LESSON SCRIPTURE: Job 1:1—2:10.

PRINTED TEXT: Job 1:1-3, 8-11, 20, 21; 2:4-6, 9, 10.

Job 1:1-3, 8-11, 20, 21

1 There was a man in the land of Uz, whose name was Job; and that man was perfect and upright, and one that feared God, and eschewed evil.

2 And there were born unto him seven sons and three daughters.

3 His substance also was seven thousand sheep, and three thousand camels, and five hundred yoke of oxen, and five hundred she asses, and a very great household; so that this man was the greatest of all the men of the east.

. . . .

8 And the Lord said unto Satan, Hast thou considered my servant Job, that there is none like him in the earth, a perfect and an upright man, one that feareth God, and escheweth evil?

9 Then Satan answered the Lord, and said, Doth Job fear God for nought?

10 Hast not thou made a hedge about him, and about his house, and about all that he hath on every side? thou hast blessed the work of his hands, and his substance is increased in the land.

11 But put forth thine hand now, and touch all that he hath, and he will curse thee to thy face.

. . . .

20 Then Job arose, and rent his mantle, and shaved his head, and fell down upon the ground, and worshipped,

21 And said, Naked came I out of my mother's womb, and naked shall I return thither: the Lord gave, and the Lord hath taken away; blessed be the name of the Lord.

Job 2:4-6, 9, 10

4 And Satan answered the Lord, and said, Skin for skin, yea, all that a man hath will he give for his life.

5 But put forth thine hand now, and touch his bone and his flesh, and he will curse thee to thy face.

6 And the Lord said unto Satan, Behold, he is in thine hand; but save his life.

. . . .

9 Then said his wife unto him, Dost thou still retain thine integrity? curse God, and die.

10 But he said unto her, Thou speakest as one of the foolish women speaketh. What? shall we receive good at the hand of God, and shall we not receive evil? In all this did not Job sin with his lips.

GOLDEN TEXT: The Lord gave, and the Lord hath taken away; blessed be the name of the Lord.—Job 1:21.

Lesson Aims

After this lesson students should be able to:
1. Describe the man Job.
2. Describe the disasters that came to him.
3. Tell how Job responded to disaster.
4. Resolve to keep their own integrity and faith in God regardless of circumstances.

Lesson Outline

INTRODUCTION
  A. Rest Without an Answer
  B. Lesson Background
 I. A GODLY MAN (Job 1:1-3)
  A. The Man (v. 1)
  B. The Family (v. 2)
  C. The Property (v. 3)
    A Name That Lives
 II. A DEVILISH SCHEME (Job 1:8-11, 20, 21)
  A. God's Approval (v. 8)
  B. Satan's Scorn (vv. 9-11)
  C. Job's Loyalty (vv. 20, 21)
III. A SECOND SCHEME (Job 2:4-6, 9, 10)
  A. Persistent Scorn (vv. 4-6)
  B. Wifely Advice (v. 9)
  C. Integrity Unshaken (v. 10)
CONCLUSION
  A. Proving and Improving
  B. Who Is on Trial?
  C. Another Trial
  D. You Can Do Right
  E. Prayer
  F. Thought to Remember

Display visual 1 from the visuals/learning resources packet and let it remain before the class throughout the lesson for today. It is shown on page 14.

Introduction

Why me? Is there a Christian who has not sometime asked that question? A highway accident leaves one paralyzed, or multiple sclerosis takes the skill from his hands. A fire or flood destroys his home and property, or a loved one dies and leaves him desolate. Someone is struck with several difficult problems all at once. Even a seasonal bout with hay fever may be enough to raise the agonizing question.

A. Rest Without an Answer

Why me? What have I done to deserve this? I've tried to live right. Haven't I been honest, kind, generous, helpful? Why am I having this trouble? Is there no justice? Where is God?

Job was not the first man to raise this question, but perhaps the book of Job is the oldest extended discussion of it on record. If Job had found a complete answer, perhaps each of us could rest with that instead of asking the question again.

Job did not find an answer, but in God's revelation he found rest for his agonized mind. And along the way he gained insight and reached conclusions that can enlighten and encourage every soul in agony today.

B. Lesson Background

Job lived in Uz. We cannot mark out the boundaries of that land on the map, but we know about where it was. Job was the greatest of the men of the East. That points us to the area east of the Jordan River, but not too far out in the desert for the soil to be cultivated.

The customs pictured and the names mentioned in the book of Job suggest that Job may have lived in the time of Abraham, Isaac, and Jacob; or perhaps during the centuries after Jacob when Israel lived in Egypt. Like Jacob, Job was a tiller of the soil as well as a keeper of sheep and cattle. Like Jacob he had a big family, but unlike Jacob he had only one wife.

I. A Godly Man
(Job 1:1-3)

The description of Job reminds us of that of Noah. "Noah was a just man and perfect in his generations" (Genesis 6:9). Job was "perfect and upright" (Job 1:1). "Noah walked with God." Job "feared God, and eschewed evil." But while Noah and his family were the only good people on earth, Job was not so lonely in his goodness. The friends who came to console him were good men too, men with a steadfast faith in God. Their fault was one shared by many good men, one highly developed in the Pharisees of Jesus' time. They were quite satisfied with their goodness, and quite confident that their traditional conclusions and teachings were unquestionable. Job himself may have been a bit too smug until his confidence was shaken by his troubles—and we may wonder if that is one reason why God allows good people to be troubled. If they are driven to question their own goodness, they may find that it is not so complete as they have supposed.

A. The Man (v. 1)

1. There was a man in the land of Uz, whose name was Job; and that man was perfect and upright, and one that feared God, and eschewed evil.

The man Job is described in four ways:

1. He was *perfect*. How often we say, "Nobody's perfect"! A perfect person would have no fault and no lack. But the word *perfect* is not always used in that absolute sense. Paul says he is not perfect in that sense, but is trying to be. Then in the next breath he calls those who are perfect to be of the same mind (Philippians 3:12-15). In other words, he calls the most perfect of us to realize that we are not entirely perfect and to try to be better. So we need not take our text to mean that Job was totally perfect, with never a sin or a fault—but he was notably close to perfection.

2. Job was *upright*. The word may also be translated *straight*. Job was honest, truthful, just, dependable. He did right.

3. He *feared God*. Reverently he worshiped; sincerely he tried to do God's will.

4. He *eschewed evil*. That old-fashioned word means he avoided evil. The *American Standard Version* has he "turned away from evil."

B. The Family (v. 2)

2. And there were born unto him seven sons and three daughters.

The Lord had told men to multiply and fill the earth (Genesis 9:1). A large family was a credit to a man as well as a delight. "Lo, children are a heritage of the Lord" (Psalm 127:3).

C. The Property (v. 3)

3. His substance also was seven thousand sheep, and three thousand camels, and five hundred yoke of oxen, and five hundred she asses, and a very great household; so that this man was the greatest of all the men of the east.

Seven thousand sheep on a modern ranch can produce about thirty-five tons of wool each year. Ancient sheep may have been less productive, but still the wool was no small item. *Five hundred yoke of oxen* can plow ground enough for a huge crop of wheat. The great numbers of *camels* and *asses* suggest long caravans carrying surplus wheat to the merchants of Phoenicia, and other caravans loaded with wool for the weavers of Mesopotamia and Egypt. It took *a very great household* to care for the animals, plant and harvest, and ship the produce. Job was a big operator, *the greatest of all the men of the east.*

A NAME THAT LIVES

Cameron Townsend went to Guatemala in 1918 to sell Spanish-language Bibles. One day a man who spoke only the dialect of his own people asked Townsend, "If your God is so great, why can't He speak my language?" That simple question launched Cam Townsend on a lifetime crusade of translating the Bible into as many native languages as possible. Today, fifty-six hundred Wycliffe linguists and support personnel work in fifty-one countries, entering a new language group every nine days. Of all the languages that have a Bible today, nearly half received it through the efforts of Cameron Townsend and the organization he founded—Wycliffe Bible Translators.

Job had an outstanding name among his acquaintances. Wherever he went, his reputation for justice and godliness preceded and followed him. The people of his day knew him as a blameless, God-fearing man.

If the people who know us were to summarize our character in just a few words, what would their description be?
—V. H.

II. A Devilish Scheme (Job 1:8-11, 20, 21)

The scene shifts from the land of Uz to the court of Heaven. The angels gathered before the Lord, and Satan appeared impudently among them (Job 1:6). From a few hints the Bible gives, we suppose Satan is an angel who rebelled and was banished from Heaven.

A. God's Approval (v. 8)

8. And the Lord said unto Satan, Hast thou considered my servant Job, that there is none like him in the earth, a perfect and an upright man, one that feareth God, and escheweth evil?

God himself affirmed the goodness of Job. Here was a man the Creator could be proud of.

B. Satan's Scorn (vv. 9-11)

9. Then Satan answered the Lord, and said, Doth Job fear God for nought?

Unable to find any fault with Job's actions, Satan attacked his motives. He said Job did not do right just because it was right, but because it was profitable. Job was selfish, said Satan. He worshiped and obeyed God because God gave him riches and honor.

10a. Hast not thou made a hedge about him, and about his house, and about all that he hath on every side?

Made a hedge about him means *protected him.* God had defended Job and his family against disease and poverty and loss.

10b. Thou hast blessed the work of his hands, and his substance is increased in the land.

God not only protected Job, but He also gave a blessing that made all Job's enterprises successful. In other words, Satan said God was bribing Job with all this wealth, and that was why Job worshiped and did right.

11. But put forth thine hand now, and touch all that he hath, and he will curse thee to thy face.

Touch here means a touch that destroys. Satan was saying Job was not good at heart, but selfish and greedy. If his property and family were taken away, Job's worship would turn to cursing. So said Satan. God then agreed to a test. He gave Satan permission to take away everything Job had, but He stipulated that Job himself was not to be injured (v. 12).

Satan moved quickly. Rustlers drove off Job's cattle and donkeys, murdering the men who were working with them. Lightning destroyed the sheep and the shepherds together. Raiders stole the camels and killed the servants. As a final blow, a tornado killed all of Job's sons and daughters (vv. 13-19).

C. Job's Loyalty (vv. 20, 21)

20. Then Job arose, and rent his mantle, and shaved his head, and fell down upon the ground, and worshipped.

Tearing the clothing and shaving the head were ways of expressing shock, grief, and dismay. In a single day the greatest of the men of the East had become a pauper. He was appalled.

Last week our newspaper told of a local rich man who was forced into bankruptcy. He shot himself. We have read of others who have talked bitterly of bad luck, or blamed the competition or the system. Some have renounced their faith in God. Job neither committed suicide nor railed at the robbers nor blamed God. He *worshipped.*

21a. And said, Naked came I out of my mother's womb, and naked shall I return thither.

Job acknowledged what we acknowledge in the oft-quoted saying, "You can't take it with you." We come into the world with nothing, and we leave it with nothing. We do not literally return to the womb, of course, but we go to a realm unseen and mysterious, and we go without any of the material things we have accumulated. Then why should we be utterly devastated if we lose those things before we die?

21b. The Lord gave, and the Lord hath taken away; blessed be the name of the Lord.

Job did not understand what had happened. He did not know that Satan, not God, was the cause. When disaster strikes, we should be cautious about calling it an act of God. But that does not help us with the question of why. We do not ask, "Why is God doing this to me?" But perhaps we still ask, "Why is God letting this happen to me?" And perhaps we hear no answer. Job heard none. But even when he thought the great Giver had taken away his gifts, Job said, *Blessed be the name of the Lord.* Verse 22 summarizes thus: "In all this Job sinned not, nor charged God foolishly." Like Job we can trust God even when we do not understand.

III. A Second Scheme
(Job 2:4-6, 9, 10)

The devil is persistent. He may have to slink away in defeat (James 4:7), but he comes back. Again the angels presented themselves before God, and again the devil came boldly with them. Again God praised the goodness of Job, who now had proved steadfast. (Job 2:1-3). But Satan was not ready to give up.

A. Persistent Scorn (vv. 4-6)

4. And Satan answered the Lord, and said, Skin for skin, yea, all that a man hath will he give for his life.

In popular language we say a man will do almost anything to save his own hide, or his own skin. Probably *skin for skin* was a popular expression with a similar meaning. A person's skin, that is, his body, is more valuable to him than all his possessions. He will not risk his own skin for the sake of cattle and sheep. Satan was saying that Job could accept the loss of his possessions and family because his own person was unhurt. God had forbidden Satan to touch the man himself. Job did not care about God, Satan implied, but only about himself.

5. But put forth thine hand now, and touch his bone and his flesh, and he will curse thee to thy face.

So the devil continued to sneer. In spite of losing property and family, Job continued to bless God. But it would be a different story if Job himself were hurt. Then his blessing would turn to cursing, said Satan.

6. And the Lord said unto Satan, Behold, he is in thine hand; but save his life.

Again God consented to test what the devil said. However, Satan must not kill the man. Satan promptly inflicted terrible suffering. He "smote Job with sore boils from the sole of his foot unto his crown" (v. 7). Anyone who has suffered from boils can imagine what agony it was to be completely covered with them.

B. Wifely Advice (v. 9)

9. Then said his wife unto him, Dost thou still retain thine integrity? curse God, and die.

Perhaps it was harder for Job's wife to watch his agony than it was for him to endure it. Loving wives can understand that. Or perhaps her integrity was not so strong as her husband's was. She threw her influence on the side of Satan. She advised Job to do what Satan wanted him to do. Of course neither of them knew it was a trap of Satan. Probably both thought God was inflicting this suffering on Job. The Hebrew word for *integrity* is related to the word for *perfect* in Job 1:1. It may be translated "Do you still retain your perfection?" Since God was now doing him harm instead of good, the wife thought that it did not pay to be a perfect man and fear God. She may have thought that cursing God would bring instant death. Seeing no hope that Job could recover, she thought the best thing he could do was to die quickly.

C. Integrity Unshaken (v. 10)

10. But he said unto her, Thou speakest as one of the foolish women speaketh. What? shall we receive good at the hand of God, and shall we not receive evil? In all this did not Job sin with his lips.

Throughout the Old Testament we see that it was considered foolish to oppose God or to do wrong. It was foolish advice that Job's wife gave. Job's mind was working clearly in spite of the agony of his body. God gives us a multitude of good things, and we accept them gladly. Loyalty to Him will not let us rebel as soon as He gives us something unpleasant. God's people do not serve Him for what they can get out of it. They are people of integrity. They serve God because He is God and it is right to serve Him. Again comes the summary: *In all this did not Job sin with his lips.* Satan's worst brought out Job's best. The perfect man's integrity was unshaken.

Conclusion

Why do bad things happen to good people? Isn't God in control? Isn't He just? More than that, isn't He loving? Doesn't He care?

We have barely started our study of Job, looking briefly at two chapters out of forty-two, but

already we have one part of the answer. The devil brings evil to us. He is walking up and down in the earth, intent on making trouble. He causes bad things to happen to good people.

But that is only part of the answer. We still question. God is in control, even of Satan. The devil cannot do any bad thing unless the Lord permits it. Then why does God let bad things happen to good people?

For this question we have at least a hint of an answer. Bad things are a test of a person. They show whether good people are really good or not.

A. Proving and Improving

The devil said there was no such thing as a good person. He said every man has his price. He said Job appeared to be good because that was profitable. He said Job, and everybody else, was selfish, concerned mainly about his own welfare.

God said, "We'll see about that." He unleashed Satan and let him do his worst. Satan made it seem that there was no profit in being good, but Job insisted on being good anyway. So the devil was proved to be wrong, and God and Job were proved to be right.

Why was such a test needed? Didn't God know what the outcome would be? Yes, of course He did. But did Job know? Before the test came, did Job know how solid was his conviction, how deep his devotion?

In the testing Job's goodness was proved. More than that, it was improved. He trusted God even when it seemed that God was doing nothing good for him, and so his trust grew greater. He clung to his conviction when everything was going wrong, and so his conviction was stronger. He continued to be good when only

visual 1

bad was happening to him, and so he was better than before.

Before we are tested, do any of us know how good we are, how strong, how faithful? The testing comes when everything else seems to go wrong. If our integrity remains unshaken through the test, then we are stronger and more faithful than ever before.

B. Who Is on Trial?

The Mason family moved to our town many years ago, in the depth of the great depression. Mrs. Mason and the children came at once to church and Bible school, but Mr. Mason would not attend.

In another town, Mason had been a prosperous businessman, an elder in the church, the superintendent of the Sunday school. Then came the crash of 1929. His business failed, and he lost his home. In our town he found a job and made a living, but with a reduced standard of living.

So Mr. Mason was through with God. He thought God had treated him badly. Why should he do anything for God when God was not doing anything for him? Or was there really a God at all? As Mason saw it, God was on trial, and He failed the test because He did not do for Mason what Mason wanted Him to do.

As Job saw it, God was not on trial. God was great and good. There was no question about that. Job was on trial. Would he maintain his integrity in spite of everything?

What do you think? Who is on trial?

C. Another Trial

The Masons were not the only people who came to our town during the depression. The Millers arrived at church in a dilapidated Model T Ford, and their cheery friendliness won a cordial welcome.

Mrs. Miller was a widow, past seventy and frail. Her son Bob was past forty and afflicted with tuberculosis. In those days the desert was thought to be good for victims of that disease, so the two loaded what they could into the Model T and headed west.

At our town they did not have enough money left to fill the gas tank. Learning that there was open desert beyond the irrigation canal only a mile from town, they decided this was the place where God wanted them to stay.

With scraps of lumber and discarded metal roofing, they put together a tiny shack with corrugated cardboard walls.

Perceptive ladies of the church welcomed the newcomers with a food shower. Men chipped in with a rusty wood-burning stove and a supply of firewood. In spite of his handicap, Bob soon was finding enough odd jobs to earn a meager living, and every Sunday a tenth of his earnings went into the collection plate.

Nobody in our town was more thankful, more cheerful, or more godly than the Millers.

D. You Can Do Right

You can do right. That is the message of this lesson. Satan did his worst to Job, and Job grew better instead of worse. You can do the same.

The devil is still walking up and down in the earth, intent on making trouble. Perhaps he has robbed you of riches and family and health. On the other hand, he may have given you such an abundance of wealth that you feel secure and see no need of God. Satan's temptations come to us in many ways.

No matter what temptations come to you, you can do right. If you ever give in to temptation, it is your own fault. "God is faithful, who will not suffer you to be tempted above that ye are able; but will with the temptation also make a way to escape, that ye may be able to bear it" (1 Corinthians 10:13).

The devil is limited. God will not let him bring you any more temptation than you can resist. If you ever give in to temptation, it is not because the temptation is irresistible; it is because you do not do your best.

You can do right. Job proved it, and you can prove it again. It's up to you.

E. Prayer

Thank You for Job, our Father. Thank You for his heroic example of fortitude and unfailing integrity. As we dedicate ourselves anew to Your service, we look to You for help to maintain our integrity and to do right even though the devil does his worst.

F. Thought to Remember

O fear not in a world like this,
    And thou shalt know ere long,
Know how sublime a thing it is
    To suffer and be strong.
                                    —LONGFELLOW

Learning by Doing

*This page contains an alternate lesson plan emphasizing learning activities. Classes
desiring such student involvement will find these suggestions helpful.*

Learning Goals

Having studied today's lesson with the class,
the learner will be able to:

1. Describe both Job's material and spiritual
status.

2. Identify at least three of the ways in which
Satan works or is restrained by God.

3. Resolve some of his own confusion about
God and Satan's work in his life.

Into the Lesson

Contact the teacher of one of the children's
classes (preschool/Primary) two weeks before
today's class. Ask that the children cooperate in
recording on tape a short segment blending the
following sounds: sheep baa-ing, cows mooing,
camels snorting, donkeys braying, and children
singing. Get all the sounds separately as well as
blended into a loud cacophony.

As the class begins, play this recording; then
ask, "How does this relate to today's text in Job 1
and 2?" Be sure the answer is related to this
idea: "These are all sounds that surrounded Job
in his prosperity." See Job 1:2, 3. This will allow
you to move directly to the following activity,
which further characterizes Job.

Into the Word

The student book contains the following eight
sentences. If your class does not use this book,
write the sentences (without underlining) on the
chalkboard or an overhead transparency and
give the students these directions: "Each of
these sentences contains a 'hidden' adjective
appropriately describing Job as seen in today's
text. Find and underline the hidden words." You
may do the first as an example. Ask the class to
identify the verse in Job 1:1—2:10 that is relevant to each word found.

1. Job appeared to have God's anointing *cup
right* in his hand. (1:1)

2. Job affirmed, "We can send one co*w or ship
ful*l caravans all across the east!" (1:5)

3. I*f a mous*e came into Job's property, he
would be lost among all the animals. (1:3)

4. Job had so many animals he said, "More
than once a year *I ch*ange oases." (1:3)

5. Job was known near and *far; me*rchants
spread his name. (1:3)

6. Satan claimed, "Only your hedge, God,
en*ables sedu*lous behavior in Job." (1:10)

7. Job moaned, "The Lord has left my s*ide; so
late* He has abandoned me to poverty." (1:21)

8. But Job continued, "Yet I will no*t rue* the
day I met Him and loved Him; He is faithful, He
is God." (2:10)

After this have two of your best oral readers
stand before the class and read aloud these two
Scripture sections: (1) Job 1:1-16, and (2) Job
1:17—2:10.

If your class is not using the student book (in
which the following activity is found) distribute
blank half sheets of paper. Direct the students to
establish four columns headed Job, Job's Wife,
Satan, God. Prepare flash cards with the following words, one word to a card: *accommodating,
confident, fair, foolish, great, impudent, mistaken, perfect, persistent, presumptuous, rash,
reasonable, resolute* (or other words of your own
choice, as related to the characters of the text).
Show the words one at a time, and direct the
learners to write each word under the name(s) of
the four story characters whom the word describes. After all the words are shown and recorded, let the class share the results. Several
words could be appropriately listed under more
than one character; such placements will allow
discussion of the text and its meaning.

Into Life

Prepare the following on separate strips of
paper. Either ask for volunteers or distribute randomly. Have each read aloud, and then ask,
"How does today's text confirm this truth?" and
"How does this truth relate to your life?"

1. It is possible for one to be perfect in God's
sight.

2. Riches do not necessarily corrupt a man.

3. Loss of material possessions is not adequate reason for despair.

4. Worship is the appropriate response to difficult times.

5. Fault Satan as you will, credit him for his
persistence.

6. Watching a loved one suffer may be as
much a temptation to sin as is undergoing suffering itself.

7. Sometimes bad things happen to good people *because* they are good.

8. One cannot expect to be trouble-free simply because he lives a good life.

9. Sorrow may be the means of inner growth.

Let's Talk It Over

The questions on this page are designed to encourage review of the lesson Scriptures and to promote discussion of the lesson by the class. The answers provided are only discussion starters. Let your class talk it over from there.

1. How can suffering exist in a world created and controlled by an all-powerful, good God?

In a word, the answer emerges from one reality: *freedom.* God created mankind with the freedom to make moral choices. Only where freedom to choose exists can there be any meaning. If there is no choice, then the world is a marionette theater, God is the master puppeteer, and we all are puppets—without meaning, without life. Man's tragic history reveals the initial and the continuing choices of wrong instead of right; of sin instead of righteousness. Evil and suffering result from our abuse of freedom, in our choosing to rebel against the Creator's will and purpose for mankind. Everything God created was "good"; suffering results from man's choice of the "bad."

2. The word *perfect* doesn't mean flawless, but *mature* or *complete* (in terms of the original purpose or intention). What, then, are the characteristics of a *mature* person?

Maturity is a relative term; no one is mature all the time, in all facets of life. However, some marks of maturity can be delineated. The mature person may be characterized in the following ways: (1) Discriminating. He doesn't swallow everything. He tests, evaluates, sifts. (2) Self-motivating. He doesn't depend on external stimuli to get him to move appropriately. (3) Congruent. The "outer" is consistent with the "inner," which is to say a person's speech and behavior match one's character. (4) Integrated. The various facets of life are related in a harmonious pattern. What a person is as a Christian ties everything together; for example, work, family, leisure, finances, worship. (5) Comprehensive. This harmonious pattern includes *all* of life. Suffering, loss, and death are gathered up along with the good in one's understanding of life. (6) Self-improving. A mature person wants to improve, so he searches, learns, and grows. Check Job out—he's remarkably mature!

3. Why do bad things happen to good people?

Those who promote the cult of "health and happiness" would have us believe that if we are "right with the Lord," we will be healthy, wealthy, and wise. The Bible reveals otherwise. Bad things happen to good people because of Satan. Read the book of Job again and notice the source of Job's troubles. So today, natural disasters (tornadoes, floods) bring death and destruction without any relationship to the guilt or innocence of the persons involved. Disease strikes the good and the bad. One person's actions may impact another person adversely (the drunken driver kills the little child on the sidewalk). Bad things happen to good people because of man's sin, affecting relationships and even the environment. Bad things will continue to happen to good people until the final redemption of the creature and the created order.

4. Cite some ways in which spouses often fail each other in times of crisis.

Mrs. Job offers a prime example. Her advice stings: "Curse God, and die!" Withholding encouragement, criticizing, refusing to maintain faith, disavowing personal loyalty, and even offering well-meaning advice can constitute failure in a crisis. One who is facing a crisis needs the support, prayer, and the steady presence of his mate.

5. What are some potential positive results from suffering?

Out of suffering we can emerge bitter or better. The "better" finds expression in the following ways: (1) growth (spiritual, emotional, intellectual); (2) witness (to God's presence and power during the crisis); (3) inspiration for fellow sufferers (to respond to suffering in a similar manner); (4) identification with other sufferers (new sensitivity toward suffering and needs—essential to healthy relationships and ministry).

6. What can we learn from Job about coping with crises?

Trust is the key element of personal faith and commitment. Job didn't understand what happened to him; but still he trusted God! Isaiah 26:3 says it all: "Thou wilt keep him in perfect peace, whose mind is stayed on thee: because he trusteth in thee." We learn to draw resources from within, not just without. Job's wife and friends failed him, but his faith did not.

Job and His Friends

LESSON SCRIPTURE: Job 2:11-13; 4:1-9; 8:1-10; 11; 13:1-12.

PRINTED TEXT: Job 4:1, 7, 8; 8:1, 5-7; 11:1, 4-6; 13:1-5.

Job 4:1, 7, 8

1 Then Eliphaz the Temanite answered and said,

. . . .

7 Remember, I pray thee, who ever perished, being innocent? Or where were the righteous cut off?

8 Even as I have seen, they that plow iniquity, and sow wickedness, reap the same.

Job 8:1, 5-7

1 Then answered Bildad the Shuhite, and said,

. . . .

5 If thou wouldest seek unto God betimes, and make thy supplication to the Almighty;

6 If thou wert pure and upright; surely now he would awake for thee, and make the habitation of thy righteousness prosperous.

7 Though thy beginning was small, yet thy latter end should greatly increase.

Job 11:1, 4-6

1 Then answered Zophar the Naamathite, and said,

. . . .

4 For thou hast said, My doctrine is pure, and I am clean in thine eyes.

5 But oh that God would speak, and open his lips against thee;

6 And that he would show thee the secrets of wisdom, that they are double to that which is! Know therefore that God exacteth of thee less than thine iniquity deserveth.

Job 13:1-5

1 Lo, mine eye hath seen all this, mine ear hath heard and understood it.

2 What ye know, the same do I know also: I am not inferior unto you.

3 Surely I would speak to the Almighty, and I desire to reason with God.

4 But ye are forgers of lies, ye are all physicians of no value.

5 Oh that ye would altogether hold your peace! And it should be your wisdom.

GOLDEN TEXT: To him that is afflicted pity should be showed from his friend.
—Job 6:14.

Through Suffering to Hope
Unit 1: Job—Probing the Meaning of Suffering (Lessons 1-4)

Lesson Aims

After this lesson students should be able to:

1. Briefly summarize what Job's friends said to him and what he replied.

2. Consider the work of the Lord that is going on here and now, and find some need to meet.

3. Make a larger sacrifice of time or effort or money.

Lesson Outline

INTRODUCTION
  A. Shocked Silence
  B. Lesson Background
I. THE SPEECH OF FRIENDS (Job 4:1, 7, 8; 8:1, 5-7; 11:1, 4-6)
  A. Eliphaz (4:1, 7, 8)
  B. Bildad (8:1, 5-7)
  C. Zophar (11:1, 4-6)
II. JOB'S REPLY (Job 13:1-5)
  A. About God (vv. 1-3)
  B. About Job's Friends (vv. 4, 5)
    What to Make of It
Conclusion
  A. A Daring Thought
  B. Sowing and Reaping
  C. A Place to Sow
  D. Keep the Faith
  E. Prayer
  F. Thought to Remember

Display visual 2 from the visuals/learning resources packet. It illustrates section A under the Conclusion. It is shown on page 20.

Introduction

News had a way of getting around long before it was ever seen on TV or published in a newspaper. When sudden disaster overwhelmed Job, His three friends soon got together and went to see him and comfort him (Job 2:11).

A. Shocked Silence

Though they knew what had happened, the three were not prepared for the sight that met their eyes. They saw Job sitting abjectly in the ashes (Job 2:8, 12). His clothing was torn; his head was bald; his body was covered with hideous sores (Job 1:20; 2:7). Could that be Job?

They had come to bring comfort, but now words failed them. Weeping aloud and tearing their own garments, they sat down to share his grief. For a week they sat there speechless in the dust (Job 2:12, 13).

B. Lesson Background

Finally Job broke the silence with a long wail. What he said fills chapter 3 of his book, but the substance of it can be condensed into two sentences: "I wish I had never been born! Why can't I die and get this over with?"

I. The Speech of Friends
(Job 4:1, 7, 8; 8:1, 5-7; 11:1, 4-6)

At last the friends found their voices. One by one they poured out long chapters of instruction and advice. Our text brings us a few brief samples of their speaking.

A. Eliphaz (4:1, 7, 8)

1. Then Eliphaz the Temanite answered and said.

Teman was a place in Edom, south of the Dead Sea. *Temanite* can mean that *Eliphaz* was a citizen of that place, or it can mean that he was a member of the family or clan headed by a man named Teman. Very probably he was both.

7. Remember, I pray thee, who ever perished, being innocent? Or where were the righteous cut off?

The theme of Eliphaz' lecture is that disaster does not come to the *innocent*, but to the guilty; not to the *righteous*, but to the evil. God is just: He punishes those who do wrong. Job was having very bad troubles, therefore he must be guilty of very bad wrongdoing.

8. Even as I have seen, they that plow iniquity, and sow wickedness, reap the same.

"Whatsoever a man soweth, that shall he also reap" (Galatians 6:7). This truth is so well established that we sometimes forget a man may also reap what he does not sow. In a parable, Jesus told of one who sowed good seed, but found tares growing with the wheat (Matthew 13:24-30). "An enemy hath done this," the planter explained. Job's misery likewise was due to an enemy. But Eliphaz did not think about that possibility. He said we reap what we sow. Since Job was reaping misery in abundance, he must have sowed evil in abundance.

B. Bildad (8:1, 5-7)

1. Then answered Bildad the Shuhite, and said.

Shuhite may mean that *Bildad* came from a place called Shuah. If so, the place cannot be located exactly. It must have been in the east country, not too far from Job's home in Uz. However, Shuah may have been a man rather than a place, and the *Shuhite* may have been a member of his family or clan. Some students note that one of Abraham's later sons was called Shuah, and this son probably went to the east country (Genesis 25:2, 6). Bildad may have been of that man's family, but we cannot be sure of this. And of course Shuah may have been the name both of a clan and of the region where that clan lived.

5, 6. If thou wouldest seek unto God betimes, and make thy supplication to the Almighty; if thou wert pure and upright; surely now he would awake for thee, and make the habitation of thy righteousness prosperous.

Bildad agreed with Eliphaz' estimate of the situation. But Bildad said Job need not be without hope. God is just. If Job would stop his sinning, if he would be *pure and upright,* and if he would *seek unto God* and pray to *the Almighty,* God would still give him prosperity.

7. Though thy beginning was small, yet thy latter end should greatly increase.

Prosperity might not come to Job quickly, Bildad said, but it would grow if he would live as he ought to live. Bildad himself was righteous and prosperous. It was easy for him to conclude that anyone who was righteous would be prosperous. In fact, that was what had happened in the life of Job before disaster struck. To Bildad it seemed reasonable to conclude that Job's goodness had failed before his prosperity had departed.

C. Zophar (11:1, 4-6)

1. Then answered Zophar the Naamathite, and said.

Naamathite connects *Zophar* with Naamah. Like Teman or Shuah, this may be either a place or a tribe or both.

4. For thou hast said, My doctrine is pure, and I am clean in thine eyes.

Job refused to accept the conclusion that his great suffering was punishment for his great sin. Recalling his past life, he could not see that he had been a great sinner. He challenged his friends to show him any wrong he had done (Job 6:24). He went so far as to say that God destroys good people as well as bad (9:22). But all of Job's protests only made his friends more determined to convince him that he had sinned, that he was being punished, and that his only hope lay in repentance.

5. But oh that God would speak, and open his lips against thee.

As this friend saw it, Job was stubbornly resisting the truth of the whole matter. Zophar

---

How to Say It

BILDAD. *Bil*-dad.
ELIPHAZ. *El*-ih-faz.
NAAMATHITE. *Nay*-uh-muth-ite.
SHUAH. *Shoo*-ah.
SHUHITE. *Shoo*-hite.
TEMANITE. *Tee*-mun-ite.
ZOPHAR. *Zo*-far.

---

wished God would join in the debate, for he felt sure God would agree with him and the others who spoke against Job.

6a. And that he would show thee the secrets of wisdom, that they are double to that which is!

Since the friends had not convinced Job that he was a great sinner, Zophar was wishing that God would help them. He could show *secrets of wisdom* that were hidden from Job—perhaps some that were hidden from the friends. They felt quite sure they were right, but God with His superior wisdom might be more convincing to Job. *That they are double to that which is.* The meaning of the Hebrew here is uncertain. The *New International Version* translates it "for true wisdom has two sides." The *American Standard Version* reads, "for he is manifold in understanding." Whatever the exact meaning may be, Zophar was thinking that God could bring to the debate some deeper wisdom; and he felt sure it would confirm what he and his friends had been trying to tell Job. Of course Zophar had no way of knowing, as we do, that God had pronounced Job "a perfect and an upright man, one that feareth God, and escheweth evil" (Job 1:8).

6b. Know therefore that God exacteth of thee less than thine iniquity deserveth.

If God would explain the situation, then Job would see that he deserved even more punishment than he was getting. So thought Zophar. As he saw it, there had to be some terrible sin or sins in Job's life to bring on his terrible affliction. Zophar had not seen any such sin or sins in Job. He had no idea what they might be. But he thought he saw Job sinning again by hiding those sins and refusing to confess them even at the urging of his friends.

II. Job's Reply
(Job 13:1-5)

Our printed text for today presents only small samples from the long arguments of Job's three friends. Job gave long answers after the lectures of Eliphaz and Bildad, and our printed text has

visual 2

IF
A MAN
DIE,
SHALL HE
LIVE?

bypassed them too. Now we come to another answer from Job. It fills three chapters (12—14), but our text gives us just a five-verse sample of his speech.

A. About God (vv. 1-3)

1. Lo, mine eye hath seen all this, mine ear hath heard and understood it.

Chapter 12 sings at length about the power and wisdom of God. Job knew about these. He had seen evidence of them; he had heard and accepted the teaching of others about them.

2. What ye know, the same do I know also: I am not inferior unto you.

Job's friends praised the greatness of God. In that Job agreed. They said goodness brings good results and wickedness brings bad results, and that is true. But they were wrong in saying that Job's troubles were the result of his sin.

Why is it so hard to correct false teachers? One reason is that they tell the truth so much. If we try to contradict everything they say, we find ourselves in the wrong. We need to compare their teaching point by point with the Scripture, put a finger on what is false, and contradict that only. This may be hard to do, because even their falsehood may seem to be based on truth. Consider the reasoning of Job's friends:

1. God is in charge. *True.*
2. God is just and good. *True.*
3. God rewards those who do good. *True.*
4. God punishes those who do evil. *True.*
5. Job is being punished. *Apparently true.*
6. Therefore Job has done evil. *False.*

Certainly the friends thought the conclusion was logical, but it was not true. They had not been with Job continually. It was easy to suppose he had done evil unknown to them. But we have God's own description of Job. That man was perfect and upright.

How could they be so wrong? They oversimplified the matter. It is true that God is in charge and has all power. It is true that He does nothing wrong. But He *allows* some things that are

wrong. That is a fact, whether we understand His reason for allowing wrong or not. The friends did not take that fact into their thinking.

Whatever we do, let's keep our faith in God. Besides, let's be careful about condemning our friends.

3. Surely I would speak to the Almighty, and I desire to reason with God.

Zophar was wishing that God would enter the debate and explain things to Job (Job 11:5, 6). Fervently Job joined in that wish. He was sure his friends did not have the right explanation of his suffering, but neither did he. He longed for God to tell what it was all about.

B. About Job's Friends (vv. 4, 5)

4. But ye are forgers of lies, ye are all physicians of no value.

Racked by pain and assailed by the repeated accusations of his friends, Job had been thinking earnestly about his past life. It simply was not true that he had been a very great sinner. His life had been mostly upright and righteous, and he knew it. His friends came with a preconceived idea. They held that God is just, and therefore goodness is always rewarded and evil is always punished. Job was suffering more loss and pain than anyone else, so they thought he must have sinned more than anyone else. Vigorously they hammered away at their arguments, but they were hammering out lies. The facts were against them. Job's life had been good. They thought his claim was false; but from the information given to us, we know it was correct. By God's own estimate, Job was "a perfect and an upright man." Was there any remedy for job's pain and loss? His friends prescribed repentance. They said he should stop sinning and do right, but they were *physicians of no value.* He had been doing right all along. He could not repent of sins he had not committed.

5. Oh that ye would altogether hold your peace! And it should be your wisdom.

Job's friends were denying the facts in order to support their theory. Thus they became worthless physicians and "forgers of lies." The best and wisest and most helpful thing they could do would be to shut up!

WHAT TO MAKE OF IT

In *Romeo and Juliet* the watchman comes upon the scene at Juliet's tomb and sees the carnage. There is Juliet, freshly dead by a dagger strike. Paris is slain; Romeo is poisoned. The watchman says that he sees "the ground whereon these woes do lie; but the true ground of all these piteous woes" he cannot understand without further detail. In other words, he could see the facts before him—three dead persons and how they died—but he couldn't understand or explain.

Job's suffering brought essentially the same response from him. He and his three friends were all equally experienced in the wisdom of their time. He knew why his friends had come. He heard what they were saying. And he knew their conclusions were wrong. Nothing that was happening to him made sense. And the torture in his soul screamed for an explanation.

Just as neither Job nor his friends had the answer, neither do we. We can identify the origin of suffering; that occurred with the fall of man. We can say that positive results may come from suffering. But further we cannot go. In the end, explanations often raise as many questions as they answer. Only faith in a loving God proves equal to the test of uninvited burdens. —V. H.

Conclusion

We are far from the end of the book of Job. The next two studies will bring us some samples from its later chapters. But we can hardly close this lesson without looking beyond our text to a sublime conclusion that Job found along the way, or without noting some significant thoughts for our own problems.

A. A Daring Thought

Job was bewildered. He had tried to do right. He had been honest and kind and helpful and generous. But he had lost everything he had except his wife, and she was giving him no help. In addition, he was afflicted with a disease that was as hideous as it was painful. It wasn't fair!

Through all his agony, Job rejected the ultimate mistake: he would not doubt God. Firmly he declared, "Though he slay me, yet will I trust in him" (Job 13:15). God was wise and powerful. He was just, and yet what was happening was unjust. A good man was suffering, and seemed doomed to die. How could that be?

In Job's tortured mind this dilemma gave birth to a daring thought. He was about to die unjustly. Could it be possible that things would be made right *after* death? A tree that is cut down may grow up again (Job 14:7-9). "If a man die, shall he live again?" (Job 14:14).

Job had none of the Christian teaching that is plain to us. He could not pin his hope on the fact of Christ's resurrection. He did not even have the law and the prophets. No book of the Bible had yet been written. Yet that daring thought took root in his mind and grew.

Thinking over what he had seen through all the years of his life, Job knew that his case was

not the only one in which justice was lacking. It was not true, as his friends insisted, that goodness was always rewarded and wickedness was always punished in this world. Crooks sometimes got rich (Job 12:6); yet after all Job's goodness he was reduced to poverty and was close to death. So there *had* to be an adjustment after death, otherwise there was not justice anywhere. So Job's thinking soared to a triumphant conclusion:

> I know that my Redeemer lives,
> and that in the end he will stand upon the earth.
> And after my skin has been destroyed,
> yet in my flesh I will see God:
> I myself will see him
> with my own eyes—I, and not another.
> How my heart yearns within me!
> —Job 19:25-27, *New International Version*

With assurance made doubly sure by our Lord's triumph over death, we echo Job's words in a glorious hymn of security in Christ:

> I know, I know that Jesus liveth,
> And on the earth again shall stand;
> I know, I know that life He giveth,
> That grace and pow'r are in His hand.
> —JESSIE BROWN POUNDS

B. Sowing and Reaping

We reap what we sow. This is as plain in a tiny backyard garden as it is in the Kansas wheat fields that stretch away to the horizon, and it is confirmed in Scripture (Galatians 6:7). Yet Eliphaz was wrong when he concluded that Job's trouble was the result of Job's own sowing.

No backyard gardener expects to start picking tomatoes the day after he plants them. There is a time of waiting, and with the waiting there is a battle with weeds—a battle as old as Adam's sin (Genesis 3:17-19).

We share the error of Eliphaz if we think doing right is sure to bring instant and complete happiness. The final harvest may be a long way off. Sacrificial Christian living does have tremendous rewards here and now, Jesus said, but with the rewards it has persecution and tribulation. The final harvest is in Heaven (Mark 10:29, 30; John 16:33; Matthew 5:11).

Through centuries the prophets of God were persecuted (Matthew 5:12; 23:37; Acts 7:52). Jesus was crucified (Mark 15:25). His apostles were jailed and beaten (Acts 5:17, 18, 40). Stephen was stoned (Acts 7:59). James was killed with a sword (Acts 12:2). Paul was jailed uncounted times, whipped at least eight times, once stoned and left for dead (2 Corinthians 11:23-25; Acts 14:19). Such things can be endured because "great is your reward in heaven" (Matthew 5:12).

Not many of us are in danger of prison or beating or death because of our faith. Since we are not compelled to give up liberty or possessions or comfort, do we conclude that no sacrifice is expected of us?

In the past week, did you give up a few hours of fun in order to take some part in Christian service?

How long has it been since you deliberately decided to do without some expensive thing so you could make a generous offering to the cause of Christ?

Can you remember a time when you saw a Christian task that was distasteful to you, but took it on because it was needed?

The Bible says, "He which soweth sparingly shall reap also sparingly; and he which soweth bountifully shall reap also bountifully" (2 Corinthians 9:6). Are we sowing too sparingly, and yet hoping to reap bountifully all the benefits Christ can give in this life and the next?

C. A Place to Sow

If you survey the work Christ is doing through your church, you will see some need that you can meet or help to meet if you are willing to make the sacrifice.

One senior saint made it his special duty and joy to keep the church lawn free from dandelions.

A group of men took turns in mowing the lawn, always taking time to trim the edges and remove every weed from shrubbery and flowers.

Many good ladies and some fine couples find joy in ministering to the sick, enlisting others when they are needed to help with transportation, cooking, or housework.

The owner of a hardware store finds time to get acquainted with newcomers in the area. He does not just invite them to church; he takes his big station wagon and brings them, introducing them to congenial people.

Two or three days each week, a housewife helps with secretarial work in the church office.

A retired schoolteacher gathers a group of housewives for prayer and Bible study every Tuesday morning.

A music teacher likes to take two or three of her students together to sing cheerful songs to someone who is shut in and lonely.

D. Keep the Faith

Eliphaz remarked that "man is born unto trouble, as the sparks fly upward" (Job 5:7). Every person comes into trouble sometime. Not many are buried in it as deeply as Job was, but no one escapes it altogether.

Many of us have had financial troubles, losing a job or a business or a home. As we get along in years, most of us lose some loved ones, though few lose ten family members in a day. Many of us have been laid low by sickness or injury, some of us for a long time.

When trouble comes, many of us ask why, as Job did. It isn't fair! God is just and good; how can He let good people have trouble they do not deserve? Such questioning drives some people to doubt that God is just and good, or that He cares, or even that He exists. Job was driven the other way. Refusing to doubt God, he was driven to the sublime conclusion that even if he died the Redeemer still would make things right.

It is a fact that trouble makes us stronger *if we keep the faith.* "We also rejoice in our sufferings, because we know that suffering produces perseverance; perseverance, character; and character, hope. And hope does not disappoint us, because God has poured out his love into our hearts by the Holy Spirit, whom he has given us" (Romans 5:3-5, *New International Version*). If our troubles make us better, isn't that reason enough for God to allow them? But they make us better only if we keep the faith.

> Faith of our fathers! holy faith!
> We will be true to thee till death!

E. Prayer

Almighty God, thank You for the assurance that Your power and wisdom have no limit, and that Your justice and mercy will prevail for eternity, even beyond the grave. May this study of Your Word build up our faith, strengthen our will, and give our bodies vigor to press on with the work we have to do in Jesus' name. Amen.

F. Thought to Remember

I know that my Redeemer lives.

Home Daily Bible Readings

Monday, Sept. 5—Job's Friends Come to Him (Job 2:11—2:10)

Tuesday, Sept. 6—Job Bewails His Fate (Job 3:11-26)

Wednesday, Sept. 7—Eliphaz Consoles Job (Job 4:1-9)

Thursday, Sept. 8—Bildad Accuses Job (Job 8:1-10)

Friday, Sept. 9—Zophar Regards God as Just (Job 11:1-12)

Saturday, Sept. 10—Zophar Says Job Has Sinned (Job 11:13-20)

Sunday, Sept. 11—Job Rebukes His Friends (Job 13:1-12)

Learning by Doing

This page contains an alternate lesson plan emphasizing learning activities. Classes desiring such student involvement will find these suggestions helpful.

Learning Goals

This lesson should enable a student to:

1. Recall the attacks made on Job and point out the fallacy in each.

2. Deal with the afflictions of his friends in a more compassionate and a more Biblically correct manner.

Into the Lesson

Either use three old get-well cards or purchase three to use for the following activity. Introduce these as a new "line" of get-well cards. Open the cards and read the messages, as follows: (1) "Sorry to see you in pain and distress; But I think I know what's causing this mess. You've sinned and to all it's abundantly clear. Now, I hope soon you'll be better, my dear!" (2) "You have sinned and now you hurt. But you can soon be whole. Remember God, repent, and cry. The truth has now been told!" (3) "You may think that this is bad, But just you wait and see: If God had given what you deserve, You'd be worse by two or three!"

Assuming your class will be amused by these exaggerated accusations against Job, ask them now to listen to the speeches of Job's friends as they sought to comfort/correct him.

Into the Word

Write each of the three brief speeches below on a separate sheet of paper (minus the Scripture references). Give the speeches to three class members sometime before class so they will be prepared to read them with feeling. These are paraphrases of the speeches of Eliphaz (chapters 4, 5), Bildad (chapter 8), and Zophar (chapter 11). Put the three names on signs to be worn around the necks of the three speakers. Have a fourth class member prepared to be Job and to read Job 12:1—13:5.

To begin this drama, have Job's three friends stand over and around Job, who is seated and virtually covered by a dark blanket.

Eliphaz: "We can't help but speak to correct you, Job (4:1, 2). When others have been stricken, you've always had the right words, but now you can't take it (4:3-5). You know that what a man sows he reaps; that is God's ordained scheme of things (4:7-9). Man *is* born for trouble (5;1-7). You should be happy that God cares enough to correct you (5:17, 18). Sooner or later He is going to redeem you from your afflictions" (5:19-26).

Bildad: "Job, how long are you going to talk foolishly? (8:2). Are you accusing God of being unfair? Unjust? (8:3). All you have to do is seek God in prayer (8:5). If you *were* pure and upright, He would come right this minute and make you prosperous once again (8:6, 7). Former generations would all teach you the same thing (8:8-10): if a man forgets God, all his hope is gone (8:11-13). Job, you know God will not cast away a perfect man!" (8:20).

Zophar: "Job, you are full of lies and mocking. Talk is cheap, and the number of your words makes them no less cheap (8:2, 3). You have said, 'I am pure in doctrine; I am clean in life' (11:4). Oh, I wish God himself would come and accuse you; I wish you could be taught by words right off His lips (11:5). Then you'd understand that if God gave you what you deserved, you'd be twice as miserable as you are (11:6). You'll never understand God; His wisdom is too high, too deep, for a little mind like yours (11:7, 8). But it's not too late, Job. Repent; put away iniquity; lift your face to Him!"

Unison: "Job, you are a terrible sinner. Repent and God will make everything right."

At this, the three friends should crumple the sheets and toss them disgustedly at Job. Then Job should stand abruptly, cast aside his blanket, and read Job 12:1—13:5, preferably from a contemporary language version. You may want Job's "friends" to be seated at the front. When Job has concluded his response, examine the three friends' speeches a line at a time, asking the class to match the ideas with specific verses from the related chapters. (The Scripture references are a guide for the teacher.)

Into Life

Discuss the following general questions related to the speeches of the friends: (1) What errors did the friends make in their attempt to minister to Job? (2) How do people today make the same mistakes in dealing with friends and associates who are distressed?

Have the students examine chapters 4—12 (two chapters per student) to make a list of encouraging statements that would be appropriate for a true "get-well" card. Job 9:4a is an example. Let the students share their findings.

Let's Talk It Over

*The questions on this page are designed to encourage review of the lesson
Scriptures and to promote discussion of the lesson by the class. The answers
provided are only discussion starters. Let your class talk it over from there.*

**1. What are some characteristics of a *true*
friend?**

The true friend embodies these characteristics: (1) Loyalty. This says, "You can count on
me to stand by you, come what may. Others may
desert you, circumstances may turn against you,
but I won't." (2) Acceptance. The nonjudgmental attitude, which accepts you for who you are
and what you are, prevails. Approval or condoning of beliefs or life-style is neither relevant
nor needed. (3) Sensitivity. Empathy (entering
into another's inner world of meanings and feelings) shows sensitivity by getting in touch with
that person's experience. (4) Encouragement.
The "booster" helps tremendously, especially
when you are depressed. The true friend constitutes a one-man construction gang, building
you up. (5) Flexibility. The "no way but my
way" approach to relationship disavows real
friendship. The true friend expresses openness,
the prizing of the other, and partnership in the
relationship. (6) Availability. The one who says,
"When you need me, I'll be there for you," is the
one who counts. The true friend embodies mature love (unconditional self-giving that seeks
the highest good of the other.

**2. Cite some reasons why all of us need
friends, especially in times of crisis.**

Everyone needs a support system for these
reasons: (1) To provide strength. There is
strength in numbers, as opposed to the weakness that many persons feel when they are
alone. Wolves, in preying upon a young moose,
will isolate the victim from its mother or from
the herd. When the victim is alone, it is vulnerable. Our networks of friends can provide much-needed strength. (2) To minister to needs. God
provides resources for us through other Christians. Through them we know His love and
grace and power. In time of crisis ministry becomes potent and pertinent. (3) To short-circuit
pride and any unwarranted feelings of self-sufficiency. In acknowledging interdependence,
we admit we are not adequate in and of ourselves. We do not harbor a false independence
that asserts, "I don't need anyone." We praise
God for His people, the fellowship of concern,
the family that cares.

**3. Job accused his three friends of being
worthless physicians whose best help would be
to remain silent. What significant insight does
this suggest for those who would help suffering
friends?**

Many people feel inadequate in the face of
suffering and loss experienced by a friend.
"What should I say?" they ask themselves. They
may feel that they just don't have the right
words for the situation. Job helps us here. There
are times when the sensitive, caring, supportive
presence of a friend is needed more than words.
In many cases the sufferer doesn't remember
words that were spoken, but who was there as a
needed, supportive friend. No one is more deluded than the person who says to himself, "I'm
effective in ministering to suffering people because I know just the right words to say." Job's
friends also thought they had all the right
words, but their words only added to Job's burdens and woes. There is a silence in suffering in
which words may only offend and intrude. The
hug, the squeeze of the hand, the arm around
the shoulder, the being there (to wait, to listen
when the other wishes to share) all speak eloquently in a nonverbal way to the one who is
suffering. Remember that the nonverbal communication is far more powerful than the verbal.

**4. Why are worn-out platitudes so defective
in comforting sufferers? Give some examples of
such platitudes.**

These platitudes convey one's insensitivity to
the sufferer and expose his lack of understanding. They sound like a "stock-in-trade" that is
pulled out for situation No. 17. Here are some
examples: "I know just how you feel." (No you
don't. If you did, you wouldn't talk like this.)
"This is God's will for your life." (How do you
know? Did God give you a special revelation?)
"She lived a long, full life and was ready to go."
(That may be; but I'm not grieving for her; I'm
grieving for me. I'm the one who is suffering
significant loss.) "You'll be OK; you'll have another baby." (But I don't want another baby. I
loved this one and he's gone.) "It must be a relief
that it's all over." (Sure, caring for him was
draining; but I was *needed*. Those were such
close times, and I miss him terribly.)

Job Takes His Case to God

LESSON SCRIPTURE: Job 29:1—30:27.

PRINTED TEXT: Job 29:1-6; 30:19-26.

Job 29:1-6

1 Moreover Job continued his parable, and said,

2 Oh that I were as in months past, as in the days when God preserved me;

3 When his candle shined upon my head, and when by his light I walked through darkness;

4 As I was in the days of my youth, when the secret of God was upon my tabernacle;

5 When the Almighty was yet with me, when my children were about me;

6 When I washed my steps with butter, and the rock poured me out rivers of oil.

Job 30:19-26

19 He hath cast me into the mire, and I am become like dust and ashes.

20 I cry unto thee, and thou dost not hear me: I stand up, and thou regardest me not.

21 Thou art become cruel to me: with thy strong hand thou opposest thyself against me.

22 Thou liftest me up to the wind; thou causest me to ride upon it, and dissolvest my substance.

23 For I know that thou wilt bring me to death, and to the house appointed for all living.

24 Howbeit he will not stretch out his hand to the grave, though they cry in his destruction.

25 Did not I weep for him that was in trouble? Was not my soul grieved for the poor?

26 When I looked for good, then evil came unto me: and when I waited for light, there came darkness.

GOLDEN TEXT: Wherefore hidest thou thy face, and holdest me for thine enemy?
—Job 13:24.

Through Suffering to Hope
Unit 1: Job – Probing the Meaning of Suffering (Lessons 1-4)

Lesson Aims

After studying this lesson a student should be able to:

1. Contrast Job's prosperous condition before his disaster with his deplorable condition afterward.

2. Recall the real reason for the disasters Job experienced, and tell what Job's friends thought the reason was.

3. Admire the strength of character with which Job kept his faith in God through all his troubles.

4. Resolve to resist and defeat the devil in every encounter with him.

Lesson Outline

INTRODUCTION
   A. The Great Debate
   B. Lesson Background
I. THE GOOD OLD DAYS (Job 29:1-6)
   A. Safety (vv. 1-3)
   B. Friendship (vv. 4, 5)
   C. Prosperity (v. 6)
     Look Forward, Not Back
II. THE BAD DAYS (Job 30:19-26)
   A. Unanswered Plea (vv. 19, 20)
   B. Cruel Pressure (vv. 21-23)
   C. Destruction Undeserved (vv. 24-26)
CONCLUSION
   A. Why?
   B. It Beats the Devil
   C. For Example
   D. Prayer
   E. Thought to Remember

Display visual 3 from the visuals/learning resources packet and let it remain before the class throughout the session. It is shown on the next page.

Introduction

"Every man has his price." So says one who is himself for sale. If a man will lie or cheat or steal for his own gain, he likes to think he is no worse than others. So he says anyone will lie or cheat or steal if the price is high enough. But that is not true. There are men of integrity who cannot be bought.

In the epic story recorded in the book of Job, it was Satan who said every man has his price. Job seemed to be a very good man; Satan said he was not good but greedy. Satan said Job acted good, but only for his own gain; he worshiped God and did right because God rewarded him with riches and honor and good health.

Satan was lying. Job was genuinely good, and so he remained good when his riches and honor and good health were gone.

A. The Great Debate

Most of the book of Job is a long debate. On one side were Job's three friends, plus a fourth who entered the argument later (Job 32—37). They all said Job's loss and suffering were God's punishment, and therefore Job must be very bad. On the other side of the debate Job was alone. He was not worse than his friends and other people around him, and he knew it. He knew he had not brought all the evil on himself by his great sin. But he was handicapped in the debate because he could not see any other explanation of his troubles.

A person can stand firm even when Satan does his worst. Job demonstrated that quite clearly. If we do not stand firm, it is not because we cannot; it is because we do not do our best.

B. Lesson Background

Last week we centered our attention on a few samples of the debate between Job and his friends. In the Bible there are 211 verses devoted to the speaking of the friends. The samples in our text total only eleven verses. Job's answers are 352 verses in the Bible, and our sample from them was only five verses. Our study has been greatly enriched if we have privately read all of the first twenty-five chapters of Job.

Chapters 26—31 record a speech of Job that is longer than any single speech before it—a total of 161 verses. From these we take fourteen verses for special study. In them Job contrasts his happy condition in days gone by with his present misery and despair.

I. The Good Old Days
(Job 29:1-6)

When we come to middle age or beyond, most of us have times when we long for the good old days. Even if we now are more prosperous, we are not so vigorous nor so carefree as we were. But few of us have lost as much as Job did. Not only his health but also his property and his family were gone. The greatest of all the men of the East was now the poorest and most miserable. No wonder he longed for the good old days.

A. Safety (vv. 1-3)

1. Moreover Job continued his parable, and said.

What Job was saying was not a parable like the parables of Jesus that we read in the New Testament. It might be called simply a speech or a lecture.

2. Oh that I were as in months past, as in the days when God preserved me.

The Hebrew word for *preserved* may be translated *kept* or watched or *guarded*. It is the word used of one who stands guard on the wall at night to keep his city safe from attack. So in bygone days God had watched over Job to keep him safe from injury or loss.

3. When his candle shined upon my head, and when by his light I walked through darkness.

In the past, God had enlightened and guided Job so that everything he did was successful. Now suddenly everything was going wrong.

B. Friendship (vv. 4, 5)

4. As I was in the days of my youth, when the secret of God was upon my tabernacle.

In Hebrew as in English, a word may have several different meanings. Here *youth* may be translated *autumn*, and autumn is the time of harvest. Job was yearning for the bygone days when he was prosperous.

Secret also represents a Hebrew word of various meanings, and *tabernacle* here does not mean a special place of worship, as it often does in the Old Testament. The second line of verse 4 may be translated "when the friendship of God was over my dwelling place."

5. When the Almighty was yet with me, when my children were about me.

Job continued to lament what he had lost. The close friendship of *the Almighty* was very precious, and so was the love of his ten *children*.

C. Prosperity (v. 6)

6. When I washed my steps with butter, and the rock poured me out rivers of oil.

Some versions have *milk* instead of *butter*. Both this and *oil* are symbols of plenty. A poor man might have to be content with dry bread, but a rich man would have milk to drink and oil to anoint his hair and skin. Before disaster came, Job had good things in abundance. Speaking figuratively of his way of life, Job said his *steps* were bathed in milk; his abundance of oil was like *rivers* gushing from the rocky soil where olives grew. Read through the rest of chapter 29 for a description of the high honor given to Job by his fellowmen.

visual 3

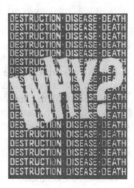

LOOK FORWARD, NOT BACK

The young city of Chicago experienced great growth due to the railroad building boom of the mid-nineteenth century. The railroad also brought greater speed, wrecks, noise, and death. One person decried the era's fast pace of life. He regretfully envisioned the time when people in balloons could float over to Europe between one sun and the next. He longed, he said, for the good old days of heavy post coaches and speed at the rate of six miles an hour.

Obviously the man's life had become burdensome. He saw advantages in his past that his current situation didn't offer. He longed to return to a time more to his liking.

Job would have understood such reverie. As he considered the pleasures he had known and the torment he was now experiencing, Job yearned for the past; for then he took great satisfaction in life: he enjoyed his family, delighted in his God, and anticipated the future.

Most of us, when undergoing trying circumstances, relive Job's desire to return to a former, better time. Retreating to a hallowed past is an attempt to escape from hardships that we feel are too heavy to bear. However, the dream cannot materialize. We may yearn for another time, but we must deal with the present. With confidence in God, we, like Job, can hold on and eventually overcome.   —V. H.

II. The Bad Days
(Job 30:19-26)

Job's new condition contrasted sharply with his earlier happiness. He had been rich; now he was poor. He had been in luxury; now he was in misery. God had blessed and exalted him; now God seemed to be oppressing him (for Job did not understand that Satan was doing it). Men had respected him; now they despised him. In all this Job was helpless, and God did not respond to his plea for help.

A. Unanswered Plea (vv. 19, 20)

19. He hath cast me into the mire, and I am become like dust and ashes.

Job had been lifted to a high and honored place. Now suddenly he was thrown down. Figuratively speaking, he was dashed into the mud like a thing of no account. Not understanding the working of Satan, he thought God had done it. That puzzled him greatly, for he could not understand why God would do such a thing. He kept asking why, and the questioning added to his agony.

Like dust and ashes may suggest also that Job was downtrodden as well as downcast, as dry dust and ashes are thrown into a mudhole to make a dry surface that can be walked upon. Some students think the dead skin of Job's boils may have been flaking off so that it looked like dust and ashes. Also, in his grief he sat in the ashes (Job 2:8). When his friends came to share his grief, they "sprinkled dust upon their heads toward heaven" (Job 2:12). Perhaps both he and they were literally covered with dust and ashes.

20. I cry unto thee, and thou dost not hear me: I stand up, and thou regardest me not.

From the beginning of his trouble Job had been pleading with God for help, but no help had come. Figuratively speaking, he had stood up to get God's attention, but apparently he had not gotten it. *Thou dost not hear me* of course does not mean that God was literally deaf. It means, "Thou dost not respond, Thou dost not do anything for me." That is the meaning also of *thou regardest me not* in the *King James Version*. Note, however, that *not* is printed in italics, which means it is not in the Hebrew text but is added by the translators to make the last part of the verse parallel to the first part. The *New International Version* does not supply the "not," but reads, "you merely look at me." With either translation the meaning is plain: Job was crying for help, but not getting any.

B. Cruel Pressure (vv. 21-23)

21. Thou art become cruel to me: with thy strong hand thou opposest thyself against me.

Again it is plain that Job did not know the devil was really the *cruel* one. He thought God was hurting him, and with such a *strong hand* that Job was helpless against Him. Since that was Job's thinking, it is the more remarkable that he was able to keep on trusting God and believing that He was holy and just.

22. Thou liftest me up to the wind; thou causest me to ride upon it, and dissolvest my substance.

To reduce this picturesque language to our less elegant modern speech, Job felt that he was being dried up and blown away. It was as if he were dissolving or evaporating in a strong wind, and he thought God was doing it to him.

23. For I know that thou wilt bring me to death, and to the house appointed for all living.

Job did not expect to survive. He had said, "Though he slay me, yet will I trust in him" (Job 13:15). He was convinced that God was going to do just that. He wished that he could die quickly and end his suffering (Job 3:20-22). *The house appointed for all living* is the grave, to which *all living* will eventually come when they stop living.

C. Destruction Undeserved (vv. 24-26)

24. Howbeit he will not stretch out his hand to the grave, though they cry in his destruction.

The Hebrew of this verse is difficult to understand. Ancient and modern versions have translated it in different ways. Let's note a few samples.

1. As we see it in the *King James Version*, the verse says God will not *stretch out his hand to the grave* to rescue the dying, even though they cry for help as He is destroying them. Job had decided that God was going to bring him to death (v. 23) in spite of his righteousness and his plea for help. That seemed very strange. Job himself had cared for the needy (v. 25), and he could not understand why God seemed to have no concern for the dying.

2. The *New International Version* reads, "Surely no one lays a hand on a broken man when he cries for help in his distress." This can be understood in either of two ways:

a. No one hits a man when he is down. On the contrary, Job himself was always ready to help the afflicted (v. 25). It seemed incredible that God was still oppressing Job, broken as he was. Yet it seemed that God was doing that (v. 21), and was going to keep on till Job was dead (v. 23). Job could not understand it.

b. No one was lending a hand to help Job when he was broken and crying for help in his distress.

3. The *New American Bible* says, "Yet should not a hand be held out to help a wretched man in his calamity?" It did not seem right or fair that no one was giving any help to Job, especially since he had been willing and ready to help others (v. 25).

4. The *American Standard Version* puts it this way: "Howbeit doth not one stretch out the hand in his fall? Or in his calamity therefore cry for help?" A falling man puts out his hand to break his fall; and if he is so injured that he cannot get up, he calls for help. In like manner Job was not accepting his disaster without protest. Unable to do anything for himself, he was crying for help. It seemed that no help was coming, and he was doomed (v. 23).

Do all these different translations have anything in common? Yes, in all of them we see Job's feeling that he was abandoned, that there was no help for him. We see also his surprise that it was so, his protest that it was not fair.

Again we may note a basic error in Job's thinking. He imagined that God was inflicting all that suffering on him. It seems that he was not aware of Satan. Is it possible that we too sometimes are puzzled and confused because we do not give the devil credit for as much power and malice as he actually has?

25. Did not I weep for him that was in trouble? Was not my soul grieved for the poor?

In his time of prosperity Job had been concerned about those who were distressed, and had expressed his concern in practical help (Job 29:11-17). Therefore it seemed the more unreasonable and unjust that there was no help for him in his time of trouble.

26. When I looked for good, then evil came unto me: and when I waited for light, there came darkness.

Job had lost all he had except his wife and his life, and these had become a burden instead of a joy. He was sunk in pain and misery, engulfed in despair. He thought he deserved better, and he did. He was a good man. We do not have to take his word for that. God himself had proclaimed that he was "a perfect and an upright man, one that feareth God, and escheweth evil" (Job 1:8). Here was a man who deserved the best, and he was getting the worst. He couldn't understand it, and that added to his misery. He was crying

for relief from pain and sorrow, but scarcely less desperately he was crying for understanding. That cry too was unanswered. There was no explanation.

Conclusion

For the conclusion we must wait till next week. This present lesson is inconclusive. We leave Job in agony, agony of body and agony of mind. Yet out of the depth of his misery comes a clear message, the message of trust. In all Job's trouble his faith never faltered. He said, "Though he slay me, yet will I trust in him" (Job 13:15). Though he could not see any reason or right in the events, he could see that they were a test. Solemnly he pledged, "When he hath tried me, I shall come forth as gold" (Job 23:10). And he did.

A. Why?

Our newspaper says a three-year-old girl has died from untreated infections. The infections followed severe beatings given by her father. San Salvador is devastated by an earthquake, and Mexico City has not yet recovered from an earlier one. Three people have died in a tornado, and others have been drowned in a flood. A bomb has exploded in a Paris store, killing dozens of innocent shoppers. A speeding car jumped the curb and charged across a playground. Two children are dead.

Why? Continually, innocent people are killed or maimed or otherwise afflicted. Is there no justice? If God is as good and as powerful as Christians say He is, why does He allow such disasters?

The question hits hardest when one is a victim, when his own home is destroyed or his wife or child is killed. That was the way it hit Job. Why were so many bad things happening to him?

His friends had a simple answer. They said Job had sinned and God was punishing him. But to Job the case was not so simple.

Were his friends right? Could he have sinned greatly without knowing it? No, that was not possible. He knew right from wrong, and he had not done any great wrong. That was a matter of fact.

Was God unjust? No, that was not possible either. God is good and right. That was a matter of faith.

Then what was the answer? As far as Job could see, there was none. But he kept his faith.

Believing in God does not depend on understanding everything that happens. That is Job's great message to us.

B. It Beats the Devil

John wrote, "This is the victory that overcometh the world, even our faith" (1 John 5:4). Job demonstrated that faith can beat the devil too.

Satan predicted that he would turn Job's worship into cursing. With God's permission he did his worst, and his worst was not enough. Job beat him completely—and Job didn't even know whom he was fighting.

Job and his friends knew God. They had lofty ideas of His power and justice and goodness. But there is no indication that they knew the devil. Does that seem strange? Remember that they lived a long time ago. There was no Bible. Knowledge of God had been handed down through the generations from Noah, but the words of Job and his friends do not indicate that knowledge of Satan had been handed down along with it.

Of course Satan is no newcomer on the earthly scene. He was busy in Eden, but he was in disguise. The record names only "the serpent." If the history handed down through the centuries did not speak of Satan, it is not surprising that Job did not know him. More surprising is the fact that the unknown writer of the book of Job did know Satan and described his part in Job's suffering. That information must have come by divine revelation, and it is convincing evidence that the book of Job is inspired of God.

As compared with Job, we are better equipped to beat the devil. We know about him. As Paul put it, "We are not ignorant of his devices" (2 Corinthians 2:11). We know how he tempted Jesus in the wilderness (Matthew 4:1-11). We know how he seduced Judas (Luke 22:3-6). We know how he was after stout Simon Peter (Luke 22:31, 32). We know he disguises himself as an angel of light (2 Corinthians 11:14). We know he is prowling like a lion in search of victims, but we know we can resist him (1 Peter 5:8, 9; James 4:7). We are without excuse if we fail to beat the devil.

C. For Example

Dick and Jane are taking a course in the book of Matthew at their community college. Politely the professor explains that this could not have been written by the apostle Matthew, as some people suppose. The book tells fantastic tales about a man who walked on water. He told the wind to stop, and it did. He even called people back from the dead. The professor says these obviously are myths that grew up after Matthew and the other apostles were dead.

Jane is impressed. The professor has been studying this for years. He is confident and pleasant and tolerant. Surely he knows what he is talking about.

Dick is not convinced. He says, "I believe the Bible."

Joe was just a passenger in a friend's car when another car came through a red light and hit it broadside. Certainly Joe had no fault in the matter, but he is paralyzed from the waist down. An unbelieving friend comes in to cheer him up, but can't resist a bit of a sneer. "Where's your God now?" he asks.

Joe smiles. "Don't you know? He's right here. How could I stand this without Him?"

An agnostic lecturer likes to begin his speech with a favorite joke. He says an American asked a man of Israel, "Why don't you Jews and Moslems sit down and settle your differences like Christians?"

"Like Christians?" said the Israeli. "You mean like they're doing in North Ireland?"

The lecturer goes on to speak of many wars. In Ireland Christians are fighting Christians. Jews and Moslems are continuing to struggle in their part of the world. In Lebanon there are so many violent factions that the rest of the world can hardly tell who is doing what. Iraq and Iran are locked in deadly conflict. Troops from Cuba are helping in Angola and Ethiopia. Soviet troops are helping Afghanistan in its effort to subdue its freedom fighters. There are rebellions in Chile and Peru. The United States is helping the government in El Salvador and the rebels in Nicaragua.

"Now," says the lecturer, "if God can't stop this killing, what is He good for? Why should anyone worship Him if He can't control what goes on in the world?"

The speaker adds, "I would stop all this bloody business if I could. If God could stop it, but chooses to let it go on, He's not even as good as I am. Why should anyone worship Him?"

Finally the lecturer concludes, "Maybe there isn't any God."

How would Job answer such reasoning?

How would you answer it?

D. Prayer

Father in Heaven, we put our trust in You. As we consider the world about us, may we never be discouraged by things we cannot explain. We know You understand. We know You are just and good. From everlasting to everlasting You are God. May Your will be done on earth as it is in Heaven, for Yours is the kingdom and the power and the glory forever. Amen.

E. Thought to Remember

"Though he slay me, yet will I trust in him."

Learning by Doing

This page contains an alternate lesson plan emphasizing learning activities. Classes desiring such student involvement will find these suggestions helpful.

Learning Goals

After studying Job 29 and 30, the adult will be able to:

1. Be able to show the contrast between Job's former status and his present condition as described in the text.

2. Be more sensitive to those with great affliction, offering comfort rather than condemnation.

Into the Lesson

On the chalkboard or other graphic display have these words written over separate columns: *Back Then* and *But Now*. As class begins, challenge your students to a "mutual commiseration session." Ask them to suggest the parallel phrases that will contrast "back then" with "now," showing that the "worse state of affairs" has arrived. (You may not personally feel that things are worse today than in years gone by, but ask your students to mention some of the things they hear others say, who bemoan the loss of "the good old days.") Expect such entries as "Back then, steak was 25¢ a pound, but now it's $2.99" (economic); and "Back then I could beat my son in tennis, but now I can't even give him competition" (Physiological); and "Back then I could handle the everyday ups and downs, but now little things tend to bother me" (emotional). Accept and record six to ten responses, then make the transition to today's Bible study by saying, "Today's text is a record of Job's thinking about his previous blessed and honored state in utter contrast to his current state of humiliation."

Into the Word

The lesson writer indicates some difficulties in translating the Hebrew wording of today's text. To help clarify the text, have four readers read aloud the verses of the printed text responsively, one verse at a time in order, with each reader using a different version of the Bible. It will be best to use literal translations rather than paraphrases. Have each verse read from the *King James Version* first. Though the choice of the other versions is optional, suggestions are *The New King James Version*, *New American Standard Bible*, and the *New International Version*. Such a procedure may enrich a discussion of the meanings of the text.

Have enough Bibles on hand so that there is at least one copy for every two persons. Ask students to examine chapter 29 and count how many times the words *when* and *then* are used. (The number will vary depending on the version.) Note that chapter 29 may be characterized as Job's remembering his "good old days," when all was right and good in his world. Now ask the class to read the first two words of chapter 30 in unison at your direction. This loud *But now* will characterize chapter 30 as Job's sad, even mournful, expression of his humiliation.

Next, read aloud the verses from chapter 29 that are given below, one group of verses at a time. After reading each verse group, which describes Job's "back then," condition, have the class examine chapter 30 to find a passage that describes an opposing "but now" side of Job's life. Some sample matches of contrasting ideas include 29:2, 3 with 30:19-21; 29:4-6 with 30:15; 29:7-11 with 30:1, 9, and others; 29:12-17 with 30:25, 26; 29:21-25 with 30:10-12. This activity should show the structure of this section of Job's defense and also reemphasize the "back then—but now" theme.

Distribute copies of the following chart. Have the students work individually to unscramble the words, which highlight the changes in Job's situation. (This activity is included in the student's book.) The words are: (1) honored, despised; (2) accompanied, alone; (3) comforted, anguished; (4) blessed, cursed; (5) active, passive; (6) happy, distressed.

FROM	TO
1. dehnoor	ddeeipss
2. aaccdeimnop	aelno
3. cedfmoort	adegihnsu
4. bdeelss	cdersu
5. aceitv	aeipssv
6. phapy	ddeeirssst

Into Life

In this study Job rehearses some of the ways he had expressed his righteousness in times past. Have the students read 29:12-17 and 30:25 to find Job's "good deeds." Write these on the chalkboard. Have each student read the list silently and ask, for each entry, "When have I done that?" Then lead a discussion of how your class can implement one or more of the ideas.

Let's Talk It Over

The questions on this page are designed to encourage review of the lesson Scriptures and to promote discussion of the lesson by the class. The answers provided are only discussion starters. Let your class talk it over from there.

1. Is the "Why?" question more theological or psychological? Explain.

The cry, "Why did God let this happen to me?" or some variation of it, arises from two different levels. In one sense it appears to be a theological question, in which one seeks to understand one of the mysteries of life. The response of most friends, and even many ministers, is to answer the question on a theological level. The attempt is made to explain how God works and doesn't work, even to the point of defending Him. But at a deeper level, "Why?" is a psychological question, laden with strong emotions. Usually it is an angry question, and the anger is directed at God. The sufferer may have trouble acknowledging the anger; after all, it seems improper to get angry with God. But, deep inside, the sufferer asks, "How could God allow this to happen? He could have intervened, but He didn't." Ministry to hurting, suffering persons gets in touch with their deep-seated negative feelings. Helping them work through these feelings is vital to their emotional and spiritual health.

2. What are some invalid feelings often experienced during times of prosperity?

Prosperity tempts us to entertain and enjoy feelings that rest on a false basis. One such feeling is security. But ultimate security isn't anchored in prosperity. Even financial security can vanish like dew from the grass. Another feeling is confidence. We may assume that what is will always be. But circumstances can and often do change very quickly. Contentment and satisfaction tend to accompany prosperity, leading a person to feel that he "has it made." Job may have felt quite secure, confident, contented, and satisfied. But all of that had been swept away, leaving him dirt poor, sitting in dust and ashes.

3. Why do people most frequently yearn for "the good old days"?

Quite simply, when the present is threatening and anxiety-producing, the temptation is to long for the past. The past is perceived as "better" through the rosy glasses of nostalgia and selective memory. Job can't be blamed for yearning for the pleasant days of the past, considering the loss he had experienced and the intense suf-

fering he was undergoing. But to long for the good old days when we face the slightest difficulty tends to blight the present in terms of the possibilities for growth and maturation that may be realized now. Such escapism sabotages the present, with its God-given potential.

4. Why do some prayers go unanswered?

Most of us at one time or another have said with Job, "I cry unto thee, and thou dost not hear me: (Job 30:20). We trust Him, and we do need help. We are desperate, yet we perceive only cosmic silence. We may feel that some prayers go unanswered because God's reply is "no" or "not yet." When He doesn't respond on our timetable with the answer we want, we accuse Him of not answering us. It is also possible that some of our prayers arise from improper motives (James 4:3). Job felt God didn't answer when he got a "not yet" response.

5. Cite some positive results of prayer that can come in negative circumstances.

(1) Prayer reinforces faith. Trust is reaffirmed in the face of opposition and disaster. (2) Prayer teaches patience. The impatient soul calls for immediate deliverance. In prayer, commitment is made to God's timetable. (3) Prayer enables one to see the experiences of this life from God's perspective, and what a difference that makes! (4) Prayer musters a Christian's resources, enabling one to continue the spiritual battle against Satan. It enables one to face trouble with renewed courage. (5) Prayer opens a person to reliance on God's provision for his need. And God's grace is all-sufficient!

6. How would you respond to someone who affirms, "If you are faithful to God, He will bless you materially"?

From at least as far back as the days of Job, some people have held this view. The teachings of Jesus, however, carry a different emphasis. He taught His followers to pray for their "daily bread." He promised that the person who seeks first the kingdom of God will have his basic needs met (Matthew 6:31-33). But greater material rewards He did not promise. The blessedness that belongs to the Christian cannot be measured materially.

God Answers Job

LESSON SCRIPTURE: Job 38:1-7; 40:1-9; 42.

PRINTED TEXT: Job 38:1-7; 40:3-5; 42:1-6, 10.

Job 38:1-7

1 Then the Lord answered Job out of the whirlwind, and said,

2 Who is this that darkeneth counsel by words without knowledge?

3 Gird up now thy loins like a man; for I will demand of thee, and answer thou me.

4 Where wast thou when I laid the foundations of the earth? Declare, if thou hast understanding.

5 Who hath laid the measures thereof, if thou knowest? Or who hath stretched the line upon it?

6 Whereupon are the foundations thereof fastened? Or who laid the corner stone thereof;

7 When the morning stars sang together, and all the sons of God shouted for joy?

Job 40:3-5

3 Then Job answered the Lord, and said,

4 Behold, I am vile; what shall I answer thee? I will lay mine hand upon my mouth.

5 Once have I spoken; but I will not answer: yea, twice; but I will proceed no further.

Job 42:1-6, 10

1 Then Job answered the Lord, and said,

2 I know that thou canst do every thing, and that no thought can be withholden from thee.

3 Who is he that hideth counsel without knowledge? Therefore have I uttered that I understood not; things too wonderful for me, which I knew not.

4 Hear, I beseech thee, and I will speak: I will demand of thee, and declare thou unto me.

5 I have heard of thee by the hearing of the ear; but now mine eye seeth thee:

6 Wherefore I abhor myself, and repent in dust and ashes.

. . . .

10 And the Lord turned the captivity of Job, when he prayed for his friends: also the Lord gave Job twice as much as he had before.

GOLDEN TEXT: I have heard of thee by the hearing of the ear; but now mine eye seeth thee.—Job 42:5.

Sep 25

Through Suffering to Hope

Unit 1: Job—Probing the Meaning
of Suffering (Lessons 1-4)

Lesson Aims

This lesson should enable the adult learner
to:

1. Briefly summarize what God said to Job.
2. Tell how Job responded to God.
3. Describe the happy ending of the book of
Job.
4. List some benefits that come from trouble.
5. Resolve to profit by his troubles.

Lesson Outline

INTRODUCTION
    A. A Cry for Knowledge
    B. Lesson Background
I. THE LORD'S CHALLENGE (Job 38:1-7)
    A. A Call to Answer (vv. 1-3)
    B. Some Questions to Answer (vv. 4-7)
    Not From Faith
II. JOB'S RESPONSE (Job 40:3-5; 42:1-6)
    A. Nothing to Say (40:3-5)
    B. Humble Confession (42:1-6)
III. HAPPY ENDING (Job 42:10)
    A. Freedom (v. 10a)
    B. Unselfish Prayer (v. 10b)
    C. Restoration (v. 10c)
CONCLUSION
    A. The Known and the Unknown
    B. Truth and Error
    C. Good Out of Bad
    D. Prayer
    E. Thought to Remember

*Display visual 4 from the visuals/learning re-
sources packet. It highlights the main points in
section C of the "Conclusion." It is shown on page
38.*

Introduction

Some years ago a reporter stirred controversy
by digging through the refuse a government official had put out for the trash collector. The reporter hoped discarded papers would reveal
some information the official did not choose to
release. Some people thought the reporter was
too nosy. He defended himself with the dictum
of the media, "The people have a right to know."

People do want to know. There's no doubt
about that. Officials employ investigators, sci-
entists spend their lives in research, and most of
the rest of us listen eagerly to gossip.

Most avidly we want to know and control
things that hurt us. We learn to predict floods
and build levees. We make our buildings fire-
proof and try to make them earthquake proof.
We spend years of time and millions of dollars
in tracking down viruses that make us sick, and
in devising vaccines to keep us well. We do not
want to be hurt.

A. A Cry for Knowledge

Job was being hurt. He longed for an end of
his pain and grief, even an end in death. But
almost as desperately he longed for information.
Why was he being hurt? His friends had a ready
explanation, but he knew it was false. He
wanted an answer from someone who knew—
from God. Over and over we hear his cry:

"Surely I would speak to the Almighty, and I
desire to reason with God" (Job 13:3).

"Wherefore hidest thou thy face, and holdest
me for thine enemy?" (Job 13:24).

"I would know the words which he would
answer me, and understand what he would say
unto me" (Job 23:5).

Job wanted to know. He thought he had a
right to know. He cried out for an explanation,
almost demanded an explanation from God.

B. Lesson Background

Two weeks ago we sampled the opinions of
Job's three friends, Eliphaz, Bildad, and Zophar.
Last week we looked at a bit of Job's longest
response. Then yet another man entered the de-
bate. Elihu delivered a long lecture (Job 32—37).
He rebuked both Job and the three friends, but
basically he agreed with the friends. He said
Job's suffering was punishment for Job's sin.

Then at last God spoke. Our lesson text begins
with a little of what He said.

I. The Lord's Challenge
(Job 38:1-7)

When at last the Lord spoke, He did not give
the answer that Job was so urgently asking. Instead, He began asking questions for Job to answer, and He kept on asking question after question without explaining why loss and suffering
had come to a good person.

A. A Call to Answer (vv. 1-3)

**1. Then the Lord answered Job out of the
whirlwind, and said.**

A *whirlwind* never fails to get attention. The
spinning current of air makes itself visible by
lifting a column of dust. It may be small, not

much bigger than a man; or it may tower majestically toward the sky. Even the black funnel of a tornado might be called a whirlwind. Many students think the Hebrew word has a still wider meaning, and some versions of the Bible have "storm" instead of *whirlwind*. This may lead us to picture a huge storm cloud riding swiftly on the wind, perhaps with lightning and thunder. Whether we picture a storm or a whirlwind, we realize that the Lord gave an impressive sign of His presence as He spoke to Job.

2. Who is this that darkeneth counsel by words without knowledge?

Someone had been talking without knowing what he was talking about, and so had brought darkness rather than light into the debate. The Lord asked who had been doing this. Was it Elihu, the one who had been talking just before the Lord came into the discussion? Was it Job, to whom the Lord spoke? (v. 1). Actually, all of them, Job, his three friends, and Elihu had been talking *without knowledge* of the real cause of Job's trouble.

3. Gird up now thy loins like a man; for I will demand of thee, and answer thou me.

To "gird up the loins" meant to get ready for action. Job was not to prepare for physical activity, but to gird up the loins of his mind (1 Peter 1:13). He was to be alert, thoughtful, ready to answer some hard questions if he could. He had been asking of God; now God would ask of him.

B. Some Questions to Answer (vv. 4-7)

4. Where wast thou when I laid the foundations of the earth? Declare, if thou hast understanding.

The factual question was *Where wast thou?* Probably Job would have answered that he was nowhere. He did not exist when God began to make the earth. But this was more than a factual question. It began to draw a contrast between God and Job. God had lived from eternity, Job for a few decades. God had wisdom and power to build the world; Job had no such ability. Then how inappropriate it would be for Job, to criticize the ways of the Eternal!

5. Who hath laid the measures thereof, if thou knowest? Or who hath stretched the line upon it?

The creation is described in human terms, as if a builder were using a measuring line to determine where the corners of his house would be. Again the factual question was simple: Who did it? Again Job could have answered. He understood that God had created earth and sky (Job 9:4-10; 12:9, 10; 26:7-13; 28:9-11, 23-27). At this point God was not trying to stump Job with questions he could not answer. God was helping

---

How to Say It
BILDAD. *Bil*-dad.
ELIHU. Ee-*lye*-hew.
ELIPHAZ. *El*-ih-faz.
ENOCH. *E*-nock.
ZOPHAR. *Zo*-far.

Job to realize that divine wisdom and power were above human criticism.

6. Whereupon are the foundations thereof fastened? Or who laid the corner stone thereof?

The question of *who laid the corner stone* is much like the question of verse 5. God did it. The question of what supports the earth's foundations is something else. This was a great puzzle to prescientific people who did not know God. But even this question could not stump Job. He understood that God had hung the earth on nothing (Job 26:7). But the question emphasized again that God is supreme, and surely above any human criticism. Job had said this before (Job 9:12), but God's questioning must have brought it to his mind more forcefully.

7. When the morning stars sang together, and all the sons of God shouted for joy.

This emphasized again that the creation was far beyond anything in Job's experience. It added that creation was begun with joy. Probably the *sons of God* then present were angels, and *morning stars* may also mean angels. A morning star is brilliant at dawn, and angels were God's bright messengers in the dawn of creation. Some students think, however, that the morning stars here are literal stars.

Read on through chapters 38 and 39 for other challenging questions the Lord asked. In all of them God's knowledge is contrasted with Job's ignorance, and God's power is contrasted with Job's weakness. Job could not understand how the Lord controlled the sea, the endless succession of day and night, the weather, the stars, the animals. Then why was he so disturbed because he did not understand the cause of suffering? It was only one of a multitude of things beyond his understanding. In a world full of mystery, why did he think he had a right to demand an explanation of that one thing?

NOT FROM FAITH

In an interview a well-known actress said she didn't want to miss anything in life, which is why she hated to die. She claimed to be very religious, though not regular in church attendance. Besides, she said, she believed that the most truly religious people are not found in church. (She didn't say where they are found). She didn't believe in an afterlife; she didn't believe in Heaven or Hell, except what one makes here on earth. And after this life is over, that's all there is for anyone.

Tailoring faith to make it acceptable to one's individual tastes is useless, and dangerous. In essence, it puts one in the place of God, and that is presumption of the highest order.

Job knew he needed divine guidance, though he was hardly ready for what he received. But those persons who develop their own theology neither desire nor have place for God's witness, since they are so busy with their own opinions. That puts them in a far more precarious position than Job!   —V. H.

II. Job's Response
(Job 40:3-5; 42:1-6)

Job saw the trend of God's questions. They were not meant to be answered, but to impress Job with God's greatness and Job's littleness. They reminded Job that his suffering was only one of many mysteries. When Job had a chance to speak again, he did not try to answer each question. He no longer demanded any explanation.

A. Nothing to Say (40:3-5)

3. Then Job answered the Lord, and said.
The Lord's closing challenge called for an answer: "Shall he that contendeth with the Almighty instruct him? He that reproveth God, let him answer it" (v. 2). So Job answered in the best way he could.

4. Behold, I am vile; what shall I answer thee? I will lay mine hand upon my mouth.
Vile does not mean evil or wicked; it means insignificant, a mere trifle. Job now was thoroughly ·convinced that he was not important enough to demand an explanation from the Almighty. He had longed to lay his case before the Lord. Now he had the opportunity, but he no longer had anything to say. He would lay his hand on his mouth to stop his talking.

5. Once have I spoken; but I will not answer: yea, twice; but I will proceed no further.
Job decided he had said too much already. He would not make matters worse by talking some more. Haven't we all felt the same way at times?

But the Lord was not through. He continued to speak of animals that He could control but Job could not (Job 40:6—41:34). One was behemoth, a huge vegetarian creature. Some students guess behemoth was the elephant; others guess he was the hippopotamus, because he liked to lie "in the covert of the reed, and fens." Besides, the elephant has been domesticated from ancient times. The hippopotamus is a more suitable example of a beast that only God controls. The other beast described at length was leviathan, perhaps the crocodile.

B. Humble Confession (42:1-6)

1, 2. Then Job answered the Lord, and said. I know that thou canst do every thing, and that no thought can be withholden from thee.
Job had known this all along, but now it had been impressed on him more forcefully.

3. Who is he that hideth counsel without knowledge? Therefore have I uttered that I understood not; things too wonderful for me, which I knew not.
Job quoted the question God had asked from the whirlwind or storm: *Who is he that hideth counsel without knowledge?* (Job 38:1, 2). Now Job was ready to acknowledge that he had done that. He did not accuse his friends. He realized that he had talked much too much about matters of which he knew much too little.

4. Hear, I beseech thee, and I will speak: I will demand of thee, and declare thou unto me.
Here Job was not renewing his earlier demand for an explanation. Rather, he was again quoting what God had said to him (Job 38:3). But with his new humility Job was not going to try to answer. He now realized that his knowledge was less than he had supposed.

5. I have heard of thee by the hearing of the ear; but now mine eye seeth thee.
From childhood Job had heard about God *by the hearing of the ear.* He had listened to the teaching that had been passed from father to son ever since Noah had taught his sons. Indeed, Job had a very fine concept of God, and held it firmly through all his distress. But now he said, *Mine eye seeth thee.* Literally speaking, his eye saw the whirlwind or storm; but he knew God was speaking from it, and it was as if he were meeting God face to face. Now he knew God better than ever before.

6. Wherefore I abhor myself, and repent in dust and ashes.
Isn't this the natural result of catching a glimpse of the Almighty? Isaiah "saw also the Lord sitting upon a throne, high and lifted up"; and Isaiah cried, "Woe is me! for I am undone; because I am a man of unclean lips" (Isaiah 6:1-5). Simon Peter saw an impressive miracle of Jesus, and "he fell down at Jesus' knees, saying, Depart from me; for I am a sinful man, O Lord" (Luke 5:1-8). The Almighty is infinite in majesty and power and holiness. How can anyone catch a glimpse of Him without abhorring himself because he is unholy? How can anyone reflect

on the boundless knowledge of God without saying, "Such knowledge is too wonderful for me; it is high, I cannot attain unto it"? (Psalm 139:6).

When first afflicted by boils, Job had sat in the ashes (Job 2:7, 8). It was a customary way of expressing grief. Probably he had sat there through all the long debate with his friends. But now he had an added reason for grief. He had grieved over his loss and pain; now he grieved over his attitude. He had been proud and presumptuous. He had thought he had a right to know the reason for his troubles. He had thought God owed him an explanation. But now he repented. He no longer thought God owed him anything. He no longer clamored for his rights. He had been "a perfect and an upright man" (Job 1:8). If he had been too proud of his perfection, he was too proud no longer. Through his trials and through God's teaching, his perfection had become more perfect.

III. Happy Ending (Job 42:10)

10. And the Lord turned the captivity of Job, when he prayed for his friends: also the Lord gave Job twice as much as he had before.

Our text takes this one verse as a summary of the eleven verses that close the book of Job. It divides neatly into three parts with three great concluding thoughts.

A. Freedom (v. 10a)

The Lord turned the captivity of Job. Loss and pain had captured Job and made him a prisoner. Or it may be said that Satan had captured Job and locked him in a prison of loss and pain. But now the Lord turned all that around. Job was

---

Home Daily Bible Readings

---

free again. Pain no longer held him, and loss was in the past. His boils disappeared, his strength returned, and his relatives gathered about him with love and gifts (v. 11).

B. Unselfish Prayer (v. 10b)

When he prayed for his friends. After speaking to Job, the Lord had a word for his three friends. He said, "Ye have not spoken of me the thing that is right." Job had been angry with them because they had come to comfort him but had only made him more miserable by saying the thing that was not right. But Job was angry no longer. He prayed for his friends, they offered the sacrifice that God prescribed, and they were forgiven (Job 42:7-9).

C. Restoration (v. 10c)

The Lord gave Job twice as much as he had before. The sheep and camels and oxen and donkeys are numbered in verse 12. Again their owner was the greatest of all the men of the East. No doubt the sons and daughters who had died were still missed, but the Lord gave Job ten more, and the girls were the prettiest ones in the country (vv. 13-15).

Conclusion

The book of Job ends without an answer to the question that burned so long in Job's tortured mind. Why do bad things happen to good people? We know, as Job did not, that the devil causes them; but that does not completely answer the question. God controls even the devil. Satan can do no more to us than God permits. Then why does God allow bad things to happen to good people?

Job longed for God's answer, but when God spoke to him out of the whirlwind and storm. He did not answer Job's questions. He raised some other questions. He called attention to a multitude of other things Job did not understand. Job lived in the midst of mysteries, and so do we.

A. The Known and the Unknown

God has left us free to learn what we can of the universe about us. We have learned much through science, and we have applied knowledge in many machines and gadgets to make life comfortable and pleasant. But there is much we do not know and much we cannot do.

We have tamed elephants, but not earthquakes. We have conquered smallpox, but not cancer. We control flooding with dams and dykes, but the flood of deadly drugs is out of control. We have learned to go swiftly by land

and sea and air, but we have not learned to avoid deadly crashes. With all our learning we have not learned to prevent hatred or greed or war or crime.

We have learned much about how things happen, but not so much about why. Think of gravitation, for example. A thing or person unsupported falls to the earth. Why? Because material things attract each other. But why do they attract? We do not know. In the ultimate analysis, it is the will of God. He built that attraction into the nature of things.

Moral laws likewise are also built in. Thou shalt not murder; thou shalt not commit adultery; thou shalt not steal; thou shalt love thy neighbor as thyself. Why? Not just because God says so, but because God designed humanity to work that way. If we violate moral laws, we not only violate God's will; we also violate our own nature. How sad it is that this is unknown to so many of us!

B. Truth and Error

God rebuked Job's friends because they did not say "the thing that is right" (Job 42:7). They insisted that God was punishing Job for doing wrong, and that slandered both Job and God. Yet they said much that was true.

It is true that God punishes the evil. In the Bible that is made plain from the time He banished Adam from Eden (Genesis 3:23) to the time when Christ will say, "Depart from me, ye cursed, into everlasting fire" (Matthew 25:41). It is true that God rewards the good. That is made plain from the time Enoch bypassed death (Genesis 5:24) to the time when Christ will say, "Come, ye blessed of my Father, inherit the kingdom prepared for you from the foundation of the world" (Matthew 25:34).

Job's friends wanted to hurry things. They thought punishment and reward must come quickly. That was their error. God can wait, Job could wait, and so can we.

C. Good Out of Bad

God did not explain just why He allowed Job to suffer. Looking at the case from a distance, however, we can see some good results.

1. Job's trust grew stronger. It was easy enough to trust when he was the greatest of the men of the East. It was pleasant to think that God was rewarding his goodness. But when he was at death's door and still declared, "Though he slay me, yet will I trust in him"—that was real trust! We too can grow more trusting through our troubles.

2. Job's character was reinforced. "Consider it pure joy, my brothers, whenever you face

visual 4

GOOD
TRUST STRENGTHENED
CHARACTER REINFORCED
THE DEVIL DEFEATED
EXAMPLE GIVEN
FUTURE ANTICIPATED
POSSESSIONS DOUBLED
RESULTS
FROM JOB'S SUFFERING

trials of many kinds, because you know that the testing of your faith develops perseverance. Perseverance must finish its work so that you may be mature and complete, not lacking anything" (James 1:2-4, *New International Version*).

3. Job defeated the devil. Wasn't it worth all his trouble to win the victory over that malicious character? "Resist the devil, and he will flee from you" (James 4:7).

4. Job provided example and encouragement for millions, including us. How joyous it is to know that we can provide similar encouragement for others!

5. Job was forced to focus on the future. Seeing no hope of justice in this world, he was driven to the conclusion that all will be made right beyond the grave. How we are blessed by having that assurance made firm in the promises and the resurrection of Christ! "Rejoice, and be exceeding glad: for great is your reward in heaven" (Matthew 5:12).

6. After his triumph over Satan, Job got more than he had lost in the beginning. So shall we, if we have to take a loss because we belong to Jesus. Peter asked bluntly what he and the other apostles would get because they had given up everything to follow Jesus. Jesus answered just as plainly: "There is no man that hath left house, or brethren, or sisters, or father, or mother, or wife, or children, or lands, for my sake, and the gospel's, but he shall receive a hundredfold now in this time, houses, and brethren, and sisters, and mothers, and children, and lands, with persecutions; and in the world to come eternal life" (Mark 10:29, 30).

Yes, our troubles can be good for us.

D. Prayer

In all our joys we thank You, Father; and in our troubles we thank You for the good they can do to us.

E. Thought to Remember

God is good.

Learning by Doing

This page contains an alternate lesson plan emphasizing learning activities. Classes desiring such student involvement will find these suggestions helpful.

Learning Goals

After this study the learner will:

1. Identify God's basic response to Job and his friends, and be able to list some of the "hard questions" God asked of Job.

2. Be able to describe Job's response to God's indictment.

3. Look forward to the time when God ultimately will make all things right for him, even as He did for Job.

Into the Lesson

Put this title on display in bold letters before the class: "Life's Most Difficult Questions." Before class begins, write the following sample questions on slips of paper, one question per slip: (1) "How could the devil believe he could have it better independent of God?" (2) "How can God be three and yet be one?" (3) "How did germs and viruses and diseases originate?" (4) "How can God who is good allow bad things to happen?" (5) "Why do the wicked sometimes prosper?" (6) "How can anything be eternal, and how can I form a concept of it?" (7) "What is the primary purpose of life?" (8) "How could God create something out of nothing?" (9) "How can I be sure there is life after death?" (10) "In what way is the devil at work in my life?" You may want to add to this list or change questions.

Distribute these questions as class members arrive. Direct the class's attention to the caption you have on display and ask those who hold the questions to read them randomly. After all the questions have been read, you may want to give opportunity for the students to suggest questions they would add to the list. Do *not* seek answers to the questions; but be sure to stress that our answers to the questions do not come from our experience or wisdom, but only from the revelation of God.

Into the Word

Give each student two index cards on which to write the following on the four sides, one per side: "I don't know," "???," "God," and "No." Select an effective oral reader and a translation of the Bible in modern English. Have the reader read from Job 38:4—40:2, stopping after every question to allow class members to select and hold up the appropriate response from their cards. This will take several minutes, but it should completely demonstrate Job's desperate situation when God finally spoke.

With your class make a list of answers to this question: "What is the probable and appropriate response of a person confronted by God?" The list should include such phrases as "He realizes his sinfulness," "He is dumbfounded," "He regrets," "He repents of pride, " "He acknowledges his ignorance." After the list is made, compare it with Job 40:3-5 and 42:1-6 to see how many of your responses were seen in Job and to see if the group list omitted some elements.

Into Life

Divide your class into four groups and assign to each respectively one of these four questions: (1) "How is the ignorance of Job's friends about God reflected in the contemporary world?" (2) "In what way(s)) is Job's self-righteousness reflected in the contemporary world?" (3) "How does God's reward of Job's faithfulness, as described in chapter 42, reflect the ultimate rewards of God's faithful?" (4) "What are the primary encouraging revelations of God, His purpose and His work, as seen in the book of Job? What difference(s)) should these make in everyday living?"

When the groups report their conclusions—after about five minutes—be certain that the following ideas are included: for group 1, "Many still blame God for the existence of evil in the world"; for group 2, "Many still believe their righteousness can be earned in personal diligence and deeds"; for group 3, "God *will* reward the faithful. Certainly our latter end will be greater than our beginning"; for group 4, "God ultimately protects His people. He is greater than Satan. There are things in His counsel we do not know."

A directed prayer will make an effective conclusion to this short study of the book of Job. Ask the class to bow reverently as you suggest the following elements for the prayer: (1) Thank God that He is in control of the universe and of our lives. (2) Thank Him for the book of Job and for the help it gives in understanding eternal truths. (3) Ask for patience and wisdom in dealing with daily distress. (4) Ask for compassionate hearts for friends beset by distress and anxiety. (5) Praise God for the hope and future glory we have in Him.

Let's Talk It Over

The questions on this page are designed to encourage review of the lesson Scriptures and to promote discussion of the lesson by the class. The answers provided are only discussion starters. Let your class talk it over from there.

1. Why do people discuss subjects about which they know little or nothing?

When God interrupted the discussion that was taking place between Job and his three friends, He raised the question, "Who is this that darkens my counsel with words without knowledge?" (Job 38:2, *New International Version*). Uninformed statements or advice will cloud instead of enlighten an issue. Yet people perpetuate the practice. Very few people will readily admit that they are ignorant. Most people wish to appear knowledgeable. At the root of this problem resides pride, the deep desire to project the image of being strong, intelligent, "sharp." Some parents have great difficulty saying, "I don't know," when questioned by their children on certain subjects. They fear that they will lose respect or even authority with an admission of ignorance. How refreshing to see someone smile and openly confess to his questioner, "I don't know"!

2. What is repentance? How is it expressed?

Repentance is neither self-loathing nor simply sorrow for sin. Sorrow according to the will of God *produces* repentance (2 Corinthians 7:10). Repentance is a change of mind that reveals itself in a changed life. Out of Job's powerful encounter with the living God he saw himself in contrast to God—on *all* points. Job's statement that he repented in "dust and ashes" (Job 42:6) doesn't mean he simply wallowed in self-loathing. Note that he demonstrated genuine repentance by appropriate actions. He retracted the presumptuous assertions that characterized him previously. He admitted his ignorance and asked God to instruct him. And he prayed for the forgiveness of his friends who had failed him in his deepest despair. Repentance was the appropriate response to really "seeing" God!

3. List some blessings that you receive when you forgive someone who has sinned against you.

(1) *Healing.* Your wounds, inflicted by another (often a friend or loved one) are cleansed and healed by God's grace, mercy, and love. Healing will not occur until forgiveness occurs. (2) *Lifting.* Your load of guilt for refusing to forgive, nursing resentment, bearing grudges, and fanning the flames of bitterness is removed. (3) *Liberation.* Until you forgive, you are a prisoner. Your jailer is the one who has wronged you. Granting forgiveness frees you from the power of the other person to blight your life. (4) *Reopening.* Until you forgive, the channel of forgiveness *to you* is blocked! Jesus said, "If you forgive men when they sin against you, your heavenly Father will also forgive you. But if you do not forgive men their sins, your Father will not forgive your sins" (Matthew 6:14, 15, *New International Version*). (5) *Growth.* In forgiving, you walk with God on the royal road of growth! Job forgave his friends when he prayed for them. He experienced all of these results of granting forgiveness.

4. What is the most appropriate personal response we can make when we become aware of God and His actions on behalf of mankind?

The most appropriate response is reverence balanced with gratitude and love, expressed in commitment. Reverence arises out of seeing God as the holy, powerful, transcendent Creator and Sustainer of all things. We see ourselves in contrast to Him. Isaiah expressed the feeling when he said, "Woe is me . . . for my eyes have seen the King, the Lord of hosts (Isaiah 6:5, *New American Standard Bible*). In God's nature, character, and activity He is holy *and* He is love. Our gratitude and love flow from seeing God clearly focused in the unique person of Jesus Christ. This healthy balance issues in our personal commitment to Him and leads us to say with Thomas, "My Lord and my God" (John 20:28).

5. God's work may be characterized by the term *restoration*. Give some examples of what God wants to restore.

For Job, God restored his fortunes; in fact, He doubled them. For all of us, He seeks to do away with sin, alienation, and death and to restore us to life and His originally intended relationship with Him. For His people who have sinned, He wants to restore the joy of His salvation (Psalm 51:12). For His church in the twentieth century, He wants to restore it to what He intended and revealed it to be in the New Testament.

A Disappointing Vineyard

LESSON SCRIPTURE: Isaiah 5:1-25.

PRINTED TEXT: Isaiah 5:1-7, 22, 23.

Isaiah 5:1-7, 22, 23

1 Now will I sing to my well-beloved a song of my beloved touching his vineyard. My well-beloved hath a vineyard in a very fruitful hill:

2 And he fenced it, and gathered out the stones thereof, and planted it with the choicest vine, and built a tower in the midst of it, and also made a winepress therein: and he looked that it should bring forth grapes, and it brought forth wild grapes.

3 And now, O inhabitants of Jerusalem, and men of Judah, judge, I pray you, betwixt me and my vineyard.

4 What could have been done more to my vineyard, that I have not done in it? Wherefore, when I looked that it should bring forth grapes, brought it forth wild grapes?

5 And now go to; I will tell you what I will do to my vineyard: I will take away the hedge thereof, and it shall be eaten up; and break down the wall thereof, and it shall be trodden down:

6 And I will lay it waste: it shall not be pruned, nor digged; but there shall come up briers and thorns: I will also command the clouds that they rain no rain upon it.

7 For the vineyard of the Lord of hosts is the house of Israel, and the men of Judah his pleasant plant: and he looked for judgment, but behold oppression; for righteousness, but behold a cry.

. . . .

22 Woe unto them that are mighty to drink wine, and men of strength to mingle strong drink:

23 Which justify the wicked for reward, and take away the righteousness of the righteous from him!

GOLDEN TEXT: He looked for judgment, but behold oppression; for righteousness, but behold a cry.—Isaiah 5:7.

Through Suffering to Hope
Unit 2: Isaiah—Interpreting a
Nation's Suffering (Lessons 5-9)

Lesson Aims

This lesson should enable a student:
1. Tell the story that is told in Isaiah's song of the vineyard, and explain its meaning.
2. Point out one example of good fruit and one of bad fruit that he can see in the world.
3. Find at least one way to improve his own service to God.

Lesson Outline

INTRODUCTION
  A. Rise and Fall of a Nation
  B. Lesson Background
I. THE VINEYARD SONG (Isaiah 5:1-4)
  A. Good Care and Bad Fruit (vv. 1, 2)
  B. The Question (vv. 3, 4)
II. THE LAST STANZA (Isaiah 5:5-7)
  A. Sentence of Doom (vv. 5, 6)
  B. Explanation (v. 7)
    Unfulfilled Expectation
III. WOE (Isaiah 5:22, 23)
  A. Drunkenness (v. 22)
  B. Injustice (v. 23)
CONCLUSION
  A. Lovers of Self
  B. Lovers of Money
  C. The Owner
    What More Could He Do?
  D. Prayer
  E. Thought to Remember

Display visual 5 in the visuals/learning resources packet. It is shown on page 43.

Introduction

The four lessons of September formed a group entitled "Probing the Meaning of Suffering." We considered the suffering of a person, Job. In his suffering his godly character was both proved and improved as ours can be.

Now we turn our attention from a person to a nation, Israel. The five October lessons form a group entitled "Interpreting a Nation's Suffering." To come to this series we leap over at least seven hundred years of history during which Israel became a nation, rose to a place of leadership among nations, and then sank down to the brink of destruction.

A. Rise and Fall of a Nation

2000—1400 B.C. Job probably lived somewhere in this span of time (Book of Job).

1400 B.C. Israel settled in the promised land after a long trip from Egypt.

1400—930 B.C. Israel lived for centuries as a loose confederation of tribes. Then it became a unified and powerful nation under Kings Saul, David, and Solomon (Judges 1:1—1 Kings 11:43).

930 B.C. Great Israel split into two little nations. The north part was still called Israel; the south part was called Judah. The power of Solomon's magnificent empire was ended (1 Kings 12:1-24).

930—721 B.C. North Israel sank into idolatry and other sins. God's law was almost forgotten. The same sin invaded Judah too, but there some of the kings resisted the invasion and tried to enforce God's law (1 Kings 12:25—2 Kings 20:21).

721 B.C. Assyrian invaders destroyed North Israel and scattered most of its people in foreign lands (2 Kings 17:1-23).

740—700 B.C. The prophet Isaiah brought God's messages to Judah during the reigns of four kings: Uzziah, Jotham, Ahaz, and Hezekiah (Isaiah 1:1).

B. Lesson Background

Generally speaking, Uzziah and Jotham were good kings. They strengthened their country greatly (2 Chronicles 26, 27). In their concern with foreign relations, however, it seems that they failed to stop the corruption of religion and morals in their own land. See 2 Kings 15:1-4, where Uzziah is called Azariah.

Ahaz was a bad king. He actively promoted false worship and evil living in Judah. In punishment God allowed surrounding nations to invade and oppress Judah. Ahaz tried to get help from the rising power of Assyria, but the alliance cost more than it was worth (2 Chronicles 28). Everything he did brought ruin upon himself and Judah because "he transgressed sore against the Lord. (v. 19).

Hezekiah was a good king. He did his best to restore both morality and true worship. God therefore defended Judah against the Assyrians who destroyed north Israel. Evil was firmly entrenched, however, and was very hard to eradicate (2 Chronicles 29—32).

The book of Isaiah collects many prophecies along with some historical data. Some of the prophecies are not dated, and not all are arranged in chronological order. Therefore we cannot tell when Isaiah sang the song in our text. However, the song itself shows that it came at a time when the people of Judah were very far from being what they ought to have been as God's people.

I. The Vineyard Song (Isaiah 5:1-4)

We are not told when or how Isaiah first presented this song. However, both Israel and Judah are named in verse 7. This suggests that the song was given before Israel was destroyed in 721 B.C. Some think its message suggests that it was given in the time when King Ahaz was promoting evil rather than a time when other kings were working for righteousness. But on the other hand, the song is placed early in Isaiah's book. This suggests that it was among Isaiah's early prophecies, given in the time of Uzziah or Jotham. Even when those kings were doing right, "the people did yet corruptly" (2 Chronicles 27:2).

A. Good Care and Bad Fruit (vv. 1, 2)

1a. Now will I sing to my well-beloved a song of my beloved touching his vineyard.

A love song and a vineyard song! How well it was designed to catch the ears of revelers at a vintage festival! The hearers did not know it yet, but Isaiah's *well-beloved* was the Lord. To Him Isaiah would sing. The song was not Isaiah's own. It was the Lord's own song, for He gave it to Isaiah by inspiration. It was a song about the *vineyard* belonging to the beloved.

1b. My well-beloved hath a vineyard in a very fruitful hill.

This *vineyard* was planted in a choice spot. The soil was rich and *fruitful*. On a *hill* it was sunlit and well drained.

2a. And he fenced it, and gathered out the stones thereof, and planted it with the choicest vine, and built a tower in the midst of it, and also made a winepress therein.

The owner meant for this vineyard to be the best. *He fenced it* to protect it from browsing cattle and sheep. He *gathered the stones* so the searching roots of the vines would find only soft, rich soil. He did not just go to a nursery and buy the first stock he saw; he searched and found *the choicest vine to plant*. When the vineyard was planted, he *built a tower in the midst of it*. In the tower the workmen could store their tools and could find shelter from

rain or sun. From the top of it they could watch for thieves. He *also made a winepress therein*. This site had everything. In addition to deep, rich soil for the vines, it had an outcrop of limestone. A trough was cut in the stone so the workers could trample the grapes. The juice would flow through a narrow outlet into a vat cut deeper in the rock. The vineyard was perfectly located, perfectly planned and planted and equipped.

2b. And he looked that it should bring forth grapes, and it brought forth wild grapes.

With the best of soil, the best of vines, and the best of care, what could a vineyard do but produce the best of grapes? But *it brought forth wild grapes*. What a letdown! Anyone who has sampled wild grapes can feel it. They are tiny, full of seeds, and incredibly sour.

B. The Question (vv. 3, 4)

3. And now, O inhabitants of Jerusalem, and men of Judah, judge, I pray you, betwixt me and my vineyard.

In this stanza of the song, the speaker is not Isaiah but Isaiah's beloved, the owner of the vineyard. Such a change of speakers is frequent in Hebrew poetry. The owner challenges the people of Jerusalem and Judah to find any fault with his treatment of the vineyard.

4. What could have been done more to my vineyard, that I have not done in it? Wherefore, when I looked that it should bring forth grapes, brought it forth wild grapes?

The question was twofold. First, who could point out one thing lacking in the owner's care for his vineyard? What advantage could have been given to it that was not given? The answer was plain. There was nothing lacking. The vineyard had every possible advantage, every reason to bear the best of fruit. Second, why didn't the vineyard do what it ought to do, what it could have done? That was not so easy to answer, but it was plain that the fault was in the vineyard itself. The owner was blameless.

GOD RIGHTFULLY EXPECTS GOOD FRUIT FROM HIS VINEYARD

visual 5

II. The Last Stanza
(Isaiah 5:5-7)

A. Sentence of Doom (vv. 5, 6)

5. And now go to; I will tell you what I will do to my vineyard: I will take away the hedge thereof, and it shall be eaten up; and break down the wall thereof, and it shall be trodden down.

Now go to is an antique English phrase somewhat like our modern *come on now*. It is an appeal for attention, a call to listen and think reasonably as the owner tells what he is going to do to the worthless vineyard. He is going to take away the protection of *hedge* and *wall*. Either of these might seem to be enough, but it seems that the owner had made his vineyard doubly secure by providing both. A heavy ox rubbing against a stone wall might possibly break it down, but a hedge of thorns would keep him from rubbing against it. With both hedge and wall removed, the sheep could browse on the vines and the cattle could both eat them and trample them into the ground.

6. And I will lay it waste: it shall not be pruned, nor digged; but there shall come up briers and thorns: I will also command the clouds that they rain no rain upon it.

The vineyard would be ruined by lack of care. No more would the owner prune the vines or cultivate the soil. *Briers and thorns* would take over the place. Furthermore the owner said, *I will also command the clouds that they rain no rain upon it.* Until this line was sung the hearers had no hint of what the parable meant. But only God can stop the rain, so now thoughtful listeners realized that He was the owner. This led into the explanation in the next verse.

B. Explanation (v. 7)

7. For the vineyard of the Lord of hosts is the house of Israel, and the men of Judah his pleasant plant: and he looked for judgment, but behold oppression; for righteousness, but behold a cry.

Now it becomes plain that the whole song is a parable. The *Lord of hosts* is the owner; *Israel* and *Judah* are the *vineyard*. From Egypt the Lord brought choice vines, the descendants of His friend Abraham, a man famous for his faith and obedience. God planted those people in the land of promise, which was a rich and fruitful land. He gave them cities that were already built by the people who had lived there before, vines and fruit trees already mature and bearing fruit. He gave them fertile soil for their grain fields and pastures of green grass for their sheep and cattle. He protected them from heathen tribes as a wall and hedge protect a vineyard. He gave them His laws to guide them in dealing with one another and with Him. What was lacking in His care? Nothing! God's provision for them was complete.

Then what kind of fruit should they produce? The Lord looked for *judgment:* that is, for justice; but He saw *oppression.* He saw unjust and cruel treatment. In any society there are some who have a talent for making money and gaining economic power. They can use their talent to help others who are not so talented, or they can use it greedily to enrich themselves and impoverish others. In Israel and Judah the rich and powerful were busy foreclosing mortgages, buying up the land of the less fortunate, building huge estates (v. 8). What then could the unsuccessful people do? They could only become serfs or slaves.

Along with all the blessings of a pleasant and fruitful land, the Lord has given His law to explain in detail how to do right. He looked *for righteousness.* But He heard *a cry*, a cry of distress from those who were oppressed and mistreated. God's law told plainly what was good; but the people in charge were calling evil good if it was profitable (v. 20). The time was near to take away the fence and let this worthless vineyard be devoured and trampled.

Unfulfilled Expectations

In 1983 a major American oil company sank a well in Alaska into a geological structure thought to hold billions of barrels of oil. It was the farthest north any U.S. oil well had ever been sunk. The effort cost $120 million. Still it was thought to hold enough oil to return many times the investment; but the hole yielded nothing but water.

Isaiah sang a song for God about His spiritual investment in Israel. God had supplied all the necessary resources for success. He orchestrated historical events in Israel's favor. He offered a constant reinforcement of goodness in their national life. But none of these had the desired effect. His investment infinitely exceeded its

---

How to Say It

AHAZ.   *A*-haz.
AZARIAH.   Az-uh-*rye*-uh.
HEZEKIAH.   Hez-uh-*kye*-uh.
ISAIAH.   Eye-*zay*-uh.
JOTHAM.   *Joe*-tham.
UZZIAH.   Uh-*zye*-uh.

return, for in Isaiah's time Israel proved to be spiritually empty.

Hasn't God provided us with better resources than He gave Israel? We live under grace, not law. The sacrifice for our sins was not a beast, but God's Son. Our hope is not in an animal carcass, but in the risen Lord. The Holy Spirit lives in us to help us yield the fruit God desires and expects to see in our lives. Are you fulfilling His expectations?   —V. H.

III. Woe
(Isaiah 5:22, 23)

A. Drunkenness (v. 22)

22. Woe unto them that are mighty to drink wine, and men of strength to mingle strong drink.

Wine is made from grapes; *strong drink* is any intoxicating drink, whether made from grapes or something else. The Hebrews may have used fermented drinks from pomegranates, dates, and barley. To *mingle strong drink* is to mix it with spices for a better flavor. What a way for a strong man to use his strength! If we are to believe what we read in modern literature, there are some among us even now who think it is a mark of manliness to drink more than anyone else does. But the result is *woe*, whether a drunken death on the highway, a lifetime of alcoholism, or just a hangover the next day. If drunkenness becomes a national habit, a nation is in danger of captivity and death (vv. 11-16).

B. Injustice (v. 23)

23. Which justify the wicked for reward, and take away the righteousness of the righteous from him!

The courts of Israel and Judah were corrupt. *The wicked* could be declared just if he was rich enough to give the judges a *reward*, a bribe. Or for a bribe the judges would convict an innocent man, and thus would falsely *take away the righteousness of the righteous from him*. Such injustice produced the cry that arose to the Lord who was looking for justice (v. 7).

Conclusion

Isaiah's beloved was the Lord of hosts, the Almighty. That was in accord with the first law of Heaven and earth: "Thou shalt love the Lord thy God with all thy heart, and with all thy soul, and with all thy mind. This is the first and great commandment" (Matthew 22:37, 38).

The Lord's vineyard was the house of Israel and the men of Judah. Planted in a choice spot and given the best of care, they should have responded with the best of fruit. But what they actually produced was sour and worthless.

What was wrong with the people of Israel and Judah? They ignored the first and great commandment that God gave them. Isaiah's beloved was not their beloved. They loved themselves, and with self-love went all the horrible sins that Paul ascribed to lovers of self in the latter days: "Men shall be lovers of their own selves, covetous, boasters, proud, blasphemers, disobedient to parents, unthankful, unholy, without natural affection, trucebreakers, false accusers, incontinent, fierce, despisers of those that are good, traitors, heady, high-minded, lovers of pleasures more than lovers of God" (2 Timothy 3:2-4). We live in the latter days. Looking at the world around us, we can see every item of that ugly list.

A. Lovers of Self

A bully on the playground terrorizes smaller children. He loves himself, and he builds his self-esteem by dominating those about him. Some executives do the same with hapless employees.

A man and woman stand up in church and vow to love, cherish, and keep each other as long as both of them shall live. Then all too soon they stand up in court to renounce their vows and demand a divorce. What is wrong? The vows are broken before they are renounced. Each of the two loves himself or herself, not the mate and certainly not God.

A slum dweller dumps his garbage on the floor of a vacant apartment across the hall. Why should he carry it downstairs and go out in the rain to set it at the curb? He loves himself too much for that.

You haven't done any of these things? All right, but what have you done because your love for self has overshadowed your love of God and others?

B. Lovers of Money

When Paul writes, "Men shall be lovers of their own selves" (2 Timothy 3:2), the next word in the *King James Version* is *covetous*. The Greek word literally means "lovers of silver," and some versions translate it "lovers of money." In another letter Paul writes, "The love of money is a root of all kinds of evil" (1 Timothy 6:10, *American Standard Version*). We quote this often, but do we really take it to heart?

Often our newspaper reports that the old "pigeon drop" has worked again. A crook on the street pretends to find some money—a lot of money. Generously he offers to share it with a bystander, only the bystander must put up some "good faith money" before the division is made. There are various ways of managing this, but the result is that the bystander loses his "good faith money" and gets nothing. The crook is a lover of money, yes. But so is the victim. Otherwise he would say, "Let's turn it over to the police. Probably the loss has been reported and they can return the money to the owner."

The owner of a gambling casino is a lover of money, and so is the customer who loses his money in the hope of multiplying it. The swindler who robs a widow of her life savings is a lover of money, but so is the widow who gives him her savings because he promises huge profits.

You haven't done any such thing? Well then, what have you done because your love of money has overshadowed your love of God?

C. The Owner

In Isaiah's song the Lord of hosts is the owner of a vineyard, which is Israel and Judah. The Lord made those people His in a special way, but at the same time He said, "All the earth is mine" (Exodus 19:5). He did not deal with Israel and Judah only. He raised up other nations and used them for His purposes, and He punished them for their sins. Notable examples are the empires of Assyria and Babylon. God used them to punish Israel and Judah, but afterward He punished Assyria and Babylon with defeat and destruction.

In recent centuries the English-speaking nations have been notably blessed with prosperity and power. Perhaps one reason is that they have acknowledged the owner, the Lord of hosts. King James I of England is famous because he authorized a translation of the Bible into the language of the people, though perhaps he did it under pressure from Puritans in his kingdom. Some influential people did not want the Bible to be so readily available to everybody, but all agreed that the Bible was God's Book. There was disagreement about how God exercises His rule. King James said that kings sit on God's throne in the earth and must answer to Him for their administration. At the same time some members of Parliament held that the voice of the people is as the voice of God. But king and Parliament agreed that God is supreme.

When some British colonies in America declared their independence, they based the declaration on the belief that God, the supreme owner, has endowed all people with "certain unalienable rights."

There is trouble ahead for any nation that loses its consciousness of God, the owner, the supreme ruler. Romans 1:28-32 gives a horrid picture of the state of people who "did not like to retain God in their knowledge." Second Timothy 3:1-8 gives a similar picture of those who are lovers of self and money and pleasure rather than lovers of God. When a nation fits such a picture, it can expect that God will take away the fence and let that nation be devoured and trampled.

What More Could He Do?

Pierre Laplace was a brilliant French mathematician and astronomer in the late eighteenth and early nineteenth centuries. Brilliant though he was, he also demonstrated a strange inconsistency that unbelievers often reveal in dealing with faith in God. He saw the fixed, orderly nature of the universe as an argument against faith in a Supreme Being.

One may be certain that if the universe were wildly disorganized and irregular, unbelievers would rage against a supposed creator who had fashioned a shabby and uncontrolled universe. Yet, finding exactly the opposite—order, regularity, and dependability—they conclude that the universe is the result, not of a Creator of wisdom and might, but of a self-organizing and perpetuating inanimate power within it.

When we think about it, Isaiah 5:4 applies strongly to the twentieth century. What more could God do to prove that He is and to encourage faith in us?

—V. H.

D. Prayer

Lord God of hosts, You have made us and we are Yours. Help us to do Your will and produce the fruit for which You created us.

E. Thought to Rememnber

Be fruitful.

Home Daily Bible Readings

Monday, Sept. 26—The Imperative to Prophesy (Amos 3:1-8)
Tuesday, Sept. 27—The Story of the Vineyard (Isaiah 5:1-7)
Wednesday, Sept. 28—Woe to Those Who Despise Righteousness (Isaiah 5:8-12)
Thursday, Sept. 29—Warnings to Those Who Sin (Isaiah 5:13-25)
Friday, Sept. 30—The Wages of Sin (Romans 6:19-23)
Saturday, Oct. 1—Jesus' Story of the Vineyard (Matthew 21:33-43)
Sunday, Oct. 2—God's Promise of Redemption (Isaiah 1:12-20)

Learning by Doing

This page contains an alternate lesson plan emphasizing learning activities. Classes desiring such student involvement will find these suggestions helpful.

Learning Goals

After this lesson the student will:

1. Be able to recall the details of the parable and its location in Scripture.

2. Contrast God's expectations with the "fruit" He received from Israel and Judah.

3. Be sensitive to unfair treatment of others around him and make a personal commitment to deal fairly with all.

Into the Lesson

If your budget, or that of the class, allows, provide introductory refreshments as the class arrives: grape juice, fresh grapes, or raisins. This should elicit some questions, which you should refuse to answer immediately.

Have written on the chalkboard or other display two columns headed "Symbol" and "Text." As class begins, indicate that you are going to write--in the first column—some of the symbolic references God uses for the relationship between himself and His people, and that you want students to identify Bible texts wherein the relationship is so characterized. (A similar matching activity is included in the student's book.) Use the following symbols of relationship; Bible texts are included for your convenience. (1) Husband-Wife, Hosea 2; (2) Shepherd-Sheep, John 10; (3) Vine-Branches, John 15; (4) Vine-dresser-Vineyard, Isaiah 5; (5) Potter-Clay, Isaiah 64. Provide concordances to two or more students, if the group needs help.

Into the Word

Plan ahead with a singer from your class or congregation to sing the following stanzas written to be sung to the tune, "Bunessan," to which Eleanor Farjeon's hymn, "Morning Has Broken" is commonly sung:

My well beloved planted a vineyard,
  Planted a vineyard on a green hill.
He dug it gently; He cleaned the stones out;
  He found the best vine, planted it well.

My well beloved, He built a tower;
  He would defend it, with holy eye.
He made a winepress, ready for good grapes,
  But the vine failed him; wild grapes would die.

My well beloved, He loved that vineyard;
  He loved that vineyard; reaching through time.
His vineyard failed Him; what could He then do?
  His heart was broken, by fruitless vine.

At the conclusion of the solo, ask your students to turn to the text. Ask them to identify elements from the song that are from the text. Then ask them to list elements in the text that were not in the song. (Basically, the stanzas deal with verses 1, 2, and 4.)

If someone in your class or congregation is a horticulturist, or simply keeps a few grapevines, ask her/him to speak briefly of the necessities of tending vines. Relate whatever is said to today's text.

Have cut out enough four-inch circles from purple (or green) construction paper so you can give one to each student; each will also need a black marker or crayon. Ask the group to examine Isaiah 5 for any specific or general sins noted in Israel or Judah. Direct each to write one sin on the "grape" he has been given. Highlight verses 7, 8, 11, 12, 13, 14, 15, 18, 20, 21, 22, 23, 24. Ask for an identification of sins found (and related verses). For example: oppression, v. 7; greed, v. 8; drunkenness, v. 11; ignoring God, v. 12; vanity, v. 14; calling evil good, v. 20; self-sufficiency, v. 21; perverted justice, v. 23; despising the word of God. v. 24. (A similar activity appears in the student book.)

Into Life

Bring pages (or whole sections) of recent newspapers—local, if available—and distribute to each class member. Provide purple crayons, if possible, and ask students to find and circle news articles that in a real sense represent "wild grapes." Ask members to identify the events and how they are "wild grapes," how they represent the opposite of God's desire for men. Also discuss how, if in any way, an individual Christian or class can nurture or prune the "wild grapes" in local society. If no one else in the class suggests it, be sure to note the need for the leaven of the gospel: the need for Christians to be salt and light in a society that has "rottenness in its roots" (see Isaiah 5:24).

If you have a small class and can afford it, distribute to each member one of the "lunch-box size" boxes of raisins. Attach to each box a sticker or masking tape on which you have written the following: "Isaiah 5—to be used as a devotional snack during the week, as a reminder of today's lesson and truth."

Close the session with prayer.

Let's Talk It Over

The questions on this page are designed to encourage review of the lesson
Scriptures and to promote discussion of the lesson by the class. The answers
provided are only discussion starters. Let your class talk it over from there.

1. Isaiah presented a song to communicate God's message to the people. Give some reasons why music can be particularly powerful in reaching people.

Music can: (1) Touch the emotions. It has the ability to stir the heart, to generate deep feeling, to move to action. Every revolution (religious or political) has been accompanied by music that aroused people's feelings. (2) Teach. Without appearing to intend to teach, music gets its message across, usually in subtle ways. It can and does influence thoughts and attitudes. Martin Luther declared his preference for writing the hymns of Christian people rather than their creeds. He knew which of the two wielded the greater power! (3) Appeal to the conscious *and* the unconscious mind. Music is in man's soul, appealing to him at the deepest levels of thought and feeling. For these reasons and more, the Christian faith is a singing faith!

2. Isaiah depicted the rich provisions God made for His people Israel. In what ways has God blessed our nation?

(1) God has blessed us with abundant natural resources. Land, water, minerals, timber, etc., all contribute to the wealth of our nation. (2) The Christian message and influence has been present from the founding of the republic. That presence has impacted our country for good. (3) Freedom and a tradition of law has guaranteed human rights and opportunities. (4) We have been blessed with natural protection by the oceans around us. Our land, people, and resources have been ravaged by war only internally. (5) Diverse and vigorous ethnic and racial mixes have been a blessing to the nation as a whole. The cultures, traditions, and heritage of these peoples have enriched our nation. (6) We are blessed with a position of influence among the nations of the world. All these blessings and privileges should endow us with a sobering and challenging sense of responsibility. As Jesus said to whom much has been given, much will be required.

3. What are some "wild grapes" (in opposition to God's intent) growing in our land?

Abortion. The destruction of fetuses on demand denies our Christian heritage and value system. God must be revulsed and saddened by the wave of abortions sweeping over our land. *Pornography.* Magazines, books, movies, television, and drama are all used to induce human minds to become moral cesspools. Filth and vulgarity pervade the land. The impact of this upon behavior and relationships is evident and adverse. *Drug abuse.* Minds and bodies that were intended to be under the control of the Spirit are dominated and enslaved by drugs. Alcohol (a drug!), "pot," cocaine, and even prescription drugs head the list. *Materialism.* "Things" dominate so many. Top priority is given to the acquisition and enjoyment of material objects. No sacrifice of time, energy, or gifts seems to be too great to satisfy the materialistic urge. *Secularism.* Indifference to and rejection of religious values and ideals leads to the downfall of a nation. "Secular" man appears to be gaining ascendancy in many circles today. *Humanism.* Giving highest elevation to human interests and values over deity (the God who created mankind) leads to the ultimate denial of reality and truth. To dethrone God or create Him in man's own image and likeness means death.

4. Cite some expressions of injustice and oppression prevalent in our society today.

(1) *Economic.* "Slum lords" gain wealth at the expense of the poor. Legal, "easy" bankruptcy has become an expression of injustice and constitutes oppression of many deserving creditors. (2) *Social.* "Age-ism" reeks as one of our newest forms of injustice and oppression. The aging are frequently discriminated against (subtly or boldly) by their families, government, and society. (3) *Legal.* Our system of justice is perverted by the wealthy who can utilize the most competent legal aid to protect themselves from the consequences of their criminal behavior. (4) *Governmental.* As in Isaiah's day, public officials often accept bribes, gaining favors for some at the expense of others. (5) *Sexual.* Females suffer inequality of pay, compared to males, for identical work. Despite legal prohibitions at this point, injustice and oppression continue.

Isaiah's Call

LESSON SCRIPTURE: Isaiah 6.

PRINTED TEXT: Isaiah 6:1-8.

Isaiah 6:1-8

1 In the year that king Uzziah died I saw also the Lord sitting upon a throne, high and lifted up, and his train filled the temple.

2 Above it stood the seraphim: each one had six wings; with twain he covered his face, and with twain he covered his feet, and with twain he did fly.

3 And one cried unto another, and said, Holy, holy, holy, is the Lord of hosts: the whole earth is full of his glory.

4 And the posts of the door moved at the voice of him that cried, and the house was filled with smoke.

5 Then said I, Woe is me! for I am undone; because I am a man of unclean lips, and I dwell in the midst of a people of unclean lips: for mine eyes have seen the King, the Lord of hosts.

6 Then flew one of the seraphim unto me, having a live coal in his hand, which he had taken with the tongs from off the altar:

7 And he laid it upon my mouth, and said, Lo, this hath touched thy lips; and thine iniquity is taken away, and thy sin purged.

8 Also I heard the voice of the Lord, saying, Whom shall I send, and who will go for us? Then said I, Here am I; send me.

GOLDEN TEXT: I heard the voice of the Lord, saying, Whom shall I send, and who will go for us? Then said I, Here am I; send me.—Isaiah 6:8.

Lesson Aims

This lesson should enable a student to:

1. Tell the story of Isaiah's call to be a prophet.

2. Give at least three possible reasons why Isaiah was called rather than some other person.

3. Include some specific Christian service in his calling.

Lesson Outline

INTRODUCTION
  A. Good and Bad in Judah
  B. Lesson Background
I. GOD AND PROPHET (Isaiah 6:1-5)
  A. The Holy Lord (vv. 1-4)
  B. The Unholy Man (v. 5)
    Admission of Guilt
II. CLEANSED FOR SERVICE (Isaiah 6:6-8)
  A. Cleansed (vv. 6, 7)
  B. A Volunteer for Service (v. 8)
    Over All the Earth
CONCLUSION
  A. Willing
  B. Able
  C. Prayer
  D. Thought to Remember

Display visual 6 from the visuals/learning resources packet. It is shown on page 52.

Introduction

Our lesson is properly titled "Isaiah's Call." It is natural to suppose that he was called before he began to prophesy, but this is not necessarily so. One may be called to service that he is already engaged in. Consider the call of Simon and Andrew (Matthew 4:18-20). They had followed Jesus for months before this (John 1:35—4:38). Likewise Isaiah may have been delivering God's messages for some time before the call recorded in chapter 6. We cannot tell.

A. Good and Bad in Judah

As noted in last week's lesson, Uzziah was a good king of Judah. "He did that which was right in the sight of the Lord. . . . And he sought God." Therefore "God made him to prosper." He strengthened the army and subdued the hostile

tribes around Judah, forcing them to pay tribute. He fortified Jerusalem and other cities, and even recovered Eloth, Solomon's ancient port on the Red Sea (2 Chronicles 26:1-15).

Like many successful people, Uzziah became too proud of himself and his success. He decided to make himself priest as well as king, personally burning incense in the temple. The priests protested that that was their duty, but Uzziah would not listen. Arrogantly he strode into the Holy Place, carrying the censer of glowing coals. At the altar of incense he felt the leprosy break out in his forehead. Terrified, he abandoned his purpose and hurried out of the temple (2 Chronicles 26:16-21).

The stricken king was isolated like any other leper, and his son Jotham managed the kingdom. Probably Uzziah in his isolation continued to direct Jotham. We know that Jotham continued his father's good policies (2 Chronicles 27:1-6). However, "the people did yet corruptly" (2 Chronicles 27:2), and their corruption was denounced in the early prophecies of Isaiah. Perhaps both Uzziah and Jotham were too engrossed with foreign affairs to give attention to the wickedness of their own people.

B. Lesson Background

Isaiah's call is dated "in the year that king Uzziah died" (Isaiah 6:1). It is hard to tell just what year that was. It may have been about 740 or 735 B.C.

It may seem that Uzziah's death would make little difference, since his son Jotham already was managing the kingdom. However, the old king had been a powerful influence for good, and his influence probably continued even when he was isolated. That influence now was gone. Isaiah knew the people in general were not so good as their kings. In particular, the wealthy landholders and moneylenders were crooked and cruel. Being well acquainted with the royal family, Isaiah doubtless knew that Jotham's son Ahaz was more in sympathy with the popular corruption than with his father's goodness. It was a dark time in Judah, and the future was to be darker still. There was urgent need for someone to proclaim God's word plainly.

I. God and Prophet
(Isaiah 6:1-5)

Isaiah wrote, "I saw the Lord." Such a statement is puzzling, for God told Moses, "There shall no man see me, and live" (Exodus 33:20). Yet Moses and others "saw the God of Israel" (Exodus 24:9-11). Stephen saw "the glory of God, and Jesus standing on the right hand of

God" (Acts 7:55). John saw a throne in Heaven, "and one sat on the throne" (Revelation 4:2).

For our limited understanding, perhaps the best explanation is the simple one God gave to Moses. Moses was shielded from the full glory of God's face, but allowed to see His back, or, as some would translate, His afterglow (Exodus 33:17-23). So at various times men have seen some part of God's glory, some manifestation or revelation of the Almighty, though the full glory of His face is too much for any man to endure.

A. The Holy Lord (vv. 1-4)

1. In the year that king Uzziah died I saw also the Lord sitting upon a throne, high and lifted up, and his train filled the temple.

The word *temple* sometimes means God's dwelling place in Heaven. See Psalm 11:4:

> The Lord is in his holy temple,
> the Lord's throne is in heaven.

Some students think Isaiah was given a vision of God enthroned in Heaven, and perhaps that is true. On the other hand, the temple in Jerusalem was known as God's dwelling place on earth, and God filled it with His glory as it was completed (1 Kings 8:10, 11). Perhaps Isaiah was in that temple when the vision came. Whatever the location, the vision was impressive. The Lord was sitting on a lofty throne, and the skirt of His long robe spread out to fill the whole temple.

2. Above it stood the seraphim: each one had six wings; with twain he covered his face, and with twain he covered his feet, and with twain he did fly.

The word *seraphim* is plural. One of the seraphim would be called a seraph. About these attendants we know only what we find in our text. The name probably means fiery or burning. They had faces and hands and feet, so we suppose they were like human beings in form, though *each one had six wings.* With one pair of wings *he did fly,* hovering in the air above the widespreading robe of the Lord. The other four wings hid the seraph from God's face. As Moses was shielded from God's full glory (Exodus 33:22), so the seraphim shielded themselves even from the glory that Isaiah was allowed to see.

3. And one cried unto another, and said, Holy, holy, holy, is the Lord of hosts: the whole earth is full of his glory.

This verse might be taken to suggest that there were only two seraphim, one of which called to the other. Mindful of the glory and majesty of the scene, however, many students picture one group calling to another, or one choir singing and another choir responding. It is usually supposed that one seraph or one group sang, *Holy,*

holy, holy, is the Lord of hosts, and another responded, *The whole earth is full of his glory.* Of course, some other division would be possible. We can imagine that one group sang the first *holy,* another echoed it in the second *holy,* and then the two together sang the third *holy.*

The primary meaning of the word *holy* is set apart, separate, distinguished. God is set apart from all other beings by His greater power and wisdom and goodness. His goodness is such a prominent part of His holiness that the word *holy* sometimes means good or righteous. God is entirely separated from anything that is wrong. In ancient times He called Israel to be likewise separated from all the wrongs and sins of the world: "Ye shall be holy: for I the Lord your God am holy" (Leviticus 19:2). Later Peter echoed that call to Christians of his time and ours: "As he which hath called you is holy, so be ye holy in all manner of conversation; because it is written, Be ye holy, for I am holy" (1 Peter 1:15, 16).

Some students suggest that the threefold repetition of *holy* refers to the Father, Son, and Holy Spirit. Possibly it does. All of them are equally holy. But certainly the repetition is emphatic. It indicates that God is completely, entirely, utterly holy.

The phrase *Lord of hosts* or *Jehovah of hosts* emphasizes the greatness and supreme power of God. He is Lord of all the angelic hosts of Heaven. He is Lord of all the hosts of His people on earth. In due time He will demonstrate that He is Lord also of all the hosts of wickedness that now defy Him.

The whole earth is full of his glory. In the song of the seraphim God's glory filled earth, not Heaven. This seems to suggest that Isaiah was seeing the Lord in His earthly temple; but of course this is only a suggestion, not a declaration. (Recall the comments on verse 1.) "The heavens declare the glory of God" (Psalm 19:1), but they declare it to the earth. For those with eyes to see, God's glory is plain in the beauty of sunrise and the heat of noonday, in the flowers that bloom and the harvest that feeds us, in towering mountains and fruitful plains, in majestic

How to Say It

AHAZ. *A*-haz.
ELOTH. *Ee*-loth.
HEZEKIAH. Hez-uh-*kye*-uh.
ISAIAH. Eye-*zay*-uh.
JOTHAM. *Joe*-tham.
SERAPHIM. *sair*-uh-fim.
UZZIAH. Uh-*zye*-uh.

forests and green pastures, in flowing rivers and trickling brooks, in rising winds and driving clouds, in flying birds and crawling animals, in flashing lightning and roaring thunder. How sad it is that some people see all these things and miss God's glory!

4. And the posts of the door moved at the voice of him that cried, and the house was filled with smoke.

Often there is some disagreement about the meaning of Hebrew architectural terms. Here the *King James Version* speaks of *the posts of the door,* but the *American Standard Version* says, "The foundations of the thresholds shook at the voice of him that cried." Isaiah probably was standing at the door, for all the floor within the temple was covered by the spreading robe of the Almighty (v. 1). He could feel the threshold tremble under his feet, for the voice of praise to God was so powerful and resonant that it shook the temple to its very foundations. This language fits well with the opinion that Isaiah was seeing this vision in the temple on earth, but of course we know little about what God's throne room in Heaven is like.

The house was filled with smoke. Students have suggested various possible meanings for this statement:

1. The smoke was white, a luminous mist like the glory of the Lord that filled the temple at its completion (1 Kings 8:10, 11).

2. The smoke was dark, intended to shield Isaiah from God's glory as the seraphim shielded themselves with their wings (v. 2).

3. The smoke was a symbol of God's anger that was going to bring destruction to Judah (vv. 11, 12).

4. The smoke was from the altar of incense (v. 6), a symbol of prayers rising to God.

5. The smoke, coupled with the trembling temple, heightened the impression of power.

If Isaiah knew what the smoke meant, he did not choose to tell us. Perhaps we shall have to be content without knowing for sure.

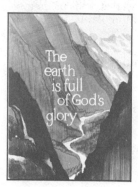

The earth is full of God's glory

visual 6

B. The Unholy Man (v. 5)

5. Then said I, Woe is me! for I am undone; because I am a man of unclean lips, and I dwell in the midst of a people of unclean lips: for mine eyes have seen the King, the Lord of hosts.

Isaiah saw the Lord "upon a throne, high and lifted up," a figure so huge that "his train filled the temple" (v. 1). With that sight before him the prophet must have felt very tiny, very weak. Then the seraphim shook the temple with their shout concerning God's holiness. At that shout Isaiah had to feel most powerfully that he was unholy. *I am a man of unclean lips.* Why did he think of his lips rather than his hands? We are not told. Perhaps the voice of the seraphim made him realize that his own voice was unworthy to speak in praise of God. Or perhaps Isaiah realized that speech is harder to control than action is. Good men who keep their hands clean may still sin with their lips (see James 3:2).

I dwell in the midst of a people of unclean lips. Isaiah was not worse than the other people of Judah, but he was the one who had seen *the King, the Lord of hosts.* Probably the prophet knew the ancient word of the Lord, "There shall no man see me, and live" (Exodus 33:20). So what could Isaiah expect but sudden death? To be *undone* is to be destroyed.

ADMISSION OF GUILT

A woman accused of breaking into a car came to court protesting her innocence. However, she quickly changed her plea to guilty, for the woman who owned the vandalized car identified the jacket worn by the defendant. The jacket had been left in the car and the defendant was wearing it as her own. To prove her case, the owner merely flipped up the collar to reveal her name stitched into it. The accused might have gotten away with her crime if she hadn't been "caught with the goods." Under the circumstances she had no choice but to admit her guilt.

Isaiah had seen God, and the sight terrified him. Suddenly, all the goodness Isaiah might have claimed vanished. Rather than pretend an innocence he didn't have, he chose to admit his sinfulness before God.

"All have sinned," the apostle says, "and come short of the glory of God" (Romans 3:23). We can be like the woman in court, feigning an innocence we don't have, or we can be like Isaiah, who freely admitted his guilt, repented, and was forgiven. If we confess and repent of our sin now, before we are forced to do so in the judgment, we too will find forgiveness and experience the joy, not the fear, of being in God's presence.

—V. H.

II. Cleansed for Service
(Isaiah 6:6-8)

Surely anyone who is aware of God's holiness must be aware of his own unholiness. Recall how Simon Peter reacted when he saw the miraculous power of Jesus at work in his own familiar fishing boat. Peter "fell down at Jesus' knees, saying, Depart from me; for I am a sinful man, O Lord" (Luke 5:8). But neither Jesus nor His Father is quick to depart from His people when they know they are unworthy. He prefers to make them more worthy for His service.

A. Cleansed (vv. 6, 7)

6, 7. Then flew one of the seraphim unto me, having a live coal in his hand, which he had taken with the tongs from off the altar: and he laid it upon my mouth, and said, Lo, this hath touched thy lips; and thine iniquity is taken away, and thy sin purged.

The fiery touch burned the uncleanness from Isaiah's lips and made them ready to serve the Lord. Of course more than the burning coal was involved in the cleansing. Isaiah had realized and confessed his sin. "If we confess our sins, he is faithful and just to forgive us our sins, and to cleanse us from all unrighteousness" (1 John 1:9).

The burning coal was taken *from off the altar*, but which altar? The temple had two. There was the small golden altar in the Holy Place where incense was burned as a symbol of prayer. Forgiveness is won in part by the burning in our hearts from which prayers arise, prayers of confession and pleading for mercy. Then there was the great altar in front of the Holy Place where sacrifices were made to atone for sin. Those sacrifices have been replaced forever by the sacrifice of Jesus on the cross (Hebrews 7:26, 27), but still there is no remission of sins without the shedding of blood (Hebrews 9:22). So both altars are involved in cleansing one for God's service: the altar of sacrifice and the altar of prayer. Christ offered himself in sacrifice for our cleansing; we offer prayers for ourselves and for one another.

B. A Volunteer for Service (v. 8)

8. Also I heard the voice of the Lord, saying, Whom shall I send, and who will go for us? Then said I, Here am I; send me.

The Lord asked a double question. He asked, *Whom shall I send?* and then *Who will go?* He was asking for a volunteer. He wanted to send someone who was willing to go and deliver His message to His people. Of course, the second question was pointed straight at Isaiah. As far as we know, he was the only human being there. So he volunteered quickly: *Here am I; send me.*

Not all of God's messengers volunteered so eagerly. Moses, for example, protested, "Not me, Lord." Insistently he offered several excuses and finally pleaded, "Send anyone you want to, but not me" (Exodus 4:10-13). But Moses was drafted, and he served magnificently.

The Lord is still asking for volunteers to speak for Him. Though we see no sublime vision, we know He is truly on the throne, high and lifted up. We know He wants His people to speak for Him, to take His gospel not only to all the world, but to every creature (Mark 16:15). His message is not only for the animist in Africa, but also for the unbeliever next door.

Some few Christians respond to God's call as eagerly as Isaiah did. They do not have Isaiah's gift of inspiration, but they have God's inspired Word in the Bible and Isaiah's willingness. With these they become swift messengers to the people next door or the people on the other side of the world. Other Christians, like Moses, wait to be drafted. Leaders of the church see their ability and urge them to take an active part in calling or teaching or ministering to the sick. Many such draftees serve as nobly as the volunteers. Then there are those who never respond to God's call, if indeed they hear it. They enjoy the blessings of salvation but never say a word for the Savior. How about you? Are you a volunteer, a draftee, or just among those present?

OVER ALL THE EARTH

In a speech delivered to the British Parliament on December 8, 1941, Winston Churchill declared that the light of hope for the Allies was only a flicker. But, he predicted, it eventually would become a flaming light shining over land

---

Home Daily Bible Readings

Monday, Oct. 3—The History of Uzziah (2 Chronicles 26:1-15)
Tuesday, Oct. 4—Uzziah's Apostasy (2 Chronicles 26:16-23)
Wednesday, Oct. 5—Isaiah's Vision of God (Isaiah 6:1-5)
Thursday, Oct. 6—Isaiah Is Charged to Prophesy (Isaiah 6:6-13)
Friday, Oct. 7—The Painful Message of the Prophets (Amos 7:10-17)
Saturday, Oct. 8—The Cost of Discipleship (Luke 9:57-62)
Sunday, Oct. 9—Jesus Expands on Isaiah (Matthew 13:10-17)

and sea. In this way he referred to the Allied military effort that would engulf Japan and Germany in its mammoth jaws.

Christianity began as a flickering light in a far-off land. Twenty centuries later it floods the world in an unparalleled spiritual illumination.

Jesus came with the truth and as the truth. He came in love expressing love. He came as one of us and met each of us at the point of our greatest need. And now, renewed, we must proclaim the acceptability and the all-sufficiency of the grace He brought us. That is the light for which those in darkness search; the hope that those in despair crave; the word of forgiveness that all the guilty need. Like Isaiah, if we have found forgiveness, we must be willing and ready to share the soul-saving message with others.   —V. H.

Conclusion

Out of all the thousands of Judah, why was Isaiah chosen to be God's prophet? Three reasons are easily seen.

1. Isaiah was willing. He said, "Here am I; send me." There was no promise of pay or popularity or success. God warned that the people would close their ears and harden their hearts. Still the message must be given until the nation's disobedience would bring its destruction (Isaiah 6:9-12). In spite of that dismal prospect, Isaiah was willing.

2. Isaiah was able. The splendid poetry of his book shows fine skill in the use of language. He was specially inspired, of course; but no doubt he was a talented speaker, singer, and writer before he was called and inspired.

3. Isaiah was in a position to do the job. Probably he was a member of the royal family. Whether he belonged to that family or not, he was in a position to talk to the rulers and be heard. King Ahaz heard but did not heed (Isaiah 7). King Hezekiah both heard and heeded, and the nation's destruction was postponed (Isaiah 36, 37). Not till Isaiah was gone did hard hearts and disobedience prevail so completely that destruction resulted (2 Chronicles 36:5-21).

A. Willing

A farm boy thought he was called to be a preacher. He said he saw the letters GPC emblazoned in the sunset sky, meaning Go Preach Christ. He therefore went away to college to study for the ministry, but after his first year his faculty adviser said he had misinterpreted the message in the sky. To this boy, GPC really meant Go Plant Corn. He was willing to be a preacher, but not able.

That story is repeated to generation after generation because something similar happens in real life in every generation. One farm boy who studied for the ministry was Tim Marston. It took more than one year, but in time he realized that he had no talent for either public speaking or private counseling.

Back home again, he was willing to be a farmer. He found that he loved the work, and was able to do it well. He made his farm the finest in the county. He was in a favored position to do this because he inherited the farm well equipped and free of debt.

Undoubtedly God called Tim to plant corn. But this successful farmer was a pillar in the church and a powerful witness for the Lord. That was part of his calling.

B. Able

Roger Long was a skilled machinist who was transferred to a new locality. There some Christian neighbors took him and his family to church. All of them were fascinated by the Christian message, which they never had really heard before. Soon they all became Christians and eagerly took part in the work of the church.

Then Roger began to feel that he was not doing enough for the Lord. Intrigued by the reports of foreign missions, he thought of becoming a missionary. Enthusiastically he talked with his wife and family, considering all the possibilities. But finally he decided that it was best to give up that ambition.

Roger was willing, even eager. He was able, or could become able with a few years of preparation. But he was not in a position to undertake the needed training. He had a family to support, and with his good job he was in an excellent position to support a family. He decided that was what God had called him to do.

So Roger devoted himself to his calling, but did not lose interest in missions. He became chairman of the missionary committee in his church. Due largely to his influence, the congregation tripled its giving to missions. Laughingly Roger says he has done more for the missionary cause than he could have done on a foreign field. Now his sons are preparing for missionary service. With an enthusiastic family and church behind them, they are in the best possible position to become missionaries.

C. Prayer

Father in Heaven, we know You have called all of us to be Your children, and we thank You. May each of us find and follow whatever calling to special service You have for him personally.

D. Thought to Remember

"Here am I; send me."

Learning by Doing

This page contains an alternate lesson plan emphasizing learning activities. Classes desiring such student involvement will find these suggestions helpful.

Learning Goals

Following a study of Isaiah's call in Isaiah 6, the learner will:

1. Be able to relate the details of the event as described.

2. Compare and contrast the specific call of Isaiah with the general call of other saints and all Christians.

3. Worship in a more reverent and submissive fashion.

Into the Lesson

At an office supply store, buy a small tablet of phone memo forms. Fill in enough of the forms to distribute one to each class member. Depending on the form used, fill in the date, time (use your Sunday-school beginning time), and message or return call with the phone number (225) 547-2424. Indicate to your class that there is a coded message in the numbers given and students are to decipher it. Display a large push-button telephone face on the chalkboard or poster board for all to see. Give students time to solve the code. If you decide a clue will help, indicate that the message is two words, and the word division is between the 5 and 4. A second clue is that the message deals with today's lesson. (The message is "Call Isaiah.") Once the message is identified, you are ready to go on to the next activity. If you are unable to purchase phone memo forms, prepare a single one on poster board, to show to the whole class.

The second introductory activity can be done on an overhead projector with transparencies, or it can be done on the chalkboard. Prepare two large cartoon-type dialogue balloons side by side, under the headings "Caller" and "Callee." Then, by overlay or by simply writing in the words, display the following Biblical confrontations and ask the class to identify the occasion and the one being called by God. (1) "Come now, I will send you to Pharaoh that you may rescue my people"/"Who am I that I should go?" (Moses, Exodus 3). (2) "Before I formed you in the womb, I knew you"/"Behold, I cannot speak; for I am a child" (Jeremiah 1). (3) "Follow me, and I will make you fishers of men"/"We will straightway leave our nets and follow you" (Simon Peter and Andrew, Matthew 4). (4) "Whom shall I send, and who will go for us?"/"Here am I; send me" (Isaiah 6).

A related activity is found in the student book that accompanies this series.

Into the Word

Have someone read aloud today's text before the class. Be sure the reader indicates the text clearly: Isaiah 6:1-8. Distribute paper and pens and ask students to number vertically one to nine. Then read the following statements one at a time and ask them to write each statement by the number to which it relates. The correct number follows each of the statements here. (1) Number of words in the two questions the voice of the Lord asked, discounting the word "and"—9. (2) Number of times the seraphim called "Holy"—3. (3) Number of letters in the word Isaiah used to describe his lips—7. (4) Number of words in Isaiah's response to the Lord's questions—5. (5) Number of seraphim directly involved in Isaiah's cleansing—1. (6) Number of wings the seraphim used for flying—2. (7) Chapter number for today's text—6. (8) Number of kings under whom Isaiah prophesied—4. (9) Number of verses in today's text—8.

On the same sheet of paper, have the students write the alphabet into a column. Mention that this text is one of the Bible's beautiful and profound revelations of God and His nature; then ask the class to take five minutes to see how many letters of the alphabet they can use for words that picture what God is or what He does. Give them two examples: *holy* (v. 3) and *exalted* (v. 1). Time them, then compile a list on the chalkboard from their findings. Be certain to ask where/how the various attributes are seen in the text. (Other words that may be suggested are *awesome, beautiful, concerned, elevated, forgiving, glorious, helper, kingly, loving, magnificent, purifying, vocal, worthy*.)

Into Life

Give each member an index card on which to write one large capital G, one small i, then a large capital G with a capital I inside. Explain the meaning as follows: when one sees how great God is, as Isaiah did, he begins to see how small he himself is, as Isaiah did. But he also realizes that living in God he is able to fulfill the ministry that God wants him to, even as Isaiah did. Suggest that the members carry the card for a week or two as a reminder.

Let's Talk It Over

The questions on this page are designed to encourage review of the lesson Scriptures and to promote discussion of the lesson by the class. The answers provided are only discussion starters. Let your class talk it over from there.

1. In what two basic ways does God reveal himself to man, and what can we learn about God from these revelations?

Essentially, God reveals himself in general and special revelation. General revelation occurs in and through the created order, that is, the heavens and the earth. These testify to the power and wisdom of the Creator. But general revelation does not tell us that God is holy and that He is love. In words (the inspired message of the prophets, apostles, and others, which are recorded in the Bible) and the Word (Jesus Christ) God reveals His holiness and His love. That is special revelation. God revealed himself to Isaiah as a holy and loving God, who cared about His people. This revelation far exceeded anything Isaiah could know through nature. Most important, God manifested himself in a way most appropriate for our understanding through the God-man, Jesus Christ.

2. How does the revelation of God's holiness fit with the concept that God is love?

The most prominent affirmation about God in contemporary Christianity is that God is love. That's a good place to start, but it doesn't give a full and balanced view of God. Many respond to this affirmation with the question, "How can a loving God allow anyone to go to Hell?" God is greater than any of our definitions or descriptions. But we can confidently affirm that He is holy and He is love. In our limited human understanding, we can classify all of God's characteristics under these two headings. As the holy God, He judges and punishes us. As the loving God, He gives of himself to forgive the sin and redeem the sinner. Isaiah saw God as holy ("Holy, holy, holy, is the Lord of hosts"—6:3) then as love personified, prophesied in the coming of Jesus into the world ("Behold, a virgin shall conceive, and bear a son, and shall call his name Immanuel"—7:14). Twentieth-century Christians, and the world, need to see God as holy *and* love.

3. Why does the primary focus of public, corporate worship need to be centered objectively in God?

Many Christians focus their worship *subjectively*—on the worshiper. Statements such as "I

didn't get anything out of that service," or "That uplifting service gave me just the help I needed" reveal this perspective. *Objective* focus centers on the One who is worshiped, rather than on the worshiper. Yet these two focuses are not to be pitted against each other. It's not "either, or" but "both, and." Balance is valid and necessary in the worship experience. But the objective focus is primary. Praise, adoration, and reverence are offered to God, because only He is worthy of it. To be sure, the worshiper will be a beneficiary of genuine worship, but that focus is secondary. Note that Isaiah's experience began with the dramatic and powerful focus on the holy God!

4. Isaiah confessed to being a man "of unclean lips." Why did his confession center on his mouth?

Jesus asserts that a man's "mouth speaks from that which fills his heart" (Luke 6:45, *New American Standard Bible*). In confessing that his lips were unclean, Isaiah was also confessing his need for spiritual cleansing. Indeed, who among us has not sinned with his lips? James says, "If any man offend not in word, the same is a perfect man, and able also to bridle the whole body" (3:2). Also, Isaiah had just heard the seraphim proclaiming the holiness of God. Perhaps this made him realize how unworthy he was even to attempt to praise God with his own voice.

5. Why do some people refuse to respond readily to God's call to service?

Here are some reasons: (1) Other concerns and values receive higher priority—"I'm too busy." (2) Feelings of inadequacy dominate—"I don't feel I can do it." "I don't have any talents." (3) Commitment is lacking—"I belong, but I'm not very active." "I don't feel I should get involved." (4) Understanding that we are "saved to serve" is lacking—"I love God and live a good life. Isn't that enough?" (5) Self-centeredness (false humility?) prevails—"I'd be embarrassed; I don't want to call attention to myself." Isaiah provides a stimulating model of appropriate responsiveness for all of us. He answered God's call with a forthright, simple expression of commitment: "Here I am. Use me!"

Words of Hope

LESSON SCRIPTURE: Isaiah 40.

PRINTED TEXT: Isaiah 40:1-5, 9-11.

Isaiah 40:1-5, 9-11

1 Comfort ye, comfort ye my people, saith your God.

2 Speak ye comfortably to Jerusalem, and cry unto her, that her warfare is accomplished, that her iniquity is pardoned: for she hath received of the Lord's hand double for all her sins.

3 The voice of him that crieth in the wilderness, Prepare ye the way of the Lord, make straight in the desert a highway for our God.

4 Every valley shall be exalted, and every mountain and hill shall be made low: and the crooked shall be made straight, and the rough places plain:

5 And the glory of the Lord shall be revealed, and all flesh shall see it together: for the mouth of the Lord hath spoken it.

. . . .

9 O Zion, that bringest good tidings, get thee up into the high mountain; O Jerusalem, that bringest good tidings, lift up thy voice with strength; lift it up, be not afraid; say unto the cities of Judah, Behold your God!

10 Behold, the Lord God will come with strong hand, and his arm shall rule for him: behold, his reward is with him, and his work before him.

11 He shall feed his flock like a shepherd: he shall gather the lambs with his arm, and carry them in his bosom, and shall gently lead those that are with young.

GOLDEN TEXT: And the glory of the Lord shall be revealed, and all flesh shall see it together: for the mouth of the Lord hath spoken it.—Isaiah 40:5.

Through Suffering to Hope
Unit 2: Isaiah—Interpreting a Nation's Suffering (Lessons 5-9)

Lesson Aims

After this lesson a student should be able to:
1. Point out the Scripture references to the return of the Jews from Babylon, to the coming of Christ, and to the second coming of Christ.
2. Tell what the released captives were called to do.
3. Resolve to tell the good news.

Lesson Outline

INTRODUCTION
  A. The Prophet's View
  B. Lesson Background
  I. COMFORT FOR JERUSALEM (Isaiah 40:1, 2)
    A. Call to Comfort (v. 1)
    B. How to Comfort (v. 2)
 II. A CRY TO GOD'S PEOPLE (Isaiah 40:3-5)
    A. Call to Prepare (v. 3)
    B. How to Prepare (vv. 4, 5)
III. A MISSION FOR JERUSALEM (Isaiah 40:9-11)
    A. Call to Proclaim (v. 9)
    B. What to Proclaim (vv. 10, 11)
       Not This God
CONCLUSION
  A. We Are There
  B. We Are Called
  C. We Have Obligations
  D. Prayer
  E. Thought to Remember

Display visual 7 from the visuals/learning resources packet. It illustrates the section "The Prophet's View" in the "Introduction." The visual is shown on page 60.

Introduction

When one looks across a wide valley at distant mountains, he seems to see but a single range, like a jagged wall with the horizon resting on its top. But when one crosses the valley to climb that mountain wall, he finds a series of ranges with valleys between. Starting up into the foothills he soon reaches a summit. From there he looks down at lower ground, with a higher summit beyond. When he gets to the next summit he sees another valley between him and a summit that is higher still. So by many ups and downs he comes to the highest summit of all.

A. The Prophet's View

R. C. Foster likened a prophet's view of the future to our view of distant mountains. Looking ahead by divine revelation, the prophet sees great events in Israel's history rising in the future like majestic mountains. There may be wide valleys of time between those outstanding events, but they are not revealed to the prophet. He sees those future events as if they were close together, though they may be separated by centuries of time.

Isaiah stood in Jerusalem while Israel and Judah both were on a slippery downward slope into captivity. He could see injustice and corruption around him, and he could see that God would send the armies of Assyria to punish His people (Isaiah 10:1-6). In the midst of Isaiah's forty-year ministry Assyria did destroy north Israel and scatter its people in foreign lands (2 Kings 17:1-6). Judah also was threatened, but Isaiah promised that God would rescue it at that time, and He did (Isaiah 37:5-7, 36-38). Nevertheless Isaiah could see that corruption in Judah would grow until Judah would be taken captive, not to Assyria, but to Babylon (Isaiah 39:5-7). That captivity came a hundred years later and lasted seventy years, but it was part of the dark valley that Isaiah could see in the near future.

Beyond the captivity of Israel and Judah Isaiah could see three great events like towering mountains: the return from captivity, the coming of Christ, and the second coming of Christ. But if Isaiah could see the wide valleys of time between those events, he did not describe them for us in his writings. In his prophecy the towering events seem to blend together like the various mountain ridges that when seen from a distance seem to blend into a single range.

B. Lesson Background

The prophecy recorded in Isaiah 40 is not dated, but probably it belongs to the latter part of Isaiah's ministry. North Israel no longer existed as a nation. Assyrian armies had crushed it and scattered its people in foreign lands. That was the Assyrian way of making sure those people would not rebel against Assyrian rule. The Assyrian invasion of Judah had been turned back, but God had revealed to Isaiah that Judah later would be captured by Babylon. The time of this captivity was not revealed to Isaiah, but later history showed that it was to begin in about a hundred years and to last for seventy years. A hundred years before the Babylonian captivity began, God called Isaiah to comfort His people by telling them what would happen after the captivity.

I. Comfort of Jerusalem
(Isaiah 40:1, 2)

Isaiah wrote his message of comfort for the future. The people of his own time saw no need for comfort because they did not believe his prophecy of disaster. The danger from Assyria was past, and the danger from Babylon had not yet arisen. Feeling secure, the people ignored Isaiah's warning of judgment (Isaiah 3). Hypocritically they went through the ceremonies of worship, and they thought God would take care of them and overlook their secret sins (Isaiah 29:13-16). All was well with them, they thought. Who needed a message of comfort? But things would be different a century later. The prophecy of Isaiah would prove to be true. Defeated and dispirited, the people of Jerusalem would be driven hundreds of weary miles to be captives in Babylon. There they would weep for their lost homeland (Psalm 137:1-6). But some among them would take the book of Isaiah with them to Babylon, and its promise of restoration would bring comfort to those in sorrow there.

A. Call to Comfort (v. 1)

1. Comfort ye, comfort ye my people, saith your God.

Disaster would come. Huge armies of Babylon would besiege Jerusalem for a year and a half. Thousands would die by starvation and disease and sword. Survivors would be taken away to the land of Babylon (2 Kings 25:1-11). Still God would call them *my people*. Leaders should be busy giving comfort, encouragement, and hope to the desolate.

B. How to Comfort (v. 2)

2. Speak ye comfortably to Jerusalem, and cry unto her, that her warfare is accomplished, that her iniquity is pardoned: for she hath received of the Lord's hand double for all her sins.

God's Word often speaks of future things as if they were present or past. So we read that Jerusalem's *warfare is accomplished*, finished, though when Isaiah said this the warfare with Babylon had not yet begun. It would start about a century later, and then Jerusalem would be subject to Babylon for seventy years. Not till the end of the seventy years would that warfare be over. But in the mind of God it was done already: that is, it was planned and decreed. The future was so sure that the message spoke as if it were already present.

Captivity was coming, and then the way to comfort the people of Jerusalem in Babylon would be to assure them that their captivity would not be forever. After seventy years of subjugation the warfare would be *accomplished*, finished. Then Jerusalem's *iniquity* would be *pardoned*. Then Jerusalem would have received *double for all her sins*. That last phrase is puzzling. The wages of sin is death (Romans 6:23). How could the people of Jerusalem die doubly? Many take this as a figure of speech meaning that the people would have been punished enough when the seventy years were over. However, the sinners who brought on the captivity were not the only ones who suffered from it. Many of the next generation also lived and died in captivity. Possibly this is what is meant by double punishment received.

II. A Cry to God's People
(Isaiah 40:3-5)

When an ancient king went traveling in his realm, a crier or herald went ahead of him, an advance man to see that everything was ready for the king. For one thing, the road had to be in good shape for his chariot. Even in our time road repairs may be hastened when someone of importance is coming. The best hotel suite is reserved, with ample room for the great man's entourage. Meetings and banquets are planned down to the last detail. Security people take elaborate precautions to prevent assassination. The advance man has the training and experience needed to see that all necessary preparations are made.

A. Call to Prepare (v. 3)

3. The voice of him that crieth in the wilderness, Prepare ye the way of the Lord, make straight in the desert a highway for our God.

By divine revelation Isaiah was looking forward about a hundred and seventy years. The Lord was coming! In the wide desert between Babylon and ruined Jerusalem, the prophet heard the voice of the crier, the advance man: *Prepare ye the way of the Lord!* He was coming to take His captive people back home.

B. How to Prepare (vv. 4, 5)

4. Every valley shall be exalted, and every mountain and hill shall be made low: and the crooked shall be made straight, and the rough places plain.

How to Say It

IMMANUEL. Ih-*man*-you-el.
ISAIAH. Eye-*zay*-uh.

It sounds like a modern road-building project, with huge earth-moving machines cutting down the hills, filling the valleys, straightening the curves, and smoothing the surface with black-top. Ancient road building was done with more men and less machinery, but it was done well. In this case, of course, the prophet was not thinking so much of a literal road as of a moral way. If God was to lead His people back to Jerusalem they must be a people made ready. High pride and stubborn rebellion had brought them to captivity; these must be cut down. On the other hand, some were so low in the valley of humiliation and despair that they had no hope. Their valley of depression must be filled with the understanding that they still were God's people. All the crooks and cheats must straighten up; the potholes of sinning must be filled with righteousness. Then the people would be ready to be returned to Jerusalem and liberty once more.

When the way would be thus prepared, God would lead His people back to Jerusalem. But this prophecy looked also to the coming of Jesus, then seven hundred years in the future. John the Baptist would be the one crying in the wilderness. He too would call for a moral way rather than a physical road. He would tell people to bring down their pride, raise up their hope, and straighten out their crooked ways (Luke 3:1-17).

5. And the glory of the Lord shall be revealed, and all flesh shall see it together: for the mouth of the Lord hath spoken it.

The glory of the Lord would be shown when Jesus would heal the sick and raise the dead and stop the storm. Multitudes would see these evidences of divine power and glory, but not *all flesh*. Our text says, *All flesh shall see it together.* This must be referring to Jesus' second coming. He will come "in the clouds of heaven with power and great glory." "Every eye shall see him, and they also which pierced him." Even as His enemies were condemning Him to death Jesus warned them that they would see Him again in power and glory. The wicked tribes of earth will mourn at His coming, but His people

will lift up their heads because He will bring redemption. His angels "shall gather together his elect from the four winds, from one end of heaven to the other" (Matthew 24:29-31; 26:64; Luke 21:25-28; Revelation 1:7). This magnificent coming is still in the future, but it is as sure as anything can be, *for the mouth of the Lord hath spoken it.* His promises are always kept. This is emphasized in Isaiah 40:6-8. Generations of people come and go like the grass of the field, "but the word of our God shall stand for ever."

III. A Mission for Jerusalem (Isaiah 40:9-11)

Good news! God will set His people free and take them home. But responsibility goes with freedom. His people liberated from Babylon must tell about it. Likewise His people freed from sin through Jesus must share the gospel, the good news of salvation. They must share also the good news that the Savior will come again and take His people home.

A. Call to Proclaim (v. 9).

9. O Zion, that bringest good tidings, get thee up into the high mountain; O Jerusalem, that bringest good tidings, lift up thy voice with strength; lift it up, be not afraid; say unto the cities of Judah, Behold your God!

Zion is another name for Jerusalem. That city, when rescued from captivity, must shout the good news from the mountaintop to all the *cities of Judah.* Jerusalem must not be timid about this. The call says, *Lift up thy voice with strength; lift it up, be not afraid.* To all of Judah Jerusalem must shout, *Behold your God!* The whole land must be called to see what God has done. Marvelously He has broken the power of mighty Babylon and set the captives free. Likewise in our time God has broken the power of sin and set the captives free, forgiving them because Christ on the cross has taken their punishment. We who are set free must shout the good news to the whole world, for God loves the whole world (John 3:16) and is eager to free all the captives of sin if they will turn to Christ.

In the Greek version of Isaiah, verse 9 is not a call to Jerusalem to proclaim the good news, but a call to the prophet to proclaim the good news to Jerusalem and the other cities of Judah. The Greek translation was made from Hebrew manuscripts older than any that are known now, and some translators think it probably has the correct reading here. Some English versions therefore follow it. For example, the *American Standard Version* reads, "O thou that tellest good

visual 7

tidings to Zion, get thee up on a high mountain; O thou that tellest good tidings to Jerusalem, lift up thy voice with strength; lift it up, be not afraid; say unto the cities of Judah, Behold, your God!" If this is the correct reading, then verse 9 is not a call to liberated Jerusalem to proclaim that God has set her free; it is a call for the prophet to proclaim to captive Jerusalem that God is about to set her free. The next two verses then continue the same proclamation.

B. What to Proclaim (vv. 10, 11)

10. Behold, the Lord God will come with strong hand, and his arm shall rule for him: behold, his reward is with him, and his work before him.

This proclamation was designed to comfort and encourage the people in captivity. The Lord Jehovah was coming *with strong hand:* with strength enough to overthrow mighty Babylon. *His arm* also may mean His strength; or the empire of the Medes and Persians, which God was going to use to conquer Babylon.

His reward is with him. To captives who have turned away from sin and have become obedient, God will bring the reward of freedom and a return to their homeland. *His work before him.* Here the Hebrew word can mean either work or payment for work. Some versions therefore make this phrase simply a repetition of the one before it: "His reward is with him, and his recompense before him" *(American Standard Version).* What the next verse describes is both Jehovah's work and his reward for His faithful people.

NOT THIS GOD

In ancient Babylonia each person had his own god, to whom he made special offerings and of whom he made requests. The god was expected to convey the worshiper's requests to higher gods who could provide the requested benefits. It was all businesslike. If the god didn't produce the desired request, a person felt it was his right to threaten his god with desertion. The people believed their gods would change their minds if the worshipers flattered them enough.

Isaiah knew better. The one, true, and living God, who revealed himself to the prophet, had nothing in common with the imaginary deities worshiped by pagans. God, for whom Isaiah spoke, could neither be wheedled nor pacified. Nor could anyone make demands of Him.

Our world needs to understand the Biblical concept of God. A lack of such understanding lies at the root of much present mischief and foolishness. Under no one's control, God instead controls all, in this world and in the next.

He issues, not takes, orders. His rule of history, the universe, and eternity remains unchanged. Before us He never bows; before Him we all shall bow. —V. H.

11. He shall feed his flock like a shepherd: he shall gather the lambs with his arm, and carry them in his bosom, and shall gently lead those that are with young.

A good shepherd leads his flock to green pastures and still waters (Psalm 23). When a ewe is pregnant, the shepherd leads slowly so she will not be too tired. When a newborn lamb cannot keep up with the flock, he carries it. So the Lord will care for His liberated people, giving each one just the help that one needs. So He cared for the people of Judah when they went back from Babylon, and so He cares for us who are Christians. We are His people, and the sheep of His pasture (Psalm 79:13). We depend on His care, but that does not excuse us from doing what we can to care for ourselves and each other.

Conclusion

One of the marvels of God's Word is its prediction of future events. In round numbers, Isaiah lived seven hundred years before Christ came. Enlightened by God's revelation, he looked ahead a hundred years to the captivity of his people in Babylon. He told also of the end of that captivity seventy years later. But that was not all. With inspired foresight he looked seven hundred years into the future to the coming of Christ. Recall the famous prediction of Isaiah 7:14: "Behold, a virgin shall conceive, and shall bear a son, and shall call his name Immanuel." *Immanuel* means God with us, and that was who Jesus was. But Isaiah's foresight was longer still. He looked to the time when Jesus will come again "and the glory of the Lord shall be revealed, and all flesh shall see it together."

A. We Are There

We are there in the prophecy of Isaiah—we who are Christians, we who have been rescued from sin and death. As the people of Judah were captives of Babylon, we were captives and slaves of sin (John 8:34). As God used the armies of Medes and Persians to break the power of Babylon and set the captives free, so by the mighty power of Jesus' death and resurrection He broke the power of sin and death and set us free. We are the people of Jerusalem. Our mother is not the old city of stone in the hills of Judah; she is the spiritual Jerusalem, "Jerusalem which is above" (Galatians 4:26).

To carry the comparison further, we are not home yet. We have been freed from sin and death, but we are on the journey between the Babylon of sin and the Heavenly Jerusalem that is our home. There are difficulties along the way—rivers to swim, mountains to climb, deserts to cross. If we press on with courage and determination, the end of our journey is the new Jerusalem. Read about it in Revelation 21.

B. We Are Called

If we are the people of Jerusalem, we are called to the mission of Jerusalem: "O Jerusalem, that bringest good tidings, lift up thy voice with strength!" We have good news. Are we stingy with it? We can tell people how to live forever. Are we telling them? Think about the people you talk with in your neighborhood, at work, at your club. How many of them are not Christians? Do you ever lift up your voice to say, "Behold your God"?

You don't know how? Many Christians don't know how to start telling about God, or Christ, or the Bible, or even the church. Here are some suggestions:

1. Think about it. How do you start talking about something you read in the newspaper? Can't you do the same with something you read in the Bible? How do you start talking about something you saw on your vacation? Can't you do the same with something you learned in Sunday school? How do you start talking about your golf or tennis or bowling? Can't you do the same with your Christian experience? If anyone is interested in how you improved your game, isn't he interested in how you became a Christian?

2. Do some studying. Look in your church library for a book on personal evangelism. If there isn't one, maybe you can borrow one from the preacher, or he can recommend one you can get at a Christian bookstore.

3. Find some companions. There are other people in your congregation who would like to be telling the good news but don't know how. Get a group to study together, using a book or finding a good personal evangelist to teach you out of his experience.

4. Be an apprentice. Go along with your minister or someone else who does know how to talk to people about the good news.

5. Just start talking. After all, your Christianity is a part of your life, as much a part as your housekeeping or your gardening or your cold. Why not make it as much a part of your conversation?

O Zion, haste, thy mission high fulfilling,
  To tell to all the world that God is Light;
That He who made all nations was not willing
  One soul should perish, lost in shades of night.
                                        —Mary A. Thomson

Home Daily Bible Readings

Monday, Oct. 10—Jeremiah's Promise of Return (Jeremiah 31:10-14)
Tuesday, Oct. 11—Isaiah Proclaims the Lord's Coming (Isaiah 40:1-5)
Wednesday, Oct. 12—Isaiah Proclaims God's Promises (Isaiah 40:6-11)
Thursday, Oct. 13—Isaiah Proclaims God's Power (Isaiah 40:12-17)
Friday, Oct. 14—Isaiah Proclaims God's Dominion (Isaiah 40:18-26)
Saturday, Oct. 15—Isaiah Proclaims God's Compassion (Isaiah 40:27-31)
Sunday, Oct. 16—The Good Shepherd (John 10:7-18)

C. We Have Obligations

Citizens have obligations. Most of us are vividly aware of that at taxpaying time, but we have obligations all the time. We are to obey the laws of our town, our state, our nation. A citizen may think it is unnecessary to drive within the speed limit, but this opinion does not release him from his obligation or save him any money when the patrolman pulls him over.

We citizens of the Heavenly Jerusalem have obligations too. Our King does not levy taxes, but He expects offerings, and He loves a cheerful giver (2 Corinthians 9:7). His Word does have commandments, but note also its requests. We read, "I beseech you." Read on through the twelfth chapter of Romans for a partial list of our obligations as citizens of Zion.

Do we neglect our obligations because there is no patrolman lurking by the roadside to pull us over and conduct us to the judge? Patrolman or not, there is a judge (2 Corinthians 5:10). It is He who will say, "Come, ye blessed of my Father, inherit the kingdom prepared for you from the foundation of the world"; and it is He who will say, "Depart from me, ye cursed, into everlasting fire, prepared for the devil and his angels" (Matthew 25:34, 41).

D. Prayer

Our Father and our shepherd, thank You for rescuing Your people from Babylon and preserving them to bring the Savior into the world. We thank You also for sending Him to rescue us from sin and death.

E. Thought to Remember

Publish glad tidings, tidings of peace;
Tidings of Jesus, redemption and release.

Learning by Doing

This page contains an alternate lesson plan emphasizing learning activities. Classes desiring such student involvement will find these suggestions helpful.

Learning Goals

After studying this lesson each adult will:

1. Be able to identify the primary elements of godly comfort.

2. Apply those in his ministry of comfort to himself and to others he finds distressed and discouraged.

3. Associate Isaiah 40 with all three of its historical realities: the return of God's people from captivity in Babylon, the birth and life of Jesus in the flesh, and the final appearance of Jesus as victor.

Into the Lesson

Mention to your class that Hosea was God's prophet to Israel (the northern kingdom) during some of the time Isaiah was prophesying to Judah (the southern kingdom). Point out that Hosea spoke of the restoration of God's people from captivity, even as Isaiah does in the text for today's lesson. Then use Hosea 14 for your introductory activity. Give students a half sheet of writing paper and ask them to number 1 through 10. Read, or have someone read, Hosea 14 *(King James Version)* omitting the following ten words: *fallen* (v. 1); *words* (v. 2); *fatherless* (v. 3); *backsliding* (v. 4); *dew* (v. 5); *olive* (v. 6); *shadow* (v. 7); *fir* (v. 8); *wise* and *right* (v. 9). Ask students to write words they believe are appropriate to the context as the text is read. At the end of the reading, compare and contrast students' answers with the text read.

Into the Word

Prepare seven cards, each with one of the letters of the word *comfort*. On the back of each card write the number(s) shown here: C (1, 2), O (3), M (4), F (5), O (9), R (10), T (11). Distribute the cards to seven volunteers. Then, on poster board or overhead transparency, reveal the following acrostic, which involves a key word of today's text.

Elements of Comfort

```
C _ _ _ _ _ _ _ _ _ _
O _ _ _ _ _ _ _
M _ _ _ _ _ _ _
F _ _ _ _ _
O _ _ _ _ _ _ _ _
R _ _ _ _ _ _ _ _ _ _
T _ _ _ _
```

In order, ask each person holding the letter cards to figure out the word that begins with his letter in the acrostic. Allow each to guess letters; fill them in if correct. (These words are to be used: *Compassion, Optimism, Ministry, Future, Outreach, Reassurance, Tears.* These represent elements of comfort. When all words are correctly revealed, ask your class to suggest ways each is demonstrated in the verses of today's text.

Distribute the following Bible references to selected class members, with the direction to find and hold them. Direct those holding the cards from the preceding activity to turn them over to reveal the number of one or two verses from today's text; if the class is large, each may give his to another student not involved to this point. As the New Testament verses are read aloud singly, ask those who are holding the cards to determine if their verse of the Isaiah text (the number on their card) matches the verses read. Here are the New Testament references and their matches from today's text: Luke 3:1-3 (v. 3); John 14:16-18 (vv. 1, 2); John 10:11, 27, 28 (v. 11); Matthew 24:29, 30 (v. 5): Luke 1:46-51 (v. 10); Matthew 21: 8-11 (v. 9); James 1:9, 10 (v. 4). Discuss how, if at all, each text read is a fulfillment of Isaiah's prophecy.

Into Life

Display a quilted comforter. Emphasize that God is our Heavenly Comforter. Mention the "Peanuts" comic strip character Linus, who needs his blanket as a "personal comforter." Ask how the comforter and Linus' blanket provide comfort as God does. Ask your class to "make a comforter" that depicts the comfort that God offers to us. Give each student a four-inch square of light-colored construction paper and a pen or marker. Let the class work in groups of four to prepare their squares. Ask them to write on each square a relevant Bible verse, a Bible reference, a key Biblical truth, or a simple drawing representing a concept at the heart of true comfort. Examples: "The wages of sin is death; the gift of God is eternal life"; "James 1:12"; a picture of an open tomb.

Collect all the "comforter squares" and attach them to a bulletin board. Have different students interpret and apply any pictures, read the Scriptures mentioned, and then let the class discuss the Biblical truths cited.

Let's Talk It Over

The questions on this page are designed to encourage review of the lesson Scriptures and to promote discussion of the lesson by the class. The answers provided are only discussion starters. Let your class talk it over from there.

1. What is prophecy? What is the importance of prophecy?

Prophecy is a "forth-telling" that, at times, involves a "foretelling." Fundamentally, prophecy is an inspired utterance. That inspired message may address the present or the future. To assume that all prophecy is prediction of future events is to misunderstand the essential nature of prophecy. In both Old and New Testaments, prophecy occupies a strategic place. How can the people of God know His truth and His will unless divinely inspired speakers (prophets) reveal it to them? The Bible reminds us again and again of the crucial role of the prophets (Acts 3:18, 20, 21; 10:43; Romans 1:1, 2; 16:25, 26; Ephesians 2:20; Hebrews 1:1; 1 Peter 1:10; 2 Peter 3:2; Revelation 10:7). Prophecy also plays an important role in its predictive mode in that the reliability and truthworthiness of divine revelation rests on the *fulfillment* of that which was predicted years, even centuries, beforehand. Isaiah's predictions concerning the restoration of God's people and the coming of Messiah were exactly and precisely fulfilled. Christians can expect God to bring to pass events still to come just as He has fulfilled prophetic predictions in the past. Be ready!

2. What is the importance of hope in daily living?

Hebrews 6:19 describes hope as "an anchor of the soul." An anchor holds the ship steady, keeping it from drifting. Life is impossible apart from hope. Hopelessness implies a lack of future, an absence of meaning to life, a despair. When hope prevails, a person can endure anything. Hope gives confidence and strength, as the psalmist indicates when he says, "Be strong, and let your heart take courage, all you who hope in the Lord" (Psalm 31:24). Such hope is not just a wish or desire ("I hope it doesn't rain"), but a confident expectation that God will act as He has promised ("I live in the hope of the resurrection of the dead"). Captives need hope in order to survive captivity. Even the dying need hope in order to cope with their experience. The Christian life cannot be lived apart from hope. Paul's trilogy affirms that which abides: "faith, hope, and love."

3. What is comfort? How can it be shared with someone in pain?

Comfort implies imparting cheer, strength, or encouragement as well as lessening pain. No wonder Paul describes the Father as the "God of all comfort"! (2 Corinthians 1:3). No wonder Paul exhorts Christians to comfort one another as well as themselves! (1 Thessalonians 3:2; 4:18; 5:11; 5:14). Comfort can be shared verbally and nonverbally. The encouraging, cheering word can comfort the hurting or the falling. When another is in pain, the loving embrace, the tender touch, the warm presence comforts. Notice in our language the use of the word "comforter" with reference to a quilt: it warms and protects. Personal warmth, expressed nonverbally and verbally, cheers, strengthens, and encourages as well as lessens the impact of pain.

4. Give some examples of contemporary "captivity" from which people need to be freed.

Three realities outside of us can foster enslavement. (1) The first is *things*. Any material object can be regarded as a master: houses, cars, money, property (real or personal). (2) The second is *circumstances*. We can become captives to what happens to us in life. We can allow disasters, successes, or uncontrollable events to determine our present condition. How many people do you know who are captives to their past (whatever it brought their way)? (3) *People*. We can become captives to relationships. Even with loving and well-meaning people we can be enslaved. Dependency, "addiction" to relationships, is a captivity. One other reality, internal to the person, can be the greatest captivity of all: to the self. Here's the root of all sin. What a small prison, to be wrapped up within one's self! Jesus offers to free us from *all* captivity.

5. Why is the "shepherd-sheep" metaphor so appealing to people?

More Christians prize the Twenty-third Psalm ("the shepherd psalm") as their favorite than any other passage in the Bible. And for good reason! "Shepherd" implies tender, loving care; protection and provisions; closeness and guidance; strength and warmth. How God-like!

The Suffering Servant

LESSON SCRIPTURE: Isaiah 52:13—53:12.

PRINTED TEXT: Isaiah 53:4-11.

Isaiah 53:4-11

4 Surely he hath borne our griefs, and carried our sorrows: yet we did esteem him stricken, smitten of God, and afflicted.

5 But he was wounded for our transgressions, he was bruised for our iniquities: the chastisement of our peace was upon him; and with his stripes we are healed.

6 All we like sheep have gone astray; we have turned every one to his own way; and the Lord hath laid on him the iniquity of us all.

7 He was oppressed, and he was afflicted, yet he opened not his mouth: he is brought as a lamb to the slaughter, and as a sheep before her shearers is dumb, so he openeth not his mouth.

8 He was taken from prison and from judgment: and who shall declare his generation? for he was cut off out of the land of the living: for the transgression of my people was he stricken.

9 And he made his grave with the wicked, and with the rich in his death; because he had done no violence, neither was any deceit in his mouth.

10 Yet it pleased the Lord to bruise him; he hath put him to grief: when thou shalt make his soul an offering for sin, he shall see his seed, he shall prolong his days, and the pleasure of the Lord shall prosper in his hand.

11 He shall see of the travail of his soul, and shall be satisfied: by his knowledge shall my righteous servant justify many; for he shall bear their iniquities.

GOLDEN TEXT: He was wounded for our transgressions, he was bruised for our iniquities: the chastisement of our peace was upon him; and with his stripes we are healed.—Isaiah 53:5.

Through Suffering to Hope

Unit 2: Isaiah — Interpreting a
Nation's Suffering (Lessons 5-9)

Lesson Aims

After this lesson a student should be able to:
1. Briefly point out how Jesus fulfilled the prophecy of our text.
2. Acknowledge his own debt to Jesus who died, and find some way to serve Him better.

Lesson Outline

INTRODUCTION
    A. Personal Suffering
    B. National Suffering
    C. A Unique Case
    D. Lesson Background
  I. SUFFERING FOR US (Isaiah 53:4-6)
    A. Suffering Misunderstood (v. 4)
    B. Suffering in our Place (vv. 5,6)
 II. SUFFERING AND DYING (Isaiah 53:7-9)
    A. Silent Suffering (v. 7)
    B. Unjust Suffering (v. 8)
    C. Suffering Unto Death (v. 9)
III. SATISFACTORY RESULT (Isaiah 53:10, 11)
    A. The Divine Plan (v. 10a)
    B. Threefold Result (v. 10b)
    C. Satisfaction (v. 11)
      As a Means to Growth
CONCLUSION
    A. Following Jesus
    B. Helping Others
    C. Prayer
    D. Thought to Remember

Display visual 8 from the visuals/learning resources packet. It is shown on page 70.

Introduction

Human suffering has many causes. In a specific case we may or may not find the cause.

A. Personal Suffering

We studied the case of Job, who suffered through no fault of his own. But some do suffer because of their own mistakes or wrongdoing. A reckless driver is injured; a heavy smoker has lung cancer; a thief is put in jail.

Job's suffering was not a punishment from God, but some suffering is. Adam and Eve were put out of Eden (Genesis 3:22-24). Uzziah became a leper (2 Chronicles 26:16-21). Herod

Antipas was eaten by worms (Acts 12:21-23).

Disasters called "natural" bring suffering to many. Often called "acts of God," they may be devices of the devil. Such were the lightning and windstorm that brought loss to Job.

Some people suffer because of the sins or mistakes of others. A person is robbed or defrauded; a pedestrian on the sidewalk is hit by a car with a drunken driver; a child is abused.

Many good people have suffered just because they were good. It was Job's goodness that provoked the devil's attack. God's prophets were persecuted in Old Testament times (Matthew 5:12; 23:37; Acts 7:52). So were Christ's apostles in New Testament times (Acts 5:17, 18; 12:1-3; 2 Corinthians 11:24-27). Paul warns, "All that will live godly in Christ Jesus shall suffer persecution" (2 Timothy 3:12).

B. National Suffering

Now we have turned our attention from personal suffering to national suffering. Israel was defeated and scattered by the Assyrians; Judah was defeated and deported by the Babylonians. In each of these cases, the suffering of the nation was God's punishment for its persistent sinning. In Judah Isaiah foretold also the punishment of other nations (Isaiah 13:17-22; 14:31; 15:1-3; 17:1; 19:1-4; 23:1-7; 30:31). In north Israel Amos likewise spoke of the punishment of other nations as well as Israel and Judah (Amos 1:3— 2:8). We cannot say that every defeated nation is punished for its sin, but it does seem probable that any nation filled with sin will sooner or later be defeated if it does not change its ways.

C. A Unique Case

This lesson brings us to a case of suffering unlike any other. The account is found in Isaiah 52:13—53:12. It tells of one whom Jehovah called "my servant" (Isaiah 52:13). This one was both exalted and despised (Isaiah 52:13; 53:3). He was oppressed and afflicted, yet He shared the spoils of victory (Isaiah 53:7, 12). Like Job, He suffered through no fault of His own. Like many people, He suffered on account of others' sins. But unlike anyone else, "he bare the sin of many" (Isaiah 53:12). He took the punishment for the sins of others so that others could escape the punishment they deserved.

Through centuries this prophecy was a puzzle. Who is this servant of Jehovah, this one whose punishment brings healing to others? Is it the prophet Isaiah himself? Is it some other prophet? Is it some godly king? Is it the whole nation of Israel? Such questions faced a thoughtful traveler with Isaiah's book before him: "Of whom speaketh the prophet this? of himself, or of some other?" A Christian had the answer, "and beginning from this scripture, preached unto him Jesus" (Acts 8:32-35, *American Standard Version*).

Our text tells of Jesus' suffering. Seven hundred years before it happened, Jehovah revealed it to Isaiah, and Isaiah wrote it down for us.

D. Lesson Background

Judah was headed for defeat and captivity. Isaiah could see that when most of his countrymen could not. Isaiah could see the end of captivity too. He even named Cyrus, the Persian ruler who would defeat Babylon and set Judah free (Isaiah 44:24—45:6). By divine revelation Isaiah could look forward through other centuries to a greater deliverance. He wrote of one born of a virgin, one who would be called "Wonderful, Counselor, The mighty God, The everlasting Father, The Prince of Peace"; one whose rule would continue forever (Isaiah 9:6, 7). Isaiah could see that God's salvation was for "all the ends of the earth" (Isaiah 45:22, 23). Wonder of wonders, Isaiah could see that the everlasting ruler would come to His glory and dominion by suffering and dying. We now look at that side of Isaiah's inspired prophecy.

I. Suffering for Us
(Isaiah 53:4-6)

"Who hath believed our report?" (Isaiah 53:1). The prophet realized that what he had to say would be thought incredible. The Savior and ruler would be "despised and rejected" (v. 3). In our violent world, power and dominion are won by slaughtering others, not by giving one's own life. But the way of Christ is not the way of our violent world. Our text goes on to explain the meaning of His suffering.

A. Suffering Misunderstood (v. 4)

4. Surely he hath borne our griefs, and carried our sorrows: yet we did esteem him stricken, smitten of God, and afflicted.

The Hebrew words translated *griefs* and *sorrows* can mean physical sickness and pain as well as mental and emotional distress. This prophecy was fulfilled in part when Jesus relieved people of sickness and demon possession (Matthew 8:16, 17). For three years Jesus "went about doing good, and healing all that were oppressed of the devil" (Acts 10:38). Everyone could see that. How unreasonable it was to think that He was *smitten of God!* Yet the rulers of His people said He was an ally of the devil, and some of the people accepted that opinion (Matthew 12:24; John 8:48, 52; 10:20). The rulers

---

How to Say It

ANTIPAS. *An*-tuh-pas.
ARIMATHEA. Air-uh-muh-*thee*-uh. (*th* as in thin)
CYRUS. *Sye*-rus.
ISAIAH. Eye-*zay*-uh.
UZZIAH. Uh-*zye*-uh.

---

condemned Him for blasphemy against God (Matthew 26:63-66). When they persuaded the Roman governor to have Him crucified, they held that He was an evil man who for His own wickedness was *stricken, smitten of God, and afflicted.*

B. Suffering in Our Place (vv. 5, 6)

5. But he was wounded for our transgressions, he was bruised for our iniquities; the chastisement of our peace was upon him; and with his stripes we are healed.

Isaiah speaks for the whole human race. Jesus suffered for *our* sins, not for any wrong that He had done. *Our transgressions* and *our iniquities* made us enemies of God (Colossians 1:21), but the punishment heaped upon Him was *the chastisement of our peace.* It atoned for our sins and made our forgiveness possible. Thus the enmity is ended and we are at peace with God. Our moral and spiritual sickness is ended: *we are healed.* Jesus made all this possible by His suffering and death; we make it actual by accepting Him as our Savior and obeying Him as our Lord.

6. All we like sheep have gone astray; we have turned every one to his own way; and the Lord hath laid on him the iniquity of us all.

All of us have been silly *like sheep.* We have turned aside from following the good shepherd, the Lord. *We have turned every one to his own way,* a selfish way, a sinful way. A lost sheep dies in the desert unless it is found and reclaimed. Jesus came to seek and save the lost (Luke 19:10). We were doomed to die for our wandering in wickedness, but *the Lord hath laid on him the iniquity of us all.* According to God's plan, Jesus took upon himself all our sin and all its punishment. He accepted the death we deserved, and made us free to live forever.

II. Suffering and Dying
(Isaiah 53:7-9)

It was no small load that Jesus took upon himself: all my sins, all your sins, the sins of hoodlums and gangsters, the sins of Nero and Stalin and Hitler, all the sins of a wicked world. So it was no small penalty He paid, no small suffering He endured. The wages of sin is death (Romans 6:23), and Jesus accepted the most painful and disgraceful death that could be devised by men of a cruel time—"even the death of the cross" (Philippians 2:8).

A. Silent Suffering (v. 7)

7. He was oppressed, and he was afflicted, yet he opened not his mouth: he is brought as a lamb to the slaughter, and as a sheep before her shearers is dumb, so he openeth not his mouth.

Jesus not only accepted our punishment; He accepted it without protest or complaint. In every phase of the legal proceedings against Him, His silence was notable. He offered no defense to the Jewish court, or to the Roman Pilate, or to King Herod of Galilee (Mark 14:60, 61; 15:3-5: Luke 23:8, 9). When pressed for an answer, He spoke briefly with true testimony and grave warning, but with no complaining (Mark 14:61, 62; John 18:33-38; 19:8-11).

B. Unjust Suffering (v. 8)

8. He was taken from prison and from judgment: and who shall declare his generation? for he was cut off out of the land of the living: for the transgression of my people was he stricken.

This verse has been puzzling to translators, and different readings are seen in popular English versions. *He was taken from prison and from judgment.* This could mean simply that Jesus was led from jail and courtroom to the cross. However, several versions translate the preposition as "by" instead of *from:* "By oppression and judgment he was taken away." Not by any just or honest judgment, but by an unjust and oppressive decision Jesus was taken from the world. *Who shall declare his generation?* Some students take *his generation* to mean "his children," those whom He generated. So the *New International Version* reads, "Who can speak of his descendants?" Jesus had no descendants because *he was cut off out of the land of the living:* that is, He was put to death at an early age. In the *American Standard Version*, however, *his generation* is taken to mean His contemporaries, the people of His time: "As for his generation, who among them considered that he was cut off out of the land of the living for the transgression of my people to whom the stroke was due?" The people of Jesus' time did not understand that He was dying for the sins of others. Soon afterward, of course, the apostles did understand that and proclaimed it vigorously. Thousands of people believed it in Jerusalem and other places, but still a majority did not understand the truth.

C. Suffering Unto Death (v. 9)

9. And he made his grave with the wicked, and with the rich in his death; because he had done no violence, neither was any deceit in his mouth.

He made his grave with the wicked. Here is another puzzle for the translator. How can it be said that Jesus *made his grave?* Literally the verb is *gave* rather than *made*, but how can it be said that Jesus "gave his grave"? As a matter of fact, His grave was not with the wicked, though His death was. He was crucified between two robbers (Mark 15:27). Perhaps the *New International Version* has solved the puzzle correctly: "He was assigned a grave with the wicked." That is, the authorities put Him to death with the wicked and intended to bury Him with them. But that intention was not carried out, and Jesus was *with the rich in his death.* Joseph of Arimathea claimed the dead body and laid it in a costly new tomb (Mark 15:42-46). Another rich man helped, and contributed a hundred pounds of myrrh and aloes for the burial (John 19:38-42). These two men knew *he had done no violence, neither was any deceit in his mouth.* Of course the disciples knew that too.

III. Satisfactory Result (Isaiah 53:10, 11)

When Jesus died, His followers were desolate. At the time they could see no good in His death. They had hoped that He would redeem Israel (Luke 24:21), but when He was dead they hoped no more.

After three days all that was changed. Despair vanished when He was alive again. The disciples remembered that He had foretold His death and resurrection (Mark 8:31; 9:9, 31; 10:32-34). They realized that He had expected to die, had intended to die. He could have avoided death by His miraculous power, could have called legions of angels to His rescue (Matthew 26:53). He was not killed against His will; He chose to give His life. As He himself said, "No man taketh it from me, but I lay it down of myself" (John 10:18). So the disciples came to see, as we do, that Jesus' death was part of the gospel, the good news (1 Corinthians 15:1-3). It was good because of its result. He died for our sins, and so we are saved from death.

A. The Divine Plan (v. 10a)

10a. Yet it pleased the Lord to bruise him; he hath put him to grief.

Surely the Lord was not happy to see the suffering of His Son. Neither was He pleased with the sin of Jesus' murderers. Marks of His displeasure were darkness at noon, and an earthquake (Matthew 27:45, 51). But the Father allowed the suffering of His Son because the result would be pleasing. By this means sinful man could be redeemed. God planned for this to happen. Not only did Jesus announce it in advance; Isaiah announced it seven hundred years earlier—and even then the plan was ancient. Jesus was "the Lamb slain from the foundation of the world" (Revelation 13:8). Before God made man, the plan was in place for his redemption by the sacrifice of God's Son.

B. Threefold Result (v. 10b)

10b. When thou shalt make his soul an offering for sin, he shall see his seed, he shall prolong his days, and the pleasure of the Lord shall prosper in his hand.

When thou shalt make his soul an offering for sin. The Hebrew word can mean either *soul* or *life.* Here it seems to mean that Jesus' life was offered in sacrifice for the sins of others. Many students prefer to translate *when he shall make* instead of *when thou shalt make*, meaning either that God was going to make Jesus' life an offering or that Jesus was going to make His own life an offering. So the *New International Version* reads, "Though the Lord makes his life a guilt offering." The *New American Standard Bible* has, "If He would render Himself as a guilt offering." From the offering of Jesus' life came the three results that are listed.

However, the reading of the *King James Version* carries a gripping thought. The good results come *when thou shalt make his soul an offering for sin:* when *you* personally accept the sacrifice of Jesus as an offering for *your* sins. The results depend not only on the offering of Jesus, but also on the acceptance of Jesus as the Savior who died so that others may live.

Then the following three results are listed:

1. *He shall see his seed.* The *seed*, the children or descendants, of a religious leader are his converts and followers. So Paul wrote to Christians in Corinth, "I have begotten you through the gospel" (1 Corinthians 4:15). By being lifted up on the cross and dying, Jesus draws us to himself (John 12:32, 33). By taking the punishment for our sins He makes it possible for us to be forgiven. Thus we are born again, becoming children of God (John 1:12, 13; 3:3-6).

2. *He shall prolong his days.* Jesus died, giving His life as an offering for sin. But Jesus is not dead. He came back to life, never to die again (Romans 6:9). His days are prolonged through all eternity. But note that the Hebrew text here does not have the word *his.* It reads simply, *He*

Home Daily Bible Readings

Monday, Oct. 17—The Promise of Redemption (Isaiah 52:1-10)
Tuesday, Oct. 18—The Servant of the Lord (Isaiah 52:18—53:3)
Wednesday, Oct. 19—The Sacrifice of the Servant (Isaiah 53:4-9)
Thursday, Oct. 20—The Fulfillment of the Servant (Isaiah 53:10-12)
Friday, Oct. 21—Peter's Proclamation of the Servant (Acts 2:14-28)
Saturday, Oct. 22—The Need for Redemption (Psalm 49:1-13)
Sunday, Oct. 23—Jesus Foretells His Servanthood (Matthew 20:20-28)

shall prolong days. If we accept Jesus as our Savior, making His life an offering for our sin and obeying Him as our Lord, he prolongs our days as well as His. We too shall live eternally.

3. *The pleasure of the Lord shall prosper in his hand.* The Lord takes pleasure in seeing people redeemed from sin and death, living godly lives, and on the way to eternal fellowship in Heaven. For this He planned from the foundation of the world. In the hand of Jesus, that is, by His work, the redemption of mankind prospers. Central in His work for redemption is the offering of His life. But note again the part we have in this. Redemption and the pleasure of the Lord prosper as we accept Jesus, as we make His life the offering for our sins, and as we lead others to do the same.

C. Satisfaction (v. 11)

11. He shall see of the travail of his soul, and shall be satisfied: by his knowledge shall my righteous servant justify many; for he shall bear their iniquities.

The travail of his soul is Jesus' suffering and death. *He shall see* may mean that He will experience all this and *be satisfied* to accept it because it will bring salvation to many. The *New American Standard Bible* says the same thing in a different way: "As a result of the anguish of His soul, He will see it and be satisfied." Because of His suffering and death He will see His seed and see the Lord's pleasure prospering (v. 10), and therefore He will be satisfied.

By his knowledge may mean that because Jesus knows the will of God and the way of salvation He is able to *justify many.* Or *his knowledge* may mean knowledge of him. When many come to know Jesus as their Savior and Lord, He justifies them by taking away their sins. With either of these interpretations the result is the same. God's *righteous servant*, Jesus, will *justify many*. he will forgive their sins and make them righteous. This is possible because *he shall bear their iniquities*. He will take upon himself the punishment they deserve.

Verse 12 adds yet another result of Jesus' suffering and death. God will give Him a victor's reward. This is stated powerfully in Philippians 2:5-11. Jesus took the form of a servant and became obedient unto death, "wherefore God also hath highly exalted him, and given him a name which is above every name: that at the name of Jesus every knee should bow, of things in heaven, and things in earth, and things under the earth; and that every tongue should confess that Jesus Christ is Lord, to the glory of God the Father."

AS A MEANS TO GROWTH

Most of the Greeks at Salamis chose not to fight the Persian Armada. Outnumbered five to one, they voted to allow each of their ships to return to its home port. Themistocles, the Greek general, determined otherwise. He sent a slave to the Persian king, Xerxes, informing him that the Greeks were trying to escape. He asked a favor of the Persian. Would he please seal the harbors to prevent escape? Xerxes obliged, playing into the hands of the wily Greek. Since the small harbors prohibited the use of the total Persian fleet at any one time, Greek mariners badly abused the enemy part by part until Xerxes had to withdraw. Themistocles forced his people to fight their way to freedom by encouraging the Persians to block all harbors to flight.

God would allow his Servant to suffer, Isaiah predicted. But not without a goal in mind, for the end of His personal suffering would be the redemption of millions of fallen humans. From His death would come a recreated life to all who would trust in His sacrifice. Thus, God didn't remove Christ's sufferings, because He had a larger purpose in mind for them.

God may also let us confront hardships as a means to growth. Undergoing trials gives us an opportunity to dramatize the power and resilience of faith. When adversity comes, let us have faith that God is able to bring blessing from it.
　　　　　　　　　　　　　　　　　　　　　　—V. H.

Conclusion

God said His righteous servant would justify many, not all (v. 11). Jesus bore the sins of many, not all (v. 12). The Savior's sacrifice is enough to atone for all the sins of the world (1 John 2:2), but some sins are not actually covered. God is

visual 8

Silent Suffering

not willing for any to perish (2 Peter 3:9), but some do perish. Why?

Jesus justifies many, but He does not justify any who prefer to be unjust. He bears the sins of many, but He does not take away the sins of those who would rather keep their sins. The salvation of sinners depends on the Savior, but it also depends on the sinners. This says two things to us who have sinned: (1) We must follow Jesus; (2) We must help others follow Him.

A. Following Jesus

Very simply Jesus said, "He that believeth and is baptized shall be saved" (Mark 16:16). But He said believing is not just saying we believe. "Not every one that saith unto me, Lord, Lord, shall enter into the kingdom of heaven; but he that doeth the will of my Father which is in heaven" (Matthew 7:21). James warned us that faith cannot live by itself (James 2:17, 20). If we believe, we must act like believers. Peter urged us to add to our faith, to build fine character and a noble way of life, "for so an entrance shall be ministered unto you abundantly into the everlasting kingdom of our Lord and Saviour Jesus Christ" (2 Peter 1:5-11). Think it over. Is your living better this year than it was last year?

B. Helping Others

Jesus will justify many by His knowledge, or by knowledge of Him. Millions of people have no knowledge of Him. What are you doing about that? Does your congregation have an adequate missionary program? Are you doing your part?

C. Prayer

How gracious You are, our Father and our God! How wonderfully You and Jesus have taken away our sins and made us Your children! May we have the wisdom and will to act today and every day as Your children ought to act.

D. Thought to Remember

"I'll live for Him who died for me."

Learning by Doing

This page contains an alternate lesson plan emphasizing learning activities. Classes desiring such student involvement will find these suggestions helpful.

Learning Goals

A study of Isaiah 53 should result in:

1. Each adult thanking God for what He did in sacrificing His only begotten Son.

2. Each being able to describe parallel elements between the chapter and descriptions of Jesus' suffering and death by the Gospel writers.

Into the Lesson

C. S. Lewis, in his children's fantasy novel *The Lion, the Witch and the Wardrobe,* uses a Christ figure, Aslan the Lion, in a scene paralleling the death of Christ for human sin. Check with church families and local libraries for a copy of the book. Have a class member read from the chapter entitled "The Triumph of the Witch." Read from the arrival of Aslan at the Stone Table (page 148 in several editions) through the end of the chapter (approximately five to six minutes' reading). Tell the class the nature of the reading; ask them to notice the elements of this fantasy segment that parallel the description of Jesus' death as recorded in the Gospels. These elements should be noted: (1) Aslan's willfulness in dying, though he could have overwhelmed his tormentors; (2) his utter lack of resistance; (3) the cutting of his flesh; (4) his total humiliation; (5) his simple look to heaven as death drew near. Contrast Lewis' writing imaginatively of such a *past* death with Isaiah's precise prediction of Jesus' death centuries *before* it occurred.

Into the Word

Have two of your effective oral readers read today's text before the class. Have the readers agree on dividing each verse and alternate the reading somewhat antiphonally. Then divide the class into groups of four. Ask one half of the groups to decide how the two readers' deed *compares* to Jesus' act on our behalf, and the other half how the two readers' deed *contrasts* with Jesus' work on the cross. Ask a representative from each group to present the list of comparisons/contrasts. Expect such elements as the following. *For the comparison group:* (1) readers acted voluntarily, when asked; (2) readers were on "public display"; (3) readers did it "for our benefit"; (4) readers worked as representatives of us all. *For the contrast group:* (1) readers did not act alone; (2) readers did not suffer; (3) readers were not taunted/jeered; (4) readers did not gain long-term consequence for the hearers. (If you need to, give each group an example to get them started.)

Many HE and WE statements are made or implied in the text. Type each of the following on separate strips, up to the approximate number in your class. (Do not put numbers on the strips.) Distribute the slips randomly; ask your students to circulate and find the person who holds the appropriate matching/contrasting statement. (They are given here as back-to-back matches, with verse numbers at the end.) HE has borne our griefs and carried our sorrows. WE considered Him stricken and afflicted by God—4. HE was wounded for our transgressions, bruised for our iniquities. WE are healed by His stripes—5. HE received from the Lord our iniquity. WE have all turned to our own way—6. HE was imprisoned and killed. WE deserved imprisonment and death—8. HE acted in a way to please the Lord: He died. WE will receive the pleasure of the Lord: eternal life—10. HE will see travail in His soul. WE will be justified by His righteousness—11. Direct those with the HE elements to take the corresponding WE elements back to their seats. Have the two statements read as pairs. Check for correctness and match-up with verses.

Into Life

Divide the class into groups of six to eight persons each and place the following prayer signs one set per group, in some circular or semicircular or consecutive pathway on walls—either in the classroom, hallway, or even outside. Direct the group to walk quietly by each sign one at a time, pausing to pray briefly at each as a response to the statement thereon.

1. "Jesus has borne my griefs and sorrows. I will praise Him for my joy." 2. "Jesus has been beaten, and I have been healed by His stripes. I will thank God for my spiritual healing in Christ." 3. "I have strayed like a foolish sheep. I will listen to the good Shepherd, asking Him to lead me." 4. "Jesus submitted in quietness and obedience. Lord, help me to be submissive and obedient." 5. "Jesus has seen His seed in me. Lord, help me be fruitful for You." 6. "God prolongs the days of His faithful servants. May I long for and enjoy Heaven with Him."

Let's Talk It Over

The questions on this page are designed to encourage review of the lesson Scriptures and to promote discussion of the lesson by the class. The answers provided are only discussion starters. Let your class talk it over from there.

1. What are some causes of human suffering?

People suffer because of the following reasons: (1) Their own sin. When a person overeats, the body suffers. Drug abuse causes both mental and physical suffering. (2) The sins of others. A drunken driver's car hits a power pole, ricocheting into a yard where children are playing. The result? Death and injury. A father sexually molests his ten-year-old daughter, and she suffers emotionally for a lifetime. (3) Disasters. A hurricane whips ashore along the Gulf Coast, wreaking havoc. An epidemic of flu hits the aging populace, bringing suffering and death to many. (4) Unknown causes. Accidents happen every day, and no one knows their causes. (5) Their stand for righteousness. God's spokesmen in both Old and New Testament times suffered persecution for opposing evil. Peter says, "If any man suffer as a Christian, let him not be ashamed; but let him glorify God on this behalf" (1 Peter 4:16).

2. Cite some of the ways people respond to suffering.

Some respond with denial. They tell themselves that this isn't happening to them, and that if they deny it long enough, it may go away. They play mental games to convince themselves and others that the suffering doesn't exist. *Some respond with complaints.* These feel that nobody knows the trouble they've seen, so they tell you about it. They bemoan their plight, wallow in misery, and grouse and gripe continually. *Some respond with anger.* They protest that they shouldn't have to suffer like this. Any available object (often a caring person who is helping them) feels the sting of their anger. *Some respond stoically.* Not all stoics lived in ancient Greece. These persons are impassive and give the impression that thy are made of steel. You won't hear a whimper out of them. *Some respond cheerfully.* If life gives them lemons, they will make lemonade out of them. Instead of getting down, they face with a smile whatever comes their way. *Some respond with resolve.* They are determined that their suffering won't whip them. They'll whip it instead. Their will to live gives them the edge on suffering. When Jesus suffered, He did so with calmness and courage, without response or retaliation.

3. How do people tend to react when they learn that a person has given up his life for another?

Every year brings new stories of heroism. A man rescues a child from in front of a speeding car, but loses his own life in the process. A boy saves his small sister from drowning in a pond, but drowns in the effort. A mother goes into a burning house to bring out her infant child, but she herself dies of smoke inhalation. The public responds with admiration, respect, honor, and praise to such heroic sacrifices. Awards are given posthumously, and memorials are erected. The survivors of tragedy, the beneficiaries of the heroism, are (most likely) deeply grateful. The sacrifice of another's life, meant the preservation of their own. When Jesus died for others, "he was despised and forsaken of men ... and we did not esteem Him" (Isaiah 53:3, *New American Standard Bible*). Today, many potential beneficiaries of His sacrifice make that same response. But, thank God, there are those who *live* today because of His death. And they are eternally grateful!

4. What results have come because Jesus died in our stead?

Look at this marvelous list found in Isaiah 53: Sinners are healed (v. 5). The offering has been made that removes our guilt (v. 10). The prolonging of our days (eternity) is possible (v. 10). Reconciliation with the Father ("the pleasure of the Lord") is made (v. 10). Jesus is satisfied (v. 11). Sins are forgiven (v. 11) The suffering servant triumphs (v. 12).

5. Cite two important places Jesus Christ has interceded for us.

The matchless fifty-third chapter of Isaiah closes with these penetrating, memorable words: he "interceded for the transgressors" (53:12, *New American Standard Bible*). His first intercession was on the cross in His death. His second (and continuing) intercession is now at the right hand of God. "Christ Jesus is He who died, yes, rather who was raised, who is at the right hand of God, who also intercedes for us" (Romans 8:34 *New American Standard Bible*). Jesus mediates and entreats the Father in our behalf. "Blessed assurance, Jesus is mine!"

Restoration of God's People

LESSON SCRIPTURE: Isaiah 65:8-25.

PRINTED TEXT: Isaiah 65:17-25.

Isaiah 65:17-25

17 For, behold, I create new heavens and a new earth: and the former shall not be remembered, nor come into mind.

18 But be ye glad and rejoice for ever in that which I create: for, behold, I create Jerusalem a rejoicing, and her people a joy.

19 And I will rejoice in Jerusalem, and joy in my people: and the voice of weeping shall be no more heard in her, nor the voice of crying.

20 There shall be no more thence an infant of days, nor an old man that hath not filled his days: for the child shall die a hundred years old; but the sinner being a hundred years old shall be accursed.

21 And they shall build houses, and inhabit them; and they shall plant vineyards, and eat the fruit of them.

22 They shall not build, and another inhabit; they shall not plant, and another eat: for as the days of a tree are the days of my people, and mine elect shall long enjoy the work of their hands.

23 They shall not labor in vain, nor bring forth for trouble; for they are the seed of the blessed of the Lord, and their offspring with them.

24 And it shall come to pass, that before they call, I will answer; and while they are yet speaking, I will hear.

25 The wolf and the lamb shall feed together, and the lion shall eat straw like the bullock: and dust shall be the serpent's meat. They shall not hurt nor destroy in all my holy mountain, saith the Lord.

GOLDEN TEXT: Behold, I create new heavens and a new earth: and the former shall not be remembered, nor come into mind.—Isaiah 65:17.

Through Suffering to Hope
Unit 2: Isaiah—Interpreting a
Nation's Suffering (Lessons 5-9)

Lesson Aims

After this lesson a student should be able to:
1. Briefly describe new Jerusalem.
2. Resolve to live here and now as a citizen of that city.
3. Tell how he can help someone else on the way to everlasting life.

Lesson Outline

INTRODUCTION
  A. Isaiah the Prophet
  B. Lesson Background
I. JOYOUS NEW CREATION (Isaiah 65:17-20)
  A. New Heavens and Earth (v. 17)
  B. New Jerusalem (vv. 18, 19)
  C. Long Life (v. 20)
II. WORK AND SUCCESS (Isaiah 65:21-23)
  A. Work Rewarded (v. 21)
  B. Security (v. 22)
  C. Blessed of the Lord (v. 23)
III. SUMMARY (Isaiah 65:24, 25)
  A. Close Contact (v. 24)
    God Still Answers Prayer
  B. Peace (v. 25)
CONCLUSION
  A. Let's Go!
  B. Let's Not Go Alone
  C. Prayer
  D. Thought to Remember

Display visual 9 from the visuals/learning resources packet. It is shown on page 77.

Introduction

History is full of allegories. Things that have happened have pictured in advance the things that are happening and will happen.

For example, Israel's journey to the promised land presents a picture of our Christian journey to Heaven. The people of Israel were slaves in Egypt till God liberated them; we were slaves of sin till He set us free by His power and grace. They entered their new life of freedom through the waters of the Red Sea; we enter ours through the waters of baptism. In their journey God led them by a pillar of cloud and fire; in our Christian journey He leads us by His Word. At the end of their journey God brought them safely into the land of promise; at the end of our journey He brings us safely into Heaven.

In a similar way the whole history of Israel resembled the whole history of the world. God brought Israel out of Egypt into freedom; He put the first people in Eden with unlimited possibilities. Almost from the beginning the people of Israel fell into sin; so did the very first people. Israel sinned through centuries till sin brought destruction; the world is sinning and will finally be destroyed. God promised that Israel would be restored; He promises also new heavens and a new earth.

A. Isaiah the Prophet

Isaiah was a prophet of Israel's destruction and restoration. He was a prophet also of the end of the world and new heavens and earth. But it seems that Isaiah saw the whole future as one picture. He said Judah would be destroyed and restored, but he did not say the destruction would come in about a hundred years and the restoration seventy years later. He said God's servant would suffer in our place and give us healing, but not that it would happen seven hundred years after he announced it. He said God would create new heavens and a new earth, but not how far in the future it would be.

History helps us understand some of Isaiah's predictions. It is easy to see that Judah fell about a hundred years after Isaiah foretold it, and was restored seventy years later. It is easy to see that Jesus fulfilled the prophecy of a suffering servant about seven hundred years after Isaiah gave it. But history does not help us to understand the prophecy of new heavens and earth. These are not yet in history; they are in the future. However, New Testament writings do help us understand what Isaiah wrote about them.

B. Lesson Background

Isaiah 65 begins with a brilliant picture of the Christian age: "I am sought of them that asked not for me; I am found of them that sought me not." Heathen Gentiles who had not cared at all about Jehovah were to find Him through the preaching of the gospel. That prophecy was fulfilled in the time when Paul wrote, "There is no difference between the Jew and the Greek . . . for whosoever shall call upon the name of the Lord shall be saved" (Romans 10:12, 13, 20). In Paul's day, as in Isaiah's own time, the people of Israel were a rebellious people to whom God stretched out His hands in vain appeal (Isaiah 65:2; Romans 10:21). Some people of Israel would be saved (Isaiah 65:8, 9; Romans 11:15). Along with the saved of the Gentiles they would enjoy God's blessing, while the disobedient would find only trouble (Isaiah 65:13-16). Our text then looks far beyond the time when a remnant of Israel would return to the land of promise, and far beyond the time when the gospel first would be received among the Gentiles. By divine revelation Isaiah writes of new heavens and a new earth.

I. Joyous New Creation
(Isaiah 65:17-20)

Judah would have a chance to return from captivity in Babylon, yes. Very clearly God gave Isaiah the promise of that. He even named the man who would overcome Babylon and set Judah free (Isaiah 44:26—45:4). However, it was only a small part of the glorious word given to Isaiah. Poetically the prophet sang to Judah that her warfare was accomplished and her iniquity pardoned, and he sang also of the coming of Jesus (Isaiah 40:1-5). Now our text takes us through other thousands of years to the time when Jesus' reign will be triumphant.

A. New Heavens and Earth (v. 17)

17. For, behold, I create new heavens and a new earth: and the former shall not be remembered, nor come into mind.

This might be taken as a poetic hyperbole describing the prosperity and joy of the people of Judah when they would be restored to the homeland, but New Testament Scriptures show that it is much more. Simon Peter rebukes those who doubt that Jesus will come back as He said He would. He may wait long, giving sinners time to repent and be saved. "But the day of the Lord will come as a thief in the night; in the which the heavens shall pass away with a great noise, and the elements shall melt with fervent heat, the earth also and the works that are therein shall be burned up." After calling us to godly living, Peter looks back to the words of Isaiah and says, "Nevertheless we, according to his promise, look for new heavens and a new earth, wherein dwelleth righteousness" (2 Peter 3:1-13). We shall see these after the present earth and sky have vanished in flame. The new will be so delightful that the earth and sky we now see will have no place in our thinking.

B. New Jerusalem (vv. 18, 19)

18. But be ye glad and rejoice for ever in that which I create: for, behold, I create Jerusalem a rejoicing, and her people a joy.

Old Jerusalem was going to be destroyed so completely that its rebuilding might well be called a new creation, and indeed there would be great joy in the rebuilding after the captivity

in Babylon. The people would rejoice in the completed temple (Ezra 6:16) and again in the completed wall of the city (Nehemiah 12:27, 43). But God's later revelation tells also of a new Jerusalem that will far surpass that restored city. Jerusalem was the heart of old Israel; Jerusalem will be the heart of the new heavens and earth. There God will live with His people, and there will be joy, joy, joy. Read of it in Revelation 21.

19. And I will rejoice in Jerusalem, and joy in my people: and the voice of weeping shall be no more heard in her, nor the voice of crying.

God would rejoice along with His people, both in earthly Jerusalem restored and in the Heavenly Jerusalem of later ages. The voice of weeping would be stilled for a time in the joy of old Jerusalem restored; it will be stilled forever in the new Jerusalem (Revelation 21:4).

C. Long Life (v. 20)

20. There shall be no more thence an infant of days, nor an old man that hath not filled his days: for the child shall die a hundred years old; but the sinner being a hundred years old shall be accursed.

Here we see four statements about Jerusalem. As they appear in the *King James Version* they may be understood as follows:

1. There will be no infant mortality: no baby will die after only a few days of life.

2. Every old man will have a long, full life.

3. One who dies at the age of a hundred will be considered a mere child.

4. Even a sinner will live a hundred years before he is accursed and dies for his sin.

This is puzzling. It comes in the midst of prophecies about earthly Jerusalem restored and Heavenly Jerusalem newly created. However, it does not seem to refer to earthly Jerusalem restored, for history does not record that it was fulfilled there. If no babies died after the Babylonian captivity, and if everybody lived a hundred years or more, wouldn't there be some record of these unusual circumstances? On the other hand, this verse does not seem to refer to the new Jerusalem described in Revelation 21, for there is no death nor sin nor curse in that fair city. Then how are we to understand this verse? Here are some possibilities:

The first two items listed above may be just a poetic way of describing everlasting life in new Jerusalem. No baby will die; every man will live the full span of life, and in new Jerusalem that is forever.

In the Greek version of the book of Isaiah, item three is translated, "the child shall be a hundred years old," rather than "the child shall die a hundred years old." If that is the correct reading, it means merely that a hundred years of a person's life is like childhood in comparison with eternal life in new Jerusalem.

The fourth item has two puzzles. First, the word used here for sin has the primary meaning of missing a mark, of failing, rather than doing wrong. It may mean failing to reach a hundred years rather than committing a sin at the age of a hundred. Another question lies in the word for *accursed*. Primarily it means light or trivial. If we give both of these words their primary meanings, we see that anything less than a hundred years is trivial in the everlasting life we shall enjoy in new Jerusalem.

II. Work and Success
(Isaiah 65:21-23)

This section seems to speak primarily of the people who would return from captivity in Babylon. Back in Judah, they would build again the ruined towns and cultivate the neglected farms. Does it speak also of those who will live in new Jerusalem? Will there be productive work for them to do? There was work for Adam in Eden (Genesis 2:15). Will there be work for the redeemed in the paradise of God? We read that "his servants shall serve him" (Revelation 22:3). Surely they will serve Him by singing His praises (Revelation 7:9, 10). Is that the only way, or will God's people in new Jerusalem have some work that may be compared with the work of God's people in restored Judah? The Bible does not answer these questions, but it assures us that life in new Jerusalem will be delightful.

A. Work Rewarded (v. 21)

21. And they shall build houses, and inhabit them; and they shall plant vineyards, and eat the fruit of them.

It takes time and work to build a house, and the reward is shelter from sun and rain and cold. It takes time and effort to clear the ground and plant a vineyard, and it takes much more time for the vines to mature and produce fruit. But all the work and waiting are rewarded when the grapes are ripe.

B. Security (v. 22)

22. They shall not build, and another inhabit; they shall not plant, and another eat: for as the days of a tree are the days of my people, and mine elect shall long enjoy the work of their hands.

Isaiah wrote this when Judah was on the way to destruction. Because of their sins the people would be evicted from their homes. The Babylonians would either destroy the houses or leave them for others. They would eat the grapes of Judah while the people who had planted the vines would be starving, besieged in Jerusalem. Then the Babylonians would leave, taking the people of Jerusalem with them, and nearby heathen would move in to enjoy the fruit of the vines. But our text tells of the time when the people of Judah would come back from Babylon and be secure. No invaders would take their homes and vineyards. Some trees do not live very long, but an oak or cedar or olive may stand for centuries. So the returned captives would have a long time of security in their homeland. In new Jerusalem, of course, the time of security will last forever.

C. Blessed of the Lord (v. 23)

23. They shall not labor in vain, nor bring forth for trouble; for they are the seed of the blessed of the Lord, and their offspring with them.

Labor was *in vain* when the crop was eaten by locusts, or when dry weather ruined it, or when invaders stole the harvest. Such calamities were ahead when Isaiah wrote this. They would reach their climax in the Babylonian captivity, but that captivity would end and the people of Judah would come back to their homeland. Then their crops would not fail, and invaders would not take the produce. Even more certainly there will be no failure nor robbery in new Jerusalem.

Bring forth here represents a Hebrew word that usually is used of giving birth to children. *Trouble* is of many kinds, ranging from fear to destruction. The *New International Version* gives it a general meaning, saying, "They will not . . . bear children doomed to misfortune." Similar is the *New American Standard Bible:* "They shall not . . . bear children for calamity." Isaiah wrote this when destruction by Babylon was about a century away. Children born in the latter part of that century would be born for trouble, born to die by starvation, to be killed in battle, or to be taken to captivity in Babylon. But the captives would come back, and then their children would not need to fear any such troubles. In new Jerusalem, of course, all troubles will be left behind forever (Revelation 21:4).

The blessed of the Lord would be those so devoted to God and His way that they would be eager to go back to Judah and rebuild a nation of God's people. After seventy years in Babylon, many of the original captives would be dead. Their children would have grown up in Babylon and would be comfortable there. Many would prefer to stay. But some would be taught the Scriptures that called them to be God's people, a people dedicated to His service and ruled by His law. Such devoted people would go back to Jerusalem, and God would bless them with peace and prosperity. This prophecy can apply to new Jerusalem. *The blessed of the Lord* are Christians. *Their offspring* are the people they bring to Christ. These will enjoy eternal peace and happiness in the Heavenly Jerusalem.

III. Summary
(Isaiah 65:24, 25)

The closing verses of our text summarize the condition of God's people, those who love Him with all their heart and soul and might (Deuteronomy 6:5), those who not only call Him Lord but also do His will (Matthew 7:21), those who seek first His kingdom and His righteousness (Matthew 6:33). In any time and place, such people are in close contact with God and are at peace with one another.

A. Close Contact (v. 24)

24. And it shall come to pass, that before they call, I will answer; and while they are yet speaking, I will hear.

Those who call to the Lord are never put on hold. He gives them His attention instantly; yes, even before they put their call into words. Jesus likewise assured His disciples, "Your Father knoweth what things ye have need of, before ye ask him" (Matthew 6:8). That does not mean we should not ask. We should (Matthew 6:9-13; 7:7-11). But our asking is not to inform God about our needs. If we pray thoughtfully, with our minds on His kingdom and His righteousness, our asking refines our wishing. If love of God is uppermost in our thoughts, and love of our fellowmen is next to it, we do not waste our time with selfish prayers that deserve only a no answer. Careless and greedy prayers can put us among those to whom James says, "Ye ask, and receive not, because ye ask amiss, that ye may spend it in your pleasures" (James 4:3, *American Standard Version*). If we do not get what we ask, it is not because God does not know what we are saying. It may be because He knows our needs better than we do. We ought to pray earnestly, "Thy will be done" (Matthew 6:10), and earnestly to shape our will according to His. "Draw nigh to God, and he will draw nigh to you" (James 4:8). Close contact with God would be available to the liberated captives who would rebuild Jerusalem. It is available to us whom Christ has set free from sin and death. It will be perfected in the Heavenly Jerusalem. There God will live with us; there His glory will so fill the city that we shall need no sun; there we shall see His face (Revelation 21:3, 23; 22:4).

GOD STILL ANSWERS PRAYER

Aleksandr Solzhenitsyn told of a brilliant astronomer who was imprisoned. He saved his sanity by praying, thinking about God, and considering the order in the universe. In this way he began to discover a new field in physics. After a time of such mental exploration he found that his progress was being hindered because he had forgotten some figures. He could build no further structures in his mind without them. So he prayed for God to help him continue his studies.

The prisoner was entitled to one book every seventy days. One half hour after his prayer a guard came and pushed a book at him. It was entitled *A Course in Astro Physics*. He was thrilled and mystified by the title. He couldn't imagine a book such as that in the prison library, but there he sat with it in his hands. He memorized everything possible in the next two days. Then a surprise inspection was held, and the book was confiscated. But its mysterious arrival had opened his mind to new dimensions and his heart to greater faith.

Isaiah predicted that God would answer prayers for His people before they were vocally uttered. No one can explain the arrival of that book at that time without a reference to Isaiah's promise. God still answers prayer.   —V. H.

B. Peace (v. 25)

25. The wolf and the lamb shall feed together, and the lion shall eat straw like the bullock: and dust shall be the serpent's meat. They shall not hurt nor destroy in all my holy mountain, saith the Lord.

When a wolf and a lamb get together, usually the wolf is the only one that is feeding. A lion's teeth are designed for tearing meat; it is hard to imagine his munching hay with the cattle. It is harder still to imagine a snake's literally lapping up dust for his dinner. Is all this a figure of speech, a poetic hyperbole meaning that greedy people no longer will prey on others, robbing

God said, "Be ye glad and rejoice for ever in that which I create."

visual 9

them by violence or trickery? Perhaps it is. Certainly the literal wolves and lions and snakes did not change their nature when the captives went home from Babylon, nor have they changed it in the Christian era. But even in a figurative sense this prophecy was not very well fulfilled in the return from Babylon. Within a century Nehemiah had to deal sternly with greedy people who were taking advantage of their fellowmen (Nehemiah 5:1-13). In the church today the prophecy is only partly fulfilled. Most Christians are fair and generous in their dealings, though a few may act like wolves or lions or snakes—and most of us act selfishly sometimes. Only in new Jerusalem will this word of the Lord be fulfilled completely. There greed and envy and enmity will be left behind with sorrow and pain. There peace will be complete.

Is it possible that the word about wolf and lion and serpent will be fulfilled literally as well as figuratively? Well, "with God all things are possible" (Mark 10:27). Sometime our earth and sky will vanish in flame, and there will be new heavens and a new earth (2 Peter 3:10-13; Revelation 21:1). If God wishes, there will be a new lion with bovine teeth and placid disposition. But to say it is possible is not to say it will be so. No animals are mentioned in the description of new Jerusalem in the closing chapters of Revelation. In time of conflict John saw the hosts of Heaven mounted on white horses (Revelation 19:11-14), but that too may be purely figurative. Then is the prophecy of wolf and lion and serpent to be taken literally, or only figuratively? Perhaps we shall not be sure till we see it in the new heavens and earth.

In any case, this closing verse of our text is summed up in its closing statement: *They shall*

Home Daily Bible Readings

Monday, Oct. 24—Blessings and Woes (Isaiah 65:1-7)

Tuesday, Oct. 25—The Gladness of the Servants (Isaiah 65:8-16)

Wednesday, Oct. 26—The Promises of the Lord (Isaiah 65:17-25)

Thursday, Oct. 27—The Promise to the Faithful (Isaiah 60:1-7)

Friday, Oct. 28—Blessings on God's People (Isaiah 60:10-14)

Saturday, Oct. 29—The Promised Restoration (Isaiah 60:15-22)

Sunday, Oct. 30—A New Heaven and Earth (Revelation 21:1-8)

not hurt nor destroy in all my holy mountain, saith the Lord. God's *holy mountain* was first the hill on which His temple stood in old Jerusalem. Now it is the church, our mother, "Jerusalem which is above" (Galatians 4:26). In time to come, God's *holy mountain* will be His perfected kingdom, which is pictured in John's vision of new Jerusalem. There we shall live in the light of God. There we no longer shall hurt one another. There at last peace and harmony will be complete.

Conclusion

In lesson 7 we noted that the prophet saw future events blended together in one picture, though they were to be widely separated in time. In this lesson predictions of Judah after the captivity are blended with predictions of the Christian era and predictions of new heavens and a new earth that are still in the future. As Christians we live in the light of God's Word, and we press on toward that eternal city where we shall live in the light of His face.

A. Let's Go!

Jesus' death and resurrection have opened the way so that we may go to the glorious new Jerusalem. Let's be traveling that way. "Be not conformed to this world: but be ye transformed by the renewing of your mind, that ye may prove what is that good, and acceptable, and perfect will of God" (Romans 12:2).

B. Let's Not Go Alone

Each of us individually makes his journey to that city where they need no sun, but none travels alone. We walk with the Lord and with His people in the church. Besides, we reach out continually to draw others into the fellowship of the saved. If you started some missionary effort last week, it may need some follow-up. If not, here is an opportunity to:

Review the church's missionary program.

Review a project and make a special offering toward it.

Begin a missionary project.

C. Prayer

Almighty God, how grateful we are for that city of light that is our destination! How grateful we are for the Savior who leads us there! May we have the courage to follow Him. In Jesus' name, amen.

D. Thought to Remember

"They shall not hurt nor destroy in all my holy mountain, saith the Lord."

Learning by Doing

This page contains an alternate lesson plan emphasizing learning activities. Classes desiring such student involvement will find these suggestions helpful.

Learning Goals

Examining today's text in Isaiah 65 will enable the adult to:

1. See the future Isaiah saw and to rejoice for the joy God has created and will create.

2. Identify parallel phrasing and concepts in New Testament texts.

3. Affirm that Isaiah's message to Judah concludes with a word of joyous hope of future restoration and glory.

Into the Lesson

Prepare six letter cards (large enough to be seen by your whole group) with the letters I, S, A, I, A, H on the front; the letters F, U, T, U, R, E on the back (with F behind I, U behind S, etc.). Display the sides reading "Isaiah" and tell your class, "If you look into *Isaiah* hard enough *(point to cards)* you can see something else." Tell them that other letters are on the reverse side. Let them guess letters; when a correct letter is guessed, turn the appropriate card over. Whenever someone guesses the word *future*, turn over all the cards and say, "Today's text shows Isaiah looking near and far into the future. Yes, if *you* look closely, you can see *future* in *Isaiah!*"

Into the Word

Prepare strips of paper bearing the following Bible text references, one per strip: Isaiah 65:17; Isaiah 65:18; Isaiah 65:19; Isaiah 65:20; Isaiah 65:21, 22; Isaiah 65:23; Isaiah 65:24; Isaiah 65:25; 2 Peter 3:13; Revelation 19:7; Revelation 7:17; 1 John 5:11; Psalm 1:3; Matthew 25:34; Matthew 6:8; Revelation 11:18. (Non-Isaiah texts match the sequence of the Isaiah verses.) If you have more than sixteen in your class, duplicate matched pairs for the activity to follow. If you have less than sixteen, decrease the number of matched pairs. Distribute a strip to each member, directing each to find and read his verse and get the phrasing in mind. Then ask everyone to stand and circulate to find the classmate with the corresponding verse. When two students find that their verses match, those students should be seated. When all are seated, you are ready to examine the text together, using the matched verses as you introduce commentary.

Now ask your class to express their views of what historical incident each idea in today's text refers to. Direct them: "If a verse refers to the time of the restoration of Judah after its captivity, raise your right hand. If the verse refers to the final coming of Jesus, raise your left hand. If the reference is to a combination of times, raise both hands." Read the verses one at a time, with the exception of 21 and 22, which should be read together. After each, ask for your show of hands. Allow those who may disagree to express their reason(s).

Into Life

Several elements of today's text are easily versified and sung. Introduce the following as short choruses; have tunes prepared in one of the following ways: (1) Give the verses to several church members—even youth—a week or two ahead of today's session and ask them to prepare a simple and singable tune; (2) Examine a hymn or chorus book for familiar and usable tunes; or (3) Introduce the verses to the class and ask for spontaneous tunes "to fit." Verses here are identified by text verse number; each has been personalized in the pronouns.

God will create new heavens;
  God will create new earth;
And we will ne'er remember
  The land of our first birth. (v. 17)

Be ye glad! Be ye glad!
  God creates rejoicing: Be ye glad!
Be ye glad! Be ye glad!
  There'll be no eye of weeping: no one sad. (v. 18)
(repeat first two lines)

We are the seed of the blessed of the Lord;
We are the seed of the blessed of the Lord;
  Our labor is not vain;
  The trouble will not reign;
  Our offspring will we bring,
For we are the blessed of the Lord. (v. 23)

Our Father knows our needs before we ask them;
He answers e'er we yet have made the call.
  While we are speaking still,
  Our blessings He does fill:
  He answers e'er we yet have made the call. (v. 24)

Teach and sing as many songs as your time allows. Suggest that one or more songs be considered for your students' personal or family devotions for the week. Provide copies of the verses, if possible. (You may want to prepare other verses to sing; you may want to assign them to small groups within your class, for development of lyrics or tune.)

Let's Talk It Over

The questions on this page are designed to encourage review of the lesson Scriptures and to promote discussion of the lesson by the class. The answers provided are only discussion starters. Let your class talk it over from there.

1. Why does the human mind, in the midst of imperfection, always envision and long for perfection?

This is a deep question, but we do have some insights. The clues are rooted deeply in mankind's original state and original nature. John Milton, seventeenth-century English poet, wrote one of the world's greatest epics, *Paradise Lost.* Four years later followed *Paradise Regained.* There's the clue: what mankind lost he longs to regain. God created us for fellowship with himself. The perfect relationship was shattered by our sin. We look back to a previous idyllic time. We also look ahead to a new paradise. This longing is planted deeply within our psyches. God spoke to this longing through the Old Testament prophets as He gave them visions of a "new age" to come. God promised restoration to His people in captivity—with a new Jerusalem, and a new life marked by peace and prosperity. New Testament prophets reveal the future of the new Israel in the Heavenly Jerusalem, and that existance will be perfect. The Christian message affirms that mankind need not just envision and long for some vague paradise; God has prepared an eternal place for those who belong to Him, who have been adopted into His family.

2. What are some beneficial results of our daily work?

Isaiah 65:21-23 depicted work for the Jews when they would return to Jerusalem after the Babylonian captivity. All of us want and need to feel that our work accomplishes something worthwhile. Some beneficial results of our daily work are these: (1) We know that we have provided for ourselves and our families. Thus, physical, intellectual, and even emotional needs are met. (2) We know that we have made a contribution to society. By our work we have helped others far beyond the confines of family. Hopefully, the world is a better place because of our contribution. (3) We feel a sense of personal satisfaction. In doing honest work (physical and/or mental) there is the feeling of being responsible, of achievement, of "a job well done." (4) We have a sense of God's blessing upon our labors. Because all of life is a stewardship, we know that if we are faithful in that stewardship, God blesses. Daily work should be more than a grind, a curse, or a treadmill, because we are the new humanity in Jesus Christ!

3. Why are people so fascinated and attracted to that which is new?

The most powerful, motivating word in modern advertising is *new,* and Madison Avenue knows what sells. *New* implies "better," advanced beyond the previous. It touches at a level of discontent with what we have. It stimulates desire. The *new* is no less powerful and attractive in the spiritual realm. We want a new life in place of the old. We long for a new sense of peace, love, and belonging. In this old world, we yearn for a new age. We see more than Isaiah saw, for we have the Revelation of John. In it shines the matchless portrait of Him who sits on the throne, saying, "Behold, I am making all things new" (Revelation 21:5 *New American Standard Bible*). There is *nothing* to compare with the new order God will one day create!

4. What will Heaven be like?

It is impossible to give a concrete, specific description of Heaven. Having known our present existence only, we cannot comprehend everything about Heaven, which is an existence on a plane different from what we have known. Thus the Bible uses objects familiar to us (such as gold, gems, and walls) to depict Heaven's richness and beauty. However, the Bible makes the following facts clear, and of them we can be confident: God will be there in our midst (that alone would make it Heaven!); no sin or imperfection will be there (what a heavenly thought); all who are therein will possess eternal life (both in quality and its unending nature).

5. What changes need to be made if a better world is to be created today?

Certain perspectives (and the policies to implement them) need to be changed: power must be used to help people, rather than to control them; people must be loved, not used; eternal values must be prized above the temporal.

Jeremiah's Call

LESSON SCRIPTURE: Jeremiah 1.

PRINTED TEXT: Jeremiah 1:4-10, 17-19.

Jeremiah 1:4-10, 17-19

4 Then the word of the Lord came unto me, saying,

5 Before I formed thee in the belly I knew thee; and before thou camest forth out of the womb I sanctified thee, and I ordained thee a prophet unto the nations.

6 Then said I, Ah, Lord God! behold, I cannot speak: for I am a child.

7 But the Lord said unto me, Say not, I am a child: for thou shalt go to all that I shall send thee, and whatsoever I command thee thou shalt speak.

8 Be not afraid of their faces: for I am with thee to deliver thee, saith the Lord.

9 Then the Lord put forth his hand, and touched my mouth. And the Lord said unto me, Behold, I have put my words in thy mouth.

10 See, I have this day set thee over the nations and over the kingdoms, to root out, and to pull down, and to destroy, and to throw down, to build, and to plant.

. . . .

17 Thou therefore gird up thy loins, and arise, and speak unto them all that I command thee: be not dismayed at their faces, lest I confound thee before them.

18 For, behold, I have made thee this day a defensed city, and an iron pillar, and brazen walls against the whole land, against the kings of Judah, against the princes thereof, against the priests thereof, and against the people of the land.

19 And they shall fight against thee; but they shall not prevail against thee; for I am with thee, saith the Lord, to deliver thee.

Nov
6

GOLDEN TEXT: The word of the Lord came unto me, saying, Before I formed thee in the belly I knew thee; and before thou camest forth out of the womb I sanctified thee, and I ordained thee a prophet unto the nations.—Jeremiah 1:4, 5.

Lesson Aims

This lesson should enable a student to:
1. Recall the facts of Jeremiah's call.
2. Tell the best way to test the truth of any religious teaching.
3. Resolve to trust God's Word, study it diligently, and share its teaching with others.

Lesson Outline

INTRODUCTION
  A. Kings and People
  B. Lesson Background
 I. CALL AND COMMISSION (Jeremiah 1:4-10)
  A. The Prophet's Predestination (vv. 4, 5)
  B. The Prophet's Protest (vv. 6-8)
  C. The Prophet's Preparation (vv. 9, 10)
    Only What Is Written
II. ENCOURAGEMENT (Jeremiah 1:17-19)
  A. The Prophet's Duty (v. 17)
  B. The Prophet's Defense (v. 18)
  C. The Prophet's Defender (v. 19)
    Overcoming
CONCLUSION
  A. Who Speaks for God?
  B. Truth Lives
  C. Don't Be Scared
  D. Prayer
  E. Thought to Remember

Display visual 10 from the visuals/learning resources packet. It is shown on page 85.

Introduction

Through centuries Judah wavered between the worship of Jehovah and the worship of imaginary gods. Heathen religions offered much that was attractive to the worldly mind. They did not demand strict moral living, discipline, or self-denial. Fraud or robbery were not objected to, if generous offerings were given to the priests. So crookedness and greed were encouraged rather than honesty and helpfulness.

A. Kings and People

Isaiah prophesied during the reigns of four kings: Uzziah, Jotham, Ahaz, and Hezekiah (Isaiah 1:1). Of these kings, only Ahaz promoted false religion (2 Chronicles 28:1-4). But while the other kings were doing their best to maintain the worship of Jehovah, "the people did yet corruptly" (2 Chronicles 27:2). King Hezekiah worked hard to restore true worship of the Lord, and the result was that God turned back the Assyrians who invaded Judah (2 Chronicles 29:1—32:23). But Hezekiah's son Manasseh ruled for fifty-five years, and encouraged all kinds of false religions (2 Chronicles 33:1-9).

In the latter part of his reign, Manasseh tried to undo the harm he had done (2 Chronicles 33:10-17). When he died, his son Amon promptly reverted to idolatry. That lasted only two years. Then Amon was assassinated by plotters in the palace, but an uprising among the people destroyed the plotters and gave the throne to Amon's son Josiah (2 Chronicles 33:21-25).

B. Lesson Background

Josiah was only eight years old when he became king. He must have had good advisers, for "he did that which was right in the sight of the Lord" (2 Chronicles 34:1, 2).

In the twelfth year of his reign, when Josiah was about twenty years old, he began a vigorous effort to wipe out idolatry and restore the true worship of the Lord (2 Chronicles 34:3-7). In the following year, Jeremiah the prophet began his work (Jeremiah 1:2). This faithful prophet continued to proclaim the word of the Lord for more than forty years, till Babylon destroyed Jerusalem and took its people away (v. 3).

I. Call and Commission (Jeremiah 1:4-10)

Marvelous are the ways of the Lord! Before Josiah and Jeremiah were born, He knew what they would be and do. He knew exactly when King Josiah would start his sweep through the land to destroy the trappings of idolatry, and He picked an unborn baby who then would be mature enough and would have the proper character and ability to support that effort by holding forth the word of God. Now the king's crusade was in full swing. Now the chosen baby was a young man. It was time he knew he was chosen.

A. The Prophet's Predestination (vv. 4, 5)

4. Then the word of the Lord came unto me, saying.

The word was quite plain. Jeremiah understood it clearly, and he knew it came from *the Lord!* It may be that some people imagine their own wish is God's call, but that was not the case here. Jeremiah did not wish to be a prophet (v. 6), but God gave him that duty anyway.

5. Before I formed thee in the belly I knew thee; and before thou camest forth out of the womb I sanctified thee, and I ordained thee a prophet unto the nations.

From the time of conception, the Lord was shaping Jeremiah within his mother's body. He was forming a person who could be a prophet. Before the child was born, God sanctified him. That means He set him apart, dedicated him to the work that would be his. To that work God *ordained* or appointed Jeremiah. *A prophet* is God's spokesman, one who receives God's message by special inspiration. Jeremiah was chosen to transmit God's word, not to Judah only but *unto the nations.*

B. The Prophet's Protest (vv. 6-8)

6. Then said I, Ah, Lord God! behold, I cannot speak: for I am a child.

Jeremiah thought he was too young for the responsibility God was giving him. We do not know how old he was. The Hebrew word translated *child* often is translated *young man.* It is used of Moses at the age of three months (Exodus 2:6), and it is used of Joseph when he was about thirty years old (Genesis 41:12). Probably some of the elder statesmen in Judah were still in sympathy with the reckless idolatry that Manasseh had promoted for many years. So were many of the common people, and priests of many idolatrous religions, and men who claimed to be prophets. Who would listen to a young fellow if he opposed all these? But the crusading king was only about twenty-one. He was overriding opposition in his effort to stamp out idolatry, and God was sending a young prophet to help him.

7. But the Lord said unto me, Say not, I am a child: for thou shalt go to all that I shall send thee, and whatsoever I command thee thou shalt speak.

What the Lord was asking would not require old age, wide experience, or great wisdom. Jeremiah was simply to go where God would send him and to say what God would tell him to say. Any young man could do that if he had two feet and a voice. Of course this does not mean Jeremiah lacked natural talent. Probably he would have been a fine speaker and writer even without inspiration. No doubt he was honest, upright, intelligent, and courageous. But God was giving him a task that would call for devotion and obedience more than anything else.

8. Be not afraid of their faces: for I am with thee to deliver thee, saith the Lord.

Young King Josiah already was destroying the heathen altars and idols in Judah. Undoubtedly he was meeting angry faces at every turn. Those

How to Say It

AHAZ. *A*-haz.
AMON. *A*-mun.
HEZEKIAH. Hez-uh-*kye*-uh.
JOSIAH. Jo-*sye*-uh.
JOTHAM. *Jo*-tham.
MANASSEH. Muh-*nas*-uh.
UZZIAH. Uh-*zye*-uh.

same faces would frown on Jeremiah. People would not want to give up the fun of heathen festivals. Pagan priests and false prophets would try to keep the evil religions that gave them their living. Bureaucrats who had been with King Manasseh and King Amon in their evil time would want to continue the graft and corruption that had been profitable to them. All of these would be furious with God's prophet, and future kings would not be on his side as Josiah was. But the prophet must not be scared. No matter who was against him, the Lord said, *I am with thee to deliver thee.* God was greater than all the opposition.

C. The Prophet's Preparation (vv. 9, 10)

9. Then the Lord put forth his hand, and touched my mouth. And the Lord said unto me, Behold, I have put my words in thy mouth.

We are not told whether Jeremiah saw any form of the Lord or not. We are not told even that he saw the Lord's hand; but he felt its touch, and the Lord told him what it meant. No more would Jeremiah decide what to say. He would simply say what Jehovah would tell him to say.

ONLY WHAT IS WRITTEN

In an interview, Philharmonic Director Zubin Mehta was asked if he felt superior to the composers whose works he directed. Not at all, he replied. In fact, Mehta thought himself a pygmy compared with the giants of composition. The maestro felt that some mistakenly attribute to the conductors the genius that truly belongs to the likes of Beethoven, Bach, and Hayden. He then explained that the single purpose of the director was to express what the composer had originally written. He didn't correct the composer, add to, or take from his work.

When God called Jeremiah as a prophet, He put His words in Jeremiah's mouth. In essence God was saying that Jeremiah was to speak only what God gave him to speak.

One who speaks for God today faces the same challenge. Within the framework of the composition—the Word of God—he can fully develop spiritual themes. But only within it. In proclaiming God's Word we expand human horizons to spiritual truth revealed in the Bible. We do not attempt to go beyond what God has revealed therein.   —V. H.

10. See, I have this day set thee over the nations and over the kingdoms, to root out, and to pull down, and to destroy, and to throw down, to build, and to plant.

Young and alone and unarmed as he was, Jeremiah was to destroy whole nations, to tear them out by the roots and smash them. Assyria had been doing this by means of vast armies. Babylon soon would be doing it the same way. But Jeremiah commanded no army and carried no spear or sword. His weapon was the word God put in his mouth. He would announce the destruction of nations, and they would be destroyed as he said. Judah would be crushed by Babylon; Babylon in turn would be destroyed; other nations would share the same fate (Jeremiah 25:8-29). But the word given to Jeremiah was not a word of destruction only. He would also *build* nations and *plant* them. Specifically, he would announce that both Israel and Judah would be liberated to be planted and built again in their homeland (Jeremiah 33). This too happened according to the word that God gave to Jeremiah. The books of Ezra and Nehemiah tell of the return from captivity.

II. Encouragement
(Jeremiah 1:17-19)

There was good reason for young Jeremiah to shrink from the task God was giving him. He would have to bring an unwelcome message. He would have to say the Lord was going to bring hostile armies from the north, armies that would flow over Judah like scalding water from a boiling kettle (Jeremiah 1:13-16). No one in Judah would want to hear that, and some would want to kill the prophet for saying it (Jeremiah 26:8). All this was discouraging to God's prophet; but on the other hand, Jeremiah's encouragement came from the Lord himself.

A. The Prophet's Duty (v. 17)

17. Thou therefore gird up thy loins, and arise, and speak unto them all that I command thee: be not dismayed at their faces, lest I confound thee before them.

In ancient times a man wore a robe down to the ankles instead of trousers. Getting ready to fight or run or work in the harvest field, he would lift the robe above his knees and secure it with a girdle or belt around his waist. This kept him from stepping on the hem of the robe or getting his feet tangled in its folds. Therefore *gird up thy loins* meant *get ready for action*, even if the preparation and action both were mental rather than physical. Jeremiah was to get ready to stand up and deliver the message God would give him. He needed to strengthen his determination to stand up and speak fearlessly. His hearers would contradict and jeer and threaten, but he must not be intimidated. *Be not dismayed* may be translated *Don't be scared*; and *confound* represents the same Hebrew word. God was saying, "Don't be scared by their faces, lest I scare you before their faces." In other words, if Jeremiah would lose his nerve and falter in giving God's message, then God would no longer support him and he would be thoroughly terrified.

B. The Prophet's Defense (v. 18)

18. For, behold, I have made thee this day a defensed city, and an iron pillar, and brazen walls against the whole land, against the kings of Judah, against the princes thereof, against the priests thereof, and against the people of the land.

Nearly everybody in Judah would oppose Jeremiah. The present king, Josiah, was on his side; but the next three *kings of Judah* would be against him, and the fourth would be a wavering weakling. The *princes* were officials not necessarily of the royal family. Some of them would favor Jeremiah at times (Jeremiah 26:16), but princes also would beat him and lock him up (Jeremiah 37:15). Probably some *priests* would support God's prophet, but other priests could be expected to oppose Jeremiah (Jeremiah 2:8; 26:8). And many *people of the land* enjoyed heathen festivals and would be annoyed when Jeremiah would denounce them. Some surely would resent his preaching against crooked business and unfair judges. But if Jeremiah would give God's message faithfully and fearlessly, no one could stop him. He would be like a city with walls of brass, too strong to be demolished by any battering ram.

C. The Prophet's Defender (v. 19)

19. And they shall fight against thee; but they shall not prevail against thee; for I am with thee, saith the Lord, to deliver thee.

Jeremiah would be beaten and jailed and starved for a time, but he would not be overcome. Princes might rule the palace, priests might rule the temple, people might fill the land, and all of them might fight against God's prophet; but Jehovah was mightier than all of them. It was the Lord God almighty who said, *They shall not prevail against thee; for I am with thee . . . to deliver thee.*

OVERCOMING

In 331 B.C. Alexander the Great and Darius of Persia met at Arbela in a decisive battle. Darius had assembled an enormous army, heavy cavalry, and many chariots. Darius even chose the field of battle: a wide plain where his troops could maneuver and where his superiority in power could be used to greatest advantage. But it was to no avail. For while Alexander's forces were outnumbered, he had one advantage—forty thousand war-hardened men accustomed to victory, fully devoted to him, conscious of his and their strength, and not afraid of any foe. The result was a smashing victory for Alexander.

When God called Jeremiah to preach, the danger of military invasion from without was beginning to loom. Within the nation a spiritual perversity brought an obstinate refusal to obey God's Word. Jeremiah's message would be rejected, and he himself would be persecuted. Yet, he was not to fear the opposition, God said, for none could prevail against him. God stood by Jeremiah as he served. That made him more than equal to the opposition.

When we stand for righteousness, we may feel that we stand alone. But it is not so. For we have Jesus' promise, "Lo, I am with you alway" (Matthew 28:20). We will overcome.   —V.H.

Conclusion

We too are called—not to be prophets like Jeremiah, but to be Christians "holding forth the word of life" (Philippians 2:16). Not having God's word put in our mouths as Jeremiah did, we must be the more eager to learn the truth in every way we can, that we may share it with others.

A. Who Speaks for God?

Jeremiah spoke for God, and what he said was infallibly true. But how could the hearers of his prophecy know that? The prophet was not approved of God as Jesus was "by miracles and wonders and signs" (Acts 2:22). He was contradicted by other men who claimed to speak for God. How could the people of Judah know who was the true prophet and who was false?

People of every time and place have a similar problem. Teachers vigorously contradict one another. Even Bible teachers have their differences. How can we tell a true teacher from a false one? Sometimes it is difficult. The Scriptures suggest three things that can help.

1. *A willing heart.* Jesus said, "If any one chooses to do God's will, he will find out whether my teaching comes from God or whether I speak on my own" (John 7:17, *New*

visual 10

International Version). Kings and princes and priests and people rejected Jeremiah's teaching because they did not want to do God's will. How many people reject the true gospel of Jesus for the same reason?

A willing heart is not infallible, however. Many people sincerely want to do God's will, but are misled by mistaken teaching. Willingness is not always enough, but it helps.

2. *The test of time.* God's law gave one test of a person who claimed to be a prophet. If he foretold an event, and then that event did not happen, obviously he was not speaking for God (Deuteronomy 18:21, 22). When the Babylonian captivity was beginning, a cheerful prophet said it would be over in a couple of years, while Jeremiah said it would last seventy years (Jeremiah 28:1-4; 29:10). It is very easy for us to see who was speaking for God, but it was not that easy for the people who heard the two men. So in our time no one believes the teachers who said Jesus would return in 1927 or in 1972, but what about those who now say He will come before the end of this century? We can only wait and see.

3. *The quicker test.* Isaiah proposed a test that does not take so much time, but takes more study. "To the law and to the testimony: if they speak not according to this word, it is because there is no light in them" (Isaiah 8:20). The book of the law was laid away in the temple and forgotten in the long and evil reign of Manasseh, but it was found in the time of King Josiah and Jeremiah the prophet (2 Chronicles 34:8-33). Now the leaders of Judah knew what God wanted them to do. They knew also that His own law said they would be crushed and taken captive if they would not obey His law (Deuteronomy 28:15-46). This confirmed the prophecy of Jeremiah, and the people should have listened to him.

Everyone could know that God's law was really His because He gave it with miraculous signs (Exodus 19:16-18). In the midst of those signs God spoke the law for all the people to hear (Deuteronomy 5:22). Likewise the teaching of Jesus and His apostles was verified by His miracles that went with it (Acts 2:22; Mark 16:20). The best test of any teaching is: Does it agree with God's written Word?

B. Truth Lives

Truth is stubborn. It has a way of living on in spite of every effort to destroy it.

Our newspaper reports that a specialist was called to talk to one of our high schools about drug abuse. The students in assembly heckled and shouted and made such a racket that the speaker gave up and left without giving his talk. But the fact remains that drugs are deadly, and some of those hecklers will have their lives ruined because they chose not to hear the truth.

That was our intellectual high school, which specializes in college preparatory courses. Perhaps the students thought they were preparing for college. Earlier a speaker had been shouted down in a prestigious university that some of those students hope to attend. But silencing a speaker does not destroy the truth.

It is not recorded that the hearers shouted Jeremiah down, but it is recorded that they put him in the stocks (Jeremiah 20: 1, 2). Still the Babylonians overwhelmed Judah just as Jeremiah said they would. The truth lived on.

In a meeting of Sunday-school teachers an editor heard his publication criticized because it taught that Jesus is coming again. "He's not coming back," the critic said confidently.

"Does the Bible say He is coming back?" asked the editor.

The critic smiled. "The Bible can be wrong."

"No," the editor corrected, "you can be wrong. The Bible is right."

That critic was repeating an opinion that has been around for centuries. Long ago the Lord's apostle brushed it aside and assured us that Jesus will indeed return (2 Peter 3). We can count on it.

There are many who do not welcome the truth. Most of them neither shout the speaker down nor put him in the stocks. They do not even contradict the truth. They just ignore it. They are aware of the teaching that all have sinned and the wages of sin is death. They have heard that a lake of fire is waiting for sinners who will not repent, and that "he that believeth and is baptized shall be saved." But they pay no attention. But truth ignored is still truth.

"All flesh is grass, and all the goodliness thereof is as the flower of the field: the grass withereth, the flower fadeth . . . but the word of our God shall stand for ever" (Isaiah 40:6-8).

C. Don't Be Scared

In our world the truth of God seems to be more and more unwelcome. Consider these indications:

Every year at Christmastime we read of efforts to keep a manger scene from being displayed in a public place.

A court ruled that the Ten Commandments may not be posted on the wall of a public school.

Christians in various places complain that the place of religion in history is being eliminated from public-school textbooks.

There is a growing movement to avoid teenage pregnancy by teaching methods of contraception, not by teaching morality.

Asked about the Bible's teaching on homosexuality, the "pastor" of a "homosexual church" replied, "We have learned not to get hung up on the Bible."

Growing numbers of fiction stories, television programs, and even serious magazine articles are designed to make us think that extramarital sex is permissible or even commendable.

A radio newsman recently reported that more and more unmarried couples are living together.

"Be not afraid of their faces." We Christians must not be intimidated. We must not silence our testimony. We must redouble our effort to keep God's truth before the world by telling and living it. God has put His truth in our minds and hearts. Who will hear it from you?

D. Prayer

Thank You for truth, Father. May our ears be open to hear it and our minds willing to obey it.

E. Thought to Remember

"The word of our God shall stand for ever."

Home Daily Bible Readings

Monday, Oct. 31—Jeremiah Protests His Youth (Jeremiah 1:1-6)

Tuesday, Nov. 1—Paul's Charge to Young Timothy (1 Timothy 4:11-16)

Wednesday, Nov. 2—The Lord Empowers Jeremiah (Jeremiah 1:7-10)

Thursday, Nov. 3—The Christian's Empowerment (Ephesians 6:10-17)

Friday, Nov. 4—Jeremiah Is Given God's Word (Jeremiah 1:13-19)

Saturday, Nov. 5—The Disciples Are Given Their Charge (Luke 9:1-6)

Sunday, Nov. 6—The Seventy Are Sent Forth (Luke 10:1-9)

Learning by Doing

This page contains an alternate lesson plan emphasizing learning activities. Classes desiring such student involvement will find these suggestions helpful.

Learning Goals

As a result of this lesson a student should:

1. Be able to describe the specifics of Jeremiah's call to be God's prophet.

2. Be assured of God's comfort and help when he answers God's call to serve Him.

Into the Lesson

As class members arrive, reveal these two rows of letters on chalkboard, overhead transparency, or poster.

G A D S S M A L L A O D E I E E I T H
W O S ' I C P L E T N J D R R M C A .

Spacing and alignment are critical. Ask the group to find the message hidden in these letters. Give them this clue: "If you can see the correct relationship between these two lines of letters, you'll discover a key truth from today's lesson." (Words are alternated between lines; begin with "G" on the top line, go to "O" on the bottom line, then to "D" on the top line, etc. The message reads, "God's call to Jeremiah was simple and direct.") Once the message is found, ask the class to contrast this coded message with God's revelation to Jeremiah in today's text. The point is that God's message was not obscure or mystical; He told Jeremiah exactly what to do and how to do it:

Into the Word

Direct the class to read silently through the text once and then to close their Bibles. Now ask for volunteers to pantomime the verses with the following suggestion notes. Let the volunteer come to the front and read silently the text and the suggestion note. As he does the pantomime, ask the class to identify the thought represented. (Distribute suggestion notes in order of the verses.) *Verse 6*—Cover mouth with hands; then indicate personal shortness by stooping. *Verse 7*—Point to a classmate; point to the door; then sweep open hand across whole class. *Verse 8*—Cross midarms as an X in front of your face; then immediately make as ugly a face as you can; repeat. *Verse 9*—Touch lips; hold out hands as an 'open book'; pretend to tear book and eat the pieces. *Verse 10*—Pick yourself up by waistband or shirt collar; seat yourself; then simulate pulling up weeds, pulling things off a shelf, stomping them as they fall; then make the motion of stacking large blocks. *Verse 17*—Sit, pretend to pull clothes on, fastening around your waist; then look as afraid as you can. *Verse 18*—Visualize building a high wall, laying blocks from the ground to above your head; "climb up" to the top of the wall; stand as a soldier, with spear in hand. *Verse 19*—Feign a boxing match between yourself and another; "land" a number of blows to yourself; but then "laugh them off." You may want to suggest some question-clues as pantomimes are given, if your class is slow to respond to some. For example, for verse 6 you might ask, "What was Jeremiah's response to God's call?"

As an alternate or additional activity for examining the text, prepare the following list of verbs as flash cards or simple slips for distribution; if you use distribution slips, number them consecutively as given here. (Flash cards need not be numbered, but you will want to keep them in order.) (1) *formed,* (2) *knew,* (3) *camest forth,* (4) *sanctified,* (5) ordained, (6) *can (not) speak,* (7) *shalt go,* (8) *shall send,* (9) *command,* (10) *shalt speak,* (11) *Be (not) afraid,* (12) *put forth,* (13) *touched,* (14) *have put,* (15) *have set,* (16) *gird up,* (17) *be (not) dismayed,* (18) *confound,* (19) *have made,* (20) *shall fight,* (21) *shall (not) prevail.* Allow the class (once again) to read the text silently, then by showing or having read each verb in the order given, ask the class to identify the following for each: who is doing, to whom, or in what manner or for what purpose.

Into Life

Give each person paper and pen and ask all to write their response to this "What if" question: "What excuse would you be most likely to give God if He called you to a ministry, which, from the human perspective, was very difficult and undesirable?" Give members a few minutes to think and write. Then collect these unsigned responses into a box. Jumble them and then read them aloud, giving opportunity for group reaction.

Ask the group collectively to list the elements of Jeremiah 1 that offer comfort and strength to the Christian messenger of 1988. Be certain these are included: (1) We are asked to speak only what God has told us to speak; (2) We have no reason to fear, if God is with us; (3) No one will prevail over us and God, ultimately.

Let's Talk It Over

The questions on this page are designed to encourage review of the lesson Scriptures and to promote discussion of the lesson by the class. The answers provided are only discussion starters. Let your class talk it over from there.

1. How can a person know that he is being called by God to an area of specialized Christian service?

Every Christian is called by God to service—we are saved to serve. Yet specialized Christian service (for example, the preaching ministry, missionary work, teaching in a Christian school, managing a Christian camp) usually, if not always, is accompanied by a personal sense of "call." Jeremiah functioned as a prophet with a vivid awareness of having been called by God. Often most, or all, of the following elements of a person's experience come together to indicate that God is calling him in a special way to some specialized service:

(1) You have a conviction that need exists and that you are the one to meet that need.

(2) You are aware that your gift or gifts match up with the need and opportunity.

(3) Circumstances cluster to open particular doors and thrust you through them.

(4) Trusted, mature Christian friends or advisers confirm their awareness of your gift that matches with yours.

You may not be able to *know* (in the accurate, semantic use of that term) that you have been called by the Lord. But, on the bases cited here, you can believe that God is calling you, and you can entrust yourself to doing His will wholeheartedly.

2. How can fear potentially impact God's messenger with negative attitudes? What is the antidote for fear?

Fear can cause the following attitudes and actions: (1) It may bring on a failure of "nerve," causing one to retreat from a courageous stance. (2) It may cause one to dilute the message, to "water it down" in an endeavor to make it less offensive to an intimidating audience. (3) It may lead one to compromise ethical demands in order to soften harsh reactions of opposition. (4) It may cause one to increase his reliance upon God. Thus turning to God, one may find strength and guidance to achieve God's purposes. Notice two realities in the above: Possibilities (2) and (3) are expressions (outgrowths) of (1), and the first three are negative. But the positive potential as seen in (4) stands before all of God's servants.

The antidote for Jeremiah's fear was God's repeated reminder, "I am with thee" (Jeremiah 1:8, 19). Believers today have that same assurance: as Jesus commissioned His followers for world evangelism (an awesome task!) He promised, "I am with you alway" (Matthew 28:20).

3. Why would God send His prophet to root out, pull down, destroy, and throw down?

Two reasons predominate: punishment and preparation. *Punishment* was being meted out to kingdoms that had disobeyed God and resisted His purpose. Frequently God's messengers were instructed to deliver messages concerning the punishment of other nations (see Isaiah 13—19; Amos 1:3—2:3). *Preparation* for building often requires a razing. It is commonplace in erecting new structures on existing sites that previous structures (often dilapidated and defective) must be torn down. What appears to be negative must occur before that which is positive can take place. Note that Jeremiah 1:10 concludes this "destructive" list with two "constructive" intentions: to build and to plant.

4. Cite some ways a person may prepare to share God's message.

Jeremiah was commanded to "gird up his loins," that is, to get ready for action. Preparation for service is extremely important. Inadequate preparation may result in defective or limited service. Preparation for sharing God's message involves at least these three essentials: prayer, study, and practice. *Prayer* constitutes the most appropriate starting point. It precedes all else and permeates the entire process. In prayer we lift up to God all of our efforts for His empowerment and guidance. *Study* focuses on understanding the content of God's Word and ways to share it. You can't share what you don't know. *Practice* commends itself for the sharpening of skills. Prayer and study need to be combined in the doing of the task. Obviously, all three of these elements need to be present in preparing one to share God's message through a sermon, a lesson, or an evangelistic call. Commitment to thorough preparation does not mean reliance upon self rather than God, but it offers God your best through which He will accomplish His purpose.

The Sins of the Nation

LESSON SCRIPTURE: Jeremiah 7.

PRINTED TEXT: Jeremiah 7:1-15.

Jeremiah 7:1-15

1 The word that came to Jeremiah from the Lord, saying,

2 Stand in the gate of the Lord's house, and proclaim there this word, and say, Hear the word of the Lord, all ye of Judah, that enter in at these gates to worship the Lord.

3 Thus saith the Lord of hosts, the God of Israel, Amend your ways and your doings, and I will cause you to dwell in this place.

4 Trust ye not in lying words, saying, The temple of the Lord, The temple of the Lord, The temple of the Lord, are these.

5 For if ye thoroughly amend your ways and your doings; if ye thoroughly execute judgment between a man and his neighbor;

6 If ye oppress not the stranger, the fatherless, and the widow, and shed not innocent blood in this place, neither walk after other gods to your hurt;

7 Then will I cause you to dwell in this place, in the land that I gave to your fathers, for ever and ever.

8 Behold, ye trust in lying words, that cannot profit.

9 Will ye steal, murder, and commit adultery, and swear falsely, and burn incense unto Baal, and walk after other gods whom ye know not;

10 And come and stand before me in this house, which is called by my name, and say, We are delivered to do all these abominations?

11 Is this house, which is called by my name, become a den of robbers in your eyes? Behold, even I have seen it, saith the Lord.

12 But go ye now unto my place which was in Shiloh, where I set my name at the first, and see what I did to it for the wickedness of my people Israel.

13 And now, because ye have done all these works, saith the Lord, and I spake unto you, rising up early and speaking, but ye heard not; and I called you, but ye answered not;

14 Therefore will I do unto this house, which is called by my name, wherein ye trust, and unto the place which I gave to you and to your fathers, as I have done to Shiloh.

15 And I will cast you out of my sight, as I have cast out all your brethren, even the whole seed of Ephraim.

Nov
13

GOLDEN TEXT: This is a nation that obeyeth not the voice of the Lord their God, nor receiveth correction: truth is perished, and is cut off from their mouth.
—Jeremiah 7:28.

Lesson Aims

This lesson should enable a student to:

1. Recall the main thoughts of the sermon Jeremiah was to deliver at the temple gate.

2. Tell how the worshipers at the temple needed to improve their ways and their doings.

3. Examine his own life and find at least one way to amend his doings.

Lesson Outline

INTRODUCTION

  A. Too Much Separation?

  B. Lesson Background

 I. AMEND! (Jeremiah 7:1-7)

  A. The Prophet's Instructions (vv. 1, 2)

  B. Do Better (v. 3)

  C. Mistaken Trust (v. 4)

  D. How to Amend (vv. 5-7)

    Breaking Them Bravely

 II. HYPOCRISY (Jeremiah 7:8-11)

  A. Lying Words (v. 8)

  B. Hypocritical Worship (vv. 9, 10)

  C. Desecration of the Temple (v. 11)

III. DOOM (Jeremiah 7:12-15)

  A. Example (v. 12)

  B. Indictment (v. 13)

  C. Destruction (vv. 14, 15)

    Not in God's Plan

CONCLUSION

  A. At the Temple Gate

  B. Checking and Changing

  C. Prayer

  D. Thought to Remember

Display visual 11 from the visuals/learning resources packet. It is shown on page 94.

Introduction

British colonists in North America brought various kinds of religion with them. The London Company that founded Virginia had no quarrel with the Church of England, but the Puritans of Massachusetts crossed the sea to get away from it. Still Massachusetts was not very tolerant. Quakers were not welcome there. Even Roger Williams had to move over to Rhode Island because his religious and political views were considered too extreme. Maryland was meant to be a refuge for persecuted Catholics, but there was such an influx of Protestants that the Catholics were a repressed minority.

A. Too Much Separation?

When the colonies became states, their citizens wanted to be sure no religion would be forced on them. The first amendment of their constitution ruled, "Congress shall make no law respecting an establishment of religion, or prohibiting the free exercise thereof."

That simple limit to the power of Congress has developed into a doctrine of separation of church and state. Probably few if any of the framers of the constitution anticipated such a separation as now exists.

Public schools are handicapped by this separation. Christianity and the Bible had a major part in shaping history. How can history be taught without them? How can reading and writing ignore anything that has so influenced literature? Ethics, sociology, philosophy, and even psychology are impoverished when the Bible is banned.

Separation of church and state may have contributed to another separation that has unfortunate results. Many people have separated religion from their business and social life. For an hour on Sunday morning it is more blessed to give than to receive; but forty hours a week are devoted to getting money, and other hours are given to getting pleasure.

Such a separation of religion and life was one of the tragic facts that Jehovah saw in Judah. Hymns and sermons and offerings at stated intervals do not constitute religion. Religion at its best is a force that shapes our lives.

B. Lesson Background

We are not told when Jeremiah gave the message that is recorded in our text. It seems probable that this was one of his early sermons, delivered while Josiah was king.

Vigorously Josiah was smashing the heathen altars and telling the people to go to Jerusalem and worship Jehovah. Josiah was the king, and he had an army to enforce his orders. Obediently the people trooped to Jerusalem.

Maybe Jehovah's feasts were not so much fun as the riotous feasts of Baal, but they were not bad either. They were neatly spaced so the farmer did not have to leave his field at a busy time, and neither did he have to travel and camp in the cold and rainy season. It was pleasant to take three vacations each year. The temple music was great, there was plenty to eat and drink, and friends could make the trip together. So the people went in great numbers.

I. Amend!
(Jeremiah 7:1-7)

This worship at the temple in Jerusalem was good as far as it went. It was what God's ancient law had commanded. But Jehovah and Jeremiah were disturbed by what was happening between the times of worship, and that was what Jeremiah's sermon was about.

A. The Prophet's Instructions (vv. 1, 2)

1. The word that came to Jeremiah from the Lord, saying.

Jeremiah wrote the following sermon, or had his secretary write it; but he made it plain that the message was not from him. It was what the Lord told him to say.

2. Stand in the gate of the Lord's house, and proclaim there this word, and say, Hear the word of the Lord, all ye of Judah, that enter in at these gates to worship the Lord.

The Lord's house was the temple Solomon had built in Jerusalem. God had accepted it and filled it with His glory when it was dedicated (2 Chronicles 7:1-3). This was the place He had chosen, to put His name there and make it the center of worship for His people (Deuteronomy 12:5-7; 1 Kings 14:21). Jeremiah was to *stand in the gate* where worshipers would go in. He was to give the Lord's message, probably many times to different groups as they arrived.

B. Do Better (v. 3)

3. Thus saith the Lord of hosts, the God of Israel, Amend your ways and your doings, and I will cause you to dwell in this place.

At the very start, Jeremiah must make it plain that he was not trying to tell the people what to do. *The Lord of hosts, the God of Israel*, was telling them. Jeremiah was only a messenger.

In our modern talk we seldom use the word *amend* except to speak of amending the constitution, but it is a good word. It means to change for the better, to improve. It was good for the people to come into the temple to worship the Lord, but God wanted them to make some changes in their other *ways* and *doings*. Then, he said, *I will cause you to dwell in this place*. Here *this place* does not mean the temple, but the land of Israel. The people were dwelling there already, but they were in danger of losing their country. In giving it to them centuries earlier, God had made it plain that they could have it if they would obey Him, but would lose it if they would not obey. Chapter 28 of Deuteronomy describes at length the blessings of the obedient and the troubles of the disobedient. Among the

latter it is written, "The Lord shall scatter thee among all people, from the one end of the earth even unto the other" (Deuteronomy 28:64). The people of Judah had better take warning. They would be driven out of their homeland unless they would straighten up their way of living.

C. Mistaken Trust (v. 4)

4. Trust ye not in lying words, saying, The temple of the Lord, The temple of the Lord, The temple of the Lord, are these.

Jeremiah was to stand in the gate of the Lord's house (v. 2). The buildings and courts clustered there were indeed *the temple of the Lord*. But it was a lie to repeat that truth over and over with the assurance that Jehovah would always protect His people just because His dwelling was among them. The popular thinking was quoted by another prophet at an earlier time: "Is not the Lord among us? none evil can come upon us" (Micah 3:11). That was mistaken thinking. The presence of the Lord's temple would not protect crooked people unless they would amend their ways and their doings.

D. How to Amend (vv. 5-7)

5. For if ye thoroughly amend your ways and your doings; if ye thoroughly execute judgment between a man and his neighbor.

One thing that needed to be amended was the work of the courts of law. In his earlier indictment of Judah, Micah said, "The heads thereof judge for reward" (Micah 3:11). That is, the judges could be bribed. That had been their way for a long time, but it would bring disaster to the nation if it was not amended.

6. If ye oppress not the stranger, the fatherless, and the widow, and shed not innocent blood in this place, neither walk after other gods to your hurt.

A *stranger* in town could easily become a victim of fraud, extortion, or robbery. He had no friends to take his part, and the corrupt courts

---

How to Say It

BAAL. *Bay*-ul.
EPHRAIM. *Ee*-fray-im.
HABAKKUK. Huh-*bak*-kuk.
ISAIAH. Eye-*zay*-uh.
JEREMIAH. Jair-uh-*my*-uh.
JOSIAH. Jo-*sye*-uh.
MICAH. *My*-kuh.
PHILISTINES. *Fil*-iss-teens or Fi-*liss*-teens.
SHILOH. *Shy*-lo.
ZEPHANIAH. Zef-uh-*nye*-uh.

would give him no help. An orphan or a widow had no man for protection and no money to bribe the judges; they were easy prey for a crook without a conscience. Since judges were for sale, a rich man could even commit murder without fear of punishment. But God took note of all these injustices. If the crooks and killers would not amend their ways, disaster was ahead. The king was destroying the altars and idols of those who followed *other gods* instead of Jehovah, but there was no way he could stop secret worship. Even those who came to Jehovah's temple could go home and have a feast for Baal. But it would be to their *hurt*, not to their advantage. It would hasten the invasion and destruction of Judah.

7. Then will I cause you to dwell in this place, in the land that I gave to your fathers, for ever and ever.

There was still time to avoid disaster. If they would put a stop to injustice and murder and idolatry, they could be secure in their homeland. But going to the temple would not make them secure if they went back home to continue in their crooked and cruel ways.

BREAKING THEM BRAVELY

In *As You Like It*, Celia accuses Orlando of inconsistency in his affection for Rosalind. "O, that's a brave man!" she scolds. "He writes brave verses, speaks brave words, swears brave oaths and breaks them bravely."

So it was with the people of Judah. Publicly they claimed to be God's people, but their behavior was inconsistent with the claim. God made it clear to His people that they would be able to stay in the land only if their behavior was consistent with their profession.

Do we claim to love the Lord and then ignore the demands such love makes? For example, more than one Christian emblazons his car with stickers professing his allegiance to Christ, then drives discourteously, parks where forbidden, or changes lanes dangerously.

"Brave words" need to be spoken by the Lord's people. But having made them, let us conduct ourselves in a manner consistent with them so that only honor will come to our Lord Jesus Christ through us.   —V. H.

II. Hypocrisy
(Jeremiah 7:8-11)

Jesus gave a blessing to the pure in heart (Matthew 5:8). To be pure is to be all of one kind, to be unmixed with anything impure. God's pure people are altogether devoted to Him; but Jeremiah was looking at people like those described in Proverbs 30:12, people pure in their own

eyes, but not washed from their filthiness. They worshiped God in the temple and lived for the devil at home. They were double-minded, unstable in their ways; and so they could not expect God's blessing (James 1:5-8).

A. Lying Words (v. 8)

8. Behold, ye trust in lying words, that cannot profit.

Verse 4 describes the lying words that were deceiving the people of Judah. Over and over they were saying the temple of the Lord was among them, therefore the Lord was among them, and therefore no harm could come to them. They said they were secure whether they did right or not, and that was a lie. But misguided people were putting their trust in it. Lies *cannot profit:* they cannot do any good. To trust in them is to be disappointed.

B. Hypocritical Worship (vv. 9, 10)

9. Will ye steal, murder, and commit adultery, and swear falsely, and burn incense unto Baal, and walk after other gods whom ye know not?

All these things were flagrant violations of God's law. A little after the middle of Josiah's reign, the long-neglected book of the law was found in the temple. It was read to the people, and they promised to obey it (2 Chronicles 34:8, 14, 29-32). If Jeremiah gave this sermon after that time, and if people were still committing the sins listed in this verse, those people knew they were breaking both God's law and their own promise to keep it.

10. And come and stand before me in this house, which is called by my name, and say, We are delivered to do all these abominations?

It was rank hypocrisy to stand in the temple of the Lord and go through the motions of worship while disobeying the Lord constantly between times of worship. Because they went to worship, people might say God would deliver them from all their enemies and all their troubles; but such words were among the lying words mentioned in verse 8. God will not forever continue to deliver those guilty of such hypocrisy.

C. Desecration of the Temple (v. 11)

11. Is this house, which is called by my name, become a den of robbers in your eyes? Behold, even I have seen it, saith the Lord.

A den of robbers might be some remote cave in the mountains where a gang of bandits could hide and be safe after pillaging a peaceful village or a caravan of traders. Likewise the heartless people of Judah imagined they could find safety by going to the temple to worship, even if they carried stolen money in their hands to buy a lamb for sacrifice, and even if they were going out to steal again by fraud or by violence. The temple was dishonored in their eyes when they saw it as a cover for crookedness rather than as a house of prayer (Isaiah 56:7). In a later time Jesus pointed out that the crooked merchants doing business in the temple likewise desecrated the Lord's house (Matthew 21:12, 13).

III. Doom
(Jeremiah 7:12-15)

The temple was indeed the house of the Lord. It was built to glorify Him, and He glorified it by filling it with His glory and putting His name there (1 Kings 8). But not even the house of the Lord was safe in a land full of sin. If the people would keep on making it a den of robbers rather than a house of prayer, then temple and people would be destroyed together.

A. Example (v. 12)

12. But go ye now unto my place which was in Shiloh, where I set my name at the first, and see what I did to it for the wickedness of my people Israel.

Shiloh was the place where the tabernacle was set up when the people of Israel finished their conquest of the promised land. The center of worship remained there for a long time, but the *wickedness* of God's people *Israel* kept growing, with the high priest's sons leading the way (1 Samuel 2:12-17, 22-24). Therefore the Lord allowed the Philistines to defeat Israel and capture the ark of the covenant (1 Samuel 4:1-11). Probably the Philistines then went on to destroy Shiloh, though that fact is not recorded in the book of Samuel. Jeremiah was preaching centuries later, but still anyone going to Shiloh would find only ruins. Jerusalem and the temple would likewise be ruined unless the people would listen to Jeremiah and amend their way of living.

B. Indictment (v. 13)

13. And now, because ye have done all these works, saith the Lord, and I spake unto you, rising up early and speaking, but ye heard not; and I called you, but ye answered not.

The people of Judah now were no better than the people of Israel had been when their wickedness had brought destruction by the Philistines. People of Judah had done *all these works:* the wicked works listed in verse 9 and those that verses 5 and 6 urged them not to do. They kept on doing such things, even though they had God's law to guide them and God *spake* to them through prophets like Isaiah, Jeremiah, Micah,

Zephaniah, and Habakkuk. One gets up early when a job or a trip is urgent. Therefore *rising up early and speaking* means speaking urgently. That was what God had been doing through the prophets. Through Jeremiah He was speaking urgently still, but still the people chose to ignore what He was saying.

C. Destruction (vv. 14, 15)

14. Therefore will I do unto this house, which is called by my name, wherein ye trust, and unto the place which I gave to you and to your fathers, as I have done to Shiloh.

This house was the temple in Jerusalem. Jeremiah was to stand at its gate to tell the people it was going to be destroyed as Shiloh had been. It was the temple of God, called by His name, but that would not save it from destruction. The people were trusting in it, thinking God would take care of them just because it was there. But they were going to be disappointed. God would not take care of them unless they would amend their doings. And destruction would not come to the temple only. The whole country of Israel was the place that God gave to the people of Judah and to their fathers. Destruction would sweep over the whole land.

15. And I will cast you out of my sight, as I have cast out all your brethren, even the whole seed of Ephraim.

Of course no one is so far away that God does not see him and know what he is doing (Psalm 139:7-12). But God had been watching over Judah with special care and providence. He was going to put the people of Judah out of that land and out of His special care. *Ephraim* was the biggest of the ten tribes that had revolted and formed a separate nation in the north part of Israel, and the name of that tribe here means the people of that whole nation. They had been cast out of their land already (2 Kings 17:1-6). The ruins of Shiloh showed what was going to happen to the temple, and the scattered people of north Israel showed what was going to happen to the people of Judah. The only way they could escape that doom was to amend their ways and doings, amend them thoroughly.

NOT IN GOD'S PLAN

In one unidentified western state, only eight out of every one hundred persons arrested on felony charges were actually prosecuted in 1982. Of those eight, only five were convicted. Of the five, only two went to prison. One of the two went to prison for less than a year.

Figures such as these indicate the complex problem that law enforcement officials face. They work hard to secure the arrests of law-breakers only to find that for one reason or another the proper penalties are not imposed.

God warned the people of Judah that punishment was certain if they persisted in evil. To verify His threats, He urged them to visit the place where His tabernacle once stood and view the ruins there. Jerusalem would become like it if they didn't repent of their wickedness.

It is possible now to escape punishment for a crime. We can run away, hide among countless millions, be overlooked by the bureaucracy, or hire skilled lawyers. But no unforgiven sinner will escape punishment before God's judgment bar. Fame, fortune, and influence will receive no respect before God. Only the penitent and forgiven will be acquitted there.   —V. H.

Conclusion

The story is repeated of a young man who took pride in doing as he pleased. Then in his middle years he began to think seriously about right and wrong. After thoughtfully surveying the Ten Commandments, he said, "At least I never made a graven image."

After surveying our text, a thoughtful sinner might say, "At least I never burned incense to Baal." We have only to look at the daily paper to know that people do steal and murder and commit adultery and swear falsely. And if no one worships Baal, we read now and then of a group that worships Satan.

A. At the Temple Gate

Most of the gross sinners don't go to church, but Jeremiah preached to people going to worship. Does his sermon apply to us?

We do not steal, but do we rob God by being stingy with our offerings? (Malachi 3:8, 9).

visual 11

We do not murder—or do we? "Whosoever hateth his brother is a murderer" (1 John 3:15).

We do not commit adultery. Do we give attention to shows that excuse and even glorify it? (See Matthew 5:27-29.)

We do not swear falsely, but do we make our word so dependable that no oath is needed to show we are telling the truth? (Matthew 5:34-37).

B. Checking and Changing

As we read the Biblical instructions to Christians, perhaps it will be helpful to make some checklists of things to do and things not to do. Such listings can be made from the third chapter of Colossians. We can make such do-and-don't-do lists from Romans 12; Ephesians 5 and 6; Philippians 4:4-9; 2 Peter 1:5-11; and other familiar passages of Scripture.

Of course, checklists are useless if we do nothing but check them. We need to amend our ways. Checklists help us to see what amendments are needed, but it is up to us to make them.

Benjamin Franklin revealed that he was not satisfied with the assumption that no one can be perfect. He asked why not. We know what is good. What's to keep us from doing it?

So Franklin made a list of virtues in which many of us fall short. Daily he checked his own behavior by the list. Writing about it later he commented, "I soon found I had undertaken a task of more difficulty than I had imagined."

If we try Franklin's experiment, perhaps we shall find what he found. Perhaps we shall not become perfect, but we shall become better than we are. Isn't that worth the effort?

C. Prayer

Our Father, may Your blessing be with us as we try to be better today than we were yesterday, and better tomorrow than we are today. In Jesus' name, amen.

D. Thought to Remember

"Be ye therefore perfect, even as your Father which is in heaven is perfect" (Matthew 5:48).

Learning by Doing

This page contains an alternate lesson plan emphasizing learning activities. Classes desiring such student involvement will find these suggestions helpful.

Learning Goals

After this study a student will be able to:

1. List the sins God identified in His people.
2. Recognize and explain the contemporary validity of the principles Jeremiah presented.
3. Renew his own commitment at the points for which Judah was condemned.

Into the Lesson

Reproduce the following puzzle on posterboard, chalkboard, or an overhead transparency. Display the puzzle as the class session begins. Give this introductory note: "Jeremiah's sermon in chapter 7 is filled with the sins of Judah, just as in this puzzle. If you look carefully, you can find eight sins. However, because of the crookedness of the people, the sins are crooked in the puzzle—the last three or four letters go a direction different from the way the word begins." The sins are *adultery, idolatry, injustice, lying, murder, oppression, robbery, and stealing.*

```
Y S I N E S N P A I
R N R S C O I N D S
E I E N I S I O U N
B S D S T I L N L S
B O R I S A N S T I
N S I U L E T E N S
G I J A M I R R N S
I N E N S Y N P Y I
I T I N S I N G P S
S I N Y L S I N S O
```

Into the Word

Because this text is a sermon, consider the following activities to get your class members to examine the text.

Suggest the following as possible "sermon titles" from this text. You might like to reveal them as flash cards or on an overhead transparency. A brief explanation of each is given here, but when you reveal each title, ask the class to explain how the title fits. (1) "Fate in the Gate"—Jeremiah is announcing Judah's fate as he stands in the temple gate. (2) "The Talisman Temple"—the people thought, superstitiously, that the presence of the temple assured their safety. (3) "Shiloh Revisited"—God tells that He will destroy Jerusalem just as He did Shiloh in earlier history. (4) "Amendments to the Consti-

tution"—God wants the people to make basic amendments in their behavior. (5) "Asleep While the Lord Speaks"—see verse 13. God called early (and late) but the people did not hear. (6) "Scattered Seed of Sorrow"—God vows He will cast out all the evildoers. (7) "Free to Commit Sin?"—some claimed (v. 10) that they were free to do what they wanted. (8) "Mistrust and Misbehavior"—because the people trusted a thing (the temple) rather than the Lord, they misbehaved. (9) "The Worst Sin of Judah." For discussion, consider which sin described was the worst in God's sight.

Divide your class into groups of four to six students each. Give one of the following "sermon theses" to each group and ask them to develop a three-point outline related to today's text. (1) "Trusting a lie has predictable and certain consequences." (2) "God has good news even when He has bad news." (3) "God has 'if-then' amendments in mind for man." (4) "The temple of God can be abused in a number of ways." (5) "The house of God is so special—how special is it?" (6) "God commands; man obeys—or disobeys!" Let each group ponder its thesis statement for five to ten minutes and then ask the groups to share their outlines.

For both of the preceding activities you may want to write some of your own "sermon titles" and/or "sermon theses."

Into Life

On chalkboard or overhead transparency write the word *ourselves* in capital letters, spreading the letters to form a circle large enough to write the words *The Sins of Judah* within the circle. Ask the class, "What do you see?" When someone says, "We see the sins of Judah in ourselves," distribute a sheet you have duplicated, or use the page in the student books, with these stimulus statements: (1) "One lie I occasionally find myself believing, to the detriment of my spiritual life, is—" (2) "Occasionally I make God's house a 'den of robbers' by—" (3) "The time(s) I am most likely to ignore God's speaking to me is (are)—" (4) "The sins that I commit and that can separate me from God are—" (5) "I am most likely to take the preacher's sermon to heart when I—" Suggest that class members use these for spiritual introspection next week.

Let's Talk It Over

The questions on this page are designed to encourage review of the lesson Scriptures and to promote discussion of the lesson by the class. The answers provided are only discussion starters. Let your class talk it over from there.

1. If God were to commission a twentieth-century prophet to speak His message at the door of the church building (as Jeremiah did at the door of the temple), what would it be?

The message would be similar, if not identical, to Jeremiah's. (1) Change your ways. (2) Repentance should start with the house of God. (3) Show your faith by your works. (4) Trust in institutions, rituals, and traditions is misplaced. (5) Judgment is coming if you don't change your ways. The axiom, "The more things change, the more they stay the same," certainly rings true. Mores and manners, customs and clothing are different, but people are not. The dynamics and expressions of relationships between persons and their God are remarkably alike, then and now. And God's message, revealing himself and addressing the human situation, remains the same.

2. What is the harm when those charged with administering justice can be influenced in their decisions by the rich and powerful?

All societies are structured on the basis of law. If those laws are unjustly administered, the society tends to disintegrate. Security and confidence in living together prevails only as laws are established and administered fairly. The absence of law means anarchy and chaos. Laws are to provide protection for all citizens, especially the poor, weak, and disadvantaged. If bribery can pervert justice, then the wealthy benefit; for only they can afford the bribes. If "kangaroo" courts are established, then laws serve only the purpose of those in power, making a mockery of the principles of law and justice. It was for good reasons that Jeremiah and other true prophets attacked injustice and the abuse of law.

3. Why is lying so prevalent in our country?

A poll taken early in 1987 revealed that seventy-one percent of those polled said they were dissatisfied with current standards of honesty in this country. Only thirty percent felt that congressional leaders always or almost always tell the truth; only thirty-eight percent felt that the president does. Forty-six percent of the men thought their wives always tell them the truth, but only thirty-six percent of the women said the same of their husbands. Duplicity and de-ception, in public and private life, are substantially greater than they have been in the past. Some reasons for this are as follows: (1) Lying functions to protect the self. The idea of looking out for no.1 holds top priority in our society. (2) Lying appears to be profitable—doesn't everyone want to make an extra buck? (3) Lying is taken for granted—everyone does it, why should I be different? (4) Values have eroded—honesty isn't prized as it once was. Just as Jeremiah called for honesty and integrity in all relationships, so messengers of the Lord today need to sound that same call!

4. Why would God allow His temple to be destroyed?

The Lord would allow the destruction of His house because of the wickedness of His people. They trusted in the temple, *not* in the God of the temple. By allowing the temple to be destroyed, God would make it abundantly clear that that physical structure had no inherent power to help the people. The destruction of the temple was one more means of pointing them, hopefully, toward God, toward reliance upon Him. The penchant of mankind consistently seems to be to trust in material things, whether buildings, or armaments, or wealth, or goods.

5. Give a few reasons why some contemporary Christians do not strongly desire to live disciplined, pure lives.

That kind of life requires effort, sacrifice, and commitment. To be sure God must be at work in perfecting character in the lives of His children, but His "working in" must be accompanied by their "working out." Not many people are willing to really work for growth. Others enjoy impurity too much and are unwilling to cut loose from that in which they delight. They pamper their perversities. Many want "a touch of the holy," but they don't yearn to *be* holy. The cost is too great. Others take a flabby, undisciplined approach to life—why should spiritual growth be any different? Well has it been said, "He who finds pain in virtue and pleasure in vice is inexperienced in both." God's true messengers have always called for purity of life. A faith that does not call for holy living does not issue from a holy God.

Suffering for the Truth

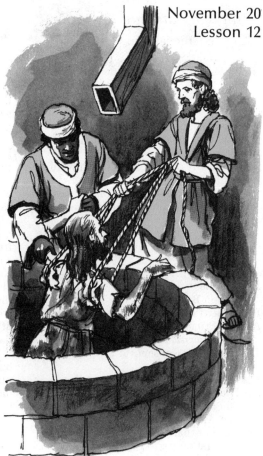

LESSON SCRIPTURE: Jeremiah 37:1—38:13.

PRINTED TEXT: Jeremiah 38:4-13.

Jeremiah 38:4-13

4 The princes said unto the king, We beseech thee, let this man be put to death: for thus he weakeneth the hands of the men of war that remain in this city, and the hands of all the people, in speaking such words unto them: for this man seeketh not the welfare of this people, but the hurt.

5 Then Zedekiah the king said, Behold, he is in your hand: for the king is not he that can do any thing against you.

6 Then took they Jeremiah, and cast him into the dungeon of Malchiah the son of Hammelech, that was in the court of the prison: and they let down Jeremiah with cords. And in the dungeon there was no water, but mire: so Jeremiah sunk in the mire.

7 Now when Ebed-melech the Ethiopian, one of the eunuchs which was in the king's house, heard that they had put Jeremiah in the dungeon; the king then sitting in the gate of Benjamin;

8 Ebed-melech went forth out of the king's house, and spake to the king, saying,

9 My lord the king, these men have done evil in all that they have done to Jeremiah the prophet, whom they have cast into the dungeon; and he is like to die for hunger in the place where he is: for there is no more bread in the city.

10 Then the king commanded Ebed-melech the Ethiopian, saying, Take from thence thirty men with thee, and take up Jeremiah

the prophet out of the dungeon, before he die.

11 So Ebed-melech took the men with him, and went into the house of the king under the treasury, and took thence old cast clouts and old rotten rags, and let them down by cords into the dungeon to Jeremiah.

12 And Ebed-melech the Ethiopian said unto Jeremiah, Put now these old cast clouts and rotten rags under thine armholes under the cords. And Jeremiah did so.

13 So they drew up Jeremiah with cords, and took him up out of the dungeon: and Jeremiah remained in the court of the prison.

Nov
20

GOLDEN TEXT: Blessed are they which are persecuted for righteousness' sake: for theirs is the kingdom of heaven.—Matthew 5:10.

Lesson Aims

This lesson should enable a student to:

1. Tell why Jeremiah was put in a pit and how he was rescued from it.

2. Explain why conditions in Judah were getting worse.

3. Point out at least one thing that makes conditions worse in our country, and suggest a way to combat that thing.

Lesson Outline

INTRODUCTION
  A. Trouble
  B. Lesson Background
 I. PUNISHMENT OF A PROPHET (Jeremiah 38:4-6)
  A. The Princes' Plea (v. 4)
    The Perversion of Disinformation
  B. The King's Consent (v. 5)
  C. The Pit (v. 6)
 II. PLEA OF A SLAVE (Jeremiah 38:7-10)
  A. The Slave (vv. 7, 8)
  B. The Plea (v. 9)
  C. The Answer (v. 10)
III. RESCUE (Jeremiah 38:11-13)
  A. Preparation (vv. 11, 12)
  B. Out of the Pit (v. 13)
    In Life and Death
CONCLUSION
  A. No Commitment
  B. No Courage
  C. No Good Judgment
  D. Prayer
  E. Thought to Remember

Display visual 12 from the visuals/learning resources packet and let it remain before the class. It is shown on page 99.

Introduction

Jeremiah began preaching while King Josiah was trying to banish idolatry and restore true worship and true righteousness. Even when people were flocking to God's temple, Jeremiah warned them that trouble was coming unless they would amend their ways and doings, unless they would establish justice and righteousness in their daily living. Apparently they paid little attention to the warning, and trouble grew.

A. Trouble

Troops from Egypt started across Judah to fight with Assyrians farther north. Josiah went out with his army to stop them, but he was defeated and killed (2 Kings 23:28-30). The people of Judah made Josiah's son Jehoahaz king, but Pharaoh of Egypt took charge of Judah and dethroned Jehoahaz. Pharaoh appointed Josiah's son Jehoiakim to be king, and required him to pay tribute to Egypt (2 Kings 23:31-35).

Then came Nebuchadnezzar of Babylon. He had defeated the Assyrians and taken their empire. Jehoiakim transferred his allegiance and sent his tribute to Babylon instead of Egypt, but after three years he rebelled. Nebuchadnezzar sent troops from other satellite nations to harass him (2 Kings 24:1, 2).

Then Nebuchadnezzar again sent his own troops to Jerusalem. Jehoiakim had died (2 Kings 24:6), and his son quickly surrendered. Nebuchadnezzar took him to Babylon. He took also the civilian and military leaders, along with the craftsmen and smiths who were able to make weapons. Nebuchadnezzar then installed another man of the royal family as king, and named him Zedekiah (2 Kings 24:10-17).

Zedekiah was loyal to Babylon for eight years, but in the ninth year he rebelled. The Babylonian army came into Judah again. Jerusalem was too well fortified to be taken by storm, but they besieged it for a year and a half (2 Kings 24:18—25:7).

B. Lesson Background

Through all these troubles Jeremiah continued his preaching. Soon after good King Josiah died, the prophet stood in the temple and gave a sermon much like the one we read in last week's lesson. Priests and false prophets and people wanted to kill him, but some of the princes rescued him—perhaps some upright officials left over from the time of Josiah (Jeremiah 26).

Jeremiah prophesied that Judah and the little nations around it would be subject to Babylon (Jeremiah 27:1-7). He said Judah's subjugation would continue for seventy years (Jeremiah 25:11), but after that time it would be ended (Jeremiah 29:10).

In the fourth and fifth years of Jehoiakim, Jeremiah compiled his prophecies and had his secretary write them on a scroll and read them to the people in the temple. When the scroll came to the attention of the king, he cut it up and burned it—but Jeremiah and his secretary could and did reproduce it (Jeremiah 36).

During the year and a half that Jerusalem was under siege, Jeremiah freely predicted that it was going to be taken and destroyed.

I. Punishment of a Prophet
(Jeremiah 38:4-6)

King Zedekiah was a weak and indecisive ruler. He did not obey God's word given through Jeremiah, but he did ask Jeremiah to pray for the nation. When Jeremiah was put in jail, accused of defecting to Babylon, the king called him for consultation. He also had the prophet released from the dungeon and kept in the prison courtyard where he could communicate with others (Jeremiah 37). Jeremiah 38:1-3 records the kind of communication that got the prophet into more trouble. He said it would be better to defect to the Babylonians than to stay in besieged Jerusalem till the city was taken.

A. The Princes' Plea (v. 4)

4. Therefore the princes said unto the king, We beseech thee, let this man be put to death: for thus he weakeneth the hands of the men of war that remain in this city, and the hands of all the people, in speaking such words unto them: for this man seeketh not the welfare of this people, but the hurt.

These were not the same princes who had rescued Jeremiah from the fury of priests and false prophets at an earlier time (Jeremiah 26). Those earlier princes had been deported to Babylon (2 Kings 24:14), and Zedekiah had replaced them with others. We can easily see why these men wanted Jeremiah killed. To them he seemed to be a traitor. They were in a struggle for survival. He was advising surrender and saying that defeat was sure. That was bad for morale. It weakened the resolve of soldiers and civilians alike. So the princes wanted the king to execute Jeremiah. That would be a warning to anyone else who might want to oppose the war effort. The princes found fault with Jeremiah's motives as well as his words. They said he wanted to hurt his people, not to help them.

The Perversion of Disinformation

US State Department officials say that a disinformation campaign carried on by the Soviet Union has caused widespread anxiety in perhaps fifty countries. The Soviets, using news stories, cartoons, and radio reports, have spread barefaced lies, saying that the AIDS epidemic is the result of US biological warfare experiments gone awry. This fabrication is believed because the Soviets persistently repeat it.

Disinformation is nothing new. Judah's leaders in Jeremiah's time were masters of it. When the prophet insisted on the coming fall of the city, the leaders raged. They wanted him silenced. They told the king that Jeremiah weakened the people's resolve, which would lead to the nation's downfall. They said, Jeremiah was to blame for the nation's troubles, not themselves or the people for falling away from God.

Evil men may misrepresent the truth now, causing the righteous to suffer. But God's word is truth, and ultimately it will be vindicated. God's people can be assured of that.   —V. H.

B. The King's Consent (v. 5)

5. Then Zedekiah the king said, Behold, he is in your hand: for the king is not he that can do any thing against you.

Again the king showed his weakness. He was convinced that Jeremiah was a man of God, or at least that he might be (Jeremiah 37:3, 17). He did not agree that the prophet ought to be killed, but he lacked the courage to overrule his subordinate officers. He left the responsibility with them. They could do whatever they wanted to.

C. The Pit (v. 6)

6. Then took they Jeremiah, and cast him into the dungeon of Malchiah the son of Hammelech, that was in the court of the prison: and they let down Jeremiah with cords. And in the dungeon there was no water, but mire: so Jeremiah sunk in the mire.

The princes wanted the king to execute Jeremiah, but they did not want the responsibility for his death. They just put him away where no one would hear his predictions of defeat. The Hebrew word for *dungeon* usually is translated *pit*, but sometimes *well* or *cistern*. The pit where Jeremiah was put probably was a cistern for storing water. Rain that fell on the paved courtyard and surrounding roofs would drain into it, carrying dust with it. The dust would settle to the bottom as mud that would remain after the water was drawn out. Jeremiah was let down by ropes, not just allowed to fall; but the mud was so soft that he sank into it. We are not told how deep it was—possibly up to his knees, or his waist, or even deeper.

GOD'S TRUTH CANNOT BE STOPPED BY SILENCING HIS SPOKESMAN

visual 12

II. Plea of a Slave
(Jeremiah 38:7-10)

Jeremiah was well known in Jerusalem. He had been preaching for thirty-eight years. News of his fate spread swiftly through the king's household, and probably through the whole city. No doubt the princes hoped it would keep anyone else from subversive talk; but with one man it had a different result.

A. The Slave (vv. 7, 8)

7. Now when Ebed-melech the Ethiopian, one of the eunuchs which was in the king's house, heard that they had put Jeremiah in the dungeon; the king then sitting in the gate of Benjamin.

Ebed-melech may be a description rather than a name. It means *king's servant*, and in this case the servant probably was a slave. He was an *Ethiopian* or Cushite, from the country south of Egypt. Male slaves in the king's house usually were *eunuchs*. This prevented sexual misconduct with any of the king's numerous wives and female servants, and perhaps eunuchs were more docile and loyal than normal men.

The tribe of Benjamin lived in the area north of Jerusalem, so *the gate of Benjamin* probably was in the north wall of the city. A gate usually was enclosed in a large tower, which provided a convenient place for judges to hold court. Apparently the king himself sometimes took his seat there to hear the people's complaints.

8. Ebed-melech went forth out of the king's house, and spake to the king, saying.

The king's slave had a complaint, and he took it straight to the king.

B. The Plea (v. 9)

9. My lord the king, these men have done evil in all that they have done to Jeremiah the prophet, whom they have cast into the dungeon; and he is like to die for hunger in the place where he is: for there is no more bread in the city.

How to Say It

EBED-MELECH. E-bed-*mee*-luhk.
HAMMELECH. *Ham*-uh-lek.
JEHOAHAZ. Jeh-*ho*-uh-haz.
JOSIAH. Jo-*sye*-uh.
MALCHIAH. Mal-*kye*-uh.
NEBUCHADNEZZAR. *Neb*-you-kud-*nezz*-er (strong accent on *nezz*).
ZEDEKIAH. Zed-uh-*kye*-uh.

Ebed-melech's complaint was twofold. First, it was unjust and evil to put Jeremiah in the cistern. Second, he was likely to starve to death there. *No more bread in the city* can hardly be taken literally. If there were absolutely no bread, Jeremiah would starve outside the cistern as quickly as in it. But the Babylonians had been around the town for months so that nothing could be brought in. Food was so scarce that no one could be expected to share with the prisoner in the pit. Earlier, when Jeremiah had been confined to the court of the prison, the king had ordered that a daily ration should be given to him (Jeremiah 37:21).

We have to admire Ebed-melech the Ethiopian. This foreigner realized that Jeremiah was telling the truth. This slave had more courage than the king. Boldly he took a stand against the princes.

C. The Answer (v. 10)

10. Then the king commanded Ebed-melech the Ethiopian, saying, Take from hence thirty men with thee, and take up Jeremiah the prophet out of the dungeon, before he die.

At last the king found courage enough to take a stand against the princes—or was it simply that he did not have courage enough to take a stand against his slave? Of course his own conscience was on the slave's side, and the princes were not there to object to the command. Zedekiah authorized Ebed-melech to go and get Jeremiah out of that hole, and *thirty men* would be enough to make sure they were not stopped.

III. Rescue
(Jeremiah 38:11-13)

Ebed-melech lost no time in carrying out his commission, but still he took time for preparation so the rescue would be as painless as possible for the prisoner.

A. Preparation (vv. 11, 12)

11. So Ebed-melech took the men with him, and went into the house of the king under the treasury, and took thence old cast clouts and old rotten rags, and let them down by cords into the dungeon to Jeremiah.

In today's English we would say *cast-off clothes* instead of *cast clouts*, and *rotten* may be interpreted as *worn out* or *torn*. Apparently *the house of the king*, like some of our houses, had a basement where discarded clothing was stored until some way was found to get rid of it. Ebed-melech and his men took some old clothes and got some ropes to lower the rags to Jeremiah in the cistern.

12. And Ebed-melech the Ethiopian said unto Jeremiah, Put now these old cast clouts and rotten rags under thine armholes under the cords. And Jeremiah did so.

Jeremiah was literally stuck in the mud. It would take a strong pull to get him out of it. The old clothes were for padding under his arms so the lifting ropes would not be abrasive.

B. Out of the Pit (v. 13)

13. So they drew up Jeremiah with cords, and took him up out of the dungeon: and Jeremiah remained in the court of the prison.

A few of the thirty men were enough to pull Jeremiah to the surface, and the rest were enough to discourage anyone who might want to interfere. The prophet was still a prisoner, but he had the freedom of *the court of the prison* instead of being confined to a cell. That court was where he had been before he was put in the cistern (Jeremiah 37:21).

IN LIFE AND DEATH

Off Guam in 1944 the submarine USS *Stingray* sought to rescue four downed airmen. She took three aboard, but had to submerge to escape fire from the Japanese. Unwilling to leave the fourth pilot, *Stingray* approached the flier at periscope depth. He seized the periscope, and the sub towed him out to sea, out of reach of the shore batteries, where she took him aboard.

The Bible, too, records noteworthy rescues. One was Jeremiah's deliverance from the miry cistern that was in the prison courtyard. Defying the influential princes, Ebed-melech, an Ethiopian servant of the king, courageously spoke to the king, urging him to save the prophet. With the king's permission the servant took thirty men and rescued Jeremiah from certain death.

God's servants have not always experienced escape from danger. Many have perished serving Him. Perhaps in dying they served His cause in a way they could not in living.

We cannot understand God's ways, but this much we know and take comfort from: In Christ, we are in God's care and keeping, now and in the life to come. —V. H.

Conclusion

In Jeremiah's time, the condition of Judah went from bad to worse. Babylon subdued the nation and compelled it to pay tribute. After a futile rebellion, the king and ten thousand of his people were taken captive, while the rest were left in Judah to keep on paying tribute (2 Kings 24). Our lesson brings us to the time of another rebellion that was to be futile. Nebuchadnez-

zar's troops surrounded Jerusalem. The people in the city were starving. Soon the Babylonians would destroy the temple and the town, and take most of the people away (2 Kings 25:1-12).

Why was all this happening to God's chosen people? The answer can be given in one word: sin. Most of the people of Judah were doing wrong, and behind the sin in their lives was the sin in their hearts. They did not love the Lord with all their heart and soul and might (Deuteronomy 6:5). They did not love their neighbors as themselves (Leviticus 19:18). They loved themselves; they loved money; they loved pleasure; they loved their idols. So they fell into the many sins that come naturally to people with such loves (2 Timothy 3:2-5).

A. No Commitment

Jeremiah and Josiah were committed to the right, but most of Judah were not. After Josiah died, each king in turn "did that which was evil in the sight of the Lord" (2 Kings 23:32, 37; 24:9, 19). The people were no better than the kings that led them. Micah briefly describes what was going on: "The heads thereof judge for reward, and the priests thereof teach for hire, and the prophets thereof divine for money" (Micah 3:11). In other words, the leaders and teachers would do and say whatever they were paid to do and say. Jeremiah adds a sad word: "And my people love to have it so" (Jeremiah 5:30, 31). With only a few exceptions, no one would take a stand for truth and right.

In our day those who make surveys are telling us that high-school students start smoking and drinking, sample illegal drugs, and experiment with sex because of "peer pressure." Some fellow brings a flask of whiskey to a class party and shares it with friends. If Joe turns it down, the others say, "You're afraid; you're a wimp." So Joe proves himself a wimp by caving in to pressure and taking a drink he doesn't want.

Are adults any better? Just because others are drinking, a man takes a drink he would rather not take. A lady listens to false and malicious gossip, and even passes it on. She can't bear to say, "That's not true!" How many Christians swell the ratings of sleazy TV shows? We need millions of people to take a firm stand for right and let their voices be heard. But when one makes a public plea for morality, he is likely to be assailed on every side. News media treat him as a crank; cartoonists and comics treat him as a joke. Even respected statesmen complain that he is trying to cram his standards down our throats. Who will dare to stand up and shout that old-fashioned moral standards are not ours but God's?

B. No Courage

King Zedekiah was not a kingly character. He had enough confidence in Jeremiah to call him from prison and ask for a word from the Lord (Jeremiah 37:16, 17). But when the princes wanted Jeremiah killed, Zedekiah consented. "The king is not he that can do any thing against you" (Jeremiah 38:5). They wanted Jeremiah dead, but they wanted the king to kill him.

In this story we see no courage in anyone except a prophet and a slave. Surely that was part of Judah's problem. Did some of the princes really object to putting Jeremiah in the cistern, but lack the courage to speak up? Do you suppose some of the judges really longed for justice, but dared not speak up against those who took bribes and gave unjust decisions? Do you suppose some priests were not greedy for money, but were afraid to rebuke those who were? Do we ourselves see wrong being done, but lack the courage to protest?

The Parent-Teacher Association was planning its annual carnival. Committees were appointed to manage the lottery, wheels of chance, and other features. A new minister in town arose with a question: "Isn't gambling illegal here?"

"Yes," he was told, "it is technically against the law; but this is for a good cause, the education of our children. We've been doing it for years, and no one has objected."

The minister was not satisfied. "You say this is for the education of our children. Do we really want to educate them in the techniques of illegal gambling? Do we want to teach them that breaking the law is OK if you can get away with it?"

No one else joined the protest, and the carnival went on. But attendance was down, the take was reduced, and the new preacher was hotly criticized. The mayor said nothing in public, but privately he said to the minister, "At least you have the satisfaction of being right. I wish I had the guts to shut that gambling down."

C. No Good Judgment

If Zedekiah was so lacking in character and courage, how did he ever dare to rebel against mighty Babylon? Well, he was only twenty-one when he became king. All the elder statesmen had been taken to Babylon, so his advisers were beginners like himself. For eight years he paid tribute to Babylon, and Babylon left him alone. By that time the might of Babylon seemed far away, and the cost of serving Babylon was very near. Zedekiah saw a big share of his national income handed over to the empire. Naturally he would like to keep that money in his own country. So at last he declared independence.

Perhaps his rebellion was due to bad judgment rather than to courage. Nebuchadnezzar's army and resources were overwhelming. Surely Zedekiah knew that. An emperor cannot let a little segment of his empire break away. If he did, other segments would try the same thing. But Zedekiah had ignored God and his word and had not been whipped into line—yet. Why couldn't he ignore Nebuchadnezzar too?

Nebuchadnezzar did what he had to do. With a huge army he besieged Jerusalem and starved it into submission. He shipped the people off to Babylon, burned the city, and smashed down the stone walls that would not burn. That not only ended the rebellion, but also discouraged any other would-be rebels.

Zedekiah should have known what would happen. But when the authority of God and his Word is cast off, good judgment vanishes along with it. When philosophers, educators, economists, and politicians turn away from God and the Bible, where can they find any absolute truth or any unchanging standards? There comes a permissive age. Children get out of hand. Selfishness takes control, and crime is multiplied. Forsaking old standards, businesses go bankrupt. Government spending goes wild, and those in control seem unable to stop it. But who will realize that all these excesses are rooted in the rejection of God and his Word?

D. Prayer

Almighty God, we thank You for our families and our friends, for Christian people, for honest officials standing for the right. Most of all, we thank You for Your own presence always.

E. Thought to Remember

Never alone.

Learning by Doing

This page contains an alternate lesson plan emphasizing learning activities. Classes desiring such student involvement will find these suggestions helpful.

Learning Goals

The following goals should be reached by your students:

1. The story of today's text will become a part of each learner's memory; he will recall the events with accuracy.

2. Appreciating the ministry and the misery of Jeremiah, each will be thankful to God for this prophet.

3. Each adult will see the universal and personal validity of the truths of today's text; each will resolve to deal with the truths as Jeremiah and Ebed-melech did.

Into the Lesson

Number pieces of stiff posterboard (9 by 6 inches each) one through sixteen. Tape them in numerical order as liftable flaps on the wall or board in front of the class, four rows of four. On half sheets of typing paper write the following words—one large word per sheet: *Blessed, are, they, which, are, persecuted, for, righteousness', sake, for, theirs, is, the, kingdom, of, heaven.* Scramble these words and tape them to the wall or board, one under each liftable flap. Tell the class there is a familiar verse of Scripture hidden and scrambled under the flaps. The goal is for someone to call all sixteen numbers in sequence to reveal the verse in correct word order. To begin, quickly lift the flaps in one-through-sixteen sequence to allow a quick glance. Then ask someone to try calling the correct number sequence, allowing him to continue until he misses. Each trier must begin again, until someone gets all the way through. When that has been done, ask the group to recite the verse in unison. Indicate that this truth well pictures the event of today's text.

Into the Word

List the following names and notations for the class to see: A—Princes, B—Zedekiah, C—Pashur, D—Jeremiah, E—Ebed-melech. Distribute paper and pens. As you read the following statements, have students decide who might have said them and identify each with the proper letter. 1. "There's always one more use for old clothes" (E, v. 11); 2. "Question Jeremiah's motives: does he want good or evil for the people?" (A, v. 4); 3. "Why will I need thirty men?" (E, v. 10); 4. "You can use my father's

cell; Jeremiah will sink right in" (C, v. 6 and 38:1); 5. "Well, do whatever you want; I can't stop you" (B, v. 5); 6. "They have not done the right thing to the prophet; he is liable to die!" (E, v. 9); 7. "My, oh, my, do I need a bath!" (D, v. 13); 8. "Anyone who interferes with military morale should be killed" (A, v. 4); 9. "I've made a mistake ... I think ... well, you go do what you think is right ... I think" (B, vv. 5, 10). Allow your students to look at the text as they write their responses. Introduce the answers, and let the class decide when each "quote" might have been said.

Label the following activity "laundry time." Display the following four lines with careful attention to the spaces:

(1) __ __ __ __ __   __ __ __ __

(2) __ __ __   __ __ __ __

(3) __ __ __ __   __-__ __ __ __

(4) __ __ __ __ __ __ __ __ __ __

Tell the class each represents a "laundry" title for an element of today's text. Then begin inserting letters into spaces in the following sequence: A, E, I, O, U, B, C, D, H, L, M, N, R, S, T, W, Y. (Write in all the A's, then all the E's, etc.) The titles are (1) DIRTY DEED, (2) MUD BATH, (3) WISHY-WASHY, (4) CLOTHESLINE. Ask students to identify each as they can. When a title is identified, ask the class to explain how the title relates to the text. Answers are (1) the princes, plan for Jeremiah, (2) Jeremiah's sinking in the mire, (3) the king's indecisiveness, and (4) Ebed-melech's use of cords to lift Jeremiah from the cistern.

Into Life

Introduce the four statements below one at a time. Let the whole class discuss them as they relate to the text. (1) "Sometimes when you speak the truth others may question your motives." See verse 4. (2) "Indecisive leadership can lead to calamity." Consider Zedekiah's behavior in regard to this. (3) "Even a person with limited influence, if he is bold enough in his conviction, can turn a bad situation around." See Ebed-melech's approach to the king. (4) "Where there's a will, there's a way." See verses 11, 12. Ask the students to cite historical or personal examples for each principle. Give each member a copy of these statements to carry as resolution statements for personal commitment.

Let's Talk It Over

The questions on this page are designed to encourage review of the lesson Scriptures and to promote discussion of the lesson by the class. The answers provided are only discussion starters. Let your class talk it over from there.

1. How many servants of the Lord today get into a figurative "pit"?

Being in the "depths," down, or depressed can issue from the following: (1) Allowing disappointment to become discouragement. Disappointment is valid and realistic, but discouragement is the devil's weapon. (2) A lack of visible results. Many workers become depressed when they can't see positive responses and growth from their efforts. (3) Opposition to proposals and programs by others within the church. Opposition is interpreted as personal rejection. (4) Personal attacks by brothers and sisters in the family of God. Character assassination against a person or his family members constitutes a heinous sin. (5) Too much stress, inappropriately handled for too long a period of time. Excessive stress becomes distress, and the "pit" can become your home. Depression among the Lord's workers is becoming more and more common.

2. What lesson may we learn from the slave who went directly to the king with his complaint about the treatment of Jeremiah?

In taking a bold stand against the princes, Ebed-melech achieved the rescue of Jeremiah from the cistern in the prison. By personally, directly appealing to King Zedekiah, the slave focused royal attention on a situation that needed correction. We may learn that the courageous appeal of one person, strategically placed, can achieve remarkable results. A slave might have said, "I don't have any clout. Who will listen to a slave? The political powers are arrayed against me. I might as well keep quiet." There was none of this. Ebed-melech acted decisively, appropriately, directly, and courageously; and Jeremiah was freed!

3. Why do people tend to resist any kind of change?

Change propels people out of their comfort zones. They feel much better with that which is familiar, easy, comfortable—almost second nature to them. Change requires adjustment and adaptation. That means one must be more flexible and less rigid in his thinking and attitudes. Effort, sometimes strenuous effort, is involved.

Change often involves the unknown; the present situation involves the known. Relatively few people are willing to launch out into the unknown, the untried, the uncertain. Change represents all of these things. The servants of the Lord are agents of change. They *will* meet with resistance as they challenge and encourage people to change the direction and goal of their lives, from serving Satan to serving Christ.

4. What are some ways a person may suffer for righteousness' sake?

In taking a stand for righteousness one may suffer: (1) Economically. Financial loss looms as a very real possibility for the person of scrupulous honesty, integrity, and strong convictions. This is not to suggest that all wealthy people are dishonest and something less than exemplary Christians. But even the wealthy would be far wealthier if they would compromise their convictions. (2) Socially. Those who are righteous may be ostracized by some people. If birds of a feather flock together, a dove will not be welcome amidst buzzards. (3) Vocationally. With some companies, promotions and career advancement will suffer when values and priorities do not match those of superiors. (4) Mentally and emotionally. One who stands for righteousness faces the possibility of harrassment in print, behind the back, over the telephone. All of these forms of suffering can be borne with the assurance of 1 Peter 3:14, "If you should suffer for the sake of righteousness, you are blessed. And do not fear their intimidation, and do not be troubled" (*New American Standard Bible*).

5. Why are people often reluctant to risk everything for what they believe?

(1) Their values are misplaced. Possessions, careers, etc., are prized more than truth. (2) Convictions are not central. That which is peripheral in our lives lacks the power to motivate us to bold action. (3) Courage is lacking. Behind that lies the absence of a faith that trusts—come what may. *If* faith were stronger, risks would be taken. Reluctance fades before mature faith, hope, and love.

The New Covenant

LESSON SCRIPTURE: Jeremiah 31:27-34.

PRINTED TEXT: Jeremiah 31:27-34.

Jeremiah 31:27-34

27 Behold, the days come, saith the Lord, that I will sow the house of Israel and the house of Judah with the seed of man, and with the seed of beast.

28 And it shall come to pass, that like as I have watched over them, to pluck up, and to break down, and to throw down, and to destroy, and to afflict; so will I watch over them, to build, and to plant, saith the Lord.

29 In those days they shall say no more, The fathers have eaten a sour grape, and the children's teeth are set on edge.

30 But every one shall die for his own iniquity: every man that eateth the sour grape, his teeth shall be set on edge.

31 Behold, the days come, saith the Lord, that I will make a new covenant with the house of Israel, and with the house of Judah:

32 Not according to the covenant that I made with their fathers, in the day that I took them by the hand to bring them out of the land of Egypt; which my covenant they brake, although I was a husband unto them, saith the Lord:

33 But this shall be the covenant that I will make with the house of Israel; After those days, saith the Lord, I will put my law in their inward parts, and write it in their hearts; and will be their God, and they shall be my people.

34 And they shall teach no more every man his neighbor, and every man his brother, saying, Know the Lord: for they shall all know me, from the least of them unto the greatest of them, saith the Lord: for I will forgive their iniquity, and I will remember their sin no more.

GOLDEN TEXT: I will put my law in their inward parts, and write it in their hearts; and will be their God, and they shall be my people.—Jeremiah 31:33.

Lesson Aims

This lesson should enable a student to:

1. Briefly tell how the New Covenant given through Christ is different from the Old Covenant given through Moses.

2. Summarize what the New Covenant promises and what it requires of us.

3. Resolve to keep the covenant.

Lesson Outline

INTRODUCTION
    A. Hope Amid Dismay
    B. Lesson Background
I. RESTORING THE NATION (Jeremiah 31:27-30)
    A. God's Care (vv. 27, 28)
    B. Man's Responsibility (vv. 29, 30)
    The One Responsible
II. REPLACING THE COVENANT (Jeremiah 31:31-34)
    A. A New Covenant (v. 31)
    B. A Different Covenant (v. 32)
    C. A Covenant in the Heart (v. 33)
    D. A Covenant of Knowledge (v. 34a)
    E. A Covenant of Forgiveness (v. 34b)
    The Same Father
CONCLUSION
    A. Our Schoolmaster
    B. Bypassing the Schoolmaster
    C. Keeping the Covenant
    D. Prayer
    E. Thought to Remember

Display visual 13 from the visuals/learning resources packet. It is shown on page 108.

Introduction

Jeremiah was a prophet of disaster. God had set him over nations "to root out, and to pull down, and to destroy, and to throw down" (Jeremiah 1:10). He promised destruction to Judah, promised it so vigorously that misguided patriots wanted to kill him (26:8; 38:4).

A. Hope Amid Dismay

Jeremiah's early prophecies had a note of hope. Disaster could be averted if the people would amend their ways and doings (Jeremiah 7:3). But they did not amend. When at last the armies of Nebuchadnezzar surrounded Jerusa-

lem and cut off its supplies, Jeremiah declared that doom was certain, and the best thing to do was to surrender (Jeremiah 38:2, 3).

Even then the message was not hopeless. The Lord had appointed Jeremiah to root out and tear down, but also to build and to plant (Jeremiah 1:10). Even as he promised seventy years of captivity, he promised also a return to the homeland (Jeremiah 23:3-8; 29:10-14). In chapters 30—33 is a collection of longer prophecies promising freedom after the captivity, and from that section we take our lesson for this week.

B. Lesson Background

Our text does not tell us when this word came from the Lord. However, the following chapter is dated in the tenth year of King Zedekiah (Jeremiah 32:1). That was when God's word gave no hope of avoiding captivity (Jeremiah 38:3), but there was hope of surviving it. Most of those who heard Jeremiah speak would not survive the long years in Babylon. Many of them would not even survive the siege and the battle that would follow it. But the nation would survive, and another generation would be liberated to return to the land of Israel.

I. Restoring the Nation
(Jeremiah 31:27-30)

It was about 606 B.C. when the Babylonians subdued Judah and forced it to pay tribute. That was the beginning of seventy years of servitude (Jeremiah 25:11), though only a few captives were taken away at that time (Daniel 1:1-7). Later a bigger group was taken away, but still the nation of Judah lived in its homeland with Zedekiah as its king (2 Kings 24:8-17). Zedekiah's tenth year was about nineteen years after the time of servitude began, and Jerusalem was destroyed the following year, twenty years after the start of servitude. Those who were taken captive at that time, about 586 B.C., would be held for fifty years before the seventy years of servitude would end.

A. God's Care (vv. 27, 28)

27. Behold, the days come, saith the Lord, that I will sow the house of Israel and the house of Judah with the seed of man, and with the seed of beast.

Jeremiah was authorized to plant. That meant Jeremiah was God's spokesman to announce God's promise to plant His people again in their own land. Both *Israel* and *Judah* were included. Israel had been uprooted more than a century earlier, and Judah now was being uprooted; but both would be planted again in the homeland.

The seed for planting would be but a handful—about fifty thousand people along with their domestic animals (Ezra 2:64-67). But it would grow to fill the land.

28. And it shall come to pass, that like as I have watched over them, to pluck up, and to break down, and to throw down, and to destroy, and to afflict; so will I watch over them, to build, and to plant, saith the Lord.

God had promised to uproot His people if they would not obey Him, and now He was doing it very diligently. But in time to come, God would be just as diligent to plant His people in their own land again. He would *watch over them*, giving them all the attention they would need.

B. Man's Responsibility (vv. 29, 30)

29. In those days they shall say no more, The fathers have eaten a sour grape, and the children's teeth are set on edge.

Captives in Babylon liked to repeat the proverb about a sour grape. It was their way of saying they were captives because of their fathers' sins, not their own. God rejected that explanation. It was true that their fathers had been sinners, but those who were taken captive had continued the sins of their fathers. God let them be defeated and captured because of their own sins (Ezekiel 18:1-20). If they had been willing to amend their ways and doings, they could have continued to live in freedom in their own country (Jeremiah 7:3). Our text looks forward to the time when the captivity would be over and the people of Israel and Judah would be back in their own land. Then they would no longer use that proverb that denied their responsibility.

30. But every one shall die for his own iniquity: every man that eateth the sour grape, his teeth shall be set on edge.

God was going to free His people, return them to their homeland, and take care of them there (vv. 27, 28). That did not mean they would be free to continue the sins that had brought on the captivity. Those who would sin would be punished; but God wanted them to understand that each person would be responsible for his own actions, and each sinner would be punished for his own sins and not anybody else's.

How to Say It

ANTIOCH. *An*-tee-ock.
NEBUCHADNEZZAR. *Neb*-you-kud-*nezz*-er (strong accent on *nezz*).
SINAI. *Sye*-nay-eye or *Sye*-nye.
ZEDEKIAH. Zed-uh-*kye*-uh.

THE ONE RESPONSIBLE

The sign above the mirror in the entryway of a state hospital's alcoholic division reads, "This is the person responsible for my being here." An alcoholic's recovery is based upon his accepting personal responsibility for his condition.

It's so easy to blame someone else for our shortcomings. The school dropout blames the teacher; the job dropout blames the boss; the home dropout blames the parents; sinners blame God. Many have developed this habit until they are unable to assume responsibility for their own failures.

God told the people of Judah that following their destruction and captivity He would one day allow them to return to their land. Then, however, they would know that each person was responsible for his own sin.

That principle still stands. Others may have influence in our lives, but we exercise the choice of alternatives. We may follow another's example, and sin; but we choose to follow. For that choice we are held accountable.   —V. H.

II. Replacing the Covenant (Jeremiah 31:31-34)

The rest of our text carries a startling announcement. God's covenant with His people was going to be replaced! The Old Covenant had been Israel's law for centuries. It had been given amid such spectacular signs of God's presence that the trembling people knew it came from God (Exodus 19:16-20; 20:18, 19). Even before it was given, they had pledged themselves to obey it (Exodus 19:8). But they had not obeyed it. Through centuries they had broken their promise. That was why many of them had been taken captive, and now Nebuchadnezzar's troops were at the gate to take the rest. But they would not be captives forever. They would come back to their own land and have another chance to live by the same Old Covenant. But they would fail again, and farther in the future God would give another covenant.

A. A New Covenant (v. 31)

31. Behold, the days come, saith the Lord, that I will make a new covenant with the house of Israel, and with the house of Judah.

The days come. Sometime in the future there would be *a new covenant.* The Lord said the captivity would last seventy years (Jeremiah 25:11), but He did not say five hundred more years would pass before the New Covenant would appear. What God predicts will surely happen, but sometimes He does not reveal when it will happen (Matthew 24:36; Acts 1:7).

The *new covenant* was to be made not only *with the house of Judah*, but also *with the house of Israel* that had been scattered a century earlier. Israel and Judah would be united again as God's people in the promised land. Here again the prophecy does not tell all. The New Covenant actually was to reach far beyond reunited Israel. It was to be offered to all mankind, as other prophecies indicated (Isaiah 42:6, 7; Acts 13:44-47; Amos 9:11, 12; Acts 15:13-19).

B. A Different Covenant (v. 32)

32. Not according to the covenant that I made with their fathers, in the day that I took them by the hand to bring them out of the land of Egypt; which my covenant they brake, although I was a husband unto them, saith the Lord.

Israel's life as a nation began when God rescued His people from slavery in Egypt. This verse pictures Him leading the infant nation *by the hand*, as a loving father leads a child just learning to walk. Compare Hosea 11:1, 3. Soon after the escape from Egypt He led them to Sinai, where He gave them the covenant that was their guide for centuries. But the New Covenant would be different, *not according* to the old one. The Old Covenant had proved to be ineffective, not because it was faulty in any way, but because the people were faulty. They had broken it almost continually through centuries. There was no excuse for that, because God *was a husband unto them*. Faithfully He kept His part of the covenant, protecting them from enemies and supplying all their needs when they were obedient. Still they disobeyed selfishly and foolishly.

C. A Covenant in the Heart (v. 33)

33. But this shall be the covenant that I will make with the house of Israel; After those days, saith the Lord, I will put my law in their inward parts, and write it in their hearts; and will be their God, and they shall be my people.

This verse goes on to explain how the New Covenant was to be different from the Old. The law of the Old Covenant was inscribed on stone and written in a book (Deuteronomy 10:1-5;

visual 13

31:24-26). The people of Israel were told to keep it in their hearts (Deuteronomy 6:6); but they failed to do this, and so they became disobedient. Anticipating their failure, the law provided judges and punishment for the disobedient (Deuteronomy 16:18-20; 25:1-3). Capital punishment was prescribed for several crimes (Deuteronomy 17:2-7; 19:11-13; 21:18-21; 22:22). With all this provision for enforcement, the law still failed because even the judges did not have it in their hearts.

The New Covenant is the one Christ instituted (Hebrews 8, 9). Of this covenant the Lord said, *I will put my law in their inward parts, and write it in their hearts.* The New Covenant is recorded in a book, the New Testament; but the book does not appoint judges and prescribe punishments. In extreme cases a stubborn sinner may be removed from the fellowship of God's people (Matthew 18:15-17; 1 Corinthians 5), but no one is whipped or stoned. We are not jailed for telling a lie or for failing to forgive (Colossians 3:9, 13). Our obedience to the New Covenant depends on our having it in our hearts. Looking for our willing obedience the Lord said, *[I] will be their God, and they shall be my people.*

It must be confessed that we sometimes fail to obey, even as the people of Israel did. Anger or pride or malice or selfishness invades our hearts and turns us from obedience. But we look for our Father's forgiveness (v. 34) to take away our sin and make us finally pure in heart (Matthew 5:8). By His grace, not our merit, we shall come at last to be His people as truly as He is our God (Revelation 21:1-3).

D. A Covenant of Knowledge (v. 34a)

34a. And they shall teach no more every man his neighbor, and every man his brother, saying, Know the Lord: for they shall all know me, from the least of them unto the greatest of them, saith the Lord.

According to the Old Covenant, each Israelite was born as one of the covenant people. He was bound by the Lord's covenant even when he knew neither the covenant nor the Lord. When he was old enough to understand, he had to be taught to *know the Lord* and the terms of the covenant.

According to the New Covenant, the situation is very different. We do not come under this covenant by being born, but by being born again (John 3:3-6). We are not born again till we know the Lord well enough to choose to obey Him and to live according to His covenant. Therefore all the people of the New Covenant know the Lord, *from the least of them unto the greatest of them.*

This does not mean we should stop our Christian teaching. All of us know the Lord, but we are learning to know Him better and understand His will more thoroughly. We are introduced to the Lord before we are born again; we know Him. Still we are born as babes in Christ (1 Corinthians 3:1, 2). We need to be nourished by the milk of God's Word (1 Peter 2:2). The written Word helps us grow, and we are happy and grateful to be taught by neighbors and brothers who know it better than we do. Though we know the Lord already, we constantly learn to know Him better, and love Him better, and obey Him better. Thus we grow in grace and in the knowledge of our Lord (2 Peter 3:18).

E. A Covenant of Forgiveness (v. 34b)

34b. For I will forgive their iniquity, and I will remember their sin no more.

This is the crowning feature of the New Covenant. All our sins are taken away, forgiven and forgotten. It is true that the Old Covenant prescribed a system of sacrifices to be made for the forgiveness of sins. See Leviticus 4. But an inspired writer of later times pointed out that the lives of animals cannot really atone for the sins of human beings (Hebrews 10:4). The sacrifices of the Old Covenant were predictions of the greater sacrifice, the sacrifice that can atone for all the sins of mankind. This is Christ's sacrifice of His own life (Hebrews 10:5-18).

THE SAME FATHER

In *As You Like It*, Orlando and his older brother Oliver are talking. Orlando says he knows that according to the customs of the time the older brother is considered the better of the two. But Orlando declares that that takes nothing from his blood. If there were twenty brothers between them, Orlando contends, he has as much of his father in him as does Oliver.

A new covenant was coming, God promised through Jeremiah. That covenant would stress the opportunity each person would have to be God's child. God's grace would flow not just to one nation, but to all mankind.

Instruction would need to be given concerning this new covenant, and Christian leaders would provide that. But the blood of Calvary would cleanse leader and follower alike.

Whatever differences separate us in life—talents, race, looks, economy, size—each Christian has the same Heavenly Father, and each is as important to Him as any other.   —V. H.

Conclusion

"Known unto God are all his works from the beginning of the world" (Acts 15:18). So said James as he quoted the prophecy of Amos to show that God meant for the gospel to be preached to Gentiles as well as to Jews (Acts 15:13-18). Since the beginning there have been many things contrary to God's will, from Eve's sin to your sin and mine; but nothing has taken God by surprise. From the beginning He knew what would happen and what He would do about it. The Old Covenant appeared many centuries after creation, but God had it in mind from the beginning. He knew also that it would fail because His people would fail to keep it, and from the beginning He had in mind the New Covenant that would replace it. In fact, the Old Covenant was designed to lead to the New.

A. Our Schoolmaster

"The law was our schoolmaster to bring us unto Christ, that we might be justified by faith" (Galatians 3:24). The New Covenant was offered first to people of the Old Covenant, and preachers of the gospel used the ancient Scriptures to lead the hearers to the New Covenant in which they would be saved by faith. Peter quoted from the Psalms to show that Jesus was both Lord and Christ, and three thousand people were convinced (Acts 2:22-41). He quoted from Deuteronomy to warn that destruction waited for those who would reject the Lord (Acts 3:11-26). Stephen confronted enemies of the New Covenant by summarizing the history of Israel and quoting from the prophets (Acts 7). Philip started with the prophecy of Isaiah and preached Christ (Acts 8:26-38). Paul used writings of historians and psalmists and prophets to convince the Jews of Antioch, and in the book of Isaiah he found God's order to preach to the Gentiles (Acts 13:13-47).

In all these cases and more, the Old Covenant was shown to lead straight to the New. But some hearers rejected the New Covenant and responded with fury; but they could not respond with reason. The demonstration was too plain to be disputed logically.

B. Bypassing the Schoolmaster

It is possible, of course, to bypass the schoolmaster and come straight to Jesus. Speaking to heathen philosophers in Athens, Paul did not cite the law and the prophets. He began with the inscription of an idolatrous altar, and he quoted a pagan poet. But he strongly asserted the truths taught in the Old Testament, and from them he went on to present the claims of Christ (Acts 17:22-31). Likewise in our time many come to Christ when they know little about the Old Covenant. They know their sin, and they hear the offer of salvation. However, it seems that only a few of the Athenian heathen became Christians, and often we are dismayed because so few modern heathen respond to the gospel. The people of the Old Covenant had a head start. To those who were open-minded, the Old Covenant pointed unmistakably to the New.

If we have bypassed the schoolmaster and come straight to Christ, if we have been justified by faith without reference to the earlier Scriptures, then what is the Old Testament good for?

Take a minute to think about the Ten Commandments, for example (Exodus 20:1-17). This is not to slight other Scriptures. Remember that Jesus pointed out the two greatest commandments, and neither of them is among the ten (Matthew 22:36-40). Nevertheless, the ten are so concise and direct that they have long been regarded as an outline of the moral law. Most of us Christians adhere scrupulously to "Thou shalt not kill" and "Thou shalt not steal." But even some Christians now regard adultery lightly. Do they realize that they are taking a light view of God's Word and God himself? And one Commandment reads, "Thou shalt not take the name of the Lord thy God in vain: for the Lord will not hold him guiltless that taketh his name in vain." How we wish that could be impressed on all the people who say "O God!" when they mean no more than "wow" or "zowie" or "ouch!"

Yes, the inspired Scriptures are profitable—all of them—if we know them and use them.

C. Keeping the Covenant

Both Isaiah and Jeremiah kept declaring that disaster was ahead because the people were not keeping the covenant. Events proved that they were right. In Isaiah's time north Israel was defeated and scattered; in Jeremiah's time the people of Judah were driven to Babylon, and Jerusalem was destroyed. This is one of the things recorded for our admonition (1 Corinthians 10:11). We too have a covenant to keep.

In promising the New Covenant, the Lord said, "I will forgive their iniquity, and I will remember their sin no more" (Jeremiah 31:34). Blessed promise! In His forgiveness is our hope. But that does not excuse us from keeping the covenant.

Joyfully we sing of wonderful grace, "grace that is greater than all our sin." That is true. Paul wrote, "Where sin abounded, grace did much more abound." But he added a warning: "What shall we say then? Shall we continue in sin, that grace may abound? God forbid. How shall we, that are dead to sin, live any longer therein?" (Romans 5:20—6:2).

When we die, all our earthly associations are ended. When we become Christians, we die to sin: our association with it is ended. Dead to sin we are buried in baptism and rise to walk in newness of life (Romans 6:3, 4). We are through with sin (Romans 6:12-14). That is our duty in the New Covenant.

"If we sin wilfully after that we have received the knowledge of the truth, there remaineth no more sacrifice for sins, but a certain fearful looking for of judgment and fiery indignation, which shall devour the adversaries" (Hebrews 10:26, 27). We must keep our covenant. If we do not, disaster is ahead for us as surely as it was for the covenant-breakers of Judah (Hebrews 10:28-31).

Does this mean that one sin by a Christian cancels the covenant and dooms the sinner forever? Not necessarily. "If we confess our sins, he is faithful and just to forgive us our sins, and to cleanse us from all unrighteousness" (1 John 1:9). God's grace still is greater than all our sin. If we confess our sin and turn away from it, the sin is canceled and the covenant stands. God said, "I will forgive their iniquity, and I will remember their sin no more." "Thanks be unto God for his unspeakable gift!" (2 Corinthians 9:15).

D. Prayer

Our Father and our God, how good it is to know that You have never failed to keep your promise! We must admit that we have broken ours at times, that we have not kept the covenant as fully as You have. Forgive our failures and our sins, we pray, and lead us on in the way of the New Covenant, the way of life eternal.

E. Thought to Remember

We have a covenant to keep.

Learning by Doing

This page contains an alternate lesson plan emphasizing learning activities. Classes desiring such student involvement will find these suggestions helpful.

Learning Goals

As a result of this lesson a student will:

1. Be able to identify the distinctions between the New Covenant and the Old.

2. Have and express a greater appreciation for the New Covenant in Christ through which we have forgiveness of our sins.

Into the Lesson

In the devotional text of today's lesson (Jeremiah 32:36-41) God says, "I will give them [my people in the New Covenant] one heart." The following activity is based on that verse. Cut out six large hearts and write one word of the verse affirmation on each of the hearts. Make the lettering as large as you can so as to fill as much interior space of each heart as possible. Cut each of the hearts into jigsaw-type pieces so that the total number of pieces for the six hearts is approximately the number of students who attend your class. (For example, if normally you have about twenty students, cut each heart into four pieces.) Cut each heart differently. On a table at the front of your classroom, leave one piece of each heart on display, then mix up the remaining pieces. Hand a piece to each person as he or she arrives and direct the person to go to the table and add the piece to the correct heart. If you have pieces left over, either add them yourself or ask for volunteers. Ask the group to identify the statement; then reveal the source (Jeremiah 32:39). Relate the truth to today's study: that all will be unified in the New Covenant, unified in the heart of God. Read Jeremiah 32:41.

Into the Word

Prepare flash cards large enough to use in your classroom, each bearing the first word of one of the following pairs on the front and the second word on the back: old—new, stone—heart, blame—responsibility, national—personal, taught—known, punishment—forgiveness, federation—union, plucked—planted. One at a time show each of the sides related to the Old Covenant (the first word of each pair above). Ask your class members to guess the word pertaining to the New Covenant that this word suggests (the word on the other side of the card). Ask them also to explain the relationship of both words to their respective covenants.

They should be encouraged to look at today's text and the devotional text, and to consider their general knowledge of Scripture as they respond. The lesson writer's comments will help explain some of the contrasts; brief notes are given here for several. Some were ready to *blame* others for their predicament, but in the New Covenant each person takes *responsibility* for his own sins; for whereas the Old Covenant was *national*, the New is entirely *personal*. In the Old, all born into the covenant had to be *taught* its meaning, but in the New all born into the covenant *know* its meaning. The legal nature of the Old necessitated *punishment*, but the grace of the New results in *forgiveness*. Whereas those under the former were a loose *federation* of tribal groups, those under the New Covenant have absolute *union* with "one heart."

Either prepare copies of the following (or use the segment included in the pupil's book) or simply have members write it as you proceed. Explain that you want them to fill in at least one, possibly two words or phrases after each preposition given, which describe the New Covenant of which God speaks in Jeremiah.

"The New Covenant of God is a covenant

of _____

by _____

in _____

with _____

Continue with other prepositions: *about, between, unlike, for, etc.* Let members share their responses and discuss them.

Into Life

Lead your class in a short period of directed prayer, using the list prepared above as a stimulus list: for example, direct the class to "Thank the Lord that ours is a covenant *of* grace, not law."

Ask your class to scan the first five chapters of Acts to find verses/occasions wherein the people of the "brand-new New Covenant" reflected the "one heart" God promised through Jeremiah. (See 1:14; 2:1; 2:46; 4:32; 5:12.) Have one or more of your students who pray effectively in public lead the group in prayer for a greater oneness in heart in keeping the covenant.

Have small cut-out hearts or heart stickers to distribute to class members as a reminder of the "unity of heart" we all share in Christ.

Let's Talk It Over

The questions on this page are designed to encourage review of the lesson Scriptures and to promote discussion of the lesson by the class. The answers provided are only discussion starters. Let your class talk it over from there.

1. What negative forces may parents pass on to their children?

Discuss the following ways parents may have negative influences on their children: (1) The impact of poor modeling. Sinful behavior, poor relationships, and a non-Christian life-style teach children powerfully. When husbands and wives mistreat each other in the presence of their children, and when they mistreat their children, such negative behavior often has an effect on how the children will behave when they themselves marry and become parents. (2) The influence of defective values. Children take note when they see that their parents prize material things over persons and profits over integrity. These parental choices teach children negatively about what matters most in life. (3) The influence of misplaced priorities. When work consistently takes precedence over family life, and when leisure takes precedence over corporate worship, a negative influence is operative. (4) Ill health and disease. Not only grown children but even newborn babies may be affected by their parents' conduct involving substance abuse or immoral behavior. (5) Bad reputations. Children may struggle for years against the legacy of their parents' bad reputations. Other negative forces exist, but these are sufficient to highlight how crucial are the *positive* legacies that faithful parents give their children.

2. Are parents responsible for how their children turn out? Give some reasons for your answer.

No. Although most parents seem to feel that they are responsible for how their children turn out, the Bible and psychology both teach us they are not. Children are a gift from the Lord. The Bible teaches that what God requires of all His gifts is faithful stewardship. Parents are stewards, not owners. First Corinthians 4:2 teaches that God requires faithfulness of stewards. Thus parents are responsible for properly teaching their children and for conducting their own lives in a manner that is consistent with their teaching. When children become adults, they answer to God for their own decisions and choices, their own thoughts and actions, their own values and belief-systems. They are responsible for accepting or rejecting Jesus Christ as Lord of their lives. Children are not extensions of their parents' personalities or egos. Because of pride, parents often desire to regard their children that way, especially when the children excel. But as adults, children become persons in their own right, with their own personalities, gifts, and capacities, *plus* their own responsibility before God.

3. Compare the Old and New Covenants.

The Old	The New
Inscribed on stone	Written in hearts
From Sinai	From Calvary
Entered by physical birth	Entered by spiritual birth
Circumcision the sign	Baptism the sign
Sacrifices were animals	Sacrifice is the Lamb of God
Etched in law	Etched in grace
Levites were priests	Christians are priests
Passover the covenant meal	Lord's Supper the covenant meal

4. What was the basic purpose of the Old Covenant?

Paul affirms in Galatians 3:24 that the Old Covenant was our "schoolmaster to bring us unto Christ." He also asserts in Romans 7:13 that the Old Covenant demonstrated the exceeding sinfulness of sin. It showed that no one could live up to the law, that all of us are in need of righteousness that would come from a source other than any human achievement. Thus the Old Covenant pointed to the Christ, prepared the way for Christ, and showed us that He is the source of the righteousness we need.

5. What is the destiny of "covenant-breakers"?

In Romans 1:31 Paul lists "covenant-breakers" ("untrustworthy" and "faithless" in some translations) among those who are "worthy of death" (v. 32). In the context, this statement does not appear to mean that anyone who breaks a covenant is automatically doomed. Rather, it characterizes one whose life consistently demonstrates this trait, and also gives hearty approval to others who practice the same. Covenant-breaking is treated seriously!

Winter Quarter, 1988-89

Theme: Scenes of Love and Compassion

Special Features

Lessons

Unit 1: Promise and Expectations

Unit 2: Proclamation and Ministry

Unit 3: Response and Responsibility

Related Resources

The following publications give additional help for the lessons in the Winter Quarter. They may be purchased from your supplier. Prices are subject to change.

Dear Theophilus: Two Letters From Luke, by John W. Wade. Covers events from the announcement of Jesus' birth until Paul's third missionary trip. Order #41036, $4.95.

Luke (Standard Bible Studies), by Lewis Foster. This approach to Luke features an overview, a comprehensive treatment, and a summary application. Order #40103, $9.95.

Teach With Success, by Guy P. Leavitt; revised by Eleanor Daniel. This manual teaches you how to teach successfully and contains an update on today's terms and trends. Order #3232, $7.95.

The Jesus Years, by Thomas D. Thurman. A detailed study of the four Gospels. Order #40061, $5.95.

You Can Teach Adults Successfully, by Ronald G. Davis, Mark Plunkett, Daniel Schantz, Rick Shonkwiler, and Mark A. Taylor. Order #3208, $2.95.

Dec 4
Dec 11
Dec 18
Dec 25
Jan 1
Jan 8
Jan 15
Jan 22
Jan 29
Feb 5
Feb 12
Feb 19
Feb 26

A Look at Luke

by John W. Wade

START WITH A GENTILE PHYSICIAN who had become a convert to Christianity. Allow him to have several months experience traveling with the apostle Paul and his evangelizing team. Then give him a stay of about two years in Caesarea as he awaited the outcome of Paul's imprisonment there. Add to this an active curiosity and an ample amount of time to travel about Palestine and talk to people who had known Jesus. Finally, give him the leading of the Holy Spirit as he took his pen to write. The result—the Gospel of Luke, an exciting account of the life of Jesus.

Luke's Gospel shares many characteristics with those of Matthew and Mark and some with the Gospel of John. Yet he is different in some respects from the other three. After all, inspiration by the Holy Spirit does not mean that one's personality is completely blotted out.

Universality of the Good News

The thirteen lessons of this quarter take us from Jesus' birth to the point where He is ready to go to Jerusalem for His rendezvous with the cross. Since these lessons cover much of Jesus' ministry, they give us an opportunity to look at some of the major themes that Luke introduces in his Gospel. One very important theme is the universality of the good news of salvation. This should not come as a complete surprise, since Luke himself was a Gentile. The evidence of this theme is seen in the prologue to the Gospel. Luke addresses his work to Theophilus, obviously a Gentile and perhaps a government official who had been instructed in the gospel message.

The blessing of healing is offered to Samaritans as well as to Jews. In *lesson eleven* Luke makes a point of mentioning that the only one of the lepers who came back to thank Jesus for his healing was a Samaritan. In *lesson five*, we see that the good news was for the poor, not just the rich and learned. *Lesson eight* shows that forgiveness extended even to those who were considered moral outcasts by the spiritual leaders. In *lesson thirteen* we see Jesus' concern extended to Zaccheus, a despised tax collector.

Good Attitude Toward Women

Another theme that Luke stresses is a favorable attitude toward women. It stands in marked contrast to the general attitudes of that day, both Jewish and Gentile. At best, women were considered second-class citizens, but more often they were looked upon as chattel to be used as men saw fit. Luke sets the stage for this theme in *lesson one* by mentioning Elisabeth and in *lesson two* in the gentle and insightful way he tells of the angel's visit to Mary to announce that she would become the mother of Jesus. He continues the same emphasis in *lesson three* as he tells of the birth in Bethlehem and in *lesson four* by the mention of Anna. In *lesson nine* Luke relates the incident of the woman who touched Jesus' garment and was healed of an issue of blood.

Jesus and Material Possessions

Luke has a good deal to say about Jesus' teachings concerning material possessions. *Lesson ten* tells about a man who asked Jesus to settle a disagreement about a family inheritance. While Jesus refused to deal with this matter, He used it as a launching pad for an extended discussion of material possessions. It was in this context that He told the parable of the rich farmer who made careful provisions for this life but none for the life to come. Jesus then went on to point out that God in His loving concern provides for the birds of the heavens and the flowers of the field. Will He not also provide for the needs of man?

The theme of material possessions is handled again in *lesson twelve*. A rich and attractive young man approached Jesus, eagerly desiring to find eternal life. But his wealth proved to be a barrier he could not get over. But that is not the final chapter on the issue of material wealth. *Lesson thirteen* gives us the delightful account of Zaccheus. Once Zaccheus heard of the good news, he readily used his wealth to undo the wrongs he had committed and to care for the needs of the poor.

The Holy Spirit

Luke frequently mentions the Spirit, more often than either Matthew or Mark. In *lesson two* it was the Holy Spirit that would come upon Mary, making possible the miraculous conception of Jesus. *Lesson four* records the incident involving the old man Simeon. Under the influence of the Holy Spirit, he was told that he would not see death until he beheld the Lord Christ. Further, he was led by the Spirit to go up to the temple at just the right time to meet Mary and Joseph when they brought the baby Jesus there to fulfill the requirements of the law. When Jesus spoke before His home synagogue *(lesson five)*, He stated that the Spirit of the Lord was upon Him.

Applying Luke's Message to Our Lives

Other themes are present in Luke's Gospel, but these will suffice to show that he wrote from a special viewpoint with a special purpose, as did each of the Gospel writers. The important question is how these emphases bear on our lives. If they had no significance for us, they would not have been included in Luke's Gospel. Knowing their importance, we must during this quarter's study find ways to make them applicable to our lives.

Taking the Gospel to Everyone

Take, for example, Luke's emphasis on the universality of the message of salvation. We all pay lip service to this Biblical teaching, but do we really believe it? Jesus reached across socio-economic lines to extend the message to the poor and downtrodden. The spiritual leaders looked down upon these people and had as little to do with them as possible. Today, if we look around in most of our congregations, we find that the majority of the people are like us, comfortable middle class. We do not deliberately exclude the outcasts, but we make little effort to reach them with the gospel. As a result, they feel out of place when they do show up in our churches.

Jesus reached across racial lines to extend mercy to the Samaritans, and, for that matter, even to Gentiles, who were considered even more objectionable. What are our churches like today? Someone has noted that the worship hour on Sunday morning may be the most segregated hour in the week. This statement may be an exaggeration, but it does point up the fact that for the most part our churches are not integrated. This is not to suggest that every congregation has to be multi-racial in order to be Christian. But churches ought to be open to persons of every race.

The implications for Jesus' teaching about the universality of the gospel go beyond the local congregation. While the Great Commission is not covered in this quarter's lessons, it is implied throughout the Gospel of Luke. This means that we must overcome the barriers of time and space and reach out to people all over the world who are lost without the gospel. Certainly a missionary emphasis would not be out of place during the study of these lessons.

Giving Women Their Place

Let us look at another of Luke's themes—a benevolent attitude toward women. To say that Jesus lived in a male-dominated society would be to state the obvious. Yet He did not hesitate to sweep aside the conventions of His day in order to set forth woman's true position—man's equal in the spiritual realm. He did not hesitate to speak to women openly or in private and share with them the good news of the gospel. This emphasis is not Luke's alone. We see it in the other Gospel accounts too. For example, John relates how Jesus spoke to a Samaritan woman at Jacob's well (4:7-26). He also extended mercy and forgiveness to a woman taken in adultery (8:3-11).

We can rejoice that Christianity has done more than any other religion to elevate the position of women. But the battle is not yet won. In many congregations women's talents and intelligence are still not fully utilized. Women are still being exploited in the sea of pornography that swirls about us. The church has only feebly resisted the printed matter and the movies that depict women as things to be used to satisfy men's lusts. Nor have we moved decisively against abortion, the sin that encourages women to deny their God-given power to perpetuate the human race. It is ironic that this most unique of all of women's powers is being rejected in the name of women's liberation!

The Christian and Material Possessions

Let's think about some ways that Jesus' teaching about material possessions can be applied to our lives. The church finance committee is likely to think of stewardship in terms of how they can increase contributions to the church. This is, of course, an important aspect of stewardship, but Christian stewardship is not completely fulfilled when we give our money.

Christian stewardship deals with everything God has entrusted to a person—his time, his talents, and his treasure. The crucial issue is one's attitude toward these things. In *lesson twelve*, Luke gives us the account of a rich young ruler. This young man had led an exemplary life in every respect except that he had made material possessions the most important thing in his life. Zaccheus, in his attitude toward wealth, gives us a refreshing contrast to the rich young ruler *(lesson thirteen)*. These two lessons will give you an opportunity to explore with your class several aspects of Christian stewardship.

With these possibilities for good, practical teaching, the lessons should not be lukewarm this quarter.

His Heart Went Out

by W. F. Lown

I WONDER WHAT GOD'S LOVE IS REALLY LIKE. We can be sure it is far greater than man's love. It is so intense, so broad, so high and so deep that Jesus, describing God's love (John 3:16), simply said, "God *so* loved the world."

All of us have felt pangs for someone who is suffering physical, mental, or deep spiritual pain. God goes a step beyond. We see His empathy demonstrated in Jesus. As the *New International Version* puts it, "His heart went out" (Luke 7:13) to the widow of Nain and hordes of others who passed His way. *Sympathy* is one thing. *Empathy* is another. *Sympathy* is the feeling of suffering *with* another. *Empathy* is the feeling of suffering *as* another. We identify as the sufferer in empathy. God did that through Jesus.

There is an old story of a kindly minister who stood at the bedside of a dying man. On the other side of the bed stood the wife who was soon to be widowed. As the last breath came and went, the widow fell to her knees and wept. The minister likewise fell to his knees, and those nearby heard him pray, "O God, help us. We are widowed." He identified with her. "His heart went out" to her.

Compassionate Healer

Jesus' ministry was characterized by words and wonders. Wherever He went He was surrounded by people in deep need. Famine and disease were no strangers to Jesus' world. His heart was wrenched by the human condition.

We see Jesus stopping to heal Peter's mother-in-law, (Luke 4:38, 39), a leper (Luke 5:13), a paralytic (Luke 5:18), and all kinds of diseases (Luke 4:40). James must have had the tender healing of Jesus in mind when he said it was insufficient to say to the suffering, "keep warm and well fed" (James 2:15, *New International Version*). One should help the unfortunate to be warmed and fed. No doubt James recalled Jesus' brand of compassion.

Luke was a doctor, and we may safely assume that he had a wonderful bedside manner. He used the word *compassion* very naturally (Luke 7:13; 10:33; 15:20). How many people had told him the stories of Jesus' wonderful love!

The Nature of Divine Love

Jesus called it a new commandment (John 13:34). Love—the Greek word is *agape*. There has been much teaching about this term, but its deeper meaning often is not understood. Some say they just cannot bring themselves to love certain people. This suggests that they are talking about *liking* people rather than *loving* as Jesus commanded.

Agape has been defined: "intelligent good will," "unselfish compassion ready to serve." The Christian is commanded by his Savior to do whatever is in the best interests of another, whatever the cost to himself. This is to be done even for people who are unlovely.

If we wonder how the love of God works, we can see it acted out in Jesus. First of all, God met the human need (lostness) at great Heavenly expense—He sent His Son. Jesus expressed *agape* by giving His life for unworthy people. This was at ultimate cost to himself.

So Loved

There has been much discussion about how to describe God's love. John 3:16 has Jesus saying, "God *so* loved ..." The Greek word that we translate *so* is often defined as "in such a manner," "on that wise," or "with such intensity." While we cannot really define God's love, we can see what it prompts—the ultimate gift. If we are to love as God does, we will have to act toward all people—enemies and all—according to what is in their best interests. This concept is unique to Christianity.

Birth, Death, and Beyond

Everything about Jesus announced the love of deity for humanity. God's compassion for both Joseph and Mary in the days surrounding Jesus' birth pointed toward it. His teachings sounded it; even His stern admonitions were in the best interests of those He admonished; His death had only one purpose, to redeem because He loved; His resurrection and subsequent appearances gave substance to His promise; His going away was to prepare for our eternal ecstasy; His return will be the divine culmination of that love.

The Direction Love Must Take

Love (ultimate compassion for others) is neither legalism nor license. It is not slavishly carrying out the letter of the law. It is not ignoring the law to do as one pleases, regardless of God's directive.

The father of the prodigal son (Luke 15:11-32) did not approve of the behavior of *either* of his sons. He did not endorse the self-righteous indignation of the older son, nor could he condone the profligacy of the younger. He acted out of love, i.e., he continued to welcome both sons into his home, while rejecting their different wayward actions. Love is like that.

The good Samaritan (Luke 10:25-37) did not approve of neglecting people in need. The "clergymen" did not approve neglecting formal religious rituals. Both were right, and perhaps both were wrong. Each should have attended to religious duties *and* ministered to the hurting. Love is like that.

So, as He could do so well, Jesus summed it all up by saying to the self-righteous Pharisees, "You give God a tenth of your mint, rue and all other kinds of garden herbs, *but* you neglect justice and the love of God. You should have practiced the latter without leaving the former undone" (Luke 11:42, *New International Version*). Love is like that.

Love is not in liking the likeable and shunning the repugnant. It is loving both and showing it by diligent concern and ministry to both, in their best interests. Love is definitely like that. See John 13:34!

Love and Self-Denial

It is easy to think of love in terms of the "warm fuzzies" it brings to us. The satisfaction, we think, is in being loved and in all of the nice experiences this brings to us. But this is not what Jesus was talking about. He was demanding that His followers be like himself—other-oriented. "If anyone would come after me, he must deny himself and take up his cross daily and follow me. For whoever wants to save his life will lose it, but whoever loses his life for me will save it" (Luke 9:23, 24, *New International Version*). This passage sheds much light on Jesus' principle of *agape*. It is *not* a self-serving love. It is a self-giving love.

Many have misunderstood Jesus to say that we should give up a huge range of things to serve Him. To the contrary, Jesus is asking us to give up our *selves*, to deny ourselves! It is our *selves* that He desires—for our eternal good. Taking up our crosses daily demands that we give up our lives daily. We do anyway. Every day one gives up a day of one's life. Let us just be sure that it is for our Savior that we "die daily." In doing this we do not become victimized martyrs, but "living sacrifices" (Romans 12:1). When we serve "the least of these," our fellows in need, we are serving Him (Matthew 25:40). And this is our joy and fulfillment.

So denying ourselves, taking up our crosses of life-surrender, and serving—these are the imple-mentation of *agape*. *Agape* is intentionally and intelligently expressing good will for the benefit of others and at our own expense. That, is imitating the loving, compassionate Jesus.

So What?

This sub-heading is not intended to be impertinent. It is meant to be thought-provoking. Actually, it is a very valid question. I wonder if non-Christians do not have this question in their hearts every time they hear a Christian message or a Christian's testimony? I suspect that for many the Christian message is reasonably well known. It is just that many see no relevance that it could possibly have to their lives. It is therefore incumbent upon us Christians that we explain to them the "so what."

What, then, is the importance to us of the way Jesus lived and loved?

For one thing, through His teaching He helps handle everything from disappointment to tragedy. Both Christians and non-Christians have an alarming tendency to be so devastated by the failure of a Christian that they abandon Christianity. If a Christian woman's preacher is revealed to be an adulterer, she may leave the church and perhaps even forsake the Christian faith. A familiar line is "If that's Christianity, I don't want any of it." Well, the fact is, that is *not* Christianity. It is a flagrant lack of Christianity. Jesus did not commit adultery. Christianity is embracing Jesus and His teachings. It is not following a religion as long as its adherents perform as they should. We are all sinners, and when one falls a little lower than the others we should minister to him rather than throwing away the teaching that he violated.

I know a lady whose husband was killed by a drunken driver. After the funeral and the trial, she went to the jail and began to minister to the killer. Her friends thought her strange. They apparently felt she should hate him. Jesus would have loved him, hating his sin.

Jesus' example of love *(agape)* and compassion help us set in order our value system and our world view. Humanism proclaims that man is at the center of life and is his own God. Today this is the "in" religion. As someone has said, each person is his own cult. People are rejecting Jesus, ignoring human need, and narcissistically enclosing themselves in their own little cocoons. They make their own definitions of right and wrong, and their priorities pertain to their own desires—and the line outside the therapist's office grows longer.

Jesus came and showed us how to make this world work right, and so to prepare ourselves for glory, where we see that right works.

Responding to God's Love

by Ron A. Fraser

SOCIOLOGISTS HAVE CONFIRMED what Christians have generally understood: there are no given worlds, only contrived ones. That is why the world can be changed. It's also why we have difficulty responding to Jesus.

We are tempted to imagine that the world as we know it is fixed and absolute, that it has always been so and always will be. Into such a world Jesus steps. While we sometimes try to make Him fit, He refuses. And He calls us to responses that rarely seem to fit. When we respond, however, nothing stays the same. Responding to Jesus reorders our world.

The temptation to use present realities as a measuring stick is as wrong as it is seductive. In our assurance that reality is "the way things are," we create the illusion that we have arrived. But Jesus calls us to respond so that quality of life will be enhanced. The best way to improve the quality of life is to respond to Jesus, for He is the measuring stick for the way life is to be lived.

At least three characteristics of our response to Jesus are illustrated in three of Jesus' encounters: the ten lepers, Luke 17:11-19; the rich ruler, 18:18-30; and Zaccheus, 19:1-10.

Response Crosses Barriers

Of all of our contrived worlds, none is more tempting than belief that "only my kind of people can respond to Jesus." Of all of Luke's themes, none delights him more than the universal appeal of Jesus.

On His way to Jerusalem, Jesus travels a road between Samaria and Galilee. On this frontier He comes upon and heals a mixed company of lepers. The only one to respond in heart-felt gratitude is a Samaritan, a foreigner (17:18). Jesus goes to the house of a tax collector, Zaccheus. It is unheard of for a rabbi to pollute himself by associating with a publican. Jesus does in spite of complaints (19:7). Zaccheus' response to Jesus' acceptance is repentance—giving to the poor, and restoring with interest whatever he has taken through heartless extortions.

Response Touches All of Life

The Pharisees, Jesus' audience in these encounters, were men who lived a double life. For them the sacred and the secular were two watertight compartments. In the religious compartment, they had beliefs and practices by which they assured themselves of their good standing before God. The secular compartment was quite separate: in it they could afford to be lovers of money. Their attitude in such things had no bearing on their religious status.

The rich ruler's problem was not just money, but law. Despite keeping the commandments, he was uncertain about his standing before God. Jesus exposes the emptiness of those who use law to limit God's claims upon life. That is the danger of law—it reduces the living response that Jesus has won to suit our own puny vision of life. Faith is living in relationship with God in such a way that all of life is a blank check. This is not easy, especially for the wealthy. For it is easy to put faith in riches. That's why the rich ruler went away sorrowful when asked to give his money to the poor and follow Jesus (18:24). "It is easier for a camel to go through a needle's eye, than for a rich man to enter into the kingdom of God" (18:25).

Money is only a test case. The account could have featured a politician with power, an academic with brains, a preacher with eloquence—anyone with resources. Will we use these to serve God and man, or for our own self-indulgence? Our response to Jesus is to touch every area of life.

Response Changes Us and Our World

It is possible for a rich man to come to the kingdom. Zaccheus is one for whom God does the impossible. He is changed! (19:8). What is changed is not the injustice and dishonesty of the tax-gathering system, but the human heart. From that, other changes follow. The man is a collaborator, a crooked capitalist, a notorious cheat! But when he responds there are repercussions all around! He begins to serve, not use others. Can you imagine the effect when one man goes to those he has cheated with checks four times the amount? Things happen to us, and to our world, when we respond to Jesus.

It is a contrived world that believes our response to Jesus is complete. For God keeps on giving, in the face of tired selfishness that believes there are no more gifts to be given, or love to respond to. We can live differently responding to Jesus. We can live gratefully, repentantly, and with total commitment. It takes courage. But the world will be a better place when we, like Jesus, live free from its lies, for its sake!

Quarterly Quiz

The questions on this page and the next may be used in several ways: as a pretest at the beginning of the quarter; as a review at the end of the quarter; or as a review after each lesson. The questions are based on the Scripture text of each lesson (King James Version).

Lesson 1

1. Name the father and mother of John the Baptist. *Luke 1:5*
2. What was the occupation of the father? *Luke 1:5*
3. Who told the father that John would be born? *Luke 1:13, 19*
4. What sign was given to indicate that the one who made the announcement told the truth? *Luke 1:20*

Lesson 2

1. What angel gave a message to the virgin Mary? *Luke 1:26, 27*
2. What was Mary's relation to Joseph at the time the angel's message was given to her? *Luke 1:27*
3. What was the angel's main message? *Luke 1:31*
4. How could Mary become a mother without the help of a man? *Luke 1:35*
5. What other information did the angel give? *Luke 1:36*

Lesson 3

1. Cyrenius ordered a census. (true/false). *Luke 2:1*
2. Joseph went to Bethlehem because (it was the capital; he liked the climate; he was of David's family). *Luke 2:4*
3. Why did Mary use a manger for her baby's bed? *Luke 2:7*
4. Shepherds kept their flocks of sheep in a poor section of the town of Bethlehem. (true/false). *Luke 2:8*
5. The angels song spoke of glory to God. What did they mention for men on earth? *Luke 2:14*

Lesson 4

1. What were the names of two elderly people who met the baby Jesus in the temple of Jerusalem. *Luke 2:25, 26*
2. What had the Holy Spirit told Simeon before this time? *Luke 2:26*
3. For whom was God's salvation prepared? *Luke 2:31*
4. What warning did Simeon give to Mary? *Luke 2:35*

5. The ministry of Jesus would reveal the thoughts of (many hearts, nobody, the angels). *Luke 2:34, 35*

Lesson 5

1. List six things that Isaiah prophesied the Christ would do. *Luke 4:18, 19*
2. When did Jesus say Isaiah's prophecy was fulfilled? *Luke 4:21*
3. After working far into the night to heal the sick, what did Jesus do before daylight? *Luke 4:42*
4. Why did Jesus for a time stop teaching and healing in Capernaum? *Luke 4:43*

Lesson 6

1. Whose boat did Jesus use as a pulpit for one of His sermons? *Luke 5:3*
2. What did Jesus tell the owner of the boat to do when the sermon he gave was over? *Luke 5:4*
3. How many fish had been taken in a night of fishing? (none, 153, seven) baskets full? *Luke 5:5*
4. What made two fishing boats come close to sinking? *Luke 5:7*
5. What did the fishermen do after a very successful time of fishing? *Luke 5:11*

Lesson 7

1. What caused a problem for four men who were bringing a paralyzed friend to Jesus? *Luke 5:18, 19*
2. How did they solve the problem? *Luke 5:19*
3. What two things did Jesus do for the paralyzed man? *Luke 5:20, 24*
4. How did the Pharisees react to Jesus' action? *Luke 5:21*
5. How did most of the people react? *Luke 5:26*

Lesson 8

1. Jesus accepted an invitation to have dinner with a Pharisee. (true/false?) *Luke 7:36*
2. The Pharisee welcomed Jesus cordially. (true/false). *Luke 7:44-46*
3. A woman who had been a sinner came to a Pharisee's house and anointed Jesus' feet. (true/false). *Luke 7:37, 38*

4. Jesus said a sinful woman was forgiven. (true/false). *Luke 7:47, 48*

5. The Pharisees were glad Jesus forgave the woman. (true/false). *Luke 7:49*

Lesson 9

1. What emergency brought a ruler of the synagogue to Jesus? *Luke 8:41, 42*

2. What delayed Jesus' trip to the ruler's home? *Luke 8:43-48*

3. What bad news came before Jesus reached the ruler's home? *Luke 8:49*

4. When Jesus came to a sorrowing home, what made the mourners laugh? *Luke 8:52, 53*

5. What is the climax of the story of the ruler's daughter who died? *Luke 8:54, 55*

Lesson 10

1. What did Jesus say when someone asked Him to settle a dispute about an inheritance? *Luke 12:13, 14*

2. After responding to the man who asked Him to settle the dispute, what did Jesus warn the people about? *Luke 12:15*

3. What lesson did Jesus draw from ravens and lilies? *Luke 12:24-28*

4. Heathen people are much concerned about food and clothing. What do Jesus' people seek more earnestly? *Luke 12:29-31*

5. Where are treasures stored most safely? *Luke 12:33*

Lesson 11

1. On the border of Samaria and Galilee, how many lepers met Jesus? (seven, ten, twelve) *Luke 17:11, 12*

2. When a group of lepers asked Jesus for mercy, what did He say to them? (be healed, show yourselves to the priests, what do you want?) *Luke 17:14*

3. As a group of lepers followed the instructions Jesus gave them, what happened? (They lost their way; they were healed; they were stoned) *Luke 17:14*

4. When several lepers were healed, how many of them hurried to thank Jesus? (ten percent, fifty percent, ninety percent) *Luke 17:15, 16*

Lesson 12

1. What question did a rich young ruler ask of Jesus? *Luke 18:18*

2. What did the rich young ruler say about his own obedience to God's laws? *Luke 18:21*

3. What did Jesus ask the rich young ruler to do in addition to keeping the law? *Luke 18:22*

4. How did the rich young ruler respond to Jesus' big request, and why? *Luke 18:23*

Lesson 13

1. Name the man who climbed a tree to see Jesus. *Luke 19:1-4*

2. Why was it necessary for a man to climb a tree in order to see Jesus? *Luke 19:3*

3. What did Jesus first say to the man in the tree? *Luke 19:5*

4. What dramatic action did a man take after coming down from a tree and having a talk with Jesus? *Luke 19:8*

Answers

Lesson 1—1. Zechariah, Elisabeth. 2. priest. 3. the angel, Gabriel. 4. Zechariah lost his voice. *Lesson 2*—1. Gabriel. 2. espoused: that is, engaged. 3. Mary was to have a son. 4. The Holy Spirit would cause her to become pregnant without any physical contact. 5. Mary's relative Elisabeth was pregnant. *Lesson 3*—1. false; Caesar ordered it. 2. he was of David's family. 3. There was no room for them in the inn. 4. false; they were in the field. 5. peace. *Lesson 4*—1. Simeon, Anna. 2. He would not die till he had seen the Christ. 3. all people. 4. a sword would pierce her soul. 5. many hearts. *Lesson 5*—1. preach the gospel to the poor, heal the brokenhearted, preach deliverance to captives, preach recovering of sight to blind, set at liberty the bruised, preach the acceptable year of the Lord. 2. this day. 3. went to a desert place. 4. to preach in other cities. *Lesson 6*—1. Simon's. 2. let down the nets. 3. none. 4. They were filled with fish. 5. followed Jesus. *Lesson 7*—1. The crowd was so thick they could not get to Jesus. 2. They lowered their friend through a hole in the roof. 3. forgave his sins; healed his paralysis. 4. thought Jesus was blasphemous. 5. glorified God; were filled with fear. *Lesson 8*—1. true. 2. false. 3. true. 4. true. 5. false. *Lesson 9*—1. His daughter was dying. 2. He healed a woman's hemorrhage. 3. The daughter died. 4. Jesus said the dead girl was sleeping. 5. Jesus restored the dead girl to life. *Lesson 10*—1. Who made me a judge or a divider over you? 2. covetousness. 3. God cares for them and will care for His people too. 4. the kingdom of God. 5. in the heavens. *Lesson 11*—1. ten. 2. Show yourselves to the priests. 3. They were healed. 4. ten percent. *Lesson 12*—1. What shall I do to inherit eternal life? 2. All these have I kept from my youth up. 3. Sell what you have, give to the poor, follow me. 4. He went away sorrowful, for he was rich. *Lesson 13*—1. Zaccheus. 2. He was short. 3. Come down, for I must stay at your house. 4. Gave half his goods to the poor, restored fourfold whatever he had taken dishonestly.

God's Promise to Zechariah

LESSON SCRIPTURE: Luke 1:1-25, 57-80.

PRINTED TEXT: Luke 1:5-13, 18-20, 24, 25.

Luke 1:5-13, 18-20, 24, 25

5 There was in the days of Herod, the king of Judea, a certain priest named Zechariah, of the course of Abijah: and his wife was of the daughters of Aaron, and her name was Elisabeth.

6 And they were both righteous before God, walking in all the commandments and ordinances of the Lord blameless.

7 And they had no child, because that Elisabeth was barren; and they both were now well stricken in years.

8 And it came to pass, that, while he executed the priest's office before God in the order of his course,

9 According to the custom of the priest's office, his lot was to burn incense when he went into the temple of the Lord.

10 And the whole multitude of the people were praying without at the time of incense.

11 And there appeared unto him an angel of the Lord standing on the right side of the altar of incense.

12 And when Zechariah saw him, he was troubled, and fear fell upon him.

13 But the angel said unto him, Fear not, Zechariah: for thy prayer is heard; and thy wife Elisabeth shall bear thee a son, and thou shalt call his name John.

. . . .

18 And Zechariah said unto the angel, Whereby shall I know this? for I am an old man, and my wife well stricken in years.

19 And the angel answering said unto him, I am Gabriel, that stand in the presence of God; and am sent to speak unto thee, and to show thee these glad tidings.

20 And, behold, thou shalt be dumb, and not able to speak, until the day that these things shall be performed, because thou believest not my words, which shall be fulfilled in their season.

. . . .

24 And after those days his wife Elisabeth conceived, and hid herself five months, saying,

25 Thus hath the Lord dealt with me in the days wherein he looked on me, to take away my reproach among men.

Golden Text: The angel said unto him, Fear not, Zechariah: for thy prayer is heard; and thy wife Elisabeth shall bear thee a son, and thou shalt call his name John.
—Luke 1:13.

Scenes of Love and Compassion
Unit 1: Promise and Expectation
(Lessons 1-4)

Lesson Aims

After this lesson, each student should:

1. Have a better understanding of the miraculous conception of John the Baptist.

2. Appreciate the fact that God has plans for every one of us even when we are past our youth.

3. Be able to relate in order the events preceding John's birth.

Lesson Outline

INTRODUCTION
  A. The Grand Pause
  B. Lesson Background
 I. ZECHARIAH CONFRONTED (Luke 1:5-13)
  A. His Identity (vv. 5-7)
     The Reward of Righteousness
  B. His Service (vv. 8-10)
  C. His Confrontation (vv. 11-13)
 II. ZECHARIAH CONFUSED (Luke 1:18-20)
  A. His Doubt (v. 18)
  B. Gabriel's Good Tidings (v. 19)
  C. Zechariah's Punishment (v. 20)
     Seeking Proof
III. ZECHARIAH COMFORTED (Luke 1:24, 25)
  A. Elisabeth's Conception (v. 24)
  B. Elisabeth's Joy (v. 25)
     When the Timing is Off
CONCLUSION
  A. God Has Worked in History
  B. Over the Hill
  C. Let Us Pray
  D. Thought to Remember

Display visual 1 from the Adult Visual Learning Resources Packet and refer to it at the appropriate time during the lesson. It is on page 125.

Introduction

A. The Grand Pause

Occasionally in a symphony or other musical composition, the composer includes what we call a grand pause. At that point, every instrument in the orchestra is at rest. As the echoes die away in the music hall, complete silence follows, focusing every eye upon the orchestra and the conductor. Then after the grand pause, the symphony moves to its resounding climax.

In a sense that is what happened in God's dealings with His people. The book of Malachi, written more than four hundred years before the birth of Christ, closed with the prophetic word that God would send Elijah "before the coming of the great and dreadful day of the Lord." Then came the grand pause in God's revelation. When He renewed His revelation, He announced the coming of John. Then would follow the birth and ministry of Jesus, reaching a dramatic conclusion in His death and resurrection.

B. Lesson Background

In the four hundred years of silence that followed Malachi's prophecy, the Jewish people enjoyed some victories, but they also suffered much at the hands of the Syrians, the Romans, and their own leaders. Many grew weary of waiting for the coming of Elijah and the Messiah who was expected to follow him, and they abandoned their hope. But others became even more intense in their expectancy. Hope was about all they had left. Jerusalem fell to the Roman general Pompey in 63 B.C., and the wily Herod managed to become king over the Jewish people. His cruel reign only intensified the Messianic hopes.

God was not oblivious to the people's suffering or their hopes. He was preparing to send "Elijah," but in a manner that the people hardly expected. Today's lesson tells us of the events surrounding the miraculous conception of John the Baptist, who, we learn, was the fulfillment of Malachi's prophecy (Luke 1:17; Matthew 11:11-14; 17:12, 13).

I. Zechariah Confronted
(Luke 1:5-13)

The printed text gives us the background for the birth of John the Baptist. In these verses we are given the historical setting and are introduced to Zechariah (called Zacharias in some editions of the *King James Version*) and Elisabeth, the parents of John the Baptist.

A. His Identity (vv. 5-7)

5. There was in the days of Herod, the king of Judea, a certain priest named Zechariah, of the course of Abijah: and his wife was of the daughters of Aaron, and her name was Elisabeth.

Luke introduces us to king Herod, often known as Herod the Great. Although he was not a Jew, Herod by political cunning had become ruler over the Jews. His actual reign extended from 37 to 4 B.C. His reputation for cruelty, even against his own family, was well deserved.

In contrast to Herod lived an obscure priest whose life was a model of godliness and decency. Like all priests, Zechariah was from the tribe of Levi. He belonged to the *course of Abijah.* In the time of David the priests had been divided into twenty-four groups (1 Chronicles 24:1-19) so as to provide an orderly arrangement for service in the temple. The order of Abijah was eighth in the list. Each of these divisions was on duty in the temple in its turn for one week at a time. About thirty persons in the Bible bear the name Zechariah or its equivalent, which means "the Lord remembers."

His wife was also a descendant of Aaron. A priest who was married to a woman of priestly descent was considered especially blessed. The name *Elisabeth* means literally "my God is an oath." In Hebrew thought it meant that one so named was a worshiper of God and would make her vows "unto the Lord" (Numbers 30:3).

6. And they were both righteous before God, walking in all the commandments and ordinances of the Lord blameless.

Both were *righteous before God:* that is, they lived in accordance with the teachings of the Old Testament. There was no sham or pretense in their lives; they were not righteous just in the eyes of men, but before God. They observed the *commandments and ordinances of the Lord.*

THE REWARD OF RIGHTEOUSNESS

Arise at 5:30 a.m., eat breakfast at 6:15, go to class at 7:00, eat lunch at noon, get to work at 1:00 p.m. Thus the day goes at a certain Christian boarding school.

No makeup or jewelry, no caffeine or meat, no TV or radio, no dating or talking to the opposite sex without adults present.

Do all these rules really make people righteous? The secret acts of the students show that their hearts are not in keeping the rules. Pizzas, Pepsis, and portable radios regularly find their way into the dorms. Attitude is the issue here.

Zechariah and Elisabeth certainly kept the law outwardly, but this was the result of their inner virtue of seeking God's will. Forced observance of a code provokes resentment, but when a person intentionally seeks God's will, he finds the reward of righteousness. It may not be as amazing as the birth of a promised child, but it is satisfying at the deepest level of one's being.
—C. R. B.

7. And they had no child, because that Elisabeth was barren; and they both were now well stricken in years.

The couple had no children! Such a statement might be the occasion for rejoicing in our selfish

---

How to Say It

AARON. *Air*-un.
ABIJAH. Uh-*bye*-juh.
DENG XIAOPING. Dung She-ow-*ping.*
ELIJAH. Ee-*lye*-juh.
GABRIEL. *Gay*-bree-ul.
HEROD. *Hair*-ud.
JUDEA. Joo-*dee*-uh.
MALACHI. *Mal*-uh-kye.
ZACHARIAS. Zack-uh-*rye*-us.
ZECHARIAH. Zek-uh-*rye*-uh.

---

and self-centered society, but not so in ancient Israel. Children were looked upon as a special blessing of God. Barrenness, on the other hand, was thought by many to be a sign of God's disfavor. As a result, Zechariah and Elisabeth missed the joys that come with parenthood. They must also have felt that their neighbors looked down upon them. The Old Testament examples of Sarah, Rachel, and Hannah illustrate how humiliating it was to be childless.

In spite of this burden that they had to bear into their old age, we do not detect a trace of bitterness in their lives. Even this great disappointment was not allowed to become a stumbling block in their service to God. We today can very well learn a lesson from their example.

B. His Service (vv. 8-10)

8, 9. And it came to pass, that, while he executed the priest's office before God in the order of his course, according to the custom of the priest's office, his lot was to burn incense when he went into the temple of the Lord.

Since there were hundreds of priests available for service in the temple, they could not all serve at the same time. Each of the twenty-four courses served a week at a time. Within each course, the specific duties were assigned by lot. On this particular occasion, it fell to Zechariah to burn the incense. This was a rare privilege, and ordinarily a priest enjoyed this privilege only once in his lifetime.

The incense offering was made twice a day—morning and evening. Luke gives us no hint whether Zechariah served in the morning or the evening. The altar of incense stood inside the temple before the Holy of Holies. An assistant would bring some live coals from the altar of sacrifice and place these upon the altar of incense. Then the priest would sprinkle the prepared incense upon the coals, sending up a cloud of fragrant smoke. The Jews understood this to symbolize prayer that ascended to God.

10. And the whole multitude of the people were praying without at the time of incense.

When Zechariah entered the sanctuary, a crowd had assembled outside for this solemn moment. The people were bowed in silent prayer as Zechariah placed the incense upon the coals. On behalf of the people, he offered a prayer of thanksgiving for blessings received and a prayer for peace. Then the priest would return to the expectant worshipers and pronounce the Aaronic blessing (Numbers 6:24-26).

C. His Confrontation (vv. 11-13)

11. And there appeared unto him an angel of the Lord standing on the right side of the altar of incense.

Zechariah was interrupted by the appearance of an *angel of the Lord*, identified in verse 19 as Gabriel. We are not told what the angel looked like, but in other appearances mentioned in the New Testament, angels look like men with clothes white and shining (Luke 24:4; John 20:12).

12. And when Zechariah saw him, he was troubled, and fear fell upon him.

Zechariah knew at once that the angel was not another priest who had come into the Holy Place. The appearance of the angel convinced him that this intruder was not human. He was overwhelmed with fear, a common response when men are confronted by angels. Perhaps he was overcome by the realization of his sinfulness in the presence of this Heavenly messenger.

13. But the angel said unto him, Fear not, Zechariah: for thy prayer is heard; and thy wife Elisabeth shall bear thee a son, and thou shalt call his name John.

The angel's first words were to reassure Zechariah. He had come to bring joy, not judgment. Zechariah's prayer had been heard. Of course God hears every prayer that men utter. What the angel meant was that God had heard the prayer approvingly. The question is, what prayer? Did he refer to the prayer that Zechariah had just uttered before the altar of incense? Some commentators say that the evening prayer in the temple was for the salvation of Israel. If this was the case, then the angel was telling Zechariah that God would indeed save His people and that Zechariah, through the birth of a son, would have a part in fulfilling this prayer.

Or did the angel have reference to the prayer for a son that Zechariah and Elisabeth undoubtedly had made many times in the past? In light of the angel's statement, this seems most likely. Their prayer for a son would be answered. How many times had they uttered such a prayer? Even after all reasonable hope was gone, they still must have prayed, hoping against hope that God would answer them. This should remind us that the power of God is not limited and that all things are possible for Him.

The son was to be named John, which means "Jehovah is gracious." It might seem strange that one who was to pronounce God's judgment (Luke 3:7-9) should bear a name that told of God's grace. Yet we must remember that the call for judgment was but a means of calling attention to the one who would follow John with the message of grace.

II. Zechariah Confused (Luke 1:18-20)

The intervening verses record that the angel told what kind of a person John would be. He would not partake of strong spirits, but would be filled with the Holy Spirit. He would go forth in the spirit and power of Elijah to prepare the people for the coming of the Lord.

A. His Doubt (v. 18)

18. And Zechariah said unto the angel, Whereby shall I know this? for I am an old man, and my wife well stricken in years.

Like most of us at times, Zechariah prayed, and then when God promised to answer his prayer, he thought it too good to be true. By the laws of nature, Zechariah was quite right. There was no way that he and Elisabeth could have a son. Yet as a priest he should have been familiar with the case of Abraham and Sarah (Genesis 21:5).

19. And the angel answering said unto him, I am Gabriel, that stand in the presence of God; and am sent to speak unto thee, and to show thee these glad tidings.

Zechariah's statement, *I am an old man*, is answered by Gabriel's *I am Gabriel*. The name *Gabriel* means "man of God." Zechariah was old, tired, and lacking in faith; but, the angel was a man of God, standing in the presence of God and possessing power and authority. Zechariah may have had serious doubt about God's power to give him a son, but Gabriel was there to bring him good news and to reassure him.

20. And, behold, thou shalt be dumb, and not able to speak, until the day that these things shall be performed, because thou believest not my words, which shall be fulfilled in their season.

Zechariah had asked for a sign (v. 18) that the prophecy of the gift of a son would be fulfilled. On occasions in the past men under somewhat similar circumstances had asked for a sign, and that sign had been given (Gideon, for example,

THE **TEMPLE**   visual 1

PRIESTS

MOST HOLY PLACE ▢   HOLY PLACE ▢   PEOPLE

ALTAR OF INCENSE   ALTAR OF SACRIFICE

Judges 6:36-40). Why was Zechariah's request for a sign considered sinful? One reason was that the appearance of the angel should have been sign enough. Further, as a priest, Zechariah had the advantage of knowing the Scriptures and should have had a more mature faith than the persons in the Old Testament period who needed signs.

Since Zechariah had asked for a sign, he would receive it, but it would hardly be what he expected. He would be unable to speak until the prophecy was fulfilled, which would be at least nine months in the future. Such a dramatic sign would certainly be convincing, and it would also greatly hamper his ability to function as a priest.

We today have little room to be critical of Zechariah. We live in a skeptical age that demands that we prove everything by scientific standards. Some of this skepticism rubs off on us, causing our faith to waver. We can be thankful that our God is merciful. Even though He punished Zechariah, He also blessed him. We can expect blessing in spite of our lack of faith, if we are willing to allow our faith to grow.

SEEKING PROOF

In 1925, John Scopes, a Tennessee teacher, was tried for breaking a state law against teaching evolution. The court's decision was somewhat irrelevant, since partisans for each side were convinced they had proved their point.

In 1982, a court in Little Rock ruled unconstitutional an Arkansas law requiring that "creation-science" be given equal time with the teaching of evolution in public schools. Again, nobody really *proved* anything. Proof is hard to obtain when there is no eyewitness to the events of creation!

We may wish for more evidence and less need for faith in our struggle to understand life. But even when an angel spoke, Zechariah had to decide whether to believe or not.

It has always been so: God's people do not have to believe what is foolish, but we are sometimes called upon to place our trust in what cannot be clearly seen with the eyes.   —C. R. B.

III. Zechariah Comforted
(Luke 1:24, 25)

The intervening verses tell how Zechariah, after his confrontation with the angel Gabriel, returned to the worshipers outside. Since he could not speak, he attempted to convey to them what had happened to him. The people rightly understood that he had seen some kind of a vision. After Zechariah's period of service in the temple was completed, he returned to his own home, which some believe was in the hill country of Judea to the south of Jerusalem.

A. Elisabeth's Conception (v. 24)

24. And after those days his wife Elisabeth conceived, and hid herself five months, saying.

Zechariah's experience in the temple was no figment of his imagination. His being stricken speechless was a real experience, and then Elisabeth became pregnant just as the angel had predicted. His doubts were now replaced with reassuring comfort. After she realized that she was pregnant, Elisabeth kept herself in seclusion for five months. We are not told why she chose to do this, but it may be that she wanted to spend extra time in meditation and prayer.

B. Elisabeth's Joy (v. 25)

25. Thus hath the Lord dealt with me in the days wherein he looked on me, to take away my reproach among men.

It would certainly be understandable that she would send up many extra prayers of thanksgiving now that her barrenness had been removed. And thankful she must have been, for never again would she have to bear the reproach of one who had no children.

WHEN THE TIMING IS OFF

The batter misses the first pitch, a fast ball. He swings too soon at the next two pitches, a slow pitch and a curve ball. Walking back to the dugout, he mutters, "My timing must be off."

A car sputters, snorts, and backfires as it pulls into the repair shop. The mechanic's intuition is soon confirmed by the dials on his diagnostic equipment: "The timing is off."

It might have seemed to Elisabeth that God's timing was off when He gave her a child in her old age. She might have said, "Think of all those years when I wanted a child, and now when I'm too old, God does this to me. Does He know what He is doing?" Instead, she saw the event as a sign of God's favor, and accepted it as her opportunity to participate in His eternal plan.

VISUALS FOR THESE LESSONS

The *Adult Visuals/Learning Resources* packet contains classroom-size visuals designed for use with the lessons in the Winter Quarter. The packet is available from your supplier. Order no. ST 292.

Sometimes we are unprepared to deal with what life brings to us. It may seem that the timing is totally wrong. But if we seek God's will, we shall find that God can turn stumbling blocks into stepping stones. And when all is said and done, we usually find that God's timing is best after all!   —C. R. B.

Conclusion

A. God Has Worked in History

For four hundred years prior to the events recorded in today's lesson text, God had not spoken to the people through the prophetic word. Now the silence was broken by the words of Gabriel to the humble priest, Zechariah. The climax of God's plan for the human race was rapidly approaching. Man would not have planned it this way. It is likely that man would have announced the preparation for the coming of God's Son in some kind of an elaborate extravaganza, not in a secluded chamber of the temple. But God's ways are not our ways, and He proceeded to unfold His plan in His own way in His own time.

The vantage point we have in history allows us to see how God has worked in the past. This helps us to see that He continues to work in human history, in His own way and at His own pace.

B. Over the Hill

Ours is a youth-oriented society, and the most painful comment one can hear about himself is that he is "over the hill." We have mandated that at seventy or even younger one is "put out to pasture." This same attitude carries over into the churches, where a minister in his fifties is likely to be considered too old to be called to an aggressive work.

Yet this relegation of older people to the sidelines has not always been reflected in the Scriptures. God frequently used older persons—Abraham or Moses, for example—to carry out His purposes. And, for that matter, our contemporary society offers some similar examples. President Reagan, past his mid-seventies, still provides vigorous leadership to our nation; and in China, Deng Xiaoping, now in his eighties,

slowly leads the world's largest nation out of doctrinaire Marxism toward a freer society.

God demonstrated that He could use older persons when He selected Zechariah and Elisabeth to become the parents of John the Baptist. If God could use older persons in the first century, is there any reason to doubt that He can also use older persons in the twentieth century? Yet in many of our churches we have treated most of our older people as if they were "over the hill."

Many older persons, having reached the age of retirement, now have time they can give for many church activities. They have reached a level of spiritual maturity that makes them excellent counselors. Their long experience gives them a vantage point in decision making that younger persons lack. Relieved of the pressures of the business world and of family rearing, they can be more objective about many decisions. Wise indeed is the congregation that can learn how to use this large reservoir of human resources that is certain to become even larger in the years ahead.

C. Let Us Pray

Gracious Heavenly Father, we thank You that You have provided for us a way by which we may come to realize our Heavenly destiny. We do not always understand why You unfolded Your plan for us in the way that You did, but give us the faith to accept it. May we be spared the doubt that plagued Zechariah. In the name of Your Son we pray. Amen.

D. Thought to Remember

"Blessed be the Lord God of Israel; for he hath visited and redeemed his people, and hath raised up a horn of salvation for us in the house of his servant David" (Luke 1:68, 69).

Home Daily Bible Readings

Monday, Nov. 28—God's Promise to Noah (Genesis 9:8-17)

Tuesday, Nov. 29—God's Promise to Abraham (Genesis 15:1-6)

Wednesday, Nov. 30—God's Promise to Joshua (Joshua 1:1-9)

Thursday, Dec. 1—God's Promise to David (2 Samuel 7:8-16)

Friday, Dec. 2—God's Promise to Solomon (1 Kings 3:5-14)

Saturday, Dec. 3—God's Promise to Hezekiah (2 Kings 20:1-11)

Sunday, Dec. 4—God's Promise to Zechariah (Luke 1:5-19)

Learning by Doing

This page contains an alternate lesson plan emphasizing learning activities. Classes desiring such student involvement will find these suggestions helpful.

Learning Goals

After this lesson, students should be able to:

1. Explain what happened when Zechariah met the angel Gabriel in the temple.

2. Suggest some ways of dealing with disappointment.

3. List some ministry options available to older adults that may not be open to younger people.

Into the Lesson

As the students arrive, give each one a piece of paper with a vertical line down the center and this heading centered over the left-hand side of the page: DISAPPOINTMENTS I HAVE ENCOUNTERED.

Ask the students to list on the left half of the paper a few disappointments in their lives (like a missed job opportunity, or a failure to take a certain class in school, etc.) Ask them then to title the right-hand column, HOW I'VE DEALT WITH THEM, and to write in that column the appropriate responses. (This activity is also in the student book.)

Discuss some of the ideas the students suggest. Then ask them to imagine the disappointment of Zechariah and Elisabeth in having no children. (See Luke 1:5-7, and note the discussion in the commentary section to understand how significant this was in the first century.) Ask, "How do you think you would have dealt with that disappointment?"

Into the Word

Call attention to the list of events in the student book, or, reproduce this list and give each student a copy.

_____ 1. The angel Gabriel appears in the temple.

_____ 2. The people become concerned about Zechariah.

_____ 3. It is predicted that Elisabeth will have a son who will be named John.

_____ 4. Zechariah communicates with gestures.

_____ 5. John is said to be the one who will come in the spirit and power of Elijah.

_____ 6. Zechariah asks, "Whereby shall I know this?"

_____ 7. Elisabeth conceives, and her "reproach" is taken away.

_____ 8. The people offer prayer outside the temple.

_____ 9. Zechariah enters the temple to burn incense.

_____ 10. Zechariah is stricken dumb as a sign that Gabriel's words are true and as punishment for Zechariah's doubt.

Have the students read Luke 1:5-25 and arrange the events listed in the proper order. (The items should be numbered as follows: 3, 8, 4, 9, 5, 6, 10, 2, 1, 7.)

Divide the class into groups of three and let the students compare their lists. Allow each group to come to agreement on the order before discussing the list with the whole class. Make a master list on the chalkboard so that everyone sees the list arranged properly. (If you don't have a chalkboard, or if you want to make the list more quickly, prepare strips of posterboard ahead of time with one item written on each. Then post each one in order.) Discuss the items briefly as they are put in their proper order so you are sure everyone understands what is taking place. Mention any significant details that take place between some of the items listed.

Into Life

Even if Zechariah still prayed for a son, his hope of having one must have been fading, and with good reason. He and his wife were old, "too old." No doubt Elisabeth shared his feelings. Yet, through the power of God, they became the parents of John the Baptist.

Many older Christians believe they have outlived their ability to serve in a useful ministry. Use the groups of three you made earlier to discuss these questions:

1. What are some ministries older Christians—perhaps retired saints—may be able to do as well as or even more successfully than younger ones? (Include ministries for shut-ins or semi shut-ins.)

2. What kind of attitude must be present for one to take on one of these ministries?

3. Is this an attitude for just older folks, or is it the same attitude necessary for younger Christians?

4. Do you display this attitude?

Use the last question to challenge the students to apply the lesson to their own lives. All of us can serve in one way or another.

Let's Talk It Over

The questions on this page are designed to encourage review of the lesson Scriptures and to promote discussion of the lesson by the class. The answers provided are only discussion starters. Let your class talk it over from there.

1. How can we strengthen our confidence that persistent prayer will at last be answered?

For Zechariah and Elisabeth the reason why God long withheld the answer to their prayers for a son was not made clear. But for us there may be factors that delay our readiness for an answer. James leads us to examine our prayers: "When you ask, you do not receive, because you ask with wrong motives, that you may spend what you get on your pleasures" (James 4:3, *New International Version*). If we discover that we are motivated by mixed or impure aims in an area of prayer, and if we purify those motives, we will gain a richer assurance of ultimate success. Also, if we keep ourselves open to God's guidance, we may see certain steps He wants us to take in order to put ourselves in position to receive the answer we are seeking.

2. Why does our knowledge of the Scripture make it unnecessary for us to seek signs?

Some persons seek for signs to bolster their faith in the existence of God. The Bible points to the evidence nature provides of God's existence and eternal power (Psalm 19:1-6; Romans 1:18-20), and it also lays a foundation of historical proof for the resurrection of Jesus Christ—the miracle that best demonstrates the reality of God. Another reason people seek signs is to be assured that some blessing is coming to them. But the Bible is a book filled with promises of divine blessings, and it sets forth the conditions we must meet in order to obtain such blessings. People look for signs, as Gideon did with his famous fleece (Judges 6:36-40), to discover what decision they should make or direction they should follow. Christians who read their Bibles regularly can testify that God's Word is a dependable source of guidance even in regard to the direst dilemmas. When people ignore the Bible and look for guidance through unusual events or emotional experiences, they dishonor God who has given us His Word to build our faith, to communicate His promises, and to offer us His guidance.

3. Zechariah was inclined to skepticism over Gabriel's promise, and we also are tempted to be skeptical over certain aspects of our faith. How can we deal with such temptation?

Many Biblical miracles have been explained away, scoffed at, and otherwise dismissed by seemingly intelligent people, and some of their skepticism may rub off on us. As far as our own experience is concerned, we must admit that we have never seen someone part the waters of the sea or call down fire from Heaven or multiply a small amount of food into enough to feed a multitude, and we would be highly suspicious of any modern religious leader who claimed to do any of these things. But the fact that neither we nor any of the modern-day skeptics have witnessed a miracle firsthand does not prove that miracles have never happened. We need to acknowledge the limits of our own wisdom and experience, and we need to approach the Bible with a humble and open mind. When we begin with the Bible's best-established miracle—the resurrection of Jesus Christ—and make firm our faith in it, then we will see that the God who could raise His Son from the dead was quite capable of accomplishing any other miracle recorded in the Scriptures. This kind of faith can withstand the erosion of skepticism.

4. What are some practical ways in which the church can make use of the "large reservoir of human resources" represented by its older members?

They can be very effective in a ministry of visitation. Elderly people who are shut in at home or in a nursing home find great enjoyment in visits from persons their own age. Senior members of the church can also perform a vital ministry through sending cards to the sick and to other absentees. To go a little further, they can take on the challenge of a comprehensive letter-writing ministry. This may include writing letters to missionaries, notes of appreciation to those who have served faithfully in the church, epistles of encouragement to people who have been struggling with problems. Church committees benefit from the participation of older members. They bring a wealth of experience to the committee's work, and they may have time to take care of some of the small duties that are seen. Paul listed "showing hospitality" (1 Timothy 5:10, *New International Version*) among the tasks that the church's widows might perform.

God's Promise to Mary

LESSON SCRIPTURE: Luke 1:26-56.

PRINTED TEXT: Luke 1:26-38.

Luke 1:26-38

26 In the sixth month the angel Gabriel was sent from God unto a city of Galilee, named Nazareth,

27 To a virgin espoused to a man whose name was Joseph, of the house of David; and the virgin's name was Mary.

28 And the angel came in unto her, and said, Hail, thou that art highly favored, the Lord is with thee: blessed art thou among women.

29 And when she saw him, she was troubled at his saying, and cast in her mind what manner of salutation this should be.

30 And the angel said unto her, Fear not, Mary: for thou hast found favor with God.

31 And, behold, thou shalt conceive in thy womb, and bring forth a son, and shalt call his name Jesus.

32 He shall be great, and shall be called the Son of the Highest; and the Lord God shall give unto him the throne of his father David:

33 And he shall reign over the house of Jacob for ever; and of his kingdom there shall be no end.

34 Then said Mary unto the angel, How shall this be, seeing I know not a man?

35 And the angel answered and said unto her, The Holy Ghost shall come upon thee, and the power of the Highest shall overshadow thee: therefore also that holy thing which shall be born of thee shall be called the Son of God.

36 And, behold, thy cousin Elisabeth, she hath also conceived a son in her old age; and this is the sixth month with her, who was called barren.

37 For with God nothing shall be impossible.

38 And Mary said, Behold the handmaid of the Lord; be it unto me according to thy word. And the angel departed from her.

Golden Text: And Mary said, Behold the handmaid of the Lord; be it unto me according to thy word. And the angel departed from her.—Luke 1:38.

Scenes of Love and Compassion
Unit 1: Promise and Expectation
(Lessons 1-4)

Lesson Aims

After this lesson a student should be able to:

1. Have a better understanding of the miraculous conception of our Lord.

2. Appreciate both the joy and the apprehension that Mary must have felt when she learned that she would become the mother of our Lord even though she was not married.

3. Be able to relate all the details of this portion of the birth narrative of Jesus.

Lesson Outline

INTRODUCTION

    A. A Native-born Prince

    B. Lesson Background

I. ANNOUNCEMENT OF THE ANGEL (Luke 1:26-29)

    A. Time and Place (v. 26)

    B. Recipient of the Message (v. 27)

    C. Gabriel's Greeting (v. 28)

    D. Mary's Response (v. 29)

II. MESSAGE OF THE ANGEL (Luke 1:30-37)

    A. A Word of Reassurance (v. 30)

    B. Content of the Message (vv. 31-33)

       The Superbaby Syndrome

    C. Mary's Question (v. 34)

    D. Gabriel's Response (v. 35)

    E. God's Work With Elisabeth (vv. 36, 37)

III. MARY'S SUBMISSION (Luke 1:38)

       The Trouble With Being Favored

CONCLUSION

    A. "Behold the Handmaid of the Lord"

    B. A City of Galilee

    C. Let Us Pray

    D. Thought to Remember

Display visual 2 from the visuals/learning resources packet. It is shown on page 132.

Introduction

A. A Native-born Prince

Several centuries ago the king of England was engaged in a war against Wales to bring it under the control of the English crown. After several months of bloody fighting, the king sent envoys to the Welsh leaders asking them to lay down their arms. They replied that they would never submit to the rule of one who spoke English or who was not born in Wales.

The king agreed to allow them to have a ruler who was born in Wales and who spoke no English. When the Welsh had laid down their arms, they demanded to see their new ruler. The king then led them to a bedchamber in his castle where his infant son lay in a crib. The baby had been born in Wales and, since he was only a few weeks old, he spoke no English. The Welsh, realizing that they had been outwitted by the king, submitted to his rule. But to this day, the heir apparent to the British crown is known as the Prince of Wales.

In a somewhat similar fashion, God knew that the people of the world would never accept as their ruler an angelic prince who spoke only the language of Heaven. And so God sent His only Son to be born of the virgin Mary. In every respect He was human without compromising His deity. As a result, for two thousand years people have accepted Him as the Prince of Peace.

B. Lesson Background

Last week we studied about the appearance of Gabriel to Zechariah in the temple. The angel said: Elisabeth, Zechariah's wife, would bear him a son. The old priest responded to this message with unbelief, and as a result he was stricken dumb. This episode ended with Zechariah returning to his home in the hill country south of Jerusalem, where he and Elisabeth awaited the birth of the promised son.

Luke then turns our attention to the north to Galilee, where lived the virgin Mary in the village of Nazareth. Once more the angel Gabriel appeared, this time to Mary.

I. Announcement of the Angel (Luke 1:26-29)

A. Time and Place (v. 26)

26. And in the sixth month the angel Gabriel was sent from God into a city of Galilee, named Nazareth.

The *sixth month* refers to the sixth month of Elisabeth's pregnancy. In this first chapter Luke does not give us any indication of when these events took place, but at the beginning of the second chapter we do find some historical references. These things occurred during the reign of Caesar Augustus (31 B.C. – A.D. 14) and while Cyrenius (or Quirinius) was governor of Syria. While there is some question about the date of his governorship, there is reason to believe that he exercised control over the area as early as 6 B.C. Matthew 2:1 informs us that the birth of Jesus occurred during the reign of Herod the Great, who died in 4 B.C. Many scholars place the birth of Jesus between 6 and 4 B.C.

The town of Nazareth was located in the hills of southern Galilee about fifteen miles west of the Sea of Galilee and about twenty miles east of the Mediterranean. While Nazareth was not located on the great trade routes that passed through the province, these routes were not far away, and so the town was not completely isolated.

It is not likely that the world would have selected someone from such a remote place to become the mother of our Lord. Nazareth is not mentioned in the Old Testament. Nathanael asked, "Can there any good thing come out of Nazareth?" (John 1:46). This seems to indicate that the town was not highly regarded. Yet God's ways are not man's ways.

B. Recipient of the Message (v. 27)

27. To a virgin espoused to a man whose name was Joseph, of the house of David; and the virgin's name was Mary.

The Scriptures tell us little about Mary, the mother of Jesus. We don't know who her parents were or if they were living when the events in this lesson occurred. Nor do we know how old she was when Gabriel appeared to her.

In modern language we would say Mary was *engaged* rather than *espoused*. She was still a virgin. Engagement was a serious legal commitment, however. It could be broken only by divorce. Girls as young as twelve were sometimes involved in such an agreement, which might last a year or more before marriage. Sexual union did not occur until after the wedding. The woman was expected to keep her vows inviolate, and any sexual liaison with another man was considered adultery and might be harshly treated. It was for this reason that Joseph, when he learned that Mary was pregnant, sought to cancel the betrothal arrangement (Matthew 1:18-21).

The birth of Jesus to a virgin has been an important doctrine of the church for centuries. Only in recent years has it been challenged. Luke plainly teaches it, as does Matthew (1:18-25). Isaiah gives his prophetic stamp of approval to the teaching (7:14). One can deny the doctrine only by denying obvious teachings of Scripture.

Of the house of David. Some commentators connect this phrase with Mary; others believe that it applies to Joseph. It is clear that Joseph was not the physical father of Jesus (Luke 3:23; Matthew 1:18-23), yet in the eyes of the Jews he was His legal father. The fact that both Mary and Joseph were probably of the Davidic line is in keeping with many prophecies that the Messiah would be a descendant of David.

How to Say It

BABYLONIANS. Bab-uh-*low*-nee-unz.
CAESAR AUGUSTUS. *See*-zur Aw-*gus*-tus.
CYRENIUS. Sye-*ree*-nee-us.
DAVIDIC. Duh-*vid*-ick.
GABRIEL. *Gay*-bree-ul.
NAZARETH. *Naz*-uh-reth.
QUIRINIUS. Kwih-*rin*-e-us.
SYRIA. *Sear*-ee-uh.

C. Gabriel's Greeting (v. 28)

28. And the angel came in unto her, and said, Hail, thou that art highly favored, the Lord is with thee: blessed art thou among women.

This verse indicates that Gabriel appeared to Mary while she was indoors. The greeting, *Hail*, was a familiar Greek expression and might very well be translated *Greetings*. It is likely the greeting was in Aramaic or Hebrew, and Luke has given us a Greek translation for it.

Gabriel's next words commended her because she was *highly favored*. God showed His special favor by choosing her to become the mother of the Christ child. The angel assured her that God was with her. Some of the best ancient texts do not have *blessed art thou among women*, and so it is dropped from some modern translations.

D. Mary's Response (v. 29)

29. And when she saw him, she was troubled at his saying, and cast in her mind what manner of salutation this should be.

No doubt Mary was startled, but she did not react with fear as did Zechariah (Luke 1:12). Perhaps her innocence and purity made the presence of the divine messenger less threatening, or she may have been more in tune with the divine than was the old priest. But though she was not so much frightened by the angel's appearance, she was perplexed by his words. Even though she was a virtuous young woman, she did not feel that she merited such a greeting. She thought for a moment, hoping to find some meaning in the words.

II. Message of the Angel
(Luke 1:30-37)

A. A Word of Reassurance (v. 30)

30. And the angel said unto her, Fear not, Mary: for thou hast found favor with God.

Even before Mary could resolve the problem in her own mind, the angel brought comforting words. Just as Gabriel had quieted the fears of Zechariah, so he calmed Mary with the same words: *Fear not.* Then he gave a reason why she should leave her fears behind. She had found favor with God. Admirable as Mary doubtless was, she had *found favor*, not earned it. That is at the heart of what favor or grace is—unmerited, unearned, undeserved.

B. Content of the Message (vv. 31-33)

31. And, behold, thou shalt conceive in thy womb, and bring forth a son, and shalt call his name Jesus.

In three short clauses, Gabriel related to Mary the great event that would change her life. She would conceive and bear a son. If the initial words of Gabriel had caused her concern, we can only imagine how upsetting these words must have been to her. Not only was she to bear a son, but she would name Him Jesus. Joseph also was told that the baby would be named Jesus, signifying that He would save His people from their sins (Matthew 1:21). This name is the Greek form of the Hebrew name *Joshua*, meaning "Jehovah is salvation."

32. He shall be great, and shall be called the Son of the Highest; and the Lord God shall give unto him the throne of his father David.

Gabriel then provided additional information about this son Mary was to bear. He would be great, and His greatness would be based on the fact that He would be *the Son of the Highest*. This expression is but another way of saying "Son of God." The reference to God as the Highest is found about a dozen times in the New Testament, seven of them in Luke (1:32, 35, 76; 2:14; 6:35; 8:28; 19:38). Mary's child is called *Son of the Highest*, while John is called "prophet of the Highest" (Luke 1:76). It seems that Luke deliberately chose these two titles to contrast their different relationships to God. John was God's spokesman, but Jesus was His Son. This affirmation, along with His virgin conception, attests to the deity of Jesus.

The Jewish people had, in the thousand years since David had lived, suffered many things. The prophets of the Old Testament sometimes brought a message of hope that would be realized in the return of David's son to the throne. Now the fulfillment of those prophecies was at hand in the person of Jesus, Mary's divine Son. Matthew traces the genealogy of Jesus through Joseph, who, though not His physical father, was looked upon as His legal father (Matthew 1:1-16). Many commentators believe that Luke gives us Jesus' ancestry traced through Mary (Luke 3:23-38). Thus Jesus is in the lineage of David through both Mary and Joseph.

visual 2

33. And he shall reign over the house of Jacob for ever; and of his kingdom there shall be no end.

When David was the king of Israel, God promised that his house would rule forever (2 Samuel 7:12-16). However, the Davidic line was interrupted when Jerusalem fell to the Babylonians and the king was carried into captivity. The Jews looked for a descendant of David who would once more become king and rule over a physical kingdom. But the prophecy was not to have its fulfillment in the physical kingdom. Rather it would be fulfilled in the Messiah-King, who would be sovereign over a spiritual kingdom that would never end.

THE SUPERBABY SYNDROME

"I guess I'm a flop in life. I can't read." So spoke a six-year-old child suffering from the "superbaby syndrome."

"Superbaby syndrome" is a name given to the problem of young children who are finding it difficult to cope with the stress of high-pressure preschool experiences and who later suffer burnout in elementary school. Educators are expressing concern about the problem.

Teaching methods appropriate for older children, but not for preschoolers are the focus of this concern. Some examples of this are pressuring preschoolers into rote memorization of math and reading lessons, and teaching two-year-olds to play miniaturized violins or to program computers. Perhaps the real problem is not the methods, but the over-achieving parents who insist that their children excel, regardless of the cost.

If any child ever born qualified for the "superbaby" label, it was Jesus. The angel's revelation to Mary certainly put Him in that category. What a responsibility she must have felt!

It is clear that Mary handled that responsibility wisely. With such a destiny as His, Jesus could easily have fallen prey to vanity or rebelliousness. But Mary became a model for all par-

ents, helping her son grow into mature acceptance of his calling.   —C. R. B.

C. Mary's Question (v. 34)

**34. Then said Mary unto the angel, How
shall this be, seeing I know not a man?**

Quite naturally, Mary was perplexed by Gabriel's statement. She understood the conception and birth process well enough to know that
by the laws of nature she could not bear a child.
Zechariah, who raised a similar question (Luke
1:18), asked out of doubt. Mary asked not because she doubted but for information about
how this would take place.

D. Gabriel's Response (v. 35)

**35. And the angel answered and said unto
her, The Holy Ghost shall come upon thee, and
the power of the Highest shall overshadow
thee: therefore also that holy thing which shall
be born of thee shall be called the Son of God.**

Gabriel's explanation was still mysterious, but
it did assure Mary that what was to happen was
according to God's will and purpose. We today
may know a great deal more about the process of
conception and birth than was known in the
first century. Yet how a single cell can be so
activated as to become a human being still remains a sweet and precious mystery whose answer will not be found in a test tube.

E. God's Work With Elisabeth
(vv. 36, 37)

**36. And, behold, thy cousin Elisabeth, she
hath also conceived a son in her old age; and
this is the sixth month with her, who was called
barren.**

Although Mary was mystified about how she
could become the mother of Jesus, she had no
doubt that it would happen. Gabriel rewarded
her faith by giving her a sign. Elisabeth in her
old age would bear a son. This was a miracle,
although it was not a unique miracle. Hundreds
of years before, God had given Sarah a son in her
old age (Genesis 21:1, 2). From a human point of
view, a virgin bearing a child may seem a
greater miracle than a woman bearing a child in
her old age. But neither miracle could be done
without God's special intervention.

The *King James Version* calls Elisabeth Mary's
cousin. The Greek word does not indicate such a
precise relationship, and so many modern translations render it *kinswoman* or *relative.* While
we cannot be certain about it, this may indicate
that Mary had ancestors both in the tribe of Levi
and in the tribe of Judah. If this was the case, it
would mean that Jesus descended from both the
ruling tribe of Judah and the priestly tribe of

Levi. This fact would underline His dual role as
king and priest.

**37. For with God nothing shall be impos-
sible.**

These words remind us of a similar message
that God brought to Abraham and Sarah in regard to the birth of Isaac (Genesis 18:14). This
verse should not be pushed too far, of course. It
is impossible for God to lie, for example (Hebrews 6:18; Titus 1:2). But nothing that is good
and right is beyond His power.

III. Mary's Submission
(Luke 1:38)

**38. And Mary said, Behold the handmaid of
the Lord; be it unto me according to thy word.
And the angel departed from her.**

Mary was not forced to bear a child against
her will. God knew her heart and knew that she
was ready to do His will, whatever it might be.
But her decision was not without problems. She
certainly knew that she would become the subject of gossip and might even be shunned by
others in her village. She had reason also to believe that Joseph would set aside their betrothal.
To obey this unusual invitation of the Lord
threatened to bring her future crashing down
about her.

Yet she never hesitated a moment. She was the
Lord's servant, whatever He might command.
The Phillips translation puts it vividly: "I belong to the Lord, body and soul." With his mission accomplished, Gabriel left her. No doubt all
kinds of conflicting thoughts swirled through
her mind. While the angel did not state that a
visit to Elisabeth would be appropriate, his
mention of her may have suggested it. We read
later that Mary did make a trip to Judah to visit
her kinswoman.

THE TROUBLE WITH BEING FAVORED

It probably didn't happen, but the story goes
this way: The police had been called to the
scene of a domestic quarrel. They arrived to find
a woman with a gun in her hand weeping over
her husband's prostrate form, crying, "Oh, how
I loved him! Oh, I loved him *so much!*"

A veteran patrolman said to his rookie partner, "I'd rather be loved less and live longer!"

God's love and favor bring responsibility and
sometimes difficulty. When God asks us to do
something significant for Him, it will cost us
something. Mary had to face malicious gossip,
awkward silences when she appeared in a
group, furtive glances and upturned noses.

God may ask us to give up a loved one so we
can later comfort someone else who grieves, or

to struggle through adverse circumstances so we can be an example of faith to those who are spiritually weak. The favor of God may cost us something, but the honor and joy are worth the price, whatever it is.   —C. R. B.

Conclusion

A. "Behold the Handmaid of the Lord"

For two thousand years Christians have argued about the proper place of Mary. The early church apparently did not have this problem. Mary is mentioned in the birth narratives in Matthew and Luke, and then infrequently and briefly in the rest of the four Gospels. She is mentioned one more time (Acts 1:14) and then passes into obscurity. Paul states that God sent forth His Son "made of a woman" (Galatians 4:4), but he does not even mention Mary's name.

None of the other New Testament writers mention her name. Nor do any of them develop a theology concerning her part in God's plan for human redemption. But this did not keep later generations from engaging in all kinds of speculation about her. Increasingly she was mentioned in Christian writings, and by the fifth century some hailed her as the "mother of God." By the Middle Ages she had become the "perpetual virgin" and "co-redemptrix" with Christ. Prayers were lifted up to her as readily as to her Son. As recently as 1950 the pope declared the "assumption of Mary," a doctrine that teaches that Mary did not die but ascended into Heaven.

In reacting against these teachings Protestants often went to the other extreme of reducing Mary almost to a nonentity. She was rarely mentioned except in relation to the birth of Jesus or her presence at the cross. As is often the case, the truth lies between the extremes.

Note that Mary was a virtuous woman. Otherwise God would not have chosen her above all other women to become the bearer of His Son. She was a pious woman: she accepted without any reservations the word of Gabriel. Her words, "Behold, the handmaid of the Lord," epitomize her humble submission to God.

B. A City of Galilee

Nazareth is no longer the remote Galilean village it was when Mary lived there. It is now a city of several thousand, whose economy is greatly enhanced by the multitudes of tourists who throng its streets every year. Local guides are happy to show you the very spot where the angel first appeared to Mary. They can point out the spring that supplied the village with its water, and the humble workshop where Jesus plied his trade.

We are likely to view these various places with the cynical skepticism that we reserve for well-advertised tourist traps. But we ought not to allow our skepticism to blind us to the fact that Mary really did live in Nazareth, and the angel Gabriel did appear to her with the most astounding announcement that a young woman ever heard. Even if we cannot with absolute certainty locate the exact spots where these events occurred, we can affirm without any doubt that they did happen. Christianity is a historical religion grounded on historical facts, and it is thrilling to be able to stand within a few feet of where these events actually happened.

When we consider the village of Nazareth as it was when Mary lived there and when God revealed to her His plan to send His Son to earth, we are inclined to wonder why He did it that way. Accustomed as we are to Hollywood's bright lights and fanfare, we have trouble accepting the fact that God is able to work in such a subdued fashion. In this situation and in many others, we find it hard to accept the fact that God's ways are not our ways and that His ways are past finding out by our human reasoning (Romans 11:33). These events, indeed all aspects of the incarnation, force us to acknowledge that God's ways are not our ways.

C. Let Us Pray

Father, help us understand Your divine Son's birth, so we, like Mary, can say, "Behold the servant of the Lord." Amen.

D. Thought to Remember

"The Word of God, Jesus Christ, became what we are in order to make us what He is."

—Irenaeus

Home Daily Bible Readings

Monday, Dec. 5—God's Promise to a Sinful World (Isaiah 9:2-7)
Tuesday, Dec. 6—God's Promise to a Troubled Woman (Luke 1:26-34)
Wednesday, Dec. 7—Jesus' Promise to Believers (John 14:12-20)
Thursday, Dec. 8—Jesus' Promise to a Penitent Thief (Luke 23:32-43)
Friday, Dec. 9—Jesus' Promise to Abraham's Descendants (Romans 4:13-24)
Saturday, Dec. 10—The Promise of Christ's Return (2 Peter 3:3-14)
Sunday, Dec. 11—God's Promise to Those Who Love Him (James 1:12-18)

Learning by Doing

This page contains an alternate lesson plan emphasizing learning activities. Classes desiring such student involvement will find these suggestions helpful.

Learning Goals

After this lesson, a student should be able to:

1. Contrast Mary's question, "How shall this be?" with Zechariah's question, "Whereby shall I know this?"

2. Illustrate by example that "with God nothing shall be impossible" (Luke 1:37).

3. Explain how Mary's example can encourage Christians today to serve the Lord in difficult situations.

Into the Lesson

Suggest this situation to the students and ask them to respond, either orally or on paper. (This activity is included in the student book.)

Suppose you and a friend are studying the first chapter of Luke. Your friend says, "I don't understand. When Zechariah questioned Gabriel about how he and Elisabeth could have a child in their old age, Gabriel got angry and punished him. When Mary asked how she, a virgin, could have a son, Gabriel just answered the question. Why the difference?"

"How would you answer your friend's questions?"

If you have the students write answers to the question, give them just a few minutes and then discuss the answers together. Be sure the class notices the difference between the two questions. Mary simply asked, "How shall this be?" It was a request for information. Zechariah asked, "How shall I know this?" It was a demand for proof.

Into the Word

The basic questions for the journalist are who, what, when, where, and why. Have the class divide into five groups and ask them all to read the lesson text. Then assign one of these questions to each group. Ask a spokesman for each group to report the group's answer.

When these five questions have been answered, introduce a sixth, Mary's own question, "how?" Have the class consider this one together. How would God bring to pass the promise delivered to Mary on this occasion? Discuss this concept—virgin birth—together. Why is it significant? Is there really enough evidence to believe in the virgin birth of Christ? (Note Matthew's Gospel, the implications of John's prologue, and Isaiah's prophecy.) Have the class

suggest objections to the doctrine and how these objections might be answered. In view of the objections, is it any wonder that Mary asked how it would be accomplished? Discuss, "In what sense are those who raise these objections modern-day kin to Zechariah with his question of doubt?"

Gabriel's statement that Mary was "highly favored" has been a source of controversy for many years—at least since the Reformation! Assign a student to do some research on this and explain in what sense Mary was "favored" and what status Christians should accord her today. (You might share the commentary in this book with the student who receives this assignment.)

The bottom line of this lesson comes in verse 37: "For with God nothing shall be impossible." Write these words at the top of the chalkboard or a large poster. Tell the class, "Our lesson today tells how Jesus' birth illustrates this fact. In what other ways did His life illustrate it?" Make a chart of specific events from the life of Christ that illustrate the truth of this verse.

Into Life

We have said that the bottom line of this lesson is verse 37. That's the bottom line for facts. No single fact is more significant than this: God is able. Period.

The bottom line for action, however, is Mary's response to Gabriel's message: "Behold the handmaid of the Lord; be it unto me according to thy word" (Luke 1:38). Until we adopt that attitude, we will not act with faithfulness to the fact that God is able.

Ask the class to brainstorm some situations that make obeying God difficult or threatening—as it was for Mary to be with child even though she was not married, to appear as though she had broken her vows to her betrothed husband. In what situations have your students found obedience and faithfulness to be difficult?

Distribute cards to the class and ask each student to complete this statement: "Because the Lord is able to do impossible things—even to use me in His service—I will make a special effort to serve Him this week in the following ministry: ...." (If your class uses the student book, you can refer your students to this activity there instead of preparing cards.)

Let's Talk It Over

The questions on this page are designed to encourage review of the lesson Scriptures and to promote discussion of the lesson by the class. The answers provided are only discussion starters. Let your class talk it over from there.

1. Jesus grew up in the ill-regarded town of Nazareth. What does this indicate about our tendency to judge people according to their family background or the community from which they come?

The greatest person who ever lived came out of one of the humblest, least esteemed communities of His time. History is filled with instances in which other men and women have risen from conditions of poverty and obscurity to become people of mighty accomplishments. We know this, and yet we often fail to apply it to specific individuals we encounter. "He comes from a hopeless family background, and he will never amount to anything," we say. "She lives in a neighborhood where girls get into trouble, and she is pretty sure to end up the same way," we declare. But history has proved the vast potential within the human spirit to rise above negative circumstances. And when that human spirit comes under the rule of Jesus Christ, the potential for dynamic change is multiplied.

2. Gabriel announced to Mary that she was highly favored. How is this description also applicable to us?

It may seem that a human being could have no greater honor than to be the mother of God's Son, but Jesus later indicated that an equally great honor was available to all human beings. When a woman cried out to Him, "Blessed is the mother who gave you birth and nursed you," Jesus responded by saying, "Blessed rather are those who hear the word of God and obey it" (Luke 11:27, 28, *New International Version*). We are highly favored in being able to hear the Word of God, the gospel of Jesus Christ. It is an honor we tend to take for granted. It would be well for us to ponder a statement Jesus made to His disciples: "Blessed are the eyes that see what you see. For I tell you that many prophets and kings wanted to see what you see but did not see it, and to hear what you hear but did not hear it" (Luke 10:23, 24, *New International Version*).

3. Mary readily accepted God's will for her as it was revealed to her by Gabriel. Yet she was surely aware of the personal trials it would involve. What does this suggest about our attitude toward trials?

In her later visit with Elisabeth, Mary uttered the words of her famous song that begins with humble praise: "My soul praises the Lord and my spirit rejoices in God my Savior" (Luke 1:46, 47, *New International Version*). This indicates the importance of demonstrating our total acceptance of God's will by praising Him even if there are unpleasant aspects in a situation. Paul reinforces this idea when he tells us to "give thanks in all circumstances, for this is God's will for you in Christ Jesus" (1 Thessalonians 5:18, *New International Version*). It is difficult for us to express gratitude for our painful, frustrating experiences, but we need to acknowledge that God uses the bad as well as the good to draw us to greater faith, commitment, and holiness.

4. In what other ways is Mary an example to us?

First of all, she must have been a woman of faith and good works before Gabriel's visit. While we have no reason to regard her as sinless, she must have been a person of purity and godliness, or God would not have chosen her to be the mother of the Christ. If we want to be used by God to accomplish mighty works, it behooves us also to keep ourselves pure.

A second aspect of Mary's faith was her humility, indicated by her answer to Gabriel: "I am the Lord's servant" (Luke 1:38, *New International Version*). Whatever plans she had made for her life, however much she valued her reputation, she humbly submitted herself to whatever service the Lord had designed for her. We treasure our own plans and goals, and we are often very much concerned with what other people think of us. It is a lofty challenge for us to avoid thinking of ourselves more highly than we ought (see Romans 12:3). But God can work best in us and through us when we view ourselves humbly as His servants.

Finally, we think of Mary as a person of great patience. Think what she must have endured in the days before Joseph learned the truth about the baby she was carrying. But at last her patience was rewarded, as Joseph understood and accepted God's unique role for him. This illustrates how God will work out the dilemmas we face, if we learn to wait patiently for Him.

God's Promise Fulfilled

LESSON SCRIPTURE: Luke 2:1-20.

PRINTED TEXT: Luke 2:1-16.

Luke 2:1-16

1 And it came to pass in those days, that there went out a decree from Caesar Augustus, that all the world should be taxed.

2 (And this taxing was first made when Cyrenius was governor of Syria.)

3 And all went to be taxed, every one into his own city.

4 And Joseph also went up from Galilee, out of the city of Nazareth, into Judea, unto the city of David, which is called Bethlehem, (because he was of the house and lineage of David,)

5 To be taxed with Mary his espoused wife, being great with child.

6 And so it was, that, while they were there, the days were accomplished that she should be delivered.

7 And she brought forth her firstborn son, and wrapped him in swaddling clothes, and laid him in a manger; because there was no room for them in the inn.

8 And there were in the same country shepherds abiding in the field, keeping watch over their flock by night.

9 And, lo, the angel of the Lord came upon them, and the glory of the Lord shone round about them; and they were sore afraid.

10 And the angel said unto them, Fear not: for, behold, I bring you good tidings of great joy, which shall be to all people.

11 For unto you is born this day in the city of David a Saviour, which is Christ the Lord.

12 And this shall be a sign unto you; Ye

shall find the babe wrapped in swaddling clothes, lying in a manger.

13 And suddenly there was with the angel a multitude of the heavenly host praising God, and saying,

14 Glory to God in the highest, and on earth peace, good will toward men.

15 And it came to pass, as the angels were gone away from them into heaven, the shepherds said one to another, Let us now go even unto Bethlehem, and see this thing which is come to pass, which the Lord hath made known unto us.

16 And they came with haste, and found Mary and Joseph, and the babe lying in a manger.

Golden Text: She brought forth her firstborn son, and wrapped him in swaddling clothes, and laid him in a manger; because there was no room for them in the inn.
—Luke 2:7.

Scenes of Love and Compassion
Unit 1: Promise and Expectation
(Lessons 1-4)

Lesson Aims

After this lesson each student should:
1. Have a better understanding of the events surrounding the birth of Jesus.
2. Appreciate more fully the significance of the incarnation in his own life.
3. Be able to relate the account of Jesus' birth to a person who has never heard it before.

Lesson Outline

INTRODUCTION
   A. Communicating With Ants
   B. Lesson Background
I. EVENTS BEFORE THE BIRTH OF JESUS (Luke 2:1-5)
   A. Caesar's Decree (vv. 1-3)
   B. Joseph's Response to the Decree (v. 4, 5)
II. THE BIRTH OF JESUS (Luke 2:6, 7)
   A. The Birth Is at Hand (v. 6)
   B. Jesus' Birth (v. 7)
      A Vacancy Sign
III. ANNOUNCEMENT TO THE SHEPHERDS (Luke 2:8-16)
   A. The Appearance of the Angel (vv. 8, 9)
   B. The Message of the Angel (vv. 10-12)
   C. The Multitude of Angels (vv. 13, 14)
      "'Tis the Season" . . . But for What?
   D. The Shepherds' Response (vv. 15, 16)
CONCLUSION
   A. The "Luck" of Bethlehem
   B. Let Us Pray
   C. Thought to Remember

Display visual 3 from the visuals/learning resources packet and let it remain before the class throughout this session. It is on page 139.

Introduction

A. Communicating With Ants

A Christian and a Deist once were discussing religion as they strolled across a meadow. "Of course I believe in God," insisted the Deist. "He created the world and the laws that govern it and then went away and left it to run according to these laws. God doesn't intervene in the world, and there is no way that He from His lofty and remote position can communicate with man."

Then he stopped and pointed to an anthill. "See that anthill. There is no way that I can possibly communicate with those ants, no matter how much I might want to. The distance between us intellectually is just too great."

"But you could communicate with the ants," insisted the Christian, "if you could become an ant and go down and live among them."

In a sense that is what God did. God is high and holy and lifted up, remote and distant from sinful man. But He sent His Son to come down and be born as a human being, accepting the limitations that such an action involved. As a human being He shared humanity's burden, but even as He bore that burden, He was able to communicate with the human race.

B. Lesson Background

In last week's lesson we studied about Gabriel's announcement to Mary that she would become the mother of God's Son. The intervening verses tell of Mary's three-month visit to Elisabeth, which ended soon before or soon after Elisabeth's son was born. After that birth Zechariah got his voice back and uttered a prophecy about the future work of the child.

I. Events Before the Birth of Jesus (Luke 2:1-5)

A. Caesar's Decree (vv. 1-3)

1. And it came to pass in those days, that there went out a decree from Caesar Augustus, that all the world should be taxed.

Luke has already informed us that Herod was the ruler over Judea (1:5). Now he gives us further information to provide the historical setting for the birth of Jesus. The man called *Caesar Augustus* was actually named Octavius or Octavian. He was the grandnephew of Julius Caesar, who adopted him as his son. After the assassination of Caesar there was a time of turmoil, but in 31 B.C. Octavian emerged as the sole ruler of Rome. In 27 B.C., the Senate conferred upon him the title *Augustus* by which he has come to be known.

The reign of Augustus was the golden age of the Roman Empire. His benevolent rule brought peace and prosperity. God in His infinite wisdom chose this particular time ("the fulness of the time," Galatians 4:4) to send His Son into the world. Augustus certainly acted of his own free will when he ordered the taxation, yet God used this decree to place Mary and Joseph in Bethlehem at the time of Jesus' birth, thus fulfilling the prophecy of Micah 5:2.

The *King James Version* indicates that this decree ordered a tax. Actually, the decree ordered an enrollment or a census, but no doubt the emperor intended to use this for the purpose of levying a tax. *All the world.* The word literally means the inhabited world, but in common practice it had reference to the entire Roman Empire, not the whole world. Like many peoples, the Romans felt anything outside their boundaries was not worth considering.

2. (And this taxing was first made when Cyrenius was governor of Syria.)

Cyrenius is the Greek equivalent of the Latin *Quirinius,* which many modern translations use. Scholars usually date the birth of Jesus between 6 and 4 B.C. This poses a problem because, according to some scholars, Quirinius did not become governor of Syria until A.D. 6 and so he could not have been governor when Jesus was born. Some have seized upon this to question the credibility of Luke as a historian. But in the book of Acts, Luke demonstrates time and again in minute details that he was a careful and an accurate historian. There is some evidence that Quirinius exercised control over Syria at an earlier time. In view of Luke's record, it seems unfair to accuse him of getting the facts wrong. Critics should keep in mind that Luke lived closer to the events than we do, and any errors would have been quickly detected when he wrote the book.

3. And all went to be taxed, every one into his own city.

The usual Roman practice was to count people where they lived. The Jews, on the other hand, were accustomed to enroll their people by tribes and families, and the enrollment usually occurred at the place where the family records were kept. Apparently the Jewish method of enrollment was followed, even though this entailed considerable travel and inconvenience. This practice was one factor that led to Jesus' being born in Bethlehem.

B. Joseph's Response to the Decree (vv. 4, 5)

4. And Joseph also went up from Galilee, out of the city of Nazareth, into Judea, unto the city of David, which is called Bethlehem, (because he was of the house and lineage of David,).

Luke has previously introduced *Joseph,* the espoused of Mary, in 1:27. Matthew tells us that he was a just man who did not want to make Mary a public example when he learned that she was pregnant (Matthew 1:19). He was also a law-abiding citizen, willing to make the long journey to Bethlehem to register. Many in Galilee revolted rather than submit to the enrollment, and that province remained a hotbed of insurrection.

The trip from Nazareth to Bethlehem was ninety miles or more. Because the Jews wanted to avoid Samaria, they often traveled many miles out of their way, taking a route to the east of the Jordan River. This added to the distance that they had to travel, giving us an example of how expensive prejudice can be.

The name *Bethlehem* means "house of bread." The town was acknowledged in the Old Testament times as the city of David (1 Samuel 20:6). Since Joseph belonged to *the house and lineage of David,* it was there that he had to go for the enrollment.

5. To be taxed with Mary his espoused wife, being great with child.

We may wonder why *Mary* accompanied Joseph on this long trip in the advanced stages of her pregnancy. Such a trip was certainly uncomfortable and even dangerous for her. Several commentators suggest that Joseph brought her along to protect her from the slander she might have been exposed to in Nazareth had she remained there. Others believe that she too had to be enrolled in Bethlehem because she was of the house of David.

II. The Birth of Jesus (Luke 2:6, 7)

A. The Birth Is at Hand (v. 6)

6. And so it was, that, while they were there, the days were accomplished that she should be delivered.

We have no way of determining the exact date of Jesus' birth. For many centuries churches in the West have observed it on December 25, but many of the Eastern churches still celebrate it on January 6. The exact date is really not important. Otherwise, Luke would have given it.

B. Jesus' Birth (v. 7)

7. And she brought forth her firstborn son, and wrapped him in swaddling clothes, and laid him in a manger; because there was no room for them in the inn.

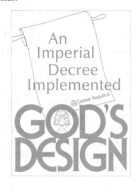

An Imperial Decree Implemented

GOD'S DESIGN

visual 3

How to Say It

ACTIUM. Ak-*she*-um or *Ak*-te-um.
CAESAR AUGUSTUS. *See*-zur Aw-*gus*-tus.
CLEOPATRA. *Klee*-o-*pa*-trah.
CYRENIUS. Sye-*ree*-nee-us.
GALILEE. *Gal*-uh-lee.
JUDEA. Joo-*dee*-uh.
NAZARETH. *Naz*-uh-reth.
OCTAVIAN. Ok-tay-vee-*an*.
OCTAVIUS. Ok-*tay*-vee-us.
QUIRINIUS. Kwih-*rin*-e-us.
SAMARIA. Suh-*meh*-ri-uh.
SEPTUAGINT. Sep-*tyoo*-uh-jint.
SYRIA. *Sear*-ee-uh.

The birth of Jesus is related in one brief sentence. Later stories of the birth add miraculous elements, but there is nothing in Luke's record to indicate that the birth was anything but normal. Scholars differ about the significance of *her firstborn son*. Some feel that since the first son enjoyed special privileges, this designation was used to show that Jesus would be the recipient of special blessings from the Heavenly Father. Others think that the term is used to show that Jesus was but the first of several of Mary's children. (See Matthew 12:46, 47; 13:55, 56.) Actually, both of these opinions may be right. Jesus was indeed very special and Mary did have other children, the younger half-brothers and half-sisters of Jesus.

Mary wrapped the newborn baby in swaddling clothes, which she probably had brought along for the occasion. Binding a baby up tightly seems strange to us, but it was the common practice in that day. Then she *laid him in a manger*. We ordinarily think of this as a trough of wood or stone in which food is placed for animals such as cattle or donkeys. This may seem rather shocking to us, but properly prepared, a manger would be a quite comfortable crib.

Because a manger was used as a bed, we suppose Mary and Joseph were sheltered in a stable. Why were they there? Luke tells us that there was *no room for them in the inn*. Apparently many people had come to Bethlehem to enroll for the taxation and had overcrowded the housing facilities, both private homes and public inns. The travelers had to camp where they could. By the middle of the second century it was believed that their stable was a cave, and eventually a succession of churches was built over the spot. The present church, the Church of the Nativity, goes back to the time of Emperor Justinian in the sixth century. Of course we have no way of knowing the exact spot where Jesus was born, but these legends will persist as long as they enhance the tourist trade.

A VACANCY SIGN

On Nob Hill in San Francisco stands one of the city's fabled luxury hotels. Anyone with three hundred dollars or so can get a room for a night there. But if you have about twenty friends, and the same number of thousand-dollar bills, you can rent the whole penthouse floor for twenty-four hours.

Included in the package are eight suites with spectacular views of the city, the finest international cuisine the hotel can provide, violinists and a pianist to entertain you, and even a quartet of Rolls-Royce limousines to bring your group to the hotel. What more could you ask for, except perhaps breakfast in bed? Well, you can have that too.

The stable in Bethlehem was not exactly Holiday Inn, nor even Motel 6. But it had a vacancy that night when it was needed, and the travelers were not too proud to accept the privacy of its humble shelter.

The baby born in that stable continues to accept whatever shelter is offered Him: He will come in and share the humble shanty of the family that lives "on the wrong side of the tracks", or the cardboard-and-rag shelter of the drifter, or the comfortable warmth of a suburban bungalow. He will gladly share the penthouse suite on Nob Hill if He is invited. But He enters only where He sees the VACANCY sign. —C. R. B.

III. Announcement to the Shepherds (Luke 2:8-16)

A. The Appearance of the Angel (vv. 8, 9)

8, 9. And there were in the same country shepherds abiding in the field, keeping watch over their flock by night. And, lo, the angel of the Lord came upon them, and the glory of the Lord shone round about them; and they were sore afraid.

Although shepherds were generally looked down upon, God found among them men of devout hearts who were ready to receive His highest revelation. Sheep and shepherds can still be seen on the hills surrounding Bethlehem. The winters are relatively mild in southern Palestine, and so it was common practice for shepherds to remain out in the fields with their flocks. At night the sheep were brought into a sheepfold or protected area. The shepherds took turns protecting the sleeping animals.

Suddenly this tranquil scene was shattered by the appearance of the angel of the Lord, whose glory must have lighted up the area. Although this angel is not identified, it is not unreasonable to suppose that he was Gabriel, who had already appeared to Zechariah and Mary (1:19, 26). The appearance of this Heavenly being struck fear into the hearts of the shepherds.

B. The Message of the Angel (vv. 10-12)

10. And the angel said unto them, Fear not: for, behold, I bring you good tidings of great joy, which shall be to all people.

Fear not! How often Scriptures have reported God's angelic beings using these words to calm the quaking hearts of those to whom they appeared! It is quite normal for a sinful human being to quail before the presence of a Heavenly messenger. But in this case there was no need to fear. The message was a joyous one, and not for them alone but for *all people.* This expression ordinarily was used to refer to all the people of Israel, and the shepherds no doubt thought of it in this sense. We today understand it to mean the true Israel, all those who surrender their lives to Jesus Christ.

11. For unto you is born this day in the city of David a Saviour, which is Christ the Lord.

Here is the good news. That very day, perhaps in that very hour, *a Saviour* had been born. In the Old Testament, God is often portrayed as the Savior of Israel. Now once again He was manifesting His saving power. The angel then further identified this *Saviour.* He *is Christ the Lord.* The designation *Christ* means one who has been anointed, an act used to set apart publicly those who served as prophets, priests, and kings. *Christ* is the Greek equivalent of the Hebrew *Messiah.*

This *Saviour* is also called *Lord.* The word used here, *Kurios,* is the Greek word that was often used to designate God in the Septuagint, the Greek translation of the Old Testament. Since the shepherds would in this situation likely understand the word in this sense, we can see that the angel was implying that the baby born in Bethlehem was divine.

12. And this shall be a sign unto you; Ye shall find the babe wrapped in swaddling clothes, lying in a manger.

Miraculous signs were often used by the messengers of God as credentials to the validity of their message, but this sign was not miraculous. It was a normal practice for a newborn child to be wrapped in swaddling clothes. It was unusual, of course, for a child to be born in a stable and placed in a manger, but it was not miraculous. The sign was certainly paradoxical. The

angel had spoken of a Savior, God's Anointed, and yet He was born in most humble surroundings.

C. The Multitude of Angels (vv. 13, 14)

13, 14. And suddenly there was with the angel a multitude of the heavenly host praising God, and saying, Glory to God in the highest, and on earth peace, good will toward men.

The Heavenly messenger was joined by a vast angelic host. The word translated *host* is a military term and could very well be translated *army.* If the appearance of one angel had brought fear to the hearts of the shepherds, what would their response have been had this whole vast army appeared first without any warning? But what an unusual army this was! It came not to bring war but to announce peace!

While Luke does not say that the Heavenly host sang their message, it is not unreasonable to suppose that they did. The joyous nature of their message was certainly appropriate to be set to music. The first phrase of their song offers praise to God, an outpouring of adoration for the Almighty that was as natural for the Heavenly host as breathing was for the human race. The second phrase proclaims peace to the world. Since the first sin, man had been at war with God, but now an end of hostilities was possible. The third phrase poses a bit of a problem. The translation that has been made familiar to us by the *King James Version* may not be the best. The *New International Version* renders this *peace to men on whom his favor rests;* the *New American Standard* has *peace among men with whom He is pleased.* This indicates that God has not promised peace indiscriminately to the whole world, but that peace is available to those who gain God's favor through their obedience to Him.

"'Tis the Season" . . . But for What?

"God-bashing," as someone has called it, has gained wide popularity. In Fresno, California, in November, 1986, the Salvation Army had posted public service ads on city buses, calling attention to its charitable work.

"Sharing is caring . . . God bless you," was the slogan on the ads. But after receiving complaints from only two people, the city attorney ordered the signs taken down. In other communities, complaints have been registered against nativity scenes or the playing of carols in public places. Of course, the objection is always raised in ostensible concern for protecting the First Amendment.

If the baby Jesus had been born in modern America, the angels would probably have been slapped with an injunction to quit violating someone's First Amendment rights!

Why is it primarily the Christian faith that arouses such opposition? Could it be because there is no peace in the hearts of those who object to observing Christmas except for its commercial value? He came to bring peace to those who please God. We should not think it strange that His presence arouses anger in those who do not!

It is unthinkable that Christians should force their faith on others. But we must also watch to see that our freedoms are not trampled on by those who would twist the constitutional guarantee of "freedom *of* religion" to mean "freedom *from* religion"!   —C. R. B.

D. The Shepherd's Response (vv. 15, 16)

15. And it came to pass, as the angels were gone away from them into heaven, the shepherds said one to another, Let us now go even unto Bethlehem, and see this thing which is come to pass, which the Lord hath made known unto us.

Once the Heavenly choir had completed its song, it returned to Heaven. The shepherds did not tarry long, but quickly decided to see for themselves what had happened in Bethlehem. They knew full well that they had not been dreaming; and set out to prove it.

16. And they came with haste, and found Mary and Joseph, and the babe lying in a manger.

Luke does not give any details about the shepherds visit to the stable, and so several questions remain unanswered. Did some of them remain behind to guard the flock? Did the angel give them more explicit instructions about how to find the stable? How long before they found it?

Since Bethlehem was a small town, finding the stable probably did not take long. It is likely that they reached it while it was still night. When they arrived, they found the situation exactly as the angel had told them.

Conclusion

A. The "Luck" of Bethlehem

Bret Harte in his famous short story, "The Luck of Roaring Camp," tells of the birth of a baby in a rude mining camp in the West. The miners gave the baby the unlikely name of Luck. The rough miners were touched by the baby, and the whole tenor of the camp changed. Violence and rowdyism subsided. People became more considerate of one another, and the camp prospered. The miners attributed their change of fortune to the baby and worked diligently to

care for him. Then the baby was killed by a flash flood that swept through the camp. With the baby gone, the fortunes of the camp took a turn for the worse, and it soon became a ghost town.

In a way Jesus may seem to have resembled Luck of Roaring Camp. His coming did bring joy and excitement to the shepherds and later to the Wise-men from the East. But in other, more important ways, the baby Jesus was quite different.

First, Jesus' birth in Bethlehem was not an accident. From the foundation of the world God had a plan to send His Son into the world to save the human race from sin. He called Abraham out of Ur to become the father of the Hebrew people, through whom would come the Savior. Seven hundred years before His birth, the prophets foretold that Immanuel, the Son of God, would be born of a virgin in the city of David. God worked through the Hebrew people for hundreds of years to bring all these things to pass. He used Caesar's census to bring Joseph and Mary to Bethlehem for Jesus' birth.

One other very important difference should be noted. The blessings did not end when Jesus died. In fact, just the opposite was the case. In His death He purchased our freedom from sin, and so as a result the blessings have multiplied and spread world wide. Jesus was certainly more than the "Luck" of Bethlehem.

B. Let Us Pray

Father, we thank You for sending Your Son to be born among us, to live among us, and to die for us. In His name we pray. Amen.

C. Thought to Remember

"God clothed Himself in man's vile flesh so that he might be weak enough to suffer woe."
     —JOHN DONNE

Learning by Doing

This page contains an alternate lesson plan emphasizing learning activities. Classes desiring such student involvement will find these suggestions helpful.

Learning Goals

After this lesson, students should be able to:
1. Retell the Christmas story in Luke.
2. Contrast the humble beginning of Jesus' earthly life with the modern drive for luxury and convenience.
3. Suggest some effective ways to spread the good news about Jesus.

Into the Lesson

Ask your students what Christmas programs they have seen in the past week or so. Ask how well those shows portrayed "the true meaning of Christmas." Most of the popular Christmas shows display good will toward others, but very few display the love and grace of God that really are the true meaning of Christmas. (This activity is included in the student book.)

Into the Word

Divide into groups of four to six. Give each one of the following assignments.

In one group, assign one person to be a reporter, another to be Caesar Augustus, another Mary, and one to three others to be shepherds. The reporter will interview the others about the events surrounding Jesus' birth. The characters will base their responses on Luke 2:1-20.

In another group, ask the students to work together to write a paraphrase of Luke 2:1-20.

A third group can work together to write a drama portraying the events of Luke 2:1-20.

If you have more than three groups, assign the same task to more than one group, or think of different ways to get other groups into the text.

After several minutes, let each group present its work to the class. This will give the students a general understanding of the passage. Then they can look at some of the particulars.

Either in the small groups or as a whole class, discuss the following questions. (See the commentary section of this book to help you explain any of these to the students. These questions are listed in the student book.)

1. What was the "taxing" by Augustus? Why do some translations call it a census?

2. Who was Cyrenius (Quirinius)? What historical problem is connected to Luke's naming him?

3. What was the "inn" mentioned? Why was there no room there?

4. Do you think Joseph and Mary lodged in the stable because of someone's hard-heartedness or because of someone's generosity?

5. How do you think Joseph and Mary felt about being in the stable? Do you suppose it was as repulsive to them as spending a night in a barn would be to most of us today?

6. What is the significance of the term *firstborn* in connection with Jesus' birth?

7. What were swaddling clothes?

8. How were shepherds viewed in that day? Why do you suppose God chose them to be the first to hear about the birth of His Son?

9. What did the shepherds do after the angels left?

10. What did the shepherds do after seeing Jesus?

Into Life

Ask students to list as many items as they can think of that are called "instant" (like instant coffee or instant replay). Then add a list of products that are designed to save time or work (like microwave ovens). It will not be hard to point out that we like luxury and convenience.

Let each student rate himself on his acceptance of this popular mindset. Use a scale of 1 to 10, on which 1 means a person is not at all interested in convenience and 10 means one is so consumed by the quest for convenience that spiritual growth is blocked.

How would the students rate Joseph an Mary? How would they rate God himself, who arranged for His Son to be born in a stable?

This is not to suggest that convenience items are evil in themselves. Discuss how one can keep such things in balance with spirituality and serving the Lord.

Point out that one aspect of serving the Lord is sharing what we know about Jesus. The quest for convenience and ease can be a handicap in that. Discuss the following:

1. How can we share the good news about Christ in new and creative ways so that people we come in contact with will listen and come to faith in Him?

2. How can we break through social barriers to share the news?

Ask students to complete this sentence: "Because I love the Lord more than personal comfort or convenience, this week I will...."

Let's Talk It Over

*The questions on this page are designed to encourage review of the lesson
Scriptures and to promote discussion of the lesson by the class. The answers
provided are only discussion starters. Let your class talk it over from there.*

**1. God used Caesar Augustus and his decree.
Does He still use human rulers? If so, how?**

It may appear that many world leaders are
governing through violence and deceit and are
therefore far removed from the divine influence.
Still God may be using them to chasten "Christian" nations as He used the rulers of Assyria
and Babylon to discipline Old Testament Israel.
We are commanded to pray for earthly rulers (1
Timothy 2:1, 2). When we do this, we should
consider what their policies and actions may
signify to us. If they are meant to discipline us,
we should pray that we will have the wisdom to
accept and apply such discipline. If they serve
to spur us to speak out and act on behalf of justice and compassion, then let us pray that God
will guide our response.

**2. Joseph did his part faithfully and well,
though in the background. Do you see any people like that in the Church?**

The church has many faithful workers in the
background: the ladies who prepare the Communion emblems and assist with baptismal services; the men who quietly take care of maintenance chores; those individuals who sing in the
choir, but never get the solos; the members who
serve on committees, but never occupy the
prominent role of chairperson; and many more.
Joseph's role, though less prominent, was nevertheless of tremendous importance. And the "Joseph's" of today make an indispensable contribution to the work of the church.

**3. The lesson writer raises the question as to
why Mary, so close to the time of her delivery,
made the difficult journey with Joseph to Bethlehem. He offers two possible answers, but can
you think of others?**

He mentions that Joseph may have wanted to
protect Mary from slanderous talk in Nazareth,
and he further notes that she also may have been
required to enroll at Bethlehem. But Mary knew
her son was to be the Christ (Luke 1:31-33). Did
she also know that the Christ would be born in
Bethlehem? (Micah 5:2). Young women did not
receive as much training in the Scriptures as
young men did, but they heard sermons and discussions in the synagogue. The Jews were aware
of the significance of Micah's prophecy (see

Matthew 2:3-6), and Mary's piety would have
made her alert to grasp any Scriptural truths
made available to her.

**4. Many decry the fact that there was no
room for Jesus in the inn of Bethlehem. Is there
an element of hypocrisy in this?**

If we are concerned about the accommodations in Bethlehem, should we not be even more
concerned about making room for Jesus in our
homes, in our jobs, in our recreation, in our financial plans, and in every other area of our
lives? Do we sing with Emily E. S. Elliott, "O
come to my heart, Lord Jesus; there is room in
my heart for Thee"?

**5. The angels announced to the shepherds
that Jesus had come to bring peace on earth.
How does the world regard this promise, and
how can we lead them into a better understanding of it?**

In our troubled world, some people ridicule
the idea that Jesus can bring peace. Others expect Him to give peace to everybody, good and
bad. We need to emphasize Scriptures that show
that Jesus' peace is related to His cross. Colossians 1:20 points out that peace is made
"through the blood of his cross." In Hebrews
13:20 we read of the God of peace working
"through the blood of the everlasting covenant."
With such an emphasis we can make clear that
Jesus offers peace to those who avail themselves
of the benefits provided through His shed blood.

**6. The angels' message spurred the shep-
herds to go into Bethlehem to investigate
Christ's birth for themselves. How can *we* motivate people to investigate the claims of Jesus
Christ?**

Whether the angels sang the words of Luke
2:14 or not, they certainly gave the message
with enthusiasm. The observation that "enthusiasm is contagious" still holds true. If we can
demonstrate with our words and acts that we are
excited about Jesus Christ, people will be drawn
to ponder the source of that excitement. Then
we need to be, as Peter exhorts us, "ready always to give an answer to every man that asketh
you a reason of the hope that is in you" (1 Peter
3:15).

God's Promise Celebrated

LESSON SCRIPTURE: Luke 2:21-40.

PRINTED TEXT: Luke 2:25-38.

Luke 2:25-38

25 And, behold, there was a man in Jerusalem, whose name was Simeon; and the same man was just and devout, waiting for the consolation of Israel: and the Holy Ghost was upon him.

26 And it was revealed unto him by the Holy Ghost, that he should not see death, before he had seen the Lord's Christ.

27 And he came by the Spirit into the temple: and when the parents brought in the child Jesus, to do for him after the custom of the law,

28 Then took he him up in his arms, and blessed God, and said,

29 Lord, now lettest thou thy servant depart in peace, according to thy word:

30 For mine eyes have seen thy salvation,

31 Which thou hast prepared before the face of all people;

32 A light to lighten the Gentiles, and the glory of thy people Israel.

33 And Joseph and his mother marveled at those things which were spoken of him.

34 And Simeon blessed them, and said unto Mary his mother, Behold, this child is set for the fall and rising again of many in Israel; and for a sign which shall be spoken against;

35 (Yea, a sword shall pierce through thy own soul also;) that the thoughts of many hearts may be revealed.

36 And there was one Anna, a prophetess, the daughter of Phanuel, of the tribe of Asher: she was of a great age, and had lived with a husband seven years from her virginity;

37 And she was a widow of about fourscore and four years, which departed not from the temple, but served God with fastings and prayers night and day.

38 And she coming in that instant gave thanks likewise unto the Lord, and spake of him to all them that looked for redemption in Jerusalem.

Golden Text: Mine eyes have seen thy salvation, which thou hast prepared before the face of all people.—Luke 2:30, 31.

Scenes of Love and Compassion
Unit 1: Promise and Expectation
(Lessons 1-4)

Lesson Aims

As a result of studying this lesson each student should be able to:

1. Identify Simeon and Anna and understand how their lives touched the life of Jesus.

2. Have a growing appreciation for the conflicting emotions that Mary must have experienced when she and Joseph took the baby Jesus to the temple.

3. Suggest ways that older persons can contribute to the spiritual growth of younger persons.

Lesson Outline

INTRODUCTION
   A. Born Under the Law
   B. Lesson Background
I. THE TESTIMONY OF SIMEON (Luke 2:25-35)
   A. Simeon's Identity (v. 25)
   B. His Vigil for the Christ (v. 26)
   C. His Meeting With the Christ (vv. 27, 28)
     No Presents for Christmas
   D. His Consolation Realized (vv. 29-32)
   E. The Response of Mary and Joseph (v. 33)
   F. His Blessing and Prediction (vv. 34, 35)
II. THE TESTIMONY OF ANNA (Luke 2:36-38)
   A. Anna's Identity (vv. 36, 37)
   B. Her Message (v. 38)
CONCLUSION
   A. People With a Mission
   B. Let Us Pray
   C. Thought to Remember

Display visual 4 from the visuals/learning resources packet and let it remain before the class throughout this session. It is shown on page 149.

Introduction

A. Born Under the Law

From time to time one hears a person criticize all religious ceremonies as "empty ritual." The church also comes under criticism as an "outmoded institution that no longer meets the needs of our day." Persons who do like to attend church regularly, especially if they also attend Sunday evening and midweek services, are looked upon as "overly pious" or perhaps even as "fanatics."

These same critics may, on the other hand, have nothing but praise for Jesus. They hail Him as a great teacher. They applaud the example of sacrificial love and service He set for us. They extoll His moral standards as the highest the world has ever known. Yet in all of this the critics fail to see the contradictions in their position. Jesus was born under the law (Galatians 4:4). Mary and Joseph, who were devout Jews, lived up to the regulations and rituals of that law. Jesus himself followed the example they had set. While He rejected some of the manmade teachings and practices of the religious teachers of His day, He nevertheless was faithful to the teachings of the Old Testament.

Granted, religious rituals may become empty and meaningless, observed only out of habit. And on rare occasions there may arise a person who really is a religious fanatic. But these situations do not have to be, as the examples of Mary, Joseph, and Jesus illustrate. Our lesson deals with an occasion when they took Jesus to the temple in observance of one of those rituals.

B. Lesson Background

Last week's lesson closed with the visit of the shepherds to Mary and the baby Jesus in the manger. They then left the mother and Son and went out to tell others about their experiences that night. Mary continued to turn over in her own mind what all these things meant.

After eight days, Jesus was circumcised in keeping with the Old Testament law (Leviticus 12:3). At that time He was also officially named. Both Mary and Joseph had already been told by the angel that His name was to be Jesus.

According to the Jewish law, a woman was considered ceremonially unclean for forty days after the birth of a son. During that time she was not permitted to attend religious services. At the conclusion of this forty-day period, Mary and Joseph, taking Jesus with them, went up to Jerusalem to the temple, where Mary offered a sacrifice for her purification. According to the law the offering was to consist of a yearling lamb and a young pigeon or turtledove; but in the case of poverty, a woman could offer two doves or two pigeons (Leviticus 12:6-8). The fact that Mary offered a pair of birds attests to the poverty of Joseph and his family.

On this same visit to the temple, Jesus was presented to God. This ceremony was based on the Old Testament teaching that every firstborn was considered holy to the Lord (Exodus 13:2). Joseph's attention to these ceremonies is clear evidence of his pious commitment to the law. The presence of the family at the temple for this occasion set the stage for today's lesson.

I. The Testimony of Simeon
(Luke 2:25-35)

A. Simeon's Identity (v. 25)

25. And, behold, there was a man in Jerusalem, whose name was Simeon; and the same man was just and devout, waiting for the consolation of Israel: and the Holy Ghost was upon him.

The Scriptures do not tell us very much about *who* Simeon was, but they do tell us *what* he was. He was *just and devout*. The term *just* may refer to his relationship with his fellow men, while the term *devout* describes his relationship with God. Although the Scriptures do not say that he was an old man, we get the impression that he was well advanced in years.

The situation was not good at that time in Judea. That little nation was under the domination of mighty Rome, who permitted the cruel and oppressive Herod the Great to rule over it. An arrogant and corrupt priesthood controlled the temple, while the legalistic and often hypocritical Pharisees provided religious leadership outside the capital. Taxes were high, and insurrections seemed always to be brewing. Yet in the midst of the most corrupt situation, God has a way of calling men to rise above it. In the days before the flood, the thought of every person was to do evil, and yet God found a Noah. The sons of Jacob were a sorry lot indeed, and yet there was a Joseph.

Simeon was one of those persons who rose above his surroundings. He was one who waited *for the consolation of Israel*—the salvation that the Messiah would bring when He came. To sustain him in his faith, he had received a special blessing from the Holy Spirit. Although Pentecost ushered in the age of the Holy Spirit, that does not mean that the Spirit could not act prior to Pentecost.

B. His Vigil for the Christ (v. 26)

26. And it was revealed unto him by the Holy Ghost, that he should not see death, before he had seen the Lord's Christ.

The Holy Spirit had revealed to Simeon that he would be permitted to see the Christ before he died. We are not told how this revelation came. It might have been through a dream or a vision, or it could have come by a direct message combined with the Scriptures.

NO PRESENTS FOR CHRISTMAS

It was just a couple of days before Christmas and the shopping mall was filled with people doing their last minute shopping. While carols extolled "peace on earth" over the public address system, crowds rustled through the mall with their packages.

One weary shopper sat down on a bench in the midst of the hubbub. He shook himself out of his stupor when he heard the words, *"That's why you ain't gettin' no presents for Christmas!"* He looked up in startled amusement to see two brothers, about eight and six years old, disappearing into the crowd.

Judging from the turmoil the world was in at the time Christ was born, one would not have expected a "Christmas present" such as Simeon had been promised. But God's promise that he would see the Messiah was far more reliable than the taunting remark of an older brother regarding a visit from Santa Claus.

The world can tease us, holding out a glimmer of hope for peace on earth and then withholding the blessing as we grasp for it. But God's promise to Simeon was fulfilled, and the giving of that first "Christmas present" has provided us all with the means to become the people we were supposed to be when God created us.

—C. R. B.

C. His Meeting With the Christ (vv. 27, 28)

27, 28. And he came by the Spirit into the temple: and when the parents brought in the child Jesus, to do for him after the custom of the law, then took he him up in his arms, and blessed God, and said.

Simeon didn't just happen to be in the temple. He had been directed to go there by the Holy Spirit. And as he made his way to the temple, he must have realized that something special was in store for him. It is likely that the meeting with the babe and His parents occurred in the outer court of the temple or in the court of women, because Mary would not have been permitted to go beyond the court of women.

Mary and Joseph had brought Jesus to the temple to present Him there in fulfillment of the law. It is likely that other parents with their children were also there. The Holy Spirit must have directed Simeon to the proper child. We can imagine the surprise of Mary and Joseph as this total stranger approached them, then took the baby in his arms and began to praise God.

D. His Consolation Realized (vv. 29-32)

29-32. Lord, now lettest thou thy servant depart in peace, according to thy word: for mine eyes have seen thy salvation, which thou hast prepared before the face of all people; a light to lighten the Gentiles, and the glory of thy people Israel.

In his ecstasy Simeon raised his voice in a hymn of praise. The word translated *Lord* in this verse is not the word usually used to address God. Rather it is the word from which our word *despot* comes. It suggests the idea of a sovereign master or owner. Simeon referred to himself as a slave who was ready to depart or be released because his goal had been achieved. He had seen the Lord's Christ (v. 26), and so there was no reason for this life to detain him any longer.

With the eyes of faith, Simeon was able to see in this baby the salvation God had promised to His people. We have no idea what kind of a Messiah Simeon had envisioned. Perhaps he had hoped for a military conqueror who would lead His people to cast off the despised yoke of the Romans. But if Simeon had anticipated a Messiah for Israel alone, verses 31 and 32 indicate that he had received an entirely different revelation. The Messiah's salvation had been *prepared before the face of all people.* In these words Simeon went well beyond the narrow Jewish nationalism. Led by the Holy Spirit, he was able to see what most others had missed in the Old Testament prophecies. Again and again in the course of human history men have laid exclusive claim to God, reserving Him for their own tribe, nation, or race. Such arrogance flies in the face of God's plan for human redemption of the world.

In verse 32, Simeon reiterates this great truth. God's salvation, mentioned in verse 30, will become a *light to lighten the Gentiles.* The idea is that the Gentiles have lived in darkness. Now that darkness will be driven away by the light of salvation. This salvation, on the other hand, will be the *glory of thy people Israel.* Israel enjoyed a covenant relationship with God that the Gentiles did not have. They had selfishly thought that this covenant was strictly for their benefit. But now they would realize their true glory when through them God's salvation would come to all nations just as He had promised when He first established the covenant with Abraham (Genesis 12:1-3).

E. The Response of Mary and Joseph
(v. 33)

33. And Joseph and his mother marveled at those things which were spoken of him.

The better manuscripts have *his father* instead of *Joseph.* In the legal sense Joseph was the father of Jesus. Luke had already clearly stated that Jesus was conceived of a virgin (1:34, 35), and so he had no reason to suppose that anyone would misunderstand the term *father* as he used it here. Yet some modern commentators have used this verse unreasonably to deny the virgin birth.

How to Say It

ASER. *A*-ser.
ASHER. *Ash*-er.
PENUEL. Pe-*nu*-el.
PHANUEL. Fuh-*nyoo*-el.
SIMEON. *Sim*-ee-un.

Mary and Joseph may have been surprised at Simeon's words for any of several reasons. The very fact that a total stranger had approached them and spoken to them as he did was enough to cause surprise. Then the fact that Jesus would be a Savior for Gentiles as well as Jews would also have occasioned surprise. Though they had experienced many strange and unusual things during the past few months, each new incident brought new wonderment. What next? they must have thought.

F. His Blessing and Prediction
(vv. 34, 35)

34. And Simeon blessed them, and said unto Mary his mother, Behold, this child is set for the fall and rising again of many in Israel; and for a sign which shall be spoken against.

Once the parents had recovered from their surprise, Simeon pronounced a blessing upon them. Perhaps it was in the form of a prayer, asking God to bless them and protect them.

Simeon followed his blessing with a somber prophetic note: *this child is set for the fall and rising again of many in Israel.* The language suggests a stone that is placed so it is a stumbling block to some and a stepping stone to others. The stone remains the same. It is the people's response to the stone that determines their fate. Some fall over it; others rise to new heights. (The word *again* is not necessary in the translation.)

Some understand this prediction in a different way. They think the same persons fall and rise again. When they first approach the stone, their pride leads them to stumble and fall. But once they have been humbled, the stone gives them the power to rise to new heights. The latter part of the verse seems to argue against this interpretation, however. The child will be *a sign which shall be spoken against.* Those who stumble and fall do so because they are unwilling to accept the sign.

35. (Yea, a sword shall pierce through thy own soul also;) that the thoughts of many hearts may be revealed.

Simeon then uttered a prophecy specifically for Mary. A sword would pierce her soul: she would suffer many griefs because of the life and ministry of her Son. How painfully that prophecy was fulfilled some thirty-three years later when she stood at the foot of the cross and watched Him die! (John 19:25). But there were other times when she must have felt anguish. She was certainly upset when Jesus at the age of twelve remained behind in the temple (Luke 2:48). And she must have been worried when Jesus was opposed and she went with her other sons to interrupt His ministry and take Him home (Mark 3:21, 31-35).

The latter part of verse 35 refers back to verse 34. The ministry of Jesus would force men to respond either for Him or against Him. God already knew the thoughts of men's hearts even though they kept them hidden from their fellow men. But with Jesus teaching among them, people would have to choose sides. Neutrality would be impossible. Some three decades later, perhaps on the very spot where Simeon stood to utter his prophecy, it would be fulfilled. Some would believe in Jesus; but others, including the religious leaders, would reject Him and cause Him to be crucified. Thus the thoughts of both groups would be revealed.

II. The Testimony of Anna
(Luke 2:36-38)

A. Anna's Identity (vv. 36, 37)

36, 37. And there was one Anna, a prophetess, the daughter of Phanuel, of the tribe of Asher: she was of a great age, and had lived with a husband seven years from her virginity; and she was a widow of about fourscore and four years, which departed not from the temple, but served God with fastings and prayers night and day.

Mary and Joseph had yet another surprise after Simeon completed his prophecy. This surprise came in the person of *Anna*, called here *a prophetess*. Of her prophesying we know only what is recorded here.

Anna is further identified as the daughter of *Phanuel*, of whom we know only that he belonged to the tribe of Aser or *Asher*. When the promised land had been divided among the tribes, Asher had been assigned to an area along the Mediterranean coast north of Mount Carmel. Although many of the people of this northern tribe had been carried away by the Assyrians, they had not completely lost their identity.

Anna was *of a great age.* Just how old is not entirely clear. She may have been eighty-four years old, or she may have been a widow for eighty-four years. If she had married as early as sixteen and had been married seven years before

visual 4

GOD'S PROMISES GIVE MOTIVATION AND MEANING FOR LIFE

she became a widow, then she would have been one hundred seven years old—of great age indeed! Luke says that she *departed not from the temple*, which may mean that she actually lived in some part of the temple complex. Luke may have meant, however, that she served constantly in the temple. Her sincere spiritual commitment is evidenced in her daily and nightly fastings and prayers.

B. Her Message (v. 38)

38. And she coming in that instant gave thanks likewise unto the Lord, and spake of him to all them that looked for redemption in Jerusalem.

Anna arrived just as Simeon was completing his message. Whether she heard the conclusion of his prophecy or whether she spoke independently of him we are not told. Her heart was filled with gratitude, and she immediately gave thanks openly and publicly. Luke's description seems to indicate that people had gathered about Simeon, and Anna took the opportunity to speak to them. Probably her inspired message, like Simeon's, was that this baby was the promised Messiah. This struck a responsive chord in the listeners who were looking for Him to bring *redemption in Jerusalem.*

The verses that follow tell how Mary and Joseph returned to Galilee. Obviously Luke is giving us an abbreviated account of this period in Jesus' life. Matthew gives us more details, telling about the flight to Egypt to escape the wrath of Herod (Matthew 2:13-23). After Herod's death the parents were able to take Jesus back to Nazareth, where he "grew" and was "filled with wisdom."

Conclusion

A. People With a Mission

Simeon was a man with a mission. He had been promised by the Holy Spirit that he would not see death until he had seen the Christ. We don't know when Simeon had received this revelation; but his mission was to wait for the Savior and perhaps to encourage others to wait for Him. That mission was the sustaining force in his life. It sustained him because it gave meaning to his life.

All of us know people whose lives have no meaning. In many cases these are people who never had any purpose in life except to satisfy their own wants. But such a selfish pursuit is an endless search for the rainbow that always proves elusive. Others may have had a purpose for their lives more noble than self, but then either fulfilled that purpose or abandoned it because it seemed that it was an impossible goal. We have known mothers who lived for their children. But when all the children left the nest, some of these mothers suddenly felt themselves without a purpose in life. They may have filled the vacuum with drugs or an extramarital affair. Or we may know a person who found meaning in his job. Then came retirement, and to his dismay he found that fishing and golfing and winter in Florida didn't quite make it. Within a few months he was dead; his empty spiritual heart had drawn the life out of his physical heart.

Simeon shared one thing with these people we have known. He too fulfilled his mission. Once that mission was fulfilled, he no longer needed nor desired to live on. "Now lettest thou thy servant depart in peace," were his words.

Yet there is one significant difference between Simeon and these others. Their goals, whether a search for self-gratification, a concern for children, or a job, were all inferior missions in comparison to Simeon's. He had been called to a divine mission, and once he had faithfully completed it, he was ready to go home where he would hear the words of the Master, "Well done, thou good and faithful servant."

Every one of us can be involved in a mission like Simeon's. While we will not be called by the Holy Spirit in quite the same way as Simeon, yet the Spirit does speak to us through God's Word. By applying His Word to our lives, we can choose among a thousand different missions that await volunteers. There may be a call to the ministry or to become a missionary on some distant shore. But our mission is likely to be closer to home: teaching a Sunday-school class, calling on the sick, giving a cup of cold water in Jesus' name.

Simeon was able to write over his career, "Mission accomplished!" But that won't be so easy for us. So long as our Lord has one job for us that we are still able to do, then our mission is not accomplished.

If we need an example of a life that was lived in continual service to God, we can find that example in the life of Anna. She was eighty or even older, and yet she continued to serve in the temple. As the years came upon her, everything she did must have been more difficult. The stairs that she once bounded up with youthful enthusiasm must have become a challenge. The waterpot she once carried readily with one hand now took both hands. Shadows may have fallen across her eyesight, or her hearing may have suffered. Yet she kept on at her job.

She must have been a strong-willed person, but this alone would not have sustained her in the thankless tasks she performed about the temple. She was sustained because she knew that what she did was to the glory of God. She, like Simeon, was on a mission; but when she was privileged to see the Christ child, her mission was not done. We have no idea how much longer she lived, but we can be sure that to her dying day she found joy in the fact that her mission was still not accomplished.

B. Let Us Pray

Dear God, we thank You that You keep Your promises. You promised to send a Savior, and You sent Him in the form of a baby. You have also promised us many things. Teach us to live in the faith that You will fulfill those promises. In Jesus' name we pray. Amen.

C. Thought to Remember

Little Jesus, wast thou shy
  Once, and just so small as I?
And what did it feel like to be
  Out of Heaven, and just like me?
                                    —FRANCIS THOMPSON

Home Daily Bible Readings

Monday, Dec. 19—Redemption in Christ's Blood (Ephesians 1:3-14)
Tuesday, Dec. 20—Peace in God's Law (Psalm 119:161-168)
Wednesday, Dec. 21—Salvation in Christ Jesus (2 Timothy 2:1-11)
Thursday, Dec. 22—Righteousness in Faith (Romans 4:1-10)
Friday, Dec. 23—Eternal Life in the Son (John 6:31-40)
Saturday, Dec. 24—Forgiveness in Waiting On the Lord (Psalm 130)
Sunday, Dec. 25—Joy in Expectation (Luke 2:21-40)

Learning by Doing

This page contains an alternate lesson plan emphasizing learning activities. Classes desiring such student involvement will find these suggestions helpful.

Learning Goals

After this lesson, students should be able to:

1. Express his own mission in life and how he is attempting to fulfill it.

2. Explain the prophecy that Jesus was set for the fall and rising again of many in Israel.

3. Relate the entire story of Jesus' presentation at the temple.

Into the Lesson

As your students arrive, ask them to imagine that they are reporters for a first-century Jerusalem newspaper. They are to write stories on the events recorded in Luke 2:22-38.

For some variety, you might assign different angles on the story. One might interview Simeon, another Anna, and another the family of Jesus. Another "reporter" could write his own observation as an eyewitness to the events, and a couple more might write commentaries on the event: one as a believer in the prophecies given and the other skeptical.

Late comers might be assigned as "editors" to write headlines for the articles and/or to arrange them in terms of priority (front-page story or stories, page-two stories, and others).

An abbreviated version of this activity is included in the student book. Have the students write headlines for stories that might be written on this event without writing the stories.

Into the Word

Provide a copy of the following lists for each of your students and ask them to match the persons or things named in the left column with the descriptive phrases on the right. (This exercise is included in the student book.)

1. Name given	a. Just and devout
2. Holy Spirit	b. Simeon was to see
3. Turtledoves	c. Mary's destiny
4. Simeon	d. Jesus
5. First-born male	e. Of eighty-four years
6. The Lord's Christ	f. Sacrifice
7. Pierced soul	g. Holy to the Lord
8. Anna	h. Tribe of Israel
9. Aser (Asher)	i. Sent Simeon to temple
10. Widow	j. Prophetess

(The correct answers, from 1 to 10, are d, i, f, a, g, b, c, j, h, e.)

Discuss the following questions, either as a class or in small groups. If you use small groups, allow time for reporting the groups' conclusions to the class as a whole. (Note the comments in the commentary section of this book for helpful ideas on some of the questions.)

1. Jesus was circumcised according to the law, and He was presented at the temple according to the law. What does this suggest about our strict observance of ethical or moral principles?

2. Simeon had a clear sense of purpose in his life. Do you think most people today have such a sense of purpose? Why or why not?

3. What is the difference between a suicidal attitude and Simeon's readiness to die?

4. How would you explain the phrase "fall and rising again of many in Israel"?

5. How do you think Anna's example speaks to the tendency of many today to feel that they have done "enough" for the Lord or for the church?

Into Life

Write the letters of the word *mission* vertically on the chalkboard. Then ask the students to suggest words beginning with each letter that describe their own sense of mission in life. Some suggestions are offered below:

M ministry
I important
S soul-winning
S servanthood
I imperative
O opportunities
N never-ending

List the suggestions offered and discuss the implications of each.

Does your church have a clear sense of mission? Ask the class to discuss what they believe the mission of the church to be, both generally and specifically. (Generally, every church has the same mission, but specifically, each church must respond to the particular needs of its own.)

Provide paper for the students (or refer them to the appropriate section in the student book), and ask them to complete this statement: "As a Christian, I have a clear sense of purpose in my life. Generally speaking, my mission is to.... Specifically, this is what I am doing to accomplish this mission: ...

Let's Talk It Over

The questions on this page are designed to encourage review of the lesson Scriptures and to promote discussion of the lesson by the class. The answers provided are only discussion starters. Let your class talk it over from there.

1. Jesus' coming to the temple provided a high point in the lives of Simeon and Anna, but those two lived daily lives of quiet devotion. What lesson can we draw from that?

Special occasions, spectacular programs, big-name speakers and musicians may be very helpful; but we need also to cultivate daily prayer, regular study of God's Word, consistent presence at church services, dependable work for the Lord, generous regular giving, and steady growth in holiness. We need to gear our worship and our teaching to the task of guiding Christians in developing these aspects of a steady, day-by-day discipleship.

2. Should we seek to be known as "devout"? Why or why not?

The New Testament speaks highly of Simeon in describing him by this term. But we sometimes feel a bit uncomfortable if we are called "devout" or "pious" or "very religious." The impression is given that we are "into" religion just as other people are "into" dieting or sports. The best way to answer this is to note that however devout he was, Simeon is known because of his brief connection with the infant Jesus. We also should make it our aim that whether or not those who know us are impressed with our devoutness, they will be impressed with our connection with Jesus and be led to consider Him.

3. Being associated with Jesus brought Mary and Joseph to unexpected experiences. Is this true of us also?

What are we doing that we never thought of doing in our pre-Christian days? We may wonder that, whereas we once were horrified at the idea of speaking before crowds, we now teach a Bible class or deliver a Communion meditation. Or we may marvel that we who in the past sang sensuous, worldly songs now participate in the church choir. Perhaps we are amazed at the change in our television viewing habits or in the kind of literature we read. Are we now loving and enjoying certain people whom we once shunned? Jesus does indeed lead us into a life filled with unpredictable turns.

4. How is Jesus a stumbling block to some people and a stepping stone to others?

Paul said the crucifixion was a stumbling block to some (1 Corinthians 1:23). Such persons still exist today, scoffing at the idea that the shedding of Jesus' blood can have any connection with the forgiveness of our sins. But the cross of Christ is a stepping stone for other people. Jesus said, "I, if I be lifted up from the earth, will draw all men unto me" (John 12:32). Today we often hear of people for whom a sermon, a song, or a painting centered around Jesus' death on the cross has profoundly touched their hearts.

Some people stumble at Jesus' call to a holy life. They draw away from Him because they are not willing to live the kind of life He exemplifies. But others find His call to holiness an inspiring challenge. They want to conquer the wickedness and selfishness that has gripped them, and they see in Jesus the stepping stone to such a conquest.

5. Simeon warned Mary of the sword that would pierce her soul. What similar warnings may we give to newborn Christians'?

We can probably predict some of their early problems. If they have non-Christian family members or close friends, they may know the pain of strained relationships. If they have lived a reckless, selfish kind of life, some fruits of that life will continue to trouble them. If they expect all church members to be fully devoted to Christ and zealous for His cause, it will disturb them to encounter indifference and self-satisfaction. Of course we do not want to paint too dark a picture, but we should give them a balanced view of both the joys and the disappointments that lie ahead.

6. Just as Anna "departed not from the temple," there are Christians who are at church whenever the doors are open. In what ways are they a blessing?

To see them on Sundays and at midweek services is a source of great satisfaction for ministers, and other leaders. They provide an example for other members who need to get out of the rut of inconsistent attendance. And they surely make an impression on non-Christian friends and neighbors who see them giving priority to spiritual matters.

Anointed to Preach Good News

LESSON SCRIPTURE: Luke 4:14-44.

PRINTED TEXT: Luke 4:16-21, 40-43.

Luke 4:16-21, 40-43

16 He came to Nazareth, where he had been brought up: and, as his custom was, he went into the synagogue on the sabbath day, and stood up for to read.

17 And there was delivered unto him the book of the prophet Isaiah. And when he had opened the book, he found the place where it was written,

18 The Spirit of the Lord is upon me, because he hath anointed me to preach the gospel to the poor; he hath sent me to heal the brokenhearted, to preach deliverance to the captives, and recovering of sight to the blind, to set at liberty them that are bruised,

19 To preach the acceptable year of the Lord.

20 And he closed the book, and he gave it again to the minister, and sat down. And the eyes of all them that were in the synagogue were fastened on him.

21 And he began to say unto them, This day is this Scripture fulfilled in your ears.

. . . .

40 Now when the sun was setting, all they that had any sick with divers diseases brought them unto him; and he laid his hands on every one of them, and healed them.

41 And devils also came out of many, crying out, and saying, Thou art Christ the Son of God. And he rebuking them suffered them not to speak: for they knew that he was Christ.

42 And when it was day, he departed and went into a desert place: and the people sought him, and came unto him, and stayed him, that he should not depart from them.

43 And he said unto them, I must preach the kingdom of God to other cities also: for therefore am I sent.

Golden Text: The Spirit of the Lord is upon me, because he hath anointed me to preach the gospel to the poor.—Luke 4:18.

Scenes of Love and Compassion
Unit 2: Proclamation and Ministry
(Lessons 5-9)

Lesson Aims

After this lesson the student should:

1. Understand that some people will become angry or even violent when their religious views are challenged.

2. Appreciate the difficulty that many have in witnessing to their home community.

3. Be able to name several specific miracles of healing Jesus performed at this point in His ministry.

Lesson Outline

INTRODUCTION
  A. A Treasure Unnoticed
  B. Lesson Background
I. JESUS' MINISTRY IN NAZARETH (Luke 4:16-21)
  A. Jesus Attended Public Worship (v. 16)
  B. Jesus Participated (v. 17)
  C. Jesus Read the Scripture (vv. 18, 19)
     Messiahs and Their Ministries
  D. Jesus' Application (vv. 20, 21)
     In Plain English
II. JESUS' MINISTRY IN CAPERNAUM (Luke 4:40-43)
  A. Jesus Healed Many (v. 40)
  B. Jesus Cast Out Demons (v. 41)
  C. Jesus Sought Seclusion (vv. 42, 43)
CONCLUSION
  A. "As His Custom Was"
  B. Liberation Theology
  C. Let Us Pray
  D. Thought to Remember

Display visual 5 from the visuals/learning resources packet and let it remain on display throughout this session. It is shown on page 156.

Introduction

A. A Treasure Unnoticed

Recently a gemologist purchased an unusual looking stone for ten dollars in a gem and mineral bazaar in Tucson, Arizona. When he got the stone home and began to examine it more carefully, he realized that it was no ordinary stone. It turned out to be one of the largest star sapphires ever found, with an appraised value of over two million dollars. Scores of people had seen nothing unusual about it. Its value went unnoticed until an expert happened to examine it.

In a way Jesus' sermon in His hometown synagogue was like this. He chose as His text Isaiah 61:1, 2. The people had heard this text before. It is quite likely that they had heard some rabbi preach a sermon on it. Yet none of them had recognized its true value. Whatever interpretation they may have given to it, they failed to recognize what a gem it was because it foretold the kind of ministry the promised Messiah would conduct.

The people were so blind to the true meaning of these verses that they became upset when Jesus explained that He was the fulfillment of the prophecy. They became so angry, in fact, that they sought to kill Him (Luke 4:28-30). Let us pray that we never become so blind that we miss the true meaning of a passage of Scripture as they did.

B. Lesson Background

In last week's lesson we read that Mary and Joseph presented Jesus in the temple, where they met Simeon and Anna. For this week's lesson, we move forward thirty years to the beginning of Jesus' ministry. We pass over Luke's record that Jesus was left behind in the temple when He was twelve years old (Luke 2:41-51). We also pass over the beginning of the work of John the Baptist, the baptism of Jesus, and His forty days of temptation in the wilderness (Luke 3:1-22; 4:1-13).

John in his Gospel tells how Jesus gathered His first disciples and performed His first miracle at Cana. John also reports His first cleansing of the temple and His first Judean ministry (John 1:29—3:36). Jesus also had carried on a brief ministry in Galilee before He returned to Nazareth. News of His ministry had already preceded Him, and so when He returned home, He was something of a celebrity.

I. Jesus' Ministry in Nazareth (Luke 4:16-21)

Immediately preceding the lesson text, Luke tells us about Jesus' ministry in Galilee before He returned to Nazareth. In this brief summary statement, we learn that Jesus had taught in many of the synagogues of Galilee. He was "in the power of the Spirit," which may indicate only that He was directed by the Holy Spirit in His teaching. It may, however, suggest that His teachings were accompanied by miracles, as Luke 4:23-27 also suggests. This would account for the fact that His fame spread so quickly through the province. These things undoubtedly contributed to the excitement when Jesus returned to Nazareth.

A. Jesus Attended Public Worship
(v. 16)

16. And he came to Nazareth, where he had been brought up: and, as his custom was, he went into the synagogue on the sabbath day, and stood up for to read.

Although Jesus had been born in Bethlehem and had spent some of His early months in Egypt (Matthew 2:13-15), He had lived most of His life in Nazareth. Here He had worked as a carpenter (Mark 6:3), following the trade of Joseph. In a town the size of Nazareth in that day, Jesus undoubtedly was known by everyone.

The synagogue was the center for religious activities in a Jewish community. It is not mentioned in the Old Testament, but apparently developed during the time of the Babylonian exile or the return from the exile. It served as a schoolroom during the week, where the basics of education were taught. Then on the Sabbath it became a place of worship, but even this worship service was strongly educational in its emphasis. The Scriptures held a central place. The common practice included reading a passage from the law then a passage from the prophets. While each synagogue had its leaders, any Jewish man might share in the service.

As his custom was. Synagogue attendance was not an option among devout Jews. At the age of five a child might be admitted to the service, and at the age of thirteen attendance was expected. It is likely that Jesus arrived in Nazareth some days before the Sabbath, and when the Sabbath came He faithfully followed the practice of regular attendance He had learned as a child. If our Lord believed it essential to attend religious services regularly, we would be wise to follow this same practice today. It is especially important that children learn this practice while they are young.

If this service was typical, a selection from the law was first read. Then Jesus either volunteered or was called upon to read from the prophets. Since His fame had preceded Him, it seems likely that He was asked to take part.

B. Jesus Participated (v. 17)

17. And there was delivered unto him the book of the prophet Isaiah. And when he had opened the book, he found the place where it was written.

Jesus took His place in the front of the assembly and was handed a scroll of the book of Isaiah. These scrolls were kept in a special closet or case, and each scroll was usually covered with a cloth to protect it. Out of reverence for the Scriptures, the reader stood as he read.

How to Say It

ARAMAIC. *Air*-uh-*may*-ik (strong accent on *may).*
BABYLONIA. Bab-ih-*lo*-nih-uh.
CAPERNAUM. Kuh-*per*-nay-um.
ISAIAH. Eye-*zay*-uh.
NAZARETH. *Naz*-uh-reth.
SEPTUAGINT. Sep-*tyoo*-uh-jint.
ZAREPHATH. *Zar*-e-fath.

Since the Scriptures were in Hebrew, a tongue that many people no longer spoke in Jesus' day, the reader ordinarily would then translate the Hebrew into Aramaic, the spoken language.

Jesus took the scroll and unrolled it. We do not know whether the place He chose happened to be the regular selection from the prophets for that day, or whether He deliberately chose this passage from Isaiah because it succinctly summed up the objectives of His ministry.

C. Jesus Read the Scriptures
(vv. 18, 19)

18, 19. The Spirit of the Lord is upon me, because he hath anointed me to preach the gospel to the poor; he hath sent me to heal the brokenhearted, to preach deliverance to the captives, and recovering of sight to the blind, to set at liberty them that are bruised, to preach the acceptable year of the Lord.

What Jesus read was Isaiah 61:1, 2. It is slightly different from our version of Isaiah, but that is to be expected when we consider the several languages involved. Jesus probably translated the Hebrew into the languages of His hearers, and Luke translated into Greek. Then other translators put it into English for us.

These words penned by Isaiah were intended to give hope to those who would be captives in Babylonia. But their second application had a more far-reaching import. They brought good news not only to those who were held captive by the Babylonians, but to all people everywhere who were held captive by sin.

The opening statements of the passage give the credentials of the Messiah. The Spirit of the Lord was upon Him, and He was commissioned to preach the good news to the poor. Who were the poor? Were they only those who were financially destitute? This would have constituted quite a large audience in Jesus' day, for most of the people were poor by our standards. However, it is worth noting that the word translated *poor* in this verse is the same word used in Matthew 5:3, where a blessing is pronounced on, "the poor in spirit," referring to those humbled and broken in spirit. It may very well be that this is the intent of the quotation from Isaiah.

He hath sent me to heal the broken-hearted. This is missing in several important New Testament manuscripts, and so it is omitted from some English translations. However, it is found both in the Hebrew text and in the Septuagint, so it is not likely that it was missing from the book Jesus read.

The Messiah would *preach deliverance to the captives.* Isaiah spoke of the captives who were carried away to Babylon, and the prophecy was fulfilled when they were allowed to return to their homeland. But the Messiah brought a far more glorious fulfillment. The Jews of Jesus' day hoped for deliverance from Roman rule, but Jesus brought freedom from a far more dangerous bondage—the bondage of sin. The word here translated *deliverance* is frequently used in the New Testament to mean forgiveness of sins.

The Messiah would give *sight to the blind.* Jesus fulfilled this prophecy literally (Matthew 9:27-30; Mark 10:46-52; Luke 7:21; John 9:1-7). However, it can also be taken figuratively to refer to removing the blindness brought by sin. The audience that Jesus was addressing certainly had need of this kind of healing.

The Messiah would also *set at liberty them that are bruised,* or oppressed. This also may mean those held and hurt by sin, but it may have another idea as well. The law of Moses with all of the additions and interpretations tacked onto it by the religious leaders had become a heavy burden for the people to bear (Matthew 23:4; Luke 11:46). The good news of the gospel is that men no longer live in bondage to the law, but under freedom brought by grace (Romans 8:1-4).

The acceptable year of the Lord may have called to mind the jubilee year, when fields and houses were returned to their original owners and slaves were set free (Leviticus 25:8-16, 39-41). Like that Jubilee year would be the victorious reign of the Messiah, when all the troubled and oppressed would be liberated.

MESSIAHS AND THEIR MINISTRIES

An obscure Latin American country grabbed the world's attention in the Spring of 1979. Jonestown, Guyana, became a place of horror with the mass suicide/murder of Jim Jones, hundreds of his followers, and an American congressional fact-finding delegation.

As a Christian minister, Jones had shown a concern for the poor and downtrodden. But somewhere along the way his altruistic mission became twisted into a grasp for messianic power.

visual 5

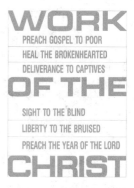

Many would-be "messiahs" try to offer humanity what Jesus came to provide? With imposters, the mission is eventually perverted by selfish ambition. But Jesus came offering real release and renewal.

Jesus offered "good news": real healings took place; spiritual slavery was destroyed, even for those who still were bound to earthly masters; true joy and hope came to those who were mired down by life's troubles. And yet people still look elsewhere for what Jesus alone can give.

What is the message for the church in this? We must make sure we present Christ to the world in such a way that His ministry is not hidden. Let us tempt no one to look elsewhere for what only Jesus can provide.   —C. R. B.

D. Jesus' Application (vv. 20, 21)

20. And he closed the book, and he gave it again to the minister, and sat down. And the eyes of all of them that were in the synagogue were fastened on him.

The book of Isaiah was written on a scroll made of papyrus or parchment. Jesus rolled up the scroll and handed it to the attendant, who placed it back in its cabinet. Then Jesus sat down, which was the normal posture assumed by a speaker in the synagogue. The synagogues were usually not furnished with chairs or benches. Everyone sat cross-legged, the people on the floor and Jesus on a raised platform.

As Jesus sat down, every eye was fixed upon Him. The people had heard of His miraculous works, and now they were ready to hear Him. No doubt they hoped He would perform a miracle in their midst. In that day, even as in our own, people were attracted to worship services by the unusual or the dramatic.

21. And he began to say unto them, This day is this Scripture fulfilled in your ears.

Even though the people were in an expectant mood, they were hardly prepared for the bombshell that Jesus dropped. The Scripture that He had just read was being fulfilled right then. This was no longer a prophecy for some distant time in the future. It was happening before their eyes!

No doubt Jesus had many more things to say about this good news. Obviously Luke gives us only a brief summary of His sermon. In the verses that follow this portion of the printed text, we get some hints about the content of His message and the people's response to it.

Their initial response was that of wonder. They marveled that such gracious words could come from one of such humble origins: "Is not this Joseph's son?" They were amazed that a person without formal training could deal with such deep theological subjects so eloquently. Yet even though they marveled at His skill, they did not accept what He said.

Indeed, before the service was over, the people became quite angry with Him. He criticized their unbelief. He used two Old Testament examples to illustrate His point. Elijah had done a miracle for a widow in Zarephath, not for one in his home town. Elisha had cured Naaman the Syrian, not one of his neighbors. Likewise Jesus' miracles were for believers in other places, not for the skeptics in Nazareth. The furious people sought to punish Jesus by throwing Him over a nearby cliff (Luke 4:22-30).

IN PLAIN ENGLISH

We all use jargon. We do it to impress people with our knowledge of technical information. We do it to camouflage our lack of knowledge. Young people do it to show their growing independence from adults. Society's elite do it to show that they are not common people. Common people do it to show that they are not snobbish intellectuals.

Doctors, lawyers, and preachers use jargon as a kind of verbal shorthand which (ideally) allows them to be more precise in communicating with their peers. Their clients and congregations sometimes feel they use jargon because they want laymen to believe their disciplines are so esoteric that the untrained will always need their service.

Jesus could take a passage from the Old Testament and say ("in plain English" as *we* would put it), "Today this Scripture is fulfilled in your hearing." The common people knew what He meant. At Nazareth they tried to kill Him, but elsewhere they "followed him gladly" (Mark 12:37). The educated leaders also knew what He meant, and they did kill Him. Thus Jesus proved that the convoluted language of theological jargon is unnecessary (except perhaps for avoiding martyrdom!)

Sometimes jargon may be justifiable. But when we are trying to communicate the good news of the gospel to our neighbors, we would do well to follow Jesus' example, and put it "in plain English."   —C. R. B.

II. Jesus' Ministry in Capernaum (Luke 4:40-43)

After Jesus' rejection at His hometown of Nazareth, He went to Capernaum, located on the northwestern shore of the Sea of Galilee. Several of the men whom Jesus later called to become His apostles lived in or near this city. For this reason and because of its convenient location, it became the center for His ministry in the province of Galilee.

In the synagogue at Capernaum, Jesus cast an unclean spirit out of a man. This brought astonishment to those who witnessed it. Visiting in the house of Peter, He healed Peter's mother-in-law of a fever. Word of these miracles quickly passed around the community, and people began to flock to Jesus (Luke 4:31-39).

A. Jesus Healed Many (v. 40)

40. Now when the sun was setting, all they that had any sick with divers diseases brought them unto him; and he laid his hands on every one of them, and healed them.

As the Sabbath Day came to an end, the people began to bring their sick and demon-possessed to Peter's house. Apparently they did not want to violate the Sabbath by bringing them before sundown, which marked the end of the Sabbath. Mark comments that "all the city was gathered together at the door" (Mark 1:33). Jesus didn't turn any of the people away, but healed them of a variety of diseases by laying His hands on them. (Matthew 8:16, 17; Mark 1:32-34).

B. Jesus Cast Out Demons (v. 41)

41. And devils also came out of many, crying out, and saying, Thou art Christ the Son of God. And he rebuking them suffered them not to speak: for they knew that he was Christ.

Demon possession seems to have been prevalent at that time. Jesus' miracle earlier in the day in the synagogue raised the hopes of others that He could cure their loved ones of this terrible affliction. As Jesus was casting these demons out, they began to acclaim Him as the Son of God. Jesus silenced them. He knew that if this were widely noised about, it might arouse the people to rise up against the Romans in hope of establishing the Messianic kingdom. Jesus had a definite timetable for His ministry, and He would not let the people force it to a climax prematurely.

C. Jesus Sought Seclusion (vv. 42, 43)

42. And when it was day, he departed and went into a desert place: and the people sought him, and came unto him, and stayed him, that he should not depart from them.

After a long and busy day that extended well into the night, Jesus quietly slipped away from Peter's house early in the morning and sought a quiet retreat in a deserted place. But He could not for long escape the people, who were soon back at Peter's door. Not finding Him there, they looked for Him until they found Him. Unlike Jesus' own townspeople, the people of Capernaum wanted Him to stay with them, and they were not hesitant about making their wishes known.

43. And he said unto them, I must preach the kingdom of God to other cities also: for therefore am I sent.

As gratifying as this invitation may have been, Jesus had no intention of allowing the people to establish His agenda. He was under obligation to preach the good news to other cities, and so He could not confine His ministry to Capernaum. But they would have an opportunity to see Him again, for He made their city His headquarters for his later work in Galilee.

For the first time Luke uses the expression the *kingdom of God* to indicate the nature of Jesus' teaching. In the broadest sense, this refers to God's sovereign reign in the hearts of men and women to the extent that they seek to do His will.

Conclusion

A. "As His Custom Was"

Jesus was reared in a pious Jewish home, where He undoubtedly received religious training from His infancy on. There is every reason to believe that He observed the regular Jewish feast days and other practices. Among these practices was the weekly attendance at the synagogue.

We will be wise and our children will be blessed if we follow the same practice today. Some adults no longer attend church, saying that they went to church too much as children and got "burned out." We need to reject this for the flimsy excuse that it is. If one checks the rosters of almost any church, he is likely to find that most of the leaders were very early introduced to the practice of regular church attendance. Jesus' custom has proved to be a very good custom indeed.

B. Liberation Theology

In recent years there has arisen in Third World countries and especially in Latin America a new theological emphasis called "Liberation Theology." Liberation Theology is a curious mixture of Marxism, the Social Gospel, and Biblical themes. One of the favorite proof texts of its proponents is Luke 4:18. One cannot deny that many persons in these Third World countries suffer a grinding poverty. And every Christian should feel a responsibility to work for adequate food, clothing, and shelter for all people.

Jesus did have a concern for the physical well-being of the people He preached to. Yet this was not His chief concern. His primary concern was always for the spiritual welfare of those who heard Him. To use His message in the synagogue of Nazareth to support a political and social revolution is to twist it completely out of its context and to miss the point of His ministry. People who hold this view are like the people of Jesus' day who wanted a Messiah who would lead them in a physical kingdom. Because they did not understand that His kingdom was not of this world, they sought to make Him a king. Jesus rejected this, choosing instead the way of the cross (John 6:15).

C. Let Us Pray

Father, we thank You for the good news that came to us through Your Son. We rejoice that the best part of that good news is that He died and was raised for us that we might be redeemed from our sins. In Jesus' name we pray. Amen.

D. Thought to Remember

"The gospel is the fulfillment of all hopes, the perfection of all philosophy, the interpreter of all revelations, and a key to all the seeming contradictions of truth in the physical and moral world."
                                              —HUGH MILLER

Home Daily Bible Readings

Monday, Dec. 26—Jesus Reads in the Synagogue (Luke 4:14-20)
Tuesday, Dec. 27—Jesus Declares His Ministry (Luke 4:21-30)
Wednesday, Dec. 28—Jesus Casts Out a Demon (Luke 4:31-37)
Thursday, Dec. 29—Jesus Ministers to the Crowds (Luke 4:38-44)
Friday, Dec. 30—"The Lord Is My Light" (Psalm 27)
Saturday, Dec. 31—Proclaiming the Lord (Psalm 40:1-10)
Sunday, Jan. 1—Jesus Proclaims His Ministry (John 18:33-37)

Learning by Doing

This page contains an alternate lesson plan emphasizing learning activities. Classes desiring such student involvement will find these suggestions helpful.

Learning Goals

As a result of studying this lesson, each student should be able to do the following:
1. Summarize the mission of Jesus.
2. Suggest some principles for listening and responding to a sermon.
3. Name some ways of keeping the spiritual and physical dimensions of ministry in balance.

Into the Lesson

Study the section under the heading "Liberation Theology" and be sure you understand this subject. Before class, write these statements on the chalkboard or on an overhead transparency. When class begins, ask the students to decide whether they agree or disagree with each one. (The statements are listed also in the student book.)
1. Jesus came to preach deliverance and liberation to the captives.
2. Jesus' concern for people was not merely spiritual, but was physical too.
3. Jesus' message often went against the grain of the established religious leadership.
4. Jesus' concern for people's needs makes it clear that He would have supported even violent attempts to win freedom from captivity.

You should get virtually unanimous agreement on the first three. Disagreement on number 4 also should be unanimous. Point out, however, that this fourth statement is the basis for liberation theology. The first three statements, liberation theologians say, naturally lead to the fourth. To refute that, note that, although Jesus was concerned for physical needs He always emphasized the spiritual over the physical, and He refused political power for himself. Liberation theology is more politics than religion—a strange mix of Marxism with the social gospel, with a little Bible thrown in. It reverses Jesus' priorities, putting the physical over the spiritual, and seeking political power even at the expense of human life.

This lesson looks at the real message of a passage often used to support liberation theology.

Into the Word

Divide the class into two groups. Ask one group to read Luke 2:16-30 and to answer the following questions. They are listed in the student book.

1. What was Jesus' custom on the Sabbath?
2. What was the basic message of the passage He read?
3. What application did Jesus make of this passage?
4. What mixed reactions did Jesus get to His message in Nazareth?
5. What truism did Jesus quote when the people began to wonder at His words?
6. How did the people respond to this?

Ask the other group to read Luke 2:31-44 and to answer these questions. They are also in the student book.
1. What first impressed the people of Capernaum about Jesus?
2. What miracles did Jesus perform there?
3. What did the evil spirits know about Jesus?
4. Where did Jesus go "when it was day"?
5. For what reason did Jesus excuse himself when the people wanted Him to stay longer with them?

After the groups have had about fifteen minutes to discuss these questions, ask for a report from each group. Together as a class, write a one-sentence summary of Jesus' mission as seen in Luke 2:16-44.

Into Life

Note again the hostile reaction of the people at Nazareth when Jesus' sermon challenged their beliefs. Discuss how people today respond to sermons. What makes a "good" sermon? Is it one that affirms ideas we already have, or is it one that challenges our thinking? List ways to listen to a sermon so that it can be applied to life.

Refer to your summary of Jesus' mission and ask the class, "Do you believe our church should have the same mission? If so, does it? If not, what should be its mission, and how well do you think it is fulfilling its mission?"

During the discussion, observe that Jesus' miracles represent one difference between Jesus' mission and ours. What can we learn from the miracles? How do they indicate Jesus' concern for the physical nature of man as well as the spiritual? How can we today keep the physical in balance with the spiritual?

Ask each student to examine his own life and to answer this question: "How am I contributing to the success of the church's mission?"

Let's Talk It Over

The questions on this page are designed to encourage review of the lesson Scriptures and to promote discussion of the lesson by the class. The answers provided are only discussion starters. Let your class talk it over from there.

1. The public reading of Scripture was a prominent feature of synagogue worship. Why should it be equally prominent in our worship services?

Many young Christians learn how to pray by listening to public prayers. They may learn how to read the Scriptures for themselves by hearing those Scriptures read aloud during a worship service. If the reading is not clear and easily understood, the hearer may conclude that the Bible is not meant to be understood. If the public reading is done in a monotone, with little expression or enthusiasm, this may reinforce the idea that the Bible is a dull and tedious book to be read out of duty rather than for delight. So it is important for the public reader to prepare well and read clearly, accurately, dramatically, and enthusiastically.

2. How can we impress upon non-Christians the fact that they are in bondage to sin and in need of deliverance?

Many people realize that they are prisoners of bad habits, such as the use of tobacco, alcohol, or drugs; they are aware of being trapped in jobs or family situations or social relationships that bring them little satisfaction; they perceive that they have little control over destructive attitudes like anger, pride, selfishness, and greed. Our task is to show them that sin is the basis of all this bondage and that Jesus Christ offers deliverance from sin. Human pride makes it difficult for people to admit that they are not in control of their lives (see John 8:33). But if we can lead them to admit that they are under the control of some undesirable force in their lives, they may be ready to acknowledge their captivity to sin and trust in a divine deliverer.

3. Jesus disrupted the worship service and made many of the worshipers angry with Him. What application, if any, does this have to our worship services?

It is unfortunate that a church's worship may be disrupted because something is said that makes worshipers angry. This usually results from a clash of personalities rather than a doctrinal or moral problem. Jesus certainly would not want any church leader to create a conflict over a matter of personal pride or selfishness. But if

worshipers become angry over the teaching of Scripture, we cannot back away from that. No doubt Jesus could have delivered a message at Nazareth that would have made every attender "feel good," but He knew He had to deal with their unbelief. And so today, not every worship service can be a calming, blissful experience to everybody. Sermons and lessons must deal with sin and repentance, with falsehood and truth, with "the whole counsel of God," even if such topics ruffle the feelings of the hearers.

4. The people of Capernaum were excited about Jesus because of what they hoped He would do for them. Do we have this attitude?

Of course we do come to Jesus because of what He can do for us. We find relief from guilt over our sins; we have victory over death and eternal punishment. We try to grow spiritually and serve faithfully so that we may continue to enjoy the blessings that result. But as we mature in Christ we should develop a love for Jesus because of who He is; we should find satisfaction in bringing honor to Him and bearing fruit that will please Him. Jesus told the apostles that they should bear much fruit "to my Father's glory" (John 15:8, *New International Version*), and that should be our aim. To put this another way, we should not say to the Lord, "What have You done for me lately?" We should be saying, "Lord, what can I do for You today?"

5. What are some reasons why Christians should practice regular, church attendance?

It is a simple way of practicing spiritual discipline. There are doubtless many church attenders who are otherwise undisciplined in their spiritual lives; nevertheless, giving priority to public worship attendance each Sunday can be a good starting-point in developing other good habits such as personal prayer and Bible study, saying no to temptations, and using opportunities for Christian witness.

Another good reason for regular attendance is the example and encouragement it gives to fellow Christians.

Regular attendance also has value as a witness to non-Christians. What will our relatives and neighbors think of our faith if they see us neglecting the services of the church?

From Fishermen to Followers

LESSON SCRIPTURE: Luke 5:1-11.

PRINTED TEXT: Luke 5:1-11.

Luke 5:1-11

1 And it came to pass, that, as the people pressed upon him to hear the word of God, he stood by the lake of Gennesaret,

2 And saw two ships standing by the lake: but the fishermen were gone out of them, and were washing their nets.

3 And he entered into one of the ships, which was Simon's, and prayed him that he would thrust out a little from the land. And he sat down, and taught the people out of the ship.

4 Now when he had left speaking, he said unto Simon, Launch out into the deep, and let down your nets for a draught.

5 And Simon answering said unto him, Master, we have toiled all the night, and have taken nothing: nevertheless at thy word I will let down the net.

6 And when they had this done, they inclosed a great multitude of fishes: and their net brake.

7 And they beckoned unto their partners, which were in the other ship, that they should come and help them. And they came, and filled both the ships, so that they began to sink.

8 When Simon Peter saw it, he fell down at Jesus' knees, saying, Depart from me; for I am a sinful man, O Lord.

9 For he was astonished, and all that were with him, at the draught of the fishes which they had taken:

10 And so was also James, and John, the sons of Zebedee, which were partners with Simon. And Jesus said unto Simon, Fear not; from henceforth thou shalt catch men.

11 And when they had brought their ships to land, they forsook all, and followed him.

Golden Text: When they had brought their ships to land, they forsook all, and followed him.—Luke 5:11.

Lesson Aims

As a result of studying this lesson each student should:

1. Understand that Jesus conducted His ministry of teaching under many different circumstances.

2. Appreciate the different methods Jesus used to recruit His disciples.

3. Be able to identify by name the disciples mentioned in this lesson who were fishermen.

Lesson Outline

Display visual 6 from the visuals/learning resources packet. It suggests that a Christian, like Simon Peter, should be willing to do whatever Jesus asks. The visual is shown on page 165.

Introduction

A. Changing Tools

There was a tribe in Africa whose very name struck fear into the hearts of neighboring tribes. They had a reputation for being murderers, a reputation that was well earned, most agree. They killed in order to rob their victims, they killed for hire, and they killed for revenge.

Then some missionaries brought the gospel to them. The missionaries were warned that they were taking their lives in their hands, but they went anyway. To everyone's surprise, some of these killers accepted the gospel and became Christians.

Later a man who was reputed to have murdered at least a dozen people was approached by a Christian from another tribe. "I am glad you have changed your occupation," he said.

"Oh, but I haven't changed my occupation," came the surprising answer. And then he quickly added, "I've just changed my tools. I used to catch men with knives and guns. Now I catch them with the Bible and the love of Christ!"

In a sense, when Jesus called the fishermen to leave their nets and boats, He wasn't asking them to change occupations. He was just asking them to change their tools—and more importantly, their quarry.

B. Lesson Background

In last week's lesson, we studied about Jesus' brief ministry in Nazareth. After His rejection there, He went to Capernaum, where He carried on a fruitful healing ministry before learning to teach in other places. However, Luke does not always record events in the order of their happening. Many students think the event of this week's lesson happened after Jesus went from Nazareth to Capernaum, but before the miracles we studied last week.

I. Teaching by the Lake (Luke 5:1-3)

In Galilee Jesus taught in the synagogues, but He also taught and performed miracles of healing in the homes and out in the streets. His fame spread so widely that He was almost mobbed by people seeking to hear Him. When the crowd was too big for a synagogue or narrow street, He taught in the open country (Mark 1:45).

A. The Crowd by the Lake (v. 1)

1. And it came to pass, that, as the people pressed upon him to hear the word of God, he stood by the lake of Gennesaret.

This scene occurs along the shores of the Sea of Galilee. This body of water, measuring about eight miles wide by thirteen miles long, lies nearly seven hundred feet below sea level. The abundant water supply and the fertile soil surrounding the lake attracted a sizeable population in ancient times. In the Old Testament this body of water bore the name Chinnereth. In the New Testament, Matthew and Mark refer to it as the Sea of Galilee (Matthew 4:18; 15:29; Mark 1:16; 7:31). John calls it the Sea of Tiberias after a city on its southwestern shore (John 6:1; 21:1). Luke calls it a lake rather than a sea, and uses the name Gennesaret, after a fertile plain located south of Capernaum. The wide beach had room for the huge crowd hungering for the Word of God, but the people pressed upon Jesus so closely that He was almost crowded into the water.

B. Teaching From a Boat (vv. 2, 3)

2, 3. And saw two ships standing by the lake: but the fishermen were gone out of them, and were washing their nets. And he entered into one of the ships, which was Simon's, and prayed him that he would thrust out a little from the land. And he sat down, and taught the people out of the ship.

Jesus saw a ready solution to the problem. There on the beach were two boats. The *King James Version* calls them ships, but they were fishing boats small enough to be drawn up on the shore so they were *standing by the lake*, as Luke puts it. The owners had just returned from fishing and were cleaning their nets, which would then be spread out to dry.

Jesus chose Simon Peter's boat to be His pulpit. He asked Peter to row out a few feet from the shore. The water then provided a barrier between Jesus and the press of the crowd. Sitting down in the boat, Jesus continued to teach. Luke doesn't give us any information about the content of Jesus' message; but obviously it met the needs of the people, else they would not have been so eager to hear it. Speaking from such a platform can be effective. Many of us have memories from camp of so-called "Galilean services," in which the speaker presented his message from a boat.

II. Fishing in the Lake
(Luke 5:4-8)

A. Putting Out Into Deep Water (v. 4)

4. Now when he had left speaking, he said unto Simon, Launch out into the deep, and let down your nets for a draught.

Once Jesus had completed His message, He dismissed the crowd and turned His attention to Simon. It was quite obvious that the men had returned without any fish, an experience that every fisherman has now and then, whether he will admit it or not. But these men were not just sportsmen who had had a disappointing night. Fishing was their profession, and empty nets meant that their livelihood was endangered. Jesus was about to solve that problem.

Jesus ordered Simon to move the boat out into deeper water and let the nets down. These were towed through the water by the boat, and then drawn up into the boat with their catch.

B. Peter's Reluctant Obedience (v. 5)

5. And Simon answering said unto him, Master, we have toiled all the night, and have taken nothing: nevertheless at thy word I will let down the net.

Simon must have been a bit surprised at the command. After all, they had fished all night and caught nothing. Besides, they were experienced fishermen, and Jesus wasn't. And so Simon voiced his feelings to Jesus. On this occasion, Simon addressed Him as *Master*, a word that means "one who stands over another." Simon's previous experience with Jesus had caused him to recognize that Jesus was a superior person.

All of Simon's fishing experience told him that this effort was a waste of time. Yet he had enough faith in Jesus to obey the order without further murmuring or delay. We often find ourselves in situations similar to Peter's. The Lord challenges us to launch out into the deep, but our experience causes us to reject such counsel. As a result we often miss the great rewards that may be ours. However, on occasion we may lay aside our reservations and follow our Lord by faith. And, as often as not, we find our nets breaking under the rich bounty He provides.

C. The Catch (vv. 6, 7)

6. And when they had this done, they inclosed a great multitude of fishes: and their net brake.

No one could have been more surprised than Simon. Experience told him that there were no fish to be had in that part of the lake. Yet here was a record catch, so great that the nets were beginning to break. This was indeed a miracle. Scholars have debated what kind of miracle it was. A few believe that Jesus may have created the fish. Others feel that He directed the fish to the spot where they could be caught. But it seems more likely that Jesus' unique powers gave Him the ability to know where the fish were and to direct Peter there.

This miracle was more than an interesting curiosity or an entertaining sideshow. Before long

---

How to Say It

GENNESARET. Geh-*ness*-uh-ret.
ZEBEDEE. *Zeb*-eh-dee.

some of the men in the group who witnessed the miracle would be called as Jesus' special disciples. He was getting them ready for the time when He would issue that call.

7. And they beckoned unto their partners, which were in the other ship, that they should come and help them. And they came, and filled both ships, so that they began to sink.

Peter and his assistants had two choices. To save their nets they had either to release the fish or call for help. No fisherman ever wants to release his catch when he gets it that close to the boat. And so they signaled to their friends in the other boat for help. Apparently they were so far away that their shouts could not be heard clearly over the sound of small waves and the noise of the people who remained on the beach, and so they resorted to signals or gestures.

We can be sure the gestures were so dramatic that those in the other boat came as quickly as they could. Perhaps they drew another net around the one that was breaking, but Luke does not pause to record such details. When Peter's boat was full, the rest of the catch was pulled into the other boat, and both boats were so full that they were almost ready to sink. On that day Peter and the others learned an important lesson: when God gives, He gives bountifully.

Perhaps there is another lesson here. In a way, this great catch of fish symbolized the great ingathering of souls that would result after Jesus called His disciples to become fishers of men.

D. Peter's Response (v. 8)

8. When Simon Peter saw it, he fell down at Jesus' knees, saying, Depart from me; for I am a sinful man, O Lord.

As the loaded boats started back toward land, waves threatening any moment to wash over the gunwales, the awesome truth of what had happened suddenly struck Peter. In the frantic effort to save the nets and keep the fish from escaping, he had had little time to think about what was happening; but now that he had caught his breath, the implications of the miracle became obvious. Peter had seen Jesus perform miracles before, but this one touched him more powerfully. Peter was a fisherman. He knew fishing, and he knew that what he had witnessed was no ordinary event. And Peter was not one to hold back his emotions. Earlier, he had called Jesus *Master*; now he called Him *Lord*. That term sometimes was used with polite respect to a superior man; but it was used also of God, and it seems that Peter was recognizing Jesus' deity. In the presence of deity, he felt himself a sinner, not worthy to be with the Lord. Obviously he did not expect Jesus to jump out of the boat and

leave him, but he was recognizing the distance that separates sinful man from sinless deity.

PARALYZED BY GUILT

A fifty-year-old man spends most of his waking moments tormenting himself for the manner in which he treated his father while his father still lived. During the father's lengthy illness, the son visited and cared for him.

However, the day his father died, he was not present, having business to attend to. He will not forgive himself for not being at his father's side at the time of death ("when he needed me most," as he phrases it). Tormented by this, he cannot live a productive life.

Paralyzed by neurotic guilt, the son refuses to recognize that he had done what could be reasonably expected of him and his presence would not have prevented his father's death.

Peter's expression of sinfulness, on the other hand, was a recognition of real guilt. It was an appropriate response as he compared himself with the Son of God, in whose presence he bowed. It is the response each of us should make, also.

But see what Jesus said to Peter. He did not say, "You are right, and don't you ever forget it, even for a moment. The rest of your days should be spent groveling before me in sorrow." Instead, Jesus urged him to leave the past behind and get on with life, spending his time in positive action. The cure for a guilty past, either real or imagined, is to live positively in the present with gratitude in the heart for God's redemptive work in Christ.   —C. R. B.

III. Jesus Calls the Fisherman (Luke 5:9-11)

A. The Fearful Fisherman (v. 9)

9. For he was astonished, and all that were with him, at the draught of the fishes which they had taken.

Peter had been astonished by the catch, but he was not alone. The others in the boat felt the same way, though they were more restrained in their response. We are not told who the other persons in the boat with Peter were. No doubt his brother Andrew was there, along with one or more of the servants who worked with them.

B. Jesus' Reassurance (v. 10)

10. And so was also James, and John, the sons of Zebedee, which were partners with Simon. And Jesus said unto Simon, Fear not; from henceforth thou shalt catch men.

When Peter and those in the boat with him called for help, Peter's partners, James and John,

visual 6

NEVERTHELESS
AT
THY WORD
I
WILL . . .

TRUST & OBEY

responded with another boat. They witnessed the miracle and must have shared Peter's feelings. But since Peter had been the first to show his fear, it was to him that Jesus addressed His words of reassurance.

"Don't be afraid," came the soothing voice of Jesus. Jesus did not deny His deity, nor did He criticize Peter for recognizing that he was a sinner. There was nothing wrong with Peter's feeling on these points. His error was in failing to realize that the Son of God had come in mercy, not to punish evildoers.

Even as Jesus reassured Peter, He also presented him a challenge. Peter had been catching fish; now he would catch men. This is a striking figure, but we must not push it too far. People catch fish in order to consume them, but Jesus catches men in order to save them. The word used for *catch* literally means *take alive*. We need also to recognize that fish are not caught because they choose to be. On the other hand, persons who are caught for the Lord come to Him of their own free will.

C. The Fishermen Become Followers (v. 11)

11. And when they had brought their ships to land, they forsook all, and followed him.

Under ordinary circumstances, the fishermen would have been celebrating their great catch and contemplating some of the rewards for their efforts. But Jesus' words confronted them with such a serious challenge that their light banter must have been subdued by the seriousness of the situation. As they rowed the loaded boats slowly to the shore, Jesus may have told them more about how they would catch men, and may have asked them plainly to leave their business and go with Him.

They forsook all, and followed him. Of course they did not just leave the fish and nets and boats to rot on the beach. There were hired men to market the fish and continue the business with the father of James and John to supervise

them (Mark 1:20). Many students think the call we are studying is the same one that is recorded in Matthew 4:18-22 and Mark 1:16-20. Others think Matthew and Mark tell of an earlier call, and the fishermen had traveled with Jesus in Galilee for a short time before the call recorded by Luke. In either case, we know that Simon Peter, Andrew, James, and John were not strangers to Jesus when He called them from their fishing. They were among the followers of John the Baptist who had turned to Jesus at an earlier time (John 1:29-42). Probably they had been with Jesus at Cana, when He did His first miracle (John 2:1-11). Probably they followed Him to Jerusalem, stayed with Him in that area for several months, and then went with Him back to Galilee (John 2:13—4:43). Back home in Galilee they were fishing again, perhaps while Jesus visited His old home in Nazareth (Luke 4:16-30) and perhaps while He was teaching and healing in some other towns. When Jesus called them to become fishers of men, they left their fishing business to go with a teacher they had been with for months, a teacher whom they knew and trusted. Apparently the father of James and John continued the fishing business with the help of hired servants. When the former fishermen went to Galilee after Jesus rose from the dead, the equipment was there for them to try their hand at fishing again (John 21:1-14).

Forsaking All

It is hard to give up everything for the prospect of an uncertain future. For example, take the case of Elvis Johnson-Idan, reported in American newspapers. He is a West African who works for the London parks department. He was surprised a few years ago when he heard that he was the new king of the Fanti kingdom in Ghana. Tribal elders had examined family lineages and found that he was next in line for the throne.

Johnson-Idan does not plan to return permanently to his kingdom. He says that his job in London is "very important." In addition, the Fantis are a very poor tribe, and their "palace" is an ordinary mud house—not a lot to entice one back to Africa, even to rule ten thousand subjects.

To be willing to give up everything—boats, nets, and livelihood in the case of Peter, Andrew, James, and John—one must have a vision, a sense of what can be accomplished by the cause one is being called to. Johnson-Idan apparently doesn't have that kind of vision for his Fanti tribe. But something about Jesus sparked that kind of vision in those four soon-to-be fishers-of-men.

Jesus couldn't even promise a mud house or ten thousand subjects. No, He would be telling them of the hardships that both He and they would suffer. But for them, it was enough to know that they would be followers of the Messiah. He hasn't promised us any more in this world, but He holds before us the same vision of the cause of God. It's worth leaving all behind, if we can share in the vision.   —C. R. B.

Conclusion

A. Fishers of Men

Our children like to sing and act out a little song, "I will make you fishers of men," based on Jesus' call of the fishermen to become disciples. It was an appropriate figure, for these men understood fishing. But it is an enlightening figure for us today, even for those who are not fishermen.

The idea of our fishing for men suggests several things. First of all, we note that a fisherman must go where the fish are. Peter did not go fishing on the top of Mount Hermon. He fished in the Sea of Galilee where the fish lived. In the same manner, if we are to catch men for Christ we must go where they are. Of course, in our increasingly crowded world, it is not difficult to find people. But if we are to be successful soul winners, we must find receptive people. Good fishermen know that fish will bite under some conditions and not under others. So we, if we are to be successful soul winners, must seek people when the conditions are right.

Good fishermen also know that they must use the right bait. Some fish will bite on worms; others prefer minnows, plugs, or flies. Men are brought to Christ by different things. Some are attracted by His love. Others are moved by the preaching of judgment. Wise is the fisherman witness who knows which will work best in each situation.

Fishermen have to be optimists. They may go out time and again with little or no success, but they are always ready to go again, dreaming of the prize catch that got away or, worse, didn't even make a pass at the bait. Soul winners have to be optimists also. Rejections will come, doors will be shut in their faces, but the soul winner must go out believing that the next time he will know the thrill of leading a person to Christ.

A good fisherman doesn't quit when he has landed his fish. He carefully preserves his catch. Once as a lad I caught several fish and placed them on a stringer in the water. Making sure that the stringer was safely tied to a tree root, I walked a hundred feet or so around the bank of the gravel pit where I was fishing. I returned a

while later to retrieve my fish. To my dismay, when I pulled them out of the water, all that I had left were bones and heads. A hungry turtle had helped himself to a tasty meal. Sometimes soul winners are so busy witnessing and winning that they don't care for the catch when it is brought in. Then Satan, like a hungry turtle, has a feast. We must protect the newly-won souls by providing church programs that will encourage them to grow in the faith.

There are all kinds of fishermen. Some fish for bluegill or crappie; others cast out their lures for bass or muskies; still others may venture out to sea to seek the big ones—marlin or sailfish. In the same way, there are all kinds of souls out there in the world who need salvation—young and old, rich and poor. Because of differences in abilities, culture, and resources, soul winners will work with different people in different situations.

The comparisons between fishermen and soul winners are numerous, but there is one very important difference. One can be a fisherman or not, as he chooses. But as Christians, we have no choice—the Master has already called us to become fishers of men.

B. Let Us Pray

Dear Father, we thank You that Your Son called those ancient fishermen to become catchers of men. We thank You also that they and others after them accepted that call. Help us also to hear that call, and like Peter, Andrew, James, and John, to accept it, leaving all to follow our Lord. Amen.

C. Thought to Remember

He will make us fishers of men if we follow Him.

Learning by Doing

This page contains an alternate lesson plan emphasizing learning activities. Classes desiring such student involvement will find these suggestions helpful.

Learning Goals

After this lesson, students should be able to:

1. Compare his own desire to hear or know God's Word with that of the crowd beside the Sea of Galilee.

2. Explain Peter's reaction to Jesus' teaching and His ability to cause the fishermen to catch a great number of fish.

3. List some characteristics of a disciple as seen in Luke 5:1-11.

Into the Lesson

Ask each student to read Luke 5:1-11, imagine he is Simon Peter, and record his thoughts and feelings as if in a diary. Provide paper, or let students use the student book.

In about five minutes, ask for volunteers to read their diary entries. Discuss the feelings Peter had at different stages during the day. How did he feel when Jesus began teaching near where he was working? How about when Jesus asked to use his boat for a pulpit? How must he have felt when Jesus said to start fishing again? How about after the catch, or when Jesus called them to follow Him?

Into the Word

Whatever Peter's feelings, it is important to note that he obeyed the Lord. Peter already knew of Jesus. His brother Andrew had introduced him earlier (John 1:35-42). They had been with Jesus in His early Judean ministry. Here, as Jesus began His Galilean ministry, He called the fishermen to follow Him again.

Assign a task force to examine Luke 5:1-11 and list the commands of Jesus that Peter obeyed.

Assign another task force to examine the text for zeal or eagerness among followers of Jesus. Have this group make a list of the actions of groups or individuals that indicate such zeal.

Assign a third task force to search for passages that record events similar to those in the lesson text. Provide them with the following list. (These assignments are in the student book.)

1. Find another occasion when Jesus preached from a boat. What was His subject on that occasion? (Matthew 13:1-52).

2. Find an occasion when Jesus gave fishing instructions to some disciples that resulted in a great catch. Describe it (John 21).

3. Some think Matthew and Mark record the same call that Luke records in our text; some think they record a different call. How is their account similar? How is it different? (Matthew 4:18-22; Mark 1:16-20).

As you discuss the first task force's results, note that Peter did not always understand the Lord, but He obeyed anyway. As the second task force reports, note the eagerness of the crowd to hear Jesus preach. Note the zeal of the fishermen, who "forsook all, and followed him."

Answers to the third group's questions follow:

1. From a boat, Jesus gave a famous sermon including several parables.

2. After the resurrection, Peter and six others were fishing when Jesus appeared and told them to cast the net on the right side. They caught 153 fish and then had breakfast with Jesus.

3. Matthew and Mark do not mention the teaching, but they record that Jesus said, "Follow me, and I will make you fishers of men." They mention that Peter and Andrew were casting a net into the sea, and that James and John were mending nets. Andrew, Zebedee, and hired servants are all mentioned as part of the business.

Into Life

Call attention to the zeal of the crowd to listen to Jesus. Ask, "How eager are we to hear or study the Word of God?" Discuss contemporary attitudes about preaching and Bible study. Are we more eager to hear the Word of God preached, or for the preacher to finish? Why is attendance at mid-week Bible studies so slim? Suggest other situations that indicate a lack of enthusiasm. Ask each student to rate his own enthusiasm as compared with the crowd's.

Ask the class to note again Peter's obedience. Are we as quick to obey commands in Scripture even when we do not fully understand them? Discuss some things in Scripture that are hard to understand but must be obeyed. Ask students to share things they have done out of a willingness to obey the Lord even when they did not fully understand why the deed or other action was necessary.

Ask, "What have we learned about discipleship?" List characteristics of a disciple as seen in this text. Ask each student to compare himself with the list.

Let's Talk It Over

The questions on this page are designed to encourage review of the lesson Scriptures and to promote discussion of the lesson by the class. The answers provided are only discussion starters. Let your class talk it over from there.

1. Jesus used a fishing boat as a pulpit. What kinds of unusual pulpits may we use today?

A seat in an airplane or on a train or bus can serve this purpose. Without making our fellow passengers a "captive audience," by engaging in friendly conversation we may gain the opportunity to speak of our faith. Another seat with similar possibilities is one in the doctor's or dentist's waiting room. Some Christians have demonstrated that a hospital bed can make an effective pulpit. On vacation we can utilize a picnic table, a beach chair, a seat at a ball park, or even a fishing boat as a means of presenting our testimony concerning Jesus Christ.

2. What are some tasks that may seem to be a waste of time, but that may have great results?

Going door-to-door to conduct a canvass or to distribute Christian literature often seems a waste of time and effort. We may meet with indifference or even hostility at several stops. But if just one contact results in a soul won to Christ, we will feel that it was all worth the effort. Teachers of children frequently wonder if they are accomplishing anything. The youngsters may seem inattentive and unresponsive in spite of the teacher's best efforts. Again, however, faithfulness in serving Christ will ultimately issue in satisfying results. Even prayer and Bible study may seem to be a waste of time. We may complain that we are not getting anything out of the Bible and that we are not seeing results from our prayers. But both of those practices fall into the category of spiritual seed-sowing. In time these practices are sure to produce a harvest (Galatians 6:7-10).

3. Why is it important for us to be frequently reminded of our unworthiness toward Jesus?

Some may think this is unhealthy, since many people are afflicted with poor self-images and feelings of inferiority. Paul called himself "less than the least of all God's people" (Ephesians 3:8, *New Internationa Version*) and said he did not deserve to be called an apostle (1 Corinthians 15:9, *New International Version*), but some may feel that we should not follow his example. But for both Peter and Paul, the recognition of their sinfulness and unworthiness served as the backdrop for their realization of the richness of God's grace. And so for us the acknowledgment of our unworthiness should not be a step toward self-hatred. It should be the prelude to a growing awareness of how much God loves us, of how wide is His mercy, and of how great a value we have in His eyes. "How great is the love the Father has lavished on us, in that we should be called children of God! And that is what we are!" (1 John 3:1, *New International Version*).

4. How can we use our occupation in fishing for men?

As important as evangelism is, we should avoid doing it on "company time." When Paul tells slaves to "serve wholeheartedly, as if you were serving the Lord" (Ephesians 6:7, *New International Version*), that indicates that modern employees are also obligated to give their employer an honest day's labor. That precludes the idea of using work time as witness time. However, it is possible to use lunch times, break times, and after-work hours to speak to fellow employees about Christ. Even then we must take care to avoid any approach that would conflict with the conducting of company business. Christians may give evangelism a bad name by neglecting their work to witness and by creating a strain in employee relationships through an unhealthy persistence.

5. For Jesus' apostles fishing was a means of livelihood; for fishermen today fishing is more often a relaxing diversion. Which of these two viewpoints is more applicable to fishing for men?

Obviously the eternal urgency of soul-winning points to the first of the above. We must share the sense of responsibility Paul reflected when he said, "I am compelled to preach. Woe to me if I do not preach the gospel!" (1 Corinthians 9:16, *New International Version*). And yet the second viewpoint also has some significance. It is important that we learn to present the gospel in a calm, relaxed manner. If we are nervous or if we come across as "high-pressure salesmen," it may affect our hearers adversely. This underscores the importance of training that will enable us to know the appropriate Scriptures, handle criticisms and excuses, and press for a decision without undue pressure.

Healed and Forgiven

LESSON SCRIPTURE: Luke 5:12-26.

PRINTED TEXT: Luke 5:17-26.

Luke 5:17-26

17 And it came to pass on a certain day, as he was teaching, that there were Pharisees and doctors of the law sitting by, which were come out of every town of Galilee, and Judea, and Jerusalem: and the power of the Lord was present to heal them.

18 And, behold, men brought in a bed a man which was taken with a palsy: and they sought means to bring him in, and to lay him before him.

19 And when they could not find by what way they might bring him in because of the multitude, they went upon the housetop, and let him down through the tiling with his couch into the midst before Jesus.

20 And when he saw their faith, he said unto him, Man, thy sins are forgiven thee.

21 And the scribes and the Pharisees began to reason, saying, Who is this which speaketh blasphemies? Who can forgive sins, but God alone?

22 But when Jesus perceived their thoughts, he answering said unto them, What reason ye in your hearts?

23 Whether is easier, to say, Thy sins be forgiven thee; or to say, Rise up and walk?

24 But that ye may know that the Son of man hath power upon earth to forgive sins, (he said unto the sick of the palsy,) I say unto thee, Arise, and take up thy couch, and go into thine house.

25 And immediately he rose up before them, and took up that whereon he lay, and departed to his own house, glorifying God.

26 And they were all amazed, and they glorified God, and were filled with fear, saying, We have seen strange things today.

Golden Text: They were all amazed, and they glorified God, and were filled with fear, saying, We have seen strange things today.—Luke 5:26.

Scenes of Love and Compassion
Unit 2: Proclamation and Ministry
(Lessons 5-9)

Lesson Aims

After studying this lesson students should:

1. Have a better understanding of the relationship between sin and physical health.

2. Have a growing appreciation of the fact that Jesus as the Son of God has power to forgive sin.

3. Be better able to help people who suffer from physical afflictions.

Lesson Outline

INTRODUCTION
  A. Critics With All the Answers.
  B. Lesson Background
I. JESUS HEALS A PALSIED MAN (Luke 5:17-24)
  A. Jesus' Continued Ministry (v. 17)
  B. The Man Brought to Jesus (vv. 18, 19)
  There Must Be a Way
  C. The Man's Sins Forgiven (v. 20)
  D. Reaction of Scribes and Pharisees (v. 21)
  E. Jesus' Response to His Critics (v. 22, 23)
  Green With Envy
  F. Jesus' Power of Healing (v. 24)
II. RESPONSE TO THE MIRACLE (Luke 5:25b, 26)
  A. The Man Is Healed (v. 25b)
  B. The Peoples' Response (v. 26)
CONCLUSION
  A. "Pneumosomatic" Healing
  B. Let Us Pray
  C. Thought to Remember

Display visual 7 from the visuals/learning resources packet and refer to it as you consider the Scripture text for the lesson. The visual is shown on page 173.

Introduction

A. Critics With All the Answers

A group of people gathered at the window of a taxidermist's shop, admiring his skill in preserving various animals in lifelike poses. One young man was critical, however, concentrating on an owl in the middle of the window. "The head feathers aren't properly arranged," he complained, "and the eyes are obviously artificial. And look at those feet! No owl grasps a branch like that." Just then the owl turned its head and blinked.

In some respects the scribes and Pharisees were like this young man. They were having trouble fitting Jesus and His teachings into their theological framework, especially because some of His teachings seemed to threaten their honored status. Instead of revising their theology, they found it more convenient to criticize Jesus, especially when He offered forgiveness for a paralytic's sins. They must have suffered no little embarrassment when the man was healed.

B. Lesson Background

In last week's lesson, we studied about a miraculous catch of fish and the subsequent call of the fishermen to become fishers of men.

After this, Luke tells us about the healing of a leper. Perhaps he does not follow a strictly chronological order here, but groups the healing of the leper with the miraculous catch of fish, and the healing of a paralytic as examples of the power of Jesus.

I. Jesus Heals a Palsied Man (Luke 5:17-24)

In the miraculous catch of fish, Luke shows us that Jesus had control over nature, a fact that brought Simon Peter to his knees. In the healing of the leper, Luke shows that Jesus also had power over the disease of leprosy. Now in the account of Jesus' healing of a palsied man, Luke shows that Jesus not only had power to heal a cripple, but also had power to forgive sin.

A. Jesus' Continued Ministry (v. 17)

17. And it came to pass on a certain day, as he was teaching, that there were Pharisees and doctors of the law sitting by, which were come out of every town of Galilee, and Judea, and Jerusalem: and the power of the Lord was present to heal them.

Luke does not give us any specific information about when or where this event took place. It is clear, however, that Jesus was attracting attention from all over the country. His ministry had gained so much popular support that the religious leaders were watching closely. They came not only from Galilee, but also from Judea and even Jerusalem, the seat of authority of the Jewish faith.

The *Pharisees* were an important religious party in the first century. They had arisen during the four hundred years between the Old Testament and the New. Many believe that their name was derived from a Hebrew word meaning *separated*. Their commitment to the law led them to live austere lives that separated them from most of the people. In their dedication to the law, they often became legalistic, paying more attention to the minute details of the law than to its real intent. They accorded great authority to the Old Testament Scriptures, especially the five books of Moses. But they had also created a large body of oral laws that became increasingly important to them.

Josephus, a Jewish historian, says there were only about six thousand Pharisees. However, they were generally respected, and wielded an influence out of proportion to their numbers. The Gospel accounts often depict them as narrow-minded hypocrites. Jesus himself condemned them on this account (Matthew 23). Yet not all Pharisees were hypocrites. After all, the apostle Paul called himself a Pharisee (Acts 26:4, 5). The Pharisees are typical of people whose very dedication causes them to put emphasis on the careful observance of externals—such things as tithing kitchen herbs and sabbath keeping. Theirs was not the sin of those shallow persons who take their religion casually. Rather, their great sin was that of spiritual pride, a sin that can come to those who take their religion seriously. This sin can lead to hypocrisy and a hardness of heart that becomes blind to human suffering. The very people studying this lesson, concerned Christians, are the ones most likely to fall into these sins. We will do well to study the activities of the Pharisees lest we become guilty of their sins.

Those whom the *King James Version* calls *doctors of the law* are more accurately called *teachers of the law* in some translations. Many scholars believe they were identical with the scribes mentioned in verse 21. They were authorities in matters of the law. They preserved the traditions that had grown up about the law and were looked to as interpreters of the law. They often held responsible positions, and some of them served as members of the Sanhedrin, the highest governing body among the Jews. They were held in high esteem by the people, and the fact that such leaders had come to check out Jesus and His teachings gives us some indication of His growing popularity.

Undoubtedly these religious leaders had heard stories about miraculous healings, since such stories would circulate very quickly among the people. Thus they felt an obligation to investigate them and either confirm the accounts or prove them false. Since Jesus had not been trained by these leaders, they probably approached this meeting with a bias against Him. If they could prove that the stories about His performing miracles were false, they would certainly do so. But their efforts were doomed to failure. The people were still bringing their sick

and infirm to Jesus *and the power of the Lord was present to heal them.* God's power is not limited just because unbelievers are present. We will do well to remember that today when unbelievers seem to challenge everything that Christianity stands for.

B. The Man Brought to Jesus
(vv. 18, 19)

18. And, behold, men brought in a bed a man which was taken with a palsy: and they sought means to bring him in, and to lay him before him.

Jesus was teaching in a house. Out-of-town visitors along with local residents had filled the building and probably also had crowded the narrow street outside it. Through this crowd four men (Mark 2:3) tried to bring the paralyzed man. Apparently the man had suffered a stroke or an injury that left him paralyzed and incapable of walking. He had to be carried on a bed, which was a pallet or stretcher.

19. And when they could not find by what way they might bring him in because of the multitude, they went upon the housetop, and let him down through the tiling with his couch into the midst before Jesus.

It seems surprising that the crowd would not make a way for the men to bring the paralytic to Jesus. How inconsiderate it was not to offer assistance so that a man in need of healing could come to Jesus! But ancient Palestinians had no monopoly on lack of consideration. Or have you never made the mistake of being caught in a department store sale? Probably some of those in the crowd were also there seeking healing, and they would not make way for one who came later.

The faith of these men was not to be thwarted by the crowd. One way or another, they were determined to get their crippled friend to Jesus. Finally they hit upon the idea of lowering him through the roof. Getting him up onto the roof was no problem, for most Palestinian homes had an outside stairway leading to the roof, which was flat. In Palestinian homes of that period, the roof was usually constructed by placing a layer of branches and twigs over heavy supporting timbers. Then mud was packed over the branches and twigs to create a roof that was adequate in an area of low rainfall. The word translated *tiling* means something made of clay, not necessarily roofing tiles such as we are familiar with now.

No doubt such a dramatic entrance immediately caught the attention of Jesus and those who were crowded about Him. It may have shocked the dignity of the visiting religious

How to Say It

GALILEE. *Gal*-uh-lee.
JUDEA. Joo-*dee*-uh.
PHARISEES. *Fair*-uh-seez.
PNEUMA (Greek). *nyoo*-muh.
PNEUMOSOMATIC. nyoo-mo-so-*mat*-ik.
SOMA (Greek). *so*-muh.

leaders, but Jesus was not offended. He quickly recognized and rewarded the faith of the paralyzed man and his friends.

THERE MUST BE A WAY

As every school-age child knows, Columbus made his first trip to the new world in 1492. However, back in 1490 he had appealed to King Ferdinand and Queen Isabella to underwrite the trip. They had asked a panel of their wisest advisers to look at Columbus' plan for a voyage to the Indies. After lengthy deliberation, the advisers listed six reasons for refusing to back the venture. One reason was that, so many centuries after the world was created, it was not likely that there were any undiscovered lands of any value.

Columbus proved them wrong, of course. His determination and persistence finally paid off, in spite of conventional wisdom.

The friends of the paralyzed man could have said, "This crowd is so big, there is just no way we can get our friend to Jesus." However, they were determined to find a way for him to be healed. Their persistence brought about a creative solution.

There is no shortage of pessimists when the church faces a problem. But if Christians are convinced of the power of Christ, creative in their thinking, and persistent in their efforts, they will find ways to open the door for God to work among them.   —C. R. B.

C. The Man's Sins Forgiven (v. 20)

20. And when he saw their faith, he said unto him, Man, thy sins are forgiven thee.

Neither the palsied man nor his friends asked for healing. But they did not have to. Their actions and the man's condition quite loudly proclaimed their reason for being there. Jesus recognized the need and their faith, and ministered to that need. But to the surprise of everyone, He did not immediately tell the man to take up his bed and walk. Instead, He forgave him his sins. Was the man's paralysis the result of some sin he had committed, or perhaps a sin that someone else had committed? It was widely believed in that day that sickness or affliction

came as a punishment for sin. This view was expressed in the book of Job.

Jesus did not hold that all suffering is the result of the sufferer's sin (John 9:3). Indeed, He made it very clear that sometimes the innocent suffer. But why did Jesus forgive the man's sins before He healed him? Two or three views are possible. First, Jesus may have known something about the man that we do not know. Maybe the man's palsy did come as the result of his sins. Or perhaps Jesus knew that the man himself believed that his affliction came as a result of his sin. In the presence of Jesus he may have been burdened with guilt, even if his sin did not cause his trouble. Until that burden was relieved, physical healing alone would not solve his problem. Jesus also seems to be telling us in this situation that spiritual health is more important than physical health. There is still another possibility. Jesus may have deliberately forgiven the man's sins in order to challenge the religious leaders who sat in the audience.

D. Reaction of Scribes and Pharisees (v. 21)

21. And the scribes and the Pharisees began to reason, saying, Who is this which speaketh blasphemies? Who can forgive sins, but God alone?

Although the scribes and Pharisees did not express their views orally, in their minds they began to accuse Jesus of blasphemy. The sin of blasphemy occurs when one deliberately insults God either by word or action. The Pharisees were correct in affirming that only God can forgive sin. Their basis for accusing Jesus of blasphemy was that He was claiming power for himself that rightly belonged only to God. There is just one weakness in their line of reasoning: *Jesus was God!* And by virtue of this fact, He has the power to forgive sins.

These men could not be expected to recognize Jesus' deity immediately. It is not easy to believe that a man can be divine. Even the closest disciples were still struggling with this idea. Yet these religious leaders had heard of Jesus' miracles. At least they could have kept their minds open and reserved judgment until more evidence was in. But we ought not to be too critical of them. Most of us are reluctant to accept new truths, especially when those truths seem to threaten our prestige or our position.

GREEN WITH ENVY

We'll call him John. He was tall, dark, and handsome when that was thought to be every young lady's ideal in a man. John was an excellent student. He had won letters in three different sports in high school, and was an outstanding forward on the college basketball team. His sonorous bass voice gave him a commanding presence, whether he was speaking or singing.

But John had one fault, according to many of his schoolmates (especially the male students). John wasn't humble enough! John was aware of his abilities, and went calmly about his life with an air of self-confidence that was the envy of many of his friends.

The envy of others was the problem, not John's imagined lack of humility. As some anonymous wit has said, "When you find yourself turning green with envy, you know you are ripe for trouble!"

The Pharisees could raise questions regarding Jesus' act of forgiving sins, but they could not hide the fact that they were jealous. *He* was the teacher drawing the crowds, and not they. *He* was the one who spoke with power and logic, not they. Faced with the choice of being critics or converts, they did as many still do: "green with envy," they got busy on their criticism.

—C. R. B.

E. Jesus' Response to His Critics (vv. 22, 23)

22, 23. But when Jesus perceived their thoughts, he answering said unto them, What reason ye in your hearts? whether is easier, to say, Thy sins be forgiven thee; or to say, Rise up and walk?

The religious leaders had not expressed their criticism aloud, but Jesus through His divine power knew exactly what they were thinking. In Matthew's account of this incident, Jesus accused His critics of harboring evil thoughts: "Wherefore think ye evil in your hearts?" (Matthew 9:4). Their thoughts were evil because they were not seeking the truth, but were seeking a basis for condemning Jesus.

The scribes and Pharisees reasoned that anyone could say "Your sins are forgiven," whether it was true or not. There was no way such a claim could be proven false. On the other hand, a claim that one could work a miracle of healing could immediately be checked. Jesus proceeded to do a miracle of healing that could be checked. Thus He proved His power to do a miracle of forgiveness that could not be checked. He accepted the critics' reasoning and used it to prove that He could make good on His claim.

F. Jesus' Power of Healing (v. 24)

24. But that ye may know that the Son of man hath power upon earth to forgive sins, (he said unto the sick of the palsy,) I say unto thee, Arise, and take up thy couch, and go into thine house.

In His response Jesus referred to himself as *the Son of man*, an expression He used often. As the Son of Abraham, His relationship to the Jewish people is stressed. As the Son of God, His divine nature is emphasized. As the Son of man, His relationship to the whole human race is underscored. Yet in Daniel's prophecy, "one like the Son of man" is given everlasting dominion over all nations (Daniel 7:13, 14). This is a clear implication of deity. It is not likely that Jesus' audience in this case caught all the implications of this title, but as time went on and He used the title more often, its meaning became clearer to His disciples.

Now Jesus was ready to answer His critics in full. He had forgiven the man's sins, but the results of that forgiveness would not be immediately obvious. However, the healing of the cripple would provide evidence of Jesus' power that could not be denied. Turning to the man, Jesus ordered him to take up his bed and carry it home. Jesus' answer was direct and to the point, with no halfway measures. The miracle was not going to be partial. The man's strength would be completely returned to him so that he could carry his bed home without any help from his friends.

II. Response to the Miracle (Luke 5:25b, 26)

A. The Man Is Healed (v. 25b)

25. And immediately he rose up before them, and took up that whereon he lay, and departed to his own house, glorifying God.

Jesus' words brought instant healing, making it obvious that supernatural rather than natural powers were involved. The man's dramatic entrance through the roof would be remembered, and his equally dramatic exit carrying his bed was certain to have a profound effect on all who witnessed it. The man himself departed, glorifying God as he went. His faith and that of his

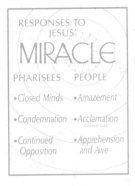

RESPONSES TO JESUS'

MIRACLE

PHARISEES   PEOPLE

• Closed Minds   • Amazement

• Condemnation   • Acclamation

• Continued   • Apprehension
  Opposition   and Awe

visual 7

friends had gained for him what otherwise would have been impossible. In the days that followed, this man's experience must have been told over a wide area.

B. The People's Response (v. 26)

26. And they were all amazed, and they glorified God, and were filled with fear, saying, We have seen strange things today.

The people had a triple response. First, *they were all amazed.* They could not understand what they had seen. Second, *they glorified God.* Jesus had made clear that His power came from God, and so the people appropriately gave God the glory. Third, the people were *filled with fear.* The reason for their fear was that they had *seen strange things.* They had seen miracles before, but this time Jesus had connected the miracle with the forgiveness of sins. This may have accounted for their fear. It helped them to realize, though only vaguely, that they were in the presence of deity. This realization often brings fear, as it did with Peter at the miraculous catch of fish (Luke 5:8).

All were amazed, but the religious leaders did not share the enthusiasm and reverence of the people. Rather, their antagonism was intensified, and they continued to oppose Jesus. Unbelievers often respond in this manner. Instead of having their hearts melted by the evidence, they are hardened.

Conclusion

A. "Pneumosomatic" Healing

Modern medical science has come to recognize that there is a strong connection between one's mental state and his physical condition. There is abundant evidence that strong emotions such as fear and anger can cause physical illness or worsen existing illness. There is evidence in the other direction too. One who is at peace with himself and the world is less susceptible to certain diseases.

A cardiologist friend of mine would take this a step further. He believes that half or more of the patients that he sees with cardiovascular diseases have spiritual problems that either cause or contribute to their ailments. We have coined the term *pneumosomatic* from the Greek *pneuma*, spirit, and *soma*, body. It designates an approach that recognizes a relationship between the spiritual and the physical in every person's makeup. Of course my friend does not claim that his theory is original. As a Christian, he is quite familiar with the teaching of Jesus.

In other situations Jesus made it quite clear that not every illness or affliction is the result of the sufferer's sins. See John 9:1-3, for example. We must not attribute every illness to the sick person's sins. But in this case Jesus healed the man spiritually by forgiving his sins before He healed him physically. Possibly his paralysis did result from his sin.

This suggests an important ministry for Christians. Unless we are physicians we cannot legally practice medicine, but we can work with physicians to promote healing. Some people become ill because they have lost hope or because they have no purpose for their life. As Christians we can give them hope and purpose that extend even beyond this life. Some persons become ill because a sense of guilt continually gnaws away at their hearts. While we cannot forgive sins as Jesus did, we can bring them to Jesus who can forgive their sins. In this sense, then, every church is a "pneumosomatic" hospital and every Christian should be practicing "pneumosomatic" medicine. The license to practice this kind of medicine is issued to every Christian by the highest authority—God's own Son, Jesus Christ.

B. Let Us Pray

We thank You, Father, that You sent Your Son into the world not only to heal sick bodies but to cure sin-sick souls. Because of that great blessing, we have Your assurance that You will forgive us our sins if we come to You with a humble and contrite heart. In Jesus' name we pray. Amen.

C. Thought to Remember

"If we confess our sins, he is faithful and just to forgive us our sins, and to cleanse us from all unrighteousness" (1 John 1:9).

Home Daily Bible Readings

Monday, Jan. 9—Jesus Heals a Leper (Luke 5:12-16)

Tuesday, Jan. 10—Jesus Even Forgives Sin (Luke 5:17-26)

Wednesday, Jan. 11—Jesus Raises the Dead (John 11:38-44)

Thursday, Jan. 12—Jesus Forgives a Sinful Woman (John 7:53—8:11)

Friday, Jan. 13—Jesus Gives the Power of Life (John 4:1-14)

Saturday, Jan. 14—Jesus Gives Hope to the Hopeless (John 5:1-9)

Sunday, Jan. 15—Jesus Promises New Life to All (John 3:16-21)

Learning by Doing

This page contains an alternate lesson plan emphasizing learning activities. Classes desiring such student involvement will find these suggestions helpful.

Learning Goals

After this lesson, students should be able to:

1. Observe the great faith of the friends of the man with palsy.

2. Evaluate the priority of spiritual healing over physical healing.

3. Glorify God for His mighty acts.

Into the Lesson

Before your students arrive, write on the chalkboard: PRAISE GOD FOR.... As each student arrives, ask him to write something on the board that will complete the statement. Invite the students to write on the board any time they feel they want to add a praise item; the writing is not limited to the time when they first come in.

When it is time to begin the lesson, review the responses on the chalkboard. Divide them between the headings **Who God Is** and **What God Does.** We praise God both for His nature (who He is) and for His actions (what He does).

Point out that today's lesson focuses on the second—God's mighty acts, done in the person of Jesus. Yet the acts show who He is. In claiming to act like God in forgiving sins, Jesus actually claimed to be God!

If you'd rather, provide paper or refer students to the student book and ask each one to write as many ways as possible to complete the statement, "Praise God for...."

Into the Word

Note that Jesus stated the purpose of His miracle of healing the paralyzed man: "that ye may know that the Son of man hath power upon earth to forgive sins" (Luke 5:24). Actually, all Jesus' miracles had the purpose of producing evidence of Jesus' deity. (See John 20:30, 31.)

Assign a small group of students to look at the miracles recorded in Luke 4 and 5. Ask them to tell what each miracle showed about Jesus. (Share with them the first paragraph under "Jesus Heals a Palsied Man" in the commentary section of this book.)

While that group is at work, ask the rest of the class to work with you to make a chart comparing the Pharisees with the friends of the palsied man. (The small group may join in this when they finish their assignment; they will report their findings later.) Make two columns on the chalkboard. Put the title PHARISEES over one, FRIENDS over the other. Then ask the following questions, which the class can answer from Luke 5:17-26.

1. Why were they there?

2. How did they deal with opposition to their ideas or their plans?

3. What evidence is here to indicate their faith or faithlessness?

4. What should have been their response to the miracle worked on the man with the palsy?

Your chart should look something like this:

PHARISEES	FRIENDS
1. They were there to discredit Jesus, or at least to criticize.	1. They believed that Jesus could help their paralyzed friend.
2. When Jesus challenged their way of thinking, they became hostile and said He had blasphemed.	2. When their way to Jesus was blocked, they found another way to reach Him.
3. Their charge of blasphemy proves they were faithless.	3. Breaking through the roof proves their faith in Jesus.
4. They should have glorified God and thought about the evidence that Jesus was divine.	4. They did glorify God. They too should have seen the evidence that Jesus was divine.

By the time you finish the chart, your task force on miracles should be ready to report. Discuss their findings briefly. Note that even though Jesus worked physical miracles. He emphasized His spiritual ministry. The miracles proved He was the Son of God.

Into Life

Ask your students to think about the men who carried their friend to Jesus. What great faith they displayed when they broke up the roof! What if Jesus hadn't helped? How would they have excused their action? But Jesus did help, as they believed He would.

Ask, "Do you have that much faith? What have you done lately that would be risky or would seem foolish except for faith in Christ?"

Let's Talk It Over

The questions on this page are designed to encourage review of the lesson Scriptures and to promote discussion of the lesson by the class. The answers provided are only discussion starters. Let your class talk it over from there.

1. Are we inclined to become like the Pharisees in their narrow-mindedness and hypocrisy? How may this be a danger to us?

We need not be disturbed if people around us say we are narrow-minded because we believe basic Biblical doctrines or adhere to God's moral standards. But we must take care not to become rigid and legalistic in regard to matters not taught in the Bible. We need not cling to an ineffective teaching method or order of worship just because it is customary. Some churches are handicapped because they continue with traditional methods that actually hinder their progress.

Our first obligation is to be faithful to God in obeying His instructions and guidelines for the church. Then we must adopt programs and procedures consistent with the Scriptures and capable of meeting the needs of what we see. If we find that a certain program is no longer affecting lives, then it is pharisaical to insist on its continuance. We do well to replace it with something that will work.

2. The friends of the paralytic were determined to bring him to Jesus. How may we relate this to our practice of praying for others?

When we have friends who are suffering, sorrowing, or otherwise in need, it is exciting to realize that our prayers can bring them to Jesus for help. It takes more than prayer to bring an unsaved friend to Jesus for salvation, but prayer can be a great help. Paul instructed Timothy: "I urge, then, first of all, that requests, prayers, intercession and thanksgiving be made for everyone" (1 Timothy 2:1, *New International Version*). God expects us to exhibit our faith in Him and dependence on Him by coming to Him with persistence regarding specific needs—our own and those of others. Satan tries to distract us from prayer and discourage us. This account of the paralytic and his determined friends illustrates well the kind of persistence that is required for effective prayer.

3. Jesus was impressed with the faith of the paralytic and his friends. How can we please Him and impress Him with our faith?

The paralytic and his friends were not afraid of risk. They risked being rejected by Jesus; they risked the anger of the man whose roof was broken. They risked the displeasure of the crowd when they interrupted Jesus talk.

What have *we* risked because of our faith? Most Christians have to admit that their faith in Christ has caused them little actual discomfort or inconvenience. Jesus is sure to be more pleased with our faith if we give more than is convenient of our income for Christian work; if we risk embarrassment or rejection by approaching strangers with our witness; if we take a heavy load of responsibility in the church.

4. Why should we often study the miracles of Jesus?

In spite of having received Jesus Christ as Savior, in spite of having prayed for forgiveness, in spite of having regularly partaken of the Lord's Supper, many Christians still are burdened with guilt over their sins. Jesus used His power to work miracles to prove His power to forgive sins. The more our minds are filled with His miracles, the greater is our assurance that He can forgive even our most terrible sins. Let's welcome the record of miracles in our Bible study. It programs our minds with the realization of God's love, mercy, and power working on our behalf.

5. What should a Christian do if he feels that his own illness may be concerned with sin?

Illness can be related to unconfessed sin or some other resistance to God's will. We need to take a personal inventory. Have we broken one of God's commands and tried to put it from our minds? Are we refusing to forgive another person who has wronged us? Are we, like Jonah, attempting to run away from something God wants us to do? If we must say yes to one of these questions, we may have discovered a cause for our illness. A prayer of repentance and an effort to correct our attitude or behavior may put us on the road to recovery. But if honest inventory reveals no such need for repentance and reformation, then we may assume that our sickness has come through carelessness or for some other reason. Even then, it may be that God has allowed it in order to teach us or mold us, as He did with Paul's famous "thorn in the flesh" (2 Corinthians 12:7-10).

Forgiveness: A Measure of Love

LESSON SCRIPTURE: Luke 7:36-50.

PRINTED TEXT: Luke 7:36-50.

Luke 7:36-50

36 One of the Pharisees desired him that he would eat with him. And he went into the Pharisee's house, and sat down to meat.

37 And, behold, a woman in the city, which was a sinner, when she knew that Jesus sat at meat in the Pharisee's house, brought an alabaster box of ointment,

38 And stood at his feet behind him weeping, and began to wash his feet with tears, and did wipe them with the hairs of her head, and kissed his feet, and anointed them with the ointment.

39 Now when the Pharisee which had bidden him saw it, he spake within himself, saying, This man, if he were a prophet, would have known who and what manner of woman this is that toucheth him; for she is a sinner.

40 And Jesus answering said unto him, Simon, I have somewhat to say unto thee. And he saith, Master, say on.

41 There was a certain creditor which had two debtors: the one owed five hundred pence, and the other fifty.

42 And when they had nothing to pay, he frankly forgave them both. Tell me therefore, which of them will love him most?

43 Simon answered and said, I suppose that he, to whom he forgave most. And he said unto him, Thou hast rightly judged.

44 And he turned to the woman, and said unto Simon, Seest thou this woman? I entered into thine house, thou gavest me no water for my feet: but she hath washed my feet with tears, and wiped them with the hairs of her head.

45 Thou gavest me no kiss: but this woman, since the time I came in, hath not ceased to kiss my feet.

46 My head with oil thou didst not anoint: but this woman hath anointed my feet with ointment.

47 Wherefore I say unto thee, Her sins, which are many, are forgiven; for she loved much: but to whom little is forgiven, the same loveth little.

48 And he said unto her, Thy sins are forgiven.

49 And they that sat at meat with him began to say within themselves, Who is this that forgiveth sins also?

50 And he said to the woman, Thy faith hath saved thee; go in peace.

Golden Text: He said to the woman, Thy faith hath saved thee; go in peace.
—Luke 7:50.

Scenes of Love and Compassion
Unit 2: Proclamation and Ministry
(Lessons 5-9)

Lesson Aims

After this lesson students should be able to:
1. Understand that God can forgive all our sins, no matter how terrible we think they are.
2. Have a growing appreciation for the fact that God loves us in spite of our sins.
3. Show others how God's forgiveness has touched his or her life.

Lesson Outline

INTRODUCTION
A. Seeing Our Sins
B. Lesson Background
I. A SINFUL WOMAN COMES TO JESUS (Luke 7:36-38)
A. The Setting for Her Coming (v. 36)
B. The Woman's Actions (vv. 37, 38)
II. REACTION TO THE WOMAN (Luke 7:39-43)
A. Simon's Problem (v. 39)
Spiritual Pride
B. Jesus' Response (vv. 40-43)
III. CONTRASTING ATTITUDES (Luke 7:44-50)
A. Negligence and Devotion (vv. 44-46)
B. Sins Forgiven (vv. 47, 48, 50)
Payment for Repentance
C. The Critic's Reaction (v. 49)
D. Jesus' Parting Words (v. 50)
CONCLUSION
A. A Limited God
B. A Friend of Sinners
C. Let Us Pray
D. Thought to Remember

Display visual 8 from the visuals/learning resources packet and refer to it as you consider the actions of the woman in this lesson. The visual is shown on page 179.

Introduction

A. Seeing Our Sins

A man who lived in the Scottish Highlands was considered by his neighbors to be a bit strange, and their judgment was not without some basis. For example, he usually wore a heavy overcoat. On the front of the coat were a number of large, brightly colored patches. The back of the coat, however, had only one small, inconspicuous patch.

When asked about his unusual coat, the man explained that the patches on the front represented the sins of his neighbors. They were large and quite obvious. The small patch on the back of the coat represented his own sins. They were quite small, and he could not even see it.

Simon, the self-righteous Pharisee, was rather like this man. He could readily see the sins of others, especially of the woman of the street. But he was so spiritually blind that he could not see sins and need for forgiveness. We suspect that in this respect the typical church member may have more in common with Simon than with the sinful woman.

B. Lesson Background

Several weeks or months passed between the events recorded in last week's lesson and the incident dealt with in today's lesson. During this time the Pharisees intensified their opposition to Jesus. They could not seriously challenge the fact that He had performed many miracles. These had been done openly and before many witnesses, and to question them would only discredit the questioners. So the critics turned to petty criticisms based on Jesus' supposed violation of the law (Luke 6:1-11).

During this time, Jesus chose twelve who would be His closest disciples or apostles (Luke 6:12-16). Also He presented the discourse we have come to call the Sermon on the Mount (Luke 6:20-49). After this sermon Jesus healed a centurion's servant, commending him for his great faith. He also raised a widow's son at Nain (Luke 7:1-17). Many other miracles are not individually recorded (Luke 6:17-19).

By this time Jesus was well known throughout the province of Galilee. It is likely that His popularity was reaching its highest level among the people. Of course, this served only to increase the antagonism of the religious leaders. As long as Jesus remained an obscure itinerant preacher, He posed no threat to the system. But now that He was being acclaimed by the people, the leaders felt compelled to do whatever they could to stop Him. The events recorded in today's lesson probably occurred in Capernaum, which Jesus had made the center for His ministry in Galilee.

Only the Gospel of Luke contains this account. It makes several important points. First of all, it illustrates Jesus' love and concern for sinners, an attitude that sharply contrasted with the attitude of the Pharisees, who sought to remove themselves as far from sinners as possible. The second lesson that this narrative teaches is that one who has been forgiven much shows greater gratitude and love than one who has been forgiven little. Still another point that this story makes is that Jesus can forgive sin, a point that had been made earlier in the account of the healing of the paralytic (Luke 5:18:26).

I. A Sinful Woman Comes to Jesus (Luke 7:36-38)

A. The Setting for Her Coming (v. 36)

36. And one of the Pharisees desired him that he would eat with him. And he went into the Pharisee's house, and sat down to meat.

We know nothing about Simon the Pharisee except what we are told in this passage. It is reasonable to suppose that he was a prominent Pharisee living in Capernaum. Since Jesus was at the height of His popularity, it is likely that He received many invitations to social functions. Luke chose to tell us about this occasion because of the lessons it teaches.

Luke does not specifically state what Simon's motives were in inviting Jesus into his house. But Simon did not extend to Jesus the usual amenities afforded a guest, so it seems likely that his motives were less than friendly. Perhaps he sought in intimate conversation some basis for criticism. Whatever his motives, he certainly did not fool Jesus.

B. The Woman's Actions (vv. 37, 38)

37, 38. And, behold, a woman in the city, which was a sinner, when she knew that Jesus sat at meat in the Pharisee's house, brought an alabaster box of ointment, and stood at his feet behind him weeping, and began to wash his feet with her tears, and did wipe them with the hairs of her head, and kissed his feet, and anointed them with the ointment.

In the midst of the meal, a surprising thing happened. A woman of the city appeared and began to lavish her gratitude upon Jesus. The woman's name is not given, and we have no way of knowing her identity. Some commentators have identified her as Mary Magdalene, but there is no basis whatever for this. She is called *a woman in the city* and *a sinner*, probably indicating that she was a well-known prostitute.

Her presence at the banquet probably was not considered an intrusion. In those days when a wealthy person gave a banquet, it was common practice to allow the poor to enter and stand about as onlookers. Instead of the privacy we usually want in a dinner served in the home, the rich enjoyed displaying their wealth by allowing outsiders to witness their lavish feasts.

The common practice was for each guest to recline on a couch with his feet pointed away from the table. Leaning on his left arm, he would then eat with his right hand. While this may seem awkward to us, it was the usual practice in that day. Understanding this, we can understand how the woman could anoint Jesus' feet without having to crawl under the table.

Probably the *alabaster box* is better called a jar or vase. The Greek is simply *an alabaster*. Precious ointments and perfumes were often sold and kept in such costly containers. What this alabaster held was most likely an expensive perfumed ointment such as rich people used to anoint their hair and skin. Poor people used cheap olive oil for that purpose. The woman seems to have been overwhelmed by her emotions of gratitude. She wept profusely, the tears falling upon Jesus' feet. She then wiped His feet with her hair and poured perfume upon them. When the woman unloosed her hair in public, an act considered disgraceful, she gave further evidence of her unrestrained appreciation for the forgiveness she had received from Jesus.

II. Reaction to the Woman (Luke 7:39-43)

A. Simon's Problem (v. 39)

39. Now when the Pharisee which had bidden him saw it, he spake within himself, saying, This man, if he were a prophet, would have known who and what manner of woman this is that toucheth him; for she is a sinner.

Simon was aghast that Jesus had allowed the woman to lavish her emotions upon Him. Pharisees attempted if possible to avoid anyone they considered to be a sinner, especially a notorious sinner. Simon's logic seemed reasonable enough to him. If Jesus really were a prophet, then He would have known that the woman was a sinner and would have avoided her.

A WOMAN'S EXAMPLE
REPENTANCE
FORGIVENESS
LOVE
SERVICE

visual 8

SPIRITUAL PRIDE

In 1987, a major scandal erupted in the world of religious television. News leaked out that the host of a religious talk show had committed adultery some seven years earlier. Charges and counter-charges of bribery, "hush money," collusion, and intimidation ran rampant.

A Christian businessman who was involved in uncovering the scandal proudly announced that it was his mission to "blow the whistle" on the sins of ministers whenever he could. (This in spite of charges pending against him for the mismanagement of a large corporation.)

A "skeleton in the closet" of the minister's wife was also revealed: she was undergoing treatment for addiction to prescription drugs. Prominent religious figures lined up on both sides of the issue, some publicly denouncing the sinners in scathingly self-righteous terms.

This has always been a problem, hasn't it? We observe both the sin and the denunciation of it by those whose sins are more genteel (or at least not yet discovered!) Thus the Pharisee could criticize Jesus for allowing himself to be touched by a "sinful woman."

We should not make light of sin when others commit it. But we should never forget that we too are sinners. God is the judge of us all. Jesus taught us that there is far more healing power in the touch of a forgiving hand than in the tirade of a "faultless" hypocrite.   —C. R. B.

B. Jesus' Response (vv. 40-43)

40-43. And Jesus answering said unto him, Simon, I have somewhat to say unto thee. And he saith, Master, say on. There was a certain creditor which had two debtors: the one owed five hundred pence, and the other fifty. And when they had nothing to pay, he frankly forgave them both. Tell me therefore, which of them will love him most? Simon answered and said, I suppose that he, to whom he forgave most. And he said unto him, Thou hast rightly judged.

Even though Simon did not speak his thoughts aloud, he could not keep them from Jesus. Knowing what Simon was thinking, Jesus proceeded to answer his objection by using a parable.

Pence is the plural of *penny*, but here it names a silver coin about halfway between an American dime and a quarter. It was called a *denarius* in Greek, and it represented a day's wages for a working man (Matthew 20:2). One debt then was nearly twenty months' pay, and the other about two months' pay. But the amount of debt is not the point that Jesus was making, but the

difference between the two debts. One debtor owed ten times as much as the other.

We should not suppose that God measures sins as a lender counts money. Without forgiveness, sins called small are as fatal as sins called big. We all stand condemned before God. But in our own minds we do make a difference between sins, and so did the Pharisee. If he acknowledged any sin of his own, he certainly thought it was slight; but he thought that woman was very bad indeed. Whether he yet saw the meaning of the parable or not, he could not avoid the right answer to Jesus' question. Jesus commended the answer and then proceeded to show how it fit the situation at hand.

III. Contrasting Attitudes (Luke 7:44-50)

A. Negligence and Devotion (vv. 44-46)

44. And he turned to the woman, and said unto Simon, Seest thou this woman? I entered into thine house, thou gavest me no water for my feet: but she hath washed my feet with tears, and wiped them with the hairs of her head.

Jesus then turned to the woman and began to contrast Simon's behavior with hers. In that day it was common practice for the host to offer a guest water and a towel to wash his feet when he entered the house, or have a servant perform this service. But Simon had not offered this common amenity. By contrast, the woman had moistened Jesus' feet with her tears and wiped them dry with her hair.

45. Thou gavest me no kiss: but this woman, since the time I came in, hath not ceased to kiss my feet.

It was also common for a host to greet his guest with a kiss. Whether out of negligence or as a direct snub, Simon had failed to do this. The woman, however, had not limited her act of devotion to a single perfunctory kiss, but had continued to kiss Jesus' feet all the evening.

46. My head with oil thou didst not anoint: but this woman hath anointed my feet with ointment.

The contrast in behavior continued. Simon had not even anointed Jesus' brow and head with a few drops of cheap olive oil, while the woman had lavishly anointed His feet with expensive perfume. Of course we cannot read Simon's heart and know his intentions. His inhospitable behavior may have been nothing more than negligence. On the other hand, he may have deliberately invited Jesus to this banquet for the purpose of insulting Him in order to gain favor with Jesus' critics. In either event, Jesus' words must have embarrassed him.

B. Sins Forgiven (vv. 47, 48)

47, 48. Wherefore I say unto thee, Her sins, which are many, are forgiven; for she loved much: but to whom little is forgiven, the same loveth little. And he said unto her, Thy sins are forgiven.

Jesus did not deny that the woman had many sins. She was a great sinner, but she had been forgiven. This forgiveness had already been granted at some point before the banquet. The love she had shown Jesus at the banquet came because He had forgiven her. It did not, as the *King James Version* may seem to indicate, produce the forgiveness. The parable that Jesus had earlier given indicates that the forgiveness was an act of grace and could not be purchased at any price.

Simon, on the other hand, had not demonstrated any love toward Jesus because he had been forgiven little. In his own mind, perhaps he was not a sinner at all and had no need of forgiveness. This issue was at the very heart of Jesus' ongoing controversy with the self-righteous Pharisees.

Turning once more to the woman, Jesus pronounced her sins forgiven. Actually this had occurred earlier, but Jesus' words gave her further assurance.

PAYMENT FOR REPENTANCE

A magazine article tells of an unusual program that is being tested in a city school system. About six hundred students in the sixth, seventh, and eighth grades are paid $3.35 per week to behave themselves in school and attend "anti-pregnancy" classes.

As you might guess, this program has met with mixed reactions. One schoolboard member who supports the program has said, "Children will do things for money. This is a money-oriented society." (So what else is new, we might ask!) A board member among the minority who opposed the program objected, "To bribe students to come to school and behave themselves goes against public education." Most Christians will probably side with the minority on this issue, don't you think?

There is a sense in which it might be said that Christians are "paid" for their repentance. But the payment is far different from getting some change in one's pocket once a week.

The payment for our repentance is forgiveness. It is a reward that cannot be spent, banked, or invested. But it is real, nonetheless.

As Jesus indicated, there is a reciprocal cause-and-effect relationship between love and forgiveness. Love comes because of forgiveness,

Home Daily Bible Readings

Monday, Jan. 16—A Woman Anoints Jesus (Luke 7:36-39)
Tuesday, Jan. 17—Jesus Tells a Parable (Luke 7:39-50)
Wednesday, Jan. 18—Abundant Redemption in God (Psalm 130)
Thursday, Jan. 19—Forgiveness Not Returned (Matthew 18:21-35)
Friday, Jan. 20—The God of Forgiveness (Nehemiah 9:16-19)
Saturday, Jan. 21—God's Offer of Forgiveness (Lamentations 3:19-26)
Sunday, Jan. 22—The Ultimate Forgiveness of Christ (Luke 23:26-34)

and forgiveness comes because of love and repentance. Those who are forgiven most understand God's love the most. Those who love God the most are the most likely to seek and find the greatest forgiveness.   —C. R. B.

C. The Critics' Reaction (v. 49)

49. And they that sat at meat with him began to say within themselves, Who is this that forgiveth sins also?

While Jesus' words brought reassurance to the woman, they struck at the heart of the Pharisees. Their response reminds us of a similar situation at the healing of the paralytic (Luke 5:21). The Pharisees were wrestling with the problem of Jesus' identity. Was He a prophet? Or was He more? Jesus' actions and words gave clear evidence that He was much more than a prophet, but their minds were closed to this truth.

All through His ministry, Jesus had step by step been revealing His identity as the Messiah, the Son of God. This revelation was done gradually because neither the people nor the religious leaders were prepared to accept it. They had built up false notions about what the Messiah would be like and what He would do. Resenting the rule of Rome, they hoped the Messiah would lead them in armed revolution. If Jesus had said plainly that He was the Messiah, they might have plunged into bloody rebellion. That was not what He wanted.

When Jesus forgave the woman's sin, He was giving one more clue to His identity. Yet the Pharisees rejected this evidence and became more hostile toward Him. Jesus came to save sinful women, but He also came to save sinful Pharisees. It must have pained Him deeply when His efforts to reach them were rebuffed.

D. Jesus' Parting Words (v. 50)

50. And he said to the woman, Thy faith hath saved thee; go in peace.

Jesus gave the woman a final word of assurance. Her faith had brought her to Him in the first place, and her trust in Him led her to believe that He could forgive her sin. Every sinner must in the same way come to Him in faith and trust Him to forgive his or her sins. Such a trusting faith will never lead to disappointment.

When Jesus bade the woman to go in peace, He conveyed everything that was implied in the Hebrew term *shalom*—prosperity in both body and soul. We have no record of what happened to the woman after this, but we cannot doubt that her life was dramatically changed.

Conclusion

A. A Limited God

In one way or another most of us reveal that we think God is limited. We limit Him by living as if Christianity were a one-day-a-week religion. On Sunday we go to church, enter into the worship, sing hymns, drop our offering in the plate, partake of communion, listen to the sermon, and then go home with a good feeling. But that's where it ends. We try to keep God in a neat box called Sunday and shut Him out of the rest of the week. We attempt to limit Him by keeping Him out of important areas of our lives—business, recreation, school.

Many people limit God by refusing to believe that He can forgive sins, really forgive even the worst of sins. Some persons go through their entire life carrying the burden of some sin that they feel God cannot forgive. Such a life is likely to be warped or contorted, missing the joy that comes from the knowledge that God can erase all sins.

The woman who poured out her gratitude to Jesus must have come from a sordid background. Her sins had made her an outcast among the upright citizens of the community. We are not told what brought her to Jesus in the first place. Perhaps she heard Him preach, or a friend may have brought her to Him. Whatever the circumstances of her introduction, she came willing to listen and accept what He had to say. In this respect, her attitude was quite different from the attitude of the Pharisees who often came to criticize. Not only did she listen to Jesus; she also believed what He had to say about forgiveness of sins. Because she believed, her burden was relieved and she could show her appreciation in ways that shocked Simon and his self-righteous friends.

If Jesus could forgive this woman, is there any reason to doubt that He can forgive our sins today? If we believe that Jesus has unlimited power, then we can be assured that He has unlimited power to forgive sin.

B. A Friend of Sinners

The Pharisees had dedicated themselves to lives of moral and religious purity. To achieve this goal they had carefully built around the law of Moses a complex code of regulations that governed their daily lives. One way to avoid contamination by the world was to avoid contact with the world as much as possible. Although they did not ordinarily retire to monasteries, they did try to avoid contact with those they deemed notorious sinners. They believed that there was some truth in the old adage that "birds of a feather flock together."

They were critical of Jesus because He did not avoid sinners. They accused Him of being "a friend of publicans and sinners" (Luke 7:34). When Jesus allowed the sinful woman to approach Him at the banquet in Simon's home, the Pharisees had additional fuel for their criticism. They reasoned that if Jesus did not know that she was a sinner, then He was not a prophet. On the other hand, if He knew she was a sinner and did not spurn her, then He was not a prophet.

They never could quite understand His real mission, which was to seek and save the lost, whoever they were and wherever they were. It is easy to criticize these Pharisees, but in so doing we ought to recognize that there is probably a bit of the Pharisee in each of us. Most of us feel uncomfortable in the presence of notorious sinners, and most of us do little evangelistic work among the prostitutes and addicts and street people—the outcasts of our society. Yet we must overcome these feelings if we are to follow our Lord into all the avenues of service in which He leads.

C. Let Us Pray

Dear God, we thank You that You sent Your Son into the world to save sinners—both the outcasts and the Pharisees. Help us to become conscious of the seriousness of our sins. Help us also to know the joy that comes from forgiveness of sins. In Jesus' saving name we pray. Amen.

D. Thought to Remember

Dear Lord and Father of mankind,
  Forgive our foolish ways!
Reclothe us in our rightful mind;
  In purer lives Thy service find,
In deeper reverence, praise.
                                    —JOHN GREENLEAF WHITTIER

Learning by Doing

This page contains an alternate lesson plan emphasizing learning activities. Classes desiring such student involvement will find these suggestions helpful.

Learning Goals

As a result of studying this lesson, each student should be able to do the following:

1. State the nature of God's forgiveness.

2. Explain the parable of the creditor.

3. Suggest ways in which contemporary Christians can follow the example of the woman in the lesson text.

Into the Lesson

As the students arrive, assign to each one a number, 1, 2, 3, or 4. When it is time to begin, ask the people with the same number to sit together. Give each group one of the following statements and ask them to decide what is wrong with it. (The statements are in the student book.)

1. God's forgiveness must be earned by careful adherence to His laws. Every sin one commits must be atoned by at least one good deed.

2. I cannot earn God's forgiveness, but I can get it if I try hard enough.

3. God forgives our past sins when we become Christians. Then He expects us to earn His favor by doing enough good to offset any sins we commit later.

4. God's forgiveness cannot be earned. He chooses some to be forgiven and some not to be, regardless of what they do.

After the groups have had a few minutes to discuss the statements, discuss them as a whole class. Note the following points:

Statement 1 indicates that forgiveness is earned. Actually it is a gift of God's grace to people who do not earn it.

Statement 2 sounds more modest, but it too bases forgiveness on human effort rather than on God's grace.

Statement 3 is another variation of 1. It indicates that the non-Christian's sins are forgiven by grace, but it fails to appreciate the continuing nature of God's grace.

Statement 4 correctly concludes that forgiveness is a gift of God's grace, but it fails to recognize the fact that man chooses to accept or reject the gift.

After some discussion of the errors in these statements, suggest the following to sum things up: "Forgiveness is a gift of God's grace. We must have faith in order to receive it, but we do not earn it either by faith or by good works."

Into the Word

Keep the groups you established earlier, and give them the following assignments:

1. Read Luke 7:36-50. Of the views of forgiveness we have discussed, which is probably closest to what the Pharisee believed? Which is more like the woman's view?

2. Read Luke 7:36-50. Explain the point of the parable of the creditors.

3. Read Luke 7:36-50. Explain the role of faith in the woman's forgiveness. Note verse 50: "Thy faith hath saved thee."

4. Read Luke 7:36-50. Try to imagine how the woman's life was different after this event.

As the groups report their conclusions, see that these thoughts are included.

1. Probably the Pharisee would have subscribed to statement 1. It seems that the woman's view was more like the summary we made.

2. The parable of the creditors reminds us that God's grace is great enough to forgive all sins, but the one who feels guilty of great sins will be more grateful.

3. It seems that the woman had been forgiven before she came to the Pharisee's house. Her gratitude and her gift were her response. At some earlier time she must have taken Him at His word when He spoke of forgiveness. She must have believed He was the Son of God, able to forgive sins, which the Pharisees refused to believe (verse 49). Specifically, she believed He could forgive *her* sins. This faith made her ready to receive the salvation Jesus offered.

4. Since it appears obvious to us that the woman's repentance was sincere, we have to imagine that she was no longer a notorious sinner. We need not suppose she was perfect (who is?), but surely her life was mostly pure and wholesome.

Into Life

Ask the class to review the text to see in how many ways the Pharisee host had been negligent in his hospitality to Jesus. List these on the chalkboard. Then ask, "Are we sometimes as self-righteously negligent in our service to the Lord?"

Similarly, look at the woman's example of unrestrained devotion and worship. Together, list some ways we today can imitate her example.

Let's Talk It Over

The questions on this page are designed to encourage review of the lesson Scriptures and to promote discussion of the lesson by the class. The answers provided are only discussion starters. Let your class talk it over from there.

1. Do Christians generally hesitate to call themselves sinners? Are they sinners?

Some Christians readily call themselves sinners, but many do not. Perhaps some hesitate to use the term because it connotes scandalous sins such as drunkenness, adultery, and murder. But unspectacular sins such as jealousy, coveteousness, speaking slanderously or spitefully, and violating traffic laws are still sins.

Some may feel that they should not call themselves sinners because they have had their sins forgiven through Christ. But the apostle Paul, long after he became a Christian, was still referring to himself as "the worst of sinners" (1 Timothy 1:15, 16, *New International Version*). John Newton, who wrote "Amazing Grace," spoke late in life of remembering two things: "That I am a great sinner, and that Christ is a great Savior." This attitude also seems fitting for us.

2. Since we are not able to anoint and kiss Jesus' feet, how may we show our gratitude to Him for bringing us forgiveness?

If we would consider what our character and our destiny would be without Jesus, it would stir us up to more fervent devotion. Perhaps we can draw a parallel between the woman's coming to Jesus while He was reclining at a table and meeting with Him regularly at the Lord's table. In each case there should be a remembrance of sinfulness. Each situation should have its emotional aspects—the shedding of tears at Communion time seems very fitting. And in each of these parallel situations there should be some definite step of devotion to Christ. The Lord's Supper offers a very appropriate occasion for dedicating ourselves to a fresh effort at holiness in thought, word, and deed.

3. We do not know exactly why Simon the Pharisee failed to extend the normal gestures of hospitality toward Jesus, but he at the least was guilty of taking Jesus for granted. What are some ways in which we take Jesus for granted?

We use the phrase "in Jesus' name" with our prayers. To use it properly we should pray for what will honor and magnify Jesus, but sometimes we use it with prayers that are selfish. In

similar fashion we occasionally invoke Jesus' teachings to attempt to prove that we are more pious or better Christians than someone else. Another way that we take Him for granted is to sing insincerely or thoughtlessly those hymns that express dedication to Him. Unlike Simon we claim to be Jesus' followers, and yet there are times we try to use Him instead of letting Him use us.

4. The lesson writer points out that Jesus' forgiveness "was an act of grace and could not be purchased even by love." Why is this important?

It seems that some believers are trying to earn forgiveness. They read the Bible and pray, but sometimes they speak as if they were earning God's favor. Their service in the church may be evidence of loving gratitude to God, or it may indicate that they are trying to make God obligated to bless them. Their financial gifts, instead of being the sign of "a cheerful giver" (2 Corinthians 9:7), may represent a subtle effort to bribe God. We ought to be generous with gifts and service, but to present them as an effort to earn forgiveness is surely an affront to God, since He has gone to such great lengths to obtain for us a forgiveness that is abundant and free.

5. Jesus told the woman in Simon's house, "Go in peace." He commanded a woman taken in adultery, "Go now and leave your life of sin" (John 8:11, *New International Version*). How are these two commands similar?

When we come to Jesus and receive forgiveness of our sins, we have a remarkable new capacity for peace. The old gnawing sense of guilt is gone; the fear of death and hell is vanquished; the pressure of resisting God's call is relieved. But if we fail to make a break with the sins of the past, the guilt, fear, and pressure will build up again and destroy our new-found peace. To put it another way, once we are forgiven we have the privilege of walking with Jesus, who "himself is our peace" (Ephesians 2:14, *New International Version*). But if we choose to walk in the old paths of sin, we forfeit the peace that comes with Jesus' companionship.

The Significance of Touch

LESSON SCRIPTURE: Luke 8:1-3, 40-56.

PRINTED TEXT: Luke 8:41-55.

Luke 8:41-55

41 And, behold, there came a man named Jairus, and he was a ruler of the synagogue; and he fell down at Jesus' feet, and besought him that he would come into his house:

42 For he had one only daughter, about twelve years of age, and she lay a dying. But as he went the people thronged him.

43 And a woman having an issue of blood twelve years, which had spent all her living upon physicians, neither could be healed of any,

44 Came behind him, and touched the border of his garment: and immediately her issue of blood stanched.

45 And Jesus said, Who touched me? When all denied, Peter and they that were with him said, Master, the multitude throng thee and press thee, and sayest thou, Who touched me?

46 And Jesus said, Somebody hath touched me: for I perceive that virtue is gone out of me.

47 And when the woman saw that she was not hid, she came trembling, and falling down before him, she declared unto him before all the people for what cause she had touched him, and how she was healed immediately.

48 And he said unto her, Daughter, be of good comfort: thy faith hath made thee whole; go in peace.

49 While he yet spake, there cometh one from the ruler of the synagogue's house, saying to him, Thy daughter is dead; trouble not the Master.

50 But when Jesus heard it, he answered him, saying, Fear not: believe only, and she shall be made whole.

51 And when he came into the house, he suffered no man to go in, save Peter, and James, and John, and the father and the mother of the maiden.

52 And all wept, and bewailed her: but he said, Weep not; she is not dead, but sleepeth.

53 And they laughed him to scorn, knowing that she was dead.

54 And he put them all out, and took her by the hand, and called, saying, Maid, arise.

55 And her spirit came again, and she arose straightway: and he commanded to give her meat.

Golden Text: He put them all out, and took her by the hand, and called, saying, Maid, arise.—Luke 8:54.

Scenes of Love and Compassion
Unit 2: Proclamation and Ministry
(Lessons 5-9)

Lesson Aims

As a result of studying this lesson each student should be able to:

1. Understand the details of the raising of Jairus' daughter and the healing of the woman with an issue of blood.

2. Appreciate the fact that God offers sources of strength to sustain us in times of personal crises.

3. Offer help and sympathy to those who suffer loss and bereavement.

Lesson Outline

INTRODUCTION
  A. "We Get Help"
  B. Lesson Background
I. A FAITH THAT CALLS FOR HELP (Luke 8:41, 42)
  A. Jairus Comes for Help (v. 41)
     Caught in the Middle
  B. His Desperate Need for Help (v. 42)
II. A FAITH THAT ACTS (Luke 8:43-48)
  A. The Woman's Problem (v. 43)
  B. Her Effort to Find Help (v. 44)
  C. Jesus' Response (vv. 45, 46)
  D. The Woman's Admission (v. 47)
  E. Jesus' Reassuring Words (v. 48)
III. A FAITH THAT IS REWARDED (Luke 8:49-55)
  A. The Bad News (v. 49)
  B. Jesus' Response (v. 50)
  C. Jesus Enters Jairus' House (vv. 51, 52)
  D. Jesus Scorned (v. 53)
  E. Jairus' Daughter Raised (vv. 54, 55)
     Pardon Me While I Laugh
CONCLUSION
  A. The Touch of His Hand
  B. Let Us Pray
  C. Thought to Remember

Display visual 9 from the visuals/learning resources packet. It correlates with the "Introduction" section below. The visual is shown on page 189.

Introduction

A. "We Get Help"

A minister was facing a serious struggle within his congregation, and at the same time was going through a crisis in his own life. Yet in the midst of his difficulties, he preached a very powerful sermon. A close friend, who knew about his problems, later spoke to him and complimented him on his sermon. And then he added, "But I don't know how you do it after all you have been through."

"When we come to the end of our own resources," came the minister's quiet reply, "we get help."

When Jairus faced a most serious crisis—his daughter lay dying—he soon came to the end of his own resources. Then he got help—he came to Jesus.

The woman with the issue of blood had exhausted all of her resources, emotional and physical. In this crisis, she did the only thing left for her to do—she got help.

At one time or another every one of us is likely to pass through a time of trouble. Certainly God expects us to use our own resources to solve our problems. Yet when we have exhausted our resources, we know that we can go to God and get help. But would it not be wiser to get help even before we come to the end of our own resources? God is not our strength just in times of extremity. He stands ready to help us even in our little everyday problems.

B. Lesson Background

Following the banquet in the house of Simon the Pharisee, Jesus continued His ministry in Galilee. Everywhere He went He was surrounded by large crowds. In the midst of this busy schedule, He and His disciples got into a boat and traveled to the land of the Gadarenes, or Gerasenes, on the southeastern shore of the Sea of Galilee. They may have taken the trip in order to get away from the crowd for a while and get some rest. As they were crossing the lake, Jesus stilled a sudden storm, and the disciples were filled with awe.

On the east side of the lake, Jesus freed a man from demons who had taken control of him, but He let the demons enter a herd of swine. The swine then ran down a steep slope and drowned in the sea. Frightened by such power, and perhaps upset by the loss of the hogs, people of that area asked Jesus to leave. In so doing, they deprived themselves of the many blessings His presence would have brought. But the Gadarenes were not much different from many today who lose countless blessings because they send Jesus away.

Since they were not welcome among the Gadarenes, Jesus and His disciples entered the boat and returned to Capernaum. Here the people welcomed Jesus enthusiastically. This provides the setting for today's lesson.

I. A Faith That Calls for Help
(Luke 8:41, 42)

A. Jairus Comes for Help (v. 41)

41. And, behold, there came a man named Jairus, and he was a ruler of the synagogue; and he fell down at Jesus' feet, and besought him that he would come into his house.

A ruler of the synagogue held a prominent position, and undoubtedly the man was highly respected and well-to-do. From the world's point of view, he had everything going for him. Yet one turn of events, the serious illness of his daughter, shoved all this into the background. In that situation the man did not hesitate to humble himself before Jesus. He must have known that his actions would earn him the scorn and rejection of some of his fellow religious leaders, but this did not deter him.

It seems obvious that Jairus knew who Jesus was and probably had heard Him preach, perhaps many times. He may have witnessed some of His miracles. He could hardly avoid the controversy that swirled about Jesus, and he may have been numbered among Jesus' critics. Yet in a moment of personal crisis, his priorities were radically rearranged. The life of his daughter was worth more than the plaudits of men.

Most of us have at one time or another faced a similar crisis. In such a situation, the things that counted most with us came to the front. But isn't it a shame that we so often wait until a crisis confronts before we finally decide what really matters?

CAUGHT IN THE MIDDLE

A tragic eighteenth-century confrontation between church and state was the subject of an excellent film, *The Mission*, which won a 1987 Oscar for the beauty of its cinematography.

By the middle of the seventeen hundreds, Jesuit missionaries to Paraguay had established thirty prosperous native Indian communities. These had raised the Indians' standard of living significantly. People of the Guarani tribe, in particular, had become skilled artisans. The musical instruments they crafted were highly desired in Europe.

The Spanish-Portuguese struggle for supremacy in the New World finally resulted in a demand that the church disband the missions and send the Indians back to their former primitive life in the jungle. The church official who had to make the decision was caught in the middle, pulled by what was good for the Indians on one side, and by what he perceived was good for the church in Europe on the other.

How to Say It

CAPERNAUM.   Kuh-*per*-nay-um.
GADARA.   *Gad*-uh-ruh.
GADARENES.   *Gad*-uh-renes.
GERASENES.   *Gur*-uh-seenz.
GETHSEMANE.   Geth-*sem*-uh-nee.
JAIRUS.   Jay-*eye*-russ or *Jay*-ih-russ.

Jairus, the ruler of the synagogue, was caught in the middle also, with his position and prestige to think of. What would people think of him if he sought out Jesus? But he also had a daughter who was dying, and Jesus was her only hope.

Jairus chose Jesus. We do not know what happened to his position. But we do know that he made the better choice. To choose Christ, regardless of what else one may lose, is never a bad choice. Then we are not caught in the middle; we are on the winning side!   —C. R. B.

B. His Desperate Need for Help (v. 42)

42. For he had one only daughter, about twelve years of age, and she lay a dying. But as he went the people thronged him.

We can understand Jairus' desperate appeal to Jesus when we learn that his only daughter was dying. While Luke does not tell us what disease she was suffering from, he does inform us that she was twelve years old. In Jewish society a twelve-year-old girl was just about ready to enter young womanhood. The loss of a child at any age is a painful experience for a parent, but to lose a daughter just as she was preparing to enter adulthood would be especially grievous.

Jesus immediately responded to this urgent request, but as He tried to make His way to Jairus' house His progress was impeded by the crowd. They had been there to greet Him when He had returned from Gadara, and now they pressed closely about Him to see if He would work a miracle.

II. A Faith That Acts
(Luke 8:43-48)

A. The Woman's Problem (v. 43)

43. And a woman having an issue of blood twelve years, which had spent all her living upon physicians, neither could be healed of any.

Even as Jesus struggled through the crowd, He was further delayed by a woman. The woman was apparently suffering from a uterine hemorrhage, a condition that had plagued her for twelve years. Not only was this ailment very debilitating, it also rendered her ceremonially unclean. The poor woman had exhausted her resources in seeking medical aid, but to no avail. Luke states the facts of the case quite candidly, even though as a physician he must have found it embarrassing to admit that practitioners of his profession could not help her.

B. Her Effort to Find Help (v. 44)

44. Came behind him, and touched the border of his garment: and immediately her issue of blood stanched.

Although the woman was too timid to ask Jesus directly for help, she had enough faith to believe that even touching Him would cure her. Desperation can sometimes be a stimulus to faith. She had lost her health, her wealth, and her religious standing in the community. She had little else to lose and everything to gain in turning to Jesus. We have no idea how much she knew about Jesus, but she certainly knew enough to believe that He could help her. It is not recorded that the touch of Jesus' garment had healed anyone before this, but out of desperation the woman was willing to try anything. And it worked immediately!

C. Jesus' Response (vv. 45, 46)

45, 46. And Jesus said, Who touched me? When all denied, Peter and they that were with him said, Master, the multitude throng thee and press thee, and sayest thou, Who touched me? And Jesus said, Somebody hath touched me: for I perceive that virtue is gone out of me.

Many people in the crowd had, no doubt, touched Jesus or brushed against Him as He started toward the house of Jairus. Realizing this, but not really understanding what was going on, Peter and the other disciples challenged Jesus' question. Jesus knew that one person had touched Him, not accidentally, but with a definite purpose. For that matter, Jesus certainly knew who that person was. He asked the question only to test that person and draw out her response. When the woman had touched Jesus, *virtue* had gone out of Him. In today's English, this word is better translated *power*. This does not necessarily mean that Jesus was weakened by this healing touch; it means that He was aware of the fact that His healing power had been activated.

D. The Woman's Admission (v. 47)

47. And when the woman saw that she was not hid, she came trembling, and falling down before him, she declared unto him before all the people for what cause she had touched him, and how she was healed immediately.

Finally the woman openly admitted her action. In getting her to do this, Jesus was not trying to embarrass her. Rather, He wanted to reassure her that what she had done met with His approval. She needed to understand that it was her faith and Jesus' divine power that had made her whole, not some impersonal magic in His garment. Further, since her illness had made her a religious outcast, the public needed to know that she was well again. Jesus, who is aware of every human need, is always sensitive to meeting that need in the most gracious manner.

E. Jesus' Reassuring Words (v. 48)

48. And he said unto her, Daughter, be of good comfort: thy faith hath made thee whole; go in peace.

On several occasions, Jesus commended the faith of those who came to Him for healing. The need of faith is reflected in Hebrews 11:6: "Without faith it is impossible to please him: for he that cometh to God must believe that he is, and that he is a rewarder of them that diligently seek him." Faith brought about miracles; but at the same time, miracles created faith and stimulated its growth. Those who came to Jesus for healing did so because the miracles they had seen or heard about led them to believe that they also might receive miraculous healing.

We need to note another aspect of faith. Had the woman done nothing but believe that she could be healed, she would not have known the blessing of health restored. She had to act on that faith by going to Jesus and touching His garment before she was made whole. Because she acted on her faith she was healed, and Jesus pronounced upon her the blessing of peace.

III. A Faith That Is Rewarded (Luke 8:49-55)

A. The Bad News (v. 49)

49. While he yet spake, there cometh one from the ruler of the synagogue's house, saying to him, Thy daughter is dead; trouble not the Master.

Bad news: the child was dead. And since she was dead, the messenger said, there was no point in bothering Jesus by having Him come to the house. The messenger believed that Jesus could heal a sick girl, even a seriously sick girl; but he did not believe that Jesus had the power to restore life once it had slipped away. Our faith is often like that. We trust God so far, but beyond that point our faith begins to waver. This news must also have been a shock to Jairus, who may have shared the messenger's feelings.

B. Jesus' Response (v. 50)

50. But when Jesus heard it, he answered him, saying, Fear not: believe only, and she shall be made whole.

If the bad news from home did cause Jairus' faith to waver, Jesus quickly strengthened it. He assured him that he had nothing to fear. No doubt Jairus needed this reassurance. He had just witnessed a miraculous healing, but raising the dead may have seemed like a far more difficult miracle. He found it hard to believe that with God all things are possible.

C. Jesus Enters Jairus' House
(vv. 51, 52)

51. And when he came into the house, he suffered no man to go in, save Peter, and James, and John, and the father and the mother of the maiden.

As the crowd followed Jesus to the home of Jairus, the people must have wondered what Jesus was going to do, now that the girl was dead. Jesus took Peter, James, and John into the house along with the parents of the girl. We don't know why Jesus chose only those to enter with Him. Perhaps the house was so crowded with mourners that it would be hard for all the disciples to get in. Three witnesses could testify to what had happened.

52. And all wept, and bewailed her: but he said, Weep not; she is not dead, but sleepeth.

Inside the house was the tumult and confusion of the wailing mourners. Some of these may have been family members or friends. Others were probably professional mourners hired for the occasion. Matthew 9:23 indicates that some were playing musical instruments, probably flutes. This further added to the din that filled the house. While the idea of hiring professional mourners to carry on as these did seems shocking to us, it was a normal practice in Jesus' day.

Jesus raised His voice above the noise, urging the mourners to cease their wailing. The girl was not dead but asleep, Jesus told them. Of course Jesus knew that the spirit had left the girl's body, but that situation was not final. Jesus was using the word *sleep* figuratively to suggest that Jairus' daughter could be aroused.

D. Jesus Scorned (v. 53)

53. And they laughed him to scorn, knowing that she was dead.

The mourners would have none of this. With scorn they laughed at Him. After all, they had been there and they knew what had happened. Perhaps their derision reflected their resentment

visual 9

When we reach the limit of our resources, we can still touch the unlimited resources of God.

as Jesus intruded into their party and told them to be quiet. Little did they know His power!

E. Jairus' Daughter Raised (vv. 54, 55)

54, 55. And he put them all out, and took her by the hand, and called, saying, Maid, arise. And her spirit came again, and she arose straightway: and he commanded to give her meat.

Jesus did not attempt to answer their scornful gibes. Instead, He ordered them out of the room, and apparently they did not attempt to challenge Him. Then He took the girl's hand, cold and lifeless, as with a word He reclaimed death's prey. As soon as He spoke, the girl's spirit returned to her body; and she arose. The miracle was instantaneous and complete.

Jesus then asked the parents to give the girl some food. Probably she had eaten little or nothing during her serious illness. Now that she was up and active again, she would need food for strength. Jesus was concerned with every human need, even a need that might be overlooked in the excitement of a great miracle.

PARDON ME WHILE I LAUGH

At eighty-four years, Beryle Kalin is still singing in the New Orleans Opera Chorus. She began singing with the chorus sixty years ago. The general director of the opera association says, "She's very good musically."

This is unusual for a person of Beryle's age, but what makes it more remarkable is that she is almost deaf! Even the director did not know it until someone told him. However, he says she always sings on pitch and with proper inflection and volume.

There is other evidence that Beryle Kalin is an unusual senior citizen. She still makes her own clothes, gardens, works for the opera guild and her political party, and regularly visits younger people who are shut-ins, although she did "slow down" a few years ago and gave up her volunteer work at several hospitals.

There are always people who are ready to say "it can't be done" and laugh at anyone who tries. Beryle has experienced some of that, but it has not deterred her a bit.

There were laughers and skeptics in the crowd that day when Jesus went to heal Jairus' daughter; but Jesus knew what He could do, and He did it. We need not listen to the doubters when we know the gifts God has given us. We experience His power in our lives, enabling us to do the difficult. That's when we can laugh—with joy at being used by God!   —C. R. B.

Verse 56, which is not included in the printed text, informs us that Jesus instructed the parents not to tell anyone about what had happened. Of course there was no way that the miracle could be hidden. Jesus probably had two reasons for restraining the parents. First, they needed some time out of the spotlight to think about the spiritual implications of what had happened. They and their daughter could have become the center of attraction in the city. Jesus wanted this to be a deep and abiding religious experience, not some circus sideshow. The other reason was that public enthusiasm was already running at a fever pitch. Further excitement might very well have convinced many that Jesus was the Messiah. Hoping that the Messiah would lead them to independence, some fervent patriots might have plunged into some violent, overt act against the Roman government. Such violence was far from the purpose of the spiritual kingdom Jesus came to establish.

Conclusion

A. The Touch of His Hand

In today's lesson we have seen examples of how Jesus touched or was touched by beneficiaries of His miracles. The Gospel accounts tell us of other examples: Jesus touched a leper as He cleansed him (Matthew 8:3); He touched the hand of Peter's mother-in-law when He healed her of a fever (Matthew 8:15); two blind men of Jericho received their sight when Jesus touched their eyes (Matthew 20:34); and when He restored the ear of the servant of the high priest, He touched it (Luke 22:51).

Modern psychologists have come to recognize the significance of the touch in interpersonal relations. With a touch of the hand, a handshake, a pat on the back, an embrace, we can convey a variety of feelings that would be difficult to convey with words alone.

Jesus' touch was not necessary for Him to perform a miracle. Several miracles are recorded that do not involve any kind of physical contact at all. A miracle could be done even when Jesus

Home Daily Bible Readings

Monday, Jan. 23—Jesus' Touch Heals a Child (Luke 8:40-42, 49-56)
Tuesday, Jan. 24—Jesus' Touch Heals a Woman (Luke 8:43-48)
Wednesday, Jan. 25—Jesus' Touch Heals a Blind Man (John 9:1-11)
Thursday, Jan. 26—Jesus' Touch Heals a Slave (Luke 22:47-53)
Friday, Jan. 27—Jesus Serves With a Touch (John 13:1-11)
Saturday, Jan. 28—Jesus Shares Himself (Mark 14:22-26)
Sunday, Jan. 29—Faith Through a Touch (John 20:19-29)

was some distance from the recipient (Matthew 8:5-13). We conclude, then, that His touch was to convey love and reassurance and His concern.

A song that used to be in many of our hymnals was "The Touch of His Hand on Mine." The author wrote,

There are days so dark that I seek in vain
    For the face of my Friend Divine;
But though darkness hide, He is there to guide
    By the touch of His hand on mine."

This song certainly has a strong emotional appeal, but obviously Jesus does not physically touch our hands today. In what sense, then, can we say that Jesus touches us? Clearly, He touches our lives through the Scriptures. As we study God's Word, we find there Christ's directions for our lives. To the extent that our lives exemplify His teachings, to that extent our lives are touched by Him. We should not suppose that our study of the Scriptures is purely an intellectual pursuit. Just as Jesus conveyed an emotional, nonverbal message of hope and assurance when He touched people, so we today receive emotional messages of peace and assurance when we study the Scriptures.

B. Let Us Pray

Dear God, we thank You that You have sent us a Savior who knows our every need. Teach us to come to Him humbly and in faith so that He may touch our lives with His wonderful saving grace. In His name we pray, Amen.

C. Thought to Remember

"There is grace and power, in the trying hour, In the touch of His hand on mine."

                              —JESSIE BROWN POUNDS

Learning by Doing

This page contains an alternate lesson plan emphasizing learning activities. Classes desiring such student involvement will find these suggestions helpful.

Learning Goals

After this lesson, students should be able to:

1. Explain the significance of touch in interpersonal relationships.

2. Relate the miracles recorded in Luke 8.

3. Suggest a personal course of action that expresses sincere faith of the type expressed in Luke 8:40-55.

Into the Lesson

Write the word *touch* vertically on the chalkboard. Ask the students to suggest words beginning with each letter that relate some messages expressed by touching another person. (This exercise is in the student book.) Some possibilities are suggested below:

T tenderness
O opposition
U understanding
C concern
H honor

After you have listed several such messages, ask for volunteers to demonstrate how a touch can communicate some of these messages. (Use one volunteer to demonstrate the touch and another to receive the touch.) For example, a student might demonstrate "concern" by putting his arm around another student; "opposition" could be demonstrated by a student's pushing away his partner. Let the students themselves think of the situations, although you might demonstrate one activity to get things started.

Into the Word

To provide some background to the lesson today, and to make a connection between last week's lesson and this one, divide the class into six groups. Each group is to take one of the following passages, study it, and then paraphrase or summarize the events or the main idea of the passage: Luke 8:1-3, 4-15, 16-18, 19-21, 22-25, 26-40.

As the groups report, make a list of facts that indicate Jesus' growing popularity. (Preaching in "every city and village," v. 1; support from women, vv. 2, 3; large crowd, v. 4; such a crowd His family could not get near, v. 19; impression made on the twelve, v. 25; report of the healed demoniac, v. 39; reception in Capernaum, v. 40.) This growing support helps explain why the two people in our text came to Him for help.

Ask each student then to read Luke 8:40-56 and to choose one of the following assignments. (They are listed in the student book.)

1. Write two diary entries in the diary of the woman who came secretly to Jesus—one before she came and one after she was healed.

2. Imagine that you are Jairus, the ruler of a synagogue. You need Jesus' help, but the other rulers have decreed that no synagogue ruler may express any support for Jesus. Write your letter of resignation.

3. Imagine you are one of the doctors who had tried to cure the woman in the text. You have seen her healed. Write a speech you will make about it to the Galilean Medical Association.

4. Imagine you are a professional mourner who was at the home of Jairus when his daughter died. Write a letter to a friend about it.

5. Write what Jairus' daughter might have said as she told a friend about her thoughts and feelings when she woke to see Jesus holding her hand and helping her rise.

Into Life

Recall to the class your earlier discussion of touching. What did Jesus communicate with His touch in this lesson? He identified with the woman who was hemorrhaging. Though she touched Him, and that secretly, He made it known that He was not afraid or embarrassed about it. He made it public. He made her problem (uncleanness) His problem (anyone who touched an unclean person was also unclean). He communicated that she was of more value than ritual. And who can imagine the depth of emotion present in Jesus' touch in taking the little girl's hand when He raised her from the dead?

On the other hand, note the faith at work in these miracles. The woman believed she could be healed even though no one had ever been healed by touching the hem of Jesus' garment. Jairus had faith enough to risk the scorn of his contemporaries, and even to believe Jesus could raise his daughter from the dead.

Distribute cards to the students and ask them to write some action they can take (a) to express the compassion Jesus expressed in His gentle touch or (b) to express the kind of faith expressed by the woman and by Jairus.

Let's Talk It Over

The questions on this page are designed to encourage review of the lesson Scriptures and to promote discussion of the lesson by the class. The answers provided are only discussion starters. Let your class talk it over from there.

1. It is possible that the crisis of his daughter's illness changed Jairus and made him open to Jesus. How can present-day unbelievers be made more receptive to the gospel through the crises they encounter?

The Bible tells of many who were led by crises to repent of sins and turn to God. In 2 Chronicles 33 we read of King Manasseh's evil career; but we also discover that he was captured by the Assyrians, and that this experience led him to turn back to God. The New Testament tells of the jailer at Philippi (Acts 16), who almost took his life when he thought his prisoners had escaped. That crisis seems to have prepared his heart to seek salvation. We do not need to pray that unbelievers will undergo such crises, but that their hearts will be so softened and their minds will be so humbled that they will be made receptive to the gospel. And we need to pray that we or some other Christian will be able to approach them wisely and lovingly with the message they need to hear.

2. Jesus required the healed woman to testify to her healing, though it embarrassed her. Why was this necessary?

Her testimony was more effective because she spoke reluctantly about matters that were very personal. Her experience has been duplicated by Christians in all eras. They have related how they were led to salvation or given victory over some problem or crisis. In so doing they have found it necessary to bare intimate aspects of their lives. Their willingness to do that has strengthened their testimony to God's wisdom, power, and love. It has also provided encouragement and hope to hearers or readers who have faced similar problems.

3. An interesting feature of Jesus' raising of Jairus' daughter was His command that she be given something to eat. How does this fit in with His miracle-working power?

This illustrates the truth that God does not do for us what we can do for ourselves. Jesus restored life and health; then the parents supplied food to maintain health. The application of this principle is summed up in the observation that we need to pray as if everything depended on God and work as if everything depended on us. If we do not get what we pray for, it may be that we are not doing our part in obtaining it.

4. What are the benefits and dangers of physical contact among Christians of the opposite sexes?

This is not an easy topic to discuss. The practice of hugging those of the opposite sex is so widely accepted in the church that one feels prudish in questioning it. But Christians are not immune to impure thoughts and intents, and such thoughts may be aroused by excessive or indiscriminate physical contact. Still a hug can be an appropriate way of expressing godly affection. It is not possible to make a list of proper and improper occasions for such physical contact. A hug may be a fitting way of welcoming a newly-baptized individual into the church, or it may be appropriate when Christians are about to be separated or when they are reunited after a long separation. When a hug is not appropriate, a warm handshake may communicate affection and encouragement. We may wonder if a modern handshake is the equivalent of the "holy kiss" in the early church (Romans 16:16; 1 Corinthians 16:20; 2 Corinthians 13:12; 1 Thessalonians 5:26); but the joining of hands can be more than a mere formality. It can be a holy, hearty, warm, and gracious way of expressing our love in Christ.

5. How can we use the Scriptures to experience a closeness to Jesus similar to the closeness experienced by those who knew Him on earth?

The Gospels give us such a vivid description of Jesus' deeds that we can use our imagination to picture ourselves as part of the scene. Some of our songs can help. "Master, the Tempest Is Raging" enables us to experience the sudden storm at sea and the drama of Jesus' "Peace, be still!" A more recent song promises, "Something Good Is Going to Happen to You," and it bases that promise on some of Jesus' acts of power and love. When we make the reading of the Gospels a regular habit, the scenes that are depicted there become so familiar to us that we come to feel that Jesus is speaking to us, touching us, walking with us, encouraging us, comforting us.

Seeking God's Kingdom

LESSON SCRIPTURE: Luke 12:13-34.

PRINTED TEXT: Luke 12:13-15, 22-34.

Luke 12:13-15, 22-34

13 One of the company said unto him, Master, speak to my brother, that he divide the inheritance with me.

14 And he said unto him, Man, who made me a judge or a divider over you?

15 And he said unto them, Take heed, and beware of covetousness: for a man's life consisteth not in the abundance of the things which he possesseth.

. . . .

22 And he said unto his disciples, Therefore I say unto you, Take no thought for your life, what ye shall eat; neither for the body, what ye shall put on.

23 The life is more than meat, and the body is more than raiment.

24 Consider the ravens: for they neither sow nor reap; which neither have storehouse nor barn; and God feedeth them: how much more are ye better than the fowls?

25 And which of you with taking thought can add to his stature one cubit?

26 If ye then be not able to do that thing which is least, why take ye thought for the rest?

27 Consider the lilies how they grow: they toil not, they spin not; and yet I say unto you, that Solomon in all his glory was not arrayed like one of these.

28 If then God so clothe the grass, which is today in the field, and tomorrow is cast into the oven; how much more will he clothe you, O ye of little faith?

29 And seek not ye what ye shall eat, or what ye shall drink, neither be ye of doubtful mind.

30 For all these things do the nations of the world seek after: and your Father knoweth that ye have need of these things.

31 But rather seek ye the kingdom of God; and all these things shall be added unto you.

32 Fear not, little flock; for it is your Father's good pleasure to give you the kingdom.

33 Sell that ye have, and give alms; provide yourselves bags which wax not old, a treasure in the heavens that faileth not, where no thief approacheth, neither moth corrupteth.

34 For where your treasure is, there will your heart be also.

Feb
5

Golden Text: Seek ye the kingdom of God; and all these things shall be added unto you.—Luke 12:31.

Lesson Aims

After this lesson students should be able to:

1. Understand that the important things of life cannot be measured in terms of dollars and cents.

2. Have a better appreciation of the nature of Christ's kingdom.

3. Distinguish between the luxuries and the necessities of life.

Lesson Outline

INTRODUCTION
  A. Writing Obituaries
  B. Lesson Background
I. AVOIDING COVETOUSNESS (Luke 12:13-15)
  A. A Man Seeks an Inheritance (v. 13)
  B. Jesus Refuses to Be a Judge (v. 14)
     The Bottom Line
  C. Jesus Warns Against Covetousness (v. 15)
II. AVOIDING ANXIETIES (Luke 12:22-30)
  A. Don't Be Anxious (vv. 22, 23)
  B. Example From the Ravens (vv. 24-26)
  C. Example From the Lilies (vv. 27, 28)
  D. God Knows Our Needs (vv. 29, 30)
     Things the World Eagerly Seeks
III. SEEKING THE KINGDOM (Luke 12:31-34)
  A. Seeking the Kingdom First (vv. 31, 32)
  B. Laying Up Treasures (v. 33)
  C. Establishing Values (v. 34)
CONCLUSION
  A. "Where Your Treasure Is"
  B. Let Us Pray
  C. Thought to Remember

Display visual 10 from the visuals/learning resources packet and let it remain before the class throughout this session. The visual is shown on page 196.

Introduction

A. Writing Obituaries

One day Alfred Nobel, the Swedish inventor of dynamite, picked up a newspaper. There to his dismay he read his own obituary. Alfred's brother had died, and a reporter had mistakenly thought that the great industrialist had passed away.

But the obituary gave Nobel an even greater shock. The reporter had described Nobel as the typical money-grubbing industrialist whose only concern was to accumulate wealth, with little consideration for the rest of society. Nobel took action to change this image. He endowed a foundation that established prizes for persons who made outstanding contribution to human culture and welfare. Perhaps the most famous of these is the Nobel Peace Price, given annually to the person who does the most to promote peace in the world.

Our world has standards by which it measures fame. Wealth is one of the most important of these, but we have others: political accomplishments, military leadership, literary contributions, theatrical and musical skills, athletic prowess. Jesus didn't mention any of these as important standards; and wealth, which He did mention, He rejected as a standard to measure one's worth.

If someone were to write your obituary, how would it read?

B. Lesson Background

In last week's lesson we studied events that occurred in the midst of Jesus' Galilean ministry. That ministry soon reached its climax in the feeding of the five thousand, Peter's good confession, and the transfiguration.

Today's lesson finds Jesus already well along in the next phase of His ministry. Luke marks that change in 9:51: "And it came to pass, when the time was come that he should be received up, he steadfastly set his face to go to Jerusalem." The time of His popular ministry in Galilee was past, and with calm resolution Jesus turned to Jerusalem, knowing that only six months ahead lay the cross.

In December, Jesus attended the feast of Dedication (Hanukkah) in Jerusalem. There He met increasingly bitter opposition from the religious leaders, so, He left Jerusalem and went to the area east of the Jordan River. There He carried on a teaching ministry for several weeks. Today's lesson has its setting during this period.

I. Avoiding Covetousness (Luke 12:13-15)

Jesus gained the trust and respect of many people, and many brought their problems to Him. The sick came to be healed; some wanted approval for the lives they were living (the rich young ruler, for example, Luke 18:18-30); some wanted a favor of one kind or another. The first part of today's lesson deals with a man who wanted a favor.

A. A Man Seeks an Inheritance (v. 13)

13. And one of the company said unto him, Master, speak to my brother, that he divide the inheritance with me.

Jesus had been talking about the hypocrisy of the Pharisees and warning His followers that they must expect persecution. He challenged them to remain faithful in the face of trials, assuring them that God would watch over them. Then a man in the crowd interrupted, asking Jesus if He would settle a dispute over an inheritance.

Obviously the man was obsessed with the importance of material things, else He would not have interrupted Jesus' discourse on spiritual things with his request. Just why the man came to Jesus we can only guess. There were legal processes open to him if he felt that his brother had unjustly deprived him of his inheritance. Perhaps he had tried those avenues, and the judgment had gone against him. Now he wanted his case tried in another court.

B. Jesus Refuses to Be a Judge (v. 14)

14. And he said unto him, Man, who made me a judge or a divider over you?

Jewish rabbis, because they were experts in the law, often gave opinions on legal matters. Since Jesus was sometimes called a rabbi, the man may have supposed that He also would give a legal opinion. Thus the man showed his complete misunderstanding about the nature of Jesus' ministry. Perhaps he thought he was honoring Jesus by asking Him to intervene; but Jesus, in no uncertain terms, made it clear that He would have no part in such a case.

THE BOTTOM LINE

In 1986, fourteen Americans became *billionaires* for the first time. We would like to think that they gained their wealth by hard work, motivated by high moral principles and a desire to become benefactors of American society.

However, from what we know about human nature, we can guess that at least some of these new billionaires may have reached their lofty perch by tricking their brothers into giving up their inheritance. Wall Street scandals of "inside dealing" remind us from time to time that the "high and mighty" are sometimes low and crafty in the way they clamber to the top.

Business corporations operate in the same fashion as such individuals when the only matter of real concern is the "bottom line" on the ledger. When the welfare of individual employees and the good of society as a whole are subordinated to the quarterly profit-and-loss statement, it indicates how thoroughly greed controls some elements of our society.

The man who asked Jesus to demand that his brother divide the inheritance may have had a legitimate claim on the money. On the other hand, he may have been inordinately interested in the money, to the exclusion of any considerations of his brother's welfare. Jesus' response indicates that, for the Christian, the bottom line can never be the bottom line!   —C. R. B.

C. Jesus Warns Against Covetousness (v. 15)

15. And he said unto them, Take heed, and beware of covetousness: for a man's life consisteth not in the abundance of the things which he possesseth.

Jesus then turned to the man's real problem—covetousness. He issued a double warning against it: *Take heed*, and *beware*. Greed is an insidious sin, coming quietly and often garbed in the cloak of respectability. It creates an appetite for more. Greed always wants more, more, more.

Greed is wrong for at least two reasons. First, it hurts others. Greed drives men to be dishonest or to bend laws to give an aura of honesty to their robbery. But greed is also wrong because of what it does to the person who has fallen into its grasp. Jesus states this as a fundamental principle rooted in man's very nature: *A man's life consisteth not in the abundance of the things which he possesseth*. Or, to put it another way, as Jesus did when Satan tempted Him with things: "Man shall not live by bread alone."

II. Avoiding Anxieties (Luke 12:22-30)

Jesus followed this condemnation of covetousness with the parable of the rich fool, which graphically illustrated the point He had made (vv. 16-21). Jesus pronounced this man a fool because he was "not rich toward God."

A. Don't Be Anxious (vv. 22, 23)

22. And he said unto his disciples, Therefore I say unto you, Take no thought for your life, what ye shall eat; neither for the body, what ye shall put on.

How to Say It

HANUKKAH. *Hahn*-uh-kuh.

Take no thought is better translated *be not anxious.* Greed and anxiety go together. Greed always wants more, and anxiety is the fear that one won't get more. Both the brother who wanted Jesus to help him gain his inheritance and the rich fool suffered from this problem. Their undue concern for food and clothing blinded them to the spiritual side of life.

23. The life is more than meat, and the body is more than raiment.

The first reason Jesus gave for not being anxious was that life is more important than food and the body is more important than clothing. He may also have suggested that it takes more than food and clothing to support life. Food and clothing may be necessary to sustain life's existence, but life is more than mere existence.

B. Example From the Ravens
(vv. 24-26)

24. Consider the ravens: for they neither sow nor reap; which neither have storehouse nor barn; and God feedeth them: how much more are ye better than the fowls?

To illustrate a second reason for not being anxious, Jesus took an example from nature. The ravens were not farmers. They did not plow, plant, or harvest; they did not store their harvest in barns. Yet God provided for their needs. If God takes care of the common birds, He will certainly take care of human beings, who were made in His very image.

25. And which of you with taking thought can add to his stature one cubit?

A third reason for not being anxious is that it doesn't work. This verse poses a bit of a problem in translation. If we take it literally as the *King James Version* has it, we can't help wondering why anyone except a child, a dwarf, or maybe a basketball player would want to be a foot and a half taller.

The word that is translated *stature* can also mean *span of life,* which is the way the *Revised Standard Version* has it. But this is illogical, for a lifetime is not measured in cubits. Jesus may have deliberately mixed these measurements just to illustrate how foolish it is to be anxious about the length of one's life.

There is no problem in understanding the point Jesus was making. We cannot increase our height or extend our life by worrying about it. In fact, fretting about how one can lengthen his life is likely to have exactly the opposite effect. Worry creates all kinds of physical problems.

26. If ye then be not able to do that thing which is least, why take ye thought for the rest?

This climaxed Jesus' argument. If one can't add even a tiny bit to the length of his life by

worrying about it, why should he be worried about greater things? The reasons Jesus gave that we should not worry are these: (1) Life is more important than food and clothing; (2) God provides for the birds and He will surely provide for man; and (3) worry won't change a thing anyway.

C. Example From the Lilies
(vv. 27, 28)

27. Consider the lilies how they grow: they toil not, they spin not; and yet I say unto you, that Solomon in all his glory was not arrayed like one of these.

Jesus next drew another example from nature. The point He made is obvious. The wild flowers are not planted or cultivated or watered by anyone, and yet year after year they appear in pleasing beauty, a beauty that surpasses the beauty of the robes of the richest king the Jews ever had.

28. If then God so clothe the grass, which is today in the field, and tomorrow is cast into the oven; how much more will he clothe you, O ye of little faith?

In a land where fuel was very scarce, even the withered flowers and grass were gathered to be used for fuel in cooking. The beautiful flowers last for only a few days, and then they are burned without a moment's hesitation. Why should God waste such beauty on such transitory things as the flowers of the field? Because He is God, that's why! The thrust of Jesus' argument is obvious. If God lavishes such beauty on something so temporary, it is certainly reasonable to believe that He will also take care of human beings.

D. God Knows Our Need (vv. 29, 30)

29. And seek not ye what ye shall eat, or what ye shall drink, neither be ye of doubtful mind.

Jesus directed this teaching pointedly at His disciples—ye! He was not suggesting that they be neglectful in providing those things that are

*God cares
for ravens
and lilies—*

*will He not
also care
for you?*

visual 10

essential for sustaining life. Such a teaching would go contrary to many Scriptures that teach that God expects people to be diligent in their work and not slothful. The emphasis that He was making is that things should not become the main concern of their lives.

This teaching of Jesus is not likely to become very popular in our society today. Our culture has become thoroughly materialistic. We are so thoroughly immersed in materialism that we are scarcely aware of how it influences our thinking. Advertising for consumer goods keeps us ever wanting more, more, more! So often our lives illustrate exactly the kind of life-style Jesus was teaching against.

We pay a price for our undue concern for things. We sometimes sacrifice our health, our integrity, and even our families to acquire money and the things that money will buy. Yet the acquisition of things is no assurance of happiness. Oh, if we could only come to understand and apply this lesson that Jesus was trying to teach!

30. For all these things do the nations of the world seek after: and your Father knoweth that ye have need of these things.

The word that is here translated *nations* is often translated "Gentiles." Jesus was chiding His disciples that in their pursuit of things they were becoming like the Gentiles. This was a verbal slap in the face that was certain to get their attention. If there was anything that a good Jew didn't want, it was to be like a Gentile.

Jesus assured them that they didn't have to be like the Gentiles in seeking after things. After all, the Father in Heaven knew of their needs even before they did. If He took care of the birds of the heavens and the flowers of the field, certainly He would take care of them.

THINGS THE WORLD EAGERLY SEEKS

A very popular television series for several seasons was "Lifestyles of the Rich and Famous."

Headlines on newsstand tabloids flaunt the vast fortunes, fast cars, palatial homes, and extravagant vacations enjoyed by the "jet set" of our society.

Full-page ads in major newspapers offer the possibility of us becoming wealthy by manipulating the stock market by using someone else's cash, or by trading in real estate with no money down.

State lotteries offer the hope of becoming an instant millionaire at the cost of only a dollar or two (and thank people when they lose for having supported the state's treasury so generously.)

Does the evidence say more about our greed or our gullibility? Is there any difference? The fact that the world so eagerly seeks material things, tells us the world is both greedy and gullible. In fact, if people were not so gullible, they would not believe the lie that life's answers are to be found in having more things.

In contrast to the world's mad scramble for wealth, Jesus puts the trust God's people place in Him for what they really need. Do you suppose that we will ever see a television program entitled "Lifestyles of the Poor and Spiritual?"
—C. R. B.

III. Seeking the Kingdom First (Luke 12:31-34)

A. Seeking the Kingdom First (vv. 31, 32)

31. But rather seek ye the kingdom of God; and all these things shall be added unto you.

The present imperative emphasizes the importance of constantly seeking the things of God. The seeking was not something they were to do only once or only now and then; it was something they were to do continually. Just as they were to hunger and thirst after righteousness (Matthew 5:6), so they were to hunger and thirst after the kingdom of God. Though the gates of God's kingdom are opened by grace, yet God expects every one of us to seek those gates with diligence.

Jesus promised that God's kingdom is available to those who earnestly seek it. But He promised more. *These things* also will be given to them. One is not to gain the things of the world by the world's method—pushing and shoving, with the resultant anxieties. Rather, the things of this world will be given when one turns his total attention to the next world. This defies the world's logic, and therefore not very many people try to apply it.

We should not interpret Jesus' teaching to mean that those who seek His kingdom will become *wealthy* in physical possessions. Rather, Jesus was saying that God will supply the *needs* of those who seek Him. Assured of this, they no longer need be anxious.

32. Fear not, little flock; for it is your Father's good pleasure to give you the kingdom.

Little flock! How apt is this description of Jesus' followers! Comparatively speaking, they were a small handful. And they were as helpless as a flock of sheep. But they need have no fear. The Father would give them the kingdom, not grudgingly, not sparingly, but graciously and with pleasure.

B. Laying Up Treasures (v. 33)

33. Sell that ye have, and give alms; provide yourselves bags which wax not old, a treasure in the heavens that faileth not, where no thief approacheth, neither moth corrupteth.

In the light of the whole New Testament teaching, we cannot conclude that Jesus wants all His people to sell everything that they own and give away the money. But He does want them to get rid of anything that keeps them from accepting the kingdom that the Father is pleased to give.

When men turn from earthly treasure to Heavenly treasure, they find safety and permanency. The bags that hold it will not become worthless with age; there will be no moths in Heaven; and no thief will be able to pick the lock on the pearly gates.

C. Establishing Values (v. 34)

34. For where your treasure is, there will be your heart also.

No X-ray is powerful enough to penetrate a person's spiritual heart and learn its motives; nor is any scalpel sharp enough to disect the spiritual heart and let us examine its workings. But we really don't need these tools. All we have to do is see where or what one's treasure is. That tells us immediately what his values are and where he places his trust.

Conclusion

A. "Where Your Treasure Is"

No other nation in all the history of the world has enjoyed the physical blessings that the United States has known. God, by giving us a wonderful combination of natural resources,

climate, and freedom, has allowed us to create unparalleled wealth. But our true wealth is not measured in terms of these physical things. It is measured by how we use these things.

When we have physical possessions, we are tempted to trust in them for security rather than in God. But even a brief glance at these things should show us how fragile they really are. We need only to look at the volatility of the stock market, where fortunes can be made or lost in a matter of minutes. Or look at what has happened in those areas whose wealth was based on maintaining high oil prices.

Wealth also tends to make people arrogant. Great wealth and humility are rarely found in the same person. The pursuit of wealth turns men's talents away from the pursuit of God's kingdom and its spiritual values. Millionaires are not often found leading prayer meetings or serving on missions committees.

If one has any doubts about where America's heart really is, let him examine how we spend our money. We spend more for pet food than we do for foreign missions. We spend much more for tobacco products than we do for Christian education. In these, as in other areas, we reveal where our heart really is. The information is not reassuring.

A minister once took his son with him to visit a rich landowner. The man took them to a vantage point on his ranch where they could look in all directions. Pointing west, he said, "It's all mine, as far as you can see." Turning to the south, he made the same statement, and then repeated it as he looked to the east and to the north. Turning to the boy, he asked, "What do you think of that?"

"Well, sir, replied the boy, "There's one direction you didn't look. I guess you don't own any land there."

"What do you mean, there's one direction we didn't look? We looked to every point of the compass."

"But, sir, you didn't look up!"

B. Let Us Pray

Dear Father, we thank You for the rich bounty You have poured out upon us. Teach us to use wisely what You have given us, that Your name may be glorified and Your kingdom enhanced. Amen.

C. Thought to Remember

"No man can tell whether he is rich or poor by turning to his ledger. It is the heart that makes a man rich. He is rich according to what he is, not according to what he has."

—HENRY WARD BEECHER

Home Daily Bible Readings

Monday, Jan. 30—More Valuable Than Sparrows (Luke 12:1-7)
Tuesday, Jan. 31—Acknowledge the Holy Spirit (Luke 12:8-12)
Wednesday, Feb. 1—Let Your Light Shine (Luke 11:33-36)
Thursday, Feb. 2—Keeping the Law Is Not Enough (Luke 11:37-44)
Friday, Feb. 3—Going Beyond the Law (Luke 11:45-52)
Saturday, Feb. 4—The Unimportance of Riches (Luke 12:13-21)
Sunday, Feb. 5—Seeking God Is Enough (Luke 12:22-34)

Learning by Doing

This page contains an alternate lesson plan emphasizing learning activities. Classes desiring such student involvement will find these suggestions helpful.

Learning Goals

After this lesson, students should be able to:

1. Portray covetousness as the dangerous evil that it is.

2. Explain what a man's life consists of.

3. List three reasons that worrying is unwarranted and suggest an alternative to worry.

4. Contrast "treasure in the heavens" with earthly treasure.

Into the Lesson

As the students arrive, give each one a pencil and a piece of paper with these words written on the top: "Draw an animal to represent the sin of *covetousness*. Below the picture, list the characteristics this animal has in common with covetousness." Ask each one to complete the assignment written on the paper.

On the chalkboard write two headings: ANIMAL and CHARACTERISTICS. When you are ready to begin, ask the students what animals they drew and what characteristics they assigned to that animal. Record their answers on the board in the proper columns. Discuss the dangers of covetousness as you discuss the answers given by the class.

Into the Word

Read aloud the section titled "Writing Obituaries" from the commentary section of this lesson. Then ask someone in the class to read Luke 12:13-21. When the Scripture has been read, have each student write two obituaries, one for the man who interrupted Jesus (Luke 12:13) and one for the farmer in the parable Jesus told (Luke 12:16-20).

In about five minutes ask for volunteers to share what they have written. Discuss what the men might have done in order to have more complimentary epitaphs.

Call attention to verse 15. Jesus said, "A man's life consisteth not in the abundance of the things which he possesseth." Ask the class, "Of what then does a man's life consist?" List the answers on the chalkboard. Then try to agree on one or two things to sum up of what man's life consists. Note how the obituaries reflect these things.

Ask a volunteer to read Luke 12:22-31. When the passage has been read, divide the class into three groups and ask each group to list the things about which they worry most. Then point out the reasons Jesus said we ought not to worry:

1. Life is more important than food and clothing.

2. God provides even for the birds, and He will surely provide for man.

3. Worrying won't help, anyway.

Assign one of these reasons to each group and ask them all to do two things:

1. Show how this truth can help keep one from worrying about the things the group named as the ones they worry about most.

2. Find an alternative to worry for such situations.

Discuss the results as you have time.

Ask another volunteer to read Luke 12:32-34. Divide the group into pairs and ask each pair to paraphrase the passage. After a few minutes, give the pairs time to read their paraphrases. Discuss the passage briefly; then decide which paraphrase best states the message of the text, or work as a class to write a new one.

Into Life

Ask the class to contrast the man in Jesus' parable (Luke 12:16-21) with Barnabas (Acts 4:32-37). Provide each one with a piece of paper with two headings: RICH MAN AND BARNABAS. They can write the contrasting aspects in columns under these names. (There is space for a similar activity in the student book.) After they have had time to work on this, you may or may not want to hear reports from volunteers. What you especially want to do with these lists is to ask each student to make a third column and write his own name at the head of it. Next to each contrast, the student is to write in this third column an R if his own behavior is more like the rich man's, or a B if he is more like Barnabas. Then ask each one to score himself 1 point for each B, and -1 for each R. This part should not be reported to the whole group, but challenge the students to consider what they can do to improve their scores.

Work together to list as many Heavenly treasures as you can. If necessary, suggest passages like Ephesians 1:3-14; Colossians 3:1, 2 to help get the students to thinking. After you have a good-sized list, close with a prayer of praise for these treasures.

Let's Talk It Over

The questions on this page are designed to encourage review of the lesson Scriptures and to promote discussion of the lesson by the class. The answers provided are only discussion starters. Let your class talk it over from there.

1. Why would it be helpful for one to write his own obituary periodically?

It could help one assess his accomplishments. If they have centered around money, possessions, or social status, one might give greater priority to helping others. An obituary showing little progress toward life's goals, might lead one to reorganize his schedule to remove fruitless pursuits. Perhaps the greatest value would be to impress one with the truth of the familiar poem: "Only one life, 'twill soon be past. Only what's done for Christ will last."

2. What is there in our society to suggest falsely that man's life *does* consist in the abundance of his possessions?

Never has the temptation to "keep up with the Joneses" been stronger than it is now. Satan led Eve to feel that she was being unfairly deprived of the fruit of Eden's forbidden tree (Genesis 3:1-5), and Satan still labors to convince us that we cannot be content unless we have the latest in automotive creations, time-saving appliances, stylish furniture, etc. The feelings of need for things is fed by advertising. The people we watch in commercials are made happier, more comfortable, healthier, and better-looking by the products they use, and we are led to believe that those products will produce similar effects in our lives. Certain religious leaders also have suggested or stated outright that God intends for His people to enjoy a life of material abundance. This gospel of "sanctified materialism" leads people to adopt goals and pursuits that are just the opposite of what Jesus prescribed. We need to speak out strongly against this reversal of Jesus' clear teaching.

3. Jesus said His disciples need not seek material things as the heathen Gentiles did, but it seems that some Christians are chasing worldly wealth as earnestly as their non-Christian neighbors are. Why is this unfortunate?

Critics of Christianity are quick to take note of any inconsistency between what Christians claim to believe and what they practice. If we talk much about the superior nature of spiritual realities and then grasp for worldly treasures just as avidly as our non-Christian neighbors, that will be noted. If we announce that Heaven is our home, but throw all our energies into gaining a more comfortable existence on earth, that also will be noted. So the effectiveness of our witness for Christ is blunted by our failure to keep "eternity's values in view." We must also ask what happens to our faith when we devote ourselves to the treasures of earth. Paul told Timothy that "some people, eager for money, have wandered from the faith and pierced themselves with many griefs" (1 Timothy 6:10, *New International Version*). That is a danger we face unless we can break away from the unending quest for more and more of this world's goods.

4. What are some practical ways of seeking the kingdom of God?

Reading the Bible is a simple way of seeking God's kingdom. But real seeking requires more than a hasty ten-minute reading so we can say we have read so many verses. If we are seeking God in His Word, then we will spend enough time and effort to show that this is an important activity in our lives. Our reading will be combined with the prayer that God's will may be accomplished in us, and with a genuine effort to incorporate Biblical principles into our daily living. A similar observation may be made regarding prayer. If we pray only as a matter of formal duty, that can hardly be called seeking God. Genuine seekers pray sincerely, earnestly, and "continually" (1 Thessalonians 5:17, *New International Version*). One of the most challenging ways of showing we are serious about seeking God's kingdom is our financial commitment. How do our gifts to God compare with our spending on material goods and recreational pursuits? This is an accurate guide to what we are really seeking.

5. How can we center our hearts on the treasures of Heaven?

Paul urged, "Set your minds on things above, not on earthly things" (Colossians 3:2, *New International Version*). But many Christians seem content to focus on earthly joys. It may be that future gates of pearl and streets of gold are less attractive than present pleasure. But one feature of Heaven should fill any believer with keen anticipation—we shall be with Jesus! Then the treasures of earth will seem unimportant.

Expressing Gratitude

LESSON SCRIPTURE: Leviticus 13:9-17, 45, 46; Luke 17:11-19.

PRINTED TEXT: Luke 17:11-19.

Luke 17:11-19

11 And it came to pass, as he went to Jerusalem, that he passed through the midst of Samaria and Galilee.

12 And as he entered into a certain village, there met him ten men that were lepers, which stood afar off:

13 And they lifted up their voices, and said, Jesus, Master, have mercy on us.

14 And when he saw them, he said unto them, Go show yourselves unto the priests. And it came to pass, that, as they went, they were cleansed.

15 And one of them, when he saw that he was healed, turned back, and with a loud voice glorified God,

16 And fell down on his face at his feet, giving him thanks: and he was a Samaritan.

17 And Jesus answering said, Were there not ten cleansed? but where are the nine?

18 There are not found that returned to give glory to God, save this stranger.

19 And he said unto him, Arise, go thy way: thy faith hath made thee whole.

Feb
12

Golden Text: One of them, when he saw that he was healed, turned back, and with a loud voice glorified God, and fell down on his face at his feet, giving him thanks: and he was a Samaritan.—Luke 17:15, 16.

| Scenes of Love and Compassion |
| Unit 3: Response and Responsibility |
| (Lessons 10-13) |

Lesson Aims

After this lesson students should:

1. Have a better understanding of his or her need to show gratitude.

2. Have a growing appreciation for the blessings for which we all should be thankful.

3. Be better able to express gratitude for the blessings he or she has received.

Lesson Outline

INTRODUCTION
   A. "Not One of Them Thanked Me!"
   B. Lesson Background
I. AN APPEAL FOR HELP (Luke 17:11-13)
   A. The Setting (v. 11)
   B. The Needy (v. 12)
   C. Their Plea (v. 13)
II. THE GRATEFUL ONE (Luke 17:14-16)
   A. The Miracle (v. 14)
   B. The Response (vv. 15, 16)
      Outcasts of Society
III. JESUS' COMMENTS (Luke 17:17-19)
   A. The Ungrateful (vv. 17, 18)
      Satisfaction Guaranteed
   B. The Grateful (v. 19)
CONCLUSION
   A. Learning Gratitude
   B. Grateful for the Good
   C. Praise in Pain
   D. Let Us Pray
   E. Thought to Remember

Visual 11 in the visuals/learning resources packet will be helpful as you present the thoughts in the "Conclusion" section. The visual is shown on page 204.

Introduction

A. "Not One of Them Thanked Me"

Today's lesson deals with the virtue of gratitude and its opposite, the sin of ingratitude. This vice, unfortunately, was not confined to Jesus' day. We still see evidence of it on every hand.

Years ago a boat was caught in a storm in Lake Michigan near Evanston, Illinois. It was so severely damaged that it began to sink. Since it was only a few hundred yards offshore from the campus of Northwestern University, some students saw the plight of the passengers on the boat and quickly responded to give help. One man, a strong swimmer, brought seventeen of the passengers to safety.

Years later a minister was using this incident as an illustration in a sermon. He was interrupted by a voice from the audience: "I'm that man." The minister then called the man to the platform.

"What stands out most in your memory of this great rescue?" he asked.

"The thing I remember most," came the man's quiet reply, "was that of the seventeen that I helped save, not one of them ever thanked me!"

B. Lesson Background

In last week's lesson, we studied about Jesus' ministry east of the Jordan following His appearance in Jerusalem at the feasts of Tabernacles and Dedication. In the east country, Jesus heard that Lazarus was seriously ill. Even though it was dangerous, Jesus returned to Bethany to raise Lazarus from the dead. Because of plots to kill Him, Jesus once more left the area of Jerusalem and "went thence unto a country near to the wilderness, into a city called Ephraim" (John 11:54). This city was located a few miles northeast of Jerusalem. Jesus did not stay there very long, however, but continued His travels. The events recorded in today's lesson text took place as He was going along the border between Samaria and Galilee.

I. An Appeal for Help (Luke 17:11-13)

A. The Setting (v. 11)

11. And it came to pass, as he went to Jerusalem, that he passed through the midst of Samaria and Galilee.

Through the midst of Samaria and Galilee is better translated *between Samaria and Galilee.* Apparently the route Jesus followed led along the border of the two provinces, down the valley past Bethshean, and across the Jordan. This was the route that many pilgrims took when they went from Galilee to Jerusalem.

B. The Needy (v. 12)

12. And as he entered into a certain village, there met him ten men that were lepers, which stood afar off.

Along the route, Jesus and His disciples approached a village that is not named. Near the village they were greeted by a pitiful sight. Ten men, victims of leprosy, stood some distance away and began to call out. Certain of the rabbis taught that a leper must stay at least four paces from other persons; but since there were several people with Jesus, these were farther away. They were not allowed to live in the village, and so they probably lived together in whatever makeshift shelter they could find or make.

The Old Testament gives a description of the symptoms that identify leprosy (Leviticus 13), but some of these may be produced by other skin diseases. When a person was suspected of having leprosy, he came before a priest, who examined him. If the priest decided that he had leprosy, he was considered unclean. He was not allowed in public gatherings, even for worship; and he was required to live away from other people. Since there was no known cure for the disease, this was the only way to keep it from becoming an epidemic.

A leper was required to wear mourning clothes, which he had torn. When anyone approached, he was to cry out, "Unclean! Unclean!"

C. Their Plea (v. 13)

13. And they lifted up their voices, and said, Jesus, Master, have mercy on us.

Together they cried to Jesus for help. In their dire circumstances, their national prejudices had been forgotten. Both Jews and Samaritans, or at least one Samaritan, were in the stricken group. At that moment, they desired healing. Nothing else really mattered. Leprosy sometimes damages the vocal cords or otherwise hampers the power of speech. The condition of these men had not deteriorated to this point. They were still able to make themselves heard. They addressed Jesus as *Master*, but just how much they knew about Him we have no way of knowing. At least they had heard enough about Him to believe that He could heal them. That is not surprising, for the whole country was talking about Jesus and His healing. Even in their isolation the lepers could hear news from relatives or friends who brought them food.

II. The Grateful One
(Luke 17:14-16))

A. The Miracle (v. 14)

14. And when he saw them, he said unto them, Go show yourselves unto the priests. And it came to pass, that, as they went, they were cleansed.

Jesus did not go to the lepers or call them to Him. He did not even tell them they would be healed. Instead He sent them to the priests, who were the public health inspectors. The priests had to give them a clean bill of health before

---

How to Say It
EPHRAIM. *Ee*-fray-im.
LAZARUS. *Laz*-uh-russ.

they could take their normal place in society. Priests served by turns in the temple of Jerusalem, but they had their homes in towns throughout the land. Thus they were available to quarantine the sick when necessary, and to end the quarantine if the sickness ended.

The men displayed considerable faith as they left Jesus and went to find the priests. They were not healed at once; the healing came only after they started on their way. Suppose they had not had enough faith to start to find a priest. Would they have been healed? Apparently not.

But they did do what Jesus commanded. They had enough faith in Him, and He spoke with such authority, that they did not tarry. In their desperate condition, perhaps they were ready to try anything. But whatever the level of their faith, it was rewarded. As they walked along, they suddenly found themselves cleansed. We can only imagine the surge of joy that must have swept over them as they felt strength return to limbs that had been weakened. They must have leaped with excitement as they examined their hands and faces and saw that they were no longer disfigured by leprosy.

B. The Response (vv. 15, 16)

15, 16. And one of them, when he saw that he was healed, turned back, and with a loud voice glorified God, and fell down on his face at his feet, giving him thanks: and he was a Samaritan.

Now comes the turning point in the story. Realizing that they had been healed, how would the men respond? We wonder if they discussed among themselves what they should do. Should they go back to thank Jesus, or go on to the priests as He had ordered? The majority decided to go on. Probably this indicated not so much in gratitude toward Jesus as an urgent desire to be officially declared clean.

One of the ten saw things differently. His first obligation was to show his gratitude. After all, saying thank you would take only a few minutes. The priests would still be there when he finished, but Jesus was just traveling through. The man might never see Him again. So he turned back.

Do we in similar situations respond like this one man or like the nine? There are people completely lacking in gratitude who believe that everything they receive from others is owed them. Certainly most of us would not be guilty of such a churlish attitude. More likely we have good intentions, but we just get too busy to carry them out.

One man came back. With joy and gratitude, he fell on his face before Jesus, thanking Him profusely. This certainly should be the response of every person who has felt the cleansing of Jesus, whether it be cleansing from a loathsome disease or the more deadly disease of sin.

Then Luke adds another deft touch to the account: *he was a Samaritan.* Luke, who was writing for a Gentile audience, perhaps injected this information as a reminder that Jesus did not confine His ministry to the Jews alone. Luke also records Jesus' parable of the good Samaritan (Luke 10:30-37). In a way, this incident of the ten lepers symbolized the rejection of Jesus by the Jewish people. Some Jews did become Christians later, but as a nation most of them rejected the gospel and still do today. Because the nine lepers failed to show gratitude for the blessing they received, they missed any further blessings that might have been theirs. In the same way, most of the Jews rejoiced in the blessing of Jesus' healing ministry among them, but later failed to show their gratitude to God by accepting the gospel. Thus they missed the greater blessing that might have been theirs.

OUTCASTS OF SOCIETY

"The Gypsies are coming!" Many years ago in the American Midwest, that cry would bring fear to the hearts of parents. As word spread from farm to farm and from town to town, children would be kept inside until the wanderers had passed. Everyone "knew" that Gypsies stole children.

In many times and places there has been strong prejudice against certain groups. In the first century many Jews despised and avoided Samaritans, but Jesus did not (John 4:1-42; Luke 9:51-56). Among ten lepers Jesus healed near the Samaritan border, a Samaritan was the only one with gratitude and courtesy enough to thank Him.

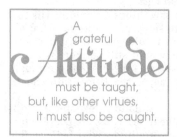

A grateful *Attitude* must be taught, but, like other virtues, it must also be caught.

visual 11

Neither social class nor national origin is a barrier to receiving Jesus' grace. Neither does it prevent a proper response to His blessing.
—C. R. B.

III. Jesus' Comments (Luke 17:17-19)

A. The Ungrateful (vv. 17, 18)

17. And Jesus answering said, Were there not ten cleansed? but where are the nine?

Jesus' words were more of a commentary than a question. He probably addressed them to the crowd, not just the man who now knelt before Him. No doubt Jesus' comments were freighted with the pain of disappointment.

Many of us at one time or another have known similar disappointment. Perhaps in a hospital room we've heard a seriously ill patient promise faithful church attendance if he should recover. But people who make promises under such circumstances don't always live up to them. This is not to suggest that these people are frivolous or insincere when they make such promises. People are not very often frivolous when they are staring death squarely in the face. They are like the nine. Once they have recovered, their own interests begin to intrude and soon take precedence over showing their gratitude to God.

SATISFACTION GUARANTEED

There have been many complaints about public education in the United States in recent years. Merchants lament that their newly-graduated clerks cannot do simple arithmetic well enough to make change. (Saved by computerized cash registers!)

College professors complain that large numbers of freshmen cannot write a business letter or a term paper expressing their thoughts in a cogent manner. Many students *do not* read their textbooks because they *are not able to* read them!

Relief is in sight. A school district in Orange County, California, is now guaranteeing its graduates! They are certified to be able to read, write, and calculate at a high-school level. If a business hires a "defective" graduate, the school system will retrain the student without charge.

Perhaps we cannot expect the majority of people to demonstrate excellence in any field of endeavor. Excellence seems to be especially rare in the spiritual realm. But is common courtesy too much to expect? When Jesus healed ten lepers, only one was thoughtful enough to come back and express his appreciation. What a commentary that is on the human race!

Since we are Christians, has Christ changed us enough to guarantee that our lives will demonstrate His excellence in all we do? —C. R. B.

18. There are not found that returned to give glory to God, save this stranger.

Jesus' heart must have been saddened as He uttered these words. The nine had not bothered to return to give thanks in spite of the great blessing they had received. The one exception was *this stranger*, this foreigner, this Samaritan, of all people. Perhaps Jesus mentioned this point in order to touch the conscience of the Jews, most of whom lumped Samaritans together as second-class persons who would not be likely to show gratitude even to one of their own, much less to a Jewish teacher.

This incident ought to be a lesson to all of us who at one time or another have prejudged and stereotyped members of other racial or religious groups. It is just easier to deal with people that way when we don't know them and don't want to take the time to get to know them. May this lesson remind us that there are persons of every race and religion who are intelligent, kind, and gracious.

B. The Grateful (v. 19)

19. And he said unto him, Arise, go thy way: thy faith hath made thee whole.

The man was now cured and he had amply shown his gratitude. He next needed to report to the priests so they could certify that he was clean. This was necessary before he could return to a normal life with his family and friends. And so Jesus told him to arise and be on his way. It took the man only a few minutes to return and thank Jesus, and yet how much better he must have felt! His friends might get to the priests first, but he would arrive with a feeling of satisfaction that they could not know.

Jesus commended him for his faith. It had made him whole. The word so translated can convey the idea of spiritual salvation, but it is clear in this situation that it refers to physical healing. The man's faith was not saving faith in the sense it would save him from his sins. He didn't know enough about Jesus yet to have this kind of faith. But he had taken the first step and under such circumstances we would expect his faith to grow and become saving faith.

Conclusion

A. Learning Gratitude

Babies are not born with hearts full of gratitude. Quite the contrary! They are selfish and grasping, without bothering to thank anyone for what they have received. Gratitude has to be learned. One does not learn gratitude on his own. It must be taught. Parents have the major responsibility for teaching it to their children. They do this in many different ways. At an early age, parents teach children to say thank you for every favor they receive from another. Many young people today are lacking in this simple grace, but the major part of the blame for their lack of thankfulness must fall upon parents.

Giving thanks for one's food at meal time is one way that children can be taught to show gratitude. Admittedly, this can become an empty ritual that carries little meaning. But still it is a ritual that can teach. An old farmer once went into the city. He had never eaten in a restaurant before, but this did not keep him from his life-long habit of saying grace over his food. As he bowed his head and quietly expressed his thanks to God, some young people saw him and began to sneer at him. One of the young men spoke out to him in derision, "Say, old man, does everyone back on the farm give thanks for their meals before they eat."

"No, son, not everybody," said the farmer with a pleasant smile. "The hogs don't!"

A grateful attitude must be taught, but it also must be caught. Some of the most important things of life we learn more readily by example than by precept. When children see their parents living lives that acknowledge God as the source of every blessing, then they too will develop grateful hearts.

B. Grateful for the Good

The lepers had many reasons to rejoice and be grateful. They should have been grateful that Jesus passed their way that day. Possibly He had never traveled that route before; or if He had, they had not been there. The men should have been grateful because they were there at just the right time when Jesus did come. Many people have missed Jesus because they were not in the right place at the right time.

The lepers should also have been grateful because they knew something about Jesus' healing power. We don't know how they knew that He could help them, but it is reasonable to suppose that word had come to them from friends or family members that Jesus was healing the afflicted. We too have many occasions when we need to stop and give thanks because someone has told us of Jesus or opened our eyes to some new blessing that we can claim from God.

Of course the lepers' greatest moment of gratitude came when they realized that they had been cleansed of their loathsome disease. Few diseases are more devastating than leprosy. It brings pain and discomfort; it is life-threatening; it is a lingering malady; and, worst of all, perhaps, it resulted in their being socially ostracized. One who has never suffered this kind of an affliction can never really appreciate the joy and relief that these men must have known when they examined themselves and found that they were clean.

But joy is not the same thing as gratitude. While all of the men must have felt some sense of gratitude, the nine were so excited from the personal relief they were experiencing that they didn't take time to go back and thank Jesus.

A writer tells about growing up in a family of the old South. During those years a black cook lived with them. Her pleasant nature made her a favorite with the children, and her simple piety made a lasting impression upon the writer. He was in the kitchen one day when she paused to eat a little snack from a dish she was preparing. Before she put it to her mouth, however, she stopped and gave thanks for it. "Auntie," he asked, "do you always give thanks for every little bite you eat?"

"Lawsy me, boy," was her reply, "don't you know that everything tastes better when you thank the Lawd for it."

What a profound truth this woman had grasped! Everything tastes better when you are thankful for it. The nine lepers certainly enjoyed their restored lives as they returned to their homes and families. Yet as they watched the tenth, who was grateful enough to return and thank Jesus, they must have seen something that they had missed. Did they, in the days that followed, begin to have a gnawing sense of guilt because they had not taken similar action? Was their joy in their restored life tempered by the knowledge that they had done nothing either to deserve this gift nor to thank the giver? Regardless of the blessings that came to them, deep down they must have realized that the grateful leper had a sense of satisfaction that they had missed. Indeed, things taste better when one is thankful!

C. Praise in Pain

It is one thing to feel a sense of gratitude when good things happen to us. It is quite another to give thanks when everything seems to go wrong. Even those who have acquired the grace of gratitude and say thanks at the appropriate time may have trouble saying those words through teeth clinched in pain or lips trembling in defeat. The apostle Paul was one of those rare souls who had reached this level of spiritual maturity. In Ephesians 5:20 he wrote, "Giving thanks always for all things unto God and the

Home Daily Bible Readings

Monday, Feb. 6—Thankful for Our History (Psalm 106:1-12)
Tuesday, Feb. 7—Thankful for Our Great God (Psalm 95:1-7a)
Wednesday, Feb. 8—Thankful for Our Righteousness (Romans 6:15-18)
Thursday, Feb. 9—Thankful for All Things (Ephesians 5:15-20)
Friday, Feb. 10—Thankful for Work (1 Thessalonians 5:12-22)
Saturday, Feb. 11—Thankful for Faith (1 Thessalonians 3:6-10)
Sunday, Feb. 12—Giving and Thanksgiving (Luke 17:11-19)

Father in the name of our Lord Jesus Christ." At the very time he wrote these lines, he was in the custody of the Roman government awaiting trial.

Under similar conditions he wrote to the Philippians a letter that vibrates with his joy. "I have learned, in whatsoever state I am, therewith to be content," he stated (Philippians 4:11). He went on to tell how he had learned to be abased and how he had learned to abound. He knew how to be full and to be hungry. This calm acceptance of whatever life had to offer, good or bad, and to be thankful was based on his firm belief that his life was totally in the hands of God. "My God shall supply all your need according to his riches in glory by Christ Jesus" (Philippians 4:19).

The writer who told about his family's black cook wrote about her death. As she lay dying, he and the other members of his family gathered about her bed. Her body was wracked by pain and every breath was agony; yet she reached out her hands to them and uttered these final words: "Much obliged, Lawd, for such fine friends."

D. Let Us Pray

Teach us, O gracious Father, how to be thankful. Teach us to see all the things that You have given us; help us to recognize that every good and perfect gift comes from You. Help us also to learn to be thankful when pain or disaster is our lot. Help us to teach others by our words and by our actions how to be grateful. In Jesus' name, amen.

E. Thought to Remember

"Blow, blow, thou winter wind!
    Thou art not so unkind
As man's ingratitude."   —WILLIAM SHAKESPEARE

Learning by Doing

*This page contains an alternate lesson plan emphasizing learning activities. Classes
desiring such student involvement will find these suggestions helpful.*

Learning Goals

After this lesson, students should be able to:

1. Recall specific individuals to whom he
needs to express gratitude.

2. List some of the blessings for which he
thanks God.

3. Suggest some ways to exhibit gratitude
daily in his life.

Into the Lesson

You'll need lots of room to write for this activity; a chalkboard just won't do. Spread some
newsprint on the wall or put up several sheets of
posterboard with this main heading: THEY'RE
THE BEST! Leaving plenty of room to write under each, write several sub-headings like
"Teacher," "Co-worker," "Friend," "Professor,"
"Christian Example," "Spiritual Advisor,"
"Christian Author," and other categories of people who often help others in notable ways.

As the students arrive, ask them to write the
names of individuals under the categories
listed. Each may write one name under as many
categories as he wishes. (If short on wall space,
write the categories on the chalkboard and provide paper for the students to write on. This
activity is also in the student book.)

While people are still writing names, discuss
some of the names listed. What do the students
find special about these people? Don't spend a
lot of time, but allow the students to explore
their memories and to feel again the reasons
they find these people "the best."

Call the class to order by saying, "Isn't it fun
to recall people who have helped to make you
what you are? We all owe a debt of gratitude to
such people. I wonder how many of them know
how we feel about them. Have we been like
some men we are going to see in our Scripture
text today—men who failed to express their
gratitude?"

Into the Word

Provide students with copies of the following
questions. Ask them to make brief notes in answer to each as you present some introductory
remarks. Use material provided in the commentary section of this book, both the "Lesson Background" and the comments on the text itself.

1. Where was Jesus when He healed the ten
lepers?

2. Where was He headed?

3. Why did the lepers stand "afar off" if they
wanted Jesus to heal them?

4. What was the reason for the seemingly unkind treatment of lepers in that day?

5. Why did Jesus send them to the priests?

6. Where would they find priests?

7. How did all ten lepers show faith?

8. What was the nationality of the one who
returned to thank Jesus?

9. What did Jesus say about the faith of the
one who returned?

10. After you present the background material, quickly review the questions. (You will find
answers in the commentary section of the lesson.)

Divide into groups of three. Ask each group to
discuss why they believe the other nine did not
return. Was it simple thoughtlessness, or was it
real ingratitude? Have them suggest reasons that
might have been behind the lepers' action.

After a few minutes, have the groups report
their findings. Write the suggested reasons on
the chalkboard. Then ask, "How many of these
same reasons do we sometimes use for not expressing gratitude to God or to others?

Into Life

Distribute thank-you cards or stationery to the
class, enough for each to write two notes. Ask
each student to choose one individual whose
name he wrote in the opening activity and to
write that person a thank you. He should choose
a person whose address he knows or can learn,
so he can actually mail the note.

Then ask the students to consider the greater
debt of thanks they owe to God. Just as the leper
returned "to give glory to God" (Luke 17:18), it
is good for us to do the same. Brainstorm for a
few minutes on some of the blessings God has
given us for which we ought to be thankful. You
might start by suggesting we ought to thank God
for the people through whom He has blessed our
lives. Let the class mention other blessings, as
time permits.

Then call attention to the second note. Ask
each student to write a thank you to God for one
of the blessings suggested. Ask the students to
take these notes home, put them someplace
where they will be seen each day, and thank God
afresh each time they see the notes.

Let's Talk It Over

The questions on this page are designed to encourage review of the lesson Scriptures and to promote discussion of the lesson by the class. The answers provided are only discussion starters. Let your class talk it over from there.

1. Why is being "too busy" a poor excuse for neglecting such Christian duties as expressing personal gratitude?

With what are we so busy? Our work, our family obligations, and our church activities occupy a sizable portion of our time, but they should not keep us so busy that we do not have time to demonstrate our loving concern for other people. The time we spend in recreational and purely social activities may be the problem. We need physical and mental relaxation, but do we need as much time as we are spending on television, sporting events, recreational reading, and socializing? In Ephesians 5:16 Paul advises us to make the most of our time *(New American Standard Version)*, or to make the most of every opportunity *(New International Version)*. We want to examine the reasons for our busyness and make appropriate adjustments if we are too busy with trivial things.

2. When we hear people make promises to God while in the midst of difficult circumstances, how can we help them to fulfill such promises?

Such promises are often vague. Someone may vow to be a better Christian, to do more for the church, to treat his family more kindly, etc. We may suggest some definite changes to fulfill those vows. We may urge him to be a better Christian by daily Bible reading and prayer; to do more for the church by regular attendance, faithful giving, and the acceptance of specific responsibility; to treat his family more kindly by scheduling some definite times to spend with them, including a regular family devotional period. If we hear a non-Christian promise to become a Christian, we may urge him to act promptly on such an intention. We should make it clear that keeping the promise is an act of gratitude, not a way of bribing God; but still the promise should be kept.

3. Why does expressing gratitude tend to make us feel better?

We speak of "owing a debt of gratitude." While that is not a Biblical expression, it is in harmony with the teaching of the Bible. Paul says something close to it in Romans 13:8: "Let no debt remain outstanding, except the continu-

ing debt to love one another" *(New International Version)*. How do we feel when we make the final payment on a car? We feel a sense of fulfillment, of relief, of joy. In a similar way we experience satisfaction in "paying off" a debt of gratitude. Paul in 2 Corinthians 9:11-15 connects thanksgiving for human acts of kindness with thanksgiving to God. Expressions of gratitude toward one another should be accompanied by prayers of thanksgiving to the Heavenly Father—and Paul makes the entire process sound like a very satisfying experience.

4. What are some principles parents should keep in mind as they endeavor to teach their children to express gratitude?

When children are taught at an early age to say thank you, they should be made to see that this is not a mere formality. Children tend, as they grow older, to discard habits that they view as being childish or pointless. We must show them that it is a matter of maturity to express thanksgiving, and that it can never become a pointless formality. When children see their parents expressing sincere gratitude, it helps them realize that saying thank you is the grown-up thing to do. The parental example can be taken a little further. Sometimes people tend to show the least respect and kindness to the members of their own families. Parents can offset this tendency by expressing gratitude to one another and to their children.

5. The lepers may have thought it was a lucky break that they were in the right place at the right time to be healed by Jesus. How is the emphasis on lucky breaks a hindrance to developing an attitude of thanksgiving?

Sometimes people thank their lucky stars. Some even indicate they are thanking God for their luck. But these may be empty expressions. If people attribute happy experiences to luck, usually they do not really thank anyone. We do not call it luck when we receive a favor or gift from a friend. Why should we label as luck a favor from the giver of "every good and perfect gift"? (James 1:17, *New International Version*). How it must grieve Him when we receive His blessings and respond with an exclamation regarding our good luck!

Wealth and Discipleship

LESSON SCRIPTURE: Luke 18:18-30.

PRINTED TEXT: Luke 18:18-30.

Luke 18:18-30

18 A certain ruler asked him, saying, Good Master, what shall I do to inherit eternal life?

19 And Jesus said unto him, Why callest thou me good? none is good, save one, that is, God.

20 Thou knowest the commandments, Do not commit adultery, Do not kill, Do not steal, Do not bear false witness, Honor thy father and thy mother.

21 And he said, All these have I kept from my youth up.

22 Now when Jesus heard these things, he said unto him, Yet lackest thou one thing: sell all that thou hast, and distribute unto the poor, and thou shalt have treasure in heaven: and come, follow me.

23 And when he heard this, he was very sorrowful: for he was very rich.

24 And when Jesus saw that he was very sorrowful, he said, How hardly shall they that have riches enter into the kingdom of God!

25 For it is easier for a camel to go through a needle's eye, than for a rich man to enter into the kingdom of God.

26 And they that heard it said, Who then can be saved?

27 And he said, The things which are impossible with men are possible with God.

28 Then Peter said, Lo, we have left all, and followed thee.

29 And he said unto them, Verily I say unto you, There is no man that hath left house, or parents, or brethren, or wife, or children, for the kingdom of God's sake,

30 Who shall not receive manifold more in this present time, and in the world to come life everlasting.

Golden Text: Sell all that thou hast, and distribute unto the poor, and thou shalt have treasure in heaven: and come, follow me.—Luke 18:22.

Scenes of Love and Compassion
Unit 3: Response and Responsibility
(Lessons 10-13)

Lesson Aims

After this lesson students should:

1. Come to realize more fully that wealth can be a stumbling block to spiritual growth.

2. Have a growing appreciation for the responsible use of wealth.

3. Be able to state one way in which he or she could use wealth more responsibly.

Lesson Outline

INTRODUCTION
   A. "Your Money or Your Life!"
   B. Lesson Background
 I. A MAN SEEKS ETERNAL LIFE (Luke 18:18-21)
   A. His Request (v. 18)
   B. Jesus' Response (vv. 19, 20)
   C. The Man's Record (v. 21)
 II. THE MAN'S WEAKNESS (Luke 18:22, 23)
   A. Jesus' Exhortation (v. 22)
      Not Quite Good Enough
   B. The Man's Sorrow (v. 23)
 III. DIVINE STANDARDS (Luke 18:24-30)
   A. Riches Can Handicap (vv. 24, 25)
      Too Heavily Laden
   B. All Things Are Possible (vv. 26, 27)
   C. Reward of the Faithful (vv. 28-30)
CONCLUSION
   A. God and Mammon
   B. Let Us Pray
   C. Thought to Remember

Visual 12 in the visuals/learning resources packet illustrates the main thoughts in the lesson text. The visual is shown on page 213.

Introduction

A. "Your Money or Your Life!"

Comedian Jack Benny got many laughs from his stage reputation of being tight-fisted, even stingy. In one well-remembered routine, he was accosted by a gunman, who leveled his weapon at him and demanded, "Your money or your life!" Benny stood motionless without batting an eye. The gunman repeated his demand, "I said your money or your life!" Still the comedian didn't move or reply. A third time the gunman made his demand, "Didn't you hear me? I said your money or your life!"

Finally Benny replied, "Don't rush me. I'm thinking, I'm thinking!"

We may chuckle at this obsession with material wealth, but Jack Benny's desire to get wealth and hold on to it is only a slight exaggeration of the attitude Jesus found in the rich young ruler. And if we are honest with ourselves, we are likely to find it in our own lives.

B. Lesson Background

In last week's lesson we read that Jesus healed ten lepers. This incident occurred somewhere along the border between Samaria and Galilee. Jesus continued to teach as He made His way through Perea, the area east of the Jordan River. His teaching included a sermon on the time of the coming of the kingdom (Luke 17:20-37), and the parable of the Pharisee and the publican (Luke 18:9-14). Then Jesus used little children as an object lesson to teach about the kind of attitude persons must have if they are to enter the kingdom of God (Luke 18:15-17).

The coming of the rich young ruler and the discussion about the dangers of wealth are recorded also in Matthew 19:16-30 and Mark 10:17-31.

I. A Man Seeks Eternal Life
(Luke 18:18-21)

A. His Request (v. 18)

18. And a certain ruler asked him, saying, Good Master, what shall I do to inherit eternal life?

Each of the three Gospel accounts gives us some information not found in the other two. Mark informs us that Jesus was leaving a village when the man ran out to speak to Him. He also says the man fell down on his knees before Jesus. It is Matthew who gives us the information that he was a young man (19:20). Luke calls him a ruler, which probably indicates that he was a leader in the local synagogue. That was an honored position, but his kneeling before Jesus indicates that he had a humble heart.

He addressed Jesus as *Good Master*, or "good teacher," indicating his respect. Apparently he had seen something in Jesus' life or heard something in His teachings to make him think the Lord had something that other teachers did not offer. No one can ask a more important question: *What shall I do to inherit eternal life?* The question deals with eternity, but it has powerful implications for the present.

Evidently the young man had been under the influence of the Pharisees. They believed in life after death, while the Sadducees did not. Further, his question reflects the Pharisees' idea that salvation is gained by good works. Recently Jesus had said one must *receive* the kingdom as a little child rather than earn it by good works (Luke 18:17). But Mark says the man ran after Jesus as Jesus was leaving the town. This suggests that he had not heard Jesus' teaching about receiving the kingdom as a little child.

No doubt the young ruler merited high marks on his moral report card. He was not uttering an idle boast when he said he had faithfully observed the law. Then why did he feel that something was missing in his life? Had he heard Jesus preach and been touched by it? Or had he on his own come to see that the law as a road to salvation led to a dead end? Regardless of the reason, he went to the right person for help.

B. Jesus' Response (vv. 19, 20)

19. And Jesus said unto him, Why callest thou me good? none is good, save one, that is, God.

It is not necessarily wrong to call a man good in a limited sense. The Bible does it (Acts 11:24). But only God is altogether good. Some students have taken Jesus' words to mean that He was not good and therefore should not be called good, but such students have missed the point. Jesus' question was designed to shock the young man into thinking about what he was saying. Was he merely trying to flatter Jesus? Did he mean Jesus was good in spite of some faults, as many men are? Or was he ready to acknowledge that Jesus was really divine, the Son of God? We all face a similar question. In what sense do we call Jesus good?

20. Thou knowest the commandments, Do not commit adultery, Do not kill, Do not steal, Do not bear false witness, Honor thy father and thy mother.

Jesus next began to examine the man, and the first part of the examination was fairly easy. Jesus quoted five of the Ten Commandments, selecting those that deal with overt actions that are to be done or not to be done. Keeping or breaking of these is easily seen. On purpose Jesus did not mention the Tenth Commandment, Thou shalt not covet, though it was the very heart of the man's problem.

Jesus did not say the ruler would gain eternal life by keeping these five commandments. To gain eternal life through the law, one would have to keep all the Ten Commandments plus all the other commands of God ... keep them faultlessly and from the heart. Even today those five Commandments provide a good place to begin, but they are only a beginning. When a person has a background in the law, as this man did, the law provides a stepping stone to the gospel.

C. The Man's Record (v. 21)

21. And he said, All these have I kept from my youth up.

Apparently in all good conscience, the young man answered that he had kept all of these commandments that dealt with outward, visible acts. What he didn't realize was that the law went beyond the obvious and the physical. Even we today are likely to view the law in that light. The apostle Paul indicates that one of the functions of the law was to bring men to a realization that they are sinners (Romans 7:7). Interestingly, the example he uses is the Tenth Commandment: "Nay, I had not known sin, but by the law: for I had not known lust, except the law had said, Thou shalt not covet."

Since the law had not opened this young man's eyes to the fact that he was a sinner, we can only conclude that he was spiritually rather superficial. Yet perhaps the law had not failed completely in its eye-opening function. Something had caused this young man to feel a need to seek out Jesus. Though in his own eyes he had observed the law, yet deep down he realized that this was not enough.

Matthew reports that the young man asked Jesus, "What good thing shall I do, that I may have eternal life?" Some students think he was hoping that one great heroic deed could insure his entrance into Heaven. But whether one attempts to gain salvation by a lifetime of good deeds or by one great deed, he is trying to earn salvation by his works. His problem is that he can never know when he has finally performed enough good deeds to merit salvation. And of course he has not. Salvation is never earned. It is a gift of God's grace.

II. The Man's Weakness
(Luke 18:22, 23)

A. Jesus' Exhortation (v. 22)

22. Now when Jesus heard these things, he said unto him, Yet lackest thou one thing: sell all that thou hast, and distribute unto the poor, and thou shalt have treasure in heaven: and come, follow me.

Now came the hard part of the exam. Jesus did not challenge the young man's estimate of his own moral life. Perhaps no one could point to an overt act that violated one of the five commandments Jesus had quoted. But Jesus had not mentioned the Tenth Commandment, which forbids covetousness. As it turned out, this was the ruler's problem. He had come to love things more than he loved his fellowman. Even worse, he had not lived up to the First Commandment, which teaches that Jehovah God must come first. Carelessly this man had placed wealth upon the throne that God should occupy.

No doubt the young man would have denied such a charge had Jesus leveled it at him. He probably paid tithes, studied the Scriptures, and attended the synagogue regularly. With such a record most of our churches would welcome him with open arms and probably make him an officer in a short time. The truth of his situation finally came out, however, when Jesus forced him to make a decision between his wealth and his "Good Master." The wealth won out.

NOT QUITE GOOD ENOUGH

On February 25, 1961, Paul Bikle flew his sailplane to a world record altitude of 46,267 feet. The record stood for twenty-five years.

Then along came Bob Harris. After years of studying meteorology, he caught the thermal wave he was looking for on February 17, 1986, and rode it to 49,009 feet. And he did it without a pressure suit to protect him from the thin air and the temperature of eighty below! Talk about having "the right stuff"! Bob Harris was *good!*

But not good enough. Harris made his flight without clearance from FAA flight controllers. As a result, his record stands under the cloud of sanctions from the FAA, which says any flight over 18,000 feet must be under their control. Harris' unauthorized flight could have placed commercial airline traffic in jeopardy.

Life is like that, isn't it? No matter how good we may be, or heroic, we are never quite good enough. We can never quite make up for the fact that we are sinners. There is always that quirk of character, that oversight, that sin (big or little), that casts a cloud over our goodness. With the rich young man, it was the power his wealth had over him. What is it that clouds your goodness?
                                                        —C. R. B.

B. The Man's Sorrow (v. 23)

23. And when he heard this, he was very sorrowful: for he was very rich.

This was not the answer the young man had expected. If Jesus had told him to go on an arduous pilgrimage or undertake some hazardous task, it is likely that he would have responded with enthusiasm. But Jesus' answer turned his excitement to sorrow. The reason is not hard to find: *he was very rich*. He possessed much

wealth, or, to put it more accurately, the wealth possessed him. The wealth had him so ensnared that he allowed it to shape the whole future of his life and his eternal destiny.

Most of us can feel somewhat aloof from this young man and his problems. After all, few of us have great wealth. But one does not need to have great possessions before they begin to take charge of his life. The young man realized that he had a conflict in his life. The dangerous thing about our enthrallment with possessions is that it may be accomplished before we are aware of the conflict.

III. Divine Standards
(Luke 18:24-30)

A. Riches Can Handicap (vv. 24, 25)

24. And when Jesus saw that he was very sorrowful, he said, How hardly shall they that have riches enter into the kingdom of God!

The young man's countenance revealed the struggle that was going on in his heart. When he turned to go away, Jesus must have been deeply pained. The man had many admirable qualities, and Mark tells us that Jesus loved him (Mark 10:21). Jesus had done His best to reach the man, but in the end he had to make up his own mind about what he would do with his life. Jesus would not make his decision for him.

The man's departure provided Jesus an opportunity to discuss further some important teachings about wealth. His first observation must have shocked many of His hearers. It was widely held that the greater the wealth, the greater God's approval of a person's life. Jesus seemed to be saying just exactly the opposite. A rich man was going to have a hard time getting into Heaven!

TOO HEAVILY LADEN

Dick Rutan and Jeana Yeager made aviation history in December, 1986. In the fragile-appearing *Voyager*, they flew around the world non-stop without refueling.

Years of planning and testing lay behind the takeoff on December 16, 1986. The plane was built of "space age" materials and weighed only 939 pounds, but when it took off with a full load of fuel, it weighed five tons!

The Voyager almost failed to get off the ground. There was so much fuel in the flexible wings that their tips scraped the runway. They were tough enough to take the scraping without much damage, however, and the rest is history.

The rich young ruler came to Jesus very heavily laden. He was attracted to Jesus and had much to commend him, but he was held down by his possessions. He could not take off with all his wealth, and he would not leave it behind, so he turned away from Jesus in sadness.

How many of us are prevented from soaring free in the realm of the spirit because our accumulation of the "necessities" of life keeps us "dragging along the ground?"   —C. R. B.

25. For it is easier for a camel to go through a needle's eye, than for a rich man to enter into the kingdom of God.

This verse is one of Jesus' most memorable sayings, made so by the fact that He resorted to an unforgettable hyperbole to make His point. Some commentators have tried to explain this startling figure by saying that the needle's eye was a small opening in the city gate through which a camel might pass with some difficulty. Others affirm that Jesus was talking about a rope instead of a camel. Since the Greek words for *rope* and *camel* are similar, they think a scribe accidentally changed the spelling to make the text read *camel*.

Such scholarly efforts miss the point Jesus was making. He fully intended to state that from the viewpoint of man it is impossible for a rich man to enter God's kingdom. The disciples understood this, and that is the reason they were so shocked.

B. All Things Are Possible (vv. 26, 27)

26. And they that heard it said, Who then can be saved?

It is interesting to note that the young man came inquiring about how he might inherit eternal life. Jesus spoke in terms of entering the kingdom of God. The disciples spoke about being saved. It is obvious that the three expressions are used interchangeably.

The different terms did not bother the disciples, but Jesus' statement did. They were used to the traditional view that the possession of riches was evidence of God's approval. If it was impossible for a rich man to be saved, the disciples reasoned, then certainly it was impossible for the less-favored to be saved.

27. And he said, The things which are impossible with men are possible with God.

The disciples' reasoning seemed logical enough. What they did not stop to consider at the moment was God's part in salvation. What may indeed be impossible with man presents no problem to Him. The disciples had not yet given up the idea of earning salvation by good works. They had not yet come to understand that salvation for everyone, rich or poor, is through God's grace. With God all things are possible! We need to remember this in troubled times when nothing seems to go right.

visual 12

ETERNAL LIFE

IN GOD

TRUST

IN ONESELF

IN MONEY

ETERNAL DEATH

C. Reward of the Faithful (vv. 28-30)

28. Then Peter said, Lo, we have left all, and followed thee.

Peter, as he so often did, acted as the spokesman for the rest of the disciples. At first they were afraid that no one could be saved. Now they wanted assurance that they would be among those entering the kingdom of God. Jesus had told the rich young ruler to give up his possessions and follow Him and thus gain treasure in Heaven. Peter wanted to remind Jesus that the disciples had already met this qualification—or at least they felt that they had.

29, 30. And he said unto them, Verily I say unto you, There is no man that hath left house, or parents, or brethren, or wife, or children, for the kingdom of God's sake, who shall not receive manifold more in this present time, and in the world to come life everlasting.

Matthew reports Jesus' reply in greater detail. Jesus assured the disciples that they would "sit upon twelve thrones, judging the twelve tribes of Israel" (Matthew 19:28). Further, they would receive back a hundredfold for everything they had given up, whether houses or family. Jesus' exaggeration for the purpose of emphasis is obvious. Speaking literally, receiving a hundred wives or a hundred children might not be considered a blessing!

The idea He intended to convey is that when one devotes himself completely to Christ, joys and blessings he receives are worth far more than what he gives up. Every mature Christian knows exactly what Jesus meant. A person may give up his family to serve the Lord, but he becomes a member of a much larger family. He may give up his house, but finds he is welcome in a thousand homes across the land and around the world. Jim Elliott, who lost his life in taking the gospel to the Auca Indians of South America, put it this way: "A man is no fool who gives up what he cannot keep to gain what he cannot lose."

But Jesus did not stop with blessings in this life alone. If we are willing to put Him first and not let things stand between us and dedicated service, we can look forward to life eternal.

Conclusion

A. God and Mammon

In His teaching Jesus made it quite clear that one cannot serve both God and mammon at the same time (Matthew 6:24; Luke 16:13). Mammon can mean wealth or anything else that comes between a person and God. Jesus did not condemn wealth as such, but it earns condemnation when it is improperly used or when it estranges man from God.

People seek wealth for various reasons. Some desire wealth because it gives them *power.* Money can be used to manipulate people. It can buy their services, their skills, and even their integrity. It cannot buy love, but it can buy flattery that some are quite happy to accept in the place of love. With enough money one can alter the nature of institutions and organizations. Even churches are not immune from power grabs engineered by money. With enough money one can manipulate voters and gain political power. A rich family member can use money to control other members of his family.

Some desire money because it will bring *prestige.* With money one can gain the plaudits of men. Since our society puts such a high premium on money, we give our highest honors to those who acquire it, often regardless of how they gain it or how they use it. Our heroes have become those who drive the biggest cars, live at the most prestigious addresses, and have their offices on the top floor. All of these things take money. A first-class airline ticket costs considerably more than a tourist class ticket. Granted, the seats in first class are larger and more comfortable, the meals better, and the liquor free, but these additional benefits hardly add up to the difference in ticket costs. Many years ago a sociologist coined a term, *conspicuous consumption*, to describe the spending of money for no other purpose than to prove that one has it to spend. Or as someone has put it more bluntly, "If you've got it, flaunt it!" Nothing in our society serves the purpose of acquiring prestige better than does money.

Let us not forget that money can buy *pleasure.* In our highly commercialized society, pleasure comes with a rather high price tag. Travel, sporting events, hobbies, even eating out all take money these days, lots of it. The simple pleasures that once brought so much joy to our lives have been all but forgotten in our mad rush

Home Daily Bible Readings

Monday, Feb. 13—Discipleship Means Endurance (Matthew 10:16-25)
Tuesday, Feb. 14—Discipleship Means Leadership (Luke 6:39-45)
Wednesday, Feb. 15—Discipleship Requires Faith and Forgiveness (Luke 17:1-5)
Thursday, Feb. 16—Discipleship Counts the Cost (Luke 14:25-35)
Friday, Feb. 17—Discipleship Comes From Within (Mark 7:1-8, 14-23)
Saturday, Feb. 18—Discipleship Demands Believing Prayer (Mark 9:14-29)
Sunday, Feb. 19—Discipleship in a Society of Achievers (Luke 18:18-30)

to do the "in thing" or visit the "in place." Remember that it was a quest for pleasure that caused the prodigal son to end up in a pig pen.

Money can also bring a sense of *security.* We must say *sense* of security, for money does not make one truly secure. Many of us have learned from experience that money, securities, and real estate can be swept away in a few brief moments. Older persons may be especially tempted to want money because it seems to bring security. Many older persons have had their share of power and found that it often leaves a bitter taste in the end. Nor is prestige very important to one whose remaining years are likely to be filled with pain and loneliness. And money-bought pleasures are likely to be too demanding physically or too fleeting to be of interest to older people. But security? That is important.

Regardless of the reason that one may seek wealth, the fact remains that one cannot serve God and mammon at the same time. Whenever one allows the pursuit of wealth to become the all-consuming purpose in his life, he has alienated himself from God, with results that can only be disastrous.

B. Let Us Pray

We thank You, Father, that You have blessed us with such a vast store of material wealth. We pray for Your help in guarding our hearts against the temptations to make wealth our god. Teach us to use carefully and wisely what You have given us. In His name, amen.

C. Thought to Remember

"A person cannot serve God and mammon, but he can serve God with mammon."

—JESSE BADER

Learning by Doing

This page contains an alternate lesson plan emphasizing learning activities. Classes desiring such student involvement will find these suggestions helpful.

Learning Goals

This lesson should enable each student to:

1. List some ways wealth can be a stumbling block to spiritual growth.

2. Suggest some ways to use wealth to enhance spiritual growth.

3. Explain how, in salvation, God does "things which are impossible with men."

Into the Lesson

Give each student a copy of this chart:

IF I HAD A MILLION DOLLARS . . .

$500,000

$400,000

$300,000

$200,000

$100,000

```
     ——————————————————————————
     1  2  3  4  5  6  7  8  9  10
```

1. _____

2. _____

3. _____

4. _____

5. _____

6. _____

7. _____

8. _____

9. _____

10. _____

Ask each student to list up to ten things for which he would spend, invest, or otherwise use the money if he suddenly received a million dollars (tax free). For each item, let him chart the expense on the graph. For example, if one decides he would have his dream home, he may list "Home" on line 1; then draw a vertical bar above the 1 on the graph to the level he would expect to spend, e.g., $250,000. He then would have $750,000 to divide among the other items on his list.

Into the Word

Ask a good reader to read Luke 18:18-30. Ask two other readers to read the parallel accounts in Matthew 19:16-30 and Mark 10:17-31. Then divide the class into three groups.

Group 1 is to consider the first part of the passage, Luke 18:18-23, and answer these questions:

a. How can wealth hinder spiritual growth?

b. What kind of answer was this man probably expecting from Jesus?

c. What was wrong with this man's understanding of salvation?

Group 2 is to focus on what happened after the man left, Luke 18:24-27, and answer these questions:

a. Why is it difficult for the rich to "enter the kingdom"?

b. Who then can be saved?

c. What was wrong with these people's understanding of salvation?

Group 3 is to look at Luke 18:28-30.

a. Peter said, "We have left all, and followed thee." Had they earned salvation?

b. Did Jesus mean a literal hundred-fold return on everything given up? If not, what?

c. What was wrong with the disciples' understanding of salvation?

As each group reports its findings, note that the rich ruler, they that heard, and the disciples all had the same misunderstanding of salvation. They were thinking of earning salvation. Rich or poor, they could not do that. Salvation is a gracious gift from God.

Into Life

Point out that the real issue is not money, but what we value or depend on most. Some of the people in our text counted on money—as a sign of God's favor. Others counted on their lack of possessions—as a sign of their devotion.

Ask the students to name the items they put on their charts earlier, and the amounts assigned to each. Does the Lord get a tithe? Just a tithe? Do the charts demonstrate that God is most important to us, or do they reveal selfish desires?

Most of your students don't have and never will have a million dollars. Work together to make a list of things on which Christians with much less can use their money for the good of the kingdom and to enhance spiritual growth.

Let's Talk It Over

The questions on this page are designed to encourage review of the lesson Scriptures and to promote discussion of the lesson by the class. The answers provided are only discussion starters. Let your class talk it over from there.

1. Are there people today who call Jesus "good" without considering the implications of that description? If so, who are they?

Jesus has been called a good man, a good leader, a good teacher. Many people who do not regard Him as the Son of God and Savior still say He is good. But if He was a good man who did good deeds, we must ask why and how He accomplished these. Jesus answered this in John 5:19: "The Son can do nothing by himself; he can do only what he sees his Father doing, because whatever the Father does the Son also does" *(New International Version)*. If we speak of His being a good leader, we must examine the behavior of His followers. They regarded Him as the Son of God and later claimed He had arisen from the grave. And if we call Him a good teacher, then we must deal with His teachings that spoke of His atonement for man's sins. Anyone who calls Jesus good and is not prepared to acknowledge His deity and His lordship has not really accepted the Gospel records.

2. How should we respond to those who claim that their religion consists in keeping the Ten Commandments?

In the Sermon on the Mount (Matthew 5:21-30) Jesus showed that outward observance of the law is inadequate; conformity to God's commands also involves the thoughts and intents of the heart. If we had only the Ten Commandments and the Sermon on the Mount, we would be bound by guilt and frustration, because we do not live up to the standards they present. They remind us of our sinfulness and our need for God's grace. And so we might tell the person who centers his religion around the Ten Commandments that he has made a good beginning. When he adds the Sermon on the Mount and sees his failure to live up to the divine standards, perhaps he will be ready to seek and find God's forgiveness.

3. How can we tell if our possessions have taken charge of our lives?

Paul wrote, "If we have food and clothing, we will be content with that" (1 Timothy 6:8, *New International Version*). Most of us need a home and car besides. But some of us are not content unless we have everything our neighbors have.

Possessions or desired possessions take charge of our lives when we cannot be happy without them. It is not a sin to have a well-kept lawn or a beautiful home or a fully-equipped car, but such items can become idols that demand too much of our time and income. Possessions take charge of our lives when we spend our resources in their service.

4. "How hardly shall they that have riches enter into the kingdom of God!" (Luke 18:24). Is that still true?

Pride, self-sufficiency, and a tendency to focus on temporal concerns are often associated with riches. All of these hinder a person's recognition of his need for God and for eternal treasures. And these attitudes are as much of a danger today as they were in Jesus' time. Though we are only average, middle-class individuals, we may be as rich as the rich young ruler. We may have more changes of clothing than he did, eat better food than he did, and live in a more comfortable home than he did. Our riches need not keep us from being concerned about spiritual blessings, but Jesus' warning is an appropriate one for us to keep in mind.

5. In what ways is the power associated with money a temptation to Christians?

Even in the church one hears the often-cynical statement, "Money talks." Church leaders may be tempted to give preferential treatment to members or visitors who have money. Those who are wealthier may expect such treatment. James issued a warning against it (James 2:1-4). Christians may be mistaken in assuming that their faith is strong enough to enable them to avoid the pitfalls of financial power. In our times the idea is frequently set forth that Christians should have as much financial power as everyone else, that the church should be economically potent enough to command respect from government and from social institutions. Paul's advice to Timothy in 1 Timothy 6:17 seems pertinent: "Command those who are rich in this present world not to be arrogant nor to put their hope in wealth, which is so uncertain, but to put their hope in God, who richly provides us with everything for our enjoyment" *(New International Version)*.

Becoming a Believer

LESSON SCRIPTURE: Luke 19:1-10.

PRINTED TEXT: Luke 19:1-10.

Luke 19:1-10

1 Jesus entered and passed through Jericho.

2 And, behold, there was a man named Zaccheus, which was the chief among the publicans, and he was rich.

3 And he sought to see Jesus who he was; and could not for the press, because he was little of stature.

4 And he ran before, and climbed up into a sycamore tree to see him; for he was to pass that way.

5 And when Jesus came to the place, he looked up, and saw him, and said unto him, Zaccheus, make haste, and come down; for today I must abide at thy house.

6 And he made haste, and came down, and received him joyfully.

7 And when they saw it, they all murmured, saying, That he was gone to be guest with a man that is a sinner.

8 And Zaccheus stood, and said unto the Lord; Behold, Lord, the half of my goods I give to the poor; and if I have taken any thing from any man by false accusation, I restore him fourfold.

9 And Jesus said unto him, This day is salvation come to this house, forasmuch as he also is a son of Abraham.

10 For the Son of man is come to seek and to save that which was lost.

Golden Text: Behold, Lord, the half of my goods I give to the poor; and if I have taken any thing from any man by false accusation, I restore him fourfold.
—Luke 19:8.

Lesson Aims

As a result of studying this lesson, each student should:

1. Understand more fully that Jesus is ready to receive and forgive any penitent sinner.

2. Have a growing appreciation for the fact that God loves him and every other sinner.

3. Be better able to share that love with others.

Lesson Outline

Display visual 13 from the visuals/learning resources packet and refer to it as you explain the Scripture text. It is shown on page 221.

Introduction

A. Repentance Tower

In a Scottish town overlooking the Solway Firth on the English border stands a square tower that bears the interesting name of "Repentance Tower." Behind the name is a story. Many years ago a bandit terrorized the border between England and Scotland. For a long time he successfully eluded the authorities. Then one day he was confronted with the claims of the gospel, and he completely surrendered his life to Christ.

His life was changed dramatically, and he spent his remaining days going about doing good and trying to make amends for the evil he had done. The tower was built as a monument to his repentance. But actually the good deeds were a far more important memorial.

So far as we know, no one ever built a monument to Zaccheus' repentance. And even if they had, it would have long since perished. But his offer to make restitution for his evil deeds is a far more lasting memorial. His offer will be remembered and spoken of as long as the Scriptures are read and studied.

B. Lesson Background

Jesus, because of the growing antagonism of the political leaders, had spent several weeks away from Jerusalem. Much of this time had been spent in Perea, the region to the east of the lower Jordan River. That was where Jesus met the rich young ruler.

Not long after this encounter, Jesus led His disciples across the Jordan and started on His last trip to Jerusalem. A few miles west of the river He came to the city of Jericho. As in other towns, the people flocked to see Him. Mark and Luke mention only one of the men, but it is clear that all three writers refer to the same incident (Mark 10:46-52; Luke 18:35-43). Word of this miracle quickly spread through the town, and soon a large crowd pressed about Jesus, hoping to see another miracle. It was this crowd that caused Zacchaeus to climb a tree in an effort to see Jesus.

I. Jesus Meets Zaccheus (Luke 19:1-5)

A. The Setting (v. 1)

1. And Jesus entered and passed through Jericho.

Jericho was located near the main road that ran from Perea to Jerusalem and other cities of Judah. Its publicans could enrich themselves by levying taxes on merchandise that passed through as well as on the local people. A copious spring made the area an oasis in the dry country, and Jericho had been a prominent town from ancient times. The earliest settlements were built around a spring, which made the spot an oasis in an otherwise quite arid area.

B. Zaccheus Identified (v. 2)

2. And, behold, there was a man named Zaccheus, which was the chief among the publicans, and he was rich.

The publicans were tax collectors. The Roman system of collecting taxes left the door open for corruption and extortion. Rulers of the empire would sell to some rich person the right to collect taxes in a province. He in turn would sell to others the right to collect taxes in parts of his province. As *chief among the publicans*, Zaccheus probably had several others making collections in parts of his area. The rate of taxation was not fixed from Rome. Each collector took what the traffic would bear. Naturally the people resented this extortion, but the tax collectors had the power of the Roman government behind them. One who refused to pay might have his property confiscated. As a result, publicans were classed with sinners (Matthew 9:10), with harlots (Matthew 21:31), and with other evildoers (Luke 18:11). As *chief among the publicans*, Zaccheus probably was hated even more than the others. Apparently he was successful at his trade, however, for *he was rich*. No doubt his neighbors envied his riches.

C. Zaccheus' Desire (v. 3)

3. And he sought to see Jesus who he was; and could not for the press, because he was little of stature.

No doubt Zaccheus had heard of Jesus. Like many others in town, he wanted to see this man who had gathered such a following. But he was foiled in his efforts even to catch a glimpse of this prophet from Galilee. The crowd compressed into the narrow streets made it impossible for him to get close to Jesus. Knowing who he was, the people may have deliberately kept him back. At least no one would help him get through the crowd, and he was too short to see over the heads of others.

D. Zaccheus' Action (v. 4)

4. And he ran before, and climbed up into a sycamore tree to see him; for he was to pass that way.

Zaccheus was short, but he was resourceful. Anticipating the route that Jesus would take, he ran on ahead and found a convenient tree. In the *King James Version* it is called a sycamore tree, but it should not be confused with the American sycamore. The Palestinian sycamore is a type of fig tree that sometimes grows thirty or forty feet

---

How to Say It

JERICHO. *Jair*-ih-ko.
PEREA. Peh-*ree*-uh.
ZACCHEUS. Zack-*kee*-us.

---

tall. It usually has a short trunk with spreading branches, making it an easy tree to climb.

Zaccheus quickly climbed the tree and waited for Jesus and the crowd. He was so eager to see the Master that he cast aside the dignity that his office and his wealth afforded him. Surely many would be quick to ridicule a chief publican perched in a tree like some curious boy.

E. Jesus' Response (v. 5)

5. And when Jesus came to the place, he looked up, and saw him, and said unto him, Zaccheus, make haste, and come down; for today I must abide at thy house.

It is likely that Zaccheus intended to remain out of sight, to see Jesus without being seen by the crowd. He certainly had no reason to expect that Jesus would pay any attention to him. What he hadn't counted on was Jesus' divine knowledge. The Master knew who was in the tree, and knew he was a good prospect for the kingdom of God.

First of all, Jesus called him by name. This must have surprised Zaccheus, but a bigger surprise was to come. Jesus invited himself to Zaccheus' house. He didn't say, "May I come to your house?" He didn't need to ask permission. He knew Zaccheus would welcome Him, but would hesitate to offer an invitation. So Jesus took the initiative. And does not Jesus deal with us in a similar fashion today? "Behold, I stand at the door, and knock" (Revelation 3:20).

Jesus knew that His going to the home of Zaccheus would alienate the religious leaders in the community. But Jesus never permitted His agenda to be determined by the religious leaders. He had associated with publicans before. Indeed, one of His chosen twelve had been a publican when He had called him (Matthew 9:9). Jesus' mission was to seek and save the lost, and certainly the religious leaders would have been quick to acknowledge that publicans were lost.

II. Jesus a Guest of Zaccheus (Luke 19:6-8)

A. Zaccheus' Joy (v. 6)

6. And he made haste, and came down, and received him joyfully.

Zaccheus must have been surprised when Jesus spoke to him. The surprise turned to shock when Jesus invited himself to his house. But Zaccheus recovered from his shock and scrambled down out of the tree. It may have been hard to believe his ears; but once he came to realize that Jesus did indeed intend to come to his house, excitement and joy flooded his heart.

The attitude of Zaccheus contrasts sharply with that of the religious leaders in Jerusalem. Even now they were plotting ways to get rid of Jesus. It is likely that some of their representatives were in Jericho, following Jesus in the hope of catching Him in some word or action that they might use against Him. If they felt joy when He went with Zaccheus, it was only because once more they could accuse Him of associating with sinful publicans.

B. The Response of the Critics (v. 7)

7. And when they saw it, they all murmured, saying, That he was gone to be guest with a man that is a sinner.

The people murmured their disapproval. Publicans were hated by everyone. They were thought to be unpatriotic, even traitors, because they worked with the Romans. They were hated also because they were thought to be extortioners, exacting taxes unfairly.

In His efforts to reach all men, even the outcasts, Jesus would not be bound by the traditions and practices of others. He had demonstrated this in reaching out to call Matthew as a disciple (Matthew 9:9). He had also shown it by associating with publicans in other situations (Matthew 9:10-13; Luke 15:1, 2). The people of Galilee had so often seen Jesus receive publicans that they probably were no longer shocked by it. But the people of Jericho had not had so many opportunities to see Him in His daily associations. They were both surprised and offended that He would go into the house of a publican.

Jesus' mission required that He be free to go to any place and speak to any person at any time. Since the gospel is for all persons, we should feel the same kind of compulsion. But when we do so act, we must at times exercise reasonable precautions. For example, a Christian may need to enter a bar to speak to someone. When he does, he needs to make sure that his action will not be misunderstood. A Christian's freedom of action must be balanced against the importance of keeping his reputation spotless.

A DIFFERENT PERSPECTIVE

White residents of Washington, D.C., rank traffic as the city's number one problem, but black residents say it is drugs.

Only twenty percent of unwed white fathers pay child support, whereas thirty-six percent of unwed black fathers do so.

Statistics such as these indicate something we ought to know: the "truths" we accept depend greatly on our point of view. "Upper-class" people may see the greatest problems in things that inconvenience them. "Lower-class" people may

be more likely to see life-and-death issues as the greatest problems.

We also tend to judge people in groups rather than individually. We call a whole group evil, irresponsible, and deserving of their problems, though some members of that group are better than some members of ours.

Those who criticized Jesus for going to Zaccheus' house grumbled that He was the guest of a "sinner." They were more troubled by Jesus' unconcern for standard social etiquette than by Zaccheus' need for salvation. Their limited perspective also blinded them to the fact that they too were sinners.

Do we grumble when some "lesser" person is blessed, saying he doesn't deserve such privileged treatment? Or do we rejoice in what God has done for him, recognizing that no sinners, not even we, deserve His grace?   —C.R.B.

C. Zaccheus' Generosity (v. 8)

8. And Zaccheus stood, and said unto the Lord; Behold, Lord, the half of my goods I give to the poor; and if I have taken any thing from any man by false accusation, I restore him fourfold.

It seems evident that Luke gives us only a brief summary of what happened after Jesus invited himself into the home of Zaccheus. It is not likely that the brief exchange between Jesus and Zaccheus at the sycamore tree could have brought about such a complete transformation in the latter. It seems more reasonable to suppose that Jesus went with Zaccheus to his home and there Jesus taught him for some time. Only after extensive teaching was he ready to make such a radical commitment.

Regardless of how much teaching it took to change Zaccheus, the change was dramatic. Immediately he was willing to give half of his wealth to the poor. So far as we know, Jesus made no demand upon Zaccheus such as He had made upon the rich young ruler. He did not need to make such a demand. Once he heard Jesus, Zaccheus was no longer dominated by his money.

Zaccheus did not stop at giving half of his wealth to the poor. He was also willing to make restitution to those whom he had wronged. The willingness to make amends is a real test of one's repentance. In returning fourfold to those whom he had unfairly taxed, Zaccheus went beyond the legal requirement. The Mosaic law required that one restore only twenty percent more than he had wrongfully taken (Leviticus 6:5; Numbers 5:6, 7). Making restitution does not remove the guilt of one's sins, but it does indicate a penitent heart. The offer to restore fourfold to any whom he had cheated indicates that Zaccheus had not cheated very many. If cheating had been his regular practice, he would not have had money enough to restore fourfold after he had given half of his wealth to the poor.

A MOUNTAINTOP EXPERIENCE

"Because it's there." That was the answer given by one of the early climbers of Mount Everest, when asked why he tried to conquer such a difficult peak. He did not prevail against the mountain, but since 1953, when Sir Edmund Hillary and Tensing Norgay made the first successful climb, two hundred people have stood on the mountaintop. In this same period, more than a hundred others have lost their lives while making the dangerous ascent.

The lure of Everest is that, at 29,028 feet, it is the world's tallest mountain. In a typical year, the government of Nepal allows three expeditions to confront the mountain, although five times that many groups will apply for permission to climb it. Perhaps Hillary had the best understanding of the challenge of Everest: "It's not the mountain we conquer, but ourselves."

Zaccheus was a little man who had long wanted to stand head-and-shoulders above other men. He had tried to achieve this by selling out to the Romans, becoming a tax-collector for them. While this brought wealth, with it came spite from his countrymen. On the day he met Jesus, Zaccheus got above their heads by climbing a tree, but that was hardly a long-term advantage over them.

When Jesus met Zaccheus and changed his life, giving him the power to conquer himself, he found the mountaintop experience he had been longing for. It's that kind of change that Jesus offers to each of us who earnestly seek Him. —C.R.B.

III. Jesus' Pronouncement (Luke 19:9, 10)

A. Salvation for Zaccheus (v. 9)

9. And Jesus said unto him, This day is salvation come to this house, forasmuch as he also is a son of Abraham.

As a result of Jesus' teaching, Zaccheus had believed and repented. These are prerequisites to salvation. Zaccheus had done everything that Jesus had told him to do. *This house* may simply be another way of saying that Zaccheus was saved. It could, however, mean that other members of his family and even his servants also received the blessings of salvation because they believed and repented. In the book of Acts, Luke

visual 13

records times when whole households believed (Acts 16:15, 31; 18:8). But in the absence of further information, we do well to avoid idle speculation about the house of Zaccheus.

The expression, *son of Abraham*, may have had either of two meanings. Jesus may have meant that Zaccheus, though other Jews considered him a sinner, was by descent a child of Abraham and upon repentance was entitled to salvation as much as any of his critics. However, Jesus may have been using the term in a different sense. He may have meant that because Zaccheus had repented and changed the whole direction of his life, he was now a true son of Abraham, whose faith and obedience won God's favor. With like faith and obedience, Zaccheus was Abraham's son in the spiritual sense, a citizen of the true Israel (Galatians 3:9, 29).

B. Jesus' Mission (v. 10)

10. For the Son of man is come to seek and to save that which was lost.

In this one brief sentence Jesus summarized His purpose for coming into the world. The picture is that of a good and faithful shepherd who leaves his comfortable abode and goes out into dangerous and rugged places to seek his lost sheep. It is a theme that Jesus used at other times to describe His mission (Luke 15:3-7; John 10:11-18). Several things are implied in this statement. First, it indicates that man is lost and can never find salvation by himself. This counters some contemporary theology that suggests man is not alienated from God, but only suffering from some minor social maladjustment. Our alienation was so complete that God had to send His Son Jesus into the world to save us.

The rest of the statement is good news. Though we were hopelessly lost, the Son of man has come to save us. We may reject the salvation that He has come to bring us, and many do; yet He still holds out the blessings of salvation to all who are willing to submit their lives to Him.

Conclusion

A. Ministering to the "Up-and-Outers"

Across the years churches have made many efforts to reach the "down-and-outers," those who have suffered both physical and material impoverishment. We have supported or worked in street rescue missions and inner city churches. More recently we have given attention to those whose lives have hit the bottom because of drug or alcohol abuse. Certainly these efforts should be continued.

But in our efforts to reach the down-and-outers, we may have neglected another very needy group, the "up-and-outers." As our society has become increasingly affluent, more of our citizens have acquired enough wealth to meet their physical needs and most of their wants. Yet their spiritual needs all too often have gone unmet.

There are probably several reasons why this important mission field has been neglected. For one thing, many of us feel uncomfortable in the presence of wealth. The trappings of wealth overawe us, and the air of confidence that wealthy people exude seems intimidating. Accumulated wealth may lead rich persons to feel that they can earn their salvation just as they have gained their wealth—by hard work and shrewd bargaining. It was exactly for this reason that Jesus warned that it is difficult for a rich man to enter the kingdom of Heaven (Luke 18:24).

If a field is difficult, that is no reason why it should be neglected or avoided. We need to recognize that many wealthy people are gracious and generous and have committed their possessions to the service of the Lord. We need also to remember that sometimes the air of confidence that some display is a facade behind which they cover their desperate hunger for something better and more important than material possessions. We need to follow the example of our Lord. In His effort to seek and save the lost, He entered every door that was opened to Him. And sometimes, as in the case of Zaccheus, He opened a door.

B. Restoring Fourfold

When Jesus led Zaccheus to realize his spiritual condition, Zaccheus responded in a most generous fashion. He indicated a willingness to give half of his fortune to care for the poor. Further, he offered to restore fourfold to anyone he had cheated. In so doing, he set an example about what repentance really means. Repentance is more than empty words; it is more than an emotional crying jag. It must involve a changed life that makes restitution for past wrongs. When the multitude came out to hear John the Baptist preach, he made it quite clear what they needed to do: "Bring forth therefore fruits worthy of repentance" (Luke 3:8)

Zaccheus offered to make restitution to those whom he had wronged. In his case that was possible, because all he had done was overcharge them on their taxes. But sometimes making restitution is impossible. A murderer does not have it in his power to restore his victim to life. One who has shattered his life and the lives of others through the use of illegal drugs cannot undo all he has done. Even one who has been guilty of a crime against property cannot completely undo his past. He may restore the money or property he has taken, but he cannot erase his police record or repair the hearts he has broken. Or how can an adulterer ever regain the good name and the trust he once enjoyed?

Yet even if complete restitution is impossible, every penitent sinner has an obligation to try. He can pick up the broken pieces of his shattered life, and with God's grace he can still make something of them. Zaccheus did.

C. Let Us Pray

We thank you, Father, for your wonderful grace that reaches down to every sinner who is willing to receive it. Show us how to accept that grace and show in our lives that we have truly repented and committed ourselves to You. In Jesus' loving name we pray. Amen.

D. Thought to Remember

"It is the duty of nations as well as of men to confess their sins and transgressions in humble sorrow, yet with assured hope that genuine repentance will lead to mercy and pardon."

—ABRAHAM LINCOLN

Home Daily Bible Readings

Monday, Feb. 20—Generous With Your Time (Matthew 20:1-16)

Tuesday, Feb. 21—Generous in Your Sharing (John 6:1-14)

Wednesday, Feb. 22—Generous in Your Good Deeds (1 Timothy 6:13-19)

Thursday, Feb.23—Generous in Your Justice (Psalm 112:1-6)

Friday, Feb.24—Generous and Cheerful in Your Giving (1 Corinthians 9:6-15)

Saturday, Feb.25—Generous to Your Neighbor (Luke 10:25-37)

Sunday, Feb. 26—Small Man With a Big Heart (Luke 19:1-10)

Learning by Doing

This page contains an alternate lesson plan emphasizing learning activities. Classes desiring such student involvement will find these suggestions helpful.

Learning Goals

After this lesson a student will be able to:

1. Arrange the events in the story of Jesus and Zaccheus in chronological order.

2. Compare Jesus' statement of purpose (Luke 19:10) with the parables recorded in Luke 15.

3. Make plans to share the gospel with one person he has previously tried to avoid.

Into the Lesson

Take twenty-two five-inch by seven-inch cards and write the letters of the following phrase on the cards, one letter per card: TO SEEK AND TO SAVE THE LOST. Before the class arrives, post these cards on the wall with the blank sides out.

When it is time to begin, announce to the class that you are going to play a game based on the popular TV game *Wheel of Fortune*. There's no wheel and there are no prizes, but the students are to call out letters they think may be in the phrase. (Tell them it is a phrase that they are trying to guess.) Everytime they guess a letter correctly, you will turn over every card on which that letter appears. As soon as someone can guess the phrase, he should call it out. Then turn over all the remaining cards so that the phrase can be seen for the rest of the class time.

Option

To provide a little competitive edge, divide the class into two teams. Have team 1 guess a letter first. If they guess correctly, allow them to guess at the phrase. Then team 2 guesses a letter and then guesses at the phrase if the letter they guess appears in the phrase. Continue until one team wins.

Into the Word

Provide each student with a copy of the following list. (It is in the student book.) Ask them to read Luke 19:1-10 (or have a good reader read it aloud first) and then arrange the events in chronological order.

_____ 1. Zaccheus climbed a sycamore tree.

_____ 2. The people murmured about Jesus, "That he was gone to be guest with a man that is a sinner."

_____ 3. Jesus passed through Jericho.

_____ 4. Zaccheus pledged half his goods to feed the poor.

_____ 5. The press of the crowd prevented Zaccheus from seeing Jesus.

_____ 6. Zaccheus came down from the tree and received Jesus joyfully.

_____ 7. Jesus said salvation had come to the house of Zaccheus.

_____ 8. Zaccheus pledged four-fold restitution of any fraudulent gain.

_____ 9. The Lord announced that He had come "to seek and to save that which was lost."

_____ 10. Jesus saw Zaccheus and told him to come down so that Jesus could abide at his house that day.

(The correct order is 3, 5, 1, 10, 6, 2, 4, 8, 7, 9.) As you review the list, make comments on the text, drawing ideas from the commentary section of this book. Point out the murmuring against associating with a publican (tax collector)—especially a "chief among the publicans"—as well as the expression "son of Abraham." (What does that mean?)

Into Life

Point out the importance of Jesus' statement in verse 10: "The Son of man is come to seek and to save that which was lost."

Divide the class into three groups. Assign group one to list as many groups, in addition to the publicans, that a "good Jew" in Jesus' day would have avoided. Then the group is to find some Scriptural record of Jesus' having associated with someone from that group.

Group 2 is to study Luke 15 and list as many ideas as possible on how Jesus does what He said He came to do in Luke 19:10.

Group three is to study what Paul says about being a son of Abraham (Romans 4). Ask them to answer this question: "Why did Jesus say 'salvation' had come to Zaccheus? Was it because of the good he did in helping the poor and making restitution, or something else? What made him a 'son of Abraham'?"

Have the groups report in reverse order, so that group 1 reports last. When that group has reported, ask students to think about what groups they generally avoid—a certain section in town, a certain racial group, a certain socio-economic group, or some other. What might they do to share the gospel with someone they know from one of these groups? Ask each one to do some of the things suggested.

Let's Talk It Over

The questions on this page are designed to encourage review of the lesson Scriptures and to promote discussion of the lesson by the class. The answers provided are only discussion starters. Let your class talk it over from there.

1. Many middle-class people harbor suspicion and even hatred toward those who are wealthy. How can we overcome such a tendency?

The suspicion is often rooted in the idea that rich people must have done something dishonest or unethical in order to gain their wealth. But that is not always true. Hard work, courage, perseverance, and thrift are often the keys to obtaining wealth, and these are virtues we can all admire. Hatred toward the rich may be based on the assumption that they scorn the common man. That may be true in some cases, but many wealthy individuals demonstrate great compassion and benevolence toward the needy. It is foolish to judge anyone's morality on the basis of his wealth or poverty.

2. The eagerness of Zaccheus is often matched by the zeal of new Christians. What can we do to keep such eagerness and zeal alive?

Too often we see newborn Christians gradually losing the spark of enthusiasm as they associate with older Christians who have become indifferent, sluggish, and cynical. How much better if the veteran believers would let the newcomers infect them with eagerness and excitement! A spark stays alive and grows when it kindles the material around it. In the same way a new Christian can keep his zeal burning warm by sharing with his friends, family, and acquaintances the faith that has brought him such excitement. And older Christians can help not only by offering encouragement and counsel, but by letting this evangelistic fervor rekindle their own eagerness to share the gospel with others.

3. Are there people in our community whom we are tempted to consider unworthy of our evangelistic efforts? How can we deal with this temptation?

While we frequently say the gospel is for everyone, we still may almost unconsciously rule out certain people. The "town drunkard" is one that some label as hopeless, but is he? Then there is the man with a violent temper and an abusive tongue. He may seem impossible to reach, but is it right for us to give up trying?

Then there are the sexually immoral: couples living together without wedlock, men and women whose adulterous activities are notorious, the individual who is an avowed homosexual. We cannot approve such practices, but neither can we deny the possibility of salvation for the practitioners. Such persons have become a part of Christ's church (1 Corinthians 6:9-11), and they still can.

4. The lesson writer states: "A Christian's freedom of action must always be balanced against the importance of keeping his reputation spotless." For example, a Christian may enter a bar for some good Christian purpose, but he had better be careful to keep his actions from being misunderstood. Can you think of other examples in which it may be difficult to maintain this balance?

One problem area is the matter of dealing with members of the opposite sex. A Christian man may properly seek to evangelize a woman other than his wife (and *vice versa*). But in choosing the time and place and the manner of approach he must exercise discretion, so as to avoid even the suggestion of misbehavior. Another sensitive area is in approaching people who hold doctrines or practices that are contrary to the Scriptures. We want to maintain contact without condoning what they teach and practice. We must proceed with prayerful caution. One more area in which this balance may be difficult is in the kinds of occupations Christians undertake. If a Christian has a job connected with tobacco, alcohol, gambling, questionable literature or entertainment, how does it affect his reputation and ability to witness? Each person must work out such problems by considering the circumstances, his own personality, and the teaching of the Scriptures.

5. Why is it important that we stress to non-Christians that they are lost without Christ?

Some people become Christians because they want to be better, or they want to overcome personal problems. Those are good aims, but are secondary to a change of relationship with God. One who is not saved needs to realize that he is lost, alienated from God, and in need of the grace provided through Jesus Christ.

Spring Quarter, 1989

Theme: Letters From Prison

Special Features

Lessons

Unit 1: Philemon—An Appeal for Acceptance

Unit 2: Colossians—Christ the Lord

Unit 3: Philippians—Life In Christ

Unit 4: Ephesians—The Christian Calling

Related Resources

The following publications are offered to give additional help for the subjects of study presented in the Spring Quarter. They may be purchased from your supplier. Prices are subject to change.

Adventures in Being a Parent, by Shirley Pollock. Order #2971, $3.95.

Check Your Homelife, by Knofel Staton. Order #39973, $4.95.

Christian Doctrine: "The Faith . . . Once Delivered," edited by William J. Richardson. Order #88588, $9.95.

Galatians/Ephesians (Standard Bible Studies), by LeRoy Lawson. Order #40109, $7.95.

Galatians/Ephesians Workbook (Standard Bible Studies), by Mike McCann and Hal Stallings. Order #40209, $1.95.

Help! I've Got Problems, by Dean Dickinson. Order #3663, $1.95.

Introduction to Christian Education (Revised), by Eleanor Daniel, John W. Wade, and Charles Gresham. Order #88591, $9.95.

Listen to Your Children, by Marie Frost. Order #3000, $2.95.

Mar 5
Mar 12
Mar 19
Mar 26
Apr 2
Apr 9
Apr 16
Apr 23
Apr 30
May 7
May 14
May 21
May 28

A Prisoner of Christ Jesus

by David Morley

A N OLD MAN and now also a prisoner of Christ Jesus." The apostle Paul described himself in this way in one of the letters that we will study this quarter (Philemon 9, *New International Version*). At the time of that writing, Paul was a prisoner in Rome, staying in his own rented house, but under constant guard. This imprisonment lasted two years. His age is uncertain, but he probably had reached what many today consider retirement age.

Paul, however, did not retire. He could not go about freely, but people were welcome to come visit him, and many did come. Some who came and heard his teaching believed, and they brought others. In this way he was able to conduct an effective ministry, even though a prisoner. Among those whom he converted to Christ during this time was a runaway slave named Onesimus. We will learn more about him and his master in lesson 1.

The apostle to the Gentiles also continued to exercise care and guidance for the churches and Christians scattered across the Roman Empire. Because he could not personally visit the various congregations, he was limited to sending representatives and writing letters. These letters furnish the material that we will study in our lessons this quarter. We should consider the advice and instructions that he gave to the first-century Christians to be equally valuable and valid for us today.

Ephesians, Philippians, Colossians, and Philemon are traditionally referred to as Paul's prison epistles. They all were written during this Roman imprisonment, which began approximately in the year A.D. 60. These epistles contain some of the most magnificent statements and explanations of our Christian doctrines and faith, as well as extended sections of instructions for practical Christian living.

The Lessons

The thirteen lessons in this quarter are divided into four units, each unit dealing with one of the letters. Unit 1 is entitled, "Philemon—An Appeal for Acceptance." Philemon, a Christian, was the owner of a slave who ran away, met Paul, became a Christian, and then returned to his owner. This is a powerful lesson in seeking and bestowing true forgiveness, and in accepting as Christian brothers those who are in social groups different from our own.

Unit 2, lessons 2-4, is entitled, "Colossians—Christ the Lord." False teachers in the area of the city of Colossae denied the lordship and supremacy of Christ, and so Paul's major theme in this epistle was to defend and explain Christ's lordship. Lesson 2 presents Christ as king and considers our responsibility to be good citizens in His kingdom. Lesson 3 deals with false teaching that attacks, denies, and seeks to replace Christ. Paul asserted that Christ is supreme over all the powers of this world. This is an important lesson in this day when the Christian faith is under such heavy attack. Lesson 4, the Easter lesson, presents Jesus Christ as the risen and glorified Lord and reaffirms His promise that Christians are risen with Him and will share in His glory.

Unit 3, "Philippians—Life in Christ," will be considered in lessons 5-8. Unit 4, lessons 9-13, is entitled "Ephesians—The Christian Calling." These units will be introduced in the following article by the author of those lessons.

Teacher, these lessons can make a difference in the lives of your students. Both the doctrinal and the practical portions of these epistles are relevant to life today. If the students obtain a good grasp of the teachings contained in these letters and learn to put them into practice, they will be well equipped to enhance the fellowship of your congregation, to detect and reject many heresies and teachings of the world, and to live dynamic Christian lives in a pagan world. Paul wrote these epistles for that express purpose, and with serious study you and your class will profit greatly from his instructions.

Each of the letters is short enough to be read in just a few minutes. You will gain a good comprehension of the material if you make it a point each day to read completely through the particular letter you are studying that week. Read different translations if you have them available. Pick out a few verses that are especially meaningful to you and memorize them. Encourage your students to read and memorize, too.

If you and your students will make these efforts to hide the Scripture in your hearts, it will work to mold and guide your lives and help you to "reach unity in the faith and in the knowledge of the Son of God and become mature, attaining to the whole measure of the fullness of Christ" (Ephesians 4:13, *New International Version*).

Tidings for Two Cities

by Edwin V. Hayden

THAT'S NOT THE WAY I heard it!"
If the story is a good one it has been told before, and probably not in exactly the same way. Several different versions may all be accurate, as each develops its own emphases, details, and style of narration.

Paul's prison epistles, all penned under the same circumstances and within a comparatively brief time, are different versions of the same story. Ephesians and Philippians provide fascinating studies in comparison and contrast, as we shall see in lessons 5-13 of this series.

Philippi and Philippians

The city of Philippi, "the chief city of that part of Macedonia" (Acts 16:12), was the site of Paul's first labors in Europe.

Originally named *Crenides*, it was a settlement near the Thracian border. Philip of Macedon, father of Alexander the Great, became interested in the city for its nearby gold mines and seized it in 358 B.C. He fortified it and renamed it for himself. Two centuries later it came under Roman rule. The Emperor Augustus (Luke 2:1) made it a Roman colony, bestowing privileges of Roman citizenship on its people.

Acts 16:12-40 tells how the church in Philippi was established. On their first Sabbath in the city, Paul and his companions joined a group that met for prayer beside the Gangites River, and taught them the gospel. As a result a businesswoman named Lydia came to believe and was baptized along with others in her household. Her home became headquarters for the new church.

"Many days" later Paul cast a "spirit of divination" out of a girl who brought gain to her masters by telling fortunes. Her owners, complaining of loss, had Paul and Silas beaten and jailed. There they sang hymns at midnight. An earthquake caused the prison doors to open and the shackles to fall from the prisoners. The terrified jailer would have killed himself, but Paul stopped him. Paul preached to the jailer who believed the gospel and was baptized, he and all his. The city fathers, keenly embarrassed when they learned that the men they had mistreated were Roman citizens, requested politely that Paul leave town. Luke remained to lead the church. Paul's stay in Philippi—whether weeks or months—had been long enough to establish deep and abiding friendships.

Luke may have been influential in securing aid for Paul while he was in Thessalonica, where he labored next (Philippians 4:15, 16), and later in Corinth (2 Corinthians 11:9).

During his third missionary journey, Paul gave major attention to gathering funds among the churches in Macedonia and Achaia (Greece) to relieve the poverty that had developed among the Christians in Judea. Philippi and its neighbors in Macedonia were remarkably generous contributors (2 Corinthians 8:1-5). When Paul stopped at Philippi on his way to Jerusalem with the gift, Luke joined him (Acts 20:3-6) and remained as his companion, with certain interruptions, throughout the time covered by the book of Acts.

Near the end of that time, while Paul was a prisoner at Rome, the Philippian church sent one of their leaders, Epaphroditus, with a generous gift to the apostle. Epaphroditus remained for a time, helping Paul in his work, but then fell gravely ill. Word of his illness reached and disturbed the brethren back home. After Epaphroditus recovered sufficiently to travel, Paul sent him back to Philippi, bearing a letter of thanks and encouragement—Paul's epistle to the Philippians.

The Philippian letter is notable for its personal warmth and friendliness. It contains more of compliment and less of rebuke than others of Paul's letters. It speaks of what was happening to Paul and what he thought about it. It includes personal admonition to some saints by name, as well as recommendation of others by name. In style it differs from Romans or Ephesians in about the same way your letter to a family at home would differ from a term paper at school.

Dominant themes in Philippians are joy and gratitude. It emphasizes also the need for harmony and unity in the church, for self-forgetful service in human relations, and for avoidance of legalism in doctrine or licentiousness in personal behavior.

Ephesus and Ephesians

Ephesus was situated at the mouth of the Cayster River on the Aegean coast of Asia Minor. For many centuries it had been a center for religious cults and a place of increasingly famous temples. The great temple to Diana (Artemis) dominated its culture when Paul arrived with the gospel.

Ephesus was also a center for trade, by sea and by land—a mixing place and radiating center for peoples, arts, literature, and cultures from all directions. It was the capital of the Roman province of Asia, probably the most important among the half dozen provinces comprising Asia Minor, or modern Turkey.

This was just the kind of city where Paul most desired to plant the gospel. So on his second missionary journey he approached it from Phrygia and Galatia, where he had planted churches earlier. He was, however, "forbidden of the Holy Ghost to preach the word in Asia" (Acts 16:6). Perhaps he was not ready yet for so severe a challenge. He went on to Troas and from there to Macedonia; hence Philippi received the gospel before Ephesus did.

As Paul returned to Judea from that second journey he stopped and taught briefly at Ephesus; then left Aquila and Priscilla there while he went on to report to the home churches. Outward bound again, he made a brief, supportive tour of the churches established on his first journey, then went on to Ephesus. There he remained for three years of tremendously influential teaching and preaching, with miracles confirming his doctrine. The story fills the nineteenth chapter of Acts.

Demetrius, a leader in the manufacture of Diana images, stirred up a riot against Paul because "not alone at Ephesus, but almost throughout all Asia, this Paul hath persuaded and turned away much people" (Acts 19:26) from the worship of Diana and the purchase of the idol-makers' wares. At about this time Paul wrote to the Corinthians that he had "fought with beasts at Ephesus" (1 Corinthians 15:32).

The apostle departed to Macedonia and Achaia, but after several months he returned to the coast of Asia on his way to Jerusalem. The elders from Ephesus met him at nearby Miletus, where he reminded them, charged them, and warned them concerning their responsibilites, and they said goodbye with prayers and tears (Acts 20:17-38). The Ephesian church had a "first love," which it later abandoned (Revelation 2:1-7).

Ephesus was becoming the "third city of the Christian world," following Jerusalem and Antioch. It was to become more notable as the scene of Timothy's leadership (1 Timothy 1:3), and of the apostle John's later ministry and writings.

City or church, Ephesus was more than a local entity. It was a gateway into all Asia, including the six other cities addressed in Revelation 2 and 3, among others. Some of these communities, such as Colossae and Laodicea, had special problems that Paul addressed in special letters (Colossians 4:16) written from his confinement at Rome. But the Ephesians were addressed in larger terms, applicable not only to the whole province of Asia, but to any place where Gentiles shared with Jews the blessings of the gospel. In fact, some ancient manuscripts of Paul's epistle do not say "at Ephesus" in the first verse. This leads some to conjecture that Ephesians was a sort of circular letter, with copies being sent to a number of churches.

That would explain some things otherwise difficult: why personal references and personal greetings, so commonly appearing in Paul's letters, are not found in one addressed to a community where he spent his longest single term of service. More of a treatise than a letter, Ephesians is theological, dealing with the unity and grandeur of Christ's body, His church.

H. H. Halley has pointed out that Paul's later ministry included two major projects designed to bind Jew and Gentile together in Christ's one body. The first project was practical, addressed to the Jewish segment. It was that major gift of money, gathered from Gentile churches and delivered to the church in Jerusalem (see Romans 15:25-27). The second was doctrinal, addressed to the Gentiles. It was the epistle to the Ephesians, declaring Gentile believers to be "no more strangers and foreigners, but fellow citizens with the saints, and of the household of God" (Ephesians 2:19).

For You in Your Town

In style and personal content, Philippians and Ephesians provide a study in contrasts. The one is almost casual; the other is carefully organized and profound. Yet the two merge in one common emphasis—"in Christ." And when the two are outlined for study and application, it is hard to distinguish one epistle from the other.

From Philippians, then, we have four lessons on one theme, "Life in Christ"—they are "To Live Is Christ"; "Serving as Christ Served"; "Pressing On in Christ"; and "Rejoicing in Christ."

From Ephesians we have the general theme, "The Christian Calling." It goes a little deeper into doctrine, but it comes out at the same place—"To the Praise of God's Glory"; "Peace With God and One Another"; "Building Up the Body of Christ"; "Called to New Life"; and "Guidelines for Family Life." (Memorial Sunday, May 28, is a good time to recognize our heritage in parents and homes where loving submission has provided a firm foundation for living).

May you and your class find great freedom in Christ through studying the letters Paul wrote while in prison!

Of Freedom and Bondage

by Lee Magness

THE ROMAN SOLDIER turned his back on the occupants of the room and gazed out the window. They were no threat. Paul, his prisoner, was an old man, slowed by a chronic illness. Besides he had the mind of a slave. He even called himself a slave, a slave of some Christos, in the letters he dictated to his companions. The companions? They weren't the soldier's problem, but they seemed to have servile attitudes as well. One, a younger man named Onesimus, had the furtive, fearful eyes of a fugitive. The others—Epaphras, Timothy, Epaphroditus, Tychicus—Paul consistently referred to as servants. What an assignment—keeping an eye on a bunch of slaves!

But now the soldier's eyes passed up and down the busy Roman street. One citizen was scurrying with her fragrances to fulfill her obligations to the gods gathered at the Pantheon. A freedman was scrubbing the doorsteps of the house of the noblewoman for whom he labored. A Roman slave trader was leading a line of young captives toward the auction block at the end of the street. A courtesan leaned down from her balcony, her necklaces sending an enticing song to the people in the street below. How free we Romans are, the soldier thought, as he turned his gaze back to his Hebrew prisoner and his companions!

Freedom and bondage—a paradoxical pair of concepts. The musings of our imaginary Roman soldier, who may have watched over Paul as he wrote what we call his prison epistles, remind us just how deceptive the concepts of liberty and slavery can be. For there is a bondage that goes about under the guise of freedom, and there is a freedom that can exist in the midst of slavery, or appear to the world as slavery. There are bondages that liberate, and there are liberties that enslave.

The Bondage of Freedom

The world on which the soldier cast his admiring gaze appeared to be free. It was a world of political power, military might, economic domination, religious liberty, and moral laxity. But the emperor was ensnared in a web of suspicions toward every theoretical threat to his throne. The soldier himself was a slave to the egotistical whims of his prideful commander. The slave trader was trapped in his own all-consuming materialism, and the woman who

was free to worship any god was bound to worship all of them. The enlightened citizens who felt no moral constraints were held captive by their own uncontrolled lusts.

Our world is much the same. Even people in a free society find ways to fashion their own chains. The governed and the governors are frequently enslaved by the governments they create to serve them. Materialism can put a stranglehold of greed on the throat of free enterprise. And moral license, which masks itself as liberty, is an ever-deepening dungeon.

The Freedom of Bondage

The world on which the soldier had turned his back, the place of detention where the prisoner Paul was held, was really a place of freedom. Yes, Paul was a prisoner, but a prisoner of Christ, not of the emperor. Yes, Paul was a servant, but a servant of the gospel, not of the empire. Yes, Paul was a slave, but a slave of God, not of himself or sin. His bondage was based on his freedom—freedom from legalism, freedom from sin, even freedom from death (see Romans 6—8).

The freedom of bondage is a good definition of the oft-used and misused phrase, religious liberty. The word *religious* comes from the Latin word *religio*, which means "bound back to." Religious people are bound to the object of their loyalty. But it is this bondage, this submission to God and complete dedication to His purposes, that liberates Christians to live fully and faithfully. Christians, even Christian slaves, are the most liberated people of the world, precisely because they are the slaves of Christ.

Bondage to Freedom

Bondage to God liberates the believer from sin and self. But there is a danger in the realm of Christian freedom, a danger that is just as enslaving as slavery to law or to sin. I call this danger "bondage *to* freedom." Paul speaks of it in Galatians 5:13. First he asserts the concept of the freedom of bondage: "For you were called to freedom, brethren." We are the called, the chosen, the committed, the children of the sovereign God;' but God's goal for us is a life of liberty within that relationship. Second, Paul warns of the danger of bondage to freedom: "only do not use your freedom as an opportunity for the flesh."

Some Christians felt that their freedom in Christ gave them absolute license, the right to reject human law, social custom, and the scruples of others with impunity. Paul tried to correct these misunderstandings. Christians were ultimately bound by God's law, not Roman law, but they had been freed to respect Roman law and honor the government willingly. Christians were not bound to keep social customs, but they had been freed to live so as not to offend the pagans they were trying to convert. Christians were not obligated to keep Jewish food laws, but they had been freed to be considerate of "weaker" Christians, even if it meant yielding some of their freedom.

We also need to beware of being in bondage to freedom itself. In a thirty miles-per-hour zone, we are free to drive a car at thirty miles per hour. But if a child runs out in front of us, we step on the brake—we willingly limit our legal right for the sake of another. So in life, we must not be so concerned for our rights in Christ that we are unwilling to yield those rights out of concern for the the welfare of others.

Bondage in Freedom

The freedom of bondage—the liberation of life that comes from allegiance to God—produces its own brand of bondage. It is positive bondage to others in the name of God. The same verse that warns us of bondage *to* freedom, also calls us to bondage *in* freedom: "For you were called to freedom, brethren; only do not use your freedom as an opportunity for the flesh, but through love be servants of one another."

The world defines freedom as freedom *from* —freedom from restraint, responsibility, regulation, and relationship. But Paul defines freedom as freedom—for submission, for service. Loneliness is terribly limiting; but love, taking responsibility for others, is wonderfully liberating. Thus the paradoxical pattern of freedom and bondage is complete. Free of moral constraint we are really under bondage to self and sin. When we become slaves of God and His will, we are truly liberated. But that freedom can become a form of bondage in which we would rather insist on our rights than yield our rights for the good of others. Instead, freedom in Christ is meant to lead to another bondage, loving service to others.

Freedom and Bondage in the Prison Epistles

As we enter into the study of the prison epistles, we would do well to look for these great principles of freedom and bondage in Christ our Lord Jesus.

Ephesians. In his letter to the Ephesians Paul mentions several types of bondage, some of which seem to be liberating and some of which truly are. There is the slavery of desire (2:1-3), which must be replaced by the liberating bondage of obedience to God's will (2:4-7). There is the slavery of separation from God (2:11, 12), which must be replaced by the liberating bondage of a relationship with God (2:13). There is the slavery of separation from the rest of God's people (2:11, 12), which must be replaced by the liberating bondage of membership in the body of Christ (2:14-16). Being rooted in love sounds limiting, but it is really the basis for life and growth (3:17). Living in darkness (5:11) makes people think they are free to act as they wish. And they are—they are free to run into obstacles and walk off cliffs. But living in the light (5:13, 14) reveals the one path that leads to the fulfilled life.

Philippians. The paradox of freedom and bondage may be illustrated best in the Philippian letter. In chapter 2 Paul reminds us that Christ himself yielded His divine prerogatives and became a slave of death, to free us from the domination of death (2:5-11). The freedom that His slavery brought us becomes the motivation for our lives of service.

Colossians and Philemon. In Colossians Paul calls on the Christians to reject the bondage of godless philosophies and legalistic applications of the Mosaic law (2:8-14). He reminds slaves to view their human slavery in the context of their status as full heirs of God's promises (3:22-24). And he reminds slave owners that they too are slaves, slaves of their Master in Heaven (4:1). Philemon, one of those Colossian slave owners, received a letter from Paul that illustrates the ambiguity of freedom and bondage. Philemon, the free man, may have been trapped in a spirit of revenge. The slave Onesimus on the other hand had become free in Christ, "serving" Paul for Philemon in the gospel ministry (v. 13).

I wonder if one day, when the Roman soldier was bored of staring at the same scene on the same street, he turned to his prisoner and said, "Just who is this Christos whose slave you are?" And I wonder if Paul would have unrolled the scroll he had just addressed to the Colossians, pointed to a place early in the letter (1:13), and said, "Christos is the Son of God, who has 'delivered us from the dominion of darkness and transferred us to the kingdom of his beloved Son.' In a sense it is from one bondage to another. But in bondage to God lies freedom."

Scripture quotations in this article are from the *Revised Standard Version* of the Bible.

Quarterly Quiz

The questions on this page and the next may be used in several ways: as a pretest at the beginning of the quarter; as a review at the end of the quarter; or as a review after each lesson. The questions are based on the Scripture text of each lesson (King James Version).

Lesson 1

1. As an apostle Paul could have ordered Philemon to receive his runaway slave, Onesimus, but instead Paul appealed to him to do so on the basis of love. (true/false). *Philemon 8, 9*

2. Paul had begotten Onesimus "in my (old age, bonds, time of distress)." *Philemon 10*

3. Paul told Philemon, "If thou count me therefore a partner, receive him [Onesimus] as (a servant of Christ, a brother beloved, myself)." *Philemon 17*

4. Who did Paul say would repay Philemon if Onesimus had wronged him or owed him anything? *Philemon 18, 19*

Lesson 2

1. Paul thanked God continually for the Colossians after learning of their faith in Christ and of their love for whom? *Colossians 1:3, 4*

2. Who was the faithful minister of Christ who brought word about the Colossian Christians to Paul when he was imprisoned in Rome? *Colossians 1:7, 8*

3. Paul said that the Father has "made us meet to be partakers of the inheritance of the saints in _____ : who hath delivered us from the power of _____ , and hath translated us into the _____ of his dear Son." *Colossians 1:12, 13*

Lesson 3

1. What did Paul warn us that some might try to do to us through philosophy and vain deceit, after the tradition of men, after the rudiments of the world? *Colossians 2:8*

2. Paul said that Christians are (complete, happy, secure) in Christ, who is the head of all principality and power. *Colossians 2:10*

3. When Christ was nailed to the cross, He blotted out the handwriting of _____ that was against us. *Colossians 2:14*

4. Some among the Colossians were teaching that the worship of _____ should be held in higher regard than the worship of Christ. *Colossians 2:18, 19*

Lesson 4

1. The two men who spoke to the women inside Jesus' sepulcher were wearing what kind of garments? *Luke 24:4*

2. What question did the two men ask the women who had entered Jesus' sepulcher? *Luke 24:5*

3. The apostle Paul affirmed that all things, both in Heaven and in earth, were created by Jesus Christ. (true/false). *Colossians 1:16*

4. Peace was made between man and God by the (shame, agony, blood) of Jesus' cross. *Colossians 1:20*

5. When Christ appears, we also shall appear with Him in glory. (true/false). *Colossians 3:4*

Lesson 5

1. Paul was certain that his imprisonment had been harmful to the spread of the gospel of Christ. (true/false). *Philippians 1:12*

2. While Paul was in prison in Rome, some preached Christ out of contention, supposing to add _____ to Paul's bonds. *Philippians 1:16*

3. Paul said, "For to me to live is _____ , and to die is _____ ." *Philippians 1:21*

4. Paul had a desire to depart this life and to be with Christ, but he knew that for him to remain in the flesh was more (comforting, needful, rewarding) for the Philippians. *Philippians 1:23, 24*

Lesson 6

1. Paul told the Philippians that to them it was given not only to believe on Christ, but also to do what for His sake? *Philippians 1:29*

2. Christians are exhorted to esteem others (beneath, as good as, better than) themselves. *Philippians 2:3*

3. Christ Jesus, who was in the form of _____ , made himself of no reputation and took upon himself the form of a _____ , and was made in the likeness of men. *Philippians 2:6, 7*

4. Becoming a man, Christ Jesus humbled himself and became obedient unto what? *Philippians 2:8*

5. Because of Jesus' complete obedience, God has highly exalted Him and given Him what kind of a name? *Philippians 2:9*

Lesson 7

1. The things that Paul had previously counted gain, he now counted what for Christ? *Philippians 3:7*

2. Desiring to be found in Christ, Paul did not want to have his own righteousness, which was of the _____ , but that which is through the _____ of Christ. *Philippians 3:9*

3. As an apostle of Jesus, Paul felt that he had already attained the degree of perfection Christ expected of him. (true/false). *Philippians 3:12*

4. When Jesus returns, He shall change our earthly body, that it may be fashioned like unto what? *Philippians 3:21*

Lesson 8

1. The peace of God, which keeps our hearts and minds through Christ Jesus, passes what? *Philippians 4:7*

2. Name the six kinds of things Paul encouraged the Philippians to think on, if there is any virture and if there is any praise. *Philippians 4:8*

3. What had Paul learned to be, regardless of the state he was in? *Philippians 4:11*

Lesson 9

1. We have redemption through the blood of Christ, and the forgiveness of sins, according to the riches of what? *Ephesians 1:7*

2. God has "abounded toward us in all wisdom and prudence, having made known unto us the _____ of his will? *Ephesians 1:8, 9*

3. Those who have believed in Jesus have been sealed with the Holy Spirit of _____ . *Ephesians 1:13*

4. The seal of the Holy Spirit is for Christians the earnest of what? *Ephesians 1:13, 14*

Lesson 10

1. Christians are God's workmanship, created in Christ Jesus unto what? *Ephesians 2:10*

2. The middle wall of partition between Jews and Gentiles was broken down by (Abraham, Moses, Christ). *Ephesians 2:13, 14*

3. Christ reconciled both Jews and Gentiles unto God in one body by (the Sermon on the Mount, the Ten Commandments, the cross). *Ephesians 2:16*

4. Through Christ both Jew and Gentile have access by one Spirit unto whom? *Ephesians 2:18*

Lesson 11

1. Paul declared himself to be the prisoner of (the Romans, the Lord, the Jews). *Ephesians 4:1*

2. List the gifts of ministries that Jesus gave to the church for the perfecting of the saints, for the work of the ministry, for the edifying of the body of Christ. *Ephesians 4:11, 12*

3. According to Paul, every spiritually alive member in Christ's body contributes something to the functioning and the development of the body. (true/false). *Ephesians 4:16*

4. The prevailing spirit in which the members of Christ's body function, supply others needs, and grow up in Him is (love, joy, peace). *Ephesians 4:16*

Lesson 12

1. In Ephesians 4:22-24 Paul says we are to "put off" something and "put on" something. What are they?

2. What are Christians not to let go down upon their wrath? *Ephesians 4:26*

3. The person who was a thief is to steal no more. Instead, he is to labor so that he may have in order to do what? *Ephesians 4:28*

4. What kind of communication should not proceed out of our mouths? *Ephesians 4:29*

5. Instead of being drunk with wine, Christians should be filled with what? *Ephesians 5:18*

Lesson 13

1. Wives are admonished to submit themselves unto their own husbands as unto whom? *Ephesians 5:22*

2. Men ought to love their wives as their own bodies. (true/false). *Ephesians 5:28*

3. Paul compares the oneness of a man and his wife with that of Christ and (the world, the church, God the Father). *Ephesians 5:31, 32*

4. The commandment for children to honor their parents is the first commandment with what? *Ephesians 6:2*

5. Fathers are not to provoke their children to (discontentment, envy, wrath). *Ephesians 6:4*

Answers

Lesson 1—1. true. 2. bonds. 3. myself. 4. Paul himself. **Lesson 2**—1. all the saints. 2. Epaphras. 3. light, darkness, kingdom. **Lesson 3**—1. spoil. 2. complete. 3. ordinances. 4. angels. **Lesson 4**—1. shining. 2. "Why seek ye the living among the dead?" 3. true. 4. blood. 5. true. **Lesson 5**—1. false. 2. affliction. 3. Christ, gain. 4. needful. **Lesson 6**—1. suffer. 2. better than. 3. God, servant. 4. death. 5. a name which is above every name. **Lesson 7**—1. loss. 2. law, faith. 3. false. 4. His glorious body. **Lesson 8**—1. all understanding. 2. true, honest, just, pure, lovely, good report. 3. content. **Lesson 9**—1. God's grace. 2. mystery. 3. promise. 4. our inheritance. **Lesson 10**—1. good works. 2. Christ. 3. the cross. 4. the Father. **Lesson 11**—1. the Lord. 2. apostles, prophets, evangelists, pastors and teachers. 3. true. 4. love. **Lesson 12**— 1. the old man, the new man. 2. the sun. 3. give to him that needeth. 4. corrupt. 5. the Spirit. **Lesson 13**—1. the Lord. 2. true. 3. the church. 4. promise. 5. wrath.

An Appeal for Acceptance

LESSON SCRIPTURE: Philemon.

PRINTED TEXT: Philemon 4-20.

Philemon 4-20

4 I thank my God, making mention of thee always in my prayers,

5 Hearing of thy love and faith, which thou hast toward the Lord Jesus, and toward all saints;

6 That the communication of thy faith may become effectual by the acknowledging of every good thing which is in you in Christ Jesus.

7 For we have great joy and consolation in thy love, because the bowels of the saints are refreshed by thee, brother.

8 Wherefore, though I might be much bold in Christ to enjoin thee that which is convenient,

9 Yet for love's sake I rather beseech thee, being such a one as Paul the aged, and now also a prisoner of Jesus Christ.

10 I beseech thee for my son Onesimus, whom I have begotten in my bonds:

11 Which in time past was to thee unprofitable, but now profitable to thee and to me:

12 Whom I have sent again: thou therefore receive him, that is, mine own bowels:

13 Whom I would have retained with me, that in thy stead he might have ministered unto me in the bonds of the gospel:

14 But without thy mind would I do nothing; that thy benefit should not be as it were of necessity, but willingly.

15 For perhaps he therefore departed for a season, that thou shouldest receive him for ever;

16 Not now as a servant, but above a servant, a brother beloved, specially to me, but how much more unto thee, both in the flesh, and in the Lord?

17 If thou count me therefore a partner, receive him as myself.

18 If he hath wronged thee, or oweth thee aught, put that on mine account;

19 I Paul have written it with mine own hand, I will repay it: albeit I do not say to thee how thou owest unto me even thine own self besides.

20 Yea, brother, let me have joy of thee in the Lord: refresh my bowels in the Lord.

GOLDEN TEXT: Perhaps he therefore departed for a season, that thou shouldest receive him for ever; not now as a servant, but above a servant, a brother beloved.
—Philemon 15, 16.

Letters From Prison

Unit 1: Philemon—an Appeal for Acceptance (Lesson 1)

Lesson Aims

As a result of this lesson students should:

1. Explain why and how Christians must forgive one another.

2. Identify people whom they have not forgiven and seek to be reconciled to them.

3. Identify people whom, for whatever reason, they have not accepted as brethren, and open their hearts to receive them.

Lesson Outline

INTRODUCTION

A. Everyone Needs to Be Accepted

B. Lesson Background

I. FOUNDATION FOR FUTURE OBEDIENCE (Philemon 4-7)

   A. Philemon, a Faithful Man (vv. 4, 5)

   B. Philemon, a Sharing Person (vv. 6, 7)

II. ACCEPT YOUR REPENTANT BROTHER (Philemon 8-17)

   A. An Appeal of Love (vv. 8, 9)

   B. An Appeal for a Precious One (vv. 10-13)

   C. An Appeal for a Tender Reception (vv. 14-17)

   Harboring Hatred

III. PROMISE AND FINAL APPEAL (Philemon 18-20)

   A. Paul's IOU to Philemon (vv. 18, 19)

   Charge My Account

   B. Joy Coming From Acceptance (v. 20)

CONCLUSION:

   A. Forgive Even Though It Is Difficult

   B. Forgive as You Are Forgiven

   C. Forgiveness Is Required

   D. Prayer for a Forgiving Heart

   E. Thought to Remember

Display visual 1 from the visuals/resources packet. It is shown on page 236. The map (visual 14) locates the places mentioned in the quarter's lessons and should be displayed also.

Introduction

A. Everyone Needs to Be Accepted

We all need acceptance. We have a strong, built-in craving for it. The desire for acceptance leads us to try to please our associates. This can be good if one associates with people of good morals and high values. It motivates us to discipline and improve ourselves. The problem is that we all make mistakes and have faults, and sometimes people of good morals and high values are very intolerant of mistakes and faults. Even Christians can be this way.

As Christians we must accept each other in spite of our errors and weaknesses. When a brother sins and then repents, we must forgive and restore him. If we don't accept him, he may seek acceptance from those outside the church.

If we remember that God accepted us in spite of our sins, then we will know why we must accept each other, imperfect as we are.

B. Lesson Background

The letter to Philemon was written by the apostle Paul while he was in prison in Rome, about A.D. 62. Philemon lived in Colossae, a city in western Asia Minor that was situated approximately one hundred miles east of Ephesus. Philemon became a Christian through the teaching of Paul, perhaps while Paul was in Ephesus (Acts 19:1-10). The two men evidently were good friends.

This letter has to do with a slave named Onesimus. Onesimus belonged to Philemon, but he had run away and made his way to Rome. In some manner he came into contact with Paul while the apostle was in prison there, and Paul led him to believe in Jesus. Onesimus remained associated with Paul for some time and was very helpful to him. Accepting Paul's advice, Onesimus determined to return to Philemon. Paul wrote this brief letter to Philemon to urge him to receive Onesimus as a Christian brother.

In this one historical event we see the place of brotherly love, forgiveness, reconciliation, honesty, generosity, kindness, and humility in the Christian life.

I. Foundation for Future Obedience (Philemon 4-7)

A. Philemon, a Faithful Man (vv. 4, 5)

4. I thank my God, making mention of thee always in my prayers.

Paul had not seen Philemon for several years, and probably had not received much news about him in that time, yet Philemon was frequently in Paul's *prayers*. This shows the affection Paul felt for Philemon. He accounted that the intervening miles and years had not diminished their friendship. The presumption is that Philemon felt the same way. This closeness was the link that allowed Paul to write in such an intimate way and make his appeal on the basis of friendship instead of apostolic authority.

5. Hearing of thy love and faith, which thou hast toward the Lord Jesus, and toward all saints.

Paul was particularly thankful for Philemon's *love and faith*, which were directed both *toward the Lord* and toward his fellow Christians. These same graces are linked elsewhere in the Bible. A good example is 1 John 3:23. John said that the possession of these attributes is the sign of a true Christian.

B. Philemon, a Sharing Person (vv. 6,7)

6. That the communication of thy faith may become effectual by the acknowledging of every good thing which is in you in Christ Jesus.

Paul prayed that Philemon would continue in the sharing that is inherent in the Christian life. Such sharing and caring among believers brings the acknowledgment that all the blessings we have are ours because of Christ. And as the world observes such behavior among God's people, they will have a clearer understanding and appreciation of the Christian life.

7. For we have great joy and consolation in thy love, because the bowels of the saints are refreshed by thee, brother.

Philemon's love for the saints was already well established, and Paul took great *joy and consolation* in it.

The ancients used the word *bowels*, meaning all of the internal body organs, in the same way that we use the word *heart* today. The meaning is that Philemon was a great encouragement to his fellow Christians, both in his words and in his deeds.

II. Accept Your Repentant Brother (Philemon 8-17)

A. An Appeal of Love (vv. 8, 9)

8. Wherefore, though I might be much bold in Christ to enjoin thee that which is convenient.

Paul had great authority as an apostle. It would have been proper for him to *enjoin* or command Philemon to do that which was *convenient*, or fitting for Philemon to do.

9. Yet for love's sake I rather beseech thee, being such a one as Paul the aged, and now also a prisoner of Jesus Christ.

For love's sake I rather beseech thee. Paul chose, however, to base his request on love, not commandment. This encompassed Paul's love for Philemon and Philemon's love for Paul and the Lord. Jesus told His disciples "If you love Me, you will keep My commandments" (John 14:15, *New American Standard Bible*.) Paul meant the same thing, that if Philemon loved him he would do what Paul asked.

Paul presented two additional reasons why Philemon should be willing to give his request special consideration. First, Paul called himself *the aged*. This adds a note of tenderness to the appeal, coming as it does from an old, gray-haired, battle-scarred man. Second, he mentioned that he was *a prisoner of Jesus Christ*, reminding Philemon that he was at that moment imprisoned for obedience to the Lord.

B. An Appeal for a Precious One (vv. 10-13)

10. I beseech thee for my son Onesimus, whom I have begotten in my bonds.

Paul called Onesimus his *son*, indicating how strongly he loved him. This is the same Greek word he used to describe Timothy (1 Timothy 1:2) and Titus (Titus 1:4). While a prisoner in *bonds* Paul had begotten Onesimus by giving him the gospel (1 Corinthians 4:15).

11. Which in time past was to thee unprofitable, but now profitable to thee and to me.

The apostle lightened his appeal by using a play on words here, for the name *Onesimus* means "profitable." In time past Onesimus had been *unprofitable*, but now that he was controlled by Christ he really lived up to his name.

Though he introduced it in a humorous way, Paul stated here the heart of the issue, the fact that would make it a real test for Philemon to accept Onesimus: Onesimus had been an unprofitable servant. There is not even a hint that Philemon had mistreated his servant and provoked him into fleeing. Onesimus was the one who had been at fault. We all know such useless people. They do as little work as they can. What work they do, they do carelessly and slowly.

How to Say It

COLOSSAE. Ko-*loss*-ee.
ONESIMUS. O-*ness*-ih-muss.
PHILEMON. Fih-*lee*-mun or Fie-*lee*-mun.

Such a servant would have been a continual headache. And to top it all off, Onesimus ran away and was a complete loss to Philemon. Some suggest that Onesimus even may have stolen from his master when he ran away.

Paul now asked Philemon to forget all the past cost and aggravation. He stated that Onesimus, since his conversion, had been very useful to him, and now he would be useful to Philemon.

12. Whom I have sent again: thou therefore receive him, that is, mine own bowels.

Whether Paul or Onesimus originated the idea of his return, Paul at least concurred in the action. He said that he *sent* Onesimus back, and plainly asked Philemon to receive him. Paul added that Onesimus was as dear to him as his own heart, and urged Philemon to treat him accordingly.

13. Whom I would have retained with me, that in thy stead he might have ministered unto me in the bonds of the gospel.

Again Paul emphasized how precious Onesimus was to him by saying he really would have liked to keep him for the help Onesimus could give him. Since Onesimus belonged to Philemon, the service he could render could be considered Philemon's contribution to Paul's work.

C. An Appeal for a Tender Reception
(vv. 14-17)

14. But without thy mind would I do nothing; that thy benefit should not be as it were of necessity, but willingly.

Though Paul wanted to keep Onesimus with him, he would not do it without Philemon's knowledge and consent. Paul wanted Philemon's *benefit*, his favor shown to Paul, to be given *willingly*, not out of constraint. Paul's feeling expressed here agrees with his teaching on giving recorded in 2 Corinthians 9:7.

15. For perhaps he therefore departed for a season, that thou shouldest receive him for ever.

*Philemon,
Please forgive your
servant, Onesimus,
and receive him as
you would me - as
a beloved brother
in Christ!
Paul*

visual 1

Philemon may have been distressed at the loss of a slave when Onesimus ran away, but Paul directed his thoughts to the result. What had happened brought good to Paul, to Onesimus, and even to Philemon. Philemon's temporary loss of his servant, therefore, was better evaluated against the consideration of both the life-long and eternal fellowship that had been gained. Paul seems to be suggesting that the defection and flight of Onesimus may not have been purposeless circumstances, but events under God's providential hand.

16. Not now as a servant, but above a servant, a brother beloved, specially to me, but how much more unto thee, both in the flesh, and in the Lord?

Onesimus returned *as a servant*, to submit himself to the will of his earthly master. But Paul urged Philemon to regard him better than a slave—as a Christian *brother*. Paul loved him in this way, and Philemon would have even more reason to do so since Onesimus was a member of his household.

It would have been hard for Philemon to accept Onesimus as more than a slave if he had any prejudice toward him as some sort of inferior person. Christians today sometimes have difficulty accepting people because of their background, status, appearance, race or other reasons. But God recognizes no such distinctions among persons, and neither should we. Christians must be willing to accept as brothers and sisters whomever God accepts as sons and daughters.

17. If thou count me therefore a partner, receive him as myself.

Philemon would have been overjoyed to see Paul at his door, safe and freed from prison. Paul urged him to give the same kind of warm reception to Onesimus, who had been freed from the prison of sin and death. However much tenderness and care Philemon would have showered on the apostle, Paul hoped he would shower it upon the servant.

In these verses Paul made it clear that he wanted Philemon to forget wrongs that were done in the past and to receive Onesimus with the greatest of joy and kindness.

HARBORING HATRED

In 1986, a seventy-two-year-old ex-convict entered an attorney's office and shot and killed him.

When the ex-convict was cornered a short time later by the police, he took a lethal dose of some poison and killed himself. This violent act of revenge was the result of a court trial thirty-one years earlier in which the attorney, then the district attorney, had prosecuted the man for a crime of arson. During his years in prison, he indicated over and over that his one purpose in life was to kill those who had prosecuted him.

What is it in the human mind and heart that refuses to forgive one who we feel has offended us? Some see it as an act of weakness to forgive and forget. The man in the account related above carried out in reality what many plan in imagination and feel in their hearts.

Paul knew Philemon was a Christian who would obey his instructions, but he wanted Philemon to act of his own will and desire and forgive Onesimus.

All of us need to search our hearts and reject any feelings of anger, resentment, or revenge that may keep us from being all God has designed us to be in Jesus Christ.   —W. P.

III. Promise and Final Appeal (Philemon 18-20)

A. Paul's IOU to Philemon (vv. 18, 19)

18. If he hath wronged thee, or oweth thee aught, put that on mine account.

Paul did not say whether Onesimus actually had stolen from Philemon or cheated him. But even if he had not done these things, Philemon could legitimately say that Onesimus owed him compensation for the period of time he was away from his master. This might amount to a few year's wages. If Philemon did feel that Onesimus owed him something, Paul said to forgive his servant the debt and charge it to Paul.

19. I Paul have written it with mine own hand, I will repay it: albeit I do not say to thee how thou owest unto me even thine own self besides.

Paul, in writing this note with his own hand, in effect signed a promissory note to pay claims Philemon had against Onesimus. But he went on to remind Philemon how much he owed to the apostle for bringing him the gospel and in this way saving his soul.

This was Paul's way of reminding Philemon of the principle that Jesus taught in the parable of the two debtors, recorded in Matthew 18:23-35. This parable teaches us that since God completely and freely forgives us, we must be willing to forgive one another. Philemon had been forgiven much; he should be willing to forgive the little that Onesimus owed him.

CHARGE MY ACCOUNT

A young man came to a professor in a Bible college with the plea that he needed a car to fulfill his desire to minister in a small country church while he studied for the ministry. After some examination the professor signed the note, assuming equal responsibility for the purchase.

All went well for a time and the student made several payments as scheduled. Then the young man made no more payments. The burden for making the payments fell on the professor who had signed the note.

Without protest or argument the professor simply made those payments until the car no longer was encumbered by debt. It would have been easy for him to feel abused, or seek to gain control of the car for its resale or his own use. Instead he chose to take a larger view and consider the reputation of the church, the college, and his own position as a Christian. To him it was more important to preserve these than to punish the young man whom he had helped.

Paul went one step further in helping the slave Onesimus: he signed a promissory note assuming Onesimus' debt, *after* he had wronged his master!

What are we willing to do to help gain acceptance for those who have wronged us or others?   —W. P.

B. Joy, Coming From Acceptance (v. 20)

20. Yea, brother, let me have joy of thee in the Lord: refresh my bowels in the Lord.

Again, Paul made a humorous reference to Onesimus' name. The Greek verb that means to *have joy* or benefit is the word from which Onesimus' name is derived.

If Philemon did as Paul requested, he would bring great joy to the apostle. Paul would be happy for Philemon, that he had grown so much in the Lord that he could exercise godly love to this extent. He would be joyful for Onesimus, who would be welcomed and cared for. All of this would *refresh* his heart, something that he doubtless needed during his stay in prison.

But Paul would not be the only one filled with joy. Onesimus obviously would be relieved and happy. Philemon himself would be joyful instead of having a heart filled with anger and resentment. The church would be joyful to welcome a new brother. A proper response by Philemon would bring gladness all around.

Conclusion

(Teacher: the following material pertains to lesson aims 1 and 2.)

Paul's letter to Philemon teaches us who are Christians the importance of forgiving and accepting one another. We do not have Christ's spirit unless we are willing to forgive as He forgave. We shatter the unity of the church if we refuse to accept each other. We alienate ourselves from Christ if we refuse to accept those whom He accepts. Faith cannot be separated from love, forgiveness, and acceptance.

A. Forgive Even Though It Is Difficult

If Onesimus had been a total stranger to Philemon, Philemon probably would have joyfully received his coming to the Lord and would have welcomed him warmly as a new Christian brother. Likewise, usually we will gladly welcome new converts, whatever past they may have. But this becomes much more difficult if that person has sinned against us personally. What if he cheated you out of a large sum of money before he became a Christian? What if she lied about you and got you fired from your job? Situations such as these make it much harder to forgive, yet forgive we must if the person repents.

Remember that sin is much more of an offense to God than it is to us. The sins of mankind led to the death of God's Son. Yet God forgives all who repent and turn to Him. If He is willing to forgive us, can we not forgive those who offend us, no matter how difficult it may be?

B. Forgive as You Are Forgiven

Forgive Freely. When we are sinned against, we tend to insist that things be set right before we forgive. But this is the thinking of the world, not of the Lord. If the offender is required to make satisfaction for all damages, then no place is left for forgiveness. By its very nature, forgiveness overlooks and forgets the offense.

The Lord is our pattern for forgiveness. He does not insist that we make full payment for our sins before He forgives us. We could not do this anyway. He gives forgiveness as a free gift to

all who have, as David said, "a broken and a contrite heart." Can we insist on more?

Forgive Without Limit. Forgiveness has no limit. Jesus said of a sinning brother, "If your brother sins, rebuke him, and if he repents, forgive him. If he sins against you seven times in a day, and seven times comes back to you and says, 'I repent,' forgive him" (Luke 17:3, 4, *New International Version*).

This sounds impossible, and perhaps ridiculous, but it is exactly how we desire God to act toward us. Who of us doesn't have some weakness, some sin which we commit time and again, for which we seek God's forgiveness?

Forgive in Your Heart. Forgiveness must come from the heart. In fact, it can occur only in the heart. If we act peaceably but harbor resentment in the heart, then we have not truly forgiven. We must restore the brother to full and tender fellowship and reestablish him in our affections. (See Matthew 18:35.)

C. Forgiveness Is Required

Christians do not have the option of refusing to forgive the repentant brother. Jesus made it very clear that we will not be forgiven unless we are willing to forgive. "For if you forgive men when they sin against you, your heavenly Father will also forgive you. But if you do not forgive men their sins, your Father will not forgive your sins" (Matthew 6:14, 15, *New International Version*.) "And when you stand praying, if you hold anything against anyone, forgive him, so that your Father in heaven may forgive you your sins" (Mark 11:25, *New International Version*).

Teacher: at this time read lesson aims 2 and 3 to your students, and challenge them to fulfill them and thus put the lesson into practice.

D. Prayer for a Forgiving Heart

Loving God, thank You for forgiving us and accepting us into Your fellowship. Thank You for continuing to forgive the sins that we have not yet conquered in our lives. Please help us to forgive those who wrong us. Help us realize that we will never be called upon to forgive as much as You have forgiven us. Help us to forgive from our hearts and learn to love those who sin against us. Amen.

E. Thought to Remember

When Onesimus became a Christian he began to live up to his name, which means: "profitable." Paul urged Philemon to live up to his name, which means "loving." Let us live up to the name *Christian*, by loving, forgiving, and accepting others as Christ accepts us.

Learning by Doing

This page contains an alternate lesson plan emphasizing learning activities. Classes desiring such student involvement will find these suggestions helpful.

Learning Goals

After examining the letter to Philemon, a student should be able to:

1. Explain *why* Philemon was asked to forgive Onesimus.

2. Explain why it is important for Christians to forgive each other.

3. Identify someone he needs to forgive and develop a plan by which he will seek to reestablish a relationship with that person.

Into the Lesson

Write the following heading and statements on the chalkboard:

AGREE OR DISAGREE?

1. Forgiving one who has wronged you is not humanly possible.

2. Forgiveness is an attribute of God that the Christian can count on with no strings attached.

As the class members arrive, direct their attention to the agree/disagree statements and ask them to make a decision about each. Have them form groups of three to five to share and discuss their responses.

After the groups have had four or five minutes to develop the discussions, ask for their responses to the statements and let them explain their reasoning. Don't judge the rightness or wrongness of a response at this time. Indicate that the letter to Philemon will provide insight by which each person may assess his responses to the statements.

Into the Word

Distribute copies of the following questions and ask students to read the text to find the answers. (If your time is limited, assign one of the three sketches to each one-third of the class.)

1. Write a brief biographical and personality sketch of Philemon as you see it developed in this letter.

2. Write a brief biographical and personality sketch of Onesimus as you see it developed in this letter.

3. Write a brief biographical and personality sketch of Paul as you see it developed in this letter.

After the sketches have been completed, present a brief background of the letter. (See "Lesson Background" in the "Introduction" section.) Then have several sketches of Philemon, Onesimus, and Paul read. Develop discussion by asking the following questions:

1. On what basis does Paul appeal to Philemon to forgive Onesimus? Why would he choose this approach rather than order him to forgive?

2. How do you think Philemon felt when he received Paul's letter? How easy would it have been to do as Paul asked?

3. What teaching can we conclude from this passage?

Into Life

Ask, How easy is it really to forgive? Then read and discuss the following situations to determine what it means to forgive.

Problem 1. Bill and Ann have been married for thirty years. Ann has trusted Bill implicitly during this time. But now Bill asks Ann to forgive his indiscretion with another woman. He tells Ann that he loves her and promises that this will never happen again. How should Ann respond? If she agrees to Bill's request, how must she respond to him in the future?

Problem 2. Paul and Ginny have a thirty-year-old son, Tom, who rebelled against them and their values when he was in his late teens. Among other things, he had stolen money from them to support his drug habit. He has now come to them to ask their forgiveness. They aren't sure whether or not he is still on drugs. How should Paul and Ginny respond? If they agree to Tom's request, how must they respond to him in the future?

Problem 3. Jane and Mary have been good friends since high school. Recently Mary attempted to undermine Jane's reputation. Now Mary has come to Jane to ask her forgiveness. How should Jane respond? If she agrees to Mary's request, how must she respond to her in the future?

It is difficult to deal with the human emotions in forgiveness. But point out these reasons why we must forgive: (1) God has forgiven us though we do not deserve forgiveness; (2) our sins will not be forgiven if we refuse to forgive others (see Matthew 18:23-35; 6:14, 15).

In closing, ask each student to identify a person whom they need to forgive and to decide how they will try to reestablish the relationship.

Let's Talk It Over

The questions on this page are designed to encourage review of the lesson Scriptures and to promote discussion of the lesson by the class. The answers provided are only discussion starters. Let your class talk it over from there.

1. How important was it to Philemon to be on the prayer list of an evangelist in prison, hundreds of miles away? How important is it to you to know that others are praying for you? Do you pray regularly for anyone outside your family circle?

It must have been great encouragement to Philemon to know that he was a subject of Paul's thanksgiving to God. If we have respect for someone who has been our teacher, we enjoy receiving that teacher's approval. Paul had taught Philemon the most important truth of life, the truth about Jesus Christ. To hear that Paul was thanking God for the work of grace in Philemon's life had to be good news to Philemon.

The Bible declares that the prayer of a righteous man is powerful and effective (James 5:16). As a Christian, Philemon surely believed in the practical benefit of Paul's prayers on his behalf.

In Ephesians 6:18 Paul instructed the believers to continue praying for "all saints" (that is, fellow Christians). That command is one of several in a section concerning spiritual warfare and how we may survive Satan's attacks. Have you deprived the Christians closest to you the benefit of your intercessory prayers? Why not covenant with one or more fellow Christians, agreeing to pray for one another daily?

2. How may Philemon have "refreshed" the hearts of the saints? (v. 7). What kind of person does it take to perform that ministry?

The key here seems to be the love Philemon was showing to the Christians of Colossae. We know from verse 2 that Philemon was host to a church that met in his house. There are other indications that Philemon was a man of some wealth. Perhaps his love had been expressed in generosity toward the needs of the church and individuals in it. Is there someone in your church who is refreshing the hearts of the saints? Giving money generously is not the only way. Refreshment may come by an act of kindness, a godly example, an encouraging word, or an occasion of forgiveness and acceptance. Paul claimed that he would be refreshed if Philemon would forgive Onesimus. (v. 20).

3. In what sense was Onesimus Paul's son? (v. 10). How may we win spiritual sons or daughters today? Why is that important?

Paul had the privilege of sharing the gospel with Onesimus, and then spending some time with him in a discipling relationship. More and more Christians are discovering the joy of leading another to Christ—not in a hit-and-run manner, but in a continuing relationship in which they show genuine love and assist the individual through decision and into maturity. This is important because it is the very thing we are commanded to do (Matthew 28:18-20).

4. In making his appeal to Philemon, did Paul depend more upon his authority as an apostle or upon his personal relationship as a friend to Philemon? What lesson is here for church leaders today?

Paul preferred not to command Philemon to obey (vv. 8, 9). Instead he suggested a course of action that he hoped Philemon would adopt willingly. In his effort to persuade, Paul leaned heavily upon the relationship of love and mutual respect that he had with Philemon (vv. 17, 19, 20). Without that relationship, this letter could not have been written. Church leaders today will do well to recognize the power of love and personal concern as they attempt to influence others to become more and more like Christ. Do you respond more willingly to the command of an authority figure or the appeal of someone whom you know loves you?

5. Discuss some possible ways that people change after Jesus Christ becomes their Lord and Savior. Is it only a matter of actions, or should there be changes of attitudes as well?

If changes occur *only* in actions (behavior), *reformation* has occurred. *Transformation* works more deeply and more thoroughly, changing the mind (that includes thoughts and attitudes). Jesus Christ calls for transformation of life. When He becomes Lord, change occurs in thoughts, attitudes, values, goals, decisions, behavior, and life-style. Change limited to overt actions may leave the heart unchanged. Herein lies the basis for trouble!

Citizens of a New Kingdom

LESSON SCRIPTURE: Colossians 1:1-14.

PRINTED TEXT: Colossians 1:1-14.

Colossians 1:1-14

1 Paul, an apostle of Jesus Christ by the will of God, and Timothy our brother,

2 To the saints and faithful brethren in Christ which are at Colossae: Grace be unto you, and peace, from God our Father and the Lord Jesus Christ.

3 We give thanks to God and the Father of our Lord Jesus Christ, praying always for you,

4 Since we heard of your faith in Christ Jesus, and of the love which ye have to all the saints,

5 For the hope which is laid up for you in heaven, whereof ye heard before in the word of the truth of the gospel;

6 Which is come unto you, as it is in all the world; and bringeth forth fruit, as it doth also in you, since the day ye heard of it, and knew the grace of God in truth:

7 As ye also learned of Epaphras our dear fellow servant, who is for you a faithful minister of Christ;

8 Who also declared unto us your love in the Spirit.

9 For this cause we also, since the day we heard it, do not cease to pray for you, and to desire that ye might be filled with the knowledge of his will in all wisdom and spiritual understanding;

10 That ye might walk worthy of the Lord unto all pleasing, being fruitful in every good work, and increasing in the knowledge of God;

11 Strengthened with all might, according to his glorious power, unto all patience and long-suffering with joyfulness;

12 Giving thanks unto the Father, which hath made us meet to be partakers of the inheritance of the saints in light:

13 Who hath delivered us from the power of darkness, and hath translated us into the kingdom of his dear Son.

14 In whom we have redemption through his blood, even the forgiveness of sins.

GOLDEN TEXT: [The Father] hath delivered us from the power of darkness, and hath translated us into the kingdom of his dear Son. In whom we have redemption through his blood, even the forgiveness of sins.—Colossians 1:13, 14.

Letters From Prison

Unit 2: Colossians—
Christ the Lord (Lessons 2-4)

Lesson Aims

Each of your students should:

1. Be able to list three characteristics of a good citizen in God's kingdom.

2. Be able to express reasons why he is grateful to the Lord.

3. Find and perform a specific task for the Lord.

Lesson Outline

INTRODUCTION

    A. Deliverance From Darkness

    B. Lesson Background

  I. PAUL'S GREETINGS (Colossians 1:1, 2)

 II. PAUL'S THANKFULNESS (Colossians 1:3-8)

    A. For the Faith and Love of the Colossians (vv. 3-5)

    B. For the Spread of the Gospel (v. 6)

    C. For a Fellow Servant (vv. 7, 8)

III. PAUL'S DESIRE FOR THE COLOSSIANS (Colossians 1:9-14)

    A. Knowledge of God's Will (v. 9)

    B. Godly, Productive Lives (vv. 10, 11)

      The Way We Live

    C. Thankful Hearts (vv. 12-14)

      New Relationships

CONCLUSION

    A. Serving the King

    B. Prayer of a Citizen

    C. Thought to Remember

Display visual 2 from the visuals/learning resources packet. It is shown on page 245.

Introduction

A. Deliverance From Darkness

Imagine yourself a citizen of the most evil kingdom conceivable. All who dwell there are murderers, liars, cheats, adulterers, brawlers, and the like. Encouraged by the wicked ruler, everyone mistreats the other in this kingdom, and you have been thrown into the darkest dungeon. You are there rightfully, because you are guilty of the vilest crimes. You spend your time just waiting for the executioner.

Now the tiny window of the door of your cell opens. An ambassador from a far country tells you that his king has taken pity on the wretched citizens of your land. The king has made a successful invasion and has overthrown the wicked ruler. You are free to leave the prison and migrate to the new kingdom if you will forsake your evil ways and loyally serve the good king. Though you can scarcely believe it possible, you pledge to obey, and the door is thrown open. You are conducted out of the prison and transported to the new kingdom. Now, as a new citizen, you must learn a whole new way of life. You must learn the laws of your new king. You must begin doing the work that he commands.

This is what happens to Christians, in a spiritual sense. We are citizens of the world, condemned by our sins. In verse 13 of our text this is called the power or dominion of darkness, over which Satan holds sway. But God sent His Son Jesus Christ to die for us, thus breaking Satan's hold on us. We are invited to come into Christ's kingdom if we will repent of our sins and follow Him as Lord. This is the kingdom of light mentioned in verse 12. When we enter Christ's kingdom, we must then learn how to live a life that is pleasing to Him.

B. Lesson Background

The apostle Paul wrote the epistles to the Ephesians, Colossians, and Philemon while he was imprisoned in Rome about A.D. 62. Tychicus, one of Paul's trusted helpers, was to deliver the Ephesian letter to the church in Ephesus, then proceed on to Colossae with the epistle to the Colossians. Onesimus, the runaway slave whom Paul was sending back to Philemon in Colossae, accompanied Tychicus (see Ephesians 6:21, 22; Colossians 4:7-9).

While Paul had not been associated personally with the church in Colossae, he was greatly concerned about its welfare (Colossians 2:1, 2). While in prison he had learned of the state of the Colossian Christians from Epaphras (Colossians 1:7, 8). Paul's "care of all the churches" made him long to see their faith maintained and their spiritual strength remain unabated.

In today's lesson text, Paul told the Colossians that they were citizens of a new kingdom. They must reject the teachings and practices of the world, and devote their full energies to becoming mature and productive citizens of the kingdom of God's Son.

I. Paul's Greetings
(Colossians 1:1, 2)

1. Paul, an apostle of Jesus Christ by the will of God, and Timothy our brother.

Paul identified himself as *an apostle of Jesus Christ*. An apostle was more than just a messenger. He possessed authority and power given him by the Lord. Christians were to give heed to the instructions of the apostles as to the Christ himself. Paul doubly stressed that his apostleship was *by the will of God*.

2. To the saints and faithful brethren in Christ which are at Colossae: Grace be unto you, and peace, from God our Father and the Lord Jesus Christ.

All Christians are *saints*. The word means set apart or separated. Christians are separated from the world.

Though false religions threatened the congregation in Colossae, they were yet *faithful*. The erroneous ideas may have confused and attracted the Colossians, but they had not yet accepted them. Because they were faithful, Paul called them *brethren in Christ*. They were all united together *in Christ*.

Grace includes all of God's freely bestowed blessings. *Peace* refers to the inner serenity and calm that naturally come to one who receives God's grace.

II. Paul's Thankfulness
(Colossians 1:3-8)

A. For the Faith and Love of the Colossians (vv. 3-5)

3. We give thanks to God and the Father of our Lord Jesus Christ, praying always for you.

Paul was thankful for the Colossian Christians. First, he was thankful to God for them. God sent His Son; God originated the gospel; God forgave and saved them.

The Father of our Lord Jesus Christ. Notice the exalted status of Jesus. He is the Son of almighty God. He is Lord. He is Jesus, which means Savior. He is Christ, God's anointed or chosen one.

4. Since we heard of your faith in Christ Jesus, and of the love which ye have to all the saints.

Paul was also thankful for the Colossians themselves. Epaphras brought a good report of the state of the church, and Paul was overjoyed by this. He particularly mentioned their *faith in Christ Jesus*. Christ was the object of their faith, as He should have been. This phrase speaks of their union with Christ, in whom they lived, and moved, and had their being.

The second thing Paul gave thanks for was the *love* the disciples had *to all the saints*. Love is the natural result of true devotion to Jesus. Indeed, their love was proof of their faith. (see 1 John 4:7-12.)

5. For the hope which is laid up for you in heaven, whereof ye heard before in the word of the truth of the gospel.

The faith and love of the Colossians are *for*, on account of, the *hope* that they have. Paul linked faith, hope, and love in 1 Corinthians 13:13. Two chapters later, in 15:12-19, he asserted that faith is futile unless it looks forward to a Heavenly hope. Hope has two parts. On the one hand is the thing that is hoped for. On the other hand is the longing and desire within the heart to receive the cherished dream. The good news of the gospel is that Jesus has made it possible for man to receive eternal life. When a person responds to the gospel it is because he accepts that offer of eternal life. Thus hope becomes the foundation and motivation for faith and love.

This hope is not in doubt; it is *laid up for you in heaven*. It already exists, and Christians have God's own promise that He will give it to us.

The phrase *whereof ye heard before* pointed the Colossians back to the time when they first heard *the word of the truth of the gospel*. The gospel is true because it is the word of God.

Christians today must heed this same message. Since the New Testament was written, men have written to explain and comment on it. Much of what men have said about the Bible is helpful and true, but men have also written many mistaken ideas and perversions of the truth. If we want to know for sure that we have the truth of the gospel, then we must continually go back to the gospel as it was originally proclaimed in the New Testament.

B. For the Spread of the Gospel (v. 6)

6. Which is come unto you, as it is in all the world; and bringeth forth fruit, as it doth also in you, since the day ye heard of it, and knew the grace of God in truth.

At that time the gospel had indeed been proclaimed throughout a large portion of the Roman world. Moreover, it was for the whole world, for people in all places and throughout the ages.

The phrase *bringeth forth fruit* should include the words "and grows." (This is how it appears in most modern translations.) A tree both grows and bears fruit. Just so the church both grows larger and continually bears fruit.

How to Say It

COLOSSAE. Ko-*loss*-ee.
EPAPHRAS. *Ep*-uh-fras.
EPHESUS. *Ef*-uh-sus.
ONESIMUS. O-*ness*-ih-muss.
TYCHICUS. *Tick*-ih-cuss.

Knew the grace of God in truth. The gospel was the true revelation of God's will. It had been faithfully proclaimed to them, and it was producing the expected results in their lives.

C. For a Fellow Servant (vv. 7, 8)

7. As ye also learned of Epaphras our dear fellow servant, who is for you a faithful minister of Christ.

The Colossians learned the gospel from *Epaphras.* It is very possible that Paul, during the time he was preaching in Ephesus, converted and trained Epaphras, and then sent him out to preach (Acts 19:1-10).

8. Who also declared unto us your love in the Spirit.

When Epaphras came to Paul in Rome, he told the apostle all about the Christians in Colossae, and especially about their *love in the Spirit.* Such godly love is true and unfeigned.

III. Paul's Desire for the Colossians (Colossians 1:9-14)

In these verses Paul taught the Colossians about their responsibilities and resources as citizens of the kingdom of God. He did it by relating a prayer that he prayed on their behalf.

(Teacher: Outline points A, B, and C are the three characteristics of a good citizen mentioned in lesson aim 1.)

A. Knowledge of God's Will (v. 9)

9. For this cause we also, since the day we heard it, do not cease to pray for you, and to desire that ye might be filled with the knowledge of his will in all wisdom and spiritual understanding.

First, Paul desired that they *might be filled with the knowledge* of God's will. As new citizens of God's kingdom, they must learn the King's will. In Greek, the word for knowledge is emphatic. It expresses "thorough participation on the part of the knower, with the object of knowledge; a knowledge that has a powerful influence on the knower" *(Bullinger's Critical Lexicon).* More than an acquaintance with the facts of God's will, it is the overriding determination to obey them. Paul prayed that the Colossians would be filled with such knowledge.

Knowledge of God's will is the indispensable foundation for faith and obedience. It is impossible to believe until one knows what to believe, or to obey until one knows what is commanded. This is the purpose of the Bible. And this is the reason for continual study of God's Word.

Wisdom and spiritual understanding. The attribute *spiritual* applies both to wisdom and to understanding. "So far as there is a distinction between the two words, wisdom is generally the knowledge of spiritual mysteries, of great theological principles; understanding is the faculty of applying them to action" *(Cook, Bible Commentary).*

B. Godly, Productive Lives (vv. 10, 11)

The second thing Paul desired of the Colossians as new citizens in the kingdom of God was that they become obedient, productive citizens.

10. That ye might walk worthy of the Lord unto all pleasing, being fruitful in every good work, and increasing in the knowledge of God.

In a disciple of the Lord, obedience follows on the heels of knowledge. As soon as we learn what to do, we should begin to put it into practice. This is how we walk *worthy of the Lord.* In one sense, of course, we are never worthy of God's love and mercy because we are always imperfect. But God does not expect perfection from us. He knows better than we do how impossible that is. What He does expect is a spirit of obedience: willingness, determination, and eagerness to do His will, even though we do it imperfectly. Everyone who loves the Lord will naturally have this attitude, and will be *pleasing* to Him.

If we have knowledge of God's will and a determination to obey, then we will become *fruitful in every good work.* This is more than abstaining from evil. It means being active in doing the positive works of the Lord, such as proclaiming the gospel or caring for the sick, widows, or orphans. Our lives will be filled with service and labor that we have offered to the Lord.

Increasing in the knowledge of God. Knowledge and obedience form a repeating cycle. First a Christian learns about some part of God's will. Then he begins to put that knowledge into practice. This experience in turn gives him a deeper knowledge and understanding of God's will, which leads him to more perfect obedience, which leads to even deeper understanding, and so on.

Do not wait until you have perfect knowledge before you begin to act on the Lord's behalf. Quite possibly, in your first efforts you may make mistakes. If you seek to help someone, you may embarrass him. If you seek to exhort someone, you may offend him. But because of your obedience, you will have learned something. One part of knowing how to do something is knowing what not to do. Continue to be obedient and you will grow in proficiency. Even the most accomplished of God's servants were inexperienced at one time, but they kept at it.

11. Strengthened with all might, according to his glorious power, unto all patience and long-suffering with joyfulness.

It was Paul's desire that the Colossians be *strengthened with all might.* Literally, this is "being made mighty with all might"; or "being strengthened with all strength." We are to be strong in the Lord, who is the source of infinite strength. His strength makes the Christian sufficient for every temptation and every task. With this in mind Paul told the Philippians, "I can do everything through him who gives me strength" (4:13, *New International Version*). To the Corinthians he made clear that he was weak, but that Christ's power worked through him (2 Corinthians 12:7-10).

(Teacher: the next three paragraphs pertain to lesson aim 3.)

The power of God enables ordinary men and women to do extraordinary things. Paul himself planted churches throughout the Roman world. Martin Luther opposed all the power of the church of Rome and prevailed through God's power. Missionaries face impossible situations, yet succeed in communicating the gospel. But a Christian doesn't have to be famous to call upon God's power. God will help every Christian to do much more than he can do by himself.

We should not be afraid to undertake some work for the Lord because we think it is beyond our capability. If the Lord presents us with a challenge, He will also give us the help we need to meet that challenge. Note, however, that the Lord does not give us talents we do not have: He helps us use to the maximum the talents we do have. Again, the Lord does not do all the work. He requires toil, dedication, and sacrifice on our part, and He then multiplies and rewards our efforts.

Average Christians are able to accomplish great and important things every day when they trust God to help, and then they press on to the work. Housewives have been able to get pornography removed from store shelves. Students have developed deaf ministries. Teachers have had great impact on their students. Every Christian can render meaningful service if only he has the will.

Paul mentioned two specific ways in which God's strength is applied. The first is *patience.* The same word is translated "endurance" in Hebrews 12:1, where it describes a runner who keeps on going until he reaches the finish line. It is the attitude or characteristic that enables one to persist uphill and down, through fair weather and foul, over all obstacles, until he reaches the finish line. The Christian life may be compared to a marathon. Read Philippians

visual 2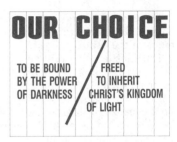

3:7-14 for Paul's description of how he ran this race.

The second way God's strength is applied is in the attitude of *long-suffering.* This refers to one's ability to endure with patience the personal attacks of others without resentment and without seeking revenge.

With joyfulness. There is some question as to whether these words describe the Christian's attitude in patience and long-suffering, or should be taken in connection with the first words of verse 12, thus reading, "with joyfulness giving thanks."

THE WAY WE LIVE

The term *life-style* was not much used until the "hippy movement" swept across America. Suddenly we were flooded with slogans such as, "Do your own thing," "Take care of number one." Each of these reflected a disregard for others and an enshrinement of self.

In his book, *In His Steps,* written nearly a century ago, Charles Sheldon took a totally different view. The story told of a man who had to make decisions relating to a number of experiences in a large city. The hero made each decision after prayerfully considering the claims of Christ on his life and studying what our Lord did or the principle He taught in a similar situation.

Our Lord always considered the best interest of others and the will of His Father in making all decisions in His earthly existence. So Paul urged the Colossians, and us, to "walk worthy of the Lord, fully pleasing him" *(The New King James Version).*

The way we live is the message most seen and heard by those all about us. We need to recommit ourselves to walking with Jesus so men can see something of Him in us.   —W. P.

C. Thankful Hearts (vv. 12-14)

The third thing that Paul desired of the Colossians, as citizens who had been delivered at the cost of the King's own Son, was gratitude. Such gratitude for His sacrifice motivates us to sacrifice for Him.

12. Giving thanks unto the Father, which hath made us meet to be partakers of the inheritance of the saints in light.

The apostle tells us that while we press along our course with endurance and bear the attacks against us with long-suffering, we should all the while give thanks to the Lord. We thank the Lord because He gives us a goal worth reaching. We thank Him because He heals sin's ultimate wound, death (1 Corinthians 15:55-57). Paul lists several of God's blessings that should motivate us to gratitude.

(Teacher: the following material relates to lesson aim 2).

Our Heavenly Father made us *meet* (that is, sufficient) *to be partakers of the inheritance.* He made us qualified to share. We could not qualify on our own merits. The inheritance includes all the promises of the gospel.

13, 14. Who hath delivered us from the power of darkness, and hath translated us into the kingdom of his dear Son: in whom we have redemption through his blood, even the forgiveness of sins.

Before He could give us an inheritance, God had to rescue us *from the power of darkness.* Darkness represents evil and all that is opposed to God. To rescue us, God sent His Son and allowed Him to be killed so we could escape (see 1 Peter 1:18, 19). He then took us from that kingdom of darkness and transferred us *into the kingdom of his dear Son.* This is a wonderful kingdom of light and life. Notice the high esteem God has toward His Son, who is very precious to Him.

In this way Christians have become citizens of a new kingdom, as our lesson title says. Christians should feel great thankfulness to the One who delivers us from spiritual bondage.

Home Daily Bible Readings

Monday, Mar. 6—Thanksgiving for Christlike Qualities (Colossians 1:1-8)
Tuesday, Mar. 7—The Quality of Faith (Hebrews 11:1-3; 12:1-2)
Wednesday, Mar. 8—The Quality of Hope (Romans 15:4-13)
Thursday, Mar. 9—The Quality of Love (1 Corinthians 13)
Friday, Mar. 10—The Quality of Wisdom (Colossians 1:9-14)
Saturday, Mar. 11—Wisdom From God (1 Corinthians 2:6-16)
Sunday, Mar. 12—Wisdom for Witnessing (Colossians 4:2-6)

NEW RELATIONSHIPS

A very gifted professor was known for his cold, harsh way of dealing with classes and students. He was always stiffly correct in everything he did. The students learned from the professor's lectures but they dreaded any personal encounter with him and avoided such. His life was so lonesome that his study and research were his only purpose for existence.

Then things began to change. The class material remained excellent and his teaching outstanding, but a new facet of existence had entered his life. He was in love!

How they ever got together was something of a mystery, but he was dating regularly a warm, happy, woman of good mind and manner. The transition was remarkable. The professor began to dress better, smile and laugh, and take a personal interest in his students.

Yes, there is a happy ending. In the spring the professor was married, and his life, now filled with love and a sense of well-being, ceased exhibiting that cold aloofness that had made him a feared man on campus.

Associations do change us. Jesus in our lives transforms daily living.   —W. P.

Conclusion

A. Serving the King

No one is a Christian against his will. God has provided the means of breaking Satan's hold on us; we can escape the power of darkness if we choose. God invites us to enter His kingdom, but He does not force us to do so. However, once we are in His kingdom, the Lord does expect us to be faithful citizens in serving Him.

Let us work tirelessly for our King. Let us call on His power to enable us to do more. Let us sacrifice for Him as He sacrificed for us.

(Teacher: At this time challenge your students with lesson aim 3.)

B. Prayer of a Citizen

Almighty God, we acknowledge You as our King. Thank You for rescuing us from the kingdom of darkness. We pledge to serve and obey You. Help us to understand Your will. Forgive us when our stubborn hearts lead us to rebel against You. In the name of Your Son we pray. Amen.

C. Thought to Remember

Christ "died for all, that those who live should no longer live for themselves but for him who died for them and was raised again" (2 Corinthians 5:15, *New International Version*).

Learning by Doing

This page contains an alternate lesson plan emphasizing learning activities. Classes desiring such student involvement will find these suggestions helpful.

Learning Goals

After examining Colossians 1:1-14, a student will be able to:

1. List three characteristics of a good citizen in God's kingdom.

2. Restate the attitude toward obedience that a Christian must have to live a life pleasing to God.

3. Identify one characteristic that a citizen of God's kingdom should have and commit himself to work on it.

Into the Lesson

Before time for the class to begin, write the words of 2 Corinthians 5:14, 15 on small index cards, one word per card. Mix the cards up and place them in an envelope. Have such an envelope prepared for every four to six students in your class.

As the class members arrive, form the groups and give each one an envelope. Tell them that when they solve the puzzle correctly, they will have discovered an important principle from today's Bible lesson. Allow the students five to seven minutes to complete this activity. Check their work.

Make the transition into the Bible study for today by stating that Paul identified some of the characteristics of a kingdom citizen in his letter to the Colossians.

Into the Word

Introduce the Scripture text for today by presenting the lesson background from the "Introduction" section. Then have a class member read the text aloud.

Have the groups who worked together on the scrambled verses continue to work together to find the answers to the following questions from Colossians 1:1-14.

1. Paul stated three things for which he was thankful. What were they? (The faith and love of the Colossians, the spread of the gospel, and a fellow servant.)

2. In verses 9-14, Paul identified three characteristics of a kingdom citizen. What are they? (Minds filled with spiritual wisdom and understanding, lives lived worthy of the Lord, and hearts overflowing with thanks to the Father.)

3. What is the motivation that compels the Christian to develop the distinctive characteristics of a kingdom citizen? (Christ has delivered us from the kingdom of darkness and has provided redemption.)

Allow the groups four to six minutes to complete this. Then briefly explain the Scripture text, using information from the commentary section.

Into Life

Paul is describing a mature Christian. Refer to Colossians 1:28.

Let the class remain in the same groups for the following activity. Ask them to examine the Scripture text and develop a blueprint for Christian maturity. Allow the groups eight to ten minutes to complete their work. Then have the groups share their finished products.

Develop a brief discussion, using the following questions.

1. How desirable is maturity in the life of a Christian? Why?

2. What percentage of Christians do you think are honestly seeking to become mature?

3. What hinders people from becoming mature in Christ?

4. What motivates people to become mature in Christ? (Refer to 2 Corinthians 5:14, 15.)

5. How mature are you? To assist the students in answering this, distribute a self-evaluation guide to each person. Ask the class members to fill it out.

HOW MATURE AM I?

Rate yourself on each of the characteristics listed below; 5 the highest.

1. I enjoy the study of God's Word.

                5 4 3 2 1

2. When I am in the midst of daily decisions, I remember principles from God's Word to help me make the decision.   5 4 3 2 1

3. My life is characterized by obedience to God.   5 4 3 2 1

4. I am a thankful person, whatever the circumstances.   5 4 3 2 1

As I examine my own maturity level, I discover that I need to—

Have class members form groups of three in which they share their aspirations for maturity. Let the groups pray together as the class is concluded. When a group is finished, the members may be dismissed.

Let's Talk It Over

The questions on this page are designed to encourage review of the lesson Scriptures and to promote discussion of the lesson by the class. The answers provided are only discussion starters. Let your class talk it over from there.

1. To whom is this message addressed? How does one qualify as a saint?

Paul addressed his letter "to the saints and faithful brethren in Christ which are at Colossae" (v. 1). In some circles saints are those canonized by the church because of their remarkable spirituality and service. In the New Testament, however, all Christians are called saints. The original word means set apart or separated. The same root word is in "sanctified" (made holy). In Christ we are sanctified, set apart as God's, and therefore saints. Thus separated from the world, we, by the character of our lives, are to bring praise to Him who redeemed us (see 1 Peter 2:9, 10).

2. What was Paul desiring for his readers when he wrote "grace be unto you, and peace"? Can we have more or less grace? Peace?

Since this letter was addressed to Christians, we know that they had already received the saving grace of God that is in Christ. Paul used the word *grace* more broadly to mean the favor or blessing of God. It is God's grace that makes up for our weakness (2 Corinthians 12:9). It is by God's grace that we are being transformed to the image of his Son (1 Corinthians 15:10). It is God's grace that we seek in time of need (Hebrews 4:16).

Peace is the contentment and security we feel, having a clear conscience before God. Peace means being rid of panic and fear, because we are trusting God (Philippians 4:6, 7).

James 4:6 assures us that God gives more grace as we humble ourselves before Him. We may experience more or less peace depending upon the level of our trust in God.

3. What is the fruit of the word of truth? (vv. 5, 6).

Jesus said "I am the way, the truth, and the life: no man cometh unto the Father, but by me" (John 14:6). Those who believe and respond to the word of truth of the gospel find the way to the Father. Jesus also said, "If ye continue in my word, then are ye my disciples indeed; and ye shall know the truth, and the truth shall make you free" (John 8:31, 32). The fruit of the word, then, is lives redeemed from bondage to sin and guilt, and set free to live in righteousness.

4. How do we become filled with the knowledge of God's will?

Some Christians pray for and yearn for insight into God's will, as though God were playing some bizarre, high stakes game with us. It is as if God were saying, "I have a preferred course of action for your life, but you must guess what it is. If you guess right, I will bless you. If you guess wrong, you are on your own." Such an attitude is uncharacteristic of His nature and His love for us.

We are fortunate to have God's revealed will recorded in the Bible. To be filled with the knowledge of His will, we need to open the Bible and read. Paul's prayer is that our knowledge may be in wisdom and spiritual understanding. Wisdom and understanding come after application of knowledge. We obey, and then we begin to understand.

5. What does it mean to "walk worthy of the Lord"?

As Christians we are given a new status. We are made the adopted children of God. We are also heirs with Jesus of eternal life and the bounty of Heaven (Galatians 4:4-7). We ought to live in a way, then, befitting the children of the King. Paul lists some qualities of a life worthy of the Lord: "being fruitful in every good work," "increasing in the knowledge of God," and being "strengthened . . . unto all patience and long-suffering with joyfulness" (Colossians 1: 10, 11).

6. What does the Bible mean by the "power of darkness"? (v. 13).

Paul tells us that Christians have been delivered from the power of darkness and have become citizens of the kingdom of Christ. That contrast helps us understand the power of darkness. Darkness is a symbol of evil and deception. Satan is a deceiver and a liar. He causes sin to appear desirable. Often, even after they begin to reap heartache and suffering, people are blind to the connection between their sin and their troubles. Even when they do see the connection, the appeal of Satan is so alluring that they choose to remain enslaved to sin. It takes the redemption that is in Christ to break that power and make us citizens of a new kingdom.

Warning Against False Teaching

LESSON SCRIPTURE: Colossians 2:6-23.

PRINTED TEXT: Colossians 2:6-19.

Colossians 2:6-19

6 As ye have therefore received Christ Jesus the Lord, so walk ye in him:

7 Rooted and built up in him, and stablished in the faith, as ye have been taught, abounding therein with thanksgiving.

8 Beware lest any man spoil you through philosophy and vain deceit, after the tradition of men, after the rudiments of the world, and not after Christ.

9 For in him dwelleth all the fulness of the Godhead bodily.

10 And ye are complete in him, which is the head of all principality and power:

11 In whom also ye are circumcised with the circumcision made without hands, in putting off the body of the sins of the flesh by the circumcision of Christ:

12 Buried with him in baptism, wherein also ye are risen with him through the faith of the operation of God, who hath raised him from the dead.

13 And you, being dead in your sins and the uncircumcision of your flesh, hath he quickened together with him, having forgiven you all trespasses;

14 Blotting out the handwriting of ordinances that was against us, which was contrary to us, and took it out of the way, nailing it to his cross;

15 And having spoiled principalities and powers, he made a show of them openly, triumphing over them in it.

16 Let no man therefore judge you in meat, or in drink, or in respect of a holy-day, or of the new moon, or of the sabbath days:

17 Which are a shadow of things to come; but the body is of Christ.

18 Let no man beguile you of your reward in a voluntary humility and worshipping of angels, intruding into those things which he hath not seen, vainly puffed up by his fleshly mind,

19 And not holding the Head, from which all the body by joints and bands having nourishment ministered, and knit together, increaseth with the increase of God.

GOLDEN TEXT: As ye have therefore received Christ Jesus the Lord, so walk ye in him: rooted and built up in him, and stablished in the faith, as ye have been taught, abounding therein with thanksgiving.—Colossians 2:6, 7.

Letters From Prison
Unit 2: Colossians—
Christ the Lord (Lessons 2-4)

Lesson Aims

You will achieve the purposes of the lesson if your students can do the following:

1. Explain why Christ has supreme authority.

2. Name at least three ways in which Christ delivers Christians from the world.

3. List several prominent teachings of the world and explain how they are opposed to Christ.

Lesson Outline

INTRODUCTION
  A. Believing and Deceiving
  B. Lesson Background
I. CHRIST IS OPPOSED TO THE WORLD (Colossians 2:6-8)
  A. Continue in Christ (vv. 6, 7)
  B. Beware of Worldly Philosophy (v. 8)
II. CHRIST HAS OVERCOME THE WORLD (Colossians 2:9-15)
  A. Christ's Authority (vv. 9, 10)
    Achieving Your Potential
  B. Christ's Deliverance (vv. 11-14)
  C. The World's Power Destroyed (v. 15)
III. CHRIST SUPERSEDES THE WORLD (Colossians 2:16-19)
  A. Shadow Replaced With Reality (vv. 16, 17)
  B. The False Replaced With the True (vv. 18, 19)
    Accepting Poor Directions
CONCLUSION
  A. Be on the Alert!
  B. Prayer of a Disciple
  C. Thought to Remember

Display visual 3 from the visuals/learning resources packet. It is shown on page 252.

Introduction

A. Believing and Deceiving

You have probably heard the riddle about the man who came to a fork in the road and didn't know which way to go to reach his destination. Two people were standing at the intersection, one of whom always told the truth, and one of whom always lied. The riddle asks how the traveler could find out which was the correct road.

Sometimes staying on the correct road to reach Heaven is just as puzzling. As we travel along we come to places where the path branches. Many people have gone each way, and we must decide which to follow. Spokesmen at the intersection try to persuade us that their way is the correct one, but only one is telling the truth. Which should the Christian believe? Who is the deceiver?

B. Lesson Background

In last week's lesson we learned that Epaphras came to Rome, bringing Paul word of the spiritual condition of the church in Colossae (Colossians 1:7, 8). Among his reasons for making the long journey was to inform the apostle concerning the false teachings that threatened the Christians at Colossae, and to receive his guidance in dealing with them. Several characteristics of these false teachings can be discerned from the content of the letter. The heretics detracted from the divine nature and authority of Christ. They denied that His work was sufficient to deliver man from sin. They tried to blend the gospel with popular philosophies of the day. They insisted on the observance of legalistic rules related to Jewish traditions. They taught the worship of angels. And they taught that the knowledge that leads to salvation is known only to a select few.

In today's lesson we will study several of these false teachings and Paul's reply to them. This is not just a dusty history lesson, however, for these heresies of old have spiritual descendants that still seek to lead Christians away from the Lord.

I. Christ Is Opposed to the World (Colossians 2:6-8)

A. Continue in Christ (vv. 6, 7)

6, 7. As ye have therefore received Christ Jesus the Lord, so walk ye in him: rooted and built up in him, and stablished in the faith, as ye have been taught, abounding therein with thanksgiving.

Christians do not subscribe to a philosophy or follow a discipline; we receive a person, *Christ Jesus*, and serve Him as Lord. All that we believe and do centers around Him. Three metaphors describe our relationship to Christ.

Christians *walk . . . in him.* This refers to the pervading manner of life. Every word, thought, and action are subjected to His will. It is as if the Christian takes the hand of Jesus and the two go everywhere together. This metaphor is an exhortation to live in constant fellowship with the Lord.

Christians are *rooted* in Christ. The first stage in the growth of a plant is the establishment of roots. All subsequent growth of the visible part of the plant depends on the nourishment it receives from the roots. If the plant is severed from its roots it will die. The first stage in the growth of a Christian is to be rooted in Christ. This happens when we believe in Jesus and fix our hearts on Him. We must then stay rooted in Christ, because if we forsake Him we will die. This metaphor is an exhortation to remain firmly connected to the Lord.

Christians are *built up in him*. This figure refers to construction, the building of life. We build our lives block by block as we cement in our personal selection of beliefs, attitudes, character traits, priorities, goals, and actions. Jesus' disciples must see that all these building blocks of life are derived from Him and harmonize with Him. This metaphor is an exhortation to incorporate into our lives only those things that come from Christ.

Speaking literally, Paul urged the Colossians to be *stablished in the faith, as ye have been taught*. He wanted them to have unwavering trust in the gospel as it was originally proclaimed to them, not as it was modified by false teachers. We obey this admonition today if we trust in the gospel as it is revealed in the Bible.

Such a person as described in these verses will naturally abound in *thanksgiving*.

B. Beware of Worldly Philosophy (v. 8)

8. Beware lest any man spoil you through philosophy and vain deceit, after the tradition of men, after the rudiments of the world, and not after Christ.

Many people, motivated by Satan, are opposed to Christ and seek to *spoil* (capture) Christians in this spiritual war. One way they do this is by entrapping Christians with deceptive *philosophy*, as they pretend to have knowledge that we don't have. Their teaching may sound plausible, but taken as a whole it is *not after Christ*. Some of it is based on the *tradition of men* and some is according to *the rudiments of the world*. That means principles and ideas that are worldly rather than godly.

One of the widespread philosophical notions of Paul's day was that the physical body is inherently evil and that the spirit is inherently good. This erroneous assumption led some early heretics to believe that Christ did not come into the world in human flesh. Many believed that men must purge themselves of the evil effects of the flesh by living a rigorously austere life. False teachers urged both of these ideas on the Colossians. (See 2:9, 23.)

How to Say It

COLOSSAE.   Ko-*loss*-ee.
EPAPHRAS.   *Ep*-uh-fras.

Teacher: The following material pertains to lesson aim 3.

Today's world does not lack for deceptive philosophies, which are only Satan's ancient lies put in new form and vocabulary. Probably the most pervasive worldly philosophy of Western civilization is the theory of evolution. As the basis for religion it produces secular humanism, which teaches that man is the supreme being in the universe. As the basis for a system of morality, it produces the law of the jungle, with every man seeking his own pleasure and prosperity at every one else's expense.

The theory of evolution contradicts all the basic teachings of the Bible. If evolution were true, it would mean that there is no Creator God, no such thing as sin or right or wrong, no purpose in the world, no life after death, and no Judgment Day.

Many other human philosophies also oppose God. The world's ideas regarding psychology, sex, power, pleasure, money, etc. are all contrary to the truth of God. Satan rules the world and fills it with his lies. He always lies. Though he may incorporate truth, he always does it in such a way as to end up with untruth. Never trust the thinking of the world. Trust Christ.

II. Christ Has Overcome the World (Colossians 2:9-15)

A. Christ's Authority (vv. 9, 10)

9. For in him dwelleth all the fulness of the Godhead bodily.

Teacher: This verse relates to lesson aim 1.

This verse asserts the incarnation of Christ in unmistakable terms. Christ is fully and completely divine, *for in him dwelleth all the fulness of the Godhead*. Godhead means the divine nature. Paul stated this thought more fully in verses 15-19 of chapter one. Because He is deity, He naturally has all the power and authority of God.

At the same time Christ is human, for He came *bodily*, that is, with a physical body. This doctrine that Christ is both divine and human corrects the false teaching that denied that Christ could have a physical body.

10. And ye are complete in him, which is the head of all principality and power.

Teacher: This verse relates to lesson aim 2.

visual 3

DECEPTIVE PHILOSOPHY·WORLDLY
LES·HUMAN TRADITION·OLD TEST
WORLDLY PRINCIPLES·DECEPTIVE
OLD TESTAME... ...ULATIONS·HU
GUARD YOUR FREEDOM IN CHRIST

reached the pinnacle of success, Hewlett-Packard chose to push ahead into the future with plans for new growth and expansion. It takes vision to make such a decision.

Paul demands this kind of vision of the Colossians. They must not be satisfied with past achievements. They are urged to enter fully into Jesus Christ who is the fullness of the Godhead bodily and so to become "complete in him."

Here is the way to achieve your full potential. You may have to forsake well-established, comfortable ways that seem beneficial and productive, but only in moving forward with Christ can you become all He wants you to be.

The future belongs to Him, and He invites you to share in all He offers.   —W. P.

Christ makes Christians *complete*. This word is replete with meanings. First, our nature is made complete. Christ restores what sin destroyed. Sin makes us spiritually incomplete because our spirits are dead within us, but Christ resurrects our spirits by infusing us with the Holy Spirit. Sin makes us rationally incomplete because our power of reason is clouded, but Christ enables us to understand the truth. Sin makes us morally incomplete because we do not know or do what is right, but Christ shows us righteousness and empowers us to do it. Sin makes us emotionally incomplete because it fills our hearts with selfishness and hatred, but Christ fills us with love. Sin makes us physically incomplete because our bodies are subject to death, but Christ conquered death and will clothe us in incorruptible bodies when He returns for us.

Second, Christ completely furnishes all the needs of Christians. He forgives and cleanses us and gives us of His righteousness. He reveals God's will to us. He gives power, hope, help, guidance, sustenance, restoration, reconciliation, and redemption.

The head of all principality and power. This refers to spiritual powers. Jesus is over them because He created them (Colossians 1:16). Anyone in a position of authority ought to be subject to Christ. If he leads us away from Christ's authority he is obviously out of place and not to be followed.

ACHIEVING YOUR POTENTIAL

Early in 1987 the giant Hewlett-Packard corporation began a reorganization process to meet the challenge of its competition in the electronics industry.

The two men who began this industrial empire could have rested on their achievements. These men with inventive genius, skill, and vision pioneered in the electronics field, and with unusual business acumen formed the company that is leader in the "chip" industry. Having

B. Christ's Deliverance (vv. 11-14)

Teacher: This section relates to lesson aim 2.

11. In whom also ye are circumcised with the circumcision made without hands, in putting off the body of the sins of the flesh by the circumcision of Christ.

Circumcision was commanded as a part of the Old Covenant between God and man. However, like so much of the Old Covenant, it was only a type, or an illustration, of the New Covenant of the gospel. Circumcision signifies separation. To the Israelites, it was a physical reminder of their separation from the peoples and idols of the world. The removal of the flesh also symbolized the fact that they were not to be ruled by their fleshly natures.

This Old Testament usage looked forward to the more complete separation from the world that is accomplished by Jesus Christ. This is a circumcision of the heart, not of the flesh. See Romans 2:28, 29. Thus it is done *without hands*. It signifies *putting off the body of the sins of the flesh*.

In Christ we undergo a spiritual circumcision, in which our spirits are freed from the bondage of the flesh. We now have the spiritual strength to resist the desires of the flesh. This is the true separation that physical circumcision anticipated but could not produce.

Since this circumcision of the heart is all that really matters, and since God no longer commands physical circumcision, the false teachers were in error to insist that the Colossians be circumcised.

12. Buried with him in baptism, wherein also ye are risen with him through the faith of the operation of God, who hath raised him from the dead.

It is *in baptism* that this circumcision, this cutting of the bondage of the flesh, occurs. Baptism is both a burial and a resurrection. Buried is the natural man who is dead in his trespasses and sins. Everything about a sinner is deathly. He is spiritually dead, morally dead, physically dying, destined for eternal death. We bury the physically dead; baptism is a burial of the spiritually dead.

But baptism also involves emerging from the water: it is resurrection. The person buried is raised to "walk in newness of life" (Romans 6:4) This transformation from a dead sinner to a living saint is not brought about by any magic in the water itself, of course. It is accomplished *through the faith of the operation of God, who hath raised him from the dead*. God supplies the power to make a Christian spiritually alive, but this power is received only when it is welcomed by the believer's faith. God supplies the strength to overcome the flesh, but the believer must decide to reject the flesh. God welcomes everyone, but one must turn to God in faith. The basis of faith is the resurrection. Since God raised Jesus from the dead, we believe that He can and will do the same for us if we come to Him.

13, 14. And you, being dead in your sins and the uncircumcision of your flesh, hath he quickened together with him, having forgiven you all trespasses; blotting out the handwriting of ordinances that was against us, which was contrary to us, and took it out of the way, nailing it to his cross.

And you is in emphatic position in the sentence. In this way Paul stressed that the spiritual circumcision, the spiritual burial and resurrection of which he spoke, had actually been accomplished in the Colossian Christians. They had been *dead* and uncircumcised, but as Christians they were *quickened*, or made alive, *together with him*, Christ. We Christians share in His resurrection and life.

Having forgiven you all trespasses. In addition to spiritual renewal, man needs renewal to the fellowship of God. This requires the forgiveness of man's sins. Paul illustrated God's forgiveness by comparing it with taking a parchment on which are listed all our violations of the law and simply wiping the handwriting clean. No record of our sins remains. Beyond this, the law itself was removed as an accuser of Christians, for God nailed it to the cross when Christ was crucified. As far as Christians are concerned, the law died with Christ.

C. The World's Power Destroyed (v. 15)

15. And having spoiled principalities and powers, he made a show of them openly, triumphing over them in it.

The imagery of this verse is that of a victorious conqueror parading his vanquished foes in a victory march. This indicates that *principalities and powers* refers to evil spiritual powers who are the enemies of God. The righteous triumph over these enemies came *in it:* that is, in Jesus' cross (v. 14). At the very moment they thought they won, Jesus defeated the power of Satan and his kingdom. In dying, Jesus abolished death and brought life and immortality to light (2 Timothy 1:10).

III. Christ Supersedes the World (Colossians 2:16-19)

A. Shadow Replaced With Reality (vv. 16, 17)

16. Let no man therefore judge you in meat, or in drink, or in respect of a holyday, or of the new moon, or of the sabbath days.

The things listed in this verse are regulations of the Old Testament law. People of Jewish heritage clung to these laws and insisted that the Christians in Colossae keep them. Paul boldly proclaimed that Christians are not to be judged on the basis of such regulations.

Let no man, whoever he may claim to be, *judge you*, or "pass judgment on you." As a Christian, do not be misguided or deluded, do not be so gullible as to believe that you must accept and follow whatever is insisted upon by whoever comes along. Rules about what to eat and drink, fasting, and the keeping of holy days—none of these are to be made binding on a Christian.

17. Which are a shadow of things to come; but the body is of Christ.

The reason that Christians are not obligated to keep the law is that the law has passed away. It was destined from the beginning to pass away because it was only a *shadow*, not the *body* or substance. It derived its existence from Christ, going before Him and revealing His form, but now that Christ has come the law has no more place. The arrival of the light of the world drove away the shadow. The purpose of the law was to show man God's will and God's nature, but Christ did that more perfectly than the law ever could. Now Christians follow a person, not a set of laws.

B. The False Replaced With the True (vv. 18, 19)

18. Let no man beguile you or your reward in a voluntary humility and worshipping of angels, intruding into those things which he hath not seen, vainly puffed up by his fleshly mind.

False teachers try to convince Christians that they cannot receive the *reward* they seek, eternal life, unless they accept the false teachings.

But accepting the false teaching is what causes a Christian to lose his reward!

Voluntary humility is false humility. It is humility put on public display. One who is truly humble will not call attention to his humility; indeed, he will not even call attention to himself. Yet false teachers are always in the limelight proclaiming their righteousness and meekness. Do not follow such people.

The second characteristic of false teaching that Paul mentioned is false worship. In the case of the false teaching that was troubling the church in Colossae, the false teachers were urging the worship *of angels.* This would be a denial of the adequacy of Christ. All false teachers put forth a system of belief that is the product of their own vain imaginations. Far from humbly accepting the revelation of God, they proudly substitute their own inventions. Do not believe anyone who claims to have knowledge of God or salvation that is not revealed in the Bible. This is the error of the many sects that have broken away from Christianity. Such groups typically have a guidebook or collection of teachings that replace the Bible.

19. And not holding the Head, from which all the body by joints and bands having nourishment ministered, and knit together, increaseth with the increase of God.

Using the figure of Christ being the *Head* and church being His *body,* Paul said that people who hold to these false teachings are like a part of the body that has lost connection with the head. Such people receive no guidance from Christ and have no connection to Him. We must not disconnect ourselves from Christ in order to join with them in their folly.

ACCEPTING POOR DIRECTIONS

Often we make mistakes unitentionally. It hurts when we fall innocently into wrongdoing, because we felt we were doing right. Consider these signs seen in different parts of the world and think about their unintentional misdirections.

In Tokyo a street sign reads, "When a passenger of the foot heave in sight, tottle the horn. Trumpet at them melodiously at first, but if they shall obstacles you passage, tottle them with vigor."

This sign is in front of a tailor shop in Jordan: "Order now your summers suit. Because a big rush we will execute customers in strict rotation."

We are amused because we know that these are innocent mistakes. They result from a misunderstanding of the proper usage of the English language.

Home Daily Bible Readings

Monday, Mar. 13—Paul Issues a Warning (Colossians 2:1-5)

Tuesday, Mar. 14—Be Rooted in Christ (Colossians 2:6-12)

Wednesday, Mar. 15—God Made You Alive (Colossians 2:13-17)

Thursday, Mar. 16—Live With Christ (Colossians 2:18-23)

Friday, Mar. 17—Put Away the Old Life (Colossians 3:5-11)

Saturday, Mar. 18—Put On the New Life (Colossians 3:12-17)

Sunday, Mar. 19—Live for Christ (Colossians 3:18—4:1)

Unfortunately, in the realm of religion too many do not know the Word of God, and they mistakenly teach as Biblical truth ideas that are foreign to God's revealed will. Paul cautions us to let no one cause us to lose our reward (we might add, whether by intention or by mistake). We must hold fast to Jesus and not be led astray by poor directions.   —W. P.

Conclusion
A. Be on the Alert

Christians today probably are beleaguered by more false teachers and proponents of the principles of the world than even the Colossian disciples were. World travel has spread every kind of religious cult to every country. Through the educational system and the media, people of all ages are constantly bombarded with the philosophies and vain, ungodly beliefs of the world.

We must be ever wary of this influence. We must constantly evaluate our attitudes and beliefs to see if they really are of God or if we have absorbed them from the world. Our only reliable means of doing this is by comparing what we believe and what others proclaim with the standard of the Bible. The Bible will always point us to God and to His Son Jesus Christ.

B. Prayer of a Disciple

Lord, we are always learning. We want to learn more about You and Your will. Give us wisdom to understand the Bible. Help us to be discerning in what we learn and believe. Help us detect and reject falsehood. Help us learn to live Your will. Amen.

C. Thought to Remember

Christ is sufficient to save us.

Learning by Doing

This page contains an alternate lesson plan emphasizing learning activities. Classes desiring such student involvement will find these suggestions helpful.

Learning Goals

After examining Colossians 2:6-19, the student will be able to:

1. Contrast the nature of the non-Christian with that of the Christian.

2. Explain why Christ has supreme authority in the life of the Christian.

3. Cite examples of legalistic requirements that are often, but mistakenly, urged upon Christians.

4. Express thanks to God for what he possesses in Christ.

Into the Lesson

Before classtime prepare the Word Find puzzle shown below. Give each person a copy.

WORD FIND

See if you can find fourteen words from the lesson text. These may be found going from left to right, right to left, top to bottom, bottom to top, or diagonally.

```
E S T A B L I S H E D P
B L O T T I N G E D P H
O U T X W D O U A A R I
E N A O E E T E A T P L
T O F A I T H P T U R O
E T A T N O A P S N I S
L Y L I D O B N A T R O
P E T F O R G I V E N P
M T U K R A R K P N P H
O R L E G D U J U O H Y
C A B A P T I S M R T O
W T R A D I T I O N S T
```

Words: *baptism, blotting, bodily, complete, established, faith, forgiven, head, judge, philosophy, rooted, sins, tradition, walk.*

After eight or ten minutes, show a completed Word Find. Remind the students that these are key words in the text for today.

Into the Word

Present the lesson background material from the "Introduction" section. Then have someone read the entire text aloud.

Form groups of three to five students each. Assign half of the groups to the first task below, and the other half to the second.

1. Advertisers often make use of "before and after" pictures as a way to entice us to buy whatever they are selling. Paul provides a striking "before and after" picture of the non-Christian/Christian in this text. Develop a chart outlining the characteristics of a non-Christian compared with a Christian.

2. The text for today contains reasons for the supremacy of Christ in the life of a Christian. List as many of these reasons as you can find.

Allow the groups eight to ten minutes to complete this task. When the groups are finished, let them report to the whole class. Use the reports and the outline provided in this book to cover the text for today.

Into Life

Ask the students whether they agree or disagree with the following statement: "Christ is sufficient to save." Let the students register their responses. Ask them why they answered as they did.

Select three pairs to develop the following role plays to examine the application of the text for today.

Role Play 1. You work with a man who has some interest in Christianity, but he has been taught many legalistic ideas about Christianity. One day he questions you about how you as a Christian feel you can go to movies. How would you use the teaching of this text to provide a response?

Role Play 2. Your neighbor has indicated some interest in Christianity. In a discussion with you, she states, "I would be willing to commit myself to Christianity if I could be assured that it makes any practical difference in a person's life." How would you respond?

Role Play 3. You are sitting beside a man on an airplane. During your conversation with him, he states, "Christianity is no different from Islam or Buddhism. Christ was another good man." How would you respond?

After each skit is presented, let the students suggest additional items that could have been mentioned.

Summarize the teaching of today's lesson. Suggest how thankful we need to be that we are new people in Christ. Distribute index cards to the students and ask them to write a prayer of thanks for their heritage in Christ.

Let's Talk It Over

The questions on this page are designed to encourage review of the lesson Scriptures and to promote discussion of the lesson by the class. The answers provided are only discussion starters. Let your class talk it over from there.

1. How have you become "rooted" in Christ and "stablished in the faith"? What provision is there in your church to make sure that happens? What more can you do, personally, to help new Christians?

Being "rooted" in Christ speaks of the quality of our faith. It means that we honestly look to Christ first as our source of truth and counsel in all matters of life. We become "stablished in the faith" as we are taught (v. 7), and as we practice Christ's teachings ("walk ye in him," v. 6).

The structured teaching programs of the church are important to this process. Preaching, Sunday school, home Bible studies, etc., all serve to increase knowledge and understanding. But at least of equal importance are the testimony and example of mature Christians. No matter what is taught in the classroom, new Christians will seldom exceed the level of faith and devotion demonstrated by those who have been Christians longer.

2. What current philosophies or ideas of man are most dangerous in terms of destroying true Christian faith? Why do you say so?

The lesson commentary (under verse 8) refers to the pervasiveness of the theory of evolution and to its detrimental effect upon the thinking and behavior of people today. Selfish materialism has made the accumulation of wealth the highest priority for many people. The idea that man is only a physical being, not answerable to any higher authority, has caused many to abandon all moral restraints. Without the prospect of eternal life stretching out before them, people are less willing to make sacrifices for the good of others.

3. What does it mean to say that we are made complete in Christ?

God's purpose in creating us was corrupted by sin. Sin destroyed our potential for fellowship with God. Sin made us subject to death. Sin blinded us to moral truth. Sin caused God's Spirit to depart from us. By His death, Christ has overcome the power of sin, and has reversed all of its deadly effects. In Christ all of God's intended purposes for us are fulfilled. Christians may be compared with the surgeon's scalpel that was used to peel potatoes, but now has been restored to its more noble purpose. We are like the old violin that everyone judged as worthless until the master musician proved it capable of producing beautiful music.

4. Looking at verses 11-14, how is our circumcision in Christ superior to the circumcision that was required of those under the Old Covenant? How do we become recipients of those blessings?

For the descendants of Abraham, circumcision was a distinguishing mark of God's ownership. It signified separation, separation from the other peoples of the world and separation from bondage to the fleshly nature. The problem was that there was no power in circumcision. It was a symbol of good intentions, but the fact is that human will is not strong enough to keep God's commands entirely.

The circumcision of Christ is a spiritual reality. In this separation the body of sin dies and is buried. We are truly set free from bondage to sin, and a new spirit is given us so that we may live in righteousness. The Bible makes our baptism the occasion for this circumcision. Baptism very aptly symbolizes death, burial, and resurrection. The receiving of this grace, however, is predicated upon our faith in the operation of God (v. 12).

5. How did Jesus spoil principalities and powers?

Principalities and powers refer to the evil spiritual powers arrayed against the purposes of God. When Jesus died on the cross, Satan seemed to have had defeated God. The promised Savior had been killed. But, that sacrificial death was the price paid that made possible the redemption of all who would believe.

6. What false standards of judgment are sometimes imposed upon Christians today?

Unfortunately, people often let matters of conscience, or even matters of preference, become tests of fellowship or measures of spirituality. Some examples are the observance (or nonobservance) of certain holidays, adherence to a particular style of worship, "acceptable" forms of dress, and participation in a time-honored agenda of services.

Risen With Christ

LESSON SCRIPTURE: Luke 24:1-7; Colossians 1:15-29; 3:1-4.

PRINTED TEXT: Luke 24:1-7; Colossians 1:15-20; 3:1-4.

Luke 24:1-7

1 Now upon the first day of the week, very early in the morning, they came unto the sepulchre, bringing the spices which they had prepared, and certain others with them.

2 And they found the stone rolled away from the sepulchre.

3 And they entered in, and found not the body of the Lord Jesus.

4 And it came to pass, as they were much perplexed thereabout, behold, two men stood by them in shining garments:

5 And as they were afraid, and bowed down their faces to the earth, they said unto them, Why seek ye the living among the dead?

6 He is not here, but is risen: remember how he spake unto you when he was yet in Galilee,

7 Saying, The Son of man must be delivered into the hands of sinful men, and be crucified, and the third day rise again.

Colossians 1:15-20

15 Who is the image of the invisible God, the firstborn of every creature:

16 For by him were all things created, that are in heaven, and that are in earth, visible and invisible, whether they be thrones, or dominions, or principalities, or powers: all things were created by him, and for him:

17 And he is before all things, and by him all things consist:

18 And he is the head of the body, the church: who is the beginning, the firstborn from the dead; that in all things he might have the preeminence.

19 For it pleased the Father that in him should all fulness dwell;

20 And, having made peace through the blood of his cross, by him to reconcile all things unto himself; by him, I say, whether they be things in earth, or things in heaven.

Colossians 3:1-4

1 If ye then be risen with Christ, seek those things which are above, where Christ sitteth on the right hand of God.

2 Set your affection on things above, not on things on the earth.

3 For ye are dead, and your life is hid with Christ in God.

4 When Christ, who is our life, shall appear, then shall ye also appear with him in glory.

GOLDEN TEXT: If ye then be risen with Christ, seek those things which are above, where Christ sitteth on the right hand of God.—Colossians 3:1.

Letters From Prison

Unit 2: Colossians— Christ the Lord (Lessons 2-4)

Lesson Aims

As a result of this lesson students should:
1. Express their belief in the fact that Jesus was raised from the dead.
2. Acknowledge Christ's authority over all creation, over life and death, and over them.
3. Name two ways in which Christians will share with Christ when He returns.
4. Explain several practical ways in which Christians can set their minds on things above.

Lesson Outline

INTRODUCTION
  A. Don't Live in the Grave
  B. Lesson Background
 I. THE RISEN CHRIST (Luke 24:1-7)
  A. The Tomb Is Empty! (vv. 1-3)
  B. The Lord Is Alive! (vv. 4-7)
      Transformation
 II. THE PREEMINENT CHRIST (Colossians 1:15-20)
  A. The Firstborn of Creation (vv. 15-17)
  B. The Firstborn of the Church
      (vv. 18-20)
 III. GUIDANCE FROM ABOVE (Colossians 3:1-4)
  A. Seek Heavenly Things (vv. 1, 2)
      Finding a "Mind-Set"
  B. Sharing Life and Glory (vv. 3, 4)
CONCLUSION
  A. Live as One Who Has Been Raised
  B. Prayer of One Risen With Christ
  C. Thought to Remember

Display visual 4 from the visuals/learning resources packet. It is shown on page 261.

Introduction

A. Don't Live in the Grave

Late in Jesus' ministry, Lazarus, one of Jesus' dearest followers and friends, became sick and died. When Jesus arrived at the place of burial, He had the tomb opened and commanded Lazarus to come forth. Immediately he returned to life and emerged from the tomb.

How much desire do you suppose Lazarus had to return to that grave? He may have taken people to see the empty tomb and to tell them the account of the miracle, but it is absurd to think that he missed being in the tomb.

This lesson is titled "Risen With Christ." One main point of the lesson is that Christians have experienced a spiritual resurrection. We who were dead in our sins have been made alive together with Christ. Now if we have been brought out of the grave of sin, we ought to look to the things that pertain to life with God.

It seems, though, that people have a strong tendency to look back fondly on the time when they were in the grave of sin. They remember the thrill of their favorite sins. They feel the urge to give in to selfishness. How absurd! Aren't these the sins that condemned us to death? Aren't these the sins that held us powerless in their grasp? We must leave these things behind. We must not live in the grave.

B. Lesson Background

Our lesson text contains selections from two books. The first is taken from the Gospel of Luke. This passage tells the story of the women who discovered Jesus' empty tomb on the resurrection morning. The purpose of this text is to introduce the historical fact of Christ's resurrection.

The other two passages continue our study from Colossians. The first of these describes Christ's preeminence: His glory, authority, and exaltation before and after His earthly mission. The second passage explains that Christians will share Christ's eternal life, and will share His glory. This being true, Paul exhorts Christians to set their thoughts and hearts on Heavenly things and not on the earthly.

I. The Risen Christ (Luke 24:1-7)

A. The Tomb Is Empty! (vv. 1-3)

Teacher: This section pertains to lesson aim 1.

1. Now upon the first day of the week, very early in the morning, they came unto the sepulchre, bringing the spices which they had prepared, and certain others with them.

Those who came to the sepulcher are identified in Luke 23:55 as the women who came with Jesus from Galilee. Luke specifically mentioned Mary Magdalene, Joanna, and Mary the mother of James, and stated that other women were there as well (Luke 24:10).

These women followed Joseph of Arimathea when he took Jesus' body from the cross and placed it in the tomb. They then went and prepared spices and perfumes to anoint Jesus' body according to their custom, but, in observance of the Fourth Commandment, they waited until the Sabbath Day was over before returning to the tomb. Because of their eagerness to perform this tender act of love, the women were on their way to the tomb *very early in the morning* on the first day of the week and arrived there at the first light of day. These women had accompanied Jesus and ministered to many of His needs and those of the apostles. Their contribution was invaluable. Their devotion was unsurpassed.

2. And they found the stone rolled away from the sepulchre.

The tomb in which Jesus was laid had been sealed by rolling a large stone in front of it. On the way to the tomb the women wondered whom they could get to remove the stone (Mark 16:3), but when they arrived they found that the stone was already rolled aside.

3. And they entered in, and found not the body of the Lord Jesus.

The women entered the tomb and found it empty: Jesus was not there!

B. The Lord Is Alive! (vv. 4-7)

4, 5a. And it came to pass, as they were much perplexed thereabout, behold, two men stood by them in shining garments: and as they were afraid, and bowed down their faces to the earth.

The women were taken by surprise to find the tomb empty, with the result that *they were much perplexed.* They did not know what to think. They had no idea what had happened to Jesus. It is not hard to imagine the mixture of surprise, dismay, and puzzlement that filled their hearts.

After a few moments, their shock was compounded as *two men stood by them in shining garments.* These were angels (Matthew 28:5). They apparently did not walk in through the door, but just appeared suddenly. The shining garments they wore revealed their Heavenly origin. The women reacted as we probably would have. They were afraid, and they dropped to the ground before the awe-inspiring beings.

5b, 6a. They said unto them, Why seek ye the living among the dead? He is not here, but is risen.

This is one of the most important announcements in the history of the world. Jesus conquered death. It had no more claim over Him. He would never die again. Jesus established His authority over death and His ability to bestow life on whomsoever He chooses.

6b, 7. Remember how he spake unto you when he was yet in Galilee, saying, The Son of man must be delivered into the hands of sinful men, and be crucified, and the third day rise again.

The angels reminded the women that Jesus had prophesied this very thing. Luke recorded three such prophecies in 9:22, 44 and 18:31-33.

How to Say It

ARIMATHEA. Air-uh-muh-*thee*-uh (*th* as in *thin*).
MAGDALENE. *Mag*-duh-leen or Mag-duh-lee-nee.

All had happened exactly according to God's plan. Christ's purpose from the beginning was to come into the world and give up His life as a sacrifice for man's sins, and then to rise from the dead to conquer death. Now the risen Christ has been exalted to God's right hand and given all the glory and authority that are His due.

How quickly the sorrows and fears of the women were turned to ecstatic, overwhelming joy, joy almost too great to believe or bear! That same transformation takes place whenever someone comes to believe in the risen Christ today. Before a person knows Christ, the end of his life is certain death. He has no hope of anything beyond it. A person may face death with calm resignation or with trembling, but in the end there is only despair. However, when a person learns and believes that Jesus Christ rose from the dead never to die again, and that He offers that same life to everyone who will follow Him, joy floods the soul. Death is not the end!

TRANSFORMATION

One of the glories of God's creation is the monarch butterfly. It begins its nine-month life as a tiny egg on a milkweed plant. That is the only food supply for the larva that emerges from the egg. In fifteen days the caterpillar increases its weight twenty-seven hundred times. At that time its skin begins to harden. Before movement becomes impossible the caterpillar attaches itself to a protected place above the ground. Within fifteen days a marvelous transformation takes place, and the beautiful black and orange monarch butterfly emerges.

Soon it is on the way back north after wintering in the Florida peninsula, the Gulf Coast, or the Monterey-Santa Cruz coastal region of California. It will mate, and the life cycle will continue for this beautiful demonstration of God's love and creative power.

Isn't this an exhibition of God's will for transformation and new life for man? Jesus lived a short life of beauty and power, and through His death and resurrection He gave to all the possibility of new life and glory in Him. We can be changed from an insignificant existence into His likeness, to live forever. He is risen, and so can we be in Him!   —W. P.

II. The Preeminent Christ
(Colossians 1:15-20)

A. The Firstborn of Creation (vv. 15-17)

Teacher: The material discussed under this point of the outline pertains to lesson aim 2.

These three verses describe the glory, authority, and power that the Son had even before the creation of the world.

15. Who is the image of the invisible God, the firstborn of every creature.

The subject of this verse is God's dear Son, Jesus Christ (v. 13). Jesus *is the image of the invisible God.* Man was created "in" the image of God, but Christ *is* the image—the exact likeness. This alone puts Christ above all. To see Jesus is to see God (John 14:8, 9). Jesus said, "He that seeth me seeth him that sent me" (John 12:45).

Jesus is also described as *the firstborn of every creature.* This does not mean that Jesus was the first created being, as some false teachers believed. Christ was not created, for Christ himself made everything that was made. He has existed eternally just as God has, for He is God (John 1:1). Paul's thought here is that Jesus existed before any of the created things and that He is in authority over them. Paul makes his meaning clear in verses 16 and 17, which are essentially a definition of the term *firstborn.*

16, 17. For by him were all things created, that are in heaven, and that are in earth, visible and invisible, whether they be thrones, or dominions, or principalities, or powers: all things were created by him, and for him: and he is before all things, and by him all things consist.

Paul listed four ways in which Christ is firstborn, preeminent, over creation.

First, Christ is the Creator of all things. This includes everyone and everything except the Father and the Holy Spirit, who have existed eternally along with the Son. *Thrones, dominions, principalities,* and *powers* likely refer to spirit-forces of the unseen world. Paul did not explain each of these terms. He simply stated that whatever ranks of spiritual beings exist, they were all originally created by the Son.

Second, Christ is the owner and ruler of all things. This is the significance of the statement that all things were created *for him.* All things were created that they might serve and glorify Him and fulfill His purposes.

Third, Christ existed *before all things.* There was a time when everything in Heaven and earth did not exist, but there has never been a time when the Son did not exist.

Fourth, Christ sustains all things: *by him all things consist.* This means that all creation owes its continued existence to the Son who created it in the first place. If He did not continue to will its existence, it would cease.

The importance of these four points is this. The Son (along with the Father and Spirit) exists eternally. He owes His existence to no one, and does not depend on anyone or anything else. He is self-sustaining and self-determining.

In contrast to this, every angelic being and every human being receives his existence from Christ and depends on Him to continue in existence. Christ is totally independent; we creatures are totally dependent on Him.

No man or woman of us can stand before Christ and say, "I owe You nothing. I am independent of You. I don't need You." All were created by the Lord, owe their very existence to Him, and depend on Him for the continuance of life. If we recognize this we will give Christ the respect that is His due. We will acknowledge our reliance on Him, and supplicate Him for our needs. We will glorify Him for His goodness to us, and we will obey Him.

B. The Firstborn of the Church
(vv. 18-20)

The previous verses described the preeminence that Christ had before creation and over creation. These three verses describe the preeminence that Christ receives because of His work in redeeming creation. One feature is that He took on human life when He came into the world. He did not have this existence prior to His conception in the virgin. As the unique God-man, Christ again receives preeminence.

18. And he is the head of the body, the church: who is the beginning, the firstborn from the dead; that in all things he might have the preeminence.

If we compare *the church* with a human body, then Christ is *the head.* All parts of the body have use and function, but all parts are directed and coordinated by the head. Indeed, if some part of the body loses connection with the head then it also loses its usefulness. This shows us the preeminence of the head in regard to the body. In the same way, Christ is preeminent over the church. He guides and directs the church and gives it life.

Every Christian must maintain the connection to his head, Jesus Christ. We must accept our orders from Him as the muscles of the body respond to the head. We do this as we obey His Word and as we follow the leaders and support the work of the church. If we refuse to do this we become a useless liability to the Lord.

Each congregation must also maintain the connection to the Lord. Churches must always

be sure that they devote their energy and resources to the works the Lord designated, such
as evangelism, spiritual nurture, encouragement, and benevolence.

Paralleling the thought of verses 15-17, Paul
next called Jesus *the beginning, the firstborn
from the dead.* When Christ died and then came
forth from the dead, He came forth as a man
whom death could never touch again. As such,
He was the first to be born from death into eternal life. He opened the way for a vast multitude
to follow Him into the eternal presence of the
Father. Because He was both the first man to
stand before the Father, and because He opened
the way for others at the cost of His own sacrifice, He fittingly has *the preeminence.*

**19. For it pleased the Father that in him
should all fulness dwell.**

This statement encompasses all the ways in
which the Father bestowed preeminence on the
Son. Jesus said that all power had been given
Him in Heaven and in earth (Matthew 28:18).
Revelation lists power, riches, wisdom,
strength, honor, glory, and blessing as some of
the things that the Son received (5:9-13).

**20. And, having made peace through the
blood of his cross, by him to reconcile all things
unto himself; by him, I say, whether they be
things in earth, or things in heaven.**

The blood of Christ, shed on the cross, produced *peace* between God and man. There was
no peace so long as man stood guilty before
God, but when Jesus paid the penalty for our
sins it allowed God to forgive all who call on the
name of the Lord. Through the work of Christ,
God was able *to reconcile all things unto himself,*
that is, restore them to His favor.

How wonderful it is to have peace with God!
Christians are not at war with God: we have surrendered to His will. We are not burdened with
guilt and shame, because Christ has cleansed
us. We do not fear His wrath, because we have
been forgiven. John said that Christians should
look forward to the judgment with confidence,
even boldness (1 John 2:28; 4:17). Jesus' sacrifice on the cross makes all this possible.

III. Guidance From Above
(Colossians 3:1-4)

A. Seek Heavenly Things (vv. 1, 2)

**1, 2. If ye then be risen with Christ, seek
those things which are above, where Christ sitteth on the right hand of God. Set your affection
on things above, not on things on the earth.**

Paul was not raising a question as to whether
the Colossian Christians were *risen with Christ*
or not; he was making a statement that they

visual 4

Raised with Christ
to share His glory,
we should no longer
seek earthly goals.

were indeed risen with Him. Though our bodies
are still perishing, our spirits have already received the quickening that Jesus offers (see Colossians 2:12).

This being the case, Paul exhorted the Colossians to *seek those things which are above,* that is,
in Heaven, where Christ is. He has in mind such
things as truth, harmony, sincerity, justice, generosity, kindness. The Heavenly things should
be the most important to us. The *things on the
earth*—such as sensual pleasure, money, luxury,
comfort, praise—should have no place in our
affections.

FINDING A "MIND-SET"

A visitor was leaning on the fence around a
field, while he watched an old farmer plowing
with a mule. After a while, the visitor said, "I
don't like to tell you how to run your business,
but you could save yourself a lot of work by
saying, 'Gee and Haw' to the mule instead of
tugging on those lines." The farmer paused and
wiped his face with his handkerchief. Then he
said, "Reckon you're right, but this mule kicked
me five years ago and I ain't said a word to it
since. Until he apologizes we're not on speaking
terms."

That's a "mind-set." It is not the one we
should have or encourage, but it is fixing one's
mind on something and holding to it.

In writing to the Colossians Paul says, "Set
your affection on the things above, not on things
on the earth" (3:2). This upward "mind-set"
could have immediately solved the old farmer's
problem. By dwelling on the hurt, he kept himself from the cure.

Some of us suffer from the same difficulty.
With our minds set on the things of the world
we cause ourselves unnecessary work, isolation,
and pain. The wrong "mind set" is disastrous
but the mind set on the Lord brings joy and spiritual maturity.   —W. P.

B. Sharing Life and Glory (vv. 3, 4)

Teacher: This section pertains to lesson aim 3.

**3. For ye are dead, and your life is hid with
Christ in God.**

Christians are *dead* to the principles and control of the world (2:20). We put our sinful natures to death when we turn to Christ and become united with Him. From that dead man Christ raises a new and living one. Paul here described that life as being *hid with Christ in God*.

While Christians are alive in this world we do enjoy to a limited extent the life that is found in Christ. We are made spiritually alive, we are alive unto God, we know and understand spiritual truth, etc. However, we do not enjoy the fullness of life as Christ will bestow it upon us in eternity. Our perfect and endless life with a perfected spirit and glorified body must await Christ's return. Until that time it is hidden with Christ in Heaven, existing in His promise and His power, and in the purposes of God. And this is the Christian's hope, which enhances his existence and lessens suffering.

4. When Christ, who is our life, shall appear, then shall ye also appear with him in glory.

Christ *is our life* because He is the one who holds the power and authority to bestow life. He is the one who has given us spiritual life. And He it is who sustains both.

Christ *shall appear* at His second coming, when He returns to gather together those who belong to Him. At that time we will *appear with him in glory*. Speaking of this same event in the letter to the Philippians, Paul said Jesus "will transform the body of our humble state into conformity with the body of His glory, by the exertion of the power that He has even to subject all things to Himself" (3:21, *New American Standard Bible*). We will both be with Him in glory, and we shall share His glory.

Conclusion

A. Live as One Who Has Been Raised

Teacher: This section pertains to lesson aim 4.

Christians have been delivered from the power of sin in many ways. In our lesson this is called being risen with Christ. This means that we are delivered from the penalty of sin, death; we are delivered from the guilt of sin; we are delivered from the control of sin. However, we are not delivered from the allurement of sin. So long as we are in this life, sin will always have some way to attract us. But we will be better able to resist sin's allurement if we remember how repulsive all sin is to God and try to gain that view of sin ourselves.

Following Paul's instruction to the Colossians will help us gain this godly point of view. He told them to set their minds and hearts on the things above. The more we think about such

Home Daily Bible Readings

Monday, Mar. 20—Jesus Appears to the Women (Luke 24:1-12)
Tuesday, Mar. 21—Discouraged Followers (Luke 24:13-27)
Wednesday, Mar. 22—Jesus Makes Himself Known (Luke 24:28-35)
Thursday, Mar. 23—Jesus Appears to His Disciples (Luke 24:36-44)
Friday, Mar. 24—Jesus Instructs His Disciples (Luke 24:45-53)
Saturday, Mar. 25—Christ's Work Continues (Colossians 1:15-20)
Sunday, Mar. 26—Raised With Christ (Colossians 1:21-29; 3:1-4)

things as purity, compassion, kindness, forgiveness, humility, truth, and love, and come to see their beauty, the less attractive such things as immorality, impurity, selfishness, anger, malice, lying, and pride will be.

Beyond this, we must fix our minds' eyes on those things that are invisible to our physical eyes, namely, the eternal life and glory that Christ will give to us when He returns. To live forever without pain or sorrow, to be exalted to reign with Christ, to share in His glory—these are of such surpassing value that nothing this world offers can begin to equal them. The more we keep this in mind, the less tempted we will be to sell our souls for the perishing things of the world.

B. Prayer of One Risen With Christ

Eternal Father, how thankful we are that Christ endured death that we might be forgiven, and that He conquered death that we might have hope. We thank You that our eternal resurrection has begun already with the raising of our spirits by the power of Your Spirit. Help us see the ugliness of sin so that we will not be lured by it. Help us to see the beauty of life with You so that we will never forsake it. In the name of Jesus we pray. Amen.

C. Thought to Remember

"It is a trustworthy statement:
  For if we died with Him, we shall also
    live with Him;
  If we endure, we shall also reign with Him;
  If we deny Him, He also will deny us;
  If we are faithless, He remains faithful;
    for He cannot deny Himself."
(2 Timothy 2:11-13, *New American Standard Bible*)

Learning by Doing

This page contains an alternate lesson plan emphasizing learning activities. Classes desiring such student involvement will find these suggestions helpful.

Learning Goals

As a result of studying this lesson based on Luke 24:1-7 and Colossians 1:15-20; 3:1-4, the pupils will be able to:

1. Explain the significance of the resurrection of Jesus Christ in establishing our hope of eternal life.

2. List reasons why Christ is preeminent in all things.

3. Select a way to live as one who has been raised from death to eternal life.

Into the Lesson

Play a cassette tape of Easter music as the pupils enter the classroom on this resurrection morning. Use the triumphant songs that create a joyful, expectant mood. As the class members arrive, call their attention to the word *risen* that you have printed vertically on a sheet of newsprint or on the chalkboard. Ask them to complete the acrostic with words they associate with the resurrection of Christ. (The words shown below are included as a teacher help.)

ACROSTIC

R—aised from the dead
I—n Heaven now
S—on of God
E—xciting
N—ew life

Allow the students five or six minutes to complete this. Then complete a master acrostic on the chalkboard using the responses of the class members.

Make the transition into the Bible study by stating that the lesson will examine the significance of the resurrection of Jesus to the Christian.

Into the Word

Briefly present the material in the "Introduction" section of the lesson. Then read Luke 24:1-7 aloud.

Give each of the students a copy of the questions below. Ask each to read Colossians 1:15-20 and 3:1-4 and jot down his answers to the questions.

1. Colossians 1:15-20 states several facts about Christ that establish His preeminence over everyone and everything. What are they? (All things were created by Him, all things were cre-

ated for Him, He existed before all things, He holds all things together, He is head of the church, He is resurrected from the dead, by Him we are reconciled to God.)

2. How significant is Christ's resurrection in establishing our hope of eternal life? (It is the basis of our hope. If Christ had not been victorious over death, we would still be dead in our sins.)

3. Colossians 3:1-4 gives a general principle regarding a Christian's conduct. What is it? (We are to set our hearts on things above, rather than on earthly things.)

4. Colossians 3:1-4 further identifies the promises that the Christian has because of Christ's resurrection. What are they? (Our lives are hidden in Christ now, and we will appear with Him in glory when He appears once again.)

Allow the students four to six minutes to complete this. Then use the questions and the commentary material to explain the meaning of the lesson text.

Into Life

Develop a discussion using the following questions.

1. Suppose that you were discussing Christian issues with a Jehovah's Witness who believes that Christ is a created son of God. How would you use this text today to establish the deity of Christ?

2. What would you say to one who states that the resurrection cannot be a possibility, and really isn't that important anyway?

3. How would you respond to one who says that being a Christian provides no benefit to the individual?

4. How do you respond to the truth of the resurrection personally?

5. What difference does the resurrection make to your hopes and aspirations?

6. How can we express our thanks to God for the hope that we have because of the resurrection?

Read 2 Timothy 2:11-13. Conclude the session by singing (or reading the texts of) Easter songs that emphasize the victory that is ours in Christ Jesus because of His resurrection. Conclude with a time of prayer. Encourage as many as will to share in their expressions of thanksgiving to God for their hope in Christ Jesus.

Let's Talk It Over

*The questions on this page are designed to encourage review of the lesson
Scriptures and to promote discussion of the lesson by the class. The answers
provided are only discussion starters. Let your class talk it over from there.*

**1. Would the stone at the opening of the tomb
have prevented Jesus from leaving the tomb?
Why was the stone rolled away?**

The apostle John reported that in the evening
of the same day Jesus arose, the disciples were
together behind closed doors, and Jesus simply
appeared among them (John 20:19). This demonstrates that His resurrected body was not con-
strained by physical barriers. It seems likely that
He could have left even a sealed tomb.

Some think the stone was rolled away so the
world could look in and see that the tomb was
empty. The empty tomb was God's eloquent sermon for the morning of that first day of the
week. "He is not here, but is risen" (Luke 24:6).

**2. Why is it not plausible that the Jewish au-
thorities moved the body of Jesus, or that the
disciples stole the body?**

The Jewish authorities were very interested in
making sure that the body was not disturbed.
They even requested that a Roman watch be
posted at the tomb, and had the tomb sealed, to
make sure that no one tampered with the body.
Even if it were possible for them to have con-
cealed the body, they certainly would have
brought forward the body, or some other evidence, to squelch the preaching of the disciples
that Jesus arose from the dead.

In order for the disciples to have stolen the
body, they would have had to overpower the
Roman guards who had been posted at the tomb.
They would have had to maneuver the large
stone away from the tomb and carry off the body
without being apprehended or even seen.
Within just fifty days these disciples would be
proclaiming publicly in the streets of Jerusalem
that Jesus arose from the dead. Many would suffer a martyr's death defending that claim. If the
disciples had stolen the body, why would they
risk death to defend a claim they would have
known was false?

**3. Is there any honor to a patriarch who is
responsible for a family's growth and material
well-being? How does this relate to Christ's preeminence as the "firstborn of every creature"?**

Think of someone such as Henry Ford, who
created a fortune that is now blessing the fourth
and fifth generations of his descendants (not to

mention the thousands of others who have been
enriched more indirectly by the work of this
man). We are glad to give honor to someone who
is the wellspring of blessing to so many.

Our text testifies to several reasons why Jesus
Christ is worthy of glory and honor. One of these
is His place of preeminence over all creation. He
is the agent of creation. He is the source of all
that we are and all that we have. If we are grateful to parents, grandparents, or others who have
contributed to our life, how much more should
we be grateful to Christ!

**4. If Christ is the head of the church, what is
the lesson for the Christians who make up the
rest of the body?**

To compare the church to the human body is
an easily understood analogy. One's head, as the
reasoning center, gives commands to the rest of
the body. The other parts of the body cooperate
in following the instructions of the head in
order to accomplish the desired result. As members of the body, we obey the Head, Christ, in
order to accomplish His objectives.

**5. What does it mean to call Jesus the "first-
born from the dead"?**

The Bible tells of several who were raised
from the dead, some prior to Jesus' resurrection.
We could say, however, that these were only re-
vived from death, since each, so far as we know,
went on to die at a later time. When Jesus arose
it was to eternal life. He arose to be glorified. He
would never die again. To call Him the "firstborn" implies that there will be others. He has
opened the way from death to eternal life for
those who accept Him as Lord.

**6. How does life change for those who "seek
those things which are above"?**

We who are "risen with Christ" see things
from the perspective of those who are living
eternal life. We fully expect to be glorified with
Christ and dwell with Him forever. With that
outlook, the cares of this world diminish in importance considerably. We can be more tolerant
of others. We can remain peaceful in the face of
trouble. We are more resistant to greed or the
coveting of material things. We are more likely
to attend to matters of eternal significance.

To Live Is Christ

LESSON SCRIPTURE: Philippians 1:1-26.

PRINTED TEXT: Philippians 1:12-26.

Apr
2

Philippians 1:12-26

12 But I would ye should understand, brethren, that the things which happened unto me have fallen out rather unto the furtherance of the gospel;

13 So that my bonds in Christ are manifest in all the palace, and in all other places;

14 And many of the brethren in the Lord, waxing confident by my bonds, are much more bold to speak the word without fear.

15 Some indeed preach Christ even of envy and strife; and some also of good will:

16 The one preach Christ of contention, not sincerely, supposing to add affliction to my bonds:

17 But the other of love, knowing that I am set for the defense of the gospel.

18 What then? notwithstanding, every way, whether in pretense, or in truth, Christ is preached; and I therein do rejoice, yea, and will rejoice.

19 For I know that this shall turn to my salvation through your prayer, and the supply of the Spirit of Jesus Christ,

20 According to my earnest expectation and my hope, that in nothing I shall be ashamed, but that with all boldness, as always, so now also Christ shall be magnified in my body, whether it be by life, or by death.

21 For to me to live is Christ, and to die is gain.

22 But if I live in the flesh, this is the fruit of my labor: yet what I shall choose I wot not.

23 For I am in a strait betwixt two, having a desire to depart, and to be with Christ; which is far better:

24 Nevertheless to abide in the flesh is more needful for you.

25 And having this confidence, I know that I shall abide and continue with you all for your furtherance and joy of faith;

26 That your rejoicing may be more abundant in Jesus Christ for me by my coming to you again.

GOLDEN TEXT: For to me to live is Christ, and to die is gain.—Philippians 1:21.

Letters From Prison
Unit 3: Philippians—
Life in Christ (Lesson 5-8)

Lesson Aims

This study should equip each student to:

1. Tell the circumstances out of which Paul wrote to the Philippians.

2. Show how some recent experience has helped, or can help, the student to serve Christ.

3. Become more free to talk about Jesus with his family, friends, and neighbors.

Lesson Outline

INTRODUCTION

    A. How Do You Stay So Cheerful?

    B. Lesson Background

 I. CHRIST IS SERVED (Philippians 1:12-18)

    A. The Military Hears of Him (vv. 12, 13)

    B. The Church Speaks of Him (v. 14)

    C. Despite Mixed Motives, the Gospel Is Preached (vv. 15-18)

II. CHRIST WILL BE SERVED (Philippians 1:19-26)

    A. Paul Will Benefit (v. 19)

    B. Christ Will Be Glorified (vv. 20, 21)

     Unconquerable

    C. Life Will Be Fulfilled (vv. 22-24)

    D. The Church Will Benefit (vv. 25, 26)

     A Purpose for Living

CONCLUSION

    A. Enjoy It Now

    B. Prayer

    C. Thought to Remember

Display visual 5 from the visuals/learning resources packet and let it remain before the class throughout this session. It is shown on page 269.

Introduction

A. How Do You Stay So Cheerful?

"How do you stay so cheerful?"

You may never have asked that question directly, because the circumstances haven't invited you to be so bold and personal. Many times, though, it has come to your mind as you have talked with someone who seemed genuinely to enjoy life, and to help others to enjoy life, in the face of serious problems with health, finances, or family.

Yet in the face of trial your friend has smiled, and not with a practiced expression put on like a garment for public display. This person really enjoys life, with an eagerness that reaches out to grasp each new day as it becomes available. How does he do it?

Obviously, he or she does not do it alone. He has help—help from God and from God's people. He has discovered that contentment, real contentment in any and all circumstances, is an important part of what he can achieve through Christ who enables him (Philippians 4:13).

The apostle Paul was that kind of person. His Christian friends at Philippi were wonderful people who helped him to be that way. His letter to them was designed, in turn, to help them toward the same accomplishment in Christ.

B. Lesson Background

"As cold water is to a thirsty soul,
so is good news from a far country."

           —Proverbs 25:25

The Christians at Philippi had been thirsty for news—any kind of news—from their beloved apostle Paul. He it was who had first brought them the good news of God's love in Christ, and had shown them His way of salvation (Acts 16:11-40). In doing so, Paul and his companions had undergone afflictions and imprisonment, along with enjoying good reception for the gospel and the establishment of a substantial church.

From Philippi Paul had gone on to Thessalonica, where he had met with more rough treatment, and the church at Philippi had sent money to help him (Philippians 4:15, 16). Afterward, when Paul had occasion to travel between Greece and Asia Minor, Philippi provided a stopping place for him.

Now, a dozen years after those first meetings, Paul was imprisoned at Rome. Word reached Philippi that he was continuing his evangelistic labors, receiving visitors in the rented dwelling where he was permitted to stay, with soldiers probably chained to him. Gifts from Philippi helped with such expenses as rental payments. One substantial gift was delivered to Paul by Epaphroditus, who stayed for a time to help Paul in his work (Philippians 4:18; 2:25-30). During that time Epaphroditus fell seriously ill, and the news of that illness reached his friends back home, to their dismay. They also seem to have heard of a new and threatening change in Paul's circumstance, such as his being moved from his own dwelling to the military guard area in the Roman praetorium.

To ease their anxieties, therefore, Paul wrote to the Philippians, sending the letter by Epaphroditus as he returned home. It is a friendly, as well as pastoral, letter, full of gratitude and warm greetings. It includes virtually no word of rebuke, but fervent exhortation that his friends live in harmony among themselves, loving one another as they have loved him. It breathes joyful confidence in Christ, and urges the same thankful joy upon its readers.

Background Scripture for our lesson begins with the beginning of the book. The first two verses express the apostle's greeting to the church with its local leaders. Verses 3 to 6 convey gratitude for the Philippians' friendship and Paul's confidence in their Christian steadfastness. Verses 7 and 8 assure them of his continuing affectionate interest in their welfare. Verses 9 to 11 constitute a prayer for the Philippians' advancement in love, understanding, purity, and fruitfulness. Then comes the report they have been so anxious to hear: how is Paul getting along?

I. Christ Is Served
(Philippians 1:12-18)

It has become evident in the earlier verses of the chapter that the supreme interest of the writer and the readers alike lay in the progress of the gospel. Personal affairs, immediately important as they were, took nonetheless a lower place in their concern.

A. The Military Hears of Him
(vv. 12, 13)

12. But I would ye should understand, brethren, that the things which happened unto me have fallen out rather unto the furtherance of the gospel.

The subject is introduced in such a way as to emphasize its importance as a purpose for Paul's writing. *The things which happened* are not named. The phrase could cover the whole range of several years' experience. It could refer to some recent change in his circumstances. It would seem to refer especially to his status as a prisoner. However that might affect him personally, it had turned to advantage for the gospel, and that was of first importance.

13. So that my bonds in Christ are manifest in all the palace, and in all other places.

"It has become known throughout the whole praetorian guard and to all the rest that my imprisonment is for Christ" *(Revised Standard Version)*. The praetorium (the word translated *palace*) was first the military headquarters of a Roman camp and then the men who were stationed there. Prisoners of state could be kept there, and soldiers could be sent from there to guard prisoners elsewhere. Paul's situation, therefore, was such as to bring him into contact with the elite of Roman soldiery. To all such,

and to all others to whom they might report, it was perfectly clear that Paul's relationship to Christ, rather than any wrongdoing on his part, was the cause of his imprisonment. That public knowledge, coupled with continuous teaching and preaching, did much to advertise the gospel.

Even the twentieth-century news media call favorable attention to Christianity at times when some hitherto unknown person is cast by accident or tragedy into the public gaze and is found by his or her reaction to be a firm and consistent believer. Tragedies are certainly not public relations gimmicks for the gospel, but the gospel does not shrink from the bright light of public attention.

B. The Church Speaks of Him (v. 14)

14. And many of the brethren in the Lord, waxing confident by my bonds, are much more bold to speak the word without fear.

While Paul was using his contacts in the praetorium to maximum effect, his brethren were carrying the message where he could no longer go. Paul had survived imprisonment. He was still alive and proclaiming the message. Perhaps they could fare as well. Paul was facing his situation with quiet courage. They could do the same, and with greater freedom. They might even do so the more easily since there were now Christians in Caesar's household (Philippians 4:22). The Christians' love of Christ and the gospel, stirred by apostolic teaching and example, had overcome their fear (compare 1 John 4:18).

C. Despite Mixed Motives, the Gospel Is Preached (vv. 15-18)

15. Some indeed preach Christ even of envy and strife; and some also of good will.

The fact of Paul's imprisonment worked in more than one way to stir the zeal of others. The differences seem to have rested more in personal attitudes toward Paul than in the message that was proclaimed. They all preached the same gospel for different reasons. Jealous brethren, perhaps irritated by the prominence Paul had gained in Rome, where he was a latecomer rather than founder of the church, saw his confinement as an opportunity to establish their own reputations for leadership. Others, who

---

How to Say It

EPAPHRODITUS. E-paf-ro-*dye*-tus.
PHILIPPI. Fuh-*lip*-pie or *Fil*-uh-pie.
THESSALONICA. *Thess*-suh-lo-*nye*-kuh.

knew the apostle better, recognized that they could please him best by setting forward the cause to which he had wholly given himself.

16, 17. The one preach Christ of contention, not sincerely, supposing to add affliction to my bonds: but the other of love, knowing that I am set for the defense of the gospel.

Most newer Bible translations present the material of these two verses in reverse order, following manuscripts apparently closer to the original. "The latter do it out of love, knowing that I am appointed for the defense of the gospel; the former proclaim Christ out of selfish ambition, rather than from pure motives, thinking to cause me distress in my imprisonment" *(New American Standard Bible)*. Those who loved Christ and the gospel supremely knew that Paul was similarly committed, and they loved him for it.

It would perhaps be wrong to say that those who belittled Paul were more in love with themselves than with Christ, but at least their motives were not pure; they were mixed. Self-promotion, especially at the expense of Paul's reputation, was prominent in them. They would *add affliction* [literally pressure] *to my bonds*. They would make his chains more galling. They assumed that he would be jealous of their successes, as they were of his. As it was, their attitude distressed him far more than did their accomplishments. He neither condemned them nor sought revenge.

18. What then? notwithstanding, every way, whether in pretense, or in truth, Christ is preached; and I therein do rejoice, yea, and will rejoice.

Here sounds again the theme of the chapter: the important question is not Paul's comfort and welfare, but the church's welfare and advancement. "But what does it matter? The important thing is that in every way, whether from false motives or true, Christ is preached" *(New International Version)*. This has to be understood in the light of Paul's other writings, such as Galatians 1:8: "Though we, or an angel from heaven, preach any other gospel unto you than that which we have preached unto you, let him be accursed." As long as the pure gospel was preached, Paul could overlook impure motives. But if the gospel were altered to admit another Lord, Mediator, or Savior, the highest and purest motives on the part of the preacher would never make up the deficit. In fact, the false gospel would be rendered doubly dangerous when presented by a winsome personality with high and holy motives.

The gospel of Christ was preached in Rome, whether by Paul, or a friend, or a rival. In that

Paul would rejoice, whatever his circumstances. No matter what happened to himself, he was engaged in a winning cause.

The apostle's attention turned sharply at this point from the advantages of the present hour to future good that would come from those advantages.

II. Christ Will Be Served (Philippians 1:19-26)

A. Paul Will Benefit (v. 19)

19. For I know that this shall turn to my salvation through your prayer, and the supply of the Spirit of Jesus Christ.

Paul would continue to rejoice in the continual preaching of Christ, but a more inclusive cause for continual rejoicing becomes immediately evident. *This*, which will eventuate in good, is the whole pattern of events noted in verses 12 to 18. "What has happened to me will turn out for my deliverance" *(New International Version)*.

What deliverance or *salvation* did Paul expect from the present happenings? Some Bible students link this statement to verse 20 and conclude that Paul had in mind his own eternal welfare. Others think he spoke of "deliverance," release from prison that would enable him again to visit and labor among his friends at Philippi.

Paul's words here seem in fact to be a quotation from Job 13:16 as it appears in the Septuagint Greek translation, rendered in the *New International Version*, "Indeed, this might turn out for my deliverance." Job was saying that his present affliction might result in great spiritual good. So Goodspeed translates Philippians 1:19, "All this will turn out for my highest welfare."

Divine help toward the ultimate benefit would be more readily available to Paul because of his friends' constant prayers.

B. Christ Will Be Glorified (vv. 20, 21)

20. According to my earnest expectation and my hope, that in nothing I shall be ashamed, but that with all boldness, as always, so now also Christ shall be magnified in my body, whether it be by life, or by death.

Earnest expectation. This graphic word speaks literally of "stretching out the head," as though to see some object in the distance. The glory of Christ, to be seen and enhanced, was the focus of Paul's attention.

Paul had told the Romans that he was not ashamed of the gospel (Romans 1:16), but he was aware of the ever-present danger of denying his Lord. He must not allow that to happen. The

visual 5

Paul's purpose
in life or death
was to magnify

CHRIST

immediate future could bring special dangers to Paul, and special temptation to avoid further trouble by exercising a prudent restraint in what he said. Instead he chose *boldness*—the freedom of clear, plain speech. It was a privilege the Roman Empire granted to its free citizens and not to others. Paul would use it to glorify Christ.

Christ shall be magnified in my body, whether it be by life, or by death. As long as Paul lived, his words and deeds would glorify His Lord. If and when he died, his acceptance of that fate for Jesus' sake would yield to Him the ultimate honor. (Compare Philippians 3:7-11).

21. For to me to live is Christ, and to die is gain.

To live is Christ. Jesus said it more fully, "I am the resurrection, and the life: he that believeth in me, though he were dead, yet shall he live: and whosoever liveth and believeth in me shall never die" (John 11:25, 26). Paul said it more fully also: "I am crucified with Christ: nevertheless I live; yet not I, but Christ liveth in me" (Galatians 2:20). The Christ life does not end with physical death. It enlarges.

To die is gain. This is not in contrast to the previous declaration; it is an extension of it. "For what is life? To me, it is Christ. Death, then, will bring more" (*Today's English Version*). That *more* is spelled out in 2 Corinthians 5:6-8, as being absent from the body and present with the Lord. Compare also 1 Thessalonians 4:17.

These passages could trouble those who seek time schedules for eternal events. One passage seems to indicate an immediate transplanting from earth to glory; the other speaks of the resurrection welcome for all saints when Christ comes in His glory. The Lord will neither move on our schedule nor show us His, except "through a glass, darkly" (1 Corinthians 13:12). That didn't bother Paul, and it shouldn't bother us. What should be of infinitely more concern is this: Until and unless we can say with Paul, "For me to live is Christ," we cannot say with him, "to die is gain"!

UNCONQUERABLE

In the early morning of January 19, 1981, armed terrorists broke into the guest house in Bogota, Colombia. Herding together the sleepy Wycliffe people, they demanded their leader. When the terrorists learned that the director was not there, they took Bible translator, Chet Bitterman, as their prisoner in the hope of gaining ransom for his release.

Then followed days of pain, prayer, anxiety, and hope for his family. Like most others, this mission was committed to the principle of no ransom for kidnapped personnel.

When Chet Bitterman was killed, the faith expressed by his family and fellow missionaries was an echo of the words of Paul in his Roman imprisonment, "For to me to live is Christ, and to die is gain." These words may be incomprehensible to unbelievers, but they express the Christian's faith in the risen Christ and hope of eternal life in Him.

We need to determine to follow Jesus today. If we do, then death, whenever it comes, can only be gain. Heaven is the home for those who serve Christ among men.   —W. P.

C. Life Will Be Fulfilled (vv. 22-24)

22. But if I live in the flesh, this is the fruit of my labor: yet what I shall choose I wot not.

For Paul, life in the flesh would postpone the experience of fulfilled life in the divine presence, but it would permit more fruitful labor for the Lord. Which, then, would be ultimately preferable? He didn't know. Was it, however, his to choose? That lay in the hands of the Roman court, which seems to have released him for further labors among the brethren, and then later to have arrested him and finally put him to death.

Paul's soliloquy was not like that of Shakespeare's Hamlet, who pondered whether or not to kill himself. The apostle would weigh his choices, and so instruct us in the values by which we are to live and face death, but he would not destroy the life that God had given.

23, 24. For I am in a strait betwixt two, having a desire to depart, and to be with Christ; which is far better: nevertheless to abide in the flesh is more needful for you.

Paul felt pressure from both sides. For himself, his desire was to *depart* this physical life, literally to loosen the tent pegs or "pull up stakes," as a nomad moving to a better location. It was an experience familiar to Paul as a tentmaker, who also wrote, "If the earthly tent we live in is destroyed, we have a building from God, an eternal house in heaven" (2 Corinthians

5:1, *New International Version*). It was not the departure, though, but the arrival; and not the better house, but the beloved Lord, that attracted Paul to be with Christ.

Paul's attraction to this present life also was affirmative, and it was wholly unselfish. He was willing to *abide* in the flesh since that was more necessary for the Philippians.

D. The Church Will Benefit (vv. 25, 26)

25. And having this confidence, I know that I shall abide and continue with you all for your furtherance and joy of faith.

Having this confidence. Paul was persuaded that his continued life would be beneficial to the Philippians, and so he felt sure that God would preserve his life at this time. Through Paul's additional teaching their faith would be advanced, and they would know greater joy in their faith because their prayers would be answered in his life and freedom.

26. That your rejoicing may be more abundant in Jesus Christ for me by my coming to you again.

Through many gifts and words of appreciation the Philippian saints had made evident their appreciation for Paul. Their joy would be *more abundant* because of his release from prison and his *coming* to be with them. His later trip to Macedonia, mentioned in 1 Timothy 1:3, no doubt included a visit to Philippi. He desired that their rejoicing be in Christ, though, rather than in him.

A PURPOSE FOR LIVING

Bumper stickers express little of the personality of the person or family on whose automobile they are placed. Few have any lasting worth, but in a limited sense they are "signs of our times."

Home Daily Bible Readings

Monday, Mar. 27—Encouragement Between the Believers (Philippians 1:1-11)
Tuesday, Mar. 28—Believers Must Sometimes Suffer (Philippians 1:12-17)
Wednesday, Mar. 29—Confidently Living in Christ (Philippians 1:18-26)
Thursday, Mar. 30—Christ Is Trustworthy (2 Timothy 1:7-12)
Friday, Mar. 31—Christ Is Faithful (2 Timothy 2:11-19)
Saturday, Apr. 1—Our Reasons to Live (John 14:12-21)
Sunday, Apr. 2—Our Source of Life (Acts 17:22-28)

Traveling billboards of American individuality and free speech, bumper stickers express everything from vulgarity to religious fervor.

Some speak of practical concerns. "Careful, Baby on Board" is an appeal for safe driving. "If you can read this, you are too close" asks for room on the highway.

One that is popular right now expresses a lifestyle. It simply reads, "Born to Shop." In our age of material acquisitiveness it tells a tale that gives meaning to life for many. But is "Born to Shop" an adequate reason for personal existence? Paul stated his reason for living when he said, "I know that I shall remain and continue with you all for your progress and joy of faith" *(New American Standard Bible)*. Serving others was the ministry of Paul as he served Christ.

If you took time to write it down, what would you say to record your purpose for living? Serving others is the example and commandment for all who follow Jesus.   —W. P.

Conclusion

A. Enjoy It Now

Today's lesson brings to mind an old rhyme:

> It's not what you'd do with a million,
>   If a million should e'er be your lot;
> It's what you're doing right now
>   With the dollar and dime that you've got.

We can learn from Paul not to wait for some distant morrow to enjoy life *in* and *with* Christ. *Today* Paul rejoiced that Christ was preached; hence *tomorrow* he could expect to rejoice in the fruits of the present circumstance (Philippians 1:18). *Today* he could affirm, "To live is Christ"; hence concerning tomorrow he could declare, "To die is gain." (v. 21).

May we, then, paraphrase the old rhyme?

> It's not in the waiting for Heaven,
>   If glory with Christ is your goal;
> It's pleasure in living for Jesus
>   Right now with your body and soul.

B. Prayer

We rejoice in Your goodness, O God our Heavenly Father. You are indeed the source of all life and living. Thank You, dear God, for Jesus, our living Lord and conqueror of death for us. Help us, please, to grasp eagerly and hold firmly and enjoy daily the life He came to be and to give. Let this be our glory forever, we pray in His name. Amen.

C. Thought to Remember

"I am the resurrection, and the life . . . whosoever liveth and believeth in me shall never die" (John 11:25, 26).

Learning by Doing

This page contains an alternate lesson plan emphasizing learning activities. Classes desiring such student involvement will find these suggestions helpful.

Learning Goals

After studying Philippians 1:12-26, a student will be able to:

1. Tell the circumstances out of which Paul wrote the letter to the Philippians.

2. Explain how Paul could maintain an attitude of optimism in the midst of his difficulties.

3. Cite circumstances in his own life when what seemed like a bad situation at the time became a blessing.

4. Select one way in which he will develop a more optimistic attitude.

Into the Lesson

As the class members arrive, have them form groups of three or four. Give each group a copy of the rhyme below. Ask them to read the rhyme, then respond to these questions: Is this true? How can we find pleasure in living for Jesus right now?

It's not in the waiting for Heaven,
    If glory with Christ is your goal;
It's pleasure in living for Jesus
    Right now with your body and soul.

Allow the groups four to six minutes to discuss this. Then let the groups share some of their thinking.

Make the transition into the Bible study for this lesson by stating that Paul experienced a tension while imprisoned in Rome: he desired to live in Heaven with Christ, yet he knew that he was needed by others here. We sometimes experience the same tensions. This lesson will provide insight about how to live with those tensions.

Into the Word

Briefly present the material from the "Introduction" section of the lesson. Then have someone read the entire text aloud. Develop the Bible study by using the following questions to direct the students' attention to the text. Encourage the students to answer the questions, but also use the commentary to provide further insight into the text if the students do not mention it.

1. What was Paul's attitude toward the fact that he had been imprisoned? (v. 12)

2. How had Paul's witness for Christ been enhanced by his imprisonment? (v. 13)

3. How had the general spread of the gospel been helped by Paul's imprisonment? (v. 14)

4. List the poor motives out of which some were preaching the gospel.

5. How did Paul respond to the fact that some teachers preached Christ out of poor motives? (vv. 15-18)

6. What was Paul's abiding hope in the midst of his circumstances? (vv. 19, 20)

7. What principle dominated Paul's attitude regarding his life and death? (v. 21)

8. How did Paul resolve the tension of longing for Heaven, yet needing to live day by day? (vv. 22-26)

9. How could Paul maintain his attitude of optimism in spite of imprisonment? What lessons can we learn from him?

Into Life

Every person must deal with less than desirable circumstances in his life, some more than others. What kind of advice can we offer to the following people who are dealing with difficult situations?

Situation 1. Tom's wife recently left him and the three children, who range in age from four to twelve. Tom has since been busy balancing the responsibilities of child care and work. How can he maintain the spirit of Paul in the midst of his difficulties? What are the possible positive outcomes of this situation?

Situation 2. Jim and Rose have always been active in the church and reared their children to love the Lord. Their son abandoned that commitment in early adulthood and experienced many difficulties. Then he committed suicide. How can Jim and Rose maintain the spirit of Paul in the midst of this tragedy? What are the possible positive outcomes of this situation?

Situation 3. Jean's husband attended church with her in the early days of their marriage. But he has since ceased to do so—and has become hostile to the church. More than that, he is insensitive to Jean, often making degrading remarks to her both privately and in the presence of others. How can Jean maintain the spirit of Paul in the midst of this tragedy? What are the possible positive outcomes of this situation?

Conclude the session by giving each person a small index card on which to complete the following sentence: As I think of myself and my circumstances, I want to follow Paul's example by—

Let's Talk It Over

The questions on this page are designed to encourage review of the lesson Scriptures and to promote discussion of the lesson by the class. The answers provided are only discussion starters. Let your class talk it over from there.

1. How had Paul's imprisonment resulted in "the furtherance of the gospel"? What does this teach us about seeing the good in bad circumstances?

If the focus of Paul's attention had been on himself, he could have become very discouraged, bemoaning his own suffering and concluding that the cause of Christ was in jeopardy, since he was not able to preach freely. But Paul's frame of reference was larger than that. He saw that his imprisonment had created an opportunity for the gospel to be spread throughout the praetorian guard. He also saw that other Christians were moved to take up the torch in his absence. Necessity and opportunity had created a new boldness in them.

When we are tempted to feel like a martyr and are filled with self-pity, maybe it is time to lift our eyes off of self. What good for God's cause may be accomplished through our suffering? Are there those around us who may benefit? A larger frame of reference may help.

2. Paul knew that some were preaching the gospel from wrong motives. How did he respond to that?

Some of those who were now preaching the gospel genuinely wanted to carry on the work of their beloved apostle. They shared his desire to see the lost reached and sinners converted. They were eager to be used to carry on the work Paul had begun. Others who had been envious of Paul's success and his prominence were now preaching with great vigor so as to add to their own reputations. They saw Paul's imprisonment as opportunity to belittle him and to exalt themselves. Paul was not naive as to their motives, but rather than become offended or pout, Paul rejoiced that, no matter the motive, Christ was being preached. Here is another lesson in looking beyond self to the larger picture.

3. What was the source of Paul's joy? How may we preserve joy in the face of adversity?

To be in prison was no cause of joy for Paul. He did not find joy in having his freedom curtailed. Yet he maintained a spirit of joy through it all. If our joy is dependent upon circumstances, we may endure a joyless existence much of the time. Paul's joy was a result of his relationship with God in Christ. Circumstances became incidental to his place in the family of God and his calling in Christ. Paul later testified, "I count all things but loss for the excellency of the knowledge of Christ Jesus my Lord" (Philippians 3:8). Paul was also aware that no set of circumstances could separate him from the love of God in Christ (Romans 8:38, 39). Possessing the same attitude toward Christ Jesus and our eternal life in Him will help us to see the relative unimportance of the momentary difficulties and suffering that we may experience in this life.

4. How may a Christian and a nonbeliever differ in their attitudes toward death?

At best the nonbeliever must consider death as the end of life, beyond which there is no hope. For those who believe only in the material/physical world, death represents the loss of everything. For the Christian, however, death is, as Paul describes it, a departure. Rather than a time of great loss, it is a time of great gain. The Christian stands to gain life without pain, life without sorrow, life without end.

The word *departure* causes one to picture an ocean liner or a large airplane filled with people eager to go to a vacation spot they have dreamed of for years. They may have some apprehension about the trip; they say good-byes to those who stay behind because of the temporary separation; but their hearts are full of expectation for what lies ahead. Death as a departure leads to the fulfillment of the Christian's long-awaited hope.

5. How could Paul say, "For to me to live is Christ"? How may that be true for you?

Paul had successfully replaced his private ambitions and desires in life for what he understood as the will and desire of Christ. Paul had given himself completely to the work of Christ. It was his aim to live as Christ would have lived had He still been walking on earth in the flesh. We can say with Paul, "For to me to live is Christ" to the extent that we have died to self and made Christ Lord of our lives (Galatians 2:20).

Serving as Christ Served

LESSON SCRIPTURE: Philippians 1:27—2:30.

PRINTED TEXT: Philippians 1:27—2:11.

Philippians 1:27-30

27 Let your conversation be as it becometh the gospel of Christ: that whether I come and see you, or else be absent, I may hear of your affairs, that ye stand fast in one spirit, with one mind striving together for the faith of the gospel;

28 And in nothing terrified by your adversaries: which is to them an evident token of perdition, but to you of salvation, and that of God.

29 For unto you it is given in the behalf of Christ, not only to believe on him, but also to suffer for his sake;

30 Having the same conflict which ye saw in me, and now hear to be in me.

Philippians 2:1-11

1 If there be therefore any consolation in Christ, if any comfort of love, if any fellowship of the Spirit, if any bowels and mercies,

2 Fulfil ye my joy, that ye be likeminded, having the same love, being of one accord, of one mind.

3 Let nothing be done through strife or vainglory; but in lowliness of mind let each esteem other better than themselves.

4 Look not every man on his own things, but every man also on the things of others.

5 Let this mind be in you, which was also in Christ Jesus:

6 Who, being in the form of God, thought it not robbery to be equal with God:

Apr 9

7 But made himself of no reputation, and took upon him the form of a servant, and was made in the likeness of men:

8 And being found in fashion as a man, he humbled himself, and became obedient unto death, even the death of the cross.

9 Wherefore God also hath highly exalted him, and given him a name which is above every name:

10 That at the name of Jesus every knee should bow, of things in heaven, and things in earth, and things under the earth;

11 And that every tongue should confess that Jesus Christ is Lord, to the glory of God the Father.

GOLDEN TEXT: Let this mind be in you, which was also in Christ Jesus: who, being in the form of God, thought it not robbery to be equal with God: but made himself of no reputation, and took upon him the form of a servant.—Philippians 2:5-7.

Lesson Aims

This lesson should equip the student to:

1. Summarize—or better, quote from a chosen Bible version—Philippians 2:5-11.

2. Explain how this exalted poetic passage appears in such an informal letter.

3. Name some service he will render to help the church in the smooth functioning of its ministry.

Lesson Outline

INTRODUCTION
  A. Evangelizing the Church
  B. World Class Competition
  I. SERVE TOGETHER (Philippians 1:27-30)
  A. Serve Faithfully (v. 27)
  B. Serve Fearlessly (v. 28)
  C. Suffer Willingly (vv. 29, 30)
  II. SERVE HARMONIOUSLY (Philippians 2:1-4)
  A. Serve With a Single Purpose (vv. 1, 2)
  B. Serve Unselfishly (vv. 3, 4)
    The Top Man
  III. FOLLOW CHRIST IN SERVICE (Philippians 2:5-11)
  A. Jesus Served Humbly (vv. 5-8)
  B. God Exalted Him Gloriously (vv. 9-11)
CONCLUSION
  A. Getting Down to Work
  B. A Servant's Prayer
  C. Thought to Remember

Display visual 6 from the visuals/learning resources packet. It is shown on page 277.

Introduction

A. Evangelizing the Church

In one of the grandest passages in all his writing, the apostle Paul evangelized the Philippian church! How can this be? They had heard the gospel already. They had believed and had turned to God. They had been baptized into Christ. They had shown by many evidences their generosity and their zeal for the spread of the gospel. How could they be—and why should they be—evangelized again?

Is not the evangel the good news concerning Jesus and the salvation He offers? The Philippian Christians needed that, and Paul gave it to

them with power and beauty in the words of Philippians 2:5-11. Even the Philippian church was not wholly mature and faultless. Tension and friction existed among them (Philippians 4:2; compare with 2:1-4). With fervent exhortation Paul urged upon them the unity of the Spirit in the bond of peace. But something more was needed to overcome their sometimes negative feelings toward one another. That supreme motivation was the gospel. They needed to remember Jesus and what He had done for them.

So Paul wrote to them again the facts of the gospel. And when Paul mentioned Jesus he never wrote casually. He wrote reverently, with awe and deep emotion. He wrote, as it were, a hymn.

The letter to the Philippians is mostly personal in style. It has not the formal grandeur of treatises such as Romans or Ephesians—until it comes to the subject of what God's Son has done for mankind. Then it glows with poetic power. Among the passages for a Christian to memorize for the enrichment of his mind forever is Philippians 2:5-11. With it firmly in place he will be equipped to meet many temptations and to answer many questions among his friends. He can then helpfully evangelize the church, saying with Paul, "Let me tell you about Jesus."

B. World Class Competition

In last week's lesson we felt the thrust of the grand truth, "To live is Christ." But the Christ life is not a solo experience. The body of Christ, continuing His ministry on earth, is composed of many members, each doing its part in coordination with all the rest. It is a team, an army, a family, and more. It succeeds or fails—as a unit made of many working parts.

Let's think of the *team* idea, and world class competition. Paul knew that kind of competition in the athletic contests among the Greeks and the Romans. We know it in Olympic Games, World Series, Super Bowls, and basketball tournaments. No one player can win by himself, and no team can win "the big one" if any player fails in his performance. The church is engaged in world class competition—Heaven versus Hell!

Occasionally we hear that a team is performing like a well-oiled machine. But there is a difference. Persons are not machine parts, uniform and interchangeable. When a machine part breaks down, the other parts do not come to its rescue, doing its work and holding it up until it can regain strength. And that is precisely what the members of a team, or a body—and especially the body of Christ—do with and for one another. Today's text begins where last week's lesson ended.

I. Serve Together
(Philippians 1:27-30)

A. Serve Faithfully (v. 27)

27. Only let your conversation be as it becometh the gospel of Christ: that whether I come and see you, or else be absent, I may hear of your affairs, that ye stand fast in one spirit, with one mind striving together for the faith of the gospel.

Let your conversation be as it becometh the gospel of Christ. Paul's words say literally, "Behave as citizens worthy...." Philippi was a special city, a colony of Rome; its people were Roman citizens, and were expected to conduct themselves accordingly. Paul reminded the Christians that they were a colony of Heaven, having citizenship there, and were expected to act like it (compare Philippians 3:20).

Whether I come and see you, or else be absent. The questions noted in Philippians 1:20-26 had not been firmly answered. Paul expected to be released from his imprisonment and to visit Philippi again; but he might not be released from prison. He would still follow news of them with vital interest however. The most important item of that news would concern their unity in contending for the revealed truth of the gospel (compare Jude 3). They were to have one controlling attitude and purpose, derived from one indwelling Spirit.

B. Serve Fearlessly (v. 28)

28. And in nothing terrified by your adversaries: which is to them an evident token of perdition, but to you of salvation, and that of God.

Paul tells the Christians not to be scared or intimidated by those who oppose them. Their fearless and staunch insistence on doing right is a sign of defeat and destruction to the opponents. Concerning this, Chrysostom said, "When they see that they cannot even scare you, they will perceive a token of their own perdition. For when the persecutors cannot prevail over the persecuted, the vanquishers over the vanquished, shall it not thence be manifest to them that they must perish?"

How to Say It

Epaphroditus. E-paf-ro-*dye*-tus.
Euodias. U-*o*-di-us.
Philippi. Fuh-*lip*-pie or *Fil*-uh-pie.
Syntyche. *Sin*-tih-key.

That of God. The divine source of the saints' help was evident to the heathen. They might not understand it, but they were impressed by it. Christians who remain cheerfully undaunted by manifold difficulties are still asked, "How do you do it?" The obvious answer is, "I have help."

C. Suffer Willingly (vv. 29, 20)

29, 30. For unto you it is given in the behalf of Christ, not only to believe on him, but also to suffer for his sake; having the same conflict which ye saw in me, and now hear to be in me.

When persecution came to the apostles during the early days of the church in Jerusalem, they did not flinch in fear or frustration, but rather rejoiced "that they were counted worthy to suffer shame" for the name of Christ (Acts 5:41). It brought them nearer to their beloved Lord. In the case of the Philippians it brought them nearer also to their beloved Paul. The Philippian Christians had seen Paul beaten and imprisoned in their city, and they knew now of his imprisonment and trials at Rome. Their own suffering is not precisely described, but it was similar. For ourselves we may ask with the hymn writer, "Must I be carried to the skies on flowery beds of ease, while others fought to win the prize, and sailed through bloody seas?"

II. Serve Harmoniously
(Philippians 2:1-4)

A. Serve With a Single Purpose
(vv. 1, 2)

1, 2. If there be therefore any consolation in Christ, if any comfort of love, if any fellowship of the Spirit, if any bowels and mercies, fulfil ye my joy, that ye be likeminded, having the same love, being of one accord, of one mind.

Paul's impassioned plea for oneness on the part of his friends suggests the presence of a problem mentioned more specifically in Philippians 4:2, with its appeal to Euodias and Syntyche to "be of the same mind in the Lord." In what church has not a similar problem at some time arisen? The very energy of the Christian faith tends to produce energetic personalities, and these sometime clash.

It is not necessary to show that the four *ifs* of verse 1 or the four pleas of verse 2 are all separately meaningful. Such fervent appeal has its own right to be repetitious. Verse 1 speaks of influences that might be expected to create and preserve unity. *Consolation* is rendered "exhortation" or "encouragement" in some newer translations. Our Lord certainly exhorted to unity in himself (John 17:20-23). *Comfort* is sometimes rendered as "incentive" and may have the force of "appeal." *Bowels and mercies* speak of emotional involvements. "So if there is any encouragement in Christ, any incentive of love, any participation in the Spirit, any affection and sympathy..." *(Revised Standard Version).* What Paul requested was the natural result of the indwelling Spirit of Christ, freed of human selfishness.

Fulfil ye my joy. The Philippian saints had been helpful to Paul in many ways. Now he pled for the one gift that would please him most of all. "Make my joy complete by being of the same mind, maintaining the same love, united in spirit, intent on one purpose" *(New American Standard Bible).* The *mind* is the inward disposition. What Paul asks is not some faceless conformity, but is a solid commitment to the same purpose and cause—a commitment sufficiently powerful to override the tendencies toward bickering and division.

B. Serve Unselfishly (vv. 3, 4)

3. Let nothing be done through strife or vainglory; but in lowliness of mind let each esteem other better than themselves.

It has been noted in the history of religions that intense earnestness frequently appears in conceit and censoriousness, like that of the Pharisees who trusted in themselves and despised others (Luke 18:9). Paul had already noted that some Christians in Rome were motivated by "envy and strife" in preaching the gospel (Philippians 1:15); hence his admonition, "Do nothing out of selfish ambition or vain conceit" *(New International Version).*

Lowliness of mind is a term that appears in the New Testament and not elsewhere in Greek writings. Pagan self-assertiveness had no place for such an idea or expression. It is the Christlike attitude that lets each one regard others as more important than himself. It finds its model in the Lord, who, equipped himself with towel and basin and washed His disciples' feet. It finds expression in the Lord's follower whose sense of self-worth does not depend on titles and places of honor, so he slips quietly into a banquet seat well removed from the speaker's table (Luke 14:7-11).

4. Look not every man on his own things, but every man also on the things of others.

Christians are not to look out for their own interests only, but also for the interests of others, too. You join a party because it represents your special interests and will bring you some personal advantage; but as a Christian you avoid narrow partisanship. You consider the larger interests of all the special interests of others. The

things of others may include others' virtues, opinions, desires, as well as interests and welfare. These all are to be considered, as well as one's own virtues, opinions, desires, and welfare. "Thou shalt love thy neighbor as thyself" (Matthew 22:38).

THE TOP MAN

"King of the Hill" was a favorite childhood game in our family. My brothers and I enjoyed the rough, tough frontier game. No holds were barred. The "hill" was just a slight rise in one corner of the school area. It was not very high but it was crowned with a smooth rock that rose about eighteen inches above the slight hill. The object was to see how long you could stay on that rock as "king of the hill" before anyone could push you off. Some of the farm girls played too, and it was humiliating to be "dethroned" by one of them.

Adult life is too often played like that childhood game. The top rung in business, club, or even charity is many times a precarious position. Ethics, Christian connections, and humanitarian concerns are often cast aside in order to stay "on top."

This is all contrary to the teaching and example of Jesus and the writings of Paul. Counting others better than self is not common in modern life, but it is Christian. I believe we could revolutionize even our church life if we quit playing "King of the Hill" and began to be concerned for "the things of others."
                                                                    —W. P.

III. Follow Christ in Service (Philippians 2:5-11)

A. Jesus Served Humbly (vv. 5-8)

5. Let this mind be in you, which was also in Christ Jesus.

The apostle turns from exhortation to motivation; and in doing so he turns from "practical teaching" to "doctrinal preaching." But Scriptural behavior is always based on Scriptural faith, just as truly as all action springs from thought and feeling. So, if the Lord's people are to exhibit Christlike behavior, they must begin with the mind—the basic attitudes—exhibited by Jesus.

For this reason Paul's review of the gospel does not deal with the words Jesus spoke or the miracles He worked. It does not even speak directly of His resurrection. It speaks rather of the attitude with which He approached His ministry. The attitude became known through His words and works; but Paul's words here strike through the externals to the spirit behind them. It is that spirit he urges upon his readers.

6. Who, being in the form of God, thought it not robbery to be equal with God.

Here is clear affirmation of the truth found in John 1:1: "In the beginning was the Word, and the Word was with God, and the Word was God." His divine status came by nature; He did not demand it nor seize it. Neither, did He grasp or "cling to His prerogatives as God's equal" (Phillips' translation).

7. But made himself of no reputation, and took upon him the form of a servant, and was made in the likeness of men.

The Lord's willing descent from celestial glory to earthly servanthood is noted in 2 Corinthians 8:9: "Ye know the grace of our Lord Jesus Christ, that, though he was rich, yet for your sakes he became poor." He "emptied himself" (*American Standard Version*); "made himself nothing" (*New International Version*). As He had been in the *form*, or very nature, of God, so now He accepted the *form*, or very nature, of a bond *servant*, or slave. In either case it was not so much the matter of physical structure or appearance; in this there was no comparison. It was rather the essential quality and purpose of His being.

Yet our Lord did not cease to be God. Assuming human form He continued to be the expression of divine love, and throughout His ministry He exercised divine power in serving. The servant Messiah had been foretold and described in Isaiah 42:1-9 and 52:13—53:12. Jesus declared plainly that He came into the world, not to be served, but to serve, and to give His life a ransom for many Matthew 20:28; He also declared just as plainly that He had been given all authority in Heaven and on earth (Matthew 28:18). In Jesus, God was serving. He wants to continue serving through the followers of Jesus.

8. And being found in fashion as a man, he humbled himself, and became obedient unto death, even the death of the cross.

Observe the continuing chain of verbs that bespeak the attitude of Jesus: He let go His claim to divine glory; He became a servant, being born as a human being; He humbled himself, and became totally obedient.

As a man. Jesus was so totally human that Scripture makes no remark about His appearance—until His appearance was changed at His transfiguration. His divine nature was, however, also complete. He consistently declared and demonstrated the power and the authority of God, but never to His own advantage as a man. His Person remained the same, always complete in its expression of love, obedience, holiness, and mercy, whether in humiliation or in glory.

visual 6

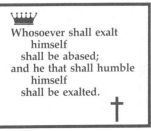

Whosoever shall exalt himself
shall be abased;
and he that shall humble himself
shall be exalted.

Jesus' obedience was first and always to the will of the Father (John 6:38; Matthew 26:39-42). That obedience led Him up to, and through, the experience of death—death in crucifixion. We may also say that Jesus became obedient to the mandate of death itself—the call that no man can refuse.

Jesus' servanthood expressed itself in at least three aspects. In relation to himself, He practiced the denial that He demanded of His followers (Matthew 16:24); self-service or self-indulgence was no part of His program. In relation to other persons, He exercised compassion, which kept Him always alert to their needs and responsive in the most helpful way. In relation to the Father He exercised total obedience, which followed every aspect of the divine will.

B. God Exalted Him Gloriously
(vv. 9-11)

9. Wherefore God also hath highly exalted him, and given him a name which is above every name.

"Whosoever exalteth himself shall be abased; and he that humbleth himself shall be exalted." On at least three occasions Jesus said that. He advised against claiming the best seats at dinner parties (Luke 14:11), or parading one's own virtues in prayer (Luke 18:14), or taking on titles of honor in religion (Matthew 23:12). Here in a sense larger than all of these, the same principle is demonstrated. To an extent beyond our comprehension Jesus humbled himself; therefore to an extent beyond description God *highly exalted him. (Direct the class's attention to visual 6.)*

The *name* is more than a title. It is reputation; it is authority; it is the symbol of oneself. God spoke from Heaven to honor Jesus (Matthew 3:17); He raised Him from the dead; He assigned to Him all authority and judgment (Matthew 28:18); He lifted Him to His own right hand in glory—glory that will be seen and acknowledged by the whole world at Christ's coming again to earth in judgment. Other men have been and will be called *Jesus*, but none can approach the glory reserved for Him whom God called "my beloved Son."

10, 11. That at the name of Jesus every knee should bow, of things in heaven, and things in earth, and things under the earth; and that every tongue should confess that Jesus Christ is Lord, to the glory of God the Father.

Those who would please God will respect the name of His Son, not speaking it carelessly nor hearing it lightly. More is involved, though, than the spoken title. Upon knowing Jesus—His Person and authority—all God's creatures will bow in humble submission. Defeated kings must ultimately bow—no matter how reluctantly—before their conquerors. So also the enemies of Christ will one day be brought to their knees before Him. It will be too late then for their salvation. The enforced acknowledgment of Him whom they have despised will only add to their humiliation; but it will add also to the future glory of those who have served humbly all their lives because of Jesus.

The acknowledgment of God's Son is to be in word and in deed. *Every tongue* is to speak His praise. To *confess* is usually to acknowledge what human pride would rather deny. It is a part of the humble servant spirit to recognize our obligation to give Him total obedience. Words alone will not suffice. Without servant deeds supporting servant words they invite the rebuke of Jesus, "Why call ye me, Lord, Lord, and do not the things which I say?" (Luke 6:46).

What, in fact, are the words of confession? "Jesus Christ is Lord!" This agrees with the confession made by Simon Peter, both personally (Matthew 16:16) and publicly (Acts 2:36). It agrees with Paul's references in Romans 10:9 and 1 Corinthians 12:3. "Confession of sin" is not necessarily Christian; it could be made in reference to any religion, or none. "Confession of faith" can be self-centered and even boastful.

A forthright declaration that Jesus Christ is Lord, on the other hand, puts the emphasis where it belongs. The man Jesus, the Jews' Messiah, is one with the God whom they called Lord; and to call Jesus "Lord" is to acknowledge that He is the one to whom we listen and render total obedience. By that confession we glorify God, who identified Jesus as His Son, and whose world-wide, eternal plan for human redemption is centered in this fact. This is the way God wants it, and will have it.

Conclusion

A. Getting Down to Work

Read again Philippians 2:5-11, without pauses for comment, and you may feel as the saints at Philippi must have felt when it was first read in their presence—or as Peter, James, and John felt at seeing Jesus' glory on the mountaintop. They wanted to linger, cheering! But that could not be. There was work to be done.

So in the following paragraphs of the Philippian letter Paul got down to work. He exhorted his friends to live so as to reflect God's light in a dark world (vv. 12-15), and so that Christians might rejoice together (vv. 16-18). Referring again to his own plans, he spoke of sending Timothy, warmly recommended as a faithful servant of Christ, to visit them (vv. 19-24); and he explained why he was sending Epaphroditus back to Philippi with this letter (vv. 25-30). Here were practical aspects of serving vigorously together for the gospel.

In summary, "We will in all things grow up into him who is the Head, that is, Christ. From him the whole body, joined and held together by every supporting ligament, grows and builds itself up in love, as each part does its work" (Ephesians 4: 15, 16, *New International Version*).

B. A Servant's Prayer

Thank You, gracious God our Heavenly Father, for Jesus our Lord, who surrendered Heaven's glory and accepted earth's suffering and sorrows to serve—to seek and to save—us. We need help now to accept more fully His way of service. Lead us, we pray, to a better understanding of Him and a humbler, more helpful spirit for His sake. Amen.

C. Thought to Remember

"Whosoever will be great among you shall be your minister: and whosoever of you will be the chiefest, shall be servant of all. For even the Son of man came not to be ministered unto, but to minister, and to give his life a ransom for many" (Mark 10:43-45).

Home Daily Bible Readings

Monday, Apr. 3—Always Ready to Give Account (Philippians 1:27—2:4)

Tuesday, Apr. 4—Christlike Humility (Philippians 2:5-11)

Wednesday, Apr. 5—Obedience in All Things (Philippians 2:12-18)

Thursday, Apr. 6—The Support of a Friend (Philippians 2:19-24)

Friday, Apr. 7—A Faithful Friend (Philippians 2:25-30)

Saturday, Apr. 8—There Is Honor in Serving (Luke 22:24-30)

Sunday, Apr. 9—A Servant Attitude Honors God (John 12:20-26)

Learning by Doing

This page contains an alternate lesson plan emphasizing learning activities. Classes desiring such student involvement will find these suggestions helpful.

Learning Goals

After examining Philippians 1:27—2:11, a student will be able to:

1. Define humility.
2. Summarize the teaching of Philippians 1:27—2:11.
3. Explain how the humility will allow for harmonious relationships within the church.
4. Identify an area of his life that he will seek to bring into conformity with the attitude of Christ.

Into the Lesson

Before class, place the word *humility* on the chalkboard. As the class members arrive, give each a small index card. Ask them to jot down words they associate with the word *humility*. Form groups of three for the participants to share their responses. Allow up to ten minutes for this. Then call the groups together and share some of the responses.

Move into the Bible study time by stating that today's text provides insights into Christlikeness that will promote personal contentment and harmony in the church.

Into the Word

Briefly present the material in the "Introduction" section of this lesson. Read the entire Scripture text aloud. Then develop the lesson as a discussion, using the following questions.

1. Paul asked the Philippians to live in a manner worthy of the gospel of Christ, contending as one man for the faith. How would his teaching in Philippians 2:1-11 help to accomplish this?
2. Paul appealed to the Philippians to be like-minded. What were the reasons given to cause the people to do as he asked? (v. 1)
3. What does it mean for Christians to be like-minded? (v. 2)
4. What attitude is to characterize the Christian's relationship to others? (v. 3)
5. Define humility. (Humility is defined as the quality or state of being humble, which is the lack of all signs of pride, arrogance, or self-assertiveness.)
6. How is Christ an example of humility? (vv. 5-11)
7. Verse 4 provides a guiding principle for the Christian life. How can this be applied?

Into Life

It is one thing to speak of living worthy of the gospel, and for the interests of others, and to live humbly, but it is something else to put it into everyday practice. Have a class member read Mark 10:43-45.

Prepare a "can of worms" and pass it around the class. The "worms" are slips of paper on which are written the following situations. Have each three or four persons draw out a situation, discuss it, and then explain how this lesson text can be applied in that situation.

1. The Bible-in-Action class wants to develop a project to remodel the church kitchen. It will cost thirty thousand dollars and will require the solicitation of funds from the entire congregation. The leaders of the church have asked the class not to do this because of other more pressing needs within the congregation. How should the class members respond?
2. The leaders of the Fidelis Class have selected curriculum topics for their class for the next year. Eloise is not at all happy with the choices, yet she wants to remain in this class. How should Eloise respond? The leaders of the class?
3. Gayle is the director of vacation Bible school. She has chosen to have the VBS at a time the children's director prefers it not be held. The dates are now on the calendar. How should the children's director respond? Gayle?
4. The Beattys have been members of First Church for many years. Their son wants to have his wedding on a date when the VBS closing program is scheduled. They asked the VBS people to move the dates for the program. This was not possible. The Beattys are hurt. How should they respond?
5. Jane has served faithfully as a teacher in the children's department for years. She is surprised at the annual teachers' banquet when her assistant, who is not very dependable, is honored for her service. How should Jane respond?

Ask the class members how their lives need to be brought into conformity with Christ's example of humility. Instruct them to use the other side of the index card given them at the beginning of the session and write a memo to themselves identifying a way to bring their lives into conformity with Christ.

Close the session with prayer.

Let's Talk It Over

The questions on this page are designed to encourage review of the lesson Scriptures and to promote discussion of the lesson by the class. The answers provided are only discussion starters. Let your class talk it over from there.

1. What recent examples can you give of your church or Sunday-school class demonstrating unity behind a project or goal? If you cannot name an example, is it for lack of unity or lack of goals? What should be done?

Some churches have a reputation for harmony and unity when, in fact, that unity has never been tested. When a church begins a new evangelistic effort, initiates a building program, or in some other way makes a new assault on the domain of Satan, it is shown if they are of one mind and one spirit.

Through prayer, Bible study, and assessment of the situation, the leaders of your class or your church should be able to identify what God is calling you to do. Churches cannot do everything at once. Choices must be made. Some worthy projects must be postponed. That is the time for showing deference, and for uniting behind your leaders and "strive together for the faith."

2. If all Christians, in humility, esteemed others better than themselves and looked out for the interests of others (vv. 3, 4), how would everyday behavior change? How would churches change?

Taking the focus off of self would result in the expression of much more genuine love. It would mean an end to envy. One could rejoice at his neighbor's success without feeling threatened. One would be a lot more generous, and find himself doing many more deeds of kindness.

At church, it means each person would stop insisting on having his own way. Churches that are growing have learned that they must program to meet the needs of the people they hope to reach, more so than the needs of the people who have been there for years. It means that members would be willing to restructure their friendship circles to include more people, or give up an office or other assignment to allow someone else a chance to serve in that capacity. It means learning to sing different songs, or otherwise modify the worship to meet the needs of other people.

3. To voluntarily defer personal rights in order to serve the need of another is a sign of strength, not weakness. Tell why you agree or disagree with that statement.

The key word here is *voluntarily*. If a person, an institution, or a government usurps our rights by force, it is because they are stronger than we are. To submit to that power, when we would choose to do otherwise, makes us feel weak.

The weak individual cannot afford to give up any rights. He guards them jealously since they are his only reassurance that he is somebody, or that he has any power. If you cut him off in traffic he will exercise his right to honk his horn, shake his fist, and maybe even swear at you. He could not respect himself if he let you get by unpunished. The strong person, confident of who he is, can give up that right and simply forgive you.

No matter what rights Jesus gave up, no matter how people abused Him, nothing changed the fact that He was the Son of God. Christians, we can afford to give up a lot, knowing that they are the adopted children of God.

4. What are some personal rights that Christians may give up for the good of others?

Many Christians give up their right to free time. Instead of spending many hours on a favorite hobby, or becoming expert at some sport, they fill their free time with meaningful service to God's work on earth. Christians give up their right to spend all of their take-home earnings. As stewards of the bounty God supplies, they give large sums for the propagation of the gospel. They also give up their right to live solitary or selfish lives in the interest of sharing the gospel with those who are lost without it.

5. Christians readily confess Jesus Christ as Lord. How does one carry that confession beyond words into actions? What about those for whom it remains only words?

Paul is writing to the Christians at Philippi. Reiterating the fact that Jesus is Lord, Paul exhorts Christians to follow Jesus' example of humble service. Like Him, we must be available to God for purposes greater than our selfish interests. Remember the words of Jesus, "Not every one that saith unto me, Lord, Lord, shall enter into the kingdom of heaven; but he that doeth the will of my Father which is in heaven" (Matthew 7:21).

Pressing On in Christ

LESSON SCRIPTURE: Philippians 3.

PRINTED TEXT: Philippians 3:7-21.

Philippians 3:7-21

7 What things were gain to me, those I counted loss for Christ.

8 Yea doubtless, and I count all things but loss for the excellency of the knowledge of Christ Jesus my Lord: for whom I have suffered the loss of all things, and do count them but dung, that I may win Christ,

9 And be found in him, not having mine own righteousness, which is of the law, but that which is through the faith of Christ, the righteousness which is of God by faith:

10 That I may know him, and the power of his resurrection, and the fellowship of his sufferings, being made conformable unto his death;

11 If by any means I might attain unto the resurrection of the dead.

12 Not as though I had already attained, either were already perfect: but I follow after, if that I may apprehend that for which also I am apprehended of Christ Jesus.

13 Brethren, I count not myself to have apprehended: but this one thing I do, forgetting those things which are behind, and reaching forth unto those things which are before,

14 I press toward the mark for the prize of the high calling of God in Christ Jesus.

15 Let us therefore, as many as be perfect, be thus minded: and if in any thing ye be otherwise minded, God shall reveal even this unto you.

16 Nevertheless, whereto we have already attained, let us walk by the same rule, let us mind the same thing.

17 Brethren, be followers together of me, and mark them which walk so as ye have us for an ensample.

18 (For many walk, of whom I have told you often, and now tell you even weeping, that they are the enemies of the cross of Christ:

19 Whose end is destruction, whose god is their belly, and whose glory is in their shame, who mind earthly things.)

20 For our conversation is in heaven; from whence also we look for the Saviour, the Lord Jesus Christ:

21 Who shall change our vile body, that it may be fashioned like unto his glorious body, according to the working whereby he is able even to subdue all things unto himself.

GOLDEN TEXT: Forgetting those things which are behind, and reaching forth unto those things which are before, I press toward the mark for the prize of the high calling of God in Christ Jesus.—Philippians 3:13, 14.

Lesson Aims

This lesson should equip students to:

1. Quote Philippians 3:13, 14.

2. Name something previously considered valuable that he is prepared to discard in order to serve Christ better.

3. Name one or more Christian role models—persons who follow Christ faithfully—whose example he accepts as valuable to himself.

Lesson Outline

INTRODUCTION

    A. More Worlds to Conquer

    B. Misplaced Confidence

I. THE CALL TO CHRIST (Philippians 3:7-11)

    A. "Assets" Became Liabilities (vv. 7, 8)

    B. Christ the Supreme Value (vv. 9-11)

II. THE COMMITMENT MADE (Philippians 3:12-14)

    Pressing On

III. THE COMPANY JOINED (Philippians 3:15-17)

IV. THOSE CONDEMNED WITH THE WORLD (Philippians 3:18, 19)

V. THE CONQUEST WITH JESUS (Philippians 3:20, 21)

    Waiting With Eagerness

CONCLUSION

    A. Winners Unlimited

    B. Prayer of Commitment

    C. Thought to Remember

Display visual 7 from the visuals/learning resources packet and refer to it as you discuss today's text. The visual is shown on page 284.

Introduction

A. More Worlds to Conquer

How would you like to be champion?

It's an attractive thought. In fact it draws and drives all kinds of people into all kinds of efforts to win at all kinds of games and contests and measured achievements. Some championships are one-time accomplishments. Having gone all the way in the state basketball tournament you take home the trophy and start preparing to fend off the next season's challengers.

Some championships are more continuously demanding. Having won the Olympic gold or the champion's belt for boxing, you have a choice. You can rest on your laurels and retire, or you can fight off the challenge of eager contenders until one of them beats you. In any case the world champion has no way to go but down; and that's not a very inspiring thought.

Today's lesson presents a different kind of championship with a different, and more inspiring conclusion. The apostle Paul, whose accomplishments in Christ already were outstanding, waves us onward and says, "Come on! There's a lot more ahead, and it's all good!"

B. Misplaced Confidence

Paul's former career offered self-satisfaction, status, influence, and security; but that wasn't enough! He had advanced in the Jews' religion more than many of his peers (Galatians 1:14), but God had something better for him in Christ.

Paul came to recognize that his family connections, his clean moral record, and his religious zeal could not earn God's favor. All these things, in fact, became liabilities, since they blinded him to his need for dependence on God's grace and forgiveness in Christ. So he abandoned them and accepted God's Son as his sole hope and basis for God's approval. He gave himself completely to serving Christ.

As a result of that service he was now a prisoner in Rome, writing to his fellow Christians at Philipppi. The Philippian church showed very few faults. But it seems that some were urging the brethren to turn to dependence on Old Testament law for their standing with God. In the opening verses of Philippians 3 Paul warned against this kind of teaching.

I. The Call to Christ (Philippians 3:7-11)

A. "Assets" Became Liabilities (vv. 7, 8)

7, 8. What things were gain to me, those I counted loss for Christ. Yea doubtless, and I count all things but loss for the excellency of the knowledge of Christ Jesus my Lord: for whom I have suffered the loss of all things, and do count them but dung, that I may win Christ.

What things were gain ... I counted loss. Paul is speaking of what may be considered the assets of his former life. Any assets—material, political, social, or even religious—that tempted him to depend on them rather than on Christ for the good life, he wrote off as liabilities.

I count all things but loss for the excellency of the knowledge of Christ Jesus my Lord. The knowledge of Christ begins with learning who He is, what He thinks and says and does, and what He desires for us. It goes on to that personal and intimate acquaintance that comes from living with Him and for Him, and leads us to rejoice in the prospect of being with Him forever. That knowledge is the pearl of great price, justifying the sale of all else one may possess in order to have it (Matthew 13:46).

For whom I have suffered the loss of all things. Accepting Christ Jesus as Lord had cost Paul the favor of the Jewish community in which his security had lain. It seems also to have cost him his home and family, with all their material and emotional support. He knew that it would probably cost his physical life, but that too was acceptable, "so that I may finish my course with joy" (Acts 20:24).

And do count them but dung, that I may win Christ. "I consider them rubbish, that I may gain Christ" *(New International Version)*. Whatever stood in the way of gaining Christ was worthless in comparison with Him.

B. Christ the Supreme Value (vv. 9-11)

9. And be found in him, not having mine own righteousness, which is of the law, but that which is through the faith of Christ, the righteousness which is of God by faith.

Righteousness—right standing or acceptability with God—is the value recognized and sought by all those who would in any way honor Him. But how is one to achieve it? Paul states that it comes only through identification with Christ. *Not having mine own righteousness.* Righteousness that would be one's own would depend on that person's perfect conformity with the law. But no one can attain it. Instead it must come through faith—first, *the faith of Christ*—God's way revealed in Christ; and then through the believer's acceptance of that way—faith in Christ. That righteousness, or right standing, comes from God and is accepted by the believer.

10, 11. That I may know him, and the power of his resurrection, and the fellowship of his sufferings, being made conformable unto his death; if by any means I might attain unto the resurrection of the dead.

The knowledge of Christ, already noted as the ultimate goal and supreme value (v. 8), involves the three elements here named. First is *the power of his resurrection;* that is where the believer makes his first contact with Christ through faith. Jesus is "declared to be the Son of God with power . . . by the resurrection from the dead" (Romans 1:4).

Thus convinced, one is prepared to participate in *the fellowship of his sufferings,* rejoicing when as a follower he is counted worthy to suffer shame in the name of his beloved Lord (Acts

---

How to Say It

PHILIPPI.   Fuh-*lip*-pie or *Fil*-uh-pie.

5:41; compare 2 Timothy 2:11, 12). That is the companionship reserved for everyone who takes up the cross daily and follows Jesus.

Being made conformable unto his death. "Becoming like him in his death" *(New International Version)* is a third element in the intimate knowledge of Christ. For Paul that would finally mean a martyr's death; but already it had meant laying down his life, day by day, and self-interest by self-interest for Christ.

Paul's statement of his goal concludes, "And so, somehow, to attain to the resurrection from the dead" *(New International Version)*. Paul had already written to the Corinthians, "We must all appear before the judgment seat of Christ; that every one may receive the things done in his body, according to that he hath done, whether it be good or bad" (2 Corinthians 5:10). The resurrection he sought would not be subject to the second death, the casting into the lake of fire those who reject the offer of life in Christ Jesus (Revelation 20:12-15).

II. The Commitment Made (Philippians 3:12-14)

12. Not as though I had already attained, either were already perfect: but I follow after, if that I may apprehend that for which also I am apprehended of Christ Jesus.

The goal still lay ahead. Paul's heroic life and ministry might cause some observers to think he "had it made," in spite of the language used in the previous verses: "that I may win Christ" (v. 8); "that I may know him" (v. 20); "if by any means I might attain . . ." (v. 11). His hope still exceeded his realization.

"But I press on to take hold of that for which Christ Jesus took hold of me" *(New International Version)*. The Lord Jesus had arrested Paul on the road to Damascus and had commissioned him to be the best possible representative for His kingdom. Paul now continued to pursue that purpose with a passion.

13, 14. Brethren, I count not myself to have apprehended: but this one thing I do, forgetting those things which are behind, and reaching forth unto those things which are before, I press toward the mark for the prize of the high calling of God in Christ Jesus.

Brethren. Apostle though he was, Paul presented himself as a normal Christian, one among equals. What he was doing could be expected also from them. Yet he knew that some were inclined to assume that their salvation was the climax, rather than the beginning, of their Christian experience. He had already exhorted them to work out their own salvation—continuing the life of service to which they had been called (Philippians 2:12). Now, with emphasis on the personal pronoun *I*, he said something like what Joshua had said to the children of Israel: "As for me and my house, we will serve the Lord" (Joshua 24:15).

I count not myself to have apprehended. The ultimate accomplishment was still beyond Paul's grasp. But he could honestly claim one thing; he was reaching for it! *I do* is not in the original, but is supplied. The broken sentence is dramatic: "But one thing at least—"

Forgetting in this circumstance is equivalent to turning away from. No longer worth consideration for Paul were the cultural assets of his Jewish heritage (vv. 4-7). He also insisted that the sufferings he had experienced in his ministry were no longer worth considering when compared to the glory that lay ahead (Romans 8:18; 2 Corinthians 4:17, 18). And certainly the failures of his pre-Christian past had to be disregarded as being no part of the new man. Even so, the Christian must say, "Forget it!" to the former assets that have no Christian value, and also to the former liabilities that have been removed by the power of Christ.

I press toward the mark. The word used here calls up the image of a runner, straining every muscle and ligament in all-out effort, focused on the finish line.

For the prize of the high calling of God in Christ Jesus. The Christian's prize, in contrast to the Greek athlete's soon-wilting laurel wreath, is an eternal and unchanging crown (1 Corinthians 9:25; 1 Peter 5:4). Described as the "crown of righteousness" it is the final acknowledgment of acceptance with God. Again, in contrast to the athlete's prize, it is available to more than one in the same race—indeed, to "all them also that love his appearing" (2 Timothy 4:8; compare 1 Corinthians 9:24).

visual 7

PRESSING ON

The rim of Broken Top didn't seem far from the campground where the youth group from an Oregon church had spent the night. Everyone was in high spirits. The day was crisp and clear. The weather promised to turn warmer. It was a great day for hiking.

Each hiker had a small pack with lunch, water, energy food, and personal things. The group set out at a quick pace, and as the trail grew steeper, the pace slowed. Stragglers began to feel the strength of the mountain grade.

It was a three-hour hike to the rim, and all made the first hour quite well. In the second hour the climb grew steeper through some lovely alpine meadows and flowers. Some decided to stay and enjoy the beauty of the area, and one sponsor remained with them.

The final hour was hard climbing. It was steep, but not dangerous. In one wide meadow a few more slowed and said it was high enough.

About ten of the group finally reached the rim and could view the towering mountains stretching north, south, and west. Lakes became jewels far below, and the vista was a glory to be remembered forever. The goal was worth the struggle and the pain of the ascent.

Pressing on in the Christian life is hard; but remember, the goal is worth the climb. —W. P.

III. The Company Joined
(Philippians 3:15-17)

15. Let us therefore, as many as be perfect, be thus minded: and if in any thing ye be otherwise minded, God shall reveal even this unto you.

Up to this point the apostle has set forth his own experience, attitude, and practice. Now he suggests that his readers join him in the same pursuit. *Perfect* here, in contrast to verse 12, signifies maturity rather than faultless holiness. Experienced Christians may be expected to know their own limitations and to have developed a sense of purpose and direction. Thus they are "no more children, tossed to and fro, and carried about with every wind of doctrine" (Ephesians 4:14).

If in any thing ye be otherwise minded, God shall reveal even this unto you. There are Christians who, like the adolescent who fervently asserts and assumes a grown-up status, are too immature to recognize or admit their immaturity (compare 1 Corinthians 10:12). God isn't through with them yet. If they and those around them will be patient, they may yet learn humility and establish a straight course. More than time is needed, though. God works through His Word and His people, as agents of His Spirit, to accomplish His purpose. The church, as the body of believers serving one another, is most important to this end.

16. Nevertheless, whereto we have already attained, let us walk by the same rule, let us mind the same thing.

We don't understand it all, but let us follow faithfully what we do understand. There can be no progress without faithfulness to what we have already achieved. By living according to the light and knowledge already gained, the Christian opens the way for new light, new knowledge, new advancements in Christ.

17. Brethren, be followers together of me, and mark them which walk so as ye have us for an ensample.

The Christian attitude and Christian life were foreign to the Gentiles. They could best understand the way of Christ by seeing it demonstrated, both in the lives of individuals and in community settings such as the church. Paul's offer of himself as a role model in his following of Christ was not boastful; it was brave! (See also 1 Corinthians 11:1.) He had to provide the necessary demonstration. It is frightening enough to know that any one of us is an example to others; but deliberately to invite that public examination is heroic.

Even Paul was not willing to stand alone in that spotlight. He urged the Philippians to "take note of those who live according to the pattern we gave you" *(New International Version)*. Pay attention to the good (Philippians 4:8)! Take full advantage of the right kind of peer influence. It is still there.

IV. Those Condemned With the World (Philippians 3:18, 19)

18, 19. (For many walk, of whom I have told you often, and now tell you even weeping, that they are the enemies of the cross of Christ: whose end is destruction, whose god is their belly, and whose glory is in their shame, who mind earthly things.)

One wonders if the church in Philippi included *many* who could be thus described. The description would certainly fit the heathen world about them, and in all his teaching the apostle warned against such worldliness. *Weeping* would probably be reserved, however, for members of the Christian community who fell so far short of their pledged discipleship. It is, as often said, necessary for the church to be in the world, but tragic when the world is in the church.

Enemies of the cross—opposers to the way of Christ—would be especially those church members whose worldly ways became a scandal in the community. They would make the gospel seem worthless, and would give occasion to some who would return to works of the law for their salvation.

Whether these people are in the church or outside, the description of them is frighteningly familiar. What, after all, claims most of our time and attention? What motivates our actions and the way we spend our money? Our Lord himself acknowledged the popularity of the broad and easy way that leads to destruction (Matthew 7: 13). May we heed His warning.

V. The Conquest With Jesus (Philippians 3:20, 21)

20. For our conversation is in heaven; from whence also we look for the Saviour, the Lord Jesus Christ.

Philippi was a Roman city (colony) within Macedonia. Its people were Roman citizens. In any emergency, they could expect Roman armies to come swiftly to their defense. Likewise, Paul said, Christians have their citizenship, their ultimate loyalty, and their hope of salvation in the commonwealth of Heaven. They expect from there the arrival of their Rescuer, who has all power and authority as Lord, but is indeed the servant-prophet from Nazareth and God's anointed Messiah. The apostle identifies Him very carefully. The message comes through, loud and clear, to Christians in all places and times: Heaven is your hometown; think about home, and not about the destruction-doomed things of the world.

21. Who shall change our vile body, that it may be fashioned like unto his glorious body, according to the working whereby he is able even to subdue all things unto himself.

The physical body is subject to destruction along with the rest of the world. It excites and overwhelms us to know that Christ "will transform the body of our humble state into conformity with the body of His glory" *(New American Standard Bible)*. Peter, James, and John had seen a preview of that transformation when Jesus was transfigured on the mountain (Matthew 17:1, 2). Peter and John recalled it in their writings (2 Peter 1:16, 17; 1 John 3:2), and Paul wrote at length about the change by which God will provide His own with glorified and indestructible spiritual bodies in the resurrection (1 Corinthians 15:42-57; 2 Corinthians 5:1-4).

According to the working whereby he is able even to subdue all things unto himself. With the power by which He created all things (John 1:3), and by which He worked miracles during His earthly ministry, and that has been extended over Heaven and earth (Matthew 28:18) the Lord of glory will be fully able to share that glory with His own.

WAITING WITH EAGERNESS

"He's coming! He's coming!" The cry had run through the crowd several times in the past hour. Each time the promise proved to be inaccurate, and the people settled back; but still in eager expectation.

We were missionaries in Jamaica, and we waited with the throng along the roadside. Having small children with us, we had brought water, iced tea, cookies, and sandwiches to ease the boredom of waiting.

The tropic sun grew hotter and beat down on the thousands along the way. Street venders were doing a record business in soda pop, ice, and other refreshments. Even with the long delay no one was in a bad mood.

The cry came again. "He's coming!" This time it was true. A slow cavalcade of cars came up the asphalt. Flags waved. The crowd cheered. There he was! Winston Churchill sat in the back seat of an open limousine with Lady Churchill at his side. His hand was raised in the V for victory sign he had made famous during World War II.

It was a great day for the Jamaican people. We cheered and waved with the multitude. It was a long wait for a moment's view, but Churchill was our hero.

The King of kings is coming! Paul wrote, "We look for the Saviour" who will make all things new. As believers, let us wait with expectation and eagerness until He appears.   —W. P.

Home Daily Bible Readings

Monday, Apr. 10—No Trust in the Flesh (Philippians 3:1-6)
Tuesday, Apr. 11—Righteous Only Through Christ (Philippians 3:7-12)
Wednesday, Apr. 12—Like-minded Believers (Philippians 3:13-21)
Thursday, Apr. 13—Strength Found in God (Psalm 18:1-6)
Friday, Apr. 14—Depend on God (Psalm 71:1-7)
Saturday, Apr. 15—Staying Close to God (Psalm 73:21-28)
Sunday, Apr. 16—Abiding in Christ (John 15:7-17)

Conclusion

A. Winners Unlimited

As a schoolboy I was never big enough, or skillful enough, to compete successfully in athletics; but as a news reporter I followed the school teams with great interest. I wonder if Paul was not in a similar situation—an athlete by interest if not by participation. To the Corinthians he wrote of the discipline necessary for an athlete to compete successfully (1 Corinthians 9:24-27); to Timothy he urged the need to follow the rules of the game (2 Timothy 2:5). Hebrews 12:1, 2 speaks of the persistence and strength required of a participant in a long race. And in today's text we have seen the intense concentration and exertion that is necessary for a successful runner.

Paul's readers knew what he was talking about. But they also knew that his real message was not about sports; it was about Jesus and the Christian's commitment to Him. "Train yourself to be godly," he exhorted Timothy. "For physical training is of some value, but godliness has value for all things, holding promise for both the present life and the life to come" (1 Timothy 4:7, 8, *New International Version*). The grand prize in godliness is not limited to any one competitor, nor to any one kind of person. At the conclusion of life's race Paul exulted, "I have fought a good fight, I have finished my course, I have kept the faith: henceforth there is laid up for me a crown of righteousness, which the Lord, the righteous judge, shall give me at that day: and not to me only, but unto all them also that love his appearing" (2 Timothy 4:7, 8). The winners' circle is limited only by the participants' willingness to press on to the goal in Christ!

B. Prayer of Commitment

We thank and praise You, our Father, for all who help us in our approach to You: for companions who encourage as we go, for teachers of the Word who show the way, for heroes such as Paul who lead us onward, and most of all, for Jesus, our Savior and the Goal of our striving. In His name we commit ourselves anew to His cause, and we plead Your ever-present help. Amen.

C. Thought to Remember

I'm pressing on the upward way,
New heights I'm gaining every day;
Still praying as I'm onward bound,
"Lord, plant my feet on higher ground."
—JOHNSON OATMAN, JR.

Learning by Doing

This page contains an alternate lesson plan emphasizing learning activities. Classes desiring such student involvement will find these suggestions helpful.

Learning Goals

After studying Philippians 3:7-21, a student will be able to:

1. Identify the chief motivation of Paul's life—and why.

2. Evaluate the motivation of his own life.

3. Identify an area of his Christian life that he will endeavor to bring into conformity with God's will.

Into the Lesson

Place the following sentence on the chalkboard before the class members arrive: "My greatest achievement up to now has been—" As the class members arrive, give each person a small index card and ask them to complete the sentence. Then have them form groups of three to share their achievements. Allow the individuals and groups six to eight minutes to work together.

Then let the groups share their answers with the entire class. (If your class members don't know each other well, you could have each person in a group introduce another person in the group, citing that person's greatest achievement.) Don't comment about the achievements—merely list them on a sheet of newsprint or on the chalkboard so that you can refer to them later in the session.

Make the transition into today's lesson by stating that Philippians 3 provides insight into Paul's assessment of his achievements and his motivations. Suggest that the students take this opportunity to evaluate themselves.

Into the Word

Present the lesson background found under the heading "Misplaced Confidence" in the "Introduction" section of this lesson. Have a class member read the text aloud.

Assign the students to groups of three (The previous groups they worked with will work well) and give each group one of the tasks below.

1. Read Philippians 3:4-21. Paul said that he considered everything loss for the sake of Christ. What in Paul's life gave him reason *not* to count it all loss for Christ? What tensions must have arisen as Paul made his decision to throw all of his efforts into gaining Christ? Was that any easier for Paul than it is for us?

2. Read Philippians 3:4-21. Paul said that he pressed on toward the goal to win the prize for which God had called him. What did he mean when he said that he forgot that which was behind? What tensions must have arisen as Paul made this decision? Why would it have been difficult for him to forget what was behind? Was his decision any easier than it would be for us?

3. Read Philippians 2:4-21. Paul pleaded for the Christians at Philippi to follow his example, rather than following the enemies of the cross. How did he contrast those who are enemies of the cross with those whose citizenship is in Heaven? Of what value is that contrast to us today?

Allow the groups six to eight minutes to complete their assignments. When you are ready to proceed, let the groups answer the questions. Fill in needed information from the comments on the text as you go.

Into Life

Refer to the class members' achievements listed on the chalkboard. Ask, How do you think Paul would have us regard these achievements? Why? Continue developing the discussion by using the following questions:

1. How can we keep our achievements in proper perspective?

2. Life is full of difficulties of various kinds. It deals us discouragement often. The pressures get to us. How, then, can we continue to press on toward the goal to win the prize in Christ Jesus?

3. How does it affect us to know that our citizenship is in Heaven?

Give each person the self-evaluation form below and ask them to complete it.

How Am I Doing?

1. I consider all of my achievements loss for the sake of Christ.   Yes   No

2. I can honestly say that I am straining toward the goal to win the prize for which God has called me.   Yes   No

3. I am well aware that my citizenship is in Heaven.   Yes   No

I want my life to follow Paul's example by—

To begin to achieve that goal, this week I will—

Close the session with prayer.

Let's Talk It Over

The questions on this page are designed to encourage review of the lesson Scriptures and to promote discussion of the lesson by the class. The answers provided are only discussion starters. Let your class talk it over from there.

1. What are some credentials in which we take pride? How can we demonstrate that our relationship with Christ is of far more value?

We may be justifiably proud of any number of accomplishments: a degree we hold, our position at work or a business we own, an office we hold in a civic organization, or our success in building a house or some other project. The apostle Paul could recall an impressive list of accomplishments in which he once took great pride. But those things had been reduced to the value of rubbish in comparison to knowing Jesus as Lord.

We testify to the value we put upon our relationship with Christ by what we let take precedence in our lives. If we complain that we have no time to serve Christ or commune with Him in prayer, what has taken precedence? If we claim to have no money to give a tithe to God, but build an addition onto the house, what has taken precedence? If we use the excuse of possessing no talent when asked to serve, but accept promotions readily at work, what has taken precedence?

2. Paul speaks of striving to "apprehend that for which also I am apprehended of Christ Jesus." What, specifically, was the calling he sought to fulfill? What is the purpose for which Christ has "apprehended" you?

Paul had the benefit of a direct word from the Lord as to his calling. When Christ appeared to him on the road to Damascus, He revealed His intention that Paul should be "a minister and a witness," delivering the Gentiles "from darkness to light, and from the power of Satan unto God" (Acts 26:16, 18).

Each Christian must discern the particulars of God's calling for his life, but the Bible places certain expectations upon every Christian. For example, we know that we are to be a light to the world (Matthew 5:14-16). We are to be God's ambassadors of reconciliation (2 Corinthians 5:17-20). We are to live pure lives (1 Peter 1:14-16). We are to employ the gifts God gives in service for the good of our brother and sister Christians (1 Peter 4:10).

3. Why is it good for all of us, like Paul, to forget what lies behind us?

If our past is marked by success and achievements in which we glory, we will be tempted to become complacent. We could go on for years celebrating the past, and daring nothing new. If the past is full of disappointments and failures, it may rob us of courage and faith to try today. Either way, we are better off to keep our focus on the goal that lies ahead, straining forward with no regard to what we accomplished, or failed to accomplish, yesterday.

4. Who is providing a current real-life example for you? Could you tell a new Christian, "follow my example"? Why or why not?

Paul knew the value of illustration in teaching. He knew that if his teaching on the Christian life remained academic, lives would not be changed. He had taken the gospel to Philippi in the first place (Acts 16), and the converts there would naturally look to see how their teacher walked his talk. Paul had committed himself to serving Christ without reservation, and he urged the Philippians to follow his example.

Most of us are influenced far more by what we see practiced than what we hear preached of the Christian life. Hopefully you have had the benefit of godly parents, a Sunday-school teacher, an elder, or a minister who has given flesh to the commands of Christ. If you are not comfortable inviting others to follow your example, you need to change your life. Someone may follow your example, whether you wish it or not.

5. Paul described some in the church at Philippi as "enemies of the cross." How may church members today fall in that category?

Verse 19 speaks volumes about those whom Paul called "enemies of the cross." They had departed from the way that leads to life. Desire to please God had been replaced with desire to satisfy the appetites of the flesh. They gloried in things for which they should have been ashamed. Their focus was on earthly pursuits and pleasures.

Unfortunately, that description fits some church members today. They wear the name Christian, but they are bad advertising. They make it appear as though Christ makes no difference. They are the hypocrites that cause the world to scorn the church.

Rejoicing in Christ

LESSON SCRIPTURE: Philippians 4.

PRINTED TEXT: Philippians 4:4-19.

Philippians 4:4-19

4 Rejoice in the Lord always: and again I say, Rejoice.

5 Let your moderation be known unto all men. The Lord is at hand.

6 Be careful for nothing; but in every thing by prayer and supplication with thanksgiving let your requests be made known unto God.

7 And the peace of God, which passeth all understanding, shall keep your hearts and minds through Christ Jesus.

8 Finally, brethren, whatsoever things are true, whatsoever things are honest, whatsoever things are just, whatsoever things are pure, whatsoever things are lovely, whatsoever things are of good report; if there be any virtue, and if there be any praise, think on these things.

9 Those things, which ye have both learned, and received, and heard, and seen in me, do: and the God of peace shall be with you.

10 But I rejoiced in the Lord greatly, that now at the last your care of me hath flourished again; wherein ye were also careful, but ye lacked opportunity.

11 Not that I speak in respect of want: for I have learned, in whatsoever state I am, therewith to be content.

12 I know both how to be abased, and I know how to abound: every where and in all things I am instructed both to be full and to be hungry, both to abound and to suffer need.

13 I can do all things through Christ which strengtheneth me.

14 Notwithstanding, ye have well done, that ye did communicate with my affliction.

15 Now ye Philippians know also, that in the beginning of the gospel, when I departed from Macedonia, no church communicated with me as concerning giving and receiving, but ye only.

16 For even in Thessalonica ye sent once and again unto my necessity.

17 Not because I desire a gift: but I desire fruit that may abound to your account.

18 But I have all, and abound: I am full, having received of Epaphroditus the things which were sent from you, an odor of a sweet smell, a sacrifice acceptable, well-pleasing to God.

19 But my God shall supply all your need according to his riches in glory by Christ Jesus.

GOLDEN TEXT: Rejoice in the Lord always: and again I say, Rejoice.—Philippians 4:4.

Letters From Prison
Unit 3: Philippians—
Life in Christ (Lessons 5-8)

Lesson Aims

This study should equip the student to:

1. Cite reasons for Paul's rejoicing in the face of his current difficulties.

2. Name some area of concern over which he will now write, "Canceled by joy in Christ."

Lesson Outline

INTRODUCTION

  A. Meaningful Last Words

  B. Saying It Again

  I. REJOICE, CONFIDING IN GOD (Philippians 4:4-7)

    A. Reflect It in Manner (vv. 4, 5)

    B. Reinforce It in Prayer (vv. 6,7)

    Overcoming Anxiety

  II. REJOICE, CONTEMPLATING THE GOOD (Philippians 4:8, 9)

    Thinking Up!

  III. REJOICE, CONTENT WITH WHAT YOU HAVE (Philippians 4:10-13)

    A. Grateful for Gifts (vv. 10, 11)

    B. Grounded in Christ (vv. 12, 13)

  IV. REJOICE, COMMUNICATING GOD'S PROVISION (Philippians 4:14-19)

    A. Partnership Acknowledged (vv. 14-17)

    B. Provision Assured (vv. 18, 19)

CONCLUSION

  A. Encore!

  B. Prayer

  C. Thought to Remember

Display visual 8 from the visuals/learning resources packet. It relates to the thoughts in verses 10-13. The visual is shown on page 294.

Introduction

A. Meaningful Last Words

What word do you use in parting from a friend? And what do you mean by it? The answer depends on language and tradition, and the meaning is sometimes lost in the habit. *Aloha* serves as a general friendly greeting in Hawaii. Among Jews the parting word is *shalom*, or *peace*.

Germans may say, "auf Wiedersehen," loosely equivalent to *I'll be seeing you*. Latins may say *adieu* or *adios*, either of which means literally

"to God"—you are committed to His care. Users of the term do not always realize or mean that.

Farewell seems a bit formal to us, but carries a general and wholesome wish for good to the one greeted. More prayerful, though less generally understood, is our *goodbye*, shortened from God by ye, and signifying "God be with you." It loses much in the translation when growled through a closing door.

The Greeks sometimes used a word with quite pleasant, but wide-ranging significance. *Chairete*, they said, meaning "rejoice" or "enjoy." And that's the word Paul used to indicate the dominant spirit and conclusion of his letter to the saints at Philippi.

The apostle made it clear that he did not advise the raucous revelry that passed for fun and rejoicing among the pagan Greeks; but neither did he advocate a grim endurance of godliness. He practiced the kind of piety that can smile through tears and can sing praises to God at midnight while shackled in a dungeon (Acts 16:25). That happened at Philippi, and so Paul encouraged those same Philippians to enjoy their life in Christ. The Lord himself had first sounded the theme: "Ye now therefore have sorrow: but I will see you again, and your heart shall rejoice, and your joy no man taketh from you.... In the world ye shall have tribulation: but be of good cheer; I have overcome the world" (John 16:22, 33).

B. Saying It Again

Paul sometimes repeated himself, and he admitted it without embarrassment (Philippians 3:1). From the repetitions, his friends might discern what he considered to be most important. Early in the Philippian letter he had urged, "Complete my joy by being of the same mind, having the same love, being in full accord and of one mind" (2:2, *Revised Standard Version*).

In his final chapter Paul returned to the same theme, addressing his plea for oneness directly to two women otherwise unknown. He added a request for others in the body of Christ to assist their leaders in all good works (vv. 2, 3). And Paul said it again, the outcome to be expected from such cooperation is rejoicing in the Lord.

I. Rejoice, Confiding in God (Philippians 4:4-7)

A. Reflect It in Manner (vv. 4, 5)

4. Rejoice in the Lord always: and again I say, Rejoice.

There was value in the traditional Greek farewell, "Rejoice," But it was a value without adequate support. That could be established only *in* the Lord. As Paul and Silas had sung praises in the Lord while in a Philippian jail, so now Paul would write from another prison in Rome, urging the same spirit on his Philippian friends. Because of *the Lord*, rejoicing was possible *always*.

5. Let your moderation be known unto all men. The Lord is at hand.

Moderation translates an adjective that is also rendered *forbearing, reasonable, gentle, considerate,* or *fair*. It describes that "sweet reasonableness" which, when confronted with difficulty, would refrain from retaliation and would even yield its own rights in the interest of peace. Such a spirit would be evident to all observers, without boast or announcement.

The Lord is at hand, or nearby. He knows what is going on and is fully capable of rendering judgment; hence personal retaliation is both unnecessary and inappropriate. He is coming in judgment and will settle all accounts.

B. Reinforce It in Prayer (vv. 6, 7)

6. Be careful for nothing; but in every thing by prayer and supplication with thanksgiving let your requests be made known unto God.

Be careful for nothing. Don't be anxious about anything. Jesus warned against all such fretfulness in His Sermon on the Mount (Matthew 6:25-34). The alternative to anxious care is believing prayer. That was Jesus' recommendation (Matthew 7:7-11); the one in need is to ask, and seek, and knock for admission at God's throne. And here it is Paul's recommendation. *Nothing* is to become an object of fearful anxiety, but *everything* is to come under the canopy of prayer. Approach God with it; recognize your need; specify your request; and bathe it all in humble gratitude for blessings already received. Glad thanksgiving and humble request are the qualities of serenity and peace.

7. And the peace of God, which passeth all understanding, shall keep your hearts and minds through Christ Jesus.

Peace indicates wholeness of being and serenity of spirit, which comes from a close relationship to the all-wise and almighty God. Jesus spoke of peace as His gift to His own followers: "Peace I leave with you, my peace I give unto you: not as the world giveth, give I unto you. Let not your heart be troubled, neither let it be afraid" (John 14:27).

Human *understanding,* or wisdom, could never formulate or invent, or even imagine, request, or comprehend the wholeness of God, which He makes available to His children. He is indeed "able to do exceeding abundantly above all that we ask or think" (Ephesians 3:20).

How to Say It

CHAIRETE. (Greek) *Ky*-ray-tay.
EPAPHRODITUS. E-paf-ro-*dye*-tus.
MACEDONIA. Mass-uh-*doe*-nee-uh.
THESSALONICA. *Thess*-suh-lo-*nye*-kuh (strong accent on nye); *th* as in *thin*.

Keep introduces a military figure of speech. God's peace "shall garrison and mount guard over" *(Amplified Version)* the spirit of the prayerful saint, as an armed escort might protect a traveler in a dangerous way.

OVERCOMING ANXIETY

Bill Kennedy, a sheriff's deputy who felt the stress of death and violence in his demanding job, found a way to overcome his anxiety; in doing so, he got a new hold on life.

Two nights a week, Bill cuddles babies. He is one of fourteen volunteers who spend spare time in the neonatal intensive care unit at Sacred Heart General Hospital in Eugene, Oregon. As a baby cuddler, Bill Kennedy gives the babies the attention they need and might not otherwise get.

Kennedy is the father of two teen-age girls, so it has been years since he has done this. With a grin he says, "You can never get too old to enjoy this. It is the opposite of what I see so much of— the death and the dying. This is the beginning, where people are starting out."

A nurse in the unit says that Kennedy is very gentle with the babies, and that they like his voice and touch. She states that loving and giving are really important in a baby's development.

In thinking of others and meeting their needs, Kennedy relieves his own anxiety.

Paul advises each of us not to be anxious, but with thanksgiving to make our requests known to God. Gratitude for blessings already received will cause us to be aware of God's constant care for us. With such assurance, we too can overcome anxiety.
—W. P.

II. Rejoice, Contemplating the Good (Philippians 4:8, 9)

8. Finally, brethren, whatsoever things are true, whatsoever things are honest, whatsoever things are just, whatsoever things are pure, whatsoever things are lovely, whatsoever things are of good report; if there be any virtue, and if there be any praise, think on these things.

Even the most fervent prayer of the most faithful saint will not immediately bring relief from every ill.

Finally, then, may be understood "as for the rest"—the things in which we have to wait awhile for the answer to our prayers. Even before the perfect peace of God takes over, one may benefit from wise mental discipline. And here the apostle uses terms that were familiar to the Greek world outside the church. Six qualities are mentioned, and they seem to fall into pairs. *True* and *honest* stand opposed to hypocrisy and deceit; *just* and *pure* contrast with confusion and pollution; *lovely* and *of good report* speak of attractive, rather than repulsive qualities. A final pair, *virtue* and *praise*, summarize the others in classical Greek, rather than peculiarly religious, terms.

A closer look at Paul's recommendation is appropriate. *True* describes that which conforms to reality. *Honest* adds the thought of being honorable, noble, and worthy of respect.

Just refers to what is upright, fair, and—for the Christian—pleasing to God. *Pure* speaks of freedom from pollution or adulteration. Mixtures of selfish ambition with promotion of "good causes" do not fit the description.

Lovely describes what is amiable and worthy of love.

Virtue. In his *Word Studies*, Vincent says, "The original classical sense of the word had no special moral import, but denoted excellence of any kind—bravery, rank, nobility; also, excellence of land, animals, things, classes of persons." The kindred word, rendered here as *praise*, indicates anything that is worthy of respect or acclaim. So, in summary of this passage, Paul says, "If anything is excellent or praiseworthy—think about such things" *(New International Version)*.

What Paul is recommending is a deliberate focus of attention and purposeful direction of one's life course toward what is good. When you realize that ultimate truth, goodness, and beauty are in the Person of Him who said, "I am the way, the truth, and the life; no man cometh unto the Father, but by me" (John 14:6), you have the Christian recipe for life and living.

THINKING UP!

The usual daily news is a discouraging array of information. Reports of murder, riots, war, family conflict, drug abuse, dishonesty in high places, etc. fill the media. Amidst all of this it is hard to keep from discouragement or despair over our human condition.

One lady revealed her method of dealing with all the disheartening events going on about her.

"I go for a walk every day," she said. "On my walk I look up to the clouds and the sky. Then I turn my eyes to the majestic hills that surround our valley. I think of God who made it all and thank Him that He cared enough to create our world, place me in it, and send Jesus as my Savior."

Her final remark was the most telling. "I just keep 'Thinking up'! If I forget to 'think up,' the evil in the world seems more than I can handle. Thinking of Jesus and His righteousness, I can go through each day successfully."

That is the sense of Paul's instruction. If we think only on the evil in the world, we can be overwhelmed. When we think on the good and holy, we cleanse both our minds and our spirits. Keep "thinking up"!   —W. P.

9. Those things, which ye have both learned, and received, and heard, and seen in me, do: and the God of peace shall be with you.

Few if any of the Philippian Christians had seen Jesus in the flesh; but they had seen Paul's reflection of Jesus under many different circumstances. They had *learned* of Christ through Paul's teaching; they had *received* the gospel as he presented it and had been baptized into Christ (Acts 16:15, 33); they had *heard* his instruction concerning their spiritual development; and they had *seen* in him a consistent demonstration of all he taught.

One thing more remained. The Philippians were to put in action what they had learned from Paul. Right thinking issues naturally in right doing, but it must never stop short of that completion. (See James 2:17-26.)

Verse 7 promised "the peace of God" in response to trustful, thankful prayer. This promises the presence of *the God of peace* in response to consistent, active faith.

III. Rejoice, Content With What You Have (Philippians 4:10-13)

A. Grateful for Gifts (vv. 10, 11)

10. But I rejoiced in the Lord greatly, that now at the last your care of me hath flourished again; wherein ye were also careful, but ye lacked opportunity.

Paul now turns to a cause for his own rejoicing. The Philippian saints had sent a gift to him by Epaphroditus, one of their members. From Philippians 2:25-30 we conclude that Epaphroditus stayed and worked with Paul in Rome for some time. He then fell seriously ill, but at last recovered sufficiently to make the journey back to Philippi. It seems natural to assume that Paul had already expressed appreciation for the gift—at least as soon as he sent word of

Home Daily Bible Readings

Monday, Apr. 17—Reasons to Rejoice (Philippians 4:1-7)

Tuesday, Apr. 18—The Secret of Contentment (Philippians 4:8-14)

Wednesday, Apr. 19—Encouragement to the Philippians (Philippians 4:15-23)

Thursday, Apr. 20—Rejoice in All Things (Romans 5:1-8)

Friday, Apr. 21—God's Chosen People (1 Peter 1:1-9)

Saturday, Apr. 22—Happy to Suffer (1 Peter 4:12-19)

Sunday, Apr. 23—Mary Rejoiced (Luke 1:46-55)

Epaphroditus' illness. So it was not necessary for him to begin the present letter with mention of their generosity. But the subject of rejoicing brought another "thank-you" for their sharing in his labors (see 1:3-8).

The Philippians' *care* for Paul was not anxiety, but was a thoughtful regard that kept him and his welfare in mind. That had never disappeared, but like a green plant in dry weather it had wilted for a time. Now with refreshing rains of opportunity, it had flourished again.

11. Not that I speak in respect of want: for I have learned, in whatsoever state I am, therewith to be content.

Paul was very careful not to imply any request for another gift. He had *learned* the key to contentment. *Content* here translates a word used by Stoic philosophers to describe self-reliance—the possession of inner resources, and independence from control by circumstances. Paul's sense of self-worth and well-being did not depend on how much he had, or where he was, or whether he was popular or well treated. There was one important difference between Paul and the Stoics. His inner resources were built upon faith in Christ. Paul had *learned* from Christ, His words and His example; and he had learned from experience with Christ that His presence was more important than any outward circumstance.

B. Grounded in Christ (vv. 12, 13)

12. I know both how to be abased, and I know how to abound: every where and in all things I am instructed both to be full and to be hungry, both to abound and to suffer need.

Paul had experienced some amazing ups and downs. He was apparently reared in moderate wealth, as indicated by his standing among the

Jews. Even as a Christian he was at times the guest of rulers. On the other hand he could name an amazing catalog of hardships suffered for the sake of Christ (2 Corinthians 11: 23-28).

He dealt here mostly with material supply, especially of food—feast or famine. He might also have spoken of contentment in solitude or in society; sickness or health; success or failure; popularity or disdain; cold climate or warm; mountain country or flatland. He carried within himself the basis of his contentment.

13. I can do all things through Christ which strengtheneth me.

At this point Paul was not talking about working miracles, or even about the remarkable accomplishments of his ministry (1 Corinthians 15:10). All these he did indeed achieve through the power of Christ in him. But for the present he had in mind something much closer to the experience of common Christians: when adjustment to difficult circumstances became necessary, he could do that with a smile of rejoicing through the enabling power of Christ.

IV. Rejoice, Communicating God's Provision (Philippians 4:14-19)

A. Partnership Acknowledged (vv. 14-17)

14. Notwithstanding, ye have well done, that ye did communicate with my affliction.

Paul's staunch independence could almost make his friends feel that their gift was unneeded and virtually unheeded. Not so. They had been partners with him in bearing his troubles, and he was grateful. The apostle expressed genuine thanks without in any way indicating a continuing dependence.

15, 16. Now ye Philippians know also, that in the beginning of the gospel, when I departed from Macedonia, no church communicated with me as concerning giving and receiving, but ye only. For even in Thessalonica ye sent once and again unto my necessity.

Paul did not stay long at Philippi on his first visit, but that was long enough to establish a strong church. From the first they established the habit that has become a permanent trademark for "the churches of Macedonia"—the godly grace of giving (2 Corinthians 8:1-5).

When no other church gave to assist Paul in his ministry, the church in Philippi did so.

Even before leaving Macedonia, Paul engaged in a difficult church planting venture at the great city of Thessalonica; and there, on more than one occasion the Philippians sent gifts to him to relieve his need. Later at Corinth, Christian brethren came from Macedonia bringing gifts to supply what he needed (see 2 Corinthians 11:9). Surely such repeated expressions of concern indicate that the Philippians possessed the motivation of which Paul spoke in 2 Corinthians 9:7: "Each man should give what he has decided in his heart to give, not reluctantly or under compulsion, for God loves a cheerful giver" *(New International Version)*.

17. Not because I desire a gift: but I desire fruit that may abound to your account.

No one must ever be allowed to say that Paul was money-hungry! His concern was for the benefit that might accrue to the giver. He used words that were common in financial accounting: "I seek for the profit which increases to your account" *(New American Standard Bible)*. By their investment in the proclamation of the gospel the Philippian Christians were laying up for themselves treasure in the dependable bank of Heaven (Matthew 6:19, 20), and Paul was glad to see interest accruing to their credit.

B. Provision Assured (vv. 18, 19)

18, 19. But I have all, and abound: I am full, having received of Epaphroditus the things which were sent from you, an odor of a sweet smell, a sacrifice acceptable, well-pleasing to God. But my God shall supply all your need according to his riches in glory by Christ Jesus.

The apostle continues in half-playful use of banking terms: "I have received full payment and even more" *(New International Version)*. What do you suppose Paul did with the surplus from the Philippians' bounty after his immediate needs were met? We may be sure that he contributed to the needs of others, but he could not easily pass along the sense of warm satisfaction that came with his friends' thoughtful provision. The *sweet smell* of an acceptable sacrifice recalls Exodus 29:18, with its description of the burnt offerings made at the consecration of Aaron to the high priesthood: "It is a sweet savor, an offering made by fire unto the Lord." Even so, the Philippians' gift to Paul had more than temporal value. It was accepted by God as a sacrifice to Him.

My God shall supply all your need. The writer of Proverbs said, "He that hath pity upon the poor lendeth unto the Lord; and that which he hath given will he pay him again" (Proverbs 19:17). How much more readily God would honor the gift to His apostle!

According to his riches in glory by Christ Jesus. God does more than supply our earthly needs. With all His riches in Christ Jesus, He has provided a Heavenly reward in which our every need shall be filled. Rejoice in the Lord!

Conclusion

A. Encore!

"Let your speech be always with grace, seasoned with salt," Paul advised the Colossians (4:6). Accordingly the apostle frequently taught with a twinkle in his eye and with salt on his tongue. Especially to the Philippian friends he not only advised rejoicing but he demonstrated the gentle humor of ultimate optimism. He flavored his letter with surprising words borrowed from philosophy, the army, and the business world—but all clustered around Christ.

Was there tension between sisters in the church? Cheer up! Demonstrate sweet reasonableness to all. The Lord is close by and will take care of all judgment.

The prayerful, thankful saint will be supplied with peace like a military escort bringing him through trouble. And if he has not yet reached high levels of spiritual attainment he may still be helped by shaping his course according to the best he can find around him.

Fellowship in Christ becomes a partnership with investment in the bank of Heaven. And Christian generosity smells good to God!

But Paul was not through when he wrote the last verse in our text. His advice to rejoicing was not complete until it was topped with an encore of grand hallelujah: "Now unto God and our Father be glory for ever and ever. Amen" (v. 20). Now we can go on our way, rejoicing in Christ.

B. Prayer

Our Heavenly Father, You have blessed us through all our days with Your smile of compassionate love and generous provision. May we learn more fully to turn our faces to You with smiles of trust and gratitude, and with songs of joyous hope in Christ Jesus, Your Son. Amen.

C. Thought to Remember

No tears can quench the eternal flame of Christian joy.

PAUL'S CONTENTMENT DID NOT DEPEND ON CIRCUMSTANCES BUT ON HIS CONFIDENCE IN CHRIST

visual 8

Learning by Doing

This page contains an alternate lesson plan emphasizing learning activities. Classes desiring such student involvement will find these suggestions helpful.

Learning Goals

After this lesson a student will be able to:

1. Define "rejoice."
2. List reasons why Paul rejoiced in spite of his difficulties.
3. List reasons why we can be content in whatever situation we find ourselves.
4. Name an area of concern that he is willing to cease worrying over.

Into the Lesson

As the class members enter the room, give each a copy of the puzzle below.

A KEY WORD

If you solve this correctly, a key word from the lesson text will appear in the row of vertical boxes. Use Philippians 4:4-19 to help you.

1. Talking to God.
2. Satisfied with things as they are.
3. Think on things that are _____ .
4. Be careful for _____ .
5. Who provides strength.
6. The God of _____ will be with you.
7. God shall supply your _____ .

1. — —|—|— — —
2. — — — —|—|— — — —
3. —|—|— — —
4. — — —|—|— — — — —
5. — — —|—|— — —
6. — — —|—|— — —
7. — —|—|— — —

Allot five to seven minutes for the students to complete this activity. (The answers are (1) prayer (2) content (3) just (4) nothing (5) Christ (6) peace (7) need.) Go over the answers together. Be sure that everyone has the word *rejoice* as the key word for the lesson.

Into the Word

Briefly present the material in the "Introduction" section. Read Philippians 4:4-19 aloud.

Develop a discussion using the following questions.

1. Summarize Paul's advice to Christians.
2. How could Paul rejoice in the midst of the circumstances in which he found himself?

3. Paul gives at least three secrets to living a life of joy in verses 4-9. What are they?
4. How can a person not be anxious when everything around him seems to be going wrong?
5. How can thanking God help us to rejoice? Does prayer really change attitudes? Give examples.
6. How does what we think about affect our attitudes?
7. What was the secret of Paul's contentment?
8. Paul had a deep conviction about the provision of his needs. What was it? As you develop the discussion, use the commentary material to fill in the areas not mentioned by the class members.

Into Life

Place the words to the following statement on small index cards, one word per card: "No tears can quench the eternal flame of Christian joy." Put the cards in an envelope. Provide an envelope for every three to five people and have the groups unscramble the message.

After the message has been deciphered, ask, "Is this true? Do you agree or disagree? Give some examples to support your answer." Have the groups share their thinking. Make sure they understand that Christian joy is not dependent on pleasurable circumstances, but rather on the hope that we possess in Christ Jesus.

Continue to apply this teaching by asking the questions below.

1. What does this have to say to us who live in an affluent society?
2. Can we find the secret of contentment in the midst of affluence? How?
3. Cite some examples of those whom you know who have learned to rejoice in spite of their circumstances.
4. Let's develop a formula for contentment. Suggest the elements and proportions of each. (Put these on the chalkboard.)

Have the students use the reverse side of the puzzle used in the opening activity to evaluate themselves in terms of contentment and rejoicing. Have them take each element in the formula on the chalkboard and judge how much they have at the present time. Then have them circle the element that they want to add during the coming week.

Let's Talk It Over

*The questions on this page are designed to encourage review of the lesson
Scriptures and to promote discussion of the lesson by the class. The answers
provided are only discussion starters. Let your class talk it over from there.*

1. Paul commands us to "Rejoice in the Lord always." How can we rejoice in circumstances that give no joy?

Many people allow their mood to be controlled by that which is occurring to them, and around them, at the moment. They simply react to events and circumstances. We can see in the word *happiness* a relationship to the word *happenstance*. Happiness (or lack of it) often depends upon what happens.

Paul is calling for a more mature response from Christians. To be able to rejoice in unpleasant circumstances we must have a frame of reference larger than the here and now. For instance, when Paul wrote these words he was in prison. That was not what he would prefer, but it did not change the most important facts of his life: he was a child of God, he was an apostle of Jesus Christ, he had a blessed future in Heaven, etc.

2. What was Paul's cure for worry?

As did Jesus, Paul taught that a believer should not be consumed with worry. (Compare our text and Matthew 6:25-34.) Each gives a very similar prescription for dealing with our worries. In a capsule it is this: trust God.

Paul recommends that we exercise our privilege to address God in prayer with our needs and fears. These prayers of supplication are to be accompanied by thanksgiving. That helps keep everything in perspective, reminding us of God's love and His power to provide. Thanking Him may also help us realize that He is already redeeming good out of the situation we fear.

3. What evidence can be given to demonstrate that many people today lack peace in their lives? How can the peace that is from God be a tool for evangelism?

The most obvious evidence that many lack peace in their lives is the number of violent crimes committed every day. Another is the number of suicides and attempted suicides. Still another is the amount of drugs taken for anxiety and depression, and the amount of illegal drugs consumed just to escape reality. The incidence of adultery, obsession with possessions, and the compulsion toward fads may also indicate lack of peace. The Christian who knows the peace of God is not likely to be involved in these things.

If we demonstrate that trust in God preserves our calm when it appears that the roof may cave in, others will be drawn to that kind of faith. If a Christian is just as anxiety-laden as anyone else, his faith will appear to be worth little as a practical help.

4. What prevalent influences cause us at times to take our focus off of things that are true, honest, just, pure, lovely, and of good report? How do we suffer when that happens?

Much of the entertainment provided by television and movies falls into this category. The themes of these are seldom the pure, just, and virtuous. They dwell upon greed, lust, crime, passion, revenge, etc. Even the news seldom concerns what is uplifting. Advertising often appeals to our base desires: pride, greed, selfishness, and our desire to be envied.

We cannot avoid all of these influences, so we must keep our guard up lest they cause us to lose our concentration on things virtuous and worthy of praise. If that happens, we will suffer from a loss of perspective. Temptations will have a stronger power over us. We will be more apt to become negative and even cynical. We may even lose our motivation altogether to try to live by God's will.

5. Paul commended the church of Philippi for their generous support of his ministry. Can you name the missionary endeavors your church supports? What is to be gained by sending money to missionaries?

It is important to be familiar with the missionaries your church supports so that you can pray for them. You may also want to send a personal note of encouragement occasionally. In order to pray for them intelligently, you will need to keep up with the progress of their work.

Paul told the Philippian Christians that their gift to him would result in fruit added to their account (v. 17). They became partners in his ministry, and could celebrate every success as their own. Completing the Great Commission of making disciples of every nation requires those who will go *and* those who will send. We should relish the opportunity of extending our witness, and of storing up treasure in Heaven, as we support missionaries.

To the Praise of God's Glory

LESSON SCRIPTURE: Ephesians 1:1-14.

PRINTED TEXT: Ephesians 1:3-14.

Ephesians 1:3-14

3 Blessed be the God and Father of our Lord Jesus Christ, who hath blessed us with all spiritual blessings in heavenly places in Christ:

4 According as he hath chosen us in him before the foundation of the world, that we should be holy and without blame before him in love:

5 Having predestinated us unto the adoption of children by Jesus Christ to himself, according to the good pleasure of his will,

6 To the praise of the glory of his grace, wherein he hath made us accepted in the beloved:

7 In whom we have redemption through his blood, the forgiveness of sins, according to the riches of his grace;

8 Wherein he hath abounded toward us in all wisdom and prudence;

9 Having made known unto us the mystery of his will, according to his good pleasure which he hath purposed in himself:

10 That in the dispensation of the fulness of times he might gather together in one all things in Christ, both which are in heaven, and which are on earth; even in him.

11 In whom also we have obtained an inheritance, being predestinated according to the purpose of him who worketh all things after the counsel of his own will:

12 That we should be to the praise of his glory, who first trusted in Christ.

13 In whom ye also trusted, after that ye heard the word of truth, the gospel of your salvation: in whom also, after that ye believed, ye were sealed with that Holy Spirit of promise,

14 Which is the earnest of our inheritance until the redemption of the purchased possession, unto the praise of his glory.

GOLDEN TEXT: We should be to the praise of his glory, who first trusted in Christ.
—Ephesians 1:12.

Letters From Prison

Unit 4: Ephesians – The Christian Calling (Lessons 9-13)

Lesson Aims

Today's study should equip a student to:

1. Show how Christians today are included in God's eternal plan.

2. Show how human choice operates within God's "predestination."

3. Bring a fresh emphasis into his appreciation and participation in songs of praise.

Lesson Outline

INTRODUCTION
  A. "In the Heavenlies"
  B. "At Ephesus"
 I. PRAISE FOR BLESSINGS (Ephesians 1:3-6)
  A. They Are Heavenly in Nature (v. 3)
  B. They Include Us by Plan (vv. 4, 5)
  C. They Reflect Glory to God (v. 6)
 II. PRAISE FOR CHRIST IN PERSON (Ephesians 1:7-10)
  A. In Him Is Salvation (v. 7)
     God's Plan
  B. In Him Is Knowledge (vv. 8, 9).
  C. In Him Is Life's Focus (v. 10)
III. PRAISE FOR ONENESS (Ephesians 1:11-14)
  A. Divine Inheritance (v. 11)
     The Household of Faith
  B. Jews Claim the Promise (v. 12)
  C. Gentiles Accept the Gospel (v. 13)
  D. The Spirit Assures Both (v. 14)
CONCLUSION
  A. Songs of Praise
  B. A Prayer of Praise
  C. Thought to Remember

Visual 9 in the visuals packet will be helpful as you consider God's blessings mentioned in the lesson text. It is shown on page 301.

Introduction

A. "In the Heavenlies"

A note of "rejoicing in Christ" sounded through our lesson last week as we concluded our study in Philippians. The same note, amplified, introduces our study in Paul's epistle to the Ephesians—"To the Praise of God's Glory." The theme of praise reaches from before creation to beyond Judgment, relating to all men everywhere, and residing in "the heavenlies."

That is Paul's term, *the heavenlies.* Most translations supply other words to complete the thought in Ephesians 1:3; 2:6; and 3:10, and so speak, for example, of "heavenly places." But the inspired apostle did not limit his thought to matters of location. He left it open to persons, and circumstances, and powers, beyond what is earthbound, temporal, and material.

You can't apply a yardstick or a calendar to the grand themes of Ephesians. As a general letter, taken up with the glory of Christ and the grandeur of His church, and without references to persons or circumstances in any one place, it could have been copied and sent alike to churches in several cities.

One name, Tychicus (Ephesians 6:21 and Colossians 4:7), ties this epistle in time and circumstance of writing to Colossians and Philemon. All came from Paul imprisoned at Rome, for delivery to the same general area in Asia Minor. Note the wide range of subject and circumstance in these letters. Philemon deals with a matter of personal concern. Colossians speaks to a local situation in which one church in one city faced a special problem in doctrinal issues. Ephesians knows no bounds of time or space.

It is appropriate, therefore, that after a friendly greeting from the apostle to his readers, the writing should burst into a hallelujah chorus-a doxology or anthem—hailing the grandeur and goodness of God to mankind. Once having entered the stream of his thought, the apostle is so carried by the force of its current that he is swept far downstream before he reaches a resting place—the end of his first sentence. Ephesians 1:3-14, our text for today, is in fact one long sentence in the Greek text. In English, the *American Standard Version* presents it faithfully as one sentence. Other translations amend the grammar a bit to change dependent clauses into sentences.

Changing the comparison, we must acknowledge a similar—and unavoidable—reduction of Paul's big beefsteak into bite-sized chunks by anyone who would provide an outline and commentary on the text. Then let the student first read the passage as a whole and gasp at its vast view of the heavenlies. Afterward he may follow us in searching out the details.

B. "At Ephesus"

As it comes to us, the letter identifies its writer, the apostle Paul, and its intended readers, "the saints which are at Ephesus." It also indicates a wider audience of "the faithful in Christ Jesus" (Ephesians 1:1). The address still carries a strong and tender feeling of family. From God, the Father of the writer and all his readers, and from Jesus, who is Messiah and Lord of all alike, it bespeaks favor and peace (v. 2). Those who belong to God in Christ are not strangers or foreigners to one another no matter where and when they may live.

Ephesus provided a suitable audience for such an all-inclusive letter to Christians. As a city of trade and influence, it brought together all the strands of culture and commerce in the Mediterranean world. Visiting there at the conclusion of his second missionary journey, and spending three years there on his third tour, Paul established the church in Ephesus and gave it his longest ministry. From him the influence of the gospel permeated the city and its broad environs, so that tradesmen felt its effect on their business. Makers and dealers in pagan idols raised a riot against Paul there (Acts 19:23-41), and unbelieving Jews from Ephesus later stirred a riot against him in Jerusalem (Acts 21:27-32).

Proud pagans and jealous Jews alike in Ephesus may have frequently asked about the church, "Is it not merely an upstart offshoot from established Judaism?" Paul's letter answers to all the world: "Before there was an Ephesus, or an Asia, or even a world, sun, or stars, the gospel and the church of Christ were in the mind, plan, and purpose of God!"

I. Praise for Blessings (Ephesians 1:3-6)

A. They Are Heavenly in Nature (v. 3)

3. Blessed be the God and Father of our Lord Jesus Christ, who hath blessed us with all spiritual blessings in heavenly places in Christ.

To *bless* is literally to "speak well of," or to "request good for," or to "do good to." This verse uses the word in the first and third ways. We are to speak well of God; in fact we are to praise Him with all we are and have, because He has done good to us in ways that only He could do. That is the theme of the entire passage before us. The rest emphasizes and specifies the ways in which God has bestowed His blessing.

First to be made clear is the relationship of *God* the *Father* to *our Lord Jesus Christ*. The eternal God, Creator and ruler of the universe, sent His one and only Son to earth in the person of *Jesus* who grew up in Nazareth of Galilee. That Son is the Messiah, or *Christ*, promised to and expected by the Jewish nation. God has given to His Son all authority to be heard and obeyed in all things by all creatures (Matthew 28:18; Acts 2:36). To Paul and his readers Jesus is *our Lord*; they had confessed and committed themselves in obedience to Him.

How to Say It

CAESAREA. Sess-uh-*ree*-uh.
EPHESUS. *Ef*-uh-sus.
TYCHICUS. *Tick*-ih-cuss.

The *blessings* promised and given to God's people in times past had been chiefly temporal and material—long life, prosperity, and a continuing family. Now *in Christ* God gave *spiritual blessings*—the eternal and imperishable gifts bestowed by the Spirit of God and received in the spirits of men. These Heavenly gifts are received in *heavenly places*—or more literally in "the heavenlies" (see above). Christ has brought the atmosphere of Heaven into life here on earth.

God works *in Christ* to make His will and purpose known. Believers become identified *in Christ* to receive the blessings of divine presence, power, and protection. *In Christ* is more than a position to be occupied; it is a life to be lived. The spiritual blessings available in Christ are otherwise impossible.

B. They Include Us by Plan (vv. 4, 5)

4, 5. According as he hath chosen us in him before the foundation of the world, that we should be holy and without blame before him in love: having predestinated us unto the adoption of children by Jesus Christ to himself, according to the good pleasure of his will.

God's people are *chosen* and *predestinated*, not by name as individuals, but generally as a people. God's eternal purpose is that none should perish, but that all should come to repentance and salvation (2 Peter 3:9). The call is to "whosoever will" (Revelation 22:17). The focus of God's purpose and the criterion of our acceptance is that we be *in him*—in Christ.

All this was in the mind and plan of God before the world was created. God's people are not left to wonder and wander an uncharted way. Our life purpose for God is bound up in His eternal purpose for us—that we should be *holy* (set apart as His possession) and *without blame* (forgiven and therefore declared innocent). We are blameless because we are saved; we are not saved because we are blameless.

In love. Love is the proper climate and motive for the Christian's holy living. It is also God's motive for choosing to adopt believers as His children. The *New International Version* includes the phrase with verse 5: "In love he predestined us to be adopted as his sons through Jesus Christ, in accordance with his pleasure and will."

John 1:12 indicates that believers become children of God, but Paul is the only New Testament writer who uses the metaphor of *adoption*. God wanted a family, and He arranged to bring sons and daughters to himself through Christ. Marvel that we can be among them!

C. They Reflect Glory to God (v. 6)

6. To the praise of the glory of his grace, wherein he hath made us accepted in the beloved.

Here sounds again the hallelujah theme of our text, to be repeated also in verses 12 and 14. The marvel of God's undeserved blessings to the children of men deserves and receives a response in praise to Him. In singing of God's amazing grace, however, we must remember that it is God, and not grace itself, that we must praise. Without God, there is no grace!

Because of this quality, we who ourselves are not acceptable have been accepted into His family, with glories beyond imagination. That acceptance is in Christ, *beloved* of God (Matthew 3:17) and commanding the love of men (John 8:42; 14:21-24; 1 Corinthians 16:22). Friends of Jesus are recognized as friends of God.

II. Praise for Christ in Person (Ephesians 1:7-10)

A. In Him Is Salvation (v. 7)

7. In whom we have redemption through his blood, the forgiveness of sins, according to the riches of his grace.

"In Christ our release is secured . . . through the shedding of his blood" *(The New English Bible)*. He paid the price to buy us back from bondage to sin and death. This was foreshadowed in the imperfect sacrifices of animals as sin and peace offerings, looking toward the perfect sacrifice of Jesus as the Lamb of God who takes away the sin of the world (John 1:29).

Forgiveness of sins is the great and needed blessing for which we are taught to pray, along with daily bread (Matthew 6:11, 12). It is neither sought nor valued by those who think they have not sinned, or can handle the sin problem for themselves. Such persons, therefore, cannot receive these *riches* of divine *grace*.

God's Plan

Two women knocked at the door of a suburban house. "Good afternoon. We would like to talk with you about your relationship with God. In this magazine is information that will tell you the events of the future. You can know what God wants you to do. Our literature is read by millions of people around the world." The plea came from the genuine desire to share their belief.

"Hey, man—this is the latest. Read this book and you can know all about the real possibilities for your life. You're a winner, and in developing your own self-image you control your own destiny. Don't let anyone fool you. Self-realization is *the answer*."

Every day, sincere people of all kinds carry their message from door to door and person to person. Radio broadcasts and TV screens flood our homes with plans for success and salvation.

What of God's plan? Paul wrote that in Christ "we have redemption through his blood, the forgiveness of sins, according to the riches of his grace" (Ephesians 1:7).

God's plan to save men is by the sacrifice of His Son Jesus. Don't be fooled by sincerity and methods of self-improvement.   —W. P.

B. In Him Is Knowledge (vv. 8, 9)

8, 9. Wherein he hath abounded toward us in all wisdom and prudence; having made known unto us the mystery of his will, according to his good pleasure which he hath purposed in himself.

God has lavished the riches of His grace upon those who will receive the same. He has done so *in all wisdom and prudence*. He does not force upon unwilling persons the spiritual blessings for which they have no desire or appreciation (compare Matthew 7:6).

The same divine wisdom directs the making known of God's purposes to men, as indicated in the *New American Standard Bible*: "In all wisdom and insight He made known to us the mystery of His will, according to His kind intention which He purposed in Him." The Heavenly Father deals with His children not as slaves but as members of His family (John 15:15). So He makes known to them eternal truths that could not be known except as He reveals them. The present revelation is this: it has been God's eternal purpose to make salvation available to Jew and Gentile alike through His Son Jesus. That is the expression of His mercy to all (Acts 10, 11; Acts 26:16-18; Ephesians 3:1-7).

C. In Him Is Life's Focus (v. 10)

10. That in the dispensation of the fulness of times he might gather together in one all things in Christ, both which are in Heaven, and which are on earth; even in him.

God's plan for human redemption was to bring all things in Heaven and earth together in Christ. In the present instance *dispensation* signifies God's arrangement for accomplishing His purpose. He sets His own time schedule (see

Galatians 4:4). When all the seasons had run out, the final revelation came.

Dispersion and confusion abound in a sin-scarred world. Paul's readers were aware that Israel had been scattered, and that hatred, distrust, and lack of understanding separated nation from nation. Even the natural world suffers from human greed (see Romans 8:22, 23). In the light of God's healing purpose all things fall into place in a single gigantic pattern brought to a focus in Christ. For each of us that includes his own personality, his family, his social life, his business or employment, and his material wealth, along with his expressions of religion. It includes the earthly, as well as the Heavenly experience (see Matthew 28:18; Philippians 2:9-11). Life is scattered and shattered until it is brought together in Him.

III. Praise for Oneness (Ephesians 1:11-14

A. Divine Inheritance (v. 11)

11. In whom also we have obtained an inheritance, being predestinated according to the purpose of him who worketh all things after the counsel of his own will.

In whom also we have obtained an inheritance. The *King James Version* here states that we who are in Christ have come into possession of what God had planned for His chosen people. Looking at the other side of the same coin, the *American Standard Version* says that we are God's inheritance. Both statements are true and both focus attention on the future blessing and glory we shall receive in Christ.

Who worketh all things after the counsel of his own will. No part of God's plan was accidental. Man has the power of free choice, yet God in His wisdom is able to cause man's freedom to work for His purposes. Those who crucified Jesus acted of their own free will, yet their very actions carried out God's purpose to offer His Son as a sacrifice for sin.

THE HOUSEHOLD OF FAITH

Paul uses a number of figures to express various aspects of the church. Four of his favorites are the church as the body of Christ, the bride of Christ, a building of God, and a household of faith. He had this latter figure in mind in two passages in our text. He mentions the means of entering this household—by adoption (v. 5)—and the outcome of that adoption—a sharing of God's inheritance (v. 11).

We Christians must not forget that our relationship to God is based on His adoption of us. We have not deserved to be adopted. Rather, it has come to us only because of God's love and grace.

The adoption we have experienced is available to all. Nor need we fear that through our Father's adding other children to His family that our inheritance will be diminished. God's great abundance is adequate to satisfy all.

We marvel that God can take us who are so dissimilar, who have such diverse backgrounds, and fashion us into one family in His Son. But that is precisely what He has done. And now we, who formerly were no people, are the people of God.

B. Jews Claim the Promise (v. 12)

12. That we should be to the praise of his glory, who first trusted in Christ.

In this verse Paul seems to turn his attention to the Jews, himself included, who had accepted Jesus as the promised Messiah. The Jews had had their hope fixed on the coming Messiah (Christ) long before any other nations came to know Him. It was fitting then, that they should rejoice and praise God for the fulfillment of their long expectation. It is fitting also that non-Jewish Christians should view with reverent awe the works of God in dealing with the Jewish nation, generously, patiently, severely, and at last triumphantly He brought them into their inheritance—and claimed their believing ones as His inheritance—in Christ.

C. Gentiles Accept the Gospel (v. 13)

13. In whom ye also trusted, after that ye heard the word of truth, the gospel of your salvation: in whom also, after that ye believed, ye were sealed with that Holy Spirit of promise.

Paul now directs his thoughts to Gentile Christians, among whom the Ephesians were numbered. They had not received the promise before Christ's coming, but they had received *the gospel* when it was brought to them, and had become partakers of the same *salvation*. The process of the Gentiles' inclusion is the same as the

visual 9

process of the Jews' inclusion in the body of Christ. The Jews first heard the truth of the gospel as preached by the apostle Peter on the Day of Pentecost after Christ's resurrection and ascension into Heaven. (Acts 2:22-36). They believed and were baptized into Christ, receiving the promised gift of the Holy Spirit (Acts 2:37-41). Gentiles had the gospel preached to them first by the same apostle Peter in the house of Cornelius at Caesarea (Acts 10:34-43); their belief was attested by a special manifestation of the Holy Spirit, and they were baptized into Christ (Acts 10:44-48).

Sealed. From ancient times seals have been used to establish the authenticity of a document, and/or to protect privacy and identify possession. *Today's English Version* says in this verse, "God put his stamp of ownership on you by giving you the Holy Spirit He had promised." The protective Spirit strengthens in difficulty and temptation.

D. The Spirit Assures Both (v. 14)

14. Which is the earnest of our inheritance until the redemption of the purchased possession, unto the praise of his glory.

The Holy Spirit is the first of God's gifts to the obedient believer in Christ, and so becomes the assurance of all promised blessings to come. In present-day business transactions "earnest money" is a part of the agreed price, a down payment indicating the buyer's pledge to pay the rest in due time. God does infinitely more: "He that spared not his own Son, but delivered him up for us all, how shall he not with him also freely give us all things?" (Romans 8:32).

Redemption—deliverance or release—from the guilt and power of sin has already been enjoyed by those who are in Christ, but not until

He comes in glory and judgment will they be finally *redeemed* from physical corruption and death. Even now, however, we are God's *purchased possession*, redeemed and bought by the precious blood of God's own Son (1 Peter 1:18-21)

God's *glory* will be seen in complete perfection only when earth—the preparatory stage for God's children—shall have been removed and the saints are with him in Heaven. Until then they will *be* to the praise of His glory (compare verse 12)! Whatever they are—family members, friends, workmen, businessmen, housewives, students, musicians, teachers—they will be that to the praise of God's glory.

Conclusion

A. Songs of Praise

A natural first way to praise the glory of God is through the singing of psalms, hymns, and spiritual songs, used either alone or accompanied by other Christians.

What songs of praise do you sing? We think readily of songs *about* praising. Some are addressed to ourselves and others, urging praise: "Praise God From Whom All Blessings Flow," or "O Worship the King." We may sing about our own rendering of praise: "I Sing the Mighty Power of God," or "I Will Sing of My Redeemer." These lead into others, *describing* God as being worthy of our praise: "All Praise to Him Who Reigns Above," or "Crown Him With Many Crowns."

Some hymns *address God* himself in praise for His creative power: "For the Beauty of the Earth," or "How Great Thou Art." Closest, though, to Paul's hallelujahs for God's eternal plan for human redemption would seem to be those hymns that praise God as our changeless Redeemer through Christ: "Joyful, Joyful, We Adore Thee," or "Great Is Thy Faithfulness, O God My Father." As Christ is the focus of creation, so He may well be the center of our singing praise to God the Father. Use your hymnbook, use your hymns, and use your voice to the glory of God.

B. A Prayer of Praise

"We praise Thee, O God, for the Son of Thy love,
For Jesus who died and is now gone above.
Hallelujah! Thine the glory, Hallelujah! amen;
Hallelujah! Thine the glory; Revive us again."

C. Thought to Remember

"Thanks be unto God for his unspeakable gift"   —(2 Corinthians 9:15).

Home Daily Bible Readings

Monday, Apr. 24—Special to God (Ephesians 1:3-8a)

Tuesday, Apr. 25—God's Children, God's Heirs (Romans 8:14-17)

Wednesday, Apr. 26—God Works for Our Good (Romans 8:26-32)

Thursday, Apr. 27—God's Plan for Unity (Ephesians 1:9-14)

Friday, Apr. 28—Good Gifts From God (Luke 11:9-13)

Saturday, Apr. 29—Victorious Because of God's Love (Romans 8:33-38)

Sunday, Apr. 30—Prayer for God's People (Ephesians 1:15-23)

Learning by Doing

This page contains an alternate lesson plan emphasizing learning activities. Classes desiring such student involvement will find these suggestions helpful.

Learning Goals

Having studied Ephesians 1:3-14, with the activity suggestions given below, a student will be able to:

1. List the blessings that God has given to the believer through Jesus Christ.

2. Explain how human choice operates within God's predestination.

3. Thank God for the blessings that God has given to him.

Into the Lesson

Prepare copies of the Word Find puzzle below as the students enter the classroom, give each one a copy and ask them to find as many of the hidden words as they can.

WORD FIND

See if you can find seventeen key words from Ephesians 1:3-14. Words may be found going from left to right, right to left, top to bottom, or bottom to top. The words are *accepted, adoption, blameless, blessed, blood, children, chosen, earnest, forgiveness, God, grace, holy, inheritance, praise, redemption, salvation, sealed.*

```
B L O O D S P C A E F E
L S E A L E D H T A O C
E S I A R P U I T R R A
S T U Y U R N L L N G R
S O S L T O O D U E I G
E C H O S E N R X S V O
D R O H A C C E P T E D
A D O P T I O N R P N U
N O I T P M E D E R E M
T M N O I T A V L A S I
R P B L A M E L E S S M
I N H E R I T A N C E T
```

Allow eight to ten minutes for the students to complete this. Let them share their results.

Make the transition into the Bible study section by stating that the words in the puzzle are key words for the person who is the recipient of God's salvation through Christ.

Into the Word

Briefly present the material in the "Introduction" section of this lesson. Then read Ephesians 1:3-14 aloud.

Divide the class members into groups of four. Ask them to read the Scripture passage again and make a list of the blessings that God has provided for the Christian. Have them write a brief definition of each of the blessings. Allow eight to ten minutes for them to complete this assignment.

After the groups have finished their work, make a master list of the blessings that they have identified. Then work through the definitions with the groups. Be sure that the following are included in your discussion: holy, blameless, adoption, redemption, forgiveness of sins, God has made known to us the mystery of His will, chosen, predestinated, salvation, sealed with the Holy Spirit of promise. Use the material in the commentary section of this lesson to help you be prepared with definitions, explanations, and illustrations as you go over this material with the class. Be sure to clarify the meaning of predestination: some of your class members may have some misconceptions about what this means.

Into Life

Emphasize the reality of God's blessings to us. Develop a brief discussion, using the following two questions.

1. How do you respond when you read and understand this list of blessings that God has provided for you?

2. What is an appropriate day-by-day response to God for these blessings?

Then ask those who worked together in a group earlier to do so again to write a song, a poem, or a prayer to express their response to the marvelous blessings that God has given. Assign one-third of the groups to write a song, another one-third to write a poem, and the other one-third to write a prayer. Each should express praise and thanks to God for the wonderful things He has done.

Allow the groups eight to ten minutes to complete their assigned tasks. When the groups are finished, let each share its work with the whole class. Make this a time of praise to God in the sharing of each other's efforts.

Close with a time of sentence prayers (the number depending upon the amount of time you have remaining) to express thanks to God for His blessings in Christ Jesus.

Let's Talk It Over

The questions on this page are designed to encourage review of the lesson Scriptures and to promote discussion of the lesson by the class. The answers provided are only discussion starters. Let your class talk it over from there.

1. How do God's blessings to us bring Him greater glory?

Paul begins his letter to the Ephesians with a doxology to the God "who hath blessed us with all spiritual blessings." If His blessings were in response to our righteous behavior, if they were the reward for our perfect obedience to His laws, then His blessing us would not be remarkable. In such a case He would be obligated to us by the terms of the covenant of law. The fact is, however, that we are all guilty of sin and deserve condemnation and death. God has provided for our pardon through Jesus Christ, and has given us spiritual blessings we do not deserve. That is the remarkable, unexpected grace that brings Him glory. He chooses to love, redeem, and forgive. Perhaps the key to this is in Ephesians 1:6. He has made us, who were unacceptable, accepted in Christ.

2. What are the "spiritual blessings in heavenly places" that we have received in Christ?

In the lesson text Paul lists many of our spiritual blessings. We have been chosen to be holy (set apart as belonging to God) and as having no blame before God (v. 4). We have received adoption as God's children (v. 5). We have been redeemed from bondage to sin and its consequences, being completely forgiven (v. 7). We are the recipients of the revelation of God's will, which remains a mystery to those who do not believe (v. 9). We are assured of an inheritance from God through Christ (v. 11). As a guarantee of that inheritance to come, we have been given the presence of the Holy Spirit in our lives. These blessings are "spiritual," but we should not construe this as meaning that these blessings have no practical value today. Brainstorm for a few minutes on the following practical benefits of these blessings: meaning, purpose, and value to life; freedom from guilt; power from the Holy Spirit to live righteously; motivating hope in the face of trouble or grief, etc.

3. How does it make you feel when friends include you in their plans? When they exclude you? How do you respond to the truth that God takes pleasure in adopting you as His own?

It is a wonderful thing to know that someone enjoys our company and genuinely wants to share experiences with us. It is gratifying to be invited to go bowling, to go fishing, or to be asked to come for dinner or just for a cup of coffee. Even if we have to decline, we would much rather be included than to hear later that our friends had a party and did not invite us. Being excluded causes us to feel rejected, unloved, and unwanted. Those feelings should cause us to appreciate the fact that God chooses us for adoption "according to the good pleasure of his will." We are included in the plans of the Sovereign of the universe, even after we have disappointed and rejected Him so often. Our hearts should be overflowing with joy for the love He has shown.

4. Why was it necessary for us to be "redeemed," the blood of Christ being the price of redemption? How does accepting Christ as Savior change our situation?

Sin in our life creates a debt of guilt toward God that we can never repay, a debt of failed obedience and misspent devotion. Because of that debt, death and condemnation have claim upon us. The debt must be paid in order for us to be free from that condemnation. Because of His sinless life of perfect devotion, Christ Jesus deserved life and honor; but He took upon himself the death and condemnation we deserved. When we accept Him as Savior and Lord, His sacrificial death is accounted to us and redeems us from condemnation.

5. What was the assurance given to Gentiles that they too were "chosen" and included in God's plans?

When the apostle Peter was summoned to the house of Cornelius, it took a vision from God to persuade him to enter the house of a Gentile. Once there, Peter began to explain the gospel, and God gave an undeniable sign of His acceptance of those devout Gentiles—the Holy Spirit came upon them, just as upon the disciples on the Day of Pentecost (see Acts 1:44-46; 2:1-4). The gift of the Holy Spirit continued to be God's affirmation to believers of their share in salvation, although not accompanied with the same manifestations. The Holy Spirit's continuing work of renewal in the life of the Christian is the down payment of glory to come.

Peace With God and One Another

LESSON SCRIPTURE: Ephesians 2.

PRINTED TEXT: Ephesians 2:8-22.

Ephesians 2:8-22

8 For by grace are ye saved through faith; and that not of yourselves: it is the gift of God:

9 Not of works, lest any man should boast.

10 For we are his workmanship, created in Christ Jesus unto good works, which God hath before ordained that we should walk in them.

11 Wherefore remember, that ye being in time past Gentiles in the flesh, who are called Uncircumcision by that which is called the Circumcision in the flesh made by hands;

12 That at that time ye were without Christ, being aliens from the commonwealth of Israel, and strangers from the covenants of promise, having no hope, and without God in the world:

13 But now, in Christ Jesus, ye who sometime were far off are made nigh by the blood of Christ.

14 For he is our peace, who hath made both one, and hath broken down the middle wall of partition between us;

15 Having abolished in his flesh the enmity, even the law of commandments contained in ordinances; for to make in himself of twain one new man, so making peace;

16 And that he might reconcile both unto God in one body by the cross, having slain the enmity thereby:

17 And came and preached peace to you which were afar off, and to them that were nigh.

18 For through him we both have access by one Spirit unto the Father.

19 Now therefore ye are no more strangers and foreigners, but fellow citizens with the saints, and of the household of God;

20 And are built upon the foundation of the apostles and prophets, Jesus Christ himself being the chief corner stone;

21 In whom all the building fitly framed together groweth unto a holy temple in the Lord:

22 In whom ye also are builded together for a habitation of God through the Spirit.

GOLDEN TEXT: Ye are no more strangers and foreigners, but fellow citizens with the saints, and of the household of God.—Ephesians 2:19.

Lesson Aims

The study of this lesson should equip the student to:

1. Explain how faith and good works are related to our salvation in Christ.

2. Describe some "walls of partition" in his own community that have been broken down or need to be broken down by the gospel.

3. Plan a more effective application of the gospel to at least one of these barriers.

Lesson Outline

Display visual 10 from the visuals/learning resources packet and let it remain before the class. It is shown on page 309.

Introduction

A. Gift of God's Love

> There comes to my heart one sweet strain,
>   A glad and a joyous refrain;
> I sing it again and again,
>   Sweet peace, the gift of God's love.
>
> Peace, peace, sweet peace!
>   Wonderful gift from above!
> O wonderful, wonderful peace!
>   Sweet peace, the gift of God's love!

The lines of Peter Bilhorn's hymn express the Christian's love for peace, and his recognition that it is a priceless gift from the hand of God. But what, after all, is peace?

Peace, as used in our text, translates the Greek *eirene.* The word describes that which is friendly and gentle, free from anger and quarrelsomeness. It denotes harmonious relations, whether between persons, or between nations, or between a man and God. It also indicates freedom from molestation, or good order in government.

Christ made peace, Paul wrote, by breaking down the spiritual walls that stood between men and men and between nation and nation. But walls are sometimes built for the purpose of "keeping peace" between neighbors who otherwise might be inclined to harm one another. Peace depends more on attitudes than it does on circumstances. Hatred and jealousy have to be removed before it is even safe to try to remove the other walls.

Wall removal does, however, suggest another aspect of *peace* that is prominent in the Hebrew *shalom*, the greeting of peace by which Jewish people have traditionally wished one another well. *Shalom* speaks of wholeness, completeness, that is near to a blend of perfectness and unity. A life that is torn by conflicting passions, or a city divided by walls, or a person separated from God by disbelief or rebellion, cannot be described with *shalom*.

Healing and wholeness, on the other hand, come and remain not with wishing or with human effort alone. Peace is still the gift of God's love.

B. Lesson Background

A hymn of praise to the glory of God dominates the first chapter of Ephesians, which we studied last week. The chapter includes also a paragraph of appreciation and prayer for the Ephesian Christians to whom the epistle was addressed.

In chapter 2 we begin to find ourselves included, at least by frequent implication. Some before-and-after photos are presented. The first deal especially with morals. "You . . . were dead in trespasses and sins" (vv. 1-3). "But God . . . hath quickened us [made us alive] together with Christ" (vv. 4-7). A similar before-and-after sequence dominates the rest of the chapter, from which our text is taken. This time, however, the emphasis is on personal relations—relations between human beings in groups and communities, and relations between men and God. In this case the "before" state is separation, and the "after" is reconciliation. The opening verses of our text deal with the means by which the miracle is accomplished.

I. God's Acceptance
(Ephesians 2:8-10)

A. It Is Given, Not Earned (vv. 8, 9)

8, 9. For by grace are ye saved through faith; and that not of yourselves: it is the gift of God: not of works, lest any man should boast.

Grace is the divine, generous loving-kindness that extends mercy and forgiveness, not only beyond any good deserved, but in spite of one's deserving only punishment. Grace is so compelling a principle that one is tempted to think of it as something complete within itself. But grace is an attribute of God. Apart from Him, there is no grace, no salvation, no blessing.

Just as the *grace* end of the salvation span must be anchored firmly in the being of God, so the *faith* end must be anchored firmly in the person whom God would receive. The gospel revealed in Christ must be heard and believed (Romans 10:8-17), and that belief is called *faith*. But *faith* is also trust and commitment growing out of that belief (1 Corinthians 2:5); and *faith* is also steadfastness and faithfulness growing out of that trust and commitment (2 Timothy 4:7, 8).

The gift of God which is *not of yourselves*, is salvation. This gift is ours *not of works*, that is, "not as a result of works" *(New American Standard Bible)*, either the works of the law prescribed in the Old Testament or the good works that result from one's faith in Christ. Yet a *gift* refused is no gift at all; it is only an offer. The outreach of faith by which one accepts God's offer must come from the believer himself. When the apostle Peter said to his hearers on the Day of Pentecost, "Repent, and be baptized every one of you in the name of Jesus Christ for the remission of sins, and ye shall receive the gift of the Holy Ghost" (Acts 2:38), he was not suggesting that their obedience would earn the gift. It was still a wholly unmerited bestowal of God, to be received through a living faith.

Lest any man should boast. Let not the unbeliever boast that his good works can save him; they can't. Let not the believer say that his good works saved him; they didn't. Christ did. Human pride poses a serious problem here. The prideful ones are reluctant to accept from God or man what they cannot claim to have earned for

---

How to Say It

EIRENE (Greek).   eye-*ray*-nay.
EPHESUS.   *Ef*-uh-sus.
SHALOM (Hebrew).   *shall*-om.

---

themselves. To say, "Thanks! I needed that," is hard enough in itself. Much more difficult is to add, "I couldn't have done it, or ever have deserved it, for myself." But that surrender of human pride is what is necessary before we can have real peace with God, with our neighbors, or even with ourselves.

B. It Results in Good Deeds

10. For we are his workmanship, created in Christ Jesus unto good works, which God hath before ordained that we should walk in them.

Workmanship translates the Greek word that signifies something made or created. God created man in His own image at the beginning (Genesis 1:26, 27); and after that image was marred by sin God set about to recreate man in His image through Christ. That creation is a work of art, an expression of the Creator's self. Redeemed man has been described as God's greatest masterpiece.

We are . . . created in Christ Jesus unto good works. The inventor knows the purpose of his creation. If it does not serve his purpose, it is of no value, no matter how attractive it may appear. But when it works, a celebration is in order. What marvelous things God can do, and frequently does, through willing lives!

We are saved to do good works; we don't do good works to be saved.

THE CRUCIAL TEST

Two elderly ladies decided to play a joke on the local county fair. For years Sue and her cousin Nellie had been winning blue ribbons for their canning and needlework entries. Everyone knew that no other contestants had a chance.

They were close friends and often cooked and did their needlework together. Both had nieces who also cooked and did lovely sewing, but neither niece had ever won a blue ribbon.

This year Sue and Nellie decided that each would enter her niece's work under the aunt's name and the aunt's own production as the girl's entry. The two older ladies kept their secret well, and to their delight the nieces received the blue ribbons.

A few days after the fair, however, the nieces discovered the switch in entries and revealed the deception, which remained a joke in the community for years.

The product was the true test. Although other names were in Sue and Nellie's entries, the quality of the products revealed that they were their true makers.

Believers are God's workmanship, created for good works. The quality of our lives reveal that we are His creation.   —W. P.

II. The Former Separation (Ephesians 2:11, 12)

11. Wherefore remember, that ye being in time past Gentiles in the flesh, who are called Uncircumcision by that which is called Circumcision in the flesh made by hands.

Reminded of the means by which they were saved, the readers next are exhorted to remember the condition from which they were rescued. Most of the Christians in and around Ephesus had come from Gentile backgrounds. Their natural heritage involved not only moral decay (vv. 1-3), but also religious and social ostracism.

Gentiles in the flesh. By a natural heritage of worldliness, the Gentiles were traditionally carnal rather than spiritual.

Called Uncircumcision. As spoken by the Jews this was not a compliment. God commanded Abraham to circumcise his male offspring as a mark of their covenant relationship with God (Genesis 17:9-14). David's disdainful reference to Goliath as an "uncircumcised Philistine" (1 Samuel 17:26, 36), and the vigor with which Peter was accused of going "in to men uncircumcised" (Acts 11:3) demonstrate the traditional Jewish use of the term. It was not mere name-calling; it was an expression of the Jews' perception of their superior standing as God's chosen people.

Circumcision in the flesh made by hands. The fleshly mark had been commanded by God as a sign of commitment to Him and His way. Many Jews in Paul's day, however, regarded it simply as a badge of their own preferred status. The apostle strongly rebuked this attitude (Romans 2:28, 29).

12. That at that time ye were without Christ, being aliens from the commonwealth of Israel, and strangers from the covenants of promise, having no hope, and without God in the world.

The Gentiles' sad state had involved not only social scorn and separation, but exclusion also from all the benefits available through God's special dealing with Israel.

Without Christ. This phrase stands in stark contrast with Paul's characteristic reference to blessedness—"in Christ." Gentiles, as such, had not even any expectation of Messiah.

Aliens from the commonwealth of Israel. As strangers and foreigners, Gentiles had no citizens' rights in the community to which God sent His law and His messengers.

The covenants of promise, the covenants God had made with Abraham (Genesis 15:8-21; 17:1-21) and Moses (Exodus 19:3-6; 24:1-11). Gentiles had no part in these.

Having no hope for a better future in this world or in life to come (see 1 Thessalonians 4:13).

Without God in the world. It is little wonder, then, that heathen Gentiles sank into the appalling sins listed in Romans 1:28-32.

III. The Healing Sacrifice (Ephesians 2:13-18)

A. Reconciled Man to Man (vv. 13-15)

13. But now, in Christ Jesus, ye who sometime were far off are made nigh by the blood of Christ.

Here is the triumphant turnaround from the tragic past to the glad present and the glorious future. Hopeless without Christ, the believers are victorious *in Christ Jesus.* Previously far from God, they are brought near to Him through acceptance of Christ's sacrifice. In the same action they are brought near to others who are brought near to Him. *The blood of Christ* is His sacrificial death, available to all.

14, 15. For he is our peace, who hath made both one, and hath broken down the middle wall of partition between us; having abolished in his flesh the enmity, even the law of commandments contained in ordinances; for to make in himself of twain one new man, so making peace.

Peace, like salvation, is a provision of divine grace, it is not achieved by human effort. Like salvation also, it is a treasure worth any cost beyond price.

He is our peace. Healing and wholeness in human relations reside in a Person, Jesus Christ, the Prince of Peace (Isaiah 9:6). Bound to Him in faith individually, and bound together *in* Him by mutual faith, we have peace with each other in spite of other disagreements. On the other hand, if we have no common commitment to Him, we have no basis for lasting peace, in spite of other human ties and common interests. Peace that does not center in Christ Jesus is not peace at all!

Christ *made both one* and broke down *the middle wall of partition between us.* Paul was a Jew and most of the Ephesians were Gentiles, but that no longer made any difference. Both were in Christ, and so they were one. The ancient hostility between them no longer existed. Jews and Gentiles out of Christ might still hate each other, but to be in Christ is to be in peace. How many other walls of partition come tumbling down when people are in Christ! No longer is there animosity between black and white, European and Asian, old and young. Christ's people are one.

In his flesh—by giving His body in death on the cross—Jesus *abolished*, or nullified, the law given to Israel at Mount Sinai. The law had been the basis of *enmity* between Jew and Gentile. Because the ritual law was superseded and its separating influence removed, the two branches of humanity might become *one new man*, a united humanity in the church, the body of Christ (1 Corinthians 12:12, 13).

B. Reconciled Men to God (vv. 16-18)

16, 17. And that he might reconcile both unto God in one body by the cross, having slain the enmity thereby: and came and preached peace to you which were afar off, and to them that were nigh.

Amazingly, the gospel is presented as the means of reconciling sinners to the God whom they have offended by their rebellion (2 Corinthians 5:18-20). Ought not the offender to take the initiative in making peace with the one he has hurt? But the foolishness of God is wiser than men. The cross of Christ is His great "I love you," both to the Jews and to the Gentiles: "Having made peace through the blood of his cross, by him to reconcile all things unto himself" (Colossians 1:20). By the cross of His Son God "put to death their hostility" *(New International Version)*.

18. For through him we both have access by one Spirit unto the Father.

Through the sacrifice of Christ both Jews and Gentiles are accorded the high privilege of admission to the throne room of the Almighty. The Holy Spirit, promised and given to believers at their baptism into Christ (Acts 2:38), enables each one to know and address the Creator as "Abba, Father" (Romans 8:15).

INSTANT ACCESS

The bank secretary was explaining the new electronic teller: "All you need is this plastic card and your own personal entry code. When you place your card in the machine, just punch

visual 10

in your code letters; then enter the deposits and withdrawals you want to make." Somehow that electronic teller could tell how much you had in your account and keep everything in order.

The electronic age has now become part of our everyday life. Computers of all kinds work for us to store and retrieve information vital to industry, agriculture, government, and many other facets of our lives.

The key to all these marvels of computerization is *access*. No matter how much your bank balance may be, without your access code, nothing is available to you.

All the riches, blessings, and promises of God are available to man, but we must have the access code to tap into the things God has prepared for His new creation. Paul gave us the key in these words: "For through him [Christ] we . . . have access by one Spirit unto the Father." Without Jesus there is no way in!   —W. P.

IV. The One Growing Body (Ephesians 2:19-22)

A. Community and Family (v. 19)

19. Now therefore ye are no more strangers and foreigners, but fellow citizens with the saints, and of the household of God.

The apostle uses three different metaphors to describe the single entity or unit into which believers are brought by their union with Christ. The first is a state or nation, including diverse and previously hostile elements. Now in Christ, however, they are citizens of the same state, the kingdom of God, with equal rights and responsibilities.

The second metaphor is that of the family or household. All are children of the same Father, even God. Again, they may have been adopted from many different backgrounds, but in the family relationship they are equals, brothers and sisters, not by their choice of one another, but by their common parentage.

B. A Temple for God's Dwelling (vv. 20-22)

The third metaphor describing the unit into which believers are brought together is a building.

20. And are built upon the foundation of the apostles and prophets, Jesus Christ himself being the chief corner stone.

To the Ephesians Paul said that the church is *built upon the foundation of the apostles and prophets*. This is true because it is through them that we know Jesus and His will. The Lord's *apostles*—the twelve and their companions—were the first public proclaimers of the risen

Lord. They were joined by New Testament *prophets*, whose inspired words confirmed the message.

In another letter Paul said, "Other foundation can no man lay than that is laid, which is Jesus Christ" (1 Corinthians 3:11). This does not contradict his statement in the verse before us. The present apostles and prophets of old rest on Jesus just as the rest of us do. Paul indicates Christ's primary position in the building by picturing Him as *the chief corner stone*. The cornerstone was the focal point of the foundation, governing the placement of all the foundation stones and thus the position of the whole building. Christ is the cornerstone, perfect in every detail. The apostles and prophets, inspired by the Holy Spirit, line up with Him. The church that rests on them is therefore resting on the one foundation, Jesus Christ.

21. In whom all the building fitly framed together groweth unto a holy temple in the Lord.

In Christ "the whole building is joined together and rises to become a holy temple in the Lord" *(New International Version)*. When properly related to the Cornerstone, each part fits properly with its neighbor, and the whole structure, planned and blessed by God, is brought to completion. It is a perfect, holy piece of architecture. It is God's house!

What the apostle Paul has written here of the all-inclusive whole is true also of individual congregations and Christians individually. Christ is the focus that keeps the various members—and the various elements of one's personality—from going off in all directions and from clashing one with another.

22. In whom ye also are builded together for a habitation of God through the Spirit.

Home Daily Bible Readings

Monday, May 1—Salvation—God's Gift (Ephesians 2:4-10)
Tuesday, May 2—The Happiness of Being Forgiven (Psalm 32)
Wednesday, May 3—The Joy of Right Relationships (Psalm 51:10-17)
Thursday, May 4—Peace With God (Psalm 85)
Friday, May 5—Made One in Christ (Ephesians 2:11-18)
Saturday, May 6—Love One Another (1 John 4:7-12)
Sunday, May 7—Forgiveness and Fellowship (1 John 1:5—2:2

This is the spiritual house, built up of living stones, described in 1 Peter 2:5. God lives, not in great cathedrals nor in little chapels (Acts 7:48; 17:24), but among and within those who are committed to Him (Matthew 18:20). His true dwelling place is in the life and community of the redeemed. And we have a vital part in making and keeping the house fit for His habitation. Speaking of the church Paul wrote, "Know ye not that ye are the temple of God, and that the Spirit of God dwelleth in you? If any man defile the temple of God, him shall God destroy; for the temple of God is holy" (1 Corinthians 3:16, 17). And speaking of the Christian person the same apostle said, "Know ye not that your body is the temple of the Holy Ghost which is in you. . . . Therefore glorify God in your body, and in your spirit, which are God's" (1 Corinthians 6:19, 20).

Conclusion

A. No Peace Factories

In a masterpiece of understatement Jesus said, "Blessed are the peacemakers: for they shall be called the children of God" (Matthew 5:9). Indeed they shall, for they must be very like God himself! Peace is His to fashion and His to produce. No factory will ever come up with even a poor imitation of peace.

God has never made any secret of His formula for peace. It is Jesus Christ, His Son, our Lord. In prophecy Isaiah said of Him, "The chastisement of our peace was upon him" (53:5). At Jesus' coming, angels announced, "Glory to God in the highest, and on earth peace, good will toward men" (Luke 2:14). At Jesus' farewell to His friends He said, "Peace I leave with you, my peace I give unto you: not as the world giveth, give I unto you" (John 14:27).

Sustained by the Holy Spirit whom He has sent, we have the peace He promised (Galatians 5:22).

B. Prayer

As perplexed people in a warring world, O God, we acknowledge You as our one source and hope for peace. Quiet the rebel spirit within us, that we may live as Your children. Help us to live as brothers and sisters with Your other children, in the peace He came to give. We plead in His name. Amen.

C. Thought to Remember

"Peace I leave with you, my peace I give unto you: not as the world giveth, give I unto you. Let not your heart be troubled, neither let it be afraid" (John 14:27).

Learning by Doing

*This page contains an alternate lesson plan emphasizing learning activities. Classes
desiring such student involvement will find these suggestions helpful.*

Learning Goals

After this lesson students should be able to:
1. Define grace.
2. Explain how faith and good works are compatible within the concept of grace.
3. List some "walls of partition" in his own congregation or community that need to be broken down by the gospel.
4. Develop a plan for the application of the gospel to at least one of these barriers.

Into the Lesson

Before the class members arrive, write the agree/disagree statement below on the chalkboard or a sheet of newsprint so everyone can see it.

Agree or Disagree?

Peace will come to mankind when each person puts the other's welfare above his own.

As the class members arrive, direct their attention to the statement. Ask them to find at least three other people who have answered as they have. The four of them are to develop an explanation to the entire class for why they have answered as they have. Allow the groups three to five minutes to do this. Then open this up to a discussion in the larger group.

Make the transition into the Bible study by stating that today's lesson will provide insight into the statement.

Into the Word

Read Ephesians 2:8-22 aloud. Then briefly present the material in the "Introduction" section.

Lead the students in a guided discussion to examine the meaning of the text. Use the questions below to develop the discussion.

1. What is a workable definition for grace? (A commonly used definition is "unmerited favor.")
2. Ephesians 2:9 states that our salvation is "not of works." Yet verse 10 says that we are God's workmanship created to do good works. How can we reconcile these two statements? ("Not of works" means "not as a result of works." Be sure to emphasize that we cannot earn salvation. Nevertheless, our lives are to be characterized by good works that model after Christ once we are Christians. Those works

don't earn salvation; they demonstrate our thankfulness to God for the salvation He has given us. They improve the lot and make the world a better place in which to live. They are also a means by which we bring glory to God, our Father. See Matthew 16.)

3. What was the spiritual condition of Gentiles before Christ came? Verses 11 and 12 outline these. (Separated from Christ, excluded from citizenship in God's kingdom, unacquainted with the covenant of promise, without hope, without God.)

4. According to verses 13-18, what barriers has Christ broken down? (He has removed the barrier of sin that separated us from God. He has broken down walls of hostility between opposing groups, making them one in Him.)

5. According to verses 19-22, what conditions are true of all believers at this time? (Citizens of God's kingdom, members of God's family, a dwelling for God's Spirit.)

6. What is the believer's part in breaking down the barriers cited in the text?

The commentary material will help you be prepared to lead the students to develop good answers to the questions above. It will also provide adequate material to fill in any gaps left by the answers of the class members.

Into Life

Ask the following questions:
1. What barriers exist in our community or congregation that ought to be broken down in Jesus Christ?
2. Should Christians really involve themselves in breaking down these barriers? Why?
3. If Christians do involve themselves in breaking down the barriers mentioned, what should be the motivating factor in doing so?

Now assign one of the barriers mentioned to each pair of class members. Ask each pair to think of ways that Christians could help to break down this barrier. Urge them to be specific in their suggestions. Allow five to seven minutes for this, and develop a general discussion based upon the results.

Give each person a small index card with the following sentence, which they are to complete:

"I want to become involved in breaking down the barriers mentioned by—"

Close the session with prayer.

Let's Talk It Over

The questions on this page are designed to encourage review of the lesson Scriptures and to promote discussion of the lesson by the class. The answers provided are only discussion starters. Let your class talk it over from there.

1. To be saved carries the meaning of rescue from perilous circumstances, it implies the concept of being stored or preserved, and the lesson text speaks of it as our being restored to our created purpose. How do each of the figures apply to our salvation in Christ.

When we are saved by Christ, we are rescued from condemnation to eternal separation from God, the judgment against sin. We are rescued from darkness—the deception of Satan that enslaves us to sin. In Christ we are designated as holy, belonging to God, and we have a future hope of being glorified with Christ and reigning with Him eternally. As sinners, we had defiled the image of God, but in Christ we are given power to complete the will of God and participate in His purposes.

2. How may we describe the advantages of being in Christ so as to interest an unbeliever? What things could we include?

We must remember that the theological language Christians sometimes use to describe salvation will have little or no meaning to non-Christians. *Redemption, atonement,* and *justification* need a lot of explaining. Jesus gave us an excellent example of the use of metaphors to illustrate salvation. To Nicodemus He spoke of being born again (the need to begin a new life generated by the Holy Spirit). To the woman at the well He spoke of living water (the satisfaction of our deepest needs for identity and purpose). He also told the very powerful story of the prodigal son (the need for repentance, the joy of forgiveness and restoration by the father). In our text, Paul speaks in terms of walls of separation being broken down (the blessing of renewed fellowship with God and the breaking down of enmity between men). All of these continue to have appeal in the twentieth century.

3. How did the traditional relationship between Jew and Gentile differ after both were in Christ? What should we learn from this concerning relationships today?

God had chosen the people of Israel to be His special people and had given them the law at Mount Sinai. This became a barrier between Jew and Gentile. The Jews were proud that God had chosen them to receive it, and they looked down on the Gentiles who had not received it. The Gentiles, on the other hand, were inclined to scoff at the Jews because they considered themselves bound by all the minute regulations of the law. And they despised the Jews because of their attitude of superiority toward all other people. Through the death of Christ, forgiveness of sins was extended to Jew and Gentile alike. When all received forgiveness, the law ceased to be a barrier; and the enmity associated with it was no more. The gospel excludes no one; its provisions are the same for all. Our commission as Christians is to make disciples of all nations (Matthew 28:19). We need to discover how best to communicate the gospel to the nations, but also to the ethnics in our own community.

4. If the fellowship of Christians is meant to be a "holy temple in the Lord," what qualities of today's churches give evidence of that? What qualities of some churches belie their identity as the temple of God?

If God indwells a church as His holy temple, we might expect to see some of the character of God shining through that fellowship of believers. We know that God is love, so we might look for love practiced by the church. Other qualities in evidence might be joy, peace, patience, goodness, kindness, gentleness, and self-control (see Galatians 5:22, 23). Since God hates sin, we might look for moral purity in the church, with heartfelt repentance when sin occurs. Unfortunately, there are churches in which certain "works of the flesh" are all too evident (Galatians 5:19-21).

5. When someone tries to live his life in genuine purity and honor to God, he may be criticized as a "super saint." To what extent should Christians be seen as different from sinners? Is there a danger in being too holy?

Christians have separated themselves from the ways of the world and have dedicated themselves to God. Being born again they are to demonstrate a new nature. If Christians cannot be distinguished from sinners, then something is radically wrong. We'll never be "too holy" in God's eyes. However, if we try to make a display of holiness, we are doing as the Pharisees did and are deserving of the same condemnation.

Building Up the Body of Christ

LESSON SCRIPTURE: Ephesians 4:1-16.

PRINTED TEXT: Ephesians 4:1-16.

Ephesians 4:1-16

1 I therefore, the prisoner of the Lord, beseech you that ye walk worthy of the vocation wherewith ye are called,

2 With all lowliness and meekness, with long-suffering, forbearing one another in love;

3 Endeavoring to keep the unity of the Spirit in the bond of peace.

4 There is one body, and one Spirit, even as ye are called in one hope of your calling;

5 One Lord, one faith, one baptism,

6 One God and Father of all, who is above all, and through all, and in you all.

7 But unto every one of us is given grace according to the measure of the gift of Christ.

8 Wherefore he saith, When he ascended up on high, he led captivity captive, and gave gifts unto men.

9 (Now that he ascended, what is it but that he also descended first into the lower parts of the earth?

10 He that descended is the same also that ascended up far above all heavens, that he might fill all things.)

11 And he gave some, apostles; and some, prophets; and some, evangelists; and some, pastors and teachers;

12 For the perfecting of the saints, for the work of the ministry, for the edifying of the body of Christ:

13 Till we all come in the unity of the faith, and of the knowledge of the Son of God,

unto a perfect man, unto the measure of the stature of the fulness of Christ:

14 That we henceforth be no more children, tossed to and fro, and carried about with every wind of doctrine, by the sleight of men, and cunning craftiness, whereby they lie in wait to deceive;

15 But speaking the truth in love, may grow up into him in all things, which is the head, even Christ:

16 From whom the whole body fitly joined together and compacted by that which every joint supplieth, according to the effectual working in the measure of every part, maketh increase of the body unto the edifying of itself in love.

GOLDEN TEXT: He gave some, apostles; and some, prophets; and some, evangelists; and some, pastors and teachers; for the perfecting of the saints, for the work of the ministry, for the edifying of the body of Christ.—Ephesians 4:11, 12.

Lesson Aims

This lesson should equip a student to:

1. Show how the principles of *love* and of *unity* relate to building up the body of Christ.

2. Show how the function of special leaders is related to service rendered by the whole membership in building the church.

3. Name a "gift of grace" that God has provided for him to use in building up the body of Christ.

Lesson Outline

INTRODUCTION
  A. Body Building
  B. Lesson Background
I. THE BODY IS ONE (Ephesians 4:1-6)
  A. Forbearance Is Needed (vv. 1-3)
    Recognizing Unity
  B. Foundations Are Provided (vv. 4-6)
II. THE BUILDERS AND THEIR GIFTS ARE MANY (Ephesians 4:7-12)
  A. Christ Is the Giver to All (vv. 7-10)
  B. Leaders Equip the Saints to Serve (vv. 11, 12)
    Using Your Gift
III. THE GOAL IS CHRISTLIKE MATURITY (Ephesians 4:13-16)
  A. The Grown-up Body (v. 13)
  B. The Unstable Past (v. 14)
  C. The Way to Grow (v. 15)
  D. The Power and the Process (v. 16)
CONCLUSION
  A. Building and Being Built
  B. Prayer
  C. Thought to Remember

Display visual 11 from the visuals/learning resources packet and let it remain before the class. It is shown on page 317.

Introduction

A. Body Building

The human race, as well as the individual person, seems naturally to desire and to achieve growth. The child hurries to grow up, and the adult yearns for the "body beautiful."

Why? Well, grown-up people with well-proportioned bodies tend to be admired and to

have influence. They appear to be more healthy, to have more pleasure, and to accomplish more than their less robust neighbors. The facts often belie the appearance, but the values of being big and beautiful are sufficient to make health spas and exercise programs profitable.

There is value in all this, but as the apostle Paul wrote to Timothy, "Physical training is of some value, but godliness has value for all things, holding promise for both the present life and the life to come" (1 Timothy 4:8, *New International Version*). Even for the present life, Christian growth and maturity certainly go beyond one's physically being big and/or beautiful.

That is not in any way to belittle care for our physical bodies. Scripture insists on its importance. But more important is the care given to our spiritual growth. Our last week's lesson introduced the church as a fellowship "built up" and growing as a structure in which God may dwell (Ephesians 2:20-22).

There are, of course, two kinds of growth— size or quantity, and efficiency or quality. How well that is known to the up-shooting teenager who finds himself possessed of awkward frame and stumbling limbs, and only later develops the coordination that brings frame and limbs into a smoothly working unit. For any kind of body to function effectively, the coordination is at least as important as the size. In the body of Christ, the coordinated working of the members is the basis for both spiritual and numerical growth.

B. Lesson Background

The book of Ephesians falls naturally into two parts. The first three chapters present all-inclusive doctrine of the church. Christ is the head of His body, the church; Christ is the foundation of His spiritual building, the church. The teaching is interlaced, however, with practical implications. The body is to glorify its Head; the building is to grow into a suitable dwelling for God's Spirit.

Chapters 4-6 deal mainly with the saints' suitable response to their calling as God's people. Chapter 4 begins, "I ... beseech you that ye walk worthy," and the rest of the book describes the worthy walk. Doctrinal and devotional passages reinforce the exhortations.

Paul was addressing believers whom he had influenced during his ministry at Ephesus. They had become "fellow citizens with the saints, and of the household of God" (2:19), but they still lived in pagan surroundings. They needed continuing Christian instruction, motivation, and encouragement. So, in fact, do we!

I. The Body Is One
(Ephesians 4:1-6)

A. Forbearance Is Needed (vv. 1-3)

1. I therefore, the prisoner of the Lord, beseech you that ye walk worthy of the vocation wherewith ye are called.

In chapter 3 Paul described his commission as apostle to the Gentiles; hence his care and prayer for the saints at Ephesus. *Therefore*, since he is now a *prisoner* and cannot minister to them in person, he addresses a written appeal for their faithfulness and consistent behavior. He beseeches, pleads, or entreats them to *walk*, or lead a life, worthy of God's upward calling.

God has issued a summons to everyone to be what He intended men to be. That call comes through the gospel of Christ; and the response becomes the Christian's true *vocation* or career, no matter what else he or she may do to finance the career. Christianity is our profession and saintliness our estate.

2. With all lowliness and meekness, with long-suffering, forbearing one another in love.

Unity and growth in the body depend on proper relationships—proper attitudes—among the members. Jesus, example and Lord, was "meek and lowly in heart" (Matthew 11:29). To the Greek mind, *meekness*, or gentleness, as opposed to self-assertion, was regarded as a second-rate virtue; and *lowliness*, or humility, as opposed to pride or haughtiness, was no virtue at all. The instruction here given would have been laughed out of court among unconverted Gentiles. It was, and is, difficult enough to achieve among believers in Christ.

Long-suffering and *forbearing one another* denote patient endurance with another's provocations, holding back the arm or the word of retaliation. *Love* is the necessary climate in which all this may occur.

3. Endeavoring to keep the unity of the Spirit in the bond of peace.

Ephesians 2:18 says, "Through him [Christ] we both [Jew and Gentile] have access by one Spirit unto the Father." That Spirit-provided unity must never be allowed to slip away. It must be kept, guarded, and maintained with all diligence. Love for Christ and His church forms a *bond* that ties the whole body together in *peace*, wholeness, and harmony.

RECOGNIZING UNITY

On his desk the teacher had three similar apples, a kitchen knife, a mixer, and a napkin. Without a word he took the first apple, cut it into small pieces, placed the pieces in the mixer, and produced a drinkable liquid of homogenized apple, seed, skin, and fruit.

He cut the second apple into halves, then quarters, eighths, and finally sixteenths. These he placed on the napkin.

The third apple he simply held complete and whole in his hand.

Then he asked, "which of these is an apple?" An argument and discussion followed. Finally the class agreed all were apples in different forms. His second question was easier. "Which is easily recognized as an apple?" All agreed it was the whole fruit in his hand.

Finally the application came. "Class," he said, "as long as the fruit is maintained in its original wholeness, anyone can recognize an apple. When the wholeness is altered, it is hard to know the fruit."

Speaking of the church, Paul urges us "to keep the unity of the Spirit in the bond of peace." When we keep the unity, the church can be recognized as the body of Christ. When we divide, the result creates confusion, argument, and doubt. —W. P.

B. Foundations Are Provided (vv. 4-6)

4. There is one body, and one Spirit, even as ye are called in one hope of your calling.

Paul now gives his attention to seven *ones*, which are the divinely supplied foundation for unity in the church. The apostle does not argue *for* the unity of body, Spirit, and hope; rather he reminds his readers that these are very obviously one each, and that they provide the basis for the oneness he urges.

If the church is truly the body of Christ (Ephesians 1:23), it cannot be more than *one body*. It is animated by *one Spirit*, the Holy Spirit, and cheered by *one hope*—the hope of life eternal in Christ. The gospel has called every hearer to that selfsame hope.

5, 6. One Lord, one faith, one baptism, one God and Father of all, who is above all, and through all, and in you all.

The church acknowledges only One as Lord: Jesus Christ. He said, "I am the way, the truth, and the life: no man cometh unto the Father, but by me" (John 14:6). "All power is given unto me in heaven and in earth" (Matthew 28:18). Those who would recognize others as Lord are simply not in His church.

The unity of the Christian gospel, or *faith*, also is a truth accepted beyond question. It is the faith once for all delivered to the saints (Jude 3). It is the one gospel—the good news of the one Christ—so exclusively right that counterfeiters or makers of alterations are worthy of condemnation (Galatians 1:6-9). The one faith is belief and trust in the one Lord, who is acknowledged in the *one baptism* (Acts 2:38; 22:16) into the one body of Christ (Galatians 3:27). Substitutes for the burial (in water) of a repentant believer in Christ for the forgiveness of sin had not yet been introduced when the apostle wrote of one baptism. The oneness of the body is established as each member is united to the one Head, even Christ, by faith and baptism.

No truth in Scripture is more universally acknowledged than the oneness of God: "The Lord our God is one Lord" (Deuteronomy 6:4). Upon this truth all else rests. So to this point the writer's emphasis falls on the *ones—one* Lord, *one* faith, *one* baptism, *one* God. These self-evident unities lead to the obvious conclusion that the community built on these must be one. But the apostle goes further in speaking of God. He is the same to *all* persons of all nations at all times. All alike are His children in Christ; all alike are under the sheltering care of Him who is *above*; all alike may experience His intimate presence, who is *through* and among them.

II. The Builders and Their Gifts Are Many (Ephesians 4:7-12)

A. Christ Is the Giver to All (vv. 7-10)

7. But unto every one of us is given grace according to the measure of the gift of Christ.

Up to this point the apostle has spoken chiefly of the whole body and its total unity. Now he turns to the individual member—*every one of us.* Whatever we have of good to contribute in the body has first been *given* to us freely by Christ. Some gifts, such as prophecy and miracles, have been special and limited. Others, such as hope and love, are universal and timeless (1 Corinthian 12:8-10; 13:13). Your gift may be as unspectacular as the ability to tell a friend what you learned in Bible school, or to use your automobile in Christian work, but the Lord expects each of us to use what he has.

8. Wherefore he saith, When he ascended up on high, he led captivity captive, and gave gifts unto men.

Psalm 68:18 is quoted as foreshadowing this divine bestowal of gifts. Some see in this psalm a reference to Moses at Mount Sinai. The psalm says, "Thou hast ascended on high, thou hast led captivity captive: thou hast received gifts for men." Moses, after he had led the captive Hebrews out of Egypt, went up into the mountain and received God's law as a gift to the people that they might live with God among them. So also Jesus, after He had descended from Heaven to earth, and then into the very grave to rescue sinners from their captivity to death and con-

demnation, arose from the grave and ascended again to Heaven. From there He bestows among His people the gifts that enable them to live at peace with God and with harmony among themselves.

9, 10. (Now that he ascended, what is it but that he also descended first into the lower parts of the earth? He that descended is the same also that ascended far up above all heavens, that he might fill all things.)

The quotation is explained in reference to Christ. John 1:1, 14 and especially Philippians 2:5-8 make clear Christ's coming from glory to earth and finally to the grave. Then, He arose from the grave, and after forty days He arose from the earth to be again with God the Father in glory (Mark 16:19; Acts 1:9). Christ ascended, not to abandon His church as an orphan (John 14:18), but to provide it with rich gifts of His spiritual presence, thus filling *all things*.

B. Leaders Equip the Saints to Serve (vv. 11, 12)

11. And he gave some, apostles; and some, prophets; and some, evangelists; and some, pastors and teachers.

The Lord's gifts, previously mentioned, are here identified. As God gave His Son to the church as its head, so the Son gave various ministries and ministers to the church for its upbuilding.

Apostles and *prophets* were specially endowed to engage in laying foundations for the church (Ephesians 2:20). As such they have no successors nor continuing office. Apostles were chosen, empowered, and sent by Christ, and were able to convey special powers to others (Acts 8:14-20). *Prophets* were endowed to speak by inspiration things that could not be known otherwise (Acts 11:27, 28; 21:10, 11). The teachings of apostles and prophets come to us now through their words preserved in the New Testament.

Evangelists . . . pastors and teachers continue as necessary servants of the Lord in His church. *Evangelists* minister especially to the unconverted, setting forth the convincing facts of the gospel. They give special attention to the first part of the Great Commission, making disciples (Matthew 28:19). *Pastors* are literally shepherds. The pastor in the New Testament was identical to the elder or bishop. (See Acts 20:17-28.) The shepherd is to lead, feed, and guard the sheep. The feeding aspect is teaching, so *pastors* and *teachers* are very often the same persons, emphasizing the second part of the Great Commission—teaching to observe Christ's commands (Matthew 28:20).

12. For the perfecting of the saints, for the work of the ministry, for the edifying of the body of Christ.

The language of this verse in Paul's Greek indicates just one purpose to be served by Christ's gifts to the church. That is "to prepare God's people for works of service, so that the body of Christ may be built up" *(New International Version)*. *Perfecting* translates a word that signifies preparing, or equipping fully. The saints are to be prepared for action, and the action is work—servant work, meeting needs in the name of Christ. The needs may be material and physical (James 1:27), emotional and social (Romans 12:15), or spiritual (Galatians 6:1, 2). The natural result of all that service is that the body of Christ is built up.

USING YOUR GIFT

Novelyn Horton is on leave from her school district to teach in the Wycliffe school in Belem, Brazil. She is a gifted teacher, but there are some gifts she does not possess. Recently she wrote of one such lack. "For some reason we had lots of frogs in our classroom. One day I opened my desk drawer, lifted up some paper, and froze. I looked down on a little three-inch frog. With all the composure I could muster, I asked for a volunteer to 'defrog' my desk. Robby immediately volunteered. After he had removed it and two others, he proudly suggested, 'Miss Horton, anytime you need someone to take frogs out of your desk, you call me.' Now where else can I get such an offer!"

Robby couldn't teach that class, but he could catch frogs. As a frog-catcher he could restore Novelyn's sense of well-being so she could continue teaching. Robby was using his gift.

God's gifts to the church provide for leadership, teaching, evangelism, and all the things needed for its proper functioning and growth. If our gift is to take care of the "frogs," let's use it for the good of the body.   —W. P.

III. The Goal Is Christlike Maturity (Ephesians 4:13-16)

A. The Grown-up Body (v. 13)

13. Till we all come in the unity of the faith, and of the knowledge of the Son of God, unto a perfect man, unto the measure of the stature of the fulness of Christ.

The abilities and the function assigned by Christ are to continue as long as the world stands, having as their purpose the growth and maturing of Christ's body, the church, in every age. What a high goal this verse presents to us: to become a perfect man like Christ. The word

visual 11

THE WORTHY WALK
HUMILITY • GENTLENESS • PATIENCE
LOVE • PEACE • UNITY • GROWTH
TO MATURITY

rendered here and elsewhere in the New Testament as *perfect* really means mature, complete, and not flawless as we actually think of its meaning. However, the goal before us is to be like Christ. We must not be satisfied with partial attainment. We may not "attain." Paul said he had not. But God has given us a man without sin, the human Jesus for our imitation. And by what means are we to strive to reach it? In the unity of the faith, the one already discussed, and the knowledge of the Son of God.

Knowledge of the Son of God—awareness of Him, information about Him, and intimacy through acquaintance with Him—grows in the growing Christian (2 Peter 3:18). It is essential to his increase in Christlike stature and maturity. And that Christlikeness becomes the complete maturity that is called *perfect*.

The fulness of Christ amazes us in its breadth and depth. He is complete man and complete God. He is Prince of peace and maker of division. He was meek in suffering and terrible in judgment. He was submissive in His death, and powerful in His resurrection.

B. The Unstable Past (v. 14)

14. That we henceforth be no more children, tossed to and fro, and carried about with every wind of doctrine, by the sleight of men, and cunning craftiness whereby they lie in wait to deceive.

One trait of an immature person is a childish lack of stability. Paul urged the saints to grow up in their knowledge and understanding of the Word, and in their steadfast commitment to a chosen course (1 Corinthians 3:1-3; Hebrews 5:13).

Changing the figure of speech, Paul would agree with James that "he that wavereth is like a wave of the sea driven with the wind and tossed" (James 1:6). Whole congregations as well as individual saints can be swept along with the fancies of some enthusiast for "new spiritual truth." The mature saint will keep a straight course, guided by his insistence on searching the Scriptures to measure the truth of what is taught (Acts 17:11).

The *sleight of men* refers literally to the rolling of dice, unpredictable in their course and deceitful in their influence. *Cunning craftiness* is translated by Goodspeed as "ingenuity in inventing error." Deceitful and crafty false teachers are always handy to mislead the weak.

C. The Way to Grow (v. 15)

15. But speaking the truth in love, may grow up into him in all things, which is the head, even Christ.

Speaking the truth translates a single verb, sometimes also translated "dealing truthfully." Truth is to dominate one's thinking, acting, following, and serving, as well as his speaking. And Jesus Christ is "the way, the truth, and the life" (John 14:6); He is the truth that makes men free (John 8:32, 36).

It is popular to suppose that some deceitfulness, or at least some obscuring of painful truth, is justifiable or even necessary in the expression of love. Not so! Love, which is a criterion of all things Christian, identifies with truth. The two are inseparable. Any failure in either truthfulness or love is a failure to *grow up into him* [Christ] *in all things.* As He is "full of grace and truth" (John 1:14) so are His mature disciples. Truth and love, translated into action, are the center of the growing Christian's exercise program for development. So, increasingly, he becomes like his Lord.

D. The Power and the Process (v. 16)

16. From whom the whole body fitly joined together and compacted by that which every joint supplieth, according to the effectual working in the measure of every part, maketh increase of the body unto the edifying of itself in love.

The *New International Version* renders this verse clearly: "From him the whole body, joined and held together by every supporting ligament, grows and builds itself up in love, as each part does its work."

Once again, Paul uses one of his favorite figures for the church—the human body. Each part or member is important to the whole, receiving direction and life force through its connection with the head, then using that direction and force in harmonious operation with the other arts, working for the strengthening of the body. *Love* enables the parts to bind and to build together. The failure of any member to do his proportionate work, or to operate in harmony with other members, will tend to cripple the body and stunt its growth.

Conclusion

A. Building and Being Built

Ephesians 4:1-16 speaks of the need for Christians to grow and mature, but our lesson topic assigned for this text is, "Building Up the Body of Christ." Is there a contradiction? Not at all!

Paul compares the church with the human body. In a body, the development of the individual parts and the growth of the body as a whole are intertwined. For example, as the legs work to carry the body where it needs to go, the legs themselves are strengthened; thereby they are enabled to serve the body to an even greater degree. So it is with each of the body's members.

It is the same in the church. We are to grow and mature in Christ, and the best way to do it is to serve the other members of His body. Spiritual growth, it seems, is one of the things that are added when a person seeks first the kingdom of God and His righteousness (Matthew 6:33).

So let's not wander around seeking a church where we may get the most out of the services for our own edification. Instead, let's settle down where we are and use the gifts we have been given so as to build up the body of Christ. We may be amazed at how we'll find ourselves built up in His likeness in the process.

B. Prayer

Thank You, Father, for the privilege of membership in the body of Christ, His church. May we have abundant joy in working with others in building that body, to His glory and to the salvation of many souls. Amen.

C. Thought to Remember

The way I do my part as a member of Christ's church makes a difference in the health and growth of His whole body!

Home Daily Bible Readings

Monday, May 8—United by Faith in Christ (Ephesians 4:1-10)

Tuesday, May 9—All Are Useful (1 Corinthians 12:14-21)

Wednesday, May 10—Using Our Gifts to Help Others (Ephesians 4:11-16)

Thursday, May 11—A Child's Gift (John 6:1-13)

Friday, May 12—Abundant Giving (Mark 14:3-9)

Saturday, May 13—The Gift of Friendship (Acts 16:11-15)

Sunday, May 14—Rekindle the Gift (2 Timothy 1:3-7)

Learning by Doing

This page contains an alternate lesson plan emphasizing learning activities. Classes desiring such student involvement will find these suggestions helpful.

Learning Goals

As a result of studying this lesson, each student should be able to do the following:

1. Explain how the principles of *love* and *unity* contribute to the building up of the body of Christ.

2. Explain the purpose for special leaders in developing unity.

3. Identify a "gift of grace" that God has provided for him to use in building up the body of Christ.

Into the Lesson

Before the class begins prepare large puzzles in the shape of the human body, one puzzle for every five or six class members. Intentionally omit one piece from each puzzle. As the class members arrive, divide them into small groups of five or six and give each group a puzzle. Ask each group to compose its puzzle, not mentioning the missing piece. Wait to find out how the groups respond.

When the groups have gone as far as they can in putting the puzzles together, discuss their work and especially their feelings about the significance of the missing pieces. Point out to them that this principle is the basis for today's Bible lesson.

Spend no more than eight to ten minutes to complete this activity.

Into the Word

Present a brief lecture using the "Introduction" section of this lesson. Ask a class member, who has been given the assignment in advance, to read Ephesians 4:1-16 aloud to the class.

Give each person a sheet containing the following questions. (Eliminate the answers, of course.) Ask each two individuals to work together to find the answers in today's text.

1. What personal characteristics contribute to a harmonious church? (Humility, gentleness, patience, love, peacefulness.)

2. Ephesians 4:4-6 suggests seven truths that are foundational for unity in the church. What are they? How does each contribute to unity? (One body [the church], one Spirit, one hope [Heaven], one Lord, one faith, one baptism, one God.)

What functional gifts has God provided to the church to achieve unity? How does each con-

tribute to unity? (Apostles, prophets, evangelists, pastors and teachers.)

4. What is the purpose of the functional gifts in the church? (To prepare Christians for service; to build up the church; to unite all in the faith and in the knowledge of Christ; to bring all to spiritual maturity.)

5. What will be the outcome when all members of the church use the gifts God has given them? (People will be grown-up Christians; the church will grow.)

Allow the students six to eight minutes to find the answers to these questions. Then lead a general discussion, using the questions to guide development of the discussion. Be prepared to fill in explanatory details as needed—but let the students take the lead in answering the questions.

Into Life

Ask the class members to look up 1 Corinthians 12:7-11, Romans 12:3-8, and 1 Peter 4:10, 11. Have the class members read them and mention the various gifts given to the church. As they do so, make a list of the gifts on the chalkboard. Ask again what the purpose of gifts is. Emphasize that gifts are to be used to prepare people for service, to perfect people in Christ, and to achieve unity—not to judge others, divide the church, or cause disunity.

Point out that some gifts, such as teaching and encouraging, are mentioned more than once. One can conclude that these are critical gifts for every congregation. Make a separate list of these gifts on the chalkboard.

Develop a further discussion by asking the following questions:

1. How important are these gifts to this congregation?

2. What gifts do you think you may be able to use for the benefit of this congregation?

3. What underlying principles should guide the use of gifts in this congregation?

Give each person a small index card and ask students to write the following sentence on it. Then ask them to complete the sentence: "I believe that God has gifted me in this way: _____ _____ and I want to use it to build up the church by _____ _____." Close with prayer.

Let's Talk It Over

The questions on this page are designed to encourage review of the lesson Scriptures and to promote discussion of the lesson by the class. The answers provided are only discussion starters. Let your class talk it over from there.

1. With the followers of Jesus fractured into so many groups, meeting under so many names, in what sense may it be said there is "one body"? How may we promote the "unity of the Spirit"?

It may be argued that there is only one body of Christ on the earth, and that its membership is not identical to any known church body. Although we cannot always distinguish true believers from impostors, Scripture testifies that "the Lord knoweth them that are his" (2 Timothy 2:19). We do well to regard ourselves as not the only Christians, but Christians only. It is not up to any of us to draw the borders of the kingdom. Christ, the righteous judge, will do that. We must live so near the Savior that we have every confidence of being included. Instead of accusing and condemning those believers with whom we differ, why not celebrate the points of faith we have in common, while continuing to adhere to our convictions based upon our understanding of the revealed will of God?

2. Some people argue that we should not send missionaries to cultures that already practice a (non-Christian) religion that suits them. What does our text say to such an idea?

While there are many religions in the world, with varying degrees of positive practical effects upon their adherents, there is only one God. That one God has made only one provision for salvation, and that is through adherence to the one faith in the one Lord. All are to be added to the one body and receiving the one Spirit. Believing in Jesus means believing that He is the one way to the Father (John 14:6), and that His is the only name under Heaven by which we may be saved (Acts 4:12).

3. What provision did Christ make for the continued expansion of His church? How does this principle work today?

The church, like a human body, is a complex organism that benefits from organization and specialization in its members. Christ has provided a scheme of organization for the church in giving the members various gifts to be employed in ministry (see 1 Corinthians 12:4-7). In our text the gifts mentioned are leadership functions, which are foundational to the growth of the church. The purpose of these, however, is for preparing or equipping every Christian for a ministry that results in the building up of the church in numbers and in spiritual strength. This is the sense of verse 12. Apostles and prophets have disappeared, but Christ still calls and provides evangelists and pastors/teachers to lead and equip Christians for personal ministry.

4. Does your church teach that every member is a minister? How many members have adopted a personal ministry? What can churches do to encourage greater participation in ministry?

Churches that saddle the salaried leader(s) with all responsibility for ministry are not only ignoring the Biblical mandate to serve, but create an impossible burden for their leader(s) and defeat any potential for growth. To include more members in ministry, there must be regular and systematic teaching on the New Testament pattern for the church (especially Ephesians 4, Romans 12, Acts 6, and 1 Corinthians 12). Members must be recruited according to their gifts for particular ministries, and trained to complete them effectively. Leaders must be willing to share ministry functions and encourage members who participate. The obligation to service should be a part of new member training.

5. What is the standard against which we gauge our progress as Christians? What is your church doing to bring your members to maturity? How can you help?

"The measure of the stature of the fulness of Christ" (v. 13) is the absolute standard for Christian growth. The aim of every church should be to bring every person to that level of maturity. We measure success in terms of direction in the lives of people, and in small increments of progress toward the goal. Ultimately no ministry of the church is excluded from involvement in this goal. The more obvious efforts are the Sunday school, personal shepherding ministries, discipling projects, small group Bible studies, prayer partners, etc. You can help by availing yourself of those ministries that will help you mature, but also by making yourself available to serve where you can contribute to the growth of another.

Called to New Life

LESSON SCRIPTURE: Ephesians 4:17—5:20.

PRINTED TEXT: Ephesians 4:22—5:4, 18-20.

Ephesians 4:22-32

22 Put off concerning the former conversation the old man, which is corrupt according to the deceitful lusts;

23 And be renewed in the spirit of your mind;

24 And that ye put on the new man, which after God is created in righteousness and true holiness.

25 Wherefore putting away lying, speak every man truth with his neighbor: for we are members one of another.

26 Be ye angry, and sin not: let not the sun go down upon your wrath:

27 Neither give place to the devil.

28 Let him that stole steal no more: but rather let him labor, working with his hands the thing which is good, that he may have to give to him that needeth.

29 Let no corrupt communication proceed out of your mouth, but that which is good to the use of edifying, that it may minister grace unto the hearers.

30 And grieve not the Holy Spirit of God, whereby ye are sealed unto the day of redemption.

31 Let all bitterness, and wrath, and anger, and clamor, and evil speaking, be put away from you, with all malice:

32 And be ye kind one to another, tenderhearted, forgiving one another, even as God for Christ's sake hath forgiven you.

Ephesians 5:1-4, 18-20

1 Be ye therefore followers of God, as dear children;

2 And walk in love, as Christ also hath loved us, and hath given himself for us an offering and a sacrifice to God for a sweet-smelling savor.

3 But fornication, and all uncleanness, or covetousness, let it not be once named among you, as becometh saints;

4 Neither filthiness, nor foolish talking, nor jesting, which are not convenient: but rather giving of thanks.

. . . .

18 And be not drunk with wine, wherein is excess; but be filled with the Spirit;

19 Speaking to yourselves in psalms and hymns and spiritual songs, singing and making melody in your heart to the Lord;

20 Giving thanks always for all things unto God and the Father in the name of our Lord Jesus Christ.

GOLDEN TEXT: Put on the new man, which after God is created in righteousness and true holiness.—Ephesians 4:24.

Lesson Aims

This study should equip the student to:

1. Name at least five areas in which the new life in Christ is different from the old life without Him.

2. Show how each of these items of behavior reflects the person and character of Jesus.

3. Identify an area in which he will give special attention to developing the new life.

Lesson Outline

INTRODUCTION

   A. It's Where We Live

   B. On Learning Christ

  I. CHANGE YOUR HABIT(S) (Ephesians 4:22-24)

 II. REPLACE WHAT IS UNACCEPTABLE (Ephesians 4:25—5:2)

   A. Truth Instead of Lying (v. 25)

   B. Patience Overruling Anger (vv. 26, 27)

     Evicting an Old Tenant

   C. Giving Instead of Taking (v. 28)

   D. Constructive Speech Instead of Corrupt Speech (vv. 29, 30)

   E. Godly Love Instead of Malice (4:31—5:2)

III. AVOID WHAT IS UNMENTIONABLE (Ephesians 5:3, 4)

IV. SING WITH SPIRIT, NOT WITH SPIRITS (Ephesians 5:18-20)

   Transformation

CONCLUSION

   A. The Law of Liberty

   B. Prayer

   C. Thought to Remember

Display visual 12 from the visuals/learning resources packet. Refer to it as you introduce the lesson, and at other times throughout the session. It is shown on page 324.

Introduction

A. It's Where We Live

"It's just a habit I picked up. I don't mean anything by it. It's really not all that important." Which of us has not heard that kind of attempt to shrug off responsibility for shady customs? But *habit* is not so lightly dismissed. It's where we live, or die!

Prepare for a jolt when you look up *habit* in the dictionary. The first definition speaks of dress, garb, or attire; then the special attire that indicates rank or occupation. Only then is *habit* identified as mental or moral makeup, and finally as established custom or activity.

Consider also those other words, such as *inhabit, habitation, and habitable.* They speak of where we live and how we live, every day.

The apostle Paul writes boldly of the Christian way as a new life—a resurrection after the self-chosen death of the "old man" of sin. The new life calls for fresh new garments to replace the sin-stained garb of former days. So "put off all these: anger, wrath, malice, blasphemy, filthy communication out of your mouth.... Put on ...kindness, humbleness of mind, meekness, long-suffering . . . and above all these things put on charity [love], which is the bond of perfectness" (Colossians 3:8-14).

B. On Learning Christ

Following his exhortation to oneness, growth, and maturity in Christ, which we studied last week, the apostle turned to the subject of moral behavior among saints: "that ye henceforth walk not as other Gentiles walk," in empty pride, ignorance of God, and greedy lust (vv. 17-19). The life-style of their unconverted neighbors was a constant, oppressive presence with the Gentile Christians. It was the social soil in which they had grown up; it was in their own roots of custom and habit. Against all this the apostle shouted urgent warning.

One sentence must suffice to turn the Ephesians from their past behavior and the present pressure of their peers: "Ye have not so learned Christ" (v. 20). In Christ was divine power to overcome the world; in Christ was demonstration of the life in which He would lead; in Christ was divine love, demanding and motivating love in return; and in Christ was victory over sin, and death, and Hell. That victory was now available to the believers—in Christ! Learn Christ, and you know the way.

I. Change Your Habit(s) (Ephesians 4:22-24)

The truth is in Jesus, Paul stated (v. 21). That truth requires that we put off the old person with his sinful habits and put on Christ with His glorious garments, or *habit.*

22. Put off concerning the former conversation the old man, which is corrupt according to the deceitful lusts.

The admonition is to *put off . . . the old man,* as one would cast off an outworn and filthy garment, which is compared to the *former conversation* or life-style. Not only the outward behavior or manifestation, but the old nature or motivation must be discarded.

Corrupt describes what is spoiled and repulsive. Such is the world's manner of life to God and His people. *Lusts* are *deceitful* in promising good and bringing evil, promising pleasure and bringing pain. Lusts also make liars out of their victims, "deceiving, and being deceived" (2 Timothy 3:13).

23. And be renewed in the spirit of your mind.

"Be ye transformed by the renewing of your mind" (Romans 12:2). This renewal is an ongoing work of God in the believer: "Though our outward man perish, yet the inward man is renewed day by day" (2 Corinthians 4:16). The new attitude and thought pattern—the mind "in you, which was also in Christ" (Philippians 2:5-8)—becomes the source of all words and actions.

24. And that ye put on the new man, which after God is created in righteousness and true holiness.

"Put on the clean fresh clothes of the new life which was made by God's design for righteousness and the holiness which is no illusion" (Philipps translation). Like the new life itself, the garments of righteousness are made and provided by God. The believer is to accept and wear them. The *holiness*, or commitment to God, and the *righteousness*, or acceptance with God, are *true* and very real—quite unlike the deceitfulness of sin, noted in verse 22.

II. Replace What Is Unacceptable (Ephesians 4:25—5:2)

The new life to which the believer is called follows actively what it has learned of Christ. The discarded old garment must be replaced with the clean and new.

A. Truth Instead of Lying (v. 25)

25. Wherefore putting away lying, speak every man truth with his neighbor: for we are members one of another.

Lying was not regarded as any great evil in the Gentile world. In fact a clever and successful liar might be admired and imitated, even as in our modern pagan society. But God sees things differently. Lies are lies, and lying belongs to the discarded past.

Speak every man truth. Here the emphasis is on verbal truth. Speech and actions should be forthright and honest, aligned with each other, without deception.

We are members one of another. Lying to a fellow member of Christ's body would be like lying to oneself. Shall the carpenter's nail-holding hand send false signals to his hammer-swinging hand concerning the location of the nail?

B. Patience Overruling Anger (vv. 26, 27)

26, 27. Be ye angry, and sin not: let not the sun go down upon your wrath: neither give place to the devil.

Here is reference to Psalm 4:4: "Stand in awe, and sin not: commune with your own heart upon your bed, and be still." He who trembles before God is not likely to fall into sin.

What do we learn of Christ concerning anger? Mark 3:5 records that Jesus looked upon certain of His critics "with anger, being grieved for the hardness of their hearts." In that hour He challenged their faultfinding by restoring a crippled hand on the Sabbath, and then withdrew to teach His disciples and the following crowd. Jesus' anger was expressed in immediate, controlled, and appropriate words and action; and it disappeared before nightfall. Christians are to be "slow to wrath" (James 1:19); to control their anger to prevent its erupting in hurtful words and actions; and to close the door on anger to prevent Satan's getting a foot into it.

EVICTING AN OLD TENANT

The skunk was a permanent resident. Every effort to remove it had been futile. The original idea was to trap it in a baited cage and carry it far into the woods.

The farm dogs thought the skunk a delightful curiosity. While keeping a respectful distance they barked wildly after it and never let it near the baited trap.

After a period of armistice, the skunk reappeared with several little editions of herself trailing behind her. Enough was enough, and this growing family of intruders was too many.

Making sure the skunk family was away, Granddad carefully closed the entry hole and any other doorways they might use to get into the house. In the evening the skunk family returned, and finding the entrance blocked they looked for other access.

This was too much for Old Blue. The hound made a wild dash at the family, received the full price of his folly, and retreated in howling disgrace in need of much cleansing. The combination of closing and combat was effective, however, and we never saw the skunks again.

It will take stern measures to keep the devil out of your life. You will have to bar the door and combat him to keep him out.　　—W. P.

visual 12

CHRIST
REQUIRES A CHANGE OF OLD
　　HEART
　　ATTITUDE
　　BEHAVIOR
　　INTERESTS
　　THOUGHTS
　　SPEECH
PUT ON THE NEW MAN!

C. Giving Instead of Taking (v. 28)

28. Let him that stole steal no more: but rather let him labor, working with his hands the thing which is good, that he may have to give to him that needeth.

The "old man" *stole* from others to supply his own desires; the "new man" *gives* to others to supply their needs. The early church clearly included some who had been thieves. But thievery, whether grand larceny or the unauthorized appropriation of public or company equipment for private use, belongs to the discarded past. For the Christian, honesty is more than a "best policy"; it is a basic principle. He will live, not by his wits, but by his work (2 Thessalonians 3:7-12). He will respect manual labor, and will not despise the "profit motive." Profit, however, will not dominate his thinking. He will not engage in hurtful enterprises to make good money. The ultimate goal is not only to support himself and his family, but to be able to help others as well.

D. Constructive Speech Instead of Corrupt Speech (vv. 29, 30)

29. Let no corrupt communication proceed out of your mouth, but that which is good to the use of edifying, that it may minister grace unto the hearers.

We are all too familiar with the corruptions of profanity and blasphemy, belittling God; or vulgarity and obscenity, besmirching man; or gossip and lying, tearing down another in a vain attempt to advance oneself. These are not for the mind or mouth of the follower of Christ. Instead, our speech is to be constructive, lifting the spirits of others by support and encouragement. Constructive speech will also include the sharing of God's Word, which is "useful for teaching, rebuking, correcting and training in righteousness" (2 Timothy 3:16, *New International Version*). God's people will talk in such a way as to *minister grace*, not disgrace, to the hearers.

30. And grieve not the Holy Spirit of God, whereby ye are sealed unto the day of redemption.

The Holy Spirit becomes the indwelling companion of the believer at his baptism (Acts 2:38, 39), and the Spirit's presence becomes the constant evidence and guarantee of our salvation as long as we live (see Ephesians 1:13, 14). The Spirit—the Holy Ghost, or Holy Guest as some prefer to call Him—comes to dwell with us and within us. At His coming He brings a generous gift, a basket filled with delectable fruit—love, joy, peace, long-suffering, gentleness, goodness, faith, meekness, self-control (Galatians 5:22, 23). There would be no surer way to *grieve*—cause pain, distress, sorrow, or offense—to such a Guest than to refuse or reject His gift. We need to provide suitable accommodations for the holy and helpful Guest residing within us (1 Corinthians 6:19, 20), and we must surely protect Him from the offense of sharing His abode with roommates such as deceit, malice, greed, and foul language. Grieved by evidence that He is not welcome, the Holy Guest may depart, with all His gifts, graces, and guarantees.

E. Godly Love Instead of Malice (4:31—5:2)

31. Let all bitterness, and wrath, and anger, and clamor, and evil speaking, be put away from you, with all malice.

The evil qualities of the "old man" comprise an unloving and unlovely syndrome, or cluster of attitudes, feelings, and expressions. *Bitterness* and *malice*, or deep-seated, established ill will, describe the dominant attitude within the person. *Wrath* and *anger*—hostility in sudden bursts or in stubborn, smoldering resentment—describe the feelings. In the "old man" these all are expressed *clamor*—the the raised and strident voice—and *evil speaking*—the words of destructive "bad mouthing."

32. And be ye kind one to another, tenderhearted, forgiving one another, even as God for Christ's sake hath forgiven you.

Here is positive attitude and action in contrast to the malicious qualities just noted. The balance is not quite precise, however. Kindness and compassion are shown in deeds more than in words, but they still include kind words of sympathy and encouragement. *Forgiveness*, which puts a time limit on anger and stops malice dead in its tracks, is the practical answer to the irritations that are inevitable where people live in close association. Not every difference of opinion can be removed by even the most careful explanation, and not every hurt can be assuaged even by the assurance that it was not intended. The only way to clear the record is to wipe it clean with forgiveness; and the strongest possible motive toward forgiveness is the ever-present knowledge that *God for Christ's sake hath forgiven you.*

All the relationships here named are *one to another* throughout the family of God. Kindness, compassion, and forgiveness are to be given to whoever needs them by whoever has them to give.

5:1, 2. Be ye therefore followers of God, as dear children; and walk in love, as Christ also hath loved us, and hath given himself for us an offering and a sacrifice to God for a sweet-smelling savor.

It is the mark of beloved children to become imitators of a loving father. So as Paul's readers were just exhorted to be like God in forgiving others, they are now urged to imitate Him in the habitual practice of love. That includes the kindness and compassion the saints are to show one another, but it also includes God's kind of goodwill and helpfulness even to one's enemies (Matthew 5:43-48; Luke 6:32-36).

The ultimate demonstration of divine love is, of course, God's gift of His Son for our salvation (John 3:16), and the Son's willing self-sacrifice for sinners (John 15:13). Jesus gave himself as an *offering and a sacrifice to God* in the sense that by His sacrifice He accomplished what God had planned. Jesus gave His sacrifice *for us* in the sense that He gave it to redeem us and give us eternal life. Genesis 8:20, 21 and Exodus 29:18 speak of God's pleasure in the odor of the burnt offerings presented by sincere worshipers. So Christians are to follow their Lord to the extent of presenting themselves as living sacrifices, holy and acceptable to the Father (Romans 12:1).

III. Avoid What Is Unmentionable (Ephesians 5:3, 4)

In the preceding verse Paul exhorts Christ's followers to "walk in love." He follows that with a clear warning against the perversion of love.

3. But fornication, and all uncleanness, or covetousness, let it not be once named among you, as becometh saints.

The bad habits named previously were offenses against other persons, and should be put away. Illicit sexual behavior is primarily a sin against God (Genesis 39:9; 1 Thessalonians 4:3-8), and is not even to be considered. *Covetousness*—greed, or the insatiable desire for wealth and the things that gratify appetite—is included here perhaps because of its association with unrestrained sexual desire. Elsewhere covetousness is called idolatry (Colossians 3:5), or the worship of substitute gods. Ephesians 5:5 says plainly that "no immoral, impure, or greedy person—such a man is an idolater—has any inheritance in the kingdom of Christ" *(New International Version).*

4. Neither filthiness, nor foolish talking, nor jesting, which are not convenient: but rather giving of thanks.

Not only dirty deeds, but dirty jokes, have no place in the Christian's habit. *Jesting* translates the Greek word that means the adjustment of words to give them two meanings; hence it refers to that kind of talk that is indecently suggestive. Such shameful conduct and language is *not convenient,* that is, it is an improper engagement of the mind and tongue for the "new man," who "after God is created in righteousness and true holiness" (Ephesians 4:24).

Against such obscene frivolity Paul contrasts the *giving of thanks.* The thankful spirit recognizes God as the source of all good; hence it will respect Him and His will in its use of sex for total self-giving in life-committed marriage, and in its use of language for helpfulness rather than degradation.

IV. Sing With Spirit, Not With Spirits (Ephesians 5:18-20)

Ephesians 5:5-17 is a passage of warnings against three things that might lead the believer back into sin and destruction: bad advice, bad company, and indifference. Then comes yet another specific reference to what a person does with his mouth.

18. And be not drunk with wine, wherein is excess; but be filled with the Spirit.

In circumstances where safe drinking water was hard to find and where wine was a staple of daily fare, New Testament writers warned constantly against the dangers of drunkenness. *Excess* here translates a word that is more often translated "riot," "profligacy," "debauchery," or "dissipation"—the scattering and wasting of one's resources. The warning against drunkenness is easy for us to follow by total abstinence from alcohol, despite its wide acceptance and promotion.

Yet the Scriptures do not describe or recommend a dull, colorless existence. Christ, the gospel, and the Holy Spirit provide joy and excitement to keep life always interesting. Don't put out the flame! (1 Thessalonians 5:19).

TRANSFORMATION

In Los Gatos Christian Church there is an active alcohol support group. No, it does not endorse or support the use of alcohol. Its members, alcoholics and their families, support each other in gaining victory over alcohol and the terrible effects it has had in their lives.

Together in prayer, concern, testimony, and confession of alcohol addiction, they deal with one of the great social problems of our age. What is being done in Los Gatos can be done anywhere.

Three basics are required. The first is confession of need and the admission of alcohol addiction by the victim of this drug. Second, family support and help is needed both to understand alcoholism and to give strength and encouragement to the addict. Third, and most important, is new power in the life of the person seeking deliverance. This new power is the presence of God that comes only when a person abandons self and accepts Jesus as Savior and Lord.

At Los Gatos new life, free from alcohol, is being experienced by those formerly enslaved to this drug. The power of Christ and the presence of His Spirit are accomplishing it. That transforming power and presence are available to anyone in bondage to sin.   —W. P.

19. Speaking to yourselves in psalms and hymns and spiritual songs, singing and making melody in your heart to the Lord.

High excitement from any source leads naturally to singing. Christians are not to indulge in ribald music any more than in ribald jests or language. They will sing, even as Paul and Silas sang at midnight in prison (Acts 16:25); their elevated moods come from a spiritual source and are expressed in spiritual terms. The songs may come from Old Testament *psalms* or from their own compositions of praise to God. *Hymns* are most natural in prayerful adoration. Any *songs* that are used are *spiritual* rather than vulgar. Christians sing alone while they work, as a natural expression of joy or as a lift to their spir-

its. They sing to others, to encourage or even to instruct. They sing to God, as a form of prayer. In all of this, they sing from the heart, and not alone from the lips.

20. Giving thanks always for all things unto God and the Father in the name of our Lord Jesus Christ.

Those who have been rescued from the grip of sin and death and brought into new life in Christ find it natural to thank God continually for the indescribable gift of His Son. And more than just words, their thanksgiving for God's infinite mercies is seen daily in their *thanksgiving*.

Conclusion

A. The Law of Liberty

It is a glorious new life to which we have been called in Christ, but one thing about it disturbs me. Where are its detailed rules of conduct? I must speak truth, control my temper, be generous, and be helpful rather than hurtful. That's fine; but in giving, for example, how much must I give, and to what causes? And in language, where is the border line between fair and foul? Why didn't God spell things out for the Christian as He did through Moses for the Jews?

But wait! The Jewish lawyers were still kept busy adding interpretive ground rules to God's game plan. And the people became so involved with rules that many of them forgot the game. In Christ, God has given new *life*, rather than new *law*—except for the law of liberty, the royal law of love (James 1:25; 2:8). Our Lord and His apostles have laid down firm principles and some specific applications. But many of the details remain to be worked out by God's people, each alone and all together, as they meet the kaleidoscopic changes in daily living.

The new life is also a new relationship with God—a relationship of children who imitate and obey their Father in love, rather than under the compulsion of law.

B. Prayer

Father, we thank and praise You for the indescribable gift of new life in Christ Jesus. For His sacrifice that saves; for His Word that teaches; for His example that leads; for the presence of the Spirit that enables, we thank You. May we never treat these as treasures to be hoarded, but always as gifts to be enjoyed and used, and shared also with others.

C. Thought to Remember

"If any man be in Christ, he is a new creature: old things are passed away; behold, all things are become new" (2 Corinthians 5:17).

Home Daily Bible Readings

Monday, May 15—A Changed Life (Galatians 1:13-24)

Tuesday, May 16—Live a New Way (Ephesians 4:20—5:2)

Wednesday, May 17—Control Your Tongue (James 3:6-12)

Thursday, May 18—Controlled by Love (2 Corinthians 6:14-21)

Friday, May 19—Be Wise, Not Foolish (Ephesians 5:15-20)

Saturday, May 20—The Way to Happiness (Psalm 1)

Sunday, May 21—Give Thanks (Psalm 136:1-9)

Learning by Doing

This page contains an alternate lesson plan emphasizing learning activities. Classes desiring such student involvement will find these suggestions helpful.

Learning Goals

After studying Ephesians 4:22—5:4, 18-20, the student will be able to:

1. Name at least five areas in which the new life in Christ is different from the old life without Him.

2. Explain how each of these items of behavior reflects the person and character of Jesus.

3. Identify an area in which he will give special attention to developing the new life.

Into the Lesson

As the class members arrive, arrange them in groups of three or four. Ask each group to write two contrasting character sketches, one of a non-Christian and one of a follower of Christ. Allow the groups five to seven minutes to do this. Then take time for the groups to share their sketches.

Make the transition into the Bible study by pointing out that the Scripture text for this lesson contrasts two styles of life: the Christians with the non-Christian.

Into the Word

Present a brief lecture using the thoughts in the "Introduction" section in this lesson. Read the lesson text aloud.

Ask the class members to work in their original groups to complete the following assignment. Each group is to read Ephesians 4:22—5:4, 18-20 again, then make a chart of what Christians are to put off and put on. The following items should be mentioned:

Put Off

Old self with its deceitful desires
Falsehood
Harboring anger
Stealing
Unwholesome talk
Grieving the Holy Spirit
Bitterness
Wrath (turbulent anger)
Anger (smoldering resentment)
Clamor (harsh speaking)
Evil speaking (abusive speech)
Malice (deep-seated ill will)
Sexual immorality
Covetousness
Obscenity
Foolish talk
Coarse joking
Drunkenness

Put On

New self
New attitudes
Speak the truth
Work
Share with those in need
Speak what is helpful in building up others
Kindness
Compassion
Forgive one another
Imitate God
Live a life of love
Give thanks
Be filled with the Spirit
Speak and sing to one another to build up in Christ
Sing praises to God

Allow the groups six to eight minutes to make their charts on a sheet of newsprint. Then display these as you lead the remainder of the class session. Use the outlines prepared by the groups to cover the text. Be sure to define each "put off" and "put on." Let class members help to do this.

Into Life

Discuss and apply the Biblical principles by using the following questions:

1. Ephesians 4:22—5:4, 18-20 makes a rather pointed contrast between the Christian and the non-Christian. Is this contrast exaggerated? Why?

2. Cite some examples from your own experience that demonstrate the contrast between the Christian and non-Christian.

3. Is it really possible for a person to "put on" all of the characteristics mentioned in the text? Why?

4. How seriously does the modern Christian take the directives given in this text?

5. How would the church—and the cause of evangelism—be affected if every Christian pursued the characteristics mentioned in this text?

Ask each person to make his own commitment to putting on the Christian life-style by writing a memo to himself stating what he will do.

Let's Talk It Over

The questions on this page are designed to encourage review of the lesson Scriptures and to promote discussion of the lesson by the class. The answers provided are only discussion starters. Let your class talk it over from there.

1. How can those who grew up in Christian families and accepted Christ at an early age relate to Paul's exhortation to "put off ... the old man?" Do such persons have an advantage or disadvantage over those converted later in life? Why?

Persons who came from Christian families may not have a sordid past of dreadful sins of which to repent. They can, however, observe the devastating effects of sin in the lives of others and realize that only the grace of God has spared them from such a condition. But even those persons who had a wholesome home environment were not isolated from the corruption of deceitful lusts. Some will insist that the advantage lies with those persons who know what it is to live without Christ, since they can more fully appreciate the redemption from sin they have received. Others believe it is a greater blessing to be a second-generation Christian, without having experienced either the momentary reward or the pain of sinful habits and attitudes. Both are right. Those in both groups have every reason to be grateful to God for rescuing them from sin's penalty, and to share the life-saving gospel with those presently enslaved by it.

2. What would you recommend that new believers do to hasten the renewing of their mind? How is this process effectively defeated in some believers?

The renewing of one's mind is a ministry of the Spirit through the Word. It requires exposure to the Bible, and especially the teachings of Jesus and His apostles recorded in the New Testament. Joining a good Sunday-school class or a Bible-study group can help. Many churches now offer discipling programs, in which a mature Christian takes personal responsibility for the instruction of a new believer. The process can be stalled if the believer does not participate in any of these, and is not open to personal study of the Scriptures.

3. How may a Christian dispel anger quickly? Are we justified in venting our anger to "get it off our chest"?

The quickest way to dispel anger is to forgive. Forgiving does not mean we approve the other's actions against us. It means we give up our per-

sonal desire to punish them by retaliation. If for no other reason, we should learn to forgive for the sake of our own well-being. Christians are to be slow in becoming angry (James 1:19). Even when angry, we have an obligation to make sure that our words are not designed to inflict wounds (Ephesians 4:29). Verse 31 puts even more severe limits on the expression of anger.

4. What kinds of speech are Christians to avoid? If our speech must always "edify," what does that include? What does it exclude?

Christians are generally agreed that profanity, obscenity, and other crude or vulgar speech is not to be used. These qualify as "corrupt communication" (Ephesians 4:29). If appropriate speech edifies and ministers grace, that must include encouragement, empathy (reflecting feelings), counsel, advice, testimony, information, discussion, warning, and prayer. Such speech will be delivered, of course, in a spirit of genuine love. The kinds of speech that are excluded from that list are harsh personal criticisms, and all negative and hurtful ideas. Can you give examples of these?

5. Give examples of behavior or attitudes that would grieve the Holy Spirit.

Since the ministry of the Spirit is to transform our character and to equip us for service, we can grieve the Spirit by failing to apply ourselves in spiritual disciplines, and by refusing to use the gift(s) we have been given in service to others. We also get a clue from the verse surrounding Ephesians 4:30 as to what grieves the Spirit: corrupt speech, bitterness, hostility, failure to love, and failure to forgive.

6. How may a Christian be filled with the Spirit? How may that filling be evidenced?

Since Ephesians 5:18 is a command given to believers, the action required must depend upon the believer. The need is not for greater measure of the Spirit to be given by God, but greater submission to the Spirit to be given by the believer. When we make every attitude and every action subject to the Spirit of God dwelling in us, then it can be said we are filled with the Spirit. The testimony of verse 19 is that this filling will result in joy and praise.

Guidelines for Family Life

LESSON SCRIPTURE: Ephesians 5:21—6:4.

PRINTED TEXT: Ephesians 5:21—6:4.

Ephesians 5:21-33

21 [Submit] yourselves one to another in the fear of God.

22 Wives, submit yourselves unto your own husbands, as unto the Lord.

23 For the husband is the head of the wife, even as Christ is the head of the church: and he is the saviour of the body.

24 Therefore as the church is subject unto Christ, so let the wives be to their own husbands in every thing.

25 Husbands, love your wives, even as Christ also loved the church, and gave himself for it;

26 That he might sanctify and cleanse it with the washing of water by the word,

27 That he might present it to himself a glorious church, not having spot, or wrinkle, or any such thing; but that it should be holy and without blemish.

28 So ought men to love their wives as their own bodies. He that loveth his wife loveth himself.

29 For no man ever yet hated his own flesh; but nourisheth and cherisheth it, even as the Lord the church:

30 For we are members of his body, of his flesh, and of his bones.

31 For this cause shall a man leave his father and mother, and shall be joined unto his wife, and they two shall be one flesh.

32 This is a great mystery: but I speak concerning Christ and the church.

33 Nevertheless, let every one of you in particular so love his wife even as himself; and the wife see that she reverence her husband.

Ephesians 6:1-4

1 Children, obey your parents in the Lord: for this is right.

2 Honor thy father and mother; which is the first commandment with promise;

3 That it may be well with thee, and thou mayest live long on the earth.

4 And, ye fathers, provoke not your children to wrath: but bring them up in the nurture and admonition of the Lord.

GOLDEN TEXT: [Submit] yourselves one to another in the fear of God.
—Ephesians 5:21.

Letters From Prison
Unit 4: Ephesians—The Christian Calling (Lessons 9-13)

Lesson Aims

This study should equip the student to:

1. Show how the teaching this week grows naturally out of the earlier doctrinal studies concerning Christ and His church.

2. Summarize the basic attitudes required of each member in a family toward the others in that family.

3. Select a verse that will be especially helpful in his own efforts to improve relationships in his family.

Lesson Outline

INTRODUCTION
   A. Paul Versus Polonius
   B. The Family of God or the Fashion of Men
   C. Lesson Background
 I. ONE ATTITUDE FOR ALL (Ephesians 5:21)
 II. BETWEEN HUSBANDS AND WIVES (Ephesians 5:22-33)
   A. For Wives (vv. 22-24)
   B. For Husbands (vv. 25-33)
      A Nurturing Relationship
III. BETWEEN PARENTS AND CHILDREN (Ephesians 6:1-4)
   A. For Children (vv. 1-3)
      Obedience Has Its Own Rewards
   B. For Parents (v. 4)
CONCLUSION
   A. Impaired Families
   B. Prayer
   C. Thought to Remember

Display visual 13 from the visuals/learning resources packet and refer to it as you proceed through the lesson. It is shown on page 332.

Introduction
A. Paul Versus Polonius

Sage advice given to a young man leaving home includes this from Shakespeare's character, Polonius, to young Laertes: "This above all: to thine own self be true, and it must follow, as the night the day, thou canst not then be false to any man."

The advice is very popular in well-meaning and scholarly circles. It has presently a host of promoters among the high priests of self-awareness, self-confidence, self-expression, and self-fulfillment. Self-preservation, we are told, is the first law of nature—preservation of one's own life, and rights, and dignity, and property—development of one's own individuality. All of this echoes something of the proud philosophical mind of the first century in the province of Asia, centering on Ephesus.

Paul's Ephesian epistle was addressed to Christians living in that environment. In his writing the apostle flung a bold challenge into the face of the entire system with an amazing demand: "Submit to one another out of reverence for Christ" (Ephesians 5:21, *New International Version*). He had already written to the Galatian Christians, similarly situated, "Ye have been called unto liberty; only use not liberty for an occasion to the flesh, but by love serve one another" (Galatians 5:13).

Free and serving? How can that be? The answer is *love*, and the source of serving love is Christ. He demonstrated the self-giving by emptying himself of Heaven's glory to enter as a humbly serving man into the world of men, at last freely giving His life and self on the cross (Philippians 2:5-8). There was nothing servile about the service Jesus rendered. He chose to serve because He loved. It is the same with those who follow Him. Paul followed, and Paul knew.

B. The Family of God or the Fashion of Men

Sociologists have invented a phrase to describe the family as today's text deals with it—father and mother bringing up children together. They call it a "nuclear family," to distinguish it from the crippled and partial families that appear all too frequently in our society. The crippling that appears in single-parent families, or children without parents, or husbands and wives without children, may be wholly unavoidable and without fault on the part of anyone. All too frequently, however, the conditions result from disregard for God's love and God's law, in what is sometimes blandly called an "alternate life-style."

Isn't it unrealistic, though, to insist on ideals of love, faithfulness, and yielding to one another's requirements in a world where these qualities are so seldom found? Don't we all have to adjust our goals to the conditions we find within and around ourselves and our families?

Jesus didn't think so. Being reminded that even Moses had permitted divorce among the children of Israel, the Lord acknowledged this as a concession to "the hardness of your hearts," but He refused to accept it as normative. For His teaching He appealed to God's original pattern—the marriage of one man and one woman, faithfully respected, for life (Matthew 19:3-12).

Neither did Paul accept the voice of the people as the voice of God in teaching about the family. The will, the word, and the way of God—himself eternally unchanging—do not depend on the changing tides of human preference or custom. And God's prescription is not to be weakened in the face of an epidemic!

C. Lesson Background

This is the last of our lesson from Ephesians, dealing with "The Christian Calling." Ephesians is mostly a doctrinal treatise, and our lessons have been mostly doctrinal, dealing with the church and the life in Christ. The later chapters contain practical expressions of Christian faith, but even these deal with general principles more than with specific instructions. Today's lesson, on the other hand, provides plain direction for the most intimate relationships in human experience—those involving the family.

There is good reason for this. God's people under the Old Covenant formed a nation built upon the family as its basic unit. So also in the New Testament, instruction about the church and the family is interwoven, with God presented as Father, and believers as His children; also with Christ presented as the bridegroom and the church as His bride. Jews and Gentiles alike are members of the same family, we are told, being called to the same spiritual life. Last week we learned of Christian attitudes in kindness and generosity, and Christian expressions in speech and song. Today's text follows immediately.

I. One Attitude for All
(Ephesians 5:21)

21. Submitting yourselves one to another in the fear of God.

In His ministry Jesus taught that each disciple should be willing to humble himself and serve others (Matthew 20:26-28). Not only so, but He embodied the very spirit of willingness to humble self to meet the needs of others (see John 13:12-16). As His disciples, we can do no less.

Christian submission, however, is not a one-way street; it is to *one another*. Each submits to the other in areas indicated by one's ability, responsibility, and position. "In lowliness of mind let each esteem other better than themselves" (Philippians 2:3).

In the fear of God. The manuscript evidence suggests a better translation would be "in the fear of Christ," or "out of reverence for Christ."

Reverence for Him will make us humble and considerate of others. Christ our Lord has exemplified the utmost in humble submission, surrendering His rights, comforts, time, and finally His life for our sakes. We are likewise submissive.

II. Between Husbands and Wives
(Ephesians 5:22-33)

A. For Wives (vv. 22-24)

22. Wives, submit yourselves unto your own husbands, as unto the Lord.

Because it is the Lord's will, the Christian wife accepts the headship of the husband in the family. The husband is leader *because* of Christ, and certainly not *instead* of Christ. Colossians 3:18 says, "Wives, submit yourselves unto your own husbands, as it is fit in the Lord."

Our text assumes that both husband and wife are Christians. First Peter 3:1, 2 suggests another reason for the Christian wife's graceful submissiveness: that she may by it serve to convert a non-Christian husband. Thus she would be marked as the superior person by her acceptance of an inferior position. So it was with Jesus.

23. For the husband is the head of the wife, even as Christ is the head of the church: and he is the saviour of the body.

In the human body the head and the body are not the same, but they are both parts of the same organism. Neither one is complete without the other, and neither could live apart from the other. Ephesians 1:22, 23 and 4:15, 16 have made clear that Christ is indeed the head of His body, the church, and hence has directive authority over it. His position has been established by the loving sacrifice He made in becoming the *saviour of the body*. Some husbands have also become physical saviors to their wives, saving them from flood or fire. But the writer seems not to include this in his reference to Christ as Savior. So the analogy is not complete. But the fact that most husbands have not in any sense been physical saviors of their wives, and the lack of Christlikeness on the part of husbands does not set aside God's plan regarding the relationship between husband and wife.

24. Therefore as the church is subject unto Christ, so let the wives be to their own husbands in every thing.

"All authority" has been given to Christ (Matthew 28:18), and therefore the church must be subject to Him. In a similar way the wife is to be in subjection to her husband. *In every thing.* That is, in every realm where the husband may rightfully exercise authority. Paul does not mean that the husband is to be above God to the wife. Her personal responsibility to God is as great as that of her husband. God's authority is higher than the husband's, and should there be any conflict, the wife is under obligation to obey God.

B. For Husbands (vv. 25-33)

The theme of the passage is still submission—of one's own pride and person to the wishes and welfare of those about him. In the case of the wife it is self-will that is surrendered. In the case of the husband it is self-interest. In both instances the necessary motivation is love.

25. Husbands, love your wives, even as Christ also loved the church, and gave himself for it.

The *love* here recommended is not sexual, romantic love. It is the kind of intense, active, thoughtful goodwill that persuaded God the Father to give His Son for our salvation (John 3:16), and led Jesus to lay down His life for His flock (John 10:10-15). The two kinds of love do dwell in the same person and bless the same marriage, but romance without devotion can be possessive and cruel. The Christian husband's role is not self-assertion, but self-sacrifice.

26, 27. That he might sanctify and cleanse it with the washing of water by the word, that he might present it to himself a glorious church, not having spot, or wrinkle, or any such thing; but that it should be holy and without blemish.

The apostle leaves for a moment the husband-wife relationship to comment further on Christ and the church. *That he might sanctify and cleanse it.* The *New American Standard Bible* has, "That He might sanctify her, having cleansed her." The church, cleansed, is set apart for the Master. *With the washing of water* bears obvious reference to the baptism of the believer into Christ. Such a one has been prepared by the *word* of the gospel preached to him (Romans 10:17), and he has been set apart (made holy) by the *word* spoken in connection with the baptism (Matthew 28:19).

The glow of bridal beauty is seen in the Lord's presenting the church to himself *a glorious*

church, not having spot, or wrinkle, or . . . blemish. The members of Jesus' bride cannot lay claim to a stainless past, but He has provided them with His own purity through the *washing with the Word.*

28. So ought men to love their wives as their own bodies. He that loveth his wife loveth himself.

In the marriage relationship the husband and wife are no longer two, but one flesh (Genesis 2:24; Mark 10:8; verse 31 below). The admonition, then, is not simply to love one's wife as much as he loves himself; it is to recognize that in loving her he is loving a part of himself. Let no one complain, then, of his or her "personality being destroyed by the marriage." That's what marriage is—the fusing of two personalities so that each loses his or her identity in the resulting new person. Anyone who is not ready for that is not ready for marriage.

A NURTURING RELATIONSHIP

Melba, a victim of cancer, lay weak and exhausted in a hospital bed in the family room at home. Each day she grew weaker, and death could not be far away. The nurses who helped care for Melba came and went in their regular shifts. Tom worked in his office every morning, but by mid-afternoon he was at her side, comforting, reading, praying, caring for his wife.

The children, late teenagers, came in from school and went directly to Melba's bed to tell her of their day and how they loved her.

Family life did not stop with the unfolding tragedy, and there was no hysteria or fear. This was a Christian home. Tom and Melba had abiding, strong faith, and they had shared that faith with their children.

Finally the parting day came. I was there as a pastor to pray and give to the family the love and concern of the entire congregation.

In those last hours Tom held Melba's now tiny form in his arms and whispered his love to her. His warmth could not stop the chill of death. I thought of Paul's words as Melba, lying in her husband's arms, went home to God. "Husbands ought to love their wives as their own bodies. He who loves his wife loves himself" (Ephesians 5:28, *New International Version*).   —W. P.

29, 30. For no man ever yet hated his own flesh; but nourisheth and cherisheth it, even as the Lord the church: for we are members of his body, of his flesh, and of his bones.

There are, of course, those mentally ill persons who take pleasure in hurting their own bodies. The clinical name for their disease is *masochism*. But masochists are not whole persons. Neither are those who take pleasure in

HUSBANDS...be willing to sacrifice...*LIKE CHRIST!*

WIVES...have a spirit of submission...*LIKE CHRIST!*

KEY TO A HAPPY HOME

CHILDREN...be subject to parents...*LIKE CHRIST!*

visual 13

hurting their spouses, who are a part of their very selves. Normal people feel and care for their bodies, and wise people pay attention to giving good nourishment and care to their whole selves—including their spouses.

Again, our role model is Christ, who not only gave himself for the church, His body, but even now continues to give himself for her, making pleas on her behalf with the Father in glory (Romans 8:34-39; Hebrews 7:25; 1 John 2:1, 2).

We are members of his body, and are subject to His care, just as Eve was declared to be of Adam, of his flesh and bones (Genesis 2:18-24). And so the loving husband suffers with his wife's illness and aches with her pain.

31. For this cause shall a man leave his father and mother, and shall be joined unto his wife, and they two shall be one flesh.

Reference to the first couple in Eden is followed naturally by this quotation from Genesis 2:24. Because the wife is to become so genuinely a part of the husband's self, the marriage has to include a cutting loose from all competing relationships. The leaving has to be accomplished before the new identity can be established. The man who is still a "mamma's boy" can never be a satisfactory husband. A wise mother kept this constantly before her children. "When you marry," she said, "your home is with your partner, and not here with us. You and your partner will be equally welcome to visit us, but the old home has to be left behind when the new one is established."

32. This is a great mystery: but I speak concerning Christ and the church.

In this declaration there is a profound truth. *Mystery,* in the New Testament sense, indicates the revelation of something that could not be known by the unaided human mind. The mys-

tery discussed in verses 25-33 is twofold and intertwined: the relationship of Christ and the church, the relationship of husband and wife. The inspired apostle could not discuss one without the other. For Christians, marriage must be rooted in commitment to Christ.

33. Nevertheless, let every one of you in particular so love his wife even as himself; and the wife see that she reverence her husband.

Here is repetition and wrap-up of the exhortation to mutual submissiveness in marriage. The husband is to surrender selfish ambition or indulgence because his wife is an integral part of himself; the wife is to surrender self-will and self-determination because she respects her husband. The wife's attitude is not to be fright, dread, or awe, but honor and respect. Submission in either direction without love would be slavish and most difficult to maintain.

III. Between Parents and Children (Ephesians 6:1-4)

A. For Children (vv. 1-3)

1. Children, obey your parents in the Lord: for this is right.

Most of Ephesians is material for mature minds, but these epistles were to be read in the churches (Colossians 4:16; 1 Thessalonians 5:27), and children would be present. The simplicity of this command recommends it to a child's thoughtful attention. Colossians 3:20 says, "Children, obey your parents in all things: for this is well-pleasing unto the Lord." If a child loves and respects God, he will seek to please Him by obeying his parents. That is no violation of the child's will or crippling of his personality. Instead, as the course chosen because of love, it becomes the flowering of the best and freest personality. Once again Jesus is our example (see Luke 2:51).

The sin of disobedience to parents is vigorously condemned in Scripture. The incorrigibly disobedient son was not to be allowed to grow up in Israel, but was to be stoned to death; "So shalt thou put evil away from among you" (Deuteronomy 21:18-21). New Testament teaching is no less positive, but without prescribing the immediate punishment (Romans 1:30; 2 Timothy 3:2).

2, 3. Honor thy father and mother; which is the first commandment with promise; that it may be well with thee, and that thou mayest live long on the earth.

The fifth of the Ten Commandments (Exodus 20:12) is repeated for application to Christians. Honor includes obedience, but it goes farther and lasts longer. It suggests the kind of behavior

---

Home Daily Bible Readings

Monday, May 22—Two Becoming One (Ephesians 5:21-33)

Tuesday, May 23—A Child From the Lord (1 Samuel 1:9-20)

Wednesday, May 24—Concern for a Child (Exodus 2:1-9)

Thursday, May 25—A Good Wife (Proverbs 31:10-17, 25-31)

Friday, May 26—For Children and Parents (Ephesians 6:1-4)

Saturday, May 27—Learning About God (Deuteronomy 6:4-9)

Sunday, May 28—Hallmarks of a Happy Home (Galatians 5:16-26)

that makes parents proud: "A wise son maketh a glad father: but a foolish son is the heaviness of his mother" (Proverbs 10:1). It includes material support for aged parents (Matthew 15:3-6; 1 Timothy 5:3, 8).

This fifth Commandment is *the first commandment with promise.* It is the only one of the ten that names benefits deriving from obedience.

That it may be well with thee. The obedient child will eat nourishing food, brush his teeth, and wear adequate clothing. He will get along well in school and in the community, respecting authority. *That thou mayest live long on the earth.* The parent-honoring child will generally avoid accidents with poisons, matches, and traffic; will stay away from life-shortening drugs; and will be less susceptible to conflicts, physical and emotional.

OBEDIENCE HAS ITS OWN REWARDS

Should they or should they not? That was the unspoken question. Jim and Dan looked hungrily at the orchard beckoning with its luscious fruit just across the fence. "Boys, you know how Mr. Hibbard feels about his peaches. Stay out of his orchard until the harvest is over." "OK, Mom," had been their cheery answer.

But that was morning. Now it was late afternoon. Mom had gone to the store. Dad wasn't home from work. Mr. and Mrs. Hibbard were gone too. Those peaches did look good!

With a deep sigh both boys backed away from the orchard fence and trudged dejectedly home. Had they made the right decision?

At that precise moment Mr. and Mrs. Hibbard drove by and into their own yard. Mom's car turned the corner and came toward the garage. Dad followed her in, home early from work.

Jim and Dan just looked at each other and grinned. It had been a good decision! Both thought of the punishment they would have received if they had been caught in the orchard. With clear conscience both boys helped Mom carry in her groceries.

Jim still likes to tell this story and laughs when he says, "Obedience to parents has always been blessed, and Dan and I knew it." —W. P.

B. For Parents (v. 4)

4. And, ye fathers, provoke not your children to wrath: but bring them up in the nurture and admonition of the Lord.

The need for subordinating one's own interests to the welfare of others is nowhere more demanding than in the rearing of children. Parental authority is for the sake of the child, and not for the convenience, will, or whim of the parent. *Fathers,* rather than mothers, are addressed here, probably because of their greater responsibility and temptation to harsh severity.

Provoke not your children to wrath. "You ... must not goad your children to resentment" *(The New English Bible).* Resentment in children comes when parents fail to treat them with respect, making foolish and unreasonable demands just to show their authority. Disciplining is necessary, but generous praise and affection will reduce the tensions associated with it.

What is the alternative? It is definitely not a weak abandonment of responsibility, but is rather a firm, patient, and loving program of training and instruction in the Lord. *Nurture* means literally the training of a child, and is translated "chastening" in Hebrews 12:5, 7, 8). Remembering that the "fear of the Lord is the beginning of knowledge" (Proverbs 1:7), the Christian parent will make the Word of God central in the teaching of his children.

Conclusion

A. Impaired Families

Not all families in your community or your church are blessed with the normal quota of family members. In some the normal family relationships are not possible. That does not mean that these families are beyond help from the apostle's teaching, or that the Christian principle, "Submit to one another out of reverence for Christ" *(New International Version),* does not apply to them. In fact, Ephesians 6:5-9 goes on to apply the same principle to servants and masters beyond the immediate family circle. It is needed wherever Christians live.

An incomplete family is a little like an incomplete, or impaired, human body. None must ever be discarded or disregarded. The impaired ones—families and persons—are to be helped in every possible way to achieve their utmost under the hindering circumstances. And that can be amazingly great!

B. Prayer

We praise You, O God, that You are our Father, in Heaven. In the deep and sometimes tragic needs of our homes and our families, we can't thank You enough for Jesus, Your Son, who alone can make us into the right kind of family members. Use us, we pray, in the expression of Your love to our loved ones. So may our homes come to reflect something of Heaven, where Christ reigns supreme. Amen.

C. Thought to Remember

"By love serve one another" (Galatians 5:13).

Learning by Doing

*This page contains an alternate lesson plan emphasizing learning activities. Classes
desiring such student involvement will find these suggestions helpful.*

Learning Goals

After studying the Biblical directives for family relationships given in Ephesians 5:21—6:4, the students will be able to:

1. Summarize the basic attitudes required of each member in a family toward the others in that family.

2. Explain how the relationships defined in this Scripture text contribute to a successful family.

3. Select a way that he will begin to apply the teaching of this text to improve relationships in his family.

Into the Lesson

Before the class begins, place the following incomplete statement on the chalkboard or a sheet of newsprint: "A family is—" As the class members arrive, give each a small index card and ask them to write as many endings for the statement as they can. When everyone has had adequate time to complete the statement, share the responses and put them on the chalkboard or a sheet of newsprint.

Make the transition into the Bible study by stating that each of us has positive and/or negative memories of our families when we were children growing up. In all likelihood, most of our positive memories resulted from the application of certain Biblical principles, whether or not the family was Christian. Today's lesson will examine those principles.

Into the Word

Briefly present the material in the "Introduction" section of the lesson. Read Ephesians 5:21—6:4 aloud. Then develop a discussion using the following questions:

1. Ephesians 5:21 presents the basic principle for successful family relationships. What is it? How does this principle affect every relationship?

2. If a husband wants to have a successful family, what attitudes must he have? (Selfless love, commitment, healthy self-esteem that results in healthy love for his wife.)

3. If a wife wants to have a successful family, what attitudes must she have? (Commitment to her husband's leadership, and the willingness to follow his leadership in the same way that she follows Christ.)

4. If parents want to have a successful family, what attitudes and actions must they have? (Understanding of the needs and capabilities of a child; commitment to instruct their child in the ways of the Lord.)

5. If a child wants to be part of a successful family, what attitudes and actions must he(she) have? (Obedience.)

6. Explain how the characteristics of the various members of the family are interdependent. How is the wife's response dependent upon the husband's? The husband's upon the wife's? The children's upon the parents'? The parents' upon the children's?

Into Life

Divide the class members into groups of three to five each. Give each of the groups one of the following statements and ask the members to respond in light of the Biblical principles mentioned today.

Group 1. Families would function better in today's society if women would stay home and rear the children instead of working.

Group 2. A husband has the right to expect his wife to respond to his commands.

Group 3. Women should not be involved in any decision-making in the family. That is the prerogative of the husband.

Group 4. Children are to obey their parents regardless of the demands placed upon them.

Group 5. A family cannot be truly successful unless it is Christian.

Group 6. Children's obedience or lack of it is an indication of parental attitudes, example and teaching.

Allow each group five to seven minutes to consider each statement and provide a response. Each statement has some truth in it, but ignores other important principles. Be sure that each group considers all of these facets. After you have dealt with these questions thoroughly, ask this question: How would family life in our society change if each member applied the principles mentioned in this chapter?

Conclude the session by asking, How would your family be different if you were to take these principles seriously? Ask each person to write down one way in which he will begin to apply the principles this week. Close with a prayer of commitment.

Let's Talk It Over

The questions on this page are designed to encourage review of the lesson Scriptures and to promote discussion of the lesson by the class. The answers provided are only discussion starters. Let your class talk it over from there.

1. "A Christian cannot be a hermit." Do you agree or disagree with that statement? Tell why.

Ephesians 5:21 is just one of more than a dozen "one another" commands to Christians in the New Testament. To submit to one another assumes relationships in community. The commands to love one another, pray for one another, forgive one another, etc. can be carried out only in community. We have all heard of those religious persons who have withdrawn to a solitary life of contemplation. While there may be value to be gained in the hermit's life, much is lost as well. The Christian pilgrimage is made easier when shared with sincere companions. Try listing all the obligations and the blessings of the Christian life that require community.

2. What could you say to the Christian who has difficulty with the principle of submission?

God hates rebellion and pride. "God resisteth the proud, but giveth grace unto the humble" (James 4:6). "For rebellion is as the sin of witchcraft, and stubbornness is as iniquity and idolatry" (1 Samuel 15:23). The very first sin was a sin of rebellion against the authority of God. One of the first conditions to becoming a Christian is repentance. To repent means to turn from your own stubborn, willful choices and to submit to Jesus as Lord. Our Lord requires of us submission, not only to himself but to other authorities in life (Romans 13:1, 2), and submission to certain obligations in relationships (as here in Ephesians 5, 6). Jesus provides the perfect example of submission because He willingly gave up His place in glory to take the form of a humble servant for our sake (Philippians 2:5-8).

3. If a husband loves his wife as Christ loved the church, how does that translate into behavior? Give examples.

The love of Christ for the church cost Him His life. His is a sacrificial love. Husbands, what are you willing to sacrifice for the sake of your wife? Have you bartered away time on career, hobbies, or even church work that should belong to her? Would you be willing to make the adjustments necessary so she could return to school, if she so desired? Have you been sympathetic to her desire to be a mother, or to have an additional child? Do you encourage her and assist in keeping a neat and attractive home? Do you pay her the courtesy of asking for her counsel on the decisions of your life? Do you let her know that she is precious to you, and that you need her now more than ever?

4. If husband and wife become one flesh, what does that say about their treatment of one another?

As our text reminds us, we nourish and cherish our own flesh (v. 29). Husbands and wives need to realize that as they do good for their spouse, they are ultimately doing good for themselves. Likewise, we cannot hurt our spouses, through neglect, criticism, ridicule, spite, or other abuse without hurting ourselves.

5. The obligation of children is to obey and honor parents. What provision is made for children to learn this?

Unfortunately, children are not able to read and understand the Bible for themselves until several years after birth. The lessons of obedience and honor to parents must be learned beginning in infancy. It is the role of parents to train their children in this by the consistent application of loving but firm discipline. Severe judgment came upon the sons of Eli for their wickedness, but also upon the father for failing to teach them to obey (1 Samuel 3:12, 13). Honor should also be demonstrated in the home. If children are addressed with respect and treated with good manners, they will be more likely to respond in kindness to others. They will also learn from the example of how Mom and Dad treat their own parents.

6. How can parents enforce discipline at home so as not to "provoke [their] children to wrath"?

Loving parents want to avoid breaking the spirit of their children while reshaping their will. Here are some simple guidelines. Criticize deeds, but do not condemn or ridicule the child. Make sure your rules are necessary and fair, and that you are willing to enforce them consistently. Look for ways to encourage and reward good behavior as well as punishing disobedience. Do not show favoritism.

Summer Quarter, 1989

Theme: Conquest and Challenge

Special Features

Lessons

Unit 1: Joshua—A Time of Conquest and Settlement

Unit 2: Judges—A Time of Conflict and Adjustment

Unit 3: Ruth—A Record of Commitment and Hope

Related Resources

The following publications are suggested to provide additional help on the subjects of study presented in the Summer Quarter. They may be purchased from your supplier. Prices are subject to change.

Bible Time Line. Large, colorful wall chart presents major characters and events in chronological sequence. Order #2628, $5.95.

God's Word, B.C., by John W. Wade. A comprehensive survey of the Old Testament. Order #41020, $2.95.

Old Testament Maps and Charts. Order #2607, $7.95.

Struggle for Freedom, by Knofel Staton. Parallels struggles of Israelites and modern Christians. Order #40034, $2.25.

Training for Service: a survey of the Bible, by Orrin Root, revised by Eleanor Daniel. Order #3212, $3.95.

Wonders in the Midst, by Ward Patterson. Details the major events and personalities from the exodus to the kingship in Israel. Order #40076, $2.25.

Jun 4
Jun 11
Jun 18
Jun 25
Jul 2
Jul 9
Jul 16
Jul 23
Jul 30
Aug 6
Aug 13
Aug 20
Aug 27

Successes and Failures

by James G. VanBuren

THE LESSONS of this quarter deal with the books of Joshua, Judges, and Ruth. If we were to desire a musical accompaniment describing the nature and texture of these works, it seems that the following choices would be appropriate.

The book of Joshua would be full of heroic trumpets sounding calls to arms and martial music such as is associated with soldiers advancing to battle, together with the reverberation of drums and the clashing of cymbals. At the end, the slow, sad strains of "taps" would echo over the grave of the departed general, Joshua—uncorruptible in character, undaunted in battle, and unfailing in dedication.

The book of Judges would bring a mixture of mournful tones of cellos and bass viols, with occasional flashes of trumpets and other brass instruments. These would soon die out amid the persistent and repetitive strains of a minor key.

The book of Ruth would be characterized by beautiful, simple tones—the strains of violins and the "voweled lay" of flutes. It would be calming, beautiful in its harmony, with minor chords gradually transformed into lyrical loveliness. It would close with a full orchestra presenting a concord of sweet sounds.

The Book of Joshua

This book is the record of the entrance of the Hebrew people into Canaan after their forty years of wilderness "wandering." This wandering was the penalty inflicted on the generation of Israelites who came out of Egypt and who showed their lack of faith in God at Kadesh-barnea (see Numbers 13:17—14:39). Joshua and Caleb were the only ones of that generation who were spared to enter the land. Following the death of Moses, Joshua gave Israel heroic leadership, unwavering in its devotion to the Lord and undeviating in its concentration on the task at hand.

It is significant that the book of Joshua is an almost unvarying record of victories. Joshua did what God told him to do, and the people obeyed without hesitation. The few occasions when someone departed from faithfulness were dealt with promptly and decisively. We do not read of the worship of any false gods, but only of their repudiation and destruction. God's directions concerning the treatment of conquered cities varied from time to time, but the Israelites were careful to act just as He commanded. The result was the rapid penetration and occupation of the major areas of Palestine.

The book of Joshua teaches us that all things are possible with God. The cities *did* have walls great and high, armed defending forces, and even some men of gigantic stature. But, as Joshua and the forces of Israel invaded the land, the walls fell, armies were defeated, and giants were slain. As Joshua said shortly before his death, "Ye know in all your hearts... that not one thing hath failed of all the good things which the Lord your God spake concerning you; all are come to pass" (Joshua 23:14).

We need to take these things to heart. God has made great promises to us in Christ: "All things work together for good to them that love God" (Romans 8:28); "And God is able to make... [us have] all sufficiency in all things" (2 Corinthians 9:8). God will not allow us to be tempted above our capacity to resist (1 Corinthians 10:13); God will give us wisdom if we ask Him for it (James 1:5); Jesus is with us always (Matthew 28:20). Indeed, we have been given "exceeding great and precious promises" (2 Peter 1:4) by a God who "cannot lie" (Titus 1:2). If we go forward in obedient faith as did Joshua, we shall find that bastions of evil will crumble, hosts of evildoers will scatter, godless power centers will be neutralized, and God and His people will be victorious! Truly, as Paul asserts in 2 Corinthians 10:4, 5, "The weapons we wield are... divinely potent to demolish strongholds; we demolish sophistries and all that rears its proud head against the knowledge of God; we compel every human thought to surrender in obedience to Christ" (*The New English Bible*).

The Book of Judges

Judges brings with it an amazing transition. The apostasy that Joshua had feared, and against which he had sought to guard, came about. The God who had led the Israelites and never failed them, and to whom they had solemnly pledged their continued loyalty after Joshua's death, was forgotten and abandoned. The imaginary deities represented by idols, the gods and goddesses of the surrounding people, were adopted. They were gods of lust, gods of selfishness, gods of crass material gain—cruel, insensitive, immoral, unmerciful. To these strange, sinister, and sensual gods the Hebrews bowed their knees, sacrificed their babies, and prostituted their daughters. The God who had given them high moral purpose, spiritual vision, and irresistible power against evil no longer was with them in their sinfulness and senseless idolatry.

The enemies the Israelites had subdued now began to dominate them and eventually enslaved them. As the long years of oppression wore on, some receptive persons looked up to the Lord. When this happened, God inspired, empowered, and aroused His people once more. For a time they would again call on the Lord and do victorious battle in His name. The yoke of pagan dominance was lifted, the false gods were repudiated, and a new, liberated life was begun. This continued only for a time, and then the whole cycle of regression, spiritual decline, and social and political enslavement was repeated.

The record of their regression from God and their suppression by their enemies is seen in a sort of litany of failure that recurs throughout Judges as a refrain. Notice how often the expression that they "did evil in the sight of the Lord" or "went a whoring after Baalim" is repeated (3:7, 12; 4:1; 6:1; 8:33-35; 10:6; 13:1).

The "judges," or special persons whom God empowered to lead Israel during their periods of spiritual and national revival, generally led in military conquests of their oppressors. They served as rulers during various intervals of freedom. They seem not to have instituted any new laws or rituals, but sought to return the people to the law of Moses and the religious system instituted by him as revealed by God.

In general, spiritual and moral values collapsed in Israel during large segments of time during the years covered by the period of the judges, and this was accompanied by a breakdown in the political and social order. In "The Song of Deborah," composed and sung by her after the defeat of Jabin the king of Canaan, is an especially revealing phrase telling of the conditions of travel in her era. We read that "the highways were unoccupied, and the travelers walked through byways" (Judges 5:6). That is, it was so unsafe to use the regular roads that travelers preferred to go by circuitous little paths and trails through the countryside to avoid the dangers that awaited them on the highways.

This period in Israel's history is described on several occasions by the brief, but telling, statement, "In those days there was no king in Israel, but every man did that which was right in his own eyes" (17:6; see also 18:1; 19:1; 21:25). The whole record of Judges is one of darkness relieved by flashes of light, as God helped certain ones who sought to turn Israel back to His way.

The Book of Ruth

This book, set in the days of the judges, tells of some who sought and served God during this time. The book has a rural setting. As we read, we seem to be in places where we see:

> Right against the eastern gate,
> Where the great sun begins his state,
> Robed in flames and amber light,
> The clouds in thousand liveries dight;
> While the ploughman near at hand,
> Whistles o'er the furrowed land,
> And the milkmaid singeth blithe,
> And the mower whets his scythe,
> . . . .
> Mountains on whose barren breast
> The laboring clouds do often rest;
> Meadows trim with daisies pied,
> Shallow brooks, and rivers wide.
> —John Milton, L'Allegro

In this book we are reminded of the beauty of devotion, because we observe Ruth's unwillingness to swerve from what she felt was her duty to Naomi. She also was helpful, willing to work, and teachable. Boaz demonstrated that obedience to God's way can help relationships between an employer and his labor force. Ruth and Boaz both followed God's directions for the circumstances in which they found themselves. The result was the marriage of Ruth and Boaz, and the bearing of the child who linked Ruth's life in Bethlehem with God's purposes for human redemption in the Messiah who would come later.

Ruth's career is an illustration of 1 Peter 5:6: "Humble yourselves therefore under the mighty hand of God, that he may exalt you in due time." Ruth humbled herself to go to Bethlehem with Naomi. In her own land she would have been a widow among her own people, with her own name, identity, and place. With Naomi she was going to a people with a different language, different customs, and a different God. She would just be "Naomi's daughter-in-law." Ruth humbled herself to become a worker in the fields of Boaz, just like adopting the task assigned to the poorest and most needy people in Israel. Ruth was willing to submit herself to Boaz's decision about the kinship relation, stooping to follow Naomi's directions though they seemed embarrassing.

As a result of all this she became the wife of one leading citizen in Bethlehem and the mother of a son who was in the Messianic lineage. Her transition from servant girl to a matron of high estate in Judah was remarkable. Surely this is yet another evidence of our need to trust our way to the Lord and to walk with Him in faith.

Choose You This Day

by Douglas Redford

THE BOOK OF JOSHUA describes Israel's conquest of the promised land, which fulfilled God's promise that He would give that land to Abram's descendants (Genesis 15:18). Except for a temporary setback at Ai, the campaign was highly successful. Israel's battle plan was essentially very simple: "The Lord God of Israel fought for Israel" (Joshua 10:42). At the same time, faithfulness and perseverance were required of the people: "Joshua made war a long time with all those kings" (11:18).

When at last the heathen peoples had been ousted and the land divided among the tribes, Joshua recognized that the Israelites could not rest on their laurels. Another type of battle loomed before them. It would not be as bloody as those fought earlier, but it would be just as critical. In fact, how the Israelites fared in this new conflict would determine whether they would retain possession of their land. For this second war would be waged, not on an earthly battleground, but on a spiritual one. At stake were not mountains, but minds; not hills, but hearts. The enemies were invisible forces, such as laziness, forgetfulness, apathy, and other manifestations of the one great enemy—sin. God had led His people to Canaan, not simply to give them a place to live, but for them to live in a unique covenant relationship with Him.

Joshua took pains to insure that Israel would be as faithful in waging this spiritual conflict as they had been in destroying Israel's flesh-and-blood foes. First, he gathered together the leadership of the people (Joshua 23) and charged them much as he had been charged by Moses (Deuteronomy 31:7, 8). Next, he assembled all the tribes of Israel at Shechem (Joshua 24). Here he reviewed God's dealings with the people, beginning with Abraham. He closed his message with a dramatic "invitation" (vv. 14, 15). The gist of this challenge appears in our title: "Choose you this day." Its implications are as significant for Christians, as they were for those who stood before Joshua. We are preparing to enter our "promised land" under the leadership of Jesus, the New Testament "Joshua"—"savior."

The Right to Choose

"Choose"

When Joshua said, "Choose," he was touching on one of the essential elements distinguishing man from all else in God's creation. Man's freedom of choice is part of what it means to be created in His image. Joshua knew that he could preach, exhort, and challenge as earnestly as possible. He could even tell the people what he himself had chosen. But ultimately the people had to choose for themselves.

In modern society, the right to choose is sacred. No matter what kind of item one is purchasing at a store, he usually is confronted with a multitude of choices. Restaurants that advertise with slogans such as, "You're the boss!" or "Have it your way!" cater to the power people like to exercise by deciding what *they* want.

Unfortunately, the "right to choose" has often been carried into the areas of morals and ethics, with devastating consequences. "Doing your own thing" or being "pro-choice" on issues such as abortion appears to respect a person's inherent rights. Yet the turmoil rampant throughout America indicates that something is terribly wrong. What works to build restaurants could destroy our most precious institutions.

The problem is that the modern "right to choose" is often interpreted within a philosophical context that maintains that there are no right or wrong choices. Every individual is right, simply by virtue of exercising his right to choose. But Biblically, it is not merely the right to choose that gives man his dignity; it is his ability to make a *right* choice that will result in fulfillment of the purpose for which God created him.

The Right Choice

"Whom ye will serve"

Joshua offered the Israelites a clear choice, summarized in the phrase, "whom ye will serve." The options were narrowed to two: the lifeless pagan gods or the true God, whose mighty works Joshua had just recounted. Only by making the right choice could Israel be assured of God's continued blessing.

Joshua's challenge reminds us that it is impossible to escape service to *someone*. We do not choose whether or not to serve; we choose *whom* we serve. True freedom is not obtained by insisting that we get our rights, but by seeing that God gets His rights as our Creator and Lord. God respects our right to choose by allowing to confront the same choice that Israel faced; we exercise that right most respectfully by choosing to serve Him.

It should be clear that this merits being called the "Choice of choices"—the most significant choice of any that we can make. If we choose to serve God, then many other choices are automatically made. Life becomes less complicated and more meaningful when we allow our choices to become God's. Whenever man has multiplied his gods (that is, his options) in the name of freedom, he has also multiplied his sorrows.

"This day"

Making the right choice is not a one-time commitment. It requires a daily discipline to duty. Here Joshua injects a sense of urgency in his invitation to the people. "This day" is the day of decision; thus, every day is in reality "the Lord's day." No day should be exempt from His control. There is no set of circumstances in any given day that will not be handled better as a result of God's guidance.

Godliness cannot be taken for granted or assumed, particularly when one considers the spiritual and moral darkness that permeates present society. Holiness must be asserted and maintained on a daily basis. Perhaps one made a commitment to Jesus Christ years ago, but "this day" the covenant must be renewed. The "other gods," while lifeless as ever, still challenge the authority of the one true God. Any day we become careless in spiritual matters may haunt us for eternity.

"Me and my house"

There is, furthermore, a future dimension to Joshua's challenge. While each individual must choose for himself, his choice will have inescapable consequences upon others around him, particularly within his own household or family. These are the people who see us on a daily basis and thus are able to judge whether we are taking seriously the choice we have made. This is why God has always emphasized the responsibility of parents to instruct their families in His way (see Deuteronomy 6:6-9; Psalm 78:1-8; 145:4; Ephesians 6:4).

As stated earlier, Joshua knew that conquering and dividing the promised land was only half the battle. To insure that the land would remain in Israel's possession, the fathers and mothers would have to equip and train their children as warriors to carry on the battle against sin. To fail would lead to faithlessness, thus repeating the sad mistake of the wandering generation that never saw the promised land.

Godliness is never automatic or hereditary. The faithful of the present must aid the coming generations in making choices that are good and wise, rooted in the Word of God.

Modern Gods

Every generation must deal with its own "gods," or threats to the authority of the true God. In the land in which we are living, the gods are not as easy to "throw away" as the gods of Joshua's time. Our idols are often "isms," such as humanism, hedonism, and materialism. These surround us daily, primarily through the media, compelling us to make each day a "this day" of decision. How can we survive?

Because these godless influences are so subtle, we should recognize that many of the choices we must make are not between a definite right and an undeniable wrong. Numerous areas of conduct are "grayer" than we may wish them to be. We must decide not only what is good or acceptable, but what is *better* or *best*. This was the lesson Jesus desired to teach Martha when He was the guest of her and her sister Mary (Luke 10:38-42). Martha was not doing anything wrong in preparing dinner for Jesus or in trying to be a good hostess. Mary, however, had chosen something "better," which, according to Jesus, "shall not be taken away from her."

It is all too easy in modern society for Christians simply to "fit in" with their surroundings rather than make those choices that result in a higher quality of discipleship. Such choices often provide opportunities to witness to others of the difference our faith in Christ makes. A bland and blind conformity, while appearing to keep our Christianity from being labeled "holier than thou," may have the opposite effect of making it seem "cheaper than thou."

From Heartache to Hope

We must convey clearly, by action as well as word, that "this day" belongs to the Lord. We must speak not only for ourselves but for the sake of our households. For here indeed is the critical arena where the price of neglecting "this day" is so great. Too many parents weep with remorse because "this day" was not taken seriously. There was always something more pressing to do with "this day." Children grieve for parents and loved ones no longer alive; opportunities for loving and touching, which once presented themselves on "this day," are gone.

Out of such regret, however, comes the most personal word of hope and encouragement from Joshua's invitation. Even though many such days may have been wasted, "this day" can mark the beginning of a bold new direction for your life. God will free you from your past and make you a "new creature," if you permit Him to do so. The choice is yours alone.

"Choose *you* this day!"

"Right in His Own Eyes"

by James B. North

THE AMERICAN PHILOSOPHER George Santayana is credited with the observation, "He who does not learn from history is condemned to repeat it." This statement certainly may be applied to Israel in the time period covered by the book of Judges. There is a basic pattern to the book: (1) The people sin; (2) God allows them to be oppressed by an enemy; (3) The people repent and cry for deliverance; (4) God sends a judge to deliver them from the oppressor. Unfortunately, the people failed to learn from their early experiences, so this cycle was repeated numerous times.

The basic cause of the difficulties, mentioned in both Judges 17:6 and 21:25, was that "every man did that which was right in his own eyes." This individualistic view of morality may be understandable in situations where there are no rules governing behavior. But where codes of law are already established, to do what one pleases is bound to cause trouble.

We are content to allow each person to choose his own car, his own clothes, and the carpeting for his own home. But in our society there are some things individuals cannot be allowed to do whenever they choose. For the good of all concerned, we do not allow each individual to lead a parade down a city street whenever he wants, or burn garbage in his backyard, or even build a house without meeting stipulated safety standards. Individual choice is one thing; going against established laws is something else.

God had given His people the Ten Commandments, plus numerous other laws. When the wilderness wanderings ended, and the Israelites were settled in the land of Canaan, God still expected His laws to be observed. But when "every man did that which was right in his own eyes," they violated His rules regarding worship and conduct. That was when God sent punishment upon them. God's laws must be honored.

God's Laws

God has given us laws, which regulate how we are to treat one another, how we are to conduct the affairs of His church, and how we are to respond to the authorities set over us. Disobeying these laws brings unpleasant consequences. Sometimes these consequences are the natural result of abandoning the guidelines.

There are laws of human behavior just as there are laws of physics. Some social problems are the simple cause-and-result of social sin. When a man gets drunk, he suffers the pain of his hangover. That simply is the result of breaking the law of sobriety. When a person overeats and gets sick, that is the result of gluttony. When a person physically and verbally badgers everyone around him, he can expect to be a lonely, friendless person. These are fundamental laws of behavior, and breaking them leads to a sure and predictable consequence.

Our Choice

Our society is one in which all too often "every person does what is right in his own eyes." Use of illegal drugs, termination of unwanted pregnancy, casual sexual encounters, employee theft, tax evasion—these are matters concerning which many people do what they want to do, regardless of the law or God's expectations of human behavior. As a result, we have slaughter on the highways, organized crime, escalating abortions, AIDS, corruption, and burdensome taxes. Failing to learn this lesson from history simply means that each succeeding generation must experience the difficulty all over again.

Individual freedom is, of course, a valued possession in our culture, and rightly so. But even the framers of our Constitution and its Bill of Rights knew that there were limits to individualism. Thus the government has the authority to impose laws upon the people—laws approved by the people's elected representatives.

Christians recognize the obligation to obey law—not only those laws that are derived from the will of the governed, but also God's laws revealed in His Word. "Doing one's own thing" is balanced by the admonition to "love one another." "Living for one's self" is balanced by the necessity of "bearing one another's burdens." "Making our own decision," is balanced by the command to "submit to one another."

In Christianity each has the freedom to choose, but that freedom must never become anarchy. As Paul said in Galatians 5:13, liberty is not to be used as an occasion for license.

To violate God's laws is to invite His retribution. One thing we must learn from history is that God's laws exist for valid reasons. To do only what is right in our own eyes is to spurn His will, belittle His love, and reject His blessings.

Quarterly Quiz

The questions on this page and the next may be used in several ways: as a pretest at the beginning of the quarter; as a review at the end of the quarter; or as a review after each lesson. The questions are based on the Scripture text of each lesson (King James Version).

Lesson 1

1. How many men of Israel carried stones from the Jordan River to build a memorial of the people's crossing of the river? *Joshua 4:2*
2. How many men were selected from each tribe to carry the stones for the memorial? *Joshua 4:2*
3. Who carried the ark of the testimony when Israel crossed the Jordan river to enter the promised land? *Joshua 4:16*
4. The stone memorial that commemorated Israel's crossing of the Jordan River was erected in (Jericho, Gilgal, Ai). *Joshua 4:20*

Lesson 2

1. The first city that fell to Israel after they entered the land of Canaan was (Ai, Jericho, Jerusalem). *Joshua 6:1, 2*
2. The Israelites marched around the city (one, two, three) times each day for (five, six, seven) days. *Joshua 6:3*
3. On which day did the Israelites march around the city seven times? *Joshua 6:15*
4. Rahab and her family were the only people in the city whose lives were spared. (true/false). *Joshua 6:17*

Lesson 3

1. After the Lord gave the land of Canaan to Israel according to His promise to their fathers, what did He give them round about? *Joshua 21:44*
2. Not one man of all of Israel's _____ stood before them in the land. *Joshua 21:44*
3. In Joshua's day, only one of the good things God had promised to Israel failed to come to pass. (true/false). *Joshua 21:45*
4. Name the tribes of Israel who took their portion of the promised land on the east side of the Jordan River. *Joshua 22:1, 4*
5. The tribes east of the Jordan River fulfilled their promise to fight alongside the other tribes of Israel until all Israel had taken possession of Canaan. (true/false). *Joshua 22:2, 3*

Lesson 4

1. Joshua told the Israelites to put away the gods that their fathers served on the other side of the _____, and in _____. *Joshua 24:14*

2. Israel declared it unthinkable that they should forsake the Lord to serve other gods. (true/false). *Joshua 24:16*
3. Where did Joshua make a covenant with Israel, and on that day set them a statute and an ordinance? *Joshua 24:25*
4. What did Joshua set up as a witness to the covenant between God and Israel? *Joshua 24:26, 27*

Lesson 5

1. After the death of Joshua, the people of Israel forsook the Lord and began to serve what gods of the people who were round about them? *Judges 2:13*
2. Because Israel turned from God to worship idols, God's anger against His people was (severe, hot, fierce). *Judges 2:14*
3. God delivered Israel into the hands of their enemies so that His people could no longer _____ before them. *Judges 2:14*
4. Israel wholeheartedly followed the leading of the judges by returning to God and worshiping Him only (true/false). *Judges 2:17*
5. Each succeeding generation of Israelites turned more and more from serving the Lord God, to follow after other gods (true/false). *Judges 2:19*

Lesson 6

1. Who was the king of Canaan who ruled in Hazor, and into whose hands the Lord sold Israel? *Judges 4:2*
2. Who was the captain of the armies of the Canaanites when Deborah judged Israel? *Judges 4:2*
3. How many chariots of iron did the captain of the Canaanite armies have at his command? *Judges 4:3*
4. When Israel came to Deborah for judgment, they found her (in a cave, under a palm tree, at the Lord's sanctuary). *Judges 4:5*
5. The man whom the Lord commanded to lead the Israelites in battle against the Canaanites was (Balak, Barak, Balaam). *Judges 4:6*

Lesson 7

1. When an angel of the Lord came to Ophrah, where did he find Gideon? *Judges 6:11*
2. What was Gideon doing there? *Judges 6:11*

3. Into the hands of what people had the Lord delivered Israel in the days of Gideon? *Judges 6:13*

4. Gideon was a member of a poor family of what tribe? *Judges 6:15*

5. How many men helped Gideon throw down the altar of Baal that his father had? *Judges 6:27*

Lesson 8

1. The Lord wanted to reduce the size of Gideon's army to prevent their saying that they had saved themselves from their oppressor (true/false). *Judges 7:2*

2. When Gideon announced to his army that those who were fearful could return home, how many men left and how many remained? *Judges 7:3*

3. The Lord told Gideon to bring the remaining men down to the water so he could do what to them there? *Judges 7:4*

4. How many men were in Gideon's army after the final reduction of soldiers? *Judges 7:7*

5. What three things was each of Gideon's soldiers given before the battle with their oppressors? *Judges 7:20*

Lesson 9

1. Abimelech went to the city of (Ophrah, Shechem, Millo) to get the men there to proclaim him king. *Judges 9:1*

2. Jerubbaal (Gideon) had (7, 17, 70) sons. *Judges 9:2*

3. Abimelech killed all but one of Gideon's sons (true/false). *Judges 9:5*

4. (Abimelech, Jotham, Jerubbaal) proclaimed a parable from the top of Mount Gerizim. *Judges 9:7*

5. In the parable what four trees and plants were asked to rule over the trees? *Judges 9:8-14*

Lesson 10

1. Who were the people who oppressed Israel during Samson's lifetime? *Judges 16:23*

2. The god worshiped by Israel's oppressors in Samson's time was _____. *Judges 16:23*

3. On the occasion when Samson was paraded blind and helpless before his captors, how many people watched from the roof of the building? *Judges 16:27*

4. The number of the enemies of Israel slain by Samson at his death was (a little less than, equal to, greater than) the number he had slain in his life. *Judges 16:30*

Lesson 11

1. Elimelech, Naomi, and their two sons lived in what city of Judah? *Ruth 1:1*

2. The family of Elimelech and Naomi left Judah because the land was suffering from (an enemy invasion, a plague, a famine). *Ruth 1:1*

3. The country to which Elimelech and Naomi took their family was (Ammon, Moab, Edom). *Ruth 1:1*

4. The two women married by the sons of Elimelech and Naomi were named _____ and _____. *Ruth 1:4*

5. When Naomi decided to return to her homeland, she urged her daughter-in-law to go with her (true/false). *Ruth 1:8*

Lesson 12

1. Who owned the field where Ruth went to work when she and Naomi returned to Judah? *Ruth 2:5*

2. The work of gathering the stalks of grain dropped or overlooked by the reapers at harvest was called _____. *Ruth 2:7*

3. The owner of the field where Ruth was working urged her to work only in his field (true/false). *Ruth 2:8*

4. Ruth expressed her surprise to the owner for his kindness, seeing she was a widow (true/false). *Ruth 2:10*

Lesson 13

1. The women of Bethlehem told Naomi that Ruth was better to her than (two, four, seven) sons. *Ruth 4:15*

2. What was the name of the son of Ruth and Boaz? *Ruth 4:17*

3. The son of Ruth and Boaz was the grandfather of David, king of Israel (true/false). *Ruth 4:17*

Answers

Lesson 1—1. twelve. 2. one. 3. priests 4. Gilgal. **Lesson 2**—1. Jericho. 2. one, six. 3. the seventh. 4. true. **Lesson 3**—1. rest. 2. enemies. 3. false. 4. Reuben, God, the half tribe of Manasseh. 5. true. **Lesson 4**—1. flood, Egypt. 2. true. 3. Shechem. 4. a great stone. **Lesson 5**—1. Baal and Ashtaroth. 2. hot. 3. stand. 4. false. 5. true. **Lesson 6**—1. Jabin. 2. Sisera. 3. nine hundred. 4. under a palm tree. 5. Barak. **Lesson 7**—1. by (in) the winepress. 2. threshed wheat. 3. Midianites. 4. Manasseh. 5. ten. **Lesson 8**—1. true. 2. twenty-two thousand, ten thousand. 3. try them. 4. three hundred. 5. a trumpet, a pitcher, a lamp. **Lesson 9**—1. Shechem. 2. 70. 3. true. 4. Jotham. 5. olive, fig, vine, bramble. **Lesson 10**—1. the Philistines. 2. Dagon. 3. about three thousand. 4. greater than. **Lesson 11**—1. Bethlehem. 2. a famine. 3. Moab. 4. Orpah, Ruth. 5. false. **Lesson 12**—1. Boaz. 2. gleaning. 3. true. 4. false. **Lesson 13**—1. seven. 2. Obed. 3. true.

The Crossing of Jordan Memorialized

LESSON SCRIPTURE: Joshua 1–4.

PRINTED TEXT: Joshua 4:1-3, 8, 15-24.

Joshua 4:1-3, 8, 15-24

1 And it came to pass, when all the people were clean passed over Jordan, that the Lord spake unto Joshua, saying,

2 Take you twelve men out of the people, out of every tribe a man,

3 And command ye them, saying, Take you hence out of the midst of Jordan, out of the place where the priests' feet stood firm, twelve stones, and ye shall carry them over with you, and leave them in the lodging place, where ye shall lodge this night.

. . . .

8 And the children of Israel did so as Joshua commanded, and took up twelve stones out of the midst of Jordan, as the Lord spake unto Joshua, according to the number of the tribes of the children of Israel, and carried them over with them unto the place where they lodged, and laid them down there.

. . . .

15 And the Lord spake unto Joshua, saying,

16 Command the priests that bear the ark of the testimony, that they come up out of Jordan.

17 Joshua therefore commanded the priests, saying, Come ye up out of Jordan.

18 And it came to pass, when the priests that bare the ark of the covenant of the Lord were come up out of the midst of Jordan, and the soles of the priests' feet were lifted up unto the dry land, that the waters of Jordan returned unto their place, and flowed over all his banks, as they did before.

19 And the people came up out of Jordan on the tenth day of the first month, and encamped in Gilgal, in the east border of Jericho.

20 And those twelve stones, which they took out of Jordan, did Joshua pitch in Gilgal.

21 And he spake unto the children of Israel, saying, When your children shall ask their fathers in time to come, saying, What mean these stones?

22 Then ye shall let your children know, saying, Israel came over this Jordan on dry land.

23 For the Lord your God dried up the waters of Jordan from before you, until ye were passed over, as the Lord your God did to the Red sea, which he dried up from before us, until we were gone over:

24 That all the people of the earth might know the hand of the Lord, that it is mighty: that ye might fear the Lord your God for ever.

GOLDEN TEXT: When your children shall ask their fathers in time to come, saying, What mean these stones? Then ye shall let your children know, saying, Israel came over this Jordan on dry land.—Joshua 4:21, 22.

Conquest and Challenge
Unit 1: Joshua—A Time of Conquest and Settlement (Lessons 1-4)

Lesson Aims

After this lesson students should be able to:

1. Understand the significance of Israel's crossing of the Jordan River and God's concern that it be remembered.

2. See the importance of memorials and realize how vital it is to remember Jesus.

3. Meaningfully participate in the Lord's Supper as a vital memorial act of spiritual value.

Lesson Outline

INTRODUCTION
    A. A Call for Courage
    B. Lesson Background
  I. A DIVINELY PLANNED MEMORIAL (Joshua 4:1-3)
  II. THE MEMORIAL PREPARED (Joshua 4:8)
  III. COMPLETION AND COMMEMORATION (Joshua 4:15-24)
    Meaningful Memorials
    Passing the Faith Along
CONCLUSION
    A. Don't Forget!
    B. Prayer
    C. Thought to Remember

Display visual 1 from the visuals/learning resources packet and call attention to it when appropriate. It is shown on page 349. Display the map (visual 14) throughout the quarter.

Introduction

A. A Call for Courage

A new generation of Israelites stood at the border of the promised land. God had assured them that they would be brought to a land of plenty and into a developed civilization. They were told there would be "great and goodly cities, which thou buildedst not. And houses full of all good things, which thou filledst not, and wells digged, which thou diggedst not, vineyards and olive trees, which thou plantedst not" (Deuteronomy 6:10, 11).

All this and more they found to be true. They also found that these cities were full of people who were not anxious to give their land away. The most important need facing them was the courage and determination to take what God

was giving them. This required faith in the help that God had promised to give them and confidence in the leadership that God had already made available in Joshua. God was most concerned, therefore, that Joshua himself be optimistic, hopeful, and thus be able to rally and inspire the people.

So God promised Joshua, "I will not fail thee, nor forsake thee" (Joshua 1:5). He challenged him: "Be strong and of a good courage. . . . Only be thou strong and very courageous. . . . Be strong and of a good courage" (1:6, ·7, 9).

It is not too much to say that God promises us spiritual blessings and wonderful possibilities in Christ. However, we sometimes face spiritual struggles and conflicts before we "enter into our rest." Well does Paul urge us, "Watch ye, stand fast in the faith, quit you like men, be strong" (1 Corinthians 16:13).

B. Lesson Background

The book of Joshua tells the story of the conquest of Canaan by the Hebrews. Their four decades of wilderness wandering were concluded, and the new generation stood on the borders of the long promised land of Canaan. The people's dependence on Joshua's leadership ability was now profound. God said to Joshua, "Moses my servant is dead; now therefore arise, go over this Jordan, thou, and all this people, unto the land which I do give to them" (1:2).

The land was given them, but they faced a formidable task in dispossessing the people living there. However, the new generation did not desire to return to the slavery their fathers had fled. They were attracted to the fertile and cultivated fields and lush pasturage of much of Canaan and were ready to enter it. They needed only the mature and inspiring direction that Joshua was able to supply to them to possess the land.

It was a mission that required of Joshua a sense of intrepid confidence and optimism. Thus it was that God repeatedly urged Joshua to be strong and courageous (1:6, 7, 9). Joshua communicated this spirit so thoroughly to his people that they promised earnestly to follow and support his leadership, even urging their leader, as God had, to "be strong and of a good courage" (1:18).

The first obstacle to be encountered was the Jordan River, the eastern boundary of the land of promise. God told Joshua how to arrange the people and to begin moving toward the river. The priests carrying the ark of the covenant were to lead at a distance of "about a thousand yards" ahead of the people (3:4, *New International Version*). Though the Jordan was at flood stage, the river dried up as soon as the feet of the priests touched the water. Suddenly it was dammed up a great distance upstream. Thus the whole people passed over on dry ground and entered Canaan at last.

I. A Divinely Planned Memorial (Joshua 4:1-3)

1. And it came to pass, when all the people were clean passed over Jordan, that the Lord spake unto Joshua, saying,

We have no information about how God communicated with Joshua—whether by an audible voice or through a distinct impression on his mind. In any case, there was no question as to the clarity and definiteness of the instructions given him. It was one of the features of Joshua's leadership that God made known His will to Joshua just as He had given guidance to Moses.

2. Take you twelve men out of the people, out of every tribe a man.

It was left to Joshua to select what particular men would be used in the task God had in mind. The only qualifying direction was that each of the tribes was to have a man selected from it. This would make the action of these men representative of the entire people. The task they were to do was not to be for themselves, or even their own tribes, but for the whole of Israel.

3. And command ye them, saying, Take you hence out of the midst of Jordan, out of the place where the priests' feet stood firm, twelve stones, and ye shall carry them over with you, and leave them in the lodging place, where ye shall lodge this night.

It is an interesting fact that even as the pivotal event of crossing the Jordan was being accomplished, God was preparing to create a memorial to it. This was a very significant milestone as future events proved. They had now finally ceased their desert wanderings and were on the brink of conquering and settling the land promised to their fathers. In the camp to which they were taking these stones two especially significant events occurred. The manna that had been provided during all the wilderness years now ceased (Joshua 5:12), and all the males were circumcised as a kind of renewal of their cove-

nant to be God's people (5:2-8). The Jordan crossing, done with the help of God's power, was in many ways similar to the crossing of the Red Sea during the flight from Egypt. That had been the final break with slavery and the beginning of special laws, rites, and institutions as God's people. So this was a break with the wilderness life and a fresh alignment with God's purposes so their own land and identity could at last be established.

II. The Memorial Prepared (Joshua 4:8)

8. And the children of Israel did so as Joshua commanded, and took up twelve stones out of the midst of Jordan, as the Lord spake unto Joshua, according to the number of the tribes of the children of Israel, and carried them over with them unto the place where they lodged, and laid them down there.

This incident gives us some idea of the value God places on the use of physical means to commemorate the accomplishment of His purposes. Surely those who experienced this great event would remember it and tell about it to succeeding generations. It was also considered valuable to build a stone monument that would serve as a tangible reminder of this miraculous entrance into the promised land.

Multiplied thousands of the Hebrews thronged across the river. It must have been a most exciting and perhaps confusing time. They had to control children and bring over all their possessions, including tents and cattle. It might have seemed that the preparation of a memorial could have waited until they had overcome some of the foes they were about to face. But, no; God wanted this done right in the midst of all the excitement and exultation of their new experience.

God wanted His people to have some reminder of His care for them and of their dependence on Him as they began their new life.

It is characteristic of Joshua that he was willing to obey God's commands, whatever they were. There is no indication that Joshua ever asked "Why?" or that he offered objections, qualifications, or excuses. He did what God said. What an example for us!

How to Say It

GILGAL.   *Gil*-gal.
JERICHO.   *Jair*-ih-ko.
RAHAB.   *Ray*-hab.

III. Completion and Commemoration
(Joshua 4:15-24)

15, 16. And the Lord spake unto Joshua, saying, Command the priests that bear the ark of the testimony, that they come up out of Jordan.

The *ark of the testimony* is also called "the ark of the covenant" and "the ark of the Lord" (vv. 9, 11). This was a box made of shittim wood, generally believed to be acacia wood, which was overlaid with gold within and without. It was rectangular in shape, about four feet long and about two-and-a-half feet wide and two-and-a-half feet high. It had four rings attached on the sides at the corners. Poles were put into the rings so the ark could be carried. The lid of the ark had a cherub at each end, and they faced each other with their wings outspread covering the mercy seat. Originally the ark contained the stone tables of the law (Deuteronomy 10:3-5). Later it appears a pot of manna was placed there, and Aaron's rod that had budded. (See Exodus 25:10-22; Hebrews 9:4.) When the ark was carried on the march, it could not be seen, for it was well covered (Numbers 4:5, 6).

The priests bearing the ark had stood in the river bed of Jordan all the while the Hebrews were crossing, exactly as God had told Joshua that was what they were to do.

17, 18. Joshua therefore commanded the priests, saying, Come ye up out of Jordan. And it came to pass, when the priests that bare the ark of the covenant of the Lord were come up out of the midst of Jordan, and the soles of the priests' feet were lifted up unto the dry land, that the waters of Jordan returned unto their place, and flowed over all his banks, as they did before.

The crossing was now completed, and the time for the priests to go over to the western bank had arrived. No longer was there any reason to restrain the swollen river, so the normal course of the water returned. There is an economy about God's use of His power for the help of His people. We note that after Jesus had brought a dead girl to life He directed her joyful parents to give her something to eat (Luke 8:51-55). The regular processes of life were to be resumed as soon as possible. After the feeding of the five thousand Jesus told the disciples, "Gather the pieces that are left over. Let nothing be wasted" (John 6:12, *New International Version*). While supernatural power had multiplied the supply of food, this did not excuse them from carefully utilizing the resources made available. Thus, as soon as the need for the special exercise of God's power was satisfied, its use was terminated.

Verse 18 shows the definite connection between the sudden stoppage of the river's flow and God's purpose for His people expressed in their entrance into Canaan. Before the crossing Joshua had told Israel that what they were about to witness would enable them to "know that the living God is among you" (3:10). Joshua told them that the waters of the Jordan would "stand upon a heap" as soon as the priests stepped into the river (v. 13); and the miracle occurred in just that manner. Some people like to think that a landslide temporarily blocked the Jordan upstream. If such were the case, the stoppage was no less miraculous, occurring at precisely the time the priests stepped into the river, lasting long enough for all of Israel to cross over, and ending just as the priests who carried the ark set foot on the western shore. But the living God, who is "Lord of all the earth" (v. 13), as easily could pile up the water without a slide if He wished.

19. And the people came up out of Jordan on the tenth day of the first month, and encamped in Gilgal, in the east border of Jericho.

The *first month* was called *Nisan* and, roughly, would fall between March 15 and April 15. They stopped to reorder their lives and practices, facing their first test—the strategic and fortified city of Jericho. As has been mentioned, the manna now ceased, and the people must have soon realized they needed to conquer the land before them if they were to be able to raise crops and cattle and establish a more settled style of life.

20. And those twelve stones, which they took out of Jordan, did Joshua pitch in Gilgal.

Joshua did this, of course, in response to God's instructions to him. The stones were not *useful* in the sense that they were to be used to grind grain, or as the foundation for a house. No, their value was symbolic, evocative, commemorative. They were meant as reminders of God's goodness to Israel and of His ability to help them overcome obstacles and hindrances to their achieving His purposes for and through them.

Some practices of the church may appear to have no materialistic or "practical" use. The Communion service is not something physically necessary, as is heat for a worship room, light for seeing. But the partaking of the elements of the bread and cup in memory of Jesus' death on the cross is nonetheless of great significance. Just as Israel erected the stones so that the Jordan crossing (and what it proved about God's power, presence, and care for them) might always be remembered, so we partake of Communion to remember Jesus' death for us.

MEANINGFUL MEMORIALS

In Plymouth, Massachusetts, is preserved Plymouth Rock. This boulder is traditionally recognized as the rock upon which the Pilgrims first stepped when they disembarked from the *Mayflower* in December of 1620. When tourists visit this memorial attraction, they are reminded not only of the landing of the Plymouth colonists, but also of the religious convictions that brought them here, of the courage required to cope with the hardship and sorrow of their first several months in America, and of the sacrifices they made to provide for us the legacy of freedom and prosperity we here now enjoy.

The rocks piled by the Israelites entering the promised land formed a meaningful memorial as well. Future generations were to be reminded of the people's dramatic crossing of the Jordan on dry ground. They were to remember also the faith that brought the Hebrews there, and the covenant of Jehovah that guarantees deliverance and protection to God's faithful children.

Jesus, the rock of our salvation, the cornerstone of God's kingdom, is our best reminder of God's deliverance from sin and of His Spirit's presence and power. So, the memorial of the Lord's Supper is meaningful to every generation, as we partake.   —R. W. B.

21. And he spake unto the children of Israel, saying, When your children shall ask their fathers in time to come, saying, What mean these stones?

The value of any memorial is that it calls attention to some past event or series of events considered to be of lasting significance. The generation that erects such a monument feels it is important, and its mere presence in later years helps people recall the past experience to which it directs attention. Such national memorials as the Bunker Hill Monument, the Washington Monument, or the Jefferson Memorial all point to the important place these events or persons had in the formation of our American life.

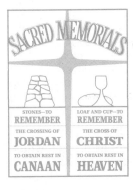

visual 1

As Joshua erected the memorial stones, it was assumed that years later children would inquire as to their meaning. This would give the older generation opportunity to tell of God's leading, intervention, and care for their life as a people.

We too must remember what God did for His people long ago, but we must be sure also that His grace toward us is memorable as well. May we so trust Him that through us He can do tremendous works that are worthy of remembering always.

22. Then ye shall let your children know, saying, Israel came over this Jordan on dry land.

It was a feat to have crossed the Jordan when there were no bridges, especially in its flood season. To enter an alien and hostile territory and to cross a river with long lines of cattle, supplies, and children, was a formidable task. However, they had walked across on *dry land*, which was a tribute to God's mighty power and protecting care.

23. For the Lord your God dried up the waters of Jordan from before you, until ye were passed over, as the Lord your God did to the Red sea, which he dried up from before us, until we were gone over.

Here the two crossings—that of the Red Sea and of the Jordan—are equated as remarkable instances of God's providential provision for Israel's success and blessing. The Red Sea crossing had accomplished their departure from Egypt and their release from slavery. The Jordan crossing ended the wilderness phase of their lives and effected the beginning of their conquest of their new land.

PASSING THE FAITH ALONG

Do you know if your great-grandfather was/is a Christian? Do you know his church affiliation? You should commend yourself if you know his *name*, let alone any knowledge about his faith. A few ambitious folk trace the roots of their family trees, but most have lost touch with ancestry beyond their grandparents.

God intended for strong links to be forged between family and faith. Children of the Hebrew children, and their children after them, were to be taught to love and obey the Lord God of Israel. Parents were to talk of their faith in the regular affairs of daily life, to impress children with God's will and way (Deuteronomy 6:1-9). The stone memorial at Gilgal was constructed to help the Israelites pass along to future generations the facts and faith connected with their miraculous crossing of the Jordan.

What will your great-grandchildren believe? Will they be Christians? With what church will they worship and affiliate? Many of these factors depend upon how you pass your faith along. We must love the Lord with all our hearts, and teach our descendants to love Him too. The chain reaction will take Christianity into the new century and beyond.   —R. W. B.

24. That all the people of the earth might know the hand of the Lord, that it is mighty: that ye might fear the Lord your God for ever.

Such a great deed as God did for His people would become known by the pagan inhabitants of the whole area. How they must have been amazed and awestruck by the evidence of the divine resources available to the Israelites. Indeed, even before this miracle, Rahab, in Jericho, told the two spies, "Your terror is fallen upon us, and ... all the inhabitants of the land faint because of you. For we have heard how the Lord dried up the water of the Red Sea for you.... And as soon as we had heard these things, our hearts did melt" (Joshua 2:9-11).

In his *Contemplations* (1634) Joseph Hall relates this to the crossing of our own Jordans of difficulty and the final river of death: "The passages into our promised Land are troublesome and perilous; and even at last, offer themselves to us the main hindrances of our salvation; which after all our hopes threaten to defeat us: for what will it avail us to have passed a Wilderness, if the waves of Jordan should swallow us up? But the same hand that hath made the way hard, hath made it sure. He that made the Wilderness comfortable, will make Jordan dry; he will master all difficulties for us; and those things which we most feared will he make most sovereign and beneficial to us. O God, as we have trusted thee with the beginning, so will we with the finishing of our glory. Faithful art thou that hast promised, which will also do it."

Home Daily Bible Readings

Monday, May 29—God Calls Joshua (Joshua 1:1-9)

Tuesday, May 30—Joshua Calls the Leaders (Joshua 1:10-18)

Wednesday, May 31—The Spies in Jericho (Joshua 2:1-15)

Thursday, June 1—Joshua Orders the Crossing (Joshua 3:1-6)

Friday, June 2—God Promises to Help (Joshua 3:7-17)

Saturday, June 3—The Israelites Cross the Sea (Exodus 14:21-31)

Sunday, June 4—Extol the Lord Our God (Psalm 99)

Conclusion

A. Don't Forget

We often tell someone not to forget some item we want him to buy at a store, or not to forget an important birthday or anniversary that is soon to be celebrated. The memorials we note in our national, civic, and religious lives are the same, though on a larger scale. They are reminders not to forget matters of great importance, whose influence still affects our lives.

For us as Christians probably the most important memorial is the one Jesus gave us during the closing days of His earthly ministry. He gave us the bread and cup of which we are to partake, He said, "in remembrance of me" (1 Corinthians 11:24). We will find it easier to live in Jesus' way, to do His will, to accept His promises, and to heed His warnings when we remember Him. It is generally true that only those realities we keep in the focus of our attention will have any marked effect in shaping our lives.

One of the most piercing admonitions given by the apostle Paul is this: "Remember Jesus Christ, raised from the dead" (2 Timothy 2:8, *New International Version*). Surely if the memorial stones at Gilgal could remind the Hebrews of God's past action in their behalf, the remembrance of Jesus, crucified and risen, can assure us of God's victory over sin, death, and all the power of evil men or Satan. This can become especially vivid for us as we hold in our hands and take into our bodies the memorials Jesus himself gave us in the loaf and the cup.

B. Prayer

O Father, we do remember the love shown us in Jesus. And we also are reminded of the power that reanimated that beaten, bruised corpse and made it arise with everlasting life and power—triumphant over death and the grave. We tend to forget, or to not remember very vividly, our loving and living Lord in the midst of all the activities of daily life. Forgive us and cleanse us and reenergize us.

We pray, O God, that we may not forget to observe often the memorial Jesus himself gave us. We are grateful for the sense of renewal and spiritual refreshment we find around the table of remembrance with our fellow believers. May all our life be a constant testimony to the fact that we *do* remember Jesus, our Lord. In His name, amen.

C. Thought to Remember

The worst kind of amnesia is that which causes us to forget all that God has done and is doing for us in Christ.

Learning by Doing

This page contains an alternate lesson plan emphasizing learning activities. Classes desiring such student involvement will find these suggestions helpful.

Learning Goals

This lesson should enable students to:

1. Trace the events in Israel's history leading up to the crossing of Jordan.

2. State the importance of the memorial stones to the Israelites.

3. Prepare a memorial stone that he will use as a reminder of God's faithfulness.

Into the Lesson

To begin, lead the class in a brainstorming session. Ask, "What are some of our national memorials?" Encourage students to call out as many memorials as they can recall. The purpose of the brainstorm is to receive as many answers as possible in a short time. As students call out their answers, write them as rapidly as you can on the chalkboard.

Next ask, "What is the purpose for each of these memorials?" Write their answers on the chalkboard. Answers include to recall sacrifice, suffering, excitement, or new beginnings. Allow three minutes for these two questions.

Connect this activity and the Bible study by saying, "Memorials are important to people for recalling past events and teaching future generations. Today we study the Israelites' crossing of the Jordan River into the promised land. God commanded them to build a memorial of that event. Let's see in our Scripture passage what that involved for Israel."

Into the Word

Divide your class into three groups of four to six individuals. If your class is larger, create more groups and give more than one group the same assignment. Assign one of the first three chapters of Joshua to each group. Each group is to write an appropriate heading for the chapter and list the significant events in the chapter. For example:

Chapter 1: Joshua's Marching Orders
1. God speaks to Joshua
2. Joshua orders the officers
3. Joshua speaks to the eastern tribes
4. The eastern tribes give assent

After ten minutes, call for the group reports.

Option: Develop a short lecture on the events leading up to our text. Use the "Lesson Background" section for information. Choose one or two events from each of chapters 1-3 of Joshua

for your overview. Be sure to emphasize how God was preparing the Israelites to enter the promised land. Use ten minutes.

Choose someone to read Joshua 3:14-17; 4:1-9; 15-24. The following questions may be duplicated so that students may answer them individually or in pairs. You may also want to use the questions to develop a whole class discussion.

1. Why do you think the Lord commanded Joshua to have the ark of the covenant brought into the Jordan ahead of the people? (To show that God was leading the way into the promised land.)

2. Why was it necessary for all of the tribes to be represented by the men who took up stones from the river bed? (The entire nation was represented in the acts of the twelve men. Thus, each individual would have a story to tell.)

3. Where were they to place these stones? (At their lodging place, Gilgal.)

4. What provision was being made to keep this event alive for future Jewish generations? (The stone memorial and its explanation would preserve the event for future generations.)

5. Why was it important for the question to be asked, "What do these stones mean to *you?*" (v. 6). (Each Israelite would then be able to tell his or her children of the personal effect of this event on his life.)

Into Life

Ask the students, "What do we learn about God in today's text?" Some possible answers are these: He is faithful, He is holy, He is mighty, He saves His people. Mention these if no one else does. Say, "Remembering is an important part of our Christian walk. What are some of the facts and events we Christians are called to remember?" Have the class read 1 Corinthians 11:24, 25; 2 Timothy 2:8, 14, 15 and list these remembrances.

Bring to class enough small stones or sheets of gray construction paper torn to look like stones so each student may have one. Have class members read 2 Timothy 2:8. Provide a felt-tipped markers, and have them write on their stones the date when they became a Christian, or today's date as a reminder of God's faithfulness to them. Ask them to place their memorial stone somewhere in their homes so that they will daily be reminded of their salvation in Jesus.

Let's Talk It Over

The questions on this page are designed to encourage review of the lesson
Scriptures and to promote discussion of the lesson by the class. The answers
provided are only discussion starters. Let your class talk it over from there.

1. The Hebrews entered Canaan with an awareness of the difficulties they would encounter in conquering it. How can we make new Christians aware of the struggles and temptations they will face?

The answer here goes back to our evangelistic methods. If in our efforts to sell a prospect on the gospel we emphasize only the benefits and advantages of being a Christian, we do that person no favor. A person should recognize at the outset that accepting Christ as Savior involves some counting the cost (Luke 14:25-33). Both before and after baptism the new believer may find it helpful to consider those passages in the New Testament that view the Christian life in military terms. He will take a more realistic view of what he is getting into when he observes that "our struggle is not against flesh and blood, but against the rulers, against the authorities, against the powers of this dark world and against the spiritual forces of evil in the heavenly realms" (Ephesians 6:12, *New International Version*). He will be challenged to cultivate personal discipline when he applies Paul's charge to Timothy: "Endure hardship with us like a good soldier of Christ Jesus" (2 Timothy 2:3, *New International Version*). And he will take courage from the description in Revelation 12:11 of those who overcame Satan "by the blood of the Lamb and by the word of their testimony; they did not love their lives so much as to shrink from death" (*New International Version*).

2. God wanted all of the people on earth to know of His power demonstrated in the miraculous crossings of the Red Sea and the Jordan River. In what ways can we let the people of our community know of how God's power is being demonstrated in our church?

Too much of the publicity the church receives is negative. If a minister is guilty of an adulterous relationship or child abuse or mishandling of money, the news media is quick to pick up on it. Ecclesiastical and doctrinal squabbles, churches that promote racism or sexism, surveys that show declining church attendance and diminishing belief in traditional doctrines—these are some of the items that qualify as religious news in the media. We must show our neighbors that God's power and God's love are still very much in evidence in God's church. And perhaps the first step in this is for church members to awaken to the demonstrations of divine power around them. If people are being won to the Lord and if their old habits and attitudes are being changed, then God's power is on display. If prayers are being answered, needy people being helped, and missionaries being supported, then we have further evidence of God's power. If Christians are learning to praise God, to be His witnesses, and to serve Him effectively, that also shows that divine power is at work within the church. The next step is to use every means available to publicize these happenings. The purpose is not to make the church or the minister look good, but to bring glory to God and to draw the attention of the entire community to His power and love.

3. What can we do to make certain that our observance of the Lord's Supper will be an occasion of remembering Jesus?

Even if the meditation, presented before the Communion service is Scriptural and thought-provoking, it is not wise to depend solely on that for our preparation. On Saturday evening or early Sunday morning we can make it a habit to read one of the Gospel accounts of the crucifixion and resurrection or one of the many other passages that speak of Christ's atoning death. And we need to pray for understanding and awareness of who Jesus is and of what He has done for us. And then as the emblems are passed to us during the worship service, we may find it helpful to use that particular passage as the focus of our meditation.

4. Why is it important to get all the people involved if a church is going to perform a major task or project?

The monument set up at Joshua's command impressed upon Israel that they were all involved in the blessings of that day. He chose one man from each tribe to erect the monument so all tribes would share in it. This promoted unity among the people. Any project for Christ will go better when unity exists within the church. Unity will not be achieved if some people feel left out, or if their opinions have not even been sought.

The Fall of Jericho

LESSON SCRIPTURE: Joshua 6.

PRINTED TEXT: Joshua 6:1-4, 15-21.

Joshua 6:1-4, 15-21

1 Now Jericho was straitly shut up because of the children of Israel: none went out, and none came in.

2 And the Lord said unto Joshua, See, I have given into thine hand Jericho, and the king thereof, and the mighty men of valor.

3 And ye shall compass the city, all ye men or war, and go round about the city once. Thus shalt thou do six days.

4 And seven priests shall bear before the ark seven trumpets of rams' horns: and the seventh day ye shall compass the city seven times, and the priests shall blow with the trumpets.

. . . .

15 And it came to pass on the seventh day, that they rose early about the dawning of the day, and compassed the city after the same manner seven times: only on that day they compassed the city seven times.

16 And it came to pass at the seventh time, when the priests blew with the trumpets, Joshua said unto the people, Shout; for the Lord hath given you the city.

17 And the city shall be accursed, even it, and all that are therein, to the Lord: only Rahab the harlot shall live, she and all that are with her in the house, because she hid the messengers that we sent.

18 And ye, in any wise keep yourselves from the accursed thing, lest ye make yourselves accursed, when ye take of the accursed thing, and make the camp of Israel a curse, and trouble it.

19 But all the silver, and gold, and vessels of brass and iron, are consecrated unto the Lord: they shall come into the treasury of the Lord.

20 So the people shouted when the priests blew with the trumpets: and it came to pass, when the people heard the sound of the trumpet, and the people shouted with a great shout, that the wall fell down flat, so that the people went up into the city, every man straight before him, and they took the city.

21 And they utterly destroyed all that was in the city, both man and woman, young and old, and ox, and sheep, and ass, with the edge of the sword.

GOLDEN TEXT: See, I have given into thine hand Jericho, and the king thereof, and the mighty men of valor.—Joshua 6:2.

Conquest and Challenge
Unit 1: Joshua—A Time of Conquest and Settlement (Lessons 1-4)

Lesson Aims

This lesson should lead the students:

1. To see that the unquestioning obedience of Joshua and the Israelites led to the overwhelming triumph at Jericho.

2. To understand that those who engage in unrestrained evil ultimately experience God's terrible wrath.

3. To select one command of the Lord Jesus to obey more fully this coming week.

Lesson Outline

INTRODUCTION

I. VICTORY VISUALIZED (Joshua 6:1-4)

II. VICTORY ACTUALIZED (Joshua 6:15-21)
   A. Final Actions and Instructions (vv. 15-19)
      The Rest of the Story
   B. The Conquest Achieved (vv. 20, 21)
      The Horrors of War

CONCLUSION
   A. Two Examples of Faith
   B. Prayer
   C. Thought to Remember

Display visual 2 from the visuals/learning resources packet and let it remain before the class throughout this session. It is shown on page 356.

Introduction

Jericho was the key city encountered by the Hebrews upon their entering the land of Canaan just north of the Dead Sea. The city was located in a subtropical region some eight hundred feet below the level of the Mediterranean Sea. Jericho was surrounded by walls that must have looked formidable to the Hebrews coming in from the desert. Forty years earlier when the twelve spies returned to the camp of Israel to report their findings concerning the land of Canaan, ten were discouraged because of the many difficulties they envisioned. One of their principal concerns was that the cities were "walled, and very great" (Numbers 13:28). Later, Moses stated that they had said, "The cities are walled up to heaven" (Deuteronomy 1:28).

God, however, told Joshua that victory over Jericho was sure. The Israelites would not need

to prepare rope ladders for an assault on the wall, or battering rams to break down the gates. The walls would collapse without Israel's attacking them if the directions that God gave were followed.

Of course we know the walls fell, but at first it must have appeared an "impossible dream" to those who received the instructions. We need to remember this when we encounter walls of defiant opposition. Many "walls" exists between social classes, between nations, between economic systems, and even between Christian groups. Often it seems as if these "walls" cannot be overcome.

Yet, if Jericho's walls could fall, so can others. There have been many cases where obedient faith in God has prevailed over seemingly impenetrable barriers. Paul speaks of Christ Jesus who made both Jew and Gentile one in His church and who therefore has "broken down the middle wall of partition between us" (Ephesians 2:14).

I. Victory Visualized (Joshua 6:1-4)

1. Now Jericho was straitly shut up because of the children of Israel: none went out, and none came in.

Jericho was undergoing what they probably considered a state of siege. It was *straitly shut up*. That is, the city gates were closed and barred. Those inside were afraid to venture out because of the hostile encampment of the Hebrews nearby.

2. And the Lord said unto Joshua, See, I have given into thine hand Jericho, and the king thereof, and the mighty men of valor.

Here was a wealthy, organized city that felt unable to send out any armed forces to drive off the Israelites in open battle. Rather, they adopted at once an attitude of defense. Their very unwillingness to go out and meet their foes was a testimony to the overpowering dread that they felt toward the Israelites. This had been reported to the two spies who had entered the city earlier and had taken refuge in the house of Rahab (Joshua 2:9-11). All of this was evident as the Jericho residents remained inside their walls, so God said, *See, I have given into thine hand Jericho.*

3. And ye shall compass the city, all ye men of war, and go round about the city once. Thus shalt thou do six days.

We sometimes have a mental picture of the entire population of the Hebrew tribes going around the city walls—men, women, and children. This, however, does not appear to be so. It seems that the armed forces made these circuits. Notice the phrase here, *all ye men of war*. Also, in verses 9 and 13 we read of *the armed men* going round the city.

This single circuit was to continue each day for six days. One can only wonder at what the guards and sentinels on Jericho's walls must have shouted to the marchers. Perhaps they taunted them as cowards. They may have cried that no matter how many times they went around they still would not find any vulnerable place to attack. It is also natural to speculate about what some of the Israelites marching around the city must have thought. Did they not wonder at this strange way of assaulting a city? Further, Joshua's command of absolute silence during the march must have been hard to understand. Couldn't they at least reply to jeers and insults that must have been audible to them from those manning the walls? No, they were told not a word was to come from them (v. 10). They must have had implicit trust in Joshua as God's leader and in God as the one who would make the victory a reality.

Many acts of obedience to God seem useless and strange to those apart from Him. Acts of worship have little "practical" meaning to those unacquainted with God's Word. Prayer, hymn singing, the Lord's Supper—all seem of little worth or significance to those unfamiliar with God's will. Spiritual victory, however, is not dependent on our being pleasing or understandable in every respect to non-Christians, but on our continued faithfulness to God's revealed will.

4. And seven priests shall bear before the ark seven trumpets of rams' horns: and the seventh day ye shall compass the city seven times, and the priests shall blow with the trumpets.

The ark was the sacred chest kept in the Most Holy Place in the tabernacle, on which the high priest was to sprinkle the blood of atonement for the sins of the people every year. Since the tabernacle and all its furnishings were to be carried about wherever the people went, the ark was

---

How to Say It

AMMONITES. *Am*-un-ites.

GOMORRAH. Guh-*mor*-uh.

JEHOSHAPHAT. Je-*hosh*-uh-fat.

JERICHO. *Jair*-ih-ko.

MOABITES. *Mo*-ub-ites.

NAAMAN. *Nay*-uh-mun.

RAHAB. *Ray*-hab.

SODOM. *Sod*-um.

---

designed with metal rings on the sides into which poles were inserted so it could be carried. Here seven priests were delegated to go before it, bearing trumpets and blowing them as they went about the walls (see verse 8). Since, as has been noted, no one was permitted to speak, the sounding of rams' horns was the only noise made by those circling the city.

II. Victory Actualized (Joshua 6:15-21)

A. Final Actions and Instructions (vv. 15-19)

15. And it came to pass on the seventh day, that they rose early about the dawning of the day, and compassed the city after the same manner seven times: only on that day they compassed the city seven times.

Everything seemed the same this *seventh day*. There was the forming into ordered ranks, the procession of the seven trumpet blowers, and the silent circling of the walls. However, instead of only walking around the city once, they made seven complete circuits. This was all according to the instructions Joshua had received from the Lord.

16. And it came to pass at the seventh time, when the priests blew with the trumpets, Joshua said unto the people, Shout; for the Lord hath given you the city.

Note that Joshua's faith was such that he proclaimed victory even before it was actually won. He was absolutely sure God's promise would come true. This reminds us of Jesus' prayer of thanks for the raising of Lazarus even prior to its accomplishment. (See John 11:41-44.)

17. And the city shall be accursed, even it, and all that are therein, to the Lord: only Rahab the harlot shall live, she and all that are with her in the house, because she hid the messengers that we sent.

The city shall be accursed, even it, and all that are therein. The Hebrew word translated *accursed* meant *under a ban, devoted*, generally to utter destruction as a result of a vow to God (see Numbers 21:2), or because of His command (see Leviticus 27:29; Deuteronomy 13:12-18; 1 Kings 20:42). At other times what was devoted to God became the property of the priest (see Leviticus 27:21; Numbers 18:14). Jericho was to be devoted to God, and Joshua was to destroy the city and everything in it, with the exceptions noted here and in verse 19.

Rahab, who had saved the two spies from capture, was to be spared as she had requested. A scarlet cord spun of threads was to be bound "in the window" (Joshua 2:18) so her house could be noted. All of her family members who were with her in this house were to be saved.

We are told that Rahab's "house" was "upon the town wall" (2:15). Often it is asked how her *house* could be there and be spared if the walls of Jericho "fell down flat" (6:20). No doubt the entire circuit of the wall fell, enabling every Israelite to enter that part of the city that was "straight before him" (6:5, 20). But it would seem that the part of the wall on which Rahab's house was built remained standing. If it had not, her house surely would have been destroyed in the general ruin. As the collapse of Jericho's walls were miraculous, so must have been the preservation of Rahab's house. That Rahab's house was on the external side of the wall doubtless made the rescue of her people much easier, since they would be on the side opposite the intense conflict in the inner city.

Rahab is an example of true faith. She believed the promise made to her by the spies she had spared. She must have displayed the scarlet cord, and this act of obedient faith was the final demonstration of her trust that assured her rescue from death. So the writer of Hebrews tells us, "By faith the prostitute Rahab, because she welcomed the spies, was not killed with those who were disobedient" (11:31, *New International Version*). We know that somehow Rahab's family was integrated into the life of the Israelites (Joshua 6:25) and that she became part of the genetic line from which Jesus, the Messiah, came according to the flesh (see Matthew 1:5).

THE REST OF THE STORY

Paul Harvey is well known for his radio broadcasts and books that tell "the rest of the story" behind items in the news. Through investigation he discovers intriguing, inspiring, and sometimes amusing sequels to events that may be reported only briefly in the media.

When we read certain passages of Scripture without considering their entire Bible context, erroneous impressions may result. For example,

WHEN THE PEOPLE ARE THE LORD'S, THE BATTLE AND THE VICTORY ARE THE LORD'S

visual 2

the report that the prostitute Rahab and her family were the only ones saved from destruction at Jericho could be confusing, if we stopped right there in our investigation. We might ask, "Why should good things happen to bad people?"

What's the rest of the story? Remember, Rahab was spared because of her helpfulness, cooperation and loyalty toward God's people. Although she was a prostitute, she obviously repented and reformed her life as a proselyte Jew. She became a direct ancestor of Jesus (Matthew 1:5). Her faith is commended by the writer of Hebrews (11:31), and James illustrates active righteousness by reference to Rahab's protection of Israel's spies (James 2:25).

The rest of the story in Rahab's case shows her to have been a person who recognized the great value of life lived under God's rule, and who took the necessary steps to achieve it.—R. W. B

18. And ye, in any wise keep yourselves from the accursed thing, lest ye make yourselves accursed, when ye take of the accursed thing, and make the camp of Israel a curse, and trouble it.

The accursed thing is that which has been devoted to God. The Israelites were strictly warned not to try to keep for themselves anything that was in the city, for it was all devoted to God. To take any of the imperishable items mentioned in verse 19 would have been to steal from God, an act nothing short of sacrilege. To take any perishable item, whether garments, tapestry, rugs, or equipage for animals, would be to make themselves part of that which was devoted to God, which in this case was to be utterly destroyed.

19. But all the silver, and gold, and vessels of brass and iron, are consecrated unto the Lord: they shall come into the treasury of the Lord.

These valuable metallic objects were to be saved that they might be used to further and support the worship of God. This worship was vital to the life of Israel, but was to be supported by offerings from the peoples' crops and herds. Until they finished their warfare and became settled it was important to provide for the priests, Levites, and the various offerings and festivals. Nothing in Jericho was to be available for the profit of individual Israelites. Whatever was not destroyed was reserved for religious uses.

B. The Conquest Achieved (vv. 20, 21)

20. So the people shouted when the priests blew with the trumpets: and it came to pass, when the people heard the sound of the trumpet, and the people shouted with a great shout, that the wall fell down flat, so that the people

went up into the city, every man straight before him, and they took the city.

The armed forces of Israel under Joshua's direction had followed God's instructions. In spite of all that might have been said about their seemingly useless marching around the walls, they had done so. This part of their task was completed. Now it was God's turn to do His part in this epic encounter. One can imagine what a tremendous volume of sound must have risen as the people's long, frustrating silence was at last broken. As they shouted there seems to have been a simultaneous collapse of large sections of the wall all around the city. The greatest barrier to the conquest of the fortress-city was now overcome, and again the completion of the victory lay in their hands. It remained for them to advance, do the fighting, and win the battle.

One can imagine the confusion and demoralization of the citizens of Jericho as their walls gave way and the shouting Hebrews poured in upon them from every side. In the city, soldiers, artisans, businessmen, women, children—all were mixed and thrown together in a huddled, terrified mass. It is not hard to see how the utter rout of Jericho's remaining resistance was accomplished. The brevity of the Biblical account, *they took the city*, gives little hint of the confused scenes of shouting, dust, flashing swords, blood, screams, and slaughter that ensued.

21. And they utterly destroyed all that was in the city, both man and woman, young and old, and ox, and sheep, and ass, with the edge of the sword.

As we noted in our comments under verse 17, the complete destruction of every living thing in Jericho was called for in Joshua's instructions prior to the assault on the city. The only lives to be spared were those of Rahab and the members of her family who were with her in her house at the time of the city's fall.

It is considered that God ordered this total destruction because of the utter wickedness of Jericho's people. The tendency of the Hebrews to be led astray from God's way by the example of these people, if they were spared, was doubtless another factor. Certainly this complete annihilation of everyone, and of all the animals, seems to be a terrible thing, as indeed it was. But the Hebrews were acting here as judicial agents of God, who thus executed His judgment upon these people.

In Genesis we read of the destruction of Sodom and Gomorrah by fire and brimstone as an act of God's wrath upon them for their total abandonment to evil. Instead of a flood, or an earthquake, or tornado, God expressed His judgment here by the swords of the invading Hebrew host. Sin's penalty is terrible. Our sins may involve not only ourselves but also our children and all related to us in any intimate way. It is noteworthy that God's judgment upon an Israelite who refused to obey His commands was also severe and included all that person's children and possessions. (See Numbers 16:25-33; Joshua 7:20-26.)

We learn much from Jericho's fall. As we have seen, the terrible price of sin is illustrated by God's using the Hebrews to utterly destroy the city. We have seen examples of the awful penalty paid by cities and countries for complicity in evil and complacency about it. In Nazi Germany frightful deeds of terror and torture were carried out by agents of the state. Millions of people were shot, mutilated, starved, gassed, and worked to death in labor and concentration camps. These crimes were committed "legally" with the express approval of government agents. Citizens were unwilling to do anything about this, or were uncaring or willfully ignorant. Later, death rained on them from bombers in their skies. Siege guns blew apart their homes and streets, and many cities were destroyed without mercy. This has ever been the result of persistent, blatant, and unrepentant sin. So Jericho was destroyed.

Throughout the whole narrative of the book of Joshua we are impressed constantly by Joshua's complete dependence upon God and obedience to Him. Sometimes he sought clarification of God's will in certain circumstances, but he never questioned it when it was revealed to him. He did what God commanded without qualification, quibbling, or complaint. He must have been a very decisive appearing leader—one everyone could see was honest and earnest. He expected others would follow God's commands as fully and as promptly as he. Moses sometimes questioned God, sometimes complained; Elijah became frightened and ran away to the wilderness; but Joshua continued always firm, faithful, and fully committed to God.

THE HORRORS OF WAR

The Vietnam War Memorial in Washington, D. C., is only the latest reminder that war is supremely costly. Americans have traditionally placed high value on human life. War memorials are only tokens of the national grief we sense when lives are lost in preserving freedom and protecting human rights.

Surely Israel too was shocked and grieved at the carnage that resulted from the many battles fought in the conquest of Canaan. They were waging battle in obedience to the command of God. The Hebrew warriors were agents of divine retribution upon those whose cup of iniquity had overflowed.

God does not delight in destruction, nor do His children, but His perfect justice requires the punishment of unrepentant and unforgiven sinners. In Joshua's day, divine punishment often came swiftly and surely in horrible military conflict. In the Christian age, most spiritual penalties seem to be deferred until the "end times." But though delayed, they must surely come.

—R. W. B.

Conclusion

A. Two Examples of Faith

In the book of Hebrews two incidents from the story of Jericho are included as examples of faith. Hebrews 11:30 tells us, "By faith the walls of Jericho fell down, after they were compassed about seven days." Also, Hebrews 11:31 says, "By faith the harlot Rahab perished not with them that believed not, when she had received the spies with peace." Both these situations reveal some valid and vital considerations in relation to faith and obedience.

The marching around Jericho's walls in silence, except for the sounding of the rams' horns, was commanded by God. The seven circuits on the seventh day and the great shout were also required. Then the walls fell as promised and the victory was secured. The walls fell "by faith" because there was no evident cause except God's action to make them fall just when the Hebrews were there, ready to attack. But it seems certain that the Hebrews' conformity to the command to march around was also essential. Theirs was a faith that obeyed a positive injunction given as a condition for the conquest. It was an obedient faith that achieved.

In the case of Rahab, she believed the spies when they said they would spare her and all her family if she would hang a scarlet cord out of her window at the time the city fell. We may be sure she did this, for Joshua sent the same spies she had saved to find and rescue her. In the midst of all the tumult and terror of the sacking of the city, they evidently found the scarlet cord as a sure sign they had the right house. So she was rescued (Joshua 6:22-25). Rahab's faith in their promise to her was proved by her conformity to their requirement that the cord be displayed. Her faith was evidenced by her actions, especially by that one act that was the outward sign of trust.

Again and again in Scripture, faith in God is confirmed by obedience to His command.

Adam and Eve's trust in God was to be shown by their not eating of the fruit of "the tree in the midst of the garden" (Genesis 3:3). Abraham's faith was validated by his readiness to offer Isaac as a sacrifice (Hebrews 11:17-19). By faith Naaman, the Syrian, dipped himself seven times in the river Jordan so his leprosy could be cleansed (2 Kings 5:1-14). It was necessary for the Israelites to apply the blood of a lamb to the lintels and doorposts of their houses so the "destroyer of the firstborn" would pass over them in Egypt (Hebrews 11:28).

Thus faith and obedience are ever linked. If we believe in Christ, we will respond to His commands in the way Joshua and these others responded to what was required of them. Only then will the victory be ours.

B. Prayer

Our God, we are thankful for the example of obedient faith Joshua presents to us. We are grateful for his unquestioning conformity to every command and his dedicated constancy in leading the people of Israel through all the conflicts they faced in Canaan. Dear Lord, forgive us for our frequent doubts and fears, our hesitancy to accept the daily challenge of our spiritual struggles with evil. Help us to believe we can overcome citadels of sin through the same unyielding devotion and unconquerable trust Joshua so powerfully manifested.

Give us, Father, a fearless faith, a dauntless dedication, and a continued conformity to Your will. May we be vigorous in our obedience that we may be victorious in reaching our objectives for our Lord. In Jesus' name, amen.

C. Thought to Remember

No results for God are achieved without obedience to Him.

Home Daily Bible Readings

Monday, June 5—The Circumcision of Israel (Joshua 5:2-9)

Tuesday, June 6—All Males Shall Be Circumcised (Genesis 17:9-14)

Wednesday, June 7—Passover Observed and a Messenger Appears (Joshua 5:10-15)

Thursday, June 8—The Song of Moses (Exodus 15:1-18)

Friday, June 9—The Lord Gives Joshua Instructions (Joshua 6:1-5)

Saturday, June 10—Joshua Gives Instructions (Joshua 6:6-10)

Sunday, June 11—Israel Circles Around Jericho (Joshua 6:11-21)

Learning by Doing

This page contains an alternate lesson plan emphasizing learning activities. Classes desiring such student involvement will find these suggestions helpful.

Learning Goals

This lesson should help a student:

1. Identify the main points of the fall of Jericho.

2. Determine in practical terms what obeying the Lord means.

3. Develop a personal strategy for obeying God.

Into the Lesson

Reproduce for each student the word puzzle below. Ask them to work individually or in pairs to find a key word in today's lesson.

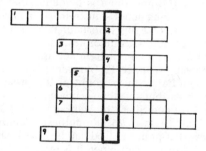

1. The first city Israel attacked in Canaan (Joshua 6:1).

2. What the priests were to do with the trumpets (v. 4).

3. Number of priests with trumpets (v. 4).

4. The company circled the city for seven of these (vv. 3, 4).

5. No noise was allowed to be made with this for six days (v. 10).

6. These men led the procession around the city (vv. 7, 9, 13).

7. The time Israel rose to march on the seventh day (v. 15).

8. What would happen to any man who would rebuild this city (v. 26).

9. Rahab and all in her _____ were spared (v. 22).

Answers: 1. Jericho. 2. blow. 3. seven. 4. days. 5. voice. 6. armed. 7. dawning. 8. cursed. 9. house.

Point out the word *obedience* formed in the heavily outlined squares. Say, "Obedience is at the center of our Christian walk. Sometimes obedience means doing things that seem ridiculous to those who are skeptics. Today's lesson looks at one such occasion in Israel's history."

Into the Word

Divide your class into groups of six. Assign one of the following projects to each group. Have each group select a leader.

Project One

Prepare a script for a radio newscast from Jericho. The newscast should be based on Joshua 6:12-14, and may have reports from those who heard Joshua 6:1-11. The final script should include a live report of the events of the seventh day of marching (Joshua 6:15-21).

Project Two

Prepare a diary entry for Rahab written on the evening after verse 25 is completed. Use Joshua 2:1-21 and Joshua 6:12-25.

Allow twenty-five minutes for these projects. Then ask the leader from each group to present his or her group's project to the class.

Into Life

Help your class members to recognize the importance of obeying God's commands. Israel began her life in the promised land committed to doing what God asked of them. But very soon disobedience occurred, and the nation suffered (Joshua 7). Like Israel, we too are tempted to disobey God. Encourage the students to focus on these thoughts as they discuss questions 1 and 2 below in the same groups they were in during their projects. Each student then is to answer questions 3 and 4 privately. These questions are included in the student book.

1. According to Deuteronomy 28:58-62, Joshua 5:6, Judges 6:10, Galatians 5:1-7, and 2 Thessalonians 3:14, what is the standard by which obedience to God is measured?

2. What truths are recorded in Galatians 5:13, 1 Peter 2:16, and 1 John 2:1 that should help us obey God? What other Scriptures are helpful in developing our obedience to Him?

3. By obeying God we demonstrate our love and appreciation to Him for what He has done for us. What areas have you struggled with most in obeying God in the past six months?

4. How can you become obedient to God in these areas? Write a personal strategy:

   a. Things I need to remember from His Word;

   b. Attitudes I need to develop or maintain;

   c. Habits I need to develop.

Close by having the students pray for strength to accomplish their plan.

Let's Talk It Over

*The questions on this page are designed to encourage review of the lesson
Scriptures and to promote discussion of the lesson by the class. The answers
provided are only discussion starters. Let your class talk it over from there.*

1. The lesson writer notes that one of the most difficult aspects of obeying God's instructions regarding the marches around Jericho must have been the maintaining of silence. How is the maintaining of appropriate silence an area of difficult obedience today?

James gives us this counsel: "Everyone should be quick to listen, slow to speak and slow to become angry" (James 1:19, *New International Version*). We tend to turn this around, so that in our eagerness to speak we often fail to hear what the other person has to say. Many misunderstandings and conflicts arise because of this human tendency. James speaks later about how a Christian needs to "keep a tight rein on his tongue" (James 1:26, *New International Version*) and this indicates how we must be willing to work to achieve obedience in this matter. Also, if it is vital for us to practice silence in order to hear what our fellow human beings are saying, it is even more important to heed Psalm 46:10: "Be still, and know that I am God." Obedience to this command has both public and private aspects. In our public worship the habit of conversing during the prelude and whispering during the remainder of the service hinders our ability to hear what God has to say to us. And in our private lives the piling up of activities in a breathtaking schedule leaves us little or no time to be silent before God with an open Bible and a bowed head.

2. We may have some difficulty understanding why God ordered the total destruction of Jericho, but we can see in it the importance of our dealing drastically with anything in our lives that can corrupt us. What are some drastic actions we may have to take to maintain our spiritual well-being?

Jesus spoke of ridding ourselves of an offending eye or hand if it causes us to sin (Matthew 5:27-30). But it is clear that we are not actually to mutilate ourselves, nor are we to physically assault people who may tempt us to sin. But we may have to act decisively and severely to cut off our association with a friend who is endeavoring to influence us toward ungodliness. It may be necessary for us to resign from a job if our superiors or fellow employees are attempting to corrupt our thinking. Our reading habits, television-watching, or selection of music may require drastic revision if we perceive that they are sowing the seeds of thorns (Mark 4:18, 19) in our minds.

3. Is there a kind of shout that Christians can utilize to claim victories in the Lord's service? If so, what kind of shout is it?

The evangelist Billy Sunday once remarked that Christians need to get the groans out of their prayers and replace them with shouts of praise. We are to offer to God the sacrifice of praise (Hebrews 13:15), and there is evidence that such praise can bring about some remarkable results. In the time of King Jehoshaphat an invading army of Moabites, Ammonites, and others was routed when Judah relied on nothing more than the power of praise (2 Chronicles 20). Much more familiar is the account of the prison-destroying earthquake that occurred in Philippi when Paul and Silas "prayed, and sang praises unto God" (Acts 16:25). From these examples it appears that praise to God can be a particularly powerful instrument when it is offered by a believer who is demonstrating faith in the midst of trial. God is not likely to make walls crumble before us or send a violent earthquake to deliver us, but when we offer Him praise instead of complaints, He may work some appropriate marvels in our situation.

4. Jesus once raised the question, "When the Son of man cometh, shall he find faith on the earth?" (Luke 18:8). Viewing faith in its inseparable connection with obedience, we can see that Jesus' question is applicable today. How is this so?

A statement that has appeared in church newsletters is appropriate here: "A faith that won't take you to church won't take you to heaven." While the New Testament does not contain an explicit, positive command regarding church attendance, it is undeniable that in order to fulfill the obligation to grow spiritually, to edify fellow Christians, and to take a proper place of service, a Christian must regularly assemble with fellow believers for study and worship. The irregular church attendance of vast numbers of church members is a form of disobedience and demonstrates a lack of faith.

Settlement of the Promised Land

LESSON SCRIPTURE: Joshua 18:1-10; 21:43—22:6.

PRINTED TEXT: Joshua 21:43—22:6.

Joshua 21:43-45

43 And the Lord gave unto Israel all the land which he sware to give unto their fathers; and they possessed it, and dwelt therein.

44 And the Lord gave them rest round about, according to all that he sware unto their fathers: and there stood not a man of all their enemies before them; the Lord delivered all their enemies into their hand.

45 There failed not aught of any good thing which the Lord had spoken unto the house of Israel; all came to pass.

Joshua 22:1-6

1 Then Joshua called the Reubenites, and the Gadites, and the half tribe of Manasseh,

2 And said unto them, Ye have kept all that Moses the servant of the Lord commanded you, and have obeyed my voice in all that I commanded you:

3 Ye have not left your brethren these many days unto this day, but have kept the charge of the commandment of the Lord your God.

4 And now the Lord your God hath given rest unto your brethren, as he promised them: therefore now return ye, and get you unto your tents, and unto the land of your possession, which Moses the servant of the Lord gave you on the other side Jordan.

5 But take diligent heed to do the commandment and the law, which Moses the servant of the Lord charged you, to love the Lord your God, and to walk in all his ways, and to keep his commandments, and to cleave unto him, and to serve him with all your heart and with all your soul.

6 So Joshua blessed them, and sent them away: and they went unto their tents.

GOLDEN TEXT: The Lord gave unto Israel all the land which he sware to give unto their fathers; and they possessed it, and dwelt therein.—Joshua 21:43.

Conquest and Challenge
Unit 1: Joshua—A Time of Conquest and Settlement (Lessons 1-4)

Lesson Aims

After this lesson students should be able to:

1. Understand that Israel conquered Canaan through obedient faith in God.

2. See the value of mutual trust in all human relations.

3. Keep the promises they make.

Lesson Outline

INTRODUCTION

I. THE CONQUEST COMPLETED (Joshua 21:43-45)
  The Reward of Rest
  Promises to Keep

II. MUTUAL PROMISES KEPT (Joshua 22:1-4)

III. PARTING ADMONITIONS (Joshua 22:5, 6)

CONCLUSION
  A. The Fruitage of Faithfulness
  B. Prayer
  C. Thought to Remember

Visual 3 will be helpful when you consider verse 45 and the Into the Lesson section of Learning by Doing. It is shown on page 365.

Introduction

The Lord had promised Israel the land of Canaan and had said they would make it their own. Under Moses' leadership they were led from Egypt to the southern border of Canaan, but were too frightened to enter it and engage in conflict with its inhabitants. As a consequence, that entire generation, except for Joshua and Caleb, were sentenced to wilderness wanderings until they died. The new generation did enter the land from the east under Joshua's dedicated leadership.

Just as their fathers had feared, there were severe conflicts and battles. But, beginning with Jericho, they found that with God's help they were constantly victorious whenever they were faithful to Him. Thus encouraged and empowered, they subdued the whole area, with few exceptions.

Many spritual parallels may be found to this situation and in our experience of developing our Christian character. It is true, in the words of 1 Corinthians 1:2, that we are "sanctified in Christ Jesus, called to be saints." We are *meant* to be devoted to the doing of God's will in Christ and are promised God's help in becoming increasingly like our Savior. But Christian character is not granted us apart from struggle and effort. This is why we have such calls as these in the apostolic writings: "Stand firm in your faith, be courageous, be strong" (1 Corinthians 16:13, *Revised Standard Version*); "fight the good fight of faith" (1 Timothy 6:12); "rid yourselves of all malice" (1 Peter 2:1, *New International Version*).

God wants us to become mature in Christ. He is "able to make all grace abound" toward us (2 Corinthians 9:8). He is "able to do exceeding abundantly above all we ask or think" (Ephesians 3:20), and is able to "comfort" our hearts and establish us "in every good word and work" (2 Thessalonians 2:17). God *can* do all this and much more. He *wants* to do all this and *will* do all this for us, His children. He wanted and promised to give Canaan to the Hebrews, but would not do so apart from their faithful submission to Him and a willingness to face opposition and conflict. So it is with us. In his hymn "Am I a Soldier of the Cross?" Isaac Watts expressed this thought as follows:

> Must I be carried to the skies
>   On flow'ry beds of ease,
> While others fought to win the prize,
>   And sailed thru bloody seas?
>
> Are there no foes for me to face?
>   Must I not stem the flood?
> Is this vile world a friend to grace,
>   To help me on to God?
>
> Sure I must fight if I would reign;
>   Increase my courage, Lord;
> I'll bear the toil, endure the pain,
>   Supported by Thy word.

I. The Conquest Completed (Joshua 21:43-45)

43. And the Lord gave unto Israel all the land which he sware to give unto their fathers; and they possessed it, and dwelt therein.

Verses 43-45 contain a general summary of the success the Hebrews achieved in occupying Canaan. God had given all this territory to them as their dwelling place. As we have seen, this did not mean it was theirs apart from the battles and struggles required to displace those already in the land. It is true the Israelites *possessed it, and dwelt therein,* but that does not mean every bit of the area was controlled completely by them. However, they did attain a dominant position so that the area was now settled by them and much of it was secure and peaceful.

44. And the Lord gave them rest round about, according to all that he sware unto their fathers: and there stood not a man of all their enemies before them; the Lord delivered all their enemies into their hand.

The great battles were fought and all the major areas were conquered. Israel had been able to defeat all the forces brought against them. None of their enemies had been able to resist them in conflict. Apparently some of the Canaanite people had fled to secluded places in the mountains or to some walled cities not strategic in location or important in size. We later learn that not all the groups from every people in the entire area had been eliminated (see Judges 1:27-34). But they no longer posed any threat to Israel at that time, so the people were given *rest round about.*

Judges 3:1-4 suggests that this partial subjugation of the inhabitants of Canaan was permitted by God so that the Israelites might be tested to see if they would continue to be obedient to Him. It is also indicated that conflict with these pagan peoples would give opportunity for the new generation of Hebrews to learn the technique of warfare. Of course, this happened years after the time of the events recorded in our lesson text. However, it is well to be aware of this so we may see the optimistic evaluation presented here in a historical perspective. A psalm written later makes this conclusion: "They did not destroy the nations, concerning whom the Lord commanded them: but were mingled among the heathen, and learned their works.... Therefore was the wrath of the Lord kindled against his people, insomuch that he abhorred his own inheritance" (Psalm 106:34, 35, 40).

THE REWARD OF REST

Rest is a gift easily taken for granted. But think of the relief and comfort of sitting in an easy chair, or stretching out on a couch after a long period of sustained exertion. What a blessing! In His grand design God has provided that our bodies, minds, and spirits can be refreshed and renewed by rest and leisure.

Israel was a weary nation. After forty years of backpacking in circles through the desert, they were required to conquer Canaan by force, facing new enemies almost daily. Battle fatigue must have set in. The promise of *rest* was an important feature of the divine covenant that kept them faithful and spurred them on to victory. What a blessed relief it would be to finally have a permanent home, unthreatened by Pharaohs, plagues, or pagans!

The rest for "New Israel," the church, is even better! Jesus invites us, "Come unto me ... and I will give you rest" (Matthew 11:28). "Anyone

How to Say It

ACHAN.   *A*-kan.
ARNON.   *Ar*-non.
CHINNERETH.   *Kin*-e-reth or *Chin*-ne-reth.
GADITES.   *Gad*-ites.
GILEAD.   *Gil*-e-ud.
JABBOK.   *Jab*-ok.
JEBUSITES.   *Jeb*-yuh-sites.
MANASSEH.   Muh-*nas*-uh.
REUBENITES.   *Roo*-ben-ites.
SHILOH.   *Shy*-lo.

who enters God's rest also rests from his own work.... Let us, therefore, make every effort to enter that rest" (Hebrews 4:10, 11, *New International Version*).   —R. W. B.

45. There failed not aught of any good thing which the Lord had spoken unto the house of Israel; all came to pass.

God had promised to bring His people to a good land and He had done so. He had said He would make their enemies afraid of them and would help them conquer the territory. He had stopped the Jordan, cast down Jericho's walls, helped them stamp out any disobedience (such as Achan's, Joshua 7), and overcome all the military forces raised against them. Thus all God's promises came true for them, His presence blessed them, His power strengthened them, and His rewards gladdened their lives.

Certainly this is an example to us. The Bible is full of God's promises, and as Christians we should be especially aware of the promises Jesus made. If we gather in His name (in His Spirit and for His glory), He has pledged to be with us (Matthew 18:20). If we scatter or go among other nations, peoples, or ethnic groups to make them His disciples, He has assured us He will be with us then also (Matthew 28:19, 20). We may well believe that we, as well as His apostles, have been given His bequest of peace, so we may have untroubled hearts (John 14:27). He has said that He gives us eternal life, that we shall never perish, and that no one shall take us out of His or His Father's hand (John 10:28, 29).

God promised His earthly people victories in military struggles and over physical enemies. We are promised nobler, higher dominance over spiritual foes. "(For the weapons of our warfare are not carnal, but mighty through God to the pulling down of strongholds;) casting down imaginations, and every high thing that exalteth itself against the knowledge of God, and bringing into captivity every thought to the obedience of Christ" (2 Corinthians 10:4, 5).

PROMISES TO KEEP

A memorable line from Robert Frost's *Stopping by Woods on a Snowy Evening* is,

I have miles to go before I sleep. . . .
And promises to keep.

Frost is lamenting the busy-ness and business of life that leaves little time for simply enjoying the wonders and beauty of God's creation. But he would forego the delight of lingering longer in an idyllic scene for quiet meditation, so that those who trusted his promises would not be disappointed.

Godly people keep their promises. We know such faithfulness is godlike, for "not one of all the Lord's good promises . . . failed; every one was fulfilled" (Joshua 21:45, *New International Version*). Israel learned that they could count on Jehovah to keep His word. Our own blessed assurance is rooted in our conviction that God is reliable and trustworthy. We share Paul's confidence which he expressed in these words to Timothy "I know whom I have believed, and am persuaded that he is able to keep that which I have committed unto him against that day" (2 Timothy 1:12).

God will keep all of His good promises to us, but we must also keep all of our promises to Him.   —R. W. B.

II. Mutual Promises Kept
(Joshua 22:1-4)

1. Then Joshua called the Reubenites, and the Gadites, and the half tribe of Manasseh.

This meeting between Joshua and the tribes mentioned took place after the majority of Canaan was controlled by Israel, and the land was divided among the tribes.

2. And said unto them, Ye have kept all that Moses the servant of the Lord commanded you, and have obeyed my voice in all that I commanded you.

All that Moses . . . commanded you. This is a reference to an agreement Moses had made with the tribes of Reuben and Gad not long before his death, just prior to Israel's crossing of the Jordan. These two tribes were interested in raising cattle and considered the land east of the Jordan ideal for their purposes. Therefore they had asked for their portions of the promised land to be given them in this area. Moses had pointed out how unfair it was for them to settle where they were while the majority of the tribes were going to have to fight for the area west of Jordan. They had agreed that their able-bodied fighting men would join the armed forces of Israel until all the land was subjugated. Then they would return to their possessions across Jordan. This is

recorded in Numbers 32:1-33. In verse 33 we learn that "half the tribe of Manasseh" was also included in this arrangement. The verse we are now considering is part of a testimony to their faithfulness in discharging, under Joshua's leadership, the obligations they had assumed while Moses was still living.

3. Ye have not left your brethren these many days unto this day, but have kept the charge of the commandment of the Lord your God.

From this it is apparent that these men had not even left their fellow fighters for even brief returns home during the lulls in the struggle to occupy the promised land. However much they may have wanted to see "how things were going" with their new possessions, they had not done so. Their constancy of purpose and dedication were now being recognized and praised.

The commandment of the Lord. The directives Moses had given them were not belittled or minimized. No one said, "This is only the opinion of a frail old man. We have our own affairs to look after, our own understanding of our duties. We cannot be bound by his counsels." Rather, they seem to have agreed with Joshua's evaluation of what their reactions to Moses' pronouncements should be. They had received a charge from God and they had regarded their conformity to it as not only a patriotic but a spiritual responsibility. So we should feel that apostolic injunctions recorded in the New Testament are not just "devout opinions" for us, but divine obligations.

4. And now the Lord your God hath given rest unto your brethren, as he promised them: therefore now return ye, and get you unto your tents, and unto the land of your possession, which Moses the servant of the Lord gave you on the other side Jordan.

Joshua indicated that the time had now come when the men from the east side of Jordan could return to their land holdings. They had been faithful to their promise to help with the conquest, and it also was important that they be discharged when that had been accomplished. Everything had gone well because the pledges of both parties had been kept.

The tribe of Reuben occupied the land directly east of the Dead Sea from the river Arnon north to a few miles above the northern end of the Dead Sea. The tribe of Gad had gained the land northward and east of Jordan to somewhat above the Jabbok river. The half tribe of Manasseh occupied the territory north and east of Jordan to somewhere in the vicinity of the southeast edge of the Sea of Galilee (then usually called "Chinnereth").

III. Parting Admonitions
(Joshua 22:5, 6)

5. But take diligent heed to do the commandment and the law, which Moses the servant of the Lord charged you, to love the Lord your God, and to walk in all his ways, and to keep his commandments, and to cleave unto him, and to serve him with all your heart and with all your soul.

The men of the tribes of Reuben, Gad, and Manasseh had diligently followed Joshua and had joined with their fellow Hebrews in the hard fighting for Palestine. As they now prepared to return to their new home on the east side of Jordan, Joshua gave them these words of counsel. He urged them not only to obey God, but to *love* Him. They were not to conform to His law out of a slavish fear, but out of sincere affection. God's way is not only right, but is full of beauty, grace, and gladness. His commands are not meant to confine or diminish us, but to liberate and fulfill our lives.

Joshua further urged these men to *serve* the Lord and to *cleave unto him. Today's English Version* renders *cleave unto him* as "be faithful to him," while the *New International Version* translates it, "hold fast to him." Joshua was urging more than obedience to God's commands. He was exhorting them to be aware of God's constant presence in their lives and to cherish His presence. It is possible to obey an order without feeling any affection for the one issuing the directive. Indeed, one may have negative feelings toward the one issuing a command and may obey sullenly and reluctantly. In contrast to these responses, Joshua urged upon these men a devotion to God based on a desire to please Him, because He is One who is worthy to be loved and trusted.

Joshua urged them to serve God with all their *heart* and *soul*. That is, their service was not to be halfhearted or partial. It is possible to engage in worship outwardly, but to be far from a devotional spirit within. In condemning the religious leaders of His day, Jesus applied to them words found in Isaiah 29:13: "You hypocrites! Isaiah was right when he prophesied about you: 'These people honor me with their lips, but their hearts are far from me'" (Matthew 15:7, 8, *New International Version*).

We all have experienced the "wandering" of our minds during worship services. While seeming to be listening to a sermon, or bowing in prayer, or singing a hymn, we may in reality be wondering about a family problem, a business decision, or a recreational project. We need to make earnest efforts to be really "present"

during worship. It is possible to do good by helping someone in need, or by writing a check for a mission or an orphanage, and still have a much less compassionate spirit than we should have. Surely such worship and benevolent works are less than pleasing to our Heavenly Father. Wholehearted submission and service are what God desires and were what Joshua urged upon his departing brethren. The thrust of one stanza of a hymn by that deeply spiritual British woman, Frances R. Havergal, catches the spirit of Joshua's ideal:

> True-hearted, whole-hearted, fullest allegiance
> Yielding henceforth to our glorious King;
> Valiant endeavor and loving obedience,
> Freely and joyously now would we bring.

6. So Joshua blessed them, and sent them away: and they went unto their tents.

The tribes from "beyond Jordan" were now dismissed. It was dangerous to be thus separated from the main body of Israel. Joshua sensed this and therefore was very urgent in his plea to them to be sincere and fervent in their dedication to God. It would not be too long before Joshua himself would be removed by death. It was all the more essential then that there be no decrease in their devotion to God. A common worship of the true God would be a bond holding all the tribes together in the years that lay ahead.

In fact, soon after these tribal warriors had gone back over Jordan into the land of Gilead, they erected a large altar just at the border between Canaan and Gilead, east of Jordan. This was done as a reminder to future generations that they were part of Israel and worshiped God just as did those on the west of Jordan. The other tribes became troubled by this altar, thinking it was designed to be a worship center in competition with the tabernacle at Shiloh. They brought their armies to Shiloh and then sent a delegation to the eastern tribes to express their displeasure and to demand an explanation for this apparent act of rebellion. However, the "separated" tribes convinced them that this was an altar of remembrance—not one for sacrifices. They wanted the children of the coming generations to realize

God fulfilled all of His **Promises** to Israel. **WILL HE DO LESS FOR US?**

visual 3

that the tribes located east of the Jordan were servants of Israel's God just as were those living to the west. This pacified all Israel and no conflict ensued. As Joshua rightly understood, a mutual dedication to the one true God was the real source of unity, blessing, and power for Israel.

Conclusion

A. The Fruitage of Faithfulness

From one point of view the book of Joshua is a long lesson on the basis, nature, and value of faithfulness to God. The foundation for all of Joshua's success as a leader of God's people was his absolute reliance upon the Lord. When he took Moses' place, as leader of Israel, he was replacing one who for forty years had guided, instructed, prayed for, and corrected the Israelites. Moses had led them from Egyptian slavery to the brink of Canaan. It was heroic task to rally, organize, and direct the Hebrews in a series of military campaigns in a hostile and strange country—the task Joshua assumed. But God encouraged Joshua and promised that He would bless and magnify. But God encouraged Joshua and promised that He would bless and magnify his leadership as he courageously confronted this great challenge.

Joshua's trust in God became manifest in the careful way he obeyed every command. No matter how strange God's orders were, such as the marching around Jericho, Joshua carried them out. Sometimes God required terrible punishment to be meted out, as in the case of Achan. At other times, utter annihilation of every living thing in a city was ordered—but whatever God commanded, Joshua did it.

Due to such absolute obedience, city after city was overthrown until Israel occupied virtually all of Canaan. Evil was put away whenever it appeared, and a large number of strong men developed who knew what it was to trust God's word, and that of Joshua, without faltering, fear, or question.

The case of the tribes of Reuben, Gad, and the half-tribe of Manasseh indicates that these men absolutely conformed to their promise to fight alongside all other Israelites until victory was won. When the time came for them to return to their homes, there was no hesitancy on Joshua's part in letting them leave as he had promised. Their mutual faithfulness to each other is a beautiful picture of the rewards of obedience and of conformity to the will of God. So the mutual trust of student and teacher is the basis on which learning is expedited. The faith of a congregation in its preacher and of a preacher in his people is a cause of spiritual growth. The faithfulness of wife to husband and of husband to wife is the stability of marriage. The children who believe in their parents and the parents who can trust their children experience a happy home, while employees who are reliable in their work, combined with employers who are fair and concerned, make for productive work places. In many ways the interrelated actions of Joshua and the tribes of Israel who settled east of Jordan exemplify a general principle of life. Continued devotion to God and conformity to His will blesses every human relationship.

B. Prayer

Our Father, we are challenged and inspired by the way Joshua was so obedient to Your directives over such a long time and under such critical conditions. Forgive us for the many times we quiver before smaller tasks. Lead us, Lord, to a renewed determination to be obedient to Your leading.

We are aware, Lord, that we face enemies to our souls and alien elements in life that must be defeated or eliminated before we can enjoy tranquillity of spirit or an opportunity to really grow in Christ. Give us courage to overcome and consistency of character to continue in our faith and to grow in our faithfulness.

We are grateful for the example of mutual trust and reliability shown by the tribes east of the Jordan and by Joshua. May we so work together for our Lord Jesus that His cause is advanced and the growth and victory of His church made more possible. In His name we pray. Amen.

C. Thought to Remember

Our victories for God that can be seen come only after His unseen victory in our hearts.

Home Daily Bible Readings

Monday, June 12—Joshua's Many Conquests (Joshua 11:16-23)
Tuesday, June 13—Joshua Told to Divide the Land (Joshua 13:1-7)
Wednesday, June 14—Beginning to Divide the Land (Joshua 13:32—14:5)
Thursday, June 15—Land Is Given to Caleb (Joshua 14:6-14)
Friday, June 16—The Allotment Ceremony at Shiloh (Joshua 18:1-10)
Saturday, June 17—The Cities of Refuge (Joshua 20:1-9)
Sunday, June 18—All the Land Is Divided (Joshua 21:41—22:6)

Learning by Doing

This page contains an alternate lesson plan emphasizing learning activities. Classes desiring such student involvement will find these suggestions helpful.

Learning Goals

This lesson should help the student:

1. Recall the basic details of Israel's conquest of the promised land.

2. Compare the fulfillment of God's promises to Israel with the fulfillment of His promises to Christians.

3. Express gratitude to God for a promise He has given.

Into the Lesson

As your class members arrive, give each a copy of the "Word Search" puzzle below. You will find the puzzle in the student book also.

Word Search

In the puzzle below are hidden twelve key words from Joshua 21:43—22:6. Read the text, then find the words. They may go up, down, forward, backward, or diagonally. The hidden words are *possessed, delivered, rest, spoken, obeyed, promised, love, walk, cleave, keep, serve, blessed.*

```
P N B E V R E S K W P
O R E S T H J Q A X O
K F O X Y A R L B F S
H A H M Z P K R L D S
N D E L I V E R E D E
E B O K W S G Y S A S
K L E G E P E J S N S
O E T F V B T D E M E
P E B D O Y M Z D A D
S Q R C L E A V E T A
P D O G I F C O B Q P
```

Allow ten minutes for this. Then go over the puzzle so all can locate the hidden words. Say, "These words are at the heart of today's account of Israel's conquest of the promised land."

Into the Word

Divide your class into groups of four. Assign one half of the groups instructions for Group 1, and the other half the directions for Group 2. Give paper to each group. Have the two sets of Scripture references already listed on the chalkboard.

Group 1. Read Joshua 21:45. Then search the following Scriptures and list the promises God made to the Israelites, which were fulfilled in the conquest of the promised land:

Genesis 12:1-3; 17:1-8; 35:11, 12; Exodus 23:20-33; 34:10-17; Deuteronomy 3:18-22; Joshua 1:3,4.

Write a summary of how God fulfilled these promises as needed in Joshua 21:45.

Group 2. Search the following Scriptures and list the promises made to Christians:

Matthew 28:20; John 3:16; 10:10; Acts 2:38; Romans 8:28; 2 Corinthians 4:16-18; Galatians 5:22, 23; James 1:5.

Allow groups to share their findings and conclusions. Move into the next section of the lesson by saying, "Let's see how we can receive the promises of God today!"

Into Life

Discuss the following questions:

1. How important were these promises to the Israelites?

2. What are the differences between the two lists of promises?

3. How are the promises to Christians better than the promises to the Israelites?

4. How does a person receive the promises given to the Christian?

Allow ten minutes for this discussion. Help your students to see the great promises they have been given in Christ. Those who have never accepted Christ should be challenged to do so as you share the answer to question 4.

Give each person a copy of the "Promise Poll" below to complete.

Promise Poll

1. I believe that God's promises are for me.
   Agree   Uncertain   Disagree
2. I have received God's promises.
   Agree   Uncertain   Disagree
3. I express thanks to God for His promises.
   Agree   Uncertain   Disagree
4. My life-style demonstrates my gratitude for God's promises
   Agree   Uncertain   Disagree
5. I want to thank God for this promise: ____
   _____.
   I will demonstrate my thankfulness for this promise by _____.

Close your session by repeating together Joshua 22:5.

Let's Talk It Over

*The questions on this page are designed to encourage review of the lesson
Scriptures and to promote discussion of the lesson by the class. The answers
provided are only discussion starters. Let your class talk it over from there.*

1. Israel's conquest of the land of Canaan illustrates the struggle that is involved in obtaining spiritual victories. Why is this a lesson that needs particular emphasis today?

The goals of comfort and convenience, so prominent in our approaches to work and entertainment, are also very much in evidence in the church. Comfortable pews and streamlined services are not in themselves objectionable, but they often seem to be the outward counterpart to an inward softness of commitment. Perhaps we feel that we have struggles enough in our jobs and our homes, and we view the church only as a place of calm and healing. But while we should find a measure of "rest unto our souls" (Matthew 11:29) in the church, the New Testament is clear that much effort and struggle is required in order to grow in Christ. Of course we can feel better about this struggle than about others we undertake. We sometimes complain that in spite of all our struggles in our employment or family life we never seem to get anywhere. But the sincere effort we put into our quest for spiritual victory is sure to bear fruit, since the Lord himself is working with us and in us. "Work out your own salvation with fear and trembling: for it is God which worketh in you both to will and to do of his good pleasure" (Philippians 2:12, 13).

2. Israel's gradual conquest of the land of Canaan illustrates the Christian's gradual progress in holiness and spiritual maturity. How does such a comparison provide encouragement for a young Christian?

Just as Israel was promised God's help in possessing the land of Canaan, we are promised the help of the indwelling Holy Spirit as we live our lives for Christ. Israel had to make the effort to "possess their possession," and we must work in harmony with the Spirit's guidance and power to achieve holiness of life. City by city, people by people, Israel progressed toward completion of their conquest. In our quest for holiness we may find it necessary to work on conquering one bad habit or attitude at a time. For example, we may aim first to eliminate a habit of speaking abusively to others, and then we may go on to grapple with the attitude that caused us to speak so. Or we may develop measures to rid ourselves of the habit of looking with lust or covetousness on what is not ours, and then may deal with the inner compulsion to so look. To gain such gradual conquests will be an encouragement to "go on to maturity" (Hebrews 6;1, *New International Version*).

3. What are some practical ways by which we can "cleave" to the Lord, or "hold tightly to him"?

To maintain the kind of closeness to the Lord those terms describe, we need to make good use of the Scriptures. Something more than a formal, cursory reading of a daily chapter is required. It is said of the spiritually blessed man of Psalm 1, "His delight is in the law of the Lord; and in his law doth he meditate day and night" (Psalm 1:2). We should aim at some approach to the Word that keeps us in regular contact with it throughout the day. Another way to "cleave" to the Lord is through prayer. To fulfill Paul's exhortation to pray continually (1 Thessalonians 5:17), we again need an approach tailored to our daily schedule that will allow us regular moments of communion with our Creator. Finally, it can be said that we cleave unto the Lord when we cleave unto His people. The fellowship we enjoy in attending regular services at our church may not be enough. Participation in a home Bible study group or cottage prayer group could be an exciting way of getting closer spiritually to man and to God.

4. If we are aware of an inclination toward being halfhearted and indifferent as far as spiritual matters are concerned, what can we do to stir ourselves up to wholehearted zeal?

If we are halfhearted about spiritual matters, it means that "the other half" of our heart is clinging to something else: material things, temporal pleasures, selfish pride, etc. That calls for repentance. We must cast out whatever we are allowing to rival God's complete rule in our hearts and restore ourselves to a wholehearted commitment to Him. We can gain a great deal of help in this endeavor through reading. Especially uplifting and challenging are biographies of outstanding Christians, including missionaries, musicians, businessmen, athletes, etc.

Joshua's Challenge to Israel

LESSON SCRIPTURE: Joshua 24.

PRINTED TEXT: Joshua 24:14-22, 26, 27.

Joshua 24:14-22, 26, 27

14 Now therefore fear the Lord, and serve him in sincerity and in truth; and put away the gods which your fathers served on the other side of the flood, and in Egypt; and serve ye the Lord.

15 And if it seem evil unto you to serve the Lord, choose you this day whom ye will serve; whether the gods which your fathers served that were on the other side of the flood, or the gods of the Amorites, in whose land ye dwell: but as for me and my house, we will serve the Lord.

16 And the people answered and said, God forbid that we should forsake the Lord, to serve other gods;

17 For the Lord our God, he it is that brought us up and our fathers out of the land of Egypt, from the house of bondage, and which did those great signs in our sight, and preserved us in all the way wherein we went, and among all the people through whom we passed:

18 And the Lord drave out from before us all the people, even the Amorites which dwelt in the land: therefore will we also serve the Lord; for he is our God.

19 And Joshua said unto the people, Ye cannot serve the Lord: for he is a holy God; he is a jealous God; he will not forgive your transgressions nor your sins.

20 If ye forsake the Lord, and serve strange gods, then he will turn and do you hurt, and consume you, after that he hath done you good.

21 And the people said unto Joshua, Nay; but we will serve the Lord.

22 And Joshua said unto the people, Ye are witnesses against yourselves that ye have chosen you the Lord, to serve him. And they said, We are witnesses.

. . . .

26 And Joshua wrote these words in the book of the law of God, and took a great stone, and set it up there under an oak, that was by the sanctuary of the Lord.

27 And Joshua said unto all the people, Behold, this stone shall be a witness unto us; for it hath heard all the words of the Lord which he spake unto us: it shall be therefore a witness unto you, lest ye deny your God.

GOLDEN TEXT: If it seem evil unto you to serve the Lord, choose you this day whom ye will serve; whether the gods which your fathers served that were on the other side of the flood, or the gods of the Amorites, in whose land ye dwell: but as for me and my house, we will serve the Lord.—Joshua 24:15.

Conquest and Challenge
Unit 1: Joshua–A Time of Conquest and Settlement (Lessons 1-4)

Lesson Aims

This lesson should help a student:
1. Understand the significance of the challenge Joshua presented to Israel.
2. Realize that a conscious choice to follow Christ must be made each day.
3. Reaffirm his loyalty to Jesus Christ.

Lesson Outline

INTRODUCTION
   A. Choosing Between Gods
   B. Lesson Background
  I. CONFRONTED WITH A CHOICE (Joshua 24:14, 15)
   Mixed Blessing
  II. CONSEQUENCES OF A CHOICE (Joshua 24:16-22)
  III. COMMEMORATION OF A CHOICE (Joshua 24:26, 27)
   Accountability
CONCLUSION
   A. Time of Decision
   B. Which Way Shall I Take?
   C. Prayer
   D. Thought to Remember

Visual 4 is designed for use with section B in the Conclusion of the lesson. The visual is shown on page 374.

Introduction

A. Choosing Between Gods

As the time for Joshua's death approached, he became increasingly concerned about the future of the people of Israel. Under his leadership they had obeyed God's directions explicitly, and they had progressed from one conquest to another. Now his presence would soon be gone, and they would face new problems without his counsel and guidance. Much of the promised land had been subdued and divided among the tribes, and the people had rest "from all their enemies round about" (Joshua 23:1). Joshua feared that in a more settled condition they would be inclined to forget their dependence on the Lord.

Remnants of the peoples they had dispossessed were still living in "pockets" in the land and in certain hill districts and isolated areas.

The various worship centers they had erected for their gods probably survived, and the Hebrews became aware of the nature and claims of these diverse deities. Joshua wanted them to confront this problem openly and to determine who would be the one they were going to worship. He certainly did not allow them to think they could just add these other gods as supplemental divinities to be adored along with Jehovah. No, a *choice* had to be made. If they were going to continue to serve the God who had led and blessed them during their days of travel and battle, then they must "put away" all others.

The gods that the Hebrews knew in their era are not competing with the true God for our devotion today. But we would be very naive if we thought there are no other gods we are tempted to serve today. For instance, we encounter the god of self-indulgence. We can spend much more than is really necessary on sleek and prestigious automobiles. We can build houses costing many thousands of dollars more than we need to spend because they are in elegant neighborhoods. Let us not forget that we follow a Savior who was born in a stable and had very few possessions, one who was "meek and lowly in heart," not proud or arrogant.

We can make a god of pleasure, or sports, or work. The list goes on. Yes, many diverse deities surround us in modern times, even though they do not wear a title as "gods." The warning of 1 John comes to us with the same force as Joshua's challenge to Israel—"Little children, keep yourselves from idols" (5:21).

B. Lesson Background

A number of years had passed since the people of Israel had settled down to peaceful living. Joshua felt that he was near death (Joshua 23:1, 14), so he called the people together at Shechem to hear his final message. He reviewed the history of their people from the time of Abraham, giving special emphasis to God's care through their journeys and through their conquest of Canaan (see Joshua 24:1-13). He then proceeded to lay before them a challenge and a choice.

I. Confronted With a Choice (Joshua 24:14, 15)

14. Now therefore fear the Lord, and serve him in sincerity and in truth: and put away the gods which your fathers served on the other side of the flood, and in Egypt; and serve ye the Lord.

Therefore looks back to the events recalled in verses 2-13. Because God had rescued and cared for His people, they ought to *fear the Lord, and* serve him, not with pretended worship, but *in sincerity and truth.* Mere outward posturing was not acceptable—neither to God nor to earnest believers such as Joshua. If truthfulness is important in one's speech and in one's relationships with other individuals, how much more is it essential in our approach to God?

The gods which your fathers served on the other side of the flood. The Hebrew word translated *flood* means a river, and in this case it refers to the Euphrates in Mesopotamia. At their home in Ur beside the Euphrates, the ancestors of Israel had worshiped idols (v. 2).

And in Egypt. Of course, worship was offered to a great many gods in Egypt. Some of the Israelites may have become worshipers of various "other gods" during the long years of slavery. There may have been a surviving reverence for these "old" divinities among some of the Hebrews. Joshua now urged them to give their complete commitment to the God who had given them this land they now occupied.

15. And if it seem evil unto you to serve the Lord, choose you this day whom ye will serve; whether the gods which your fathers served that were on the other side of the flood, or the gods of the Amorites, in whose land ye dwell: but as for me and my house, we will serve the Lord.

If it seem evil . . . to serve the Lord. Evidently some of the people worshiped Jehovah, but, for added insurance, they worshiped these other gods too. Joshua was telling them they couldn't do both. They had to choose between the two.

The Amorites, in whose land ye dwell. The Amorites were one of the "nations" that lived in Canaan before Israel came (v. 11). Rather than repeat the entire list, Joshua used the name of this one group to represent them all.

We will serve the Lord. Joshua's staunch stand for God and His way showed the uncompromising, zealous spirit of the intrepid leader of Israel. He spoke for all those within his immediate range of influence and responsibility. Whatever anyone else did, he knew where he and those close to him stood. What a challenge and inspiration he was to those he led in that day—

and what an example of faith and fervor he sets for us today! Joshua's decisiveness should speak to us about our own Christian stance. So Paul urged, "Watch ye, stand fast in the faith" (1 Corinthians 16:13); "Stand fast therefore in . . . liberty" (Galatians 5:1); "Stand fast, and hold the traditions which ye have been taught" (2 Thessalonians 2:15). As Charles Wesley wrote,

> Stand then in His great might,
>   With all His strength endued,
> And take, to arm you for the fight,
>   The panoply of God;
> That having all things done,
>   And all your conflicts past,
> Ye may o'ercome through Christ alone,
>   And stand entire at last.

MIXED BLESSING

An estimated seventy-five percent of college freshmen have no career goal, and thus are not prepared to select an academic major. That is not necessarily wrong or bad, but it is a fact. Later choice of careers and multiple changes of careers are typical in this age of unlimited options. One reason most of our ancestors decided at an earlier age what their life's work would be is that there were fewer alternatives.

We are indeed privileged to live in a time and place where opportunities abound. In the vocational realm, however, selecting a career from so many choices can be very difficult, even a burden that some people would rather avoid. *Choice* carries responsibilities.

The selection of a ruling authority in our lives carries with it grave implications. By choosing whom we will serve, we actually determine our spiritual destiny. That was the choice Joshua laid before the people of Israel. They had to come to grips with that most important decision of life, and so must we. By our daily decisions we reconfirm that choice. Joshua and Israel made the right choice: "We will serve the Lord!"
—R. W. B.

II. Consequences of a Choice
(Joshua 24:16-22)

16. And the people answered and said, God forbid that we should forsake the Lord, to serve other gods.

The people reacted with horror to the idea that they would turn from their devotion to the God who had been their deliverer and guide. The dimensions of their indebtedness to Him are seen in the next verse. This seems to suggest that they were aware of the importance of their continued reliance on the Lord. Some might say there is no need to stress how much we depend

on God to those who have a sense of devotion to
Him already. But it is vital to keep an awareness
of the reality of trust vividly before the Christian
community. It is so easy to become complacent
in our dedication, to take for granted that "we
all know and believe" certain things. But our
fervor can die down, our zeal can diminish, and
our commitment can waver. As Paul wrote in 1
Corinthians 10:12, "So, if you think you are
standing firm, be careful that you don't fall!"
(New International Version).

**17. For the Lord our God, he it is that
brought us up and our fathers out of the land of
Egypt, from the house of bondage, and which
did those great signs in our sight, and preserved us in all the way wherein we went, and
among all the people through whom we passed.**

A note of gratitude is sounded here for God's
deliverance and protection. To be rescued from
slavery to a powerful nation such as Egypt was
an almost unbelievable accomplishment. The
slaves had no economic power, no rights in law,
no way of securing military assistance. How
could a people so helpless, so controlled, so
lacking in structured organization, hope to be
freed from their bondage? Besides, their labor
was very important to numerous agricultural enterprises, to the construction of roads and buildings, and in the various activities of domestic
life in the homes of Egypt. The *land of Egypt*
was famous for its excellence in the areas of architecture, medicine, astronomy, and literature.
Its pyramids and palaces were the wonder of the
world, but to the enslaved Hebrews it had been
the house of bondage.

After Israel's initial liberation from Egypt,
God's protecting power and providential care
had been evidenced in two ways. They were
preserved . . . in all the way they went. That is,
they were helped to cross desert and arid areas,
to traverse rough, mountainous terrain and to
find water and fodder for their cattle during the
journey. Of course, their own nourishment was
provided by the manna God regularly sent.

They were also cared for *among all the people
through whom they passed.* Their dangers arose
not only from their physical environment, but
from the tribes whose areas they crossed. Sometimes these people were hostile and had to be
met in battle; sometimes they were only sullen
and threatening. Through all these situations
God had led them safely and surely.

**18. And the Lord drave out from before us all
the people, even the Amorites which dwelt in
the land: therefore will we also serve the Lord;
for he is our God.**

Even the Amorites. The Amorites are mentioned frequently as one of the most prominent

and most evil of the various peoples whom the
Hebrews dispossessed. In an unusual and significant prophetic passage in Genesis 15, Abraham was told by God that descendants of his
would be in bondage in a "land that is not
theirs" for four hundred years, but that they
would come again into Palestine. God explained
the reason for this lengthy time in this way: "the
iniquity of the Amorites is not yet full" ("the sin
of the Amorites has not yet reached its full measure." *New International Version*). (See Genesis
15:13-16.) This shows that the casting out of
these peoples was a judgment on their sin.

We note that later the sins connected with the
idolatry of the Amorites are especially mentioned. Of the wickedness of Ahab it is said, "He
did very abominably in following idols, according to all things as did the Amorites" (1 Kings
21:26). Of Manasseh it was charged, "(He) hath
done wickedly above all that the Amorites did,
which were before him, and hath made Judah
also to sin with his idols" (2 Kings 21:11).

**19. And Joshua said unto the people, Ye can-
not serve the Lord: for he is a holy God; he is a
jealous God; he will not forgive your transgressions nor your sins.**

Ye cannot serve the Lord. That is, you cannot
worship God if you continue to worship heathen
idols. This reminds us of Jesus' words in the
Sermon on the Mount: "Ye cannot serve God
and mammon" (Matthew 6:24). It is also in
keeping with Moses' words in Deuteronomy
6:13, 14, "Thou shalt fear the Lord thy God, and
serve him, and shalt swear by his name. Ye shall
not go after other gods, of the gods of the people
which are round about you." *He is a holy God.*
He is set apart, separated from all that is evil and
dedicated to all that is good. You cannot worship Him "in sincerity and in truth" unless you

are likewise set apart and dedicated (Leviticus 19:1, 2). *He is a jealous God.* He will not accept a part of your love while you distribute the rest of it among idols and worldly goods and sins. *He will not forgive your . . . sins.* Of course He will forgive them if you stop them and repent and pray for forgiveness. But He will not forgive your sins while you continue in them.

20. If ye forsake the Lord, and serve strange gods, then he will turn and do you hurt, and consume you, after that he hath done you good.

"If you forsake the Lord and worship foreign gods, he will turn and bring adversity upon you and, although he once brought you prosperity, he will make an end of you" *(The New English Bible).* We know that when Israel and Judah many years later, did indeed forsake God, He gave them into the hands of the Assyrians and Babylonians, their land was desolated, and their cities were burned.

21. And the people said unto Joshua, Nay; but we will serve the Lord.

Having heard a clear and stern statement of the situation they faced, the people strongly affirmed their dedication to Jehovah. They were willing to serve the God of their fathers. No matter what He asked, they would do it.

22. And Joshua said unto the people, Ye are witnesses against yourselves that ye have chosen you the Lord, to serve him. And they said, We are witnesses.

At first it seems rather strange that Joshua went to such lengths to encourage the people to pledge their allegiance to the Lord. Had not Joshua constantly told them what God wanted them to do, and had they not done it? Whether it was marching around Jericho's walls, or sparing Rahab and her kinfolk, or destroying Achan and his relatives, or totally destroying certain cities and certain things from others, they had been "followers" of God all the time.

This was true, but now Joshua was soon to die. He wanted the whole nation, while still together and while still looking to him, to make a commitment of continuing devotion to the true God. Because he would not be on hand to remind them of their promise, he said, *Ye are witnesses against yourselves.* That is, "Your words are duly noted, and if you should violate your solemn covenant, they will testify against you."

III. Commemoration of a Choice (Joshua 24:26, 27)

26. And Joshua wrote these words in the book of the law of God, and took a great stone, and set it up there under an oak, that was by the sanctuary of the Lord.

Joshua wrote these words. That is, he recorded what had just transpired in the renewal of the covenant at Shechem. Thus a written document would be kept as a witness against the people if ever they should be guilty of repudiating the covenant.

And took a great stone, and set it up. This was to be a memorial stone. Often a stone has been selected and set up, or a large, prominent rock has been designated, as a sign or token of some outstanding event in the history of a tribe or nation. We remember the stones placed to commemorate the crossing of the Jordan River (Joshua 4:20-22) and the stone altar erected as a sign of the membership of the tribes of Reuben, Gad, and Manasseh in Israel (Joshua 22:21-29). Still today well-to-do families set up stones in cemeteries as a means of perpetuating the names of deceased relatives.

By the sanctuary of the Lord. At this time the tabernacle was at Shiloh, so it does not seem that this is a reference to it. Many Bible scholars feel that the sanctuary at Shechem was the site where Abraham had worshiped God and where Jacob, also, had erected an altar.

27. And Joshua said unto all the people, Behold, this stone shall be a witness unto us; for it hath heard all the words of the Lord which he spake unto us: it shall be therefore a witness unto you, lest ye deny your God.

This stone shall be a witness. That is, this stone shall "stand for" the agreement you have made this day to be God's people and to worship Him alone. A great stone is a solid, enduring, visible reminder of the event it commemorates.

It hath heard all the words of the Lord. Of course, Joshua knew the stone couldn't "hear," literally, as we do. But he means to say, "This stone, having stood here when I delivered to you God's demands and requirements, will remind you continually of what was spoken before it." It would stand as a constant testimony to what they had pledged at this place. If they were faithful to their promises, it would be a consolation and an encouragement to them. If they were rebellious toward God, it would be a mute, constant witness against them.

ACCOUNTABILITY

In one episode of TV's *Newhart* show Stephanie, the generally selfish and irresponsible maid, breaks one too many promises to George, the usually easy-going, forgiving handyman. George confronts Stephanie with her broken promises and tells her he has decided that they can't be friends anymore. Not having taken their friendship seriously before, Stephanie is surprised to be held accountable for her careless commitments, and even more surprised that she is saddened by the broken relationship. Only when she demonstrates a truly penitent spirit does George forgive her and pledge restored friendship.

When vows are witnessed, accountability is implied. Joshua wanted Israel to know that God would hold them accountable for their pledge of allegiance at Shechem. Even the rocks had "heard" the covenant, the terms of agreement between God and His people. The large witness stone set up there would be a continuing reminder of Israel's accountability to God.

Accountability should keep Christians honest, faithful, and diligent. For indeed, "we must all appear before the judgment seat of Christ, that each one may receive what is due him for the things done while in the body, whether good or bad" (2 Corinthians 5:10, *New International Version*).   R. W. B.

Conclusion

A. Time of Decision

Joshua was an old man. Years earlier he had been among those who were slaves in Egypt. He had experienced the exodus, had crossed the Red Sea, and had been at Sinai when God had made His covenant with Israel. He had endured the hardships of the wilderness and had finally led his people across the Jordan into the land that God had promised them; and here again he had witnessed great victories that God had made possible. A man of deep faith, he had been a courageous leader. But now he knew that his days of leadership were near an end.

Was there anything else that Joshua could do for his people before that end came? Yes, there was one more thing, a matter of tremendous importance. He knew that the people were divided in their loyalties. He knew that they could not be partly the chosen people of God and partly pagans. He must challenge them to full commitment to the Lord.

visual 4

We are reminded of another challenge that is put to the uncommitted, to souls that are wavering at the point of decision: "Behold, now is the accepted time; behold, now is the day of salvation" (2 Corinthians 6:2). And again, "Today if ye will hear his voice, harden not your hearts" (Hebrews 3:7, 8). Obviously, no one will ever begin to walk with God unless he decides to do so. Before he laid down the reins of leadership, Joshua brought his people to this point of decision. As his final service in their behalf, he could have done nothing more significant.

B. Which Way Shall I Take?

Whether we realize it or not, every day we decide which direction our lives will take. As we step out of our doorway each morning, it is as if we were confronted with direction signs that would determine our destiny. *(Display visual 4 from the visuals packet. Point to the signs and talk a little about each as you do.)* We are tempted away from loyalty to God in many ways. Few of us decide deliberately to be unfaithful; we just drift into ways that turn us aside from our life in Christ Jesus. But when we stop to consider, one thing is certain. We cannot go in two directions at the same time. To follow any way other than the way of God is to take us away from Him. Which way shall I take? That is the question. And each of us *must* answer it decisively, or find himself drifting aimlessly into oblivion.

Teacher, point out on the signpost what people choose in the place of God, and indicate what the result of such choices must be—disappointment, disillusionment, even eternal doom. Stress that the decision to follow in the way of God must be made deliberately and thoughtfully. A person will not drift into that way. Joshua's challenge is still before us in the twentieth century: "Choose you this day whom ye will serve."

C. Prayer

Our Father, we are touched as we think of the long years of devoted service Joshua brought to his people. We are challenged by his unwavering obedience to every command he received and by his unquestioning willingness to walk in Your way. As we follow the leading of Jesus, may we be steadfast in resisting temptation, stalwart in witness, and undivided in loyalty. Grant us modesty in self-evaluation and pride in all that pertains to the victory of our Lord. In His name, amen.

D. Thought to Remember

The garb of Christian royalty,
Is the purple robe of loyalty.

Learning by Doing

This page contains an alternate lesson plan emphasizing learning activities. Classes desiring such student involvement will find these suggestions helpful.

Learning Goals

As a result of this lesson a student should:

1. List reasons why the Israelites could be expected to commit themselves to God.

2. Determine why it is wise to commit oneself to God.

3. Be motivated to accept Joshua's challenge of commitment to serve the Lord.

Into the Lesson

Display the following verse on a chalkboard, an overhead transparency, or a banner: "The fear of the Lord is the beginning of wisdom: and the knowledge of the Holy is understanding" (Proverbs 9:10). Ask the students to respond to the following questions. This activity should take no more than ten minutes.

1. What thoughts are brought to mind from this verse?

2. How does the fear of the Lord lead to wisdom?

3. How does the fear of the Lord lead to serving Him?

4. Why is this important for Christians?

Allow for a number of responses to be made to each question. Then say, "Some Christians seem to have a misunderstanding of what it means to fear the Lord. To fear Him means to reverence Him. As the children of Israel settled down to a peaceful life in their land, Joshua feared that they might forget their need for God. Thus, he called on them to renew their commitment to God. They were to fear and serve Him only. As we study today, let's look for our challenge to serve Him."

Into the Word

Joshua 24 is a dialogue between Joshua and the children of Israel. It is helpful to understand who is speaking to whom, so read the text aloud as a dialogue. Put the Scripture references on the chalkboard or on overhead to guide the reading.

Joshua (Teacher) (verses)	Israel (Class) (verses)
2-15	16-18
19, 20	21
22a	22b
23	24
27	

Next, divide the class into groups of six, and appoint a leader in each group. Give each student a copy of the questions below and have the groups work together to find the answers.

1. Why would it be wise for Israel to serve the Lord?

2. How is God described in this chapter?

3. What would be the penalty if Israel forsook God?

4. What did the people promise?

5. Why did Joshua set up a large stone at Shechem?

6. What was Joshua's purpose in speaking to Israel on this occasion?

Allow the groups twenty minutes to answer the questions; then bring them together in one group. (You may need to rearrange chairs in a circle or half-circle to facilitate discussion.) Ask this summarizing question: "What did you learn from this passage of Scripture?" Then ask, "How would you define *commitment?*" Then, "On the basis of the event described in this Scripture text, what kind of conduct may one have expected of Israel from that time forward?" Bring this section together by saying, "Commitment begins with an attitude of fear and reverence toward God. It issues in obedience to Him as we serve Him with our lives."

Into Life

Call the class's attention to the chalkboard, on which you have written this question: "What are the alternatives to living for the Lord?" Ask the group to brainstorm the question. Encourage students to call out their first impressions. Remember that during brainstorming, no attempt is made to evaluate suggestions. Write their suggestions on the chalkboard. Then brainstorm this question: "What has God done in our past that we should commit our service to Him?"

After the brainstorm, lead the students to write a "Challenge of Commitment" as they apply this lesson to their lives. They may use the sheet of paper used for the discussion questions, or you may give them another sheet. Ask them to write two or more paragraphs in which they state their desire to serve the Lord. They should also include reasons why they should serve the Lord and how they will share this decision with their "whole house."

Close with a prayer of commitment.

Let's Talk It Over

The questions on this page are designed to encourage review of the lesson Scriptures and to promote discussion of the lesson by the class. The answers provided are only discussion starters. Let your class talk it over from there.

1. Joshua seemed to be concerned that when the Israelites entered into a more settled existence, they would face the danger of forgetting God. Why does a relatively trouble-free life pose a similar danger to us?

It seems that we human beings often take the attitude that we will let God take care of the difficult things, while we can handle everything else. If we operate according to such a policy, and if the difficult things are relatively few, then we leave little room for dependence on God. Problems and painful experiences are therefore useful in reminding us of our need for God's wisdom and power. They also serve as occasions of learning and spiritual growth. The psalmist testified to this when he wrote, "It is good for me that I have been afflicted; that I might learn thy statutes" (Psalm 119:71). A practical aspect to this question involves our prayers. While it is a natural tendency for us to pray that our troubles and those of our friends be removed, we would be wiser to ask the Lord to teach us and mold our lives by means of those troubles.

2. Are there Christians whose interest in sports approaches the level of idolatry? How can we maintain a legitimate enjoyment of sporting events without allowing them to rival our wholehearted allegiance to God?

If people would keep track of the amount of time spent in attending sporting events, watching them on television, reading about them, or personally participating in them, and compare that record with the time spent in church attendance, Bible study, prayer, and Christian service, the results could be revealing. Another means of assessment would be to honestly measure the relative enthusiasm and delight exhibited in connection with sports and with spiritual activities. Many Christians would probably have to confess that their delight in athletic contests is significantly greater. These observations can remind us that we have a capacity for enthusiasm. The next step is to take inventory of all the aspects of our faith that merit enthusiasm. Then, if we sing enthusiastically, pray enthusiastically, witness enthusiastically, and serve enthusiastically, we should be able to transfer some of that time and energy expended on sports into more God-centered pursuits.

3. Should a Christian parent be able to say, "As for me and my house, we will serve the Lord"? Why or why not?

All Christian parents should aim at leading their children to become active Christians. Some parents tend to avoid this responsibility because they feel (or say they feel) that they should not unduly influence their children in such a personal matter. But in both Old and New Testaments believers are urged to bear a strong influence for godliness upon their children. Solomon advised parents to "train up a child in the way he should go: and when he is old, he will not depart from it" (Proverbs 22:6). Paul told fathers regarding their children to "bring them up in the nurture and admonition of the Lord" (Ephesians 6:4). So it is clear that the goal of a household united in worship of and service to the Lord is a worthy one. However, we recognize that salvation and discipleship are matters of individual choice. While it is quite proper for Christian parents to instruct and guide their children in the things of the Lord, it is important that the children be given room to make their own commitment to the Lord, to decide for themselves that they want to serve Him.

4. Could the stones of the church building serve a similar function as the memorial stone Joshua set up? What kinds of promises and pledges have these stones "heard"?

It might provide an incentive to renewed faithfulness to the Lord if we were to consider the words we have uttered within our church's walls. We could remember the moment we made our confession of faith in Jesus Christ, either prior to our being baptized, or when we united with our current home congregation. This remembrance could stir us up to a fresh effort to confess our Savior before our neighbors and fellow workers. As we look about at the interior of the church, we may recall the many times we have joined in the singing of hymns. Have we consistently lived up to such sentiments as "I am Thine, O Lord," "Have Thine own way, Lord," and "I will cling to the old rugged cross"? If we were married in the church we presently attend, we could think about the vows we uttered that day and ask ourselves whether or not we are faithfully fulfilling them.

Deliverance and Disobedience

LESSON SCRIPTURE: Judges 1, 2.

PRINTED TEXT: Judges 2:11-19.

Judges 2:11-19

11 And the children of Israel did evil in the sight of the Lord, and served Baalim:

12 And they forsook the Lord God of their fathers, which brought them out of the land of Egypt, and followed other gods, of the gods of the people that were round about them, and bowed themselves unto them, and provoked the Lord to anger.

13 And they forsook the Lord, and served Baal and Ashtaroth.

14 And the anger of the Lord was hot against Israel, and he delivered them into the hands of spoilers that spoiled them, and he sold them into the hands of their enemies round about, so that they could not any longer stand before their enemies.

15 Whithersoever they went out, the hand of the Lord was against them for evil, as the Lord had said, and as the Lord had sworn unto them: and they were greatly distressed.

16 Nevertheless the Lord raised up judges, which delivered them out of the hand of those that spoiled them.

17 And yet they would not hearken unto their judges, but they went a whoring after other gods, and bowed themselves unto them: they turned quickly out of the way which their fathers walked in, obeying the commandments of the Lord; but they did not so.

18 And when the Lord raised them up judges, then the Lord was with the judge, and delivered them out of the hand of their enemies all the days of the judge: for it repented the Lord because of their groanings by reason of them that oppressed them and vexed them.

19 And it came to pass, when the judge was dead, that they returned, and corrupted themselves more than their fathers, in following other gods to serve them, and to bow down unto them; they ceased not from their own doings, nor from their stubborn way.

GOLDEN TEXT: When the Lord raised them up judges, then the Lord was with the judge, and delivered them out of the hand of their enemies all the days of the judge.—Judges 2:18.

Lesson Aims

As a result of this lesson, students should:

1. Understand that the period of the judges was a time when the cycle of departure from God's way and of partial return to Him was repeated often by Israel.

2. Be able to identify the allurement of the worship of the Canaanite gods, and mention modern counterparts of that idol worship.

3. Rededicate themselves to the worship and service of the one, true, and living God only.

Lesson Outline

INTRODUCTION

I. ISRAEL'S APOSTASY (Judges 2:11-13)
   How Soon Will They Forget?

II. GOD'S ANGER AND ITS RESULTS (Judges 2:14, 15)

III. THE ANTIDOTE OF THE JUDGES (Judges 2:16-19)
   "When the Cat's Away...."

CONCLUSION

A. False Gods, Then and Now
B. Prayer
C. Thought to Remember

Display visual 5 from the visuals/learning resources packet. It correlates with the three main points of the lesson outline above. It is shown on the next page.

Introduction

In reality our lesson material today is an introduction to the book of Judges. Therefore it may be well to say something about the chronology of the book. The exact dates covered are difficult to determine, but we know the events began not too long after the death of Joshua and are depicted down to the period of Samuel. One way of arriving at an approximate date is through considering data found in the Bible itself.

One "outside" date is required for a beginning, and this is based on the period of Solomon. Practically all scholars, both liberal and conservative, agree that his reign would be dated about 974 B.C.

Taking this as our beginning point, we turn to 1 Kings 6:1, which reads, "And it came to pass in the four hundred and eightieth year after the children of Israel were come out of the land of Egypt, in the fourth year of Solomon's reign over Israel, in the month Zif, which is the second month, that he began to build the house of the Lord." If this was 970 B.C., then the exodus would be dated 1450 B.C. Because of archaeological evidence in Palestine, several modern scholars date the exodus at about 1250 B.C. This may well be modified as additional material is unearthed.

Thus the period of the judges began somewhere between 1400 and 1200 B.C. and lasted until around 1060 B.C. It will be seen that the later date (1250 B.C.) for the exodus seems to shorten the era severely.

We do not know just when Israel's decline began after Joshua, but it seems to have been distressingly soon after his death. In any case, it became a lengthy period covering scores of years. We shall find this a dark and ugly period but one in which shafts of faith and mercy penetrated the gloom like searchlights. It was indeed an era when "sin abounded" but when, in spite of everything, sometimes "grace did much more abound."

I. Israel's Apostasy
(Judges 2:11-13)

11. And the children of Israel did evil in the sight of the Lord, and served Baalim.

Evil in the sight of the Lord. The Israelites *did evil* in that they ceased to follow the faith and worship of the living God and began to worship the gods of the Canaanite peoples. Perhaps what they did was not wrong in the eyes of the people who surrounded them. The gods whose worship the Israelites adopted were those exalted by their neighbors, so they doubtless considered that the Hebrews finally were becoming sensible in their devotional exercises. It is likely the Israelites felt that they were doing the right thing in adopting more "acceptable modes of worship." However, what they were doing was evil in God's sight. They should have known this from the clear teachings of His commandments. We remember how earnestly Joshua, just before his death, had urged his hearers not to forget the Lord God. In fact, all the people vowed solemnly to be true to His way. (See last week's lesson.) But they failed to teach and exalt the way of the true God before their children, for it is said that "there arose another generation after them, which knew not the Lord" (Judges 2:10).

And served Baalim. "Baal" is a word that means "lord" or "master." Most often the word refers to the deities worshiped by the people

visual 5

who lived in and around Canaan. Each locality had a presiding deity, and he was known as "Baal." The Hebrew plural is made by the addition of "im" to a noun, so *Baalim* means Baals. Although each area had its own Baal, there was much similarity in the worship of these idols.

12. And they forsook the Lord God of their fathers, which brought them out of the land of Egypt, and followed other gods, of the gods of the people that were round about them, and bowed themselves unto them, and provoked the Lord to anger.

The first chapter of the book of Judges contains a list of the many areas in the promised land that were not completely conquered and occupied by the Hebrews. In some cases the reasons for such lack of success are given, as in verse 19, where it states that Judah could not drive out the inhabitants living in plains of the area allotted to them "because they had chariots of iron." Beginning with verse 27 there follows case after case of Israel's failure to achieve complete dominance. "Neither did Manasseh drive out the inhabitants of Beth-shean." It continues, "Neither did Ephraim . . ." (v. 29); "Neither did Zebulun . . ." (v. 30); "Neither did Asher . . ." (v. 31); "Neither did Naphtali . . ." (v. 33).

Chapter 3 gives further information about the peoples who still dwelt in the land. A summary of sorts is found in verses 5 and 6: "And the children of Israel dwelt among the Canaanites, Hittites, and Amorites, and Perizzites, and Hivites, and Jebusites. And they took their daughters to be their wives, and gave their daughters to their sons, and served their gods."

Having failed to drive the heathen peoples from the land of Canaan as they had been instructed to do, Israel settled down to coexist with them. They intermarried with them and adopted their idolatrous worship.

13. And they forsook the Lord, and served Baal and Ashtaroth.

The *Ashtaroth* were female deities, thought of as the wives or consorts of the Baals. The peoples of the eastern Mediterranean lands believed these gods controlled the forces of nations and were responsible for the processes of seedtime and harvest, fertility and reproduction. They believed that these gods would favorably affect the prosperity of those who honored and exalted them. The ceremonies by which they were worshiped were degrading, including practices both licentious and cruel. In times of peril the worshipers sacrificed their own sons and daughters to the idols (see Psalm 106:35-38). Obviously, if Israel chose to worship such gods as these, they would *have* to forsake the Lord. They could not worship both. The same choice is ours; we may serve the gods of our own age and suffer the consequences, or we may serve the Lord. As we view the gross paganism around us today, it is clear that apostasy from God is still the greatest peril our country faces.

HOW SOON WILL THEY FORGET?

All the experts agree that one causative factor for "mid-life crisis" among human beings is *confrontation with mortality*. Fear of physical death, however, is only part of the cause for anxiety among pre-senior citizens. Like Solomon, thinking persons dislike the thought that, once dead, their achievements, ideas, and ideals will die too. "For the wise man, like the fool, will not be long remembered; in days to come both will be forgotten" (Ecclesiastes 2:16, *New International Version*).

At 110, Joshua probably did not fear death; perhaps he welcomed it. More likely he would have been troubled by the fear that, after his death, his godly counsel would be forgotten. Sadly, that is exactly what happened. When Joshua and his generation had been buried, Israel forsook the God of their fathers.

Will our descendants be true to our personal convictions, faithful to Christ and His church? Each generation must choose whether or not to follow the Lord. But let us do all we can to ensure the endurance of the values and faith we hold dear. Let us live for Christ in cheerful and sincere obedience so that our instruction and example will only draw our children and grandchildren to Christ.   —R. W. B.

II. God's Anger and Its Results (Judges 2:14, 15)

14. And the anger of the Lord was hot against Israel, and he delivered them into the hands of spoilers that spoiled them, and he sold them into the hands of their enemies round about, so that they could not any longer stand before their enemies.

How to Say It

AMORITES. *Am*-uh-rites.
ASHER. *Ash*-er.
ASHTAROTH. *Ash*-ta-roth.
BAAL. *Bay*-ul.
BAALIM. *Bay*-uh-lim.
BETH-SHEAN. Beth-*she*-un.
CANAANITES. *Kay*-nan-ites.
HITTITES. *Hit*-ites or *Hit*-tites.
HIVITES. *Hi*-vites.
JEBUSITES. *Jeb*-yuh-sites.
MANASSEH. Muh-*nas*-uh.
NAPHTALI. *Naf*-tuh-lye.
PERIZZITES. *Pair*-iz-zites.
ZEBULUN. *Zeb*-you-lun.

We should not believe that men could turn from the worship of the holy God and dedicate themselves to false, imaginary deities, with all the immorality and cruelty such idolatry involved, without provoking a reaction from God. He had told the Hebrews He was a jealous God and had commanded specifically that they should worship Him alone, have no other gods before Him, and not bow down to them or serve them (Exodus 20:4, 5). But they chose to disregard His command.

He delivered them into the hands of spoilers. The *New International Version* translates this, "The Lord handed them over to raiders who plundered them." God had been with Israel's armies under Joshua. They had seen evidences of God's power and wisdom in the casting down of walls and in the strategy given for victory time after time. When they did His will and were true to Him they were irresistible and undefeated. Now, however, their mighty Defender had withdrawn from them because they had been faithless to Him.

15. Whithersoever they went out, the hand of the Lord was against them for evil, as the Lord had said, and as the Lord had sworn unto them: and they were greatly distressed.

The defeats and disasters experienced by Israel were not because of God's inability to help them, but because of their unwillingness to follow Him. Further, God had forewarned them of the dire consequences of disobedience. They had broken their covenant with their God, and He was bringing upon them those curses and calamities He had warned them would come.

In Leviticus 26, among the many fearful predictions of punishment for abandoning their God, the Israelites were told, "And I will bring a sword upon you, that shall avenge the quarrel of my covenant: . . . and ye shall be delivered into the hand of the enemy. . . . and I will destroy your high places, and cut down your images, and cast your carcasses upon the carcasses of your idols, and my soul shall abhor you. And I will make your cities waste, and bring your sanctuaries unto desolation. . . . And I will scatter you among the heathen, and will draw out a sword after you: and your land shall be desolate, and your cities waste" (vv. 25-33).

In Deuteronomy 28 the description of God's punishment for their turning from Him is even more detailed and dreadful (vv. 15-68).

Some time ago, in motoring through several states, we crossed one state line and immediately began noticing signs that said the speed limit was "strictly enforced." Surveillance by aircraft and radar was threatened more than once. Finally there was another sign about the importance of observing the speed limit, to which the following notice was added: "You have been warned!" Something similar to this had happened to the Israelites. Repeated warnings from God were given them about the dire consequences of disobedience. They could never say they had not been warned—and that in a clear and emphatic way. Nevertheless, they went boldly on in their spiritual rebellion and moral decadence.

III. The Antidote of the Judges (Judges 2:16-19)

16. Nevertheless the Lord raised up judges, which delivered them out of the hand of those that spoiled them.

Judges were not just officials who rendered judgments in matters of law. They were national leaders who enabled Israel for a time to throw off the yoke of oppression placed upon them by their enemies. For the most part they were military heroes who led Israel to victory over their oppressors. However, it is said that they "judged Israel," and the implication is that they did function in a judicial capacity.

These leaders were *raised up* by God. The conditions under which He raised them up are stated elsewhere. The people "cried unto the Lord" (3:9, 15; 4:3; 6:7). The phrase suggests their remorse for their rebellion as well as their dependence upon God. It was an acknowledgment that their only hope of salvation lay in God, whom they had rejected.

It is a matter of surprise and thanksgiving that in the midst of so much that was decadent and debased God's power could still work to bring change for the better through chosen personalities. The days of the judges show us how easy it is to forget God and fall into dissoluteness and despair. But they also demonstrate that God is always merciful and ready to respond to the cry of His people when they repent of their evil and turn to Him. How our generation needs to hear this message of God's great love!

17. And yet they would not hearken unto their judges, but they went a whoring after other gods, and bowed themselves unto them: they turned quickly out of the way which their fathers walked in, obeying the commandments of the Lord; but they did not so.

They would not hearken unto their judges. This is to be understood in the light of the remainder of the verse and of the continuing story running through the book. The people would turn to God and follow the leading of the judge during the time of the crisis, but their repentance was not permanent. As soon as the immediate crisis was past and the judge who had delivered them was dead (v. 19), they would once again turn from God's way and begin to lust after the sensuous gods of the Canaanites.

They went a whoring after other Gods. This was true both figuratively and literally. God was thought of as the "husband" of Israel by the prophets of a later day. There is no reason to believe this was not the view held from the earliest time. He was the One to whom they were linked by vows of devotion and pledges of love. To forsake Him and His way for other deities was to commit spiritual adultery. This was the view Jeremiah voiced as he looked backward at the history of his people. He said God would make a "new" covenant with His people and added, "Not according to the covenant that I made with their fathers in the day that I took them by the hand to bring them out of the land of Egypt; which my covenant they brake, although I was an husband unto them, saith the Lord" (31:32).

Earlier in the same book Jeremiah quoted God as saying to Israel, "Thou hast played the harlot with many lovers; yet return again to me, saith the Lord" (3:1). The concept of God as the "Husband of Israel" was also voiced by Isaiah: "For thy Maker is thine husband; The Lord of hosts is his name; and thy Redeemer the Holy One of Israel; The God of the whole earth shall he be called" (54:5).

But, as has been noted earlier, the *whoring after other gods*, the worship of these false gods, involved literal sexual immorality. *They turned quickly*, after each deliverance, and again disobeyed the commandments of God, unlike their fathers who had been obedient (Judges 2:7).

18. And when the Lord raised them up judges, then the Lord was with the judge, and delivered them out of the hand of their enemies all the days of the judge: for it repented the Lord because of their groanings by reason of them that oppressed them and vexed them.

The Lord was with the judge. This explains the success of these leaders who were raised up in times of national distress. The judges may be considered as great individuals, but the power by which they did their great deeds was from the Lord.

It repented the Lord because of their groanings. This does not mean that God changed His mind because they had trouble due to their sins. Rather it speaks of God's merciful concern for His people.

Numbers 23:19 indicates that God is not a man that He should repent. He had decreed that if Israel obeyed His commands, He would bring punishment upon them. God had not changed from that position. Israel had chosen to disobey Him, and consequently they were receiving the punishment He had willed. But God is compassionate and stands ready to forgive His people when *they* repent and turn to Him. In these times of severe oppression during the period of the judges, the people repented and turned back to Him. When they did, God's compassion was evident, and He blessed them as He had said He would do.

19. And it came to pass, when the judge was dead, that they returned, and corrupted themselves more than their fathers, in following other gods to serve them, and to bow down unto them; they ceased not from their own doings, nor from their stubborn way.

The recurrent pattern seen in the book of Judges is one of persistence in disobedience to God, domination by a neighboring people, and then deliverance through a judge. A period of

Home Daily Bible Readings

Monday, June 26—Judah's First Victories (Judges 1:1-7)

Tuesday, June 27—The Israelites Conquer Jerusalem (Judges 1:8-15)

Wednesday, June 28—Victories of Judah and Joseph (Judges 1:16-26)

Thursday, June 29—The Heathen Tribes in Victory (Judges 1:27-36)

Friday, June 30—The Death of Joshua (Judges 2:1-9)

Saturday, July 1—The People Do Evil (Judges 2:10-15)

Sunday, July 2—The Lord Raises Up Judges (Judges 2:16-23)

renewal and freedom would be followed by further departure from the Lord, and then another period of enslavement. The natural result of such continual backsliding was that they *corrupted themselves more than their fathers.* It seems that with each succeeding generation the spiritual conditions of Israel grew darker.

"WHEN THE CAT'S AWAY. . . ."

Two men were sitting in a restaurant awaiting their lunch to be served. The waitress overheard them laughing and telling obscene jokes.

Another man, a stranger to the waitress, entered the restaurant and sat down at their table. Abruptly the tenor of the conversation changed. No more dirty jokes were told. Shortly the new man arose, shook hands with the two, and left. The waitress could not control her curiosity. "How come you didn't share all your stories with your buddy who just left?" she asked.

"You gotta be kidding," was the reply." Don't you know he's the new preacher in town?"

The Israelites often acted like the two men in this incident. "When the cat's away, mice play," and "when the judge died, the people returned to . . . evil practices and stubborn ways" (Judges 2:19, *New International Version*).

Mature Christians behave in godly ways, even when no one is watching. What kind of a person are you when family, friends, and fellow Christians aren't around? In reality, God has put each of us on the "honor system." We are free to choose right or wrong. "On our honor, let us do our best to serve God. . . ."

Conclusion

A. False Gods, Then and Now

The Hebrews were led astray to the worship of false gods by the allurement of two major benefits—the relaxation of sexual standards and the attainment of material gain. Many varieties of sexual gratification were made available as part of the worship of the Canaanite gods. Not only was this allowed as a concession, but it was promoted as a religious experience. The exaltation of these deities and their worship was supposed to contribute to the success of stock raising, the prosperity of vintners, and the promotion of good harvests of grain, figs, and dates.

Today there are those who insist that the maintenance of virginity before marriage and of fidelity to one partner after marriage are constricting, inhibiting, and physically disorienting practices. There is an exaltation of "free love" or "self-fulfillment" without the restriction of "outdated codes" or "straightlaced Puritanism." Further, many think that a person is experiencing a successful life only if his or her property, possessions, and financial power are continually increasing. If we think of worship as a focusing of life on what we believe is of highest worth, then, indeed, modern men are really worshipers of the same deities as those before whom the Israelites bowed. Only the names and forms are different.

The terrible aspect about the Hebrews' worship of these "strange gods" was that they had a revelation of the true and living God in their possession—His law. They also had the record of God's blessings upon them as they had come from Egypt to Canaan and then into Canaan to take possession of the land and establish their lives there. All God's truth they now seemed to forget and scorn, and all God's care they either forgot or took for granted. How tragic that today we are tempted to turn from the truth—especially, in our case, the living truth in Jesus—to the deceptive fictions of men, to choose darkness rather than light and death rather than life! The result is that we find more and more to mistrust and hate, and less and less to trust and love. Well does John close his first letter with the words: "Dear children, keep yourselves from idols" (5:21, *New International Version*).

B. Prayer

Our Father, we are thankful for the record of the life of the Israelites as they began and continued their life as a people in the land of promise. We are grateful, Lord, not because it is pleasant to read, but because it is profitable for us to remember. We are saddened by their rejection of the true worship for that which was false and sinful. Father, help us to be reminded about how easily we can be led astray also. Help us not to give ourselves to the worship of the sensual and sordid rather than the spiritual and the uplifting. Enable us to see the fallacy of only seeking the increase of material goods as our most important aim in life.

We are especially grateful to see that even in dark days among people who forsake the true way of life there are still persons who are touched with awe of You and who are ready to yield to a summons to self-giving and gallantry for truth and righteousness and eternal things. Lord, may we know surrender instead of stubbornness, purity in place of stain, truth in the face of falsehood, and peace amid restlessness. Through Jesus Christ our Lord we pray. Amen.

C. Thought to Remember

The true God alone is the High and Holy One who inhabits eternity. False gods are low, sensuous, earthy, and time bound.

Learning by Doing

This page contains an alternate lesson plan emphasizing learning activities. Classes desiring such student involvement will find these suggestions helpful.

Learning Goals

This lesson should enable the student to:

1. Identify the cycle of behavior that characterized Israel in the time of the judges.

2. Explain why God continued to deliver the Israelites.

3. List some Biblical principles that can help keep him from disobeying God.

Into the Lesson

Before class write the following statement on small index cards, one word per card: "Disobeying God brings calamity; returning to Him brings deliverance." Scramble the cards and place them in an envelope. Make one such puzzle for each four students in your class.

Divide your students into groups of four and give each group an envelope. Instruct them to arrange the words into an intelligible sentence. When all have completed this, make the transition to Bible study by saying, "The book of Judges tells us of the Israelites' problems as they forsook God following the death of Joshua. We want to determine how we can keep from following their pattern of disobedience."

Into the Word

The outline below describes the cycle of Israel's experiences during the time of the judges. Write it on the chalkboard or overhead transparency.

    I. Disobedience
    II. Calamity
    III. Return to God
    IV. Deliverance

Write these four points at the top of four sheets of paper, one per sheet. Then divide your class into four groups and give each a sheet.

Ask the groups to search Judges 2:11-19 to find all they can on their particular part of the cycle. (Note that returning to God is evident in the stories of the judges.) Call the groups back together and let them report to the class. Let the whole class discuss the reports. Then use the following questions for further discussion.

1. How can we combat the tendency to fall away as the nation of Israel did?

2. How do we fall into the same traps that Israel did? Give modern examples of being too dependent on leadership, too desirous of wealth, too eager to make friends (lower God's standards), too eager to compromise (look for shortcuts).

3. What tempted the people to serve other gods? What tempts us to serve other gods?

4. How did a generation arise who knew not the Lord? What can we do to ensure that the next generation will know and serve God?

5. Why did God continue to deliver the Israelites? Will He always deliver wayward people?

Allot twenty minutes for this segment.

Into Life

Have the students return to their four groups, and give each group two of these Scriptures: Proverbs 8:13; Proverbs 27:17; Matthew 5:16; Romans 7:24, 25a; 1 Corinthians 10:13; 1 Corinthians 15:33; Colossians 3:2;1 John 1:6—2:2. Ask each group to discuss this question: "What principles do we learn from these Scriptures that could deliver us from the cycle of disobedience?" Then let them come back together and share their principles.

Close your session by having each student evaluate his level of obedience to the Lord. (Of course, we recognize that we are saved by God's grace, just as the Israelites were. Some may need to accept Christ as their Savior. Be sensitive to that need and be ready to share the gospel with those students privately. There is also a need to nurture those who are Christians. This involves obedience.) Give each student a copy of the following five statements. Ask them to consider their level of obedience and attitude toward obedience by marking the statement that most closely mirrors their understanding.

1. I will do what I want no matter what God wants.

2. If God will first give me what I want, then I'll give Him something of equal value.

3. If God will first give me what I want, then I'll do what He wants.

4. I will first give God what He wants, then in faith believe He will give me what I want.

5. I will give God what He wants, regardless of whether He gives me what I want.

Challenge each to see that number 5 is the level of obedience toward which we should strive. Ask your students to complete this sentence, which you have included on the sheet: "I thank God that He can deliver me from the cycle of disobedience by _____."

Let's Talk It Over

The questions on this page are designed to encourage review of the lesson Scriptures and to promote discussion of the lesson by the class. The answers provided are only discussion starters. Let your class talk it over from there.

1. How can we combat the constant, pervasive influence toward spiritual and moral error that our society brings to bear upon us?

It seems that someone is always trying to influence us to adopt his point of view. Certainly the entertainment world has a philosophy it is trying to get across. And individuals with whom we work, whom we meet in passing, or who come to our door are often determined to influence our religious or moral beliefs. Some of this we can avoid, but as Paul noted, we would have to leave the world in order to avoid any contact with people whose influence is unwholesome (1 Corinthians 5:10). Since we must deal with this constant assault, why not meet it with a counterassault? After all, who has any more reason for wanting to influence others than Christians? We must master the Biblical principles of theology and morality and make our voice heard in the midst of the clamor of worldly and humanistic viewpoints.

2. The lesson writer says of the Israelite armies, "When they did [God's] will and were true to Him they were irresistible and undefeated. Now, however, their mighty Defender had withdrawn from them because they had been faithless to Him." How may these statements apply to the church?

The church is meant to be "irresistible and undefeated." The book of Acts shows that the church in Jerusalem continued to conquer in spite of persecution. See also Paul's statement in Philippians 1:28. If the modern church is not experiencing this sense of being irresistible, it may be an indication of faithlessness, which undermined Israel's power. The church that is weak, unfruitful, and stagnant should examine itself. Are members guilty of "covetousness, which is idolatry"? (Colossians 3:5). Have some failed to repent of sexual and moral sins? Are leaders allowing selfishness, pride, and jealousy to destroy their effectiveness? It is tempting to attribute the church's problems to the leaders of the church, to the devil's tactics, or to the indifference of the community to the gospel. But often a church's major problem is tolerance of sin in its midst, and divine power will be blocked until that sin is dealt with.

3. One reason for Israel's downfall was their practice of intermarriage with heathen neighbors. Why is this observation one that Christians do well to consider?

Christian parents may seem narrow-minded in insisting that their teenagers date only other Christians. And Christian young people may have to wait a little longer on marriage when they determine they will marry only a faithful believer in the Lord. But these policies have often been demonstrated to be wise and safe. Of course there are occasions when a Christian dates or even marries a non-Christian and eventually leads that person to Christ. But often the opposite result occurs: the unbelieving partner influences the Christian to abandon or to become inactive in his or her faith. When we realize how important it is for Christians to marry within their faith, we can recognize one more reason to support programs that enable Christian teens to meet and form friendships. Also, while Christian colleges do not exist to provide the environment for Christian marriages, the opportunities for dating and marriage among young adult believers are a legitimate side benefit of such institutions.

4. God was viewed in the Old Testament as the "husband" of Israel, and Christ is, spiritually speaking, our husband. What are some practical implications of this truth?

Paul wrote to the Corinthians, "I am jealous over you with godly jealousy: for I have espoused you to one husband, that I may present you as a chaste virgin to Christ" (2 Corinthians 11:2). If Christ is our husband, then we owe to Him our love and devotion. No human being, no earthly goal, no amount of money or possessions should be allowed to usurp His claim to first place in our affections. Since He is our husband, we should make it our aim to please Him. Our exercise of faith, commitment to obedience, and efforts at service will accomplish that purpose. Technically, we may say that we are *to be* Christ's bride, that He will become our husband at the time of the wedding supper of the Lamb (Revelation 19:6-9). So we should keep ourselves pure for Him in anticipation of that day when we will be united with Him.

Deborah: Leader of God's People

LESSON SCRIPTURE: Judges 4, 5.

PRINTED TEXT: Judges 4:1-9, 14, 15.

Judges 4:1-9, 14, 15

1 And the children of Israel again did evil in the sight of the Lord, when Ehud was dead.

2 And the Lord sold them into the hand of Jabin king of Canaan, that reigned in Hazor; the captain of whose host was Sisera, which dwelt in Harosheth of the Gentiles.

3 And the children of Israel cried unto the Lord: for he had nine hundred chariots of iron; and twenty years he mightily oppressed the children of Israel.

4 And Deborah, a prophetess, the wife of Lapidoth, she judged Israel at that time.

5 And she dwelt under the palm tree of Deborah, between Ramah and Bethel in mount Ephraim: and the children of Israel came up to her for judgment.

6 And she sent and called Barak the son of Abinoam out of Kedesh-naphtali, and said unto him, Hath not the Lord God of Israel commanded, saying, Go and draw toward mount Tabor, and take with thee ten thousand men of the children of Naphtali and of the children of Zebulun?

7 And I will draw unto thee, to the river Kishon, Sisera the captain of Jabin's army, with his chariots and his multitude; and I will deliver him into thine hand.

8 And Barak said unto her, If thou wilt go with me, then I will go: but if thou wilt not go with me, then I will not go.

9 And she said, I will surely go with thee: notwithstanding the journey that thou takest shall not be for thine honor; for the Lord shall sell Sisera into the hand of a woman. And Deborah arose, and went with Barak to Kedesh.

. . . .

14 And Deborah said unto Barak, Up; for this is the day in which the Lord hath delivered Sisera into thine hand: is not the Lord gone out before thee? So Barak went down from mount Tabor, and ten thousand men after him.

15 And the Lord discomfited Sisera, and all his chariots, and all his host, with the edge of the sword before Barak; so that Sisera lighted down off his chariot, and fled away on his feet.

GOLDEN TEXT: Barak said unto her, If thou wilt go with her, If thou wilt go with me, then I will go: but if thou wilt not go with me, then I will not go.—Judges 4:8.

Conquest and Challenge
Unit 2: Judges—A Time of Conflict and Adjustment (Lessons 5-10)

Lesson Aims

This lesson should help a student:
1. Be aware that leaders are needed if the Lord's cause is to prosper.
2. Consider what leadership role he or she may fill in the Lord's work.
3. Determine to support those who presently lead in God's work.

Lesson Outline

INTRODUCTION—A Woman Warrior
I. SURPASSING OPPRESSION (Judges 4:1-3)
   A. Its Cause (v. 1)
   B. Its Condition (vv. 2, 3a)
   C. Its Continuance (v. 3b)
II. SURPRISING DEVELOPMENTS (Judges 4:4-9)
   A. Deborah Introduced (vv. 4, 5)
   B. Deborah's Instructions (vv. 6, 7)
   C. Deborah's Involvement (vv. 8, 9)
     Not Alone
III. SUPERLATIVE DELIVERANCE (Judges 4:14, 15)
   A. Deborah's Faith (v. 14a)
   B. Barak's Action (v. 14b)
   C. Sisera's Defeat (v. 15)
     Opening Doors of Opportunity
CONCLUSION
   A. Victory Assured
   B. Victorious Women
   C. Prayer
   D. Thought to Remember

Display visual 6 (the chart of the judges) from the visuals/learning resources packet. It will be useful in this lesson and the next four lessons in this series. It is shown on page 389.

Introduction—A Woman Warrior

Deborah is one of the most unusual women to be found in the whole scope of Biblical literature. The social climate of the civilizations of Bible times favored the confining of women to domestic roles. Some women, however, engaged in certain commercial enterprises, such as spinning, weaving, sewing, and selling garments. Priscilla of the New Testament worked with her husband in the tent-making trade.

Certain women were empowered to bring to general attention special messages from God. They were known as "prophetesses." We read of the prophetess, Huldah, in the days of Josiah (2 Chronicles 34:22-28). In Acts 21:8, 9 reference is made to four virgin daughters of Philip, the evangelist, who were prophetesses. Deborah is called a prophetess as well, one of a very few in Israel's history. However, while her prophetic gift certainly distinguishes her, it is not the most unusual thing about her.

Deborah became a revolutionary leader in Israel. It was she who approached Barak and urged him to lead an army against Israel's oppressors. Not only that, but such was her magnetism and force of leadership that Barak refused to go into battle unless she was present during the conflict.

There were women in Hebrew history who were involved with matters of state, for good or ill. The beautiful queen Esther comes to mind, as well as the wicked monarch Athaliah. Yet no woman besides Deborah is reported to have gone into battle along with men. She was an example of courage, inspiration, and challenge to the people of her era. She is an example of how gifted women, even in unusual and unfavorable circumstances, can achieve victories when they are yielded to God and unafraid to utilize the special gifts He has given them.

I. Surpassing Oppression (Judges 4:1-3)

A. Its Cause (v. 1)

1. And the children of Israel again did evil in the sight of the Lord, when Ehud was dead.

Following the liberation that Ehud wrought, Israel was free from foreign domination for eighty years (Judges 3:26-30). Now, after this long interim, Israel again repudiated God's way, worshiping of the gods of the nations round about. The deities adored were mythical and, in many cases, cruel, obscene, and dishonest—a far cry from the holy, compassionate, and ethical deity the people of Israel knew as their own. Usually such deviation in worship led to an increase in injustice, insensitivity, and instability in all the relationships of life.

B. Its Condition (vv. 2, 3a)

2, 3a. And the Lord sold them into the hand of Jabin king of Canaan, that reigned in Hazor; the captain of whose host was Sisera, which dwelt in Harosheth of the Gentiles. And the children of Israel cried unto the Lord.

Hazor was a fortress city located about ten miles due north of the Sea of Galilee. *Harosheth of the Gentiles* was about thirty five miles south and west of Hazor. Jabin lived in Hazor, which was in the area assigned to the tribe of Naphtali, while Sisera lived in an area designated as belonging to the tribe of Zebulun. Unable to rescue themselves from their oppressors, Israel, *cried unto the Lord.*

C. Its Continuance (v. 3b)

3b. For he had nine hundred chariots of iron; and twenty years he mightily oppressed the children of Israel.

We do not know just what the status of iron-mastering was in Israel at the time we are now considering. However, it seems apparent that the idea of *chariots of iron* was an especially daunting prospect. When speaking to the tribes of Ephraim and Manasseh about their prospective victories over the Canaanites, Joshua had said "Thou shalt drive out the Canaanites, though they have iron chariots, and though they be strong" (Joshua 17:17, 18). Such chariots were reinforcements and "heavy armor support" for ancient armies. Under ancient battle conditions *nine hundred chariots of iron* were a formidable threat.

II. Surprising Developments (Judges 4:4-9)

A. Deborah Introduced (vv. 4, 5)

4. And Deborah, a prophetess, the wife of Lapidoth, she judged Israel at that time.

While Israel was under subjection to the Canaanites, apparently some type of internal authority was recognized among the Hebrews. Deborah wielded no political power as far as the Canaanites were concerned. But her people sought her judgment about matters regarding their daily lives, for she was recognized as being *a prophetess.* Under the influence of the Spirit of God with which she was blessed, she settled disputes and directed the people in God's ways. Examples are seen in verses 6, 9, and 14.

5. And she dwelt under the palm tree of Deborah between Ramah and Bethel in mount Ephraim: and the children of Israel came up to her for judgment.

By *dwelt* here is meant "she sat" under the palm tree. Probably there was no building or settlement here at all, but only a pleasantly situated palm tree, easily found. Here it was, between two more settled communities, that Deborah probably pitched a tent at designated intervals and, unnoticed by the Canaanite authorities, rendered judgment. *Ramah* was about six miles north of Jerusalem, and *Bethel* was about five miles farther north. Therefore, Deborah's judgment place was a long way south of Hazor.

B. Deborah's Instructions (vv. 6, 7)

6. And she sent and called Barak the son of Abinoam out of Kedesh-naphtali, and said unto him, Hath not the Lord God of Israel commanded, saying, Go and draw toward mount Tabor, and take with thee ten thousand men of the children of Naphtali and of the children of Zebulun?

Kedesh-naphtali was a town located some four miles north of Hazor. *Tabor* was a mountain just a few miles south and west of the south end of the lake of Galilee. The order for Barak came from God. He was to muster an army of ten thousand men from the northern part of Israel and assemble them near Mount Tabor. Here Sisera's chariots would be rendered ineffective, and when the favorable moment came, Barak's army could sweep down from the heights.

7. And I will draw unto thee, to the river Kishon, Sisera the captain of Jabin's army, with his chariots and his multitude; and I will deliver him into thine hand.

The *river Kishon* flows north and west from the vicinity of Mount Tabor into the Mediterranean Sea. In her instructions to Barak, Deborah told him how many men to recruit, where to secure them, and where to deploy them. A promise was given that if these directions were followed, a victory for Israel would ensue. This was to be in the face of whatever force Sisera led and in spite of the dreaded *chariots.*

C. Deborah's Involvement (vv. 8, 9)

8. And Barak said unto her, If thou wilt go with me, then I will go: but if thou wilt not go with me, then I will not go.

Here is an unusual situation! We have a warrior of such competence and consequence he can lead ten thousand men into battle against a fierce and formidable foe. Yet, before he will even attempt to go, he requests the assurance that this woman, the wife of another, will go with him to the fray! Of course, he realized that she was no ordinary woman, but a prophetess of the eternal God. From her came words of vibrant power and vital truth. It was not just that he needed to know she was willing to share the hazards of the conflict; it would be great for the morale of the soldiers when they knew that one who lived close to God was among them. But Deborah's next words seem to suggest that Barak's faith should have been stronger.

9. And she said, I will surely go with thee: notwithstanding the journey that thou takest shall not be for thine honor; for the Lord shall sell Sisera into the hand of a woman. And Deborah arose, and went with Barak to Kedesh.

How to Say It

ABINOAM. A-*bin*-o-am.
ATHALIAH. Ath-uh-*lye*-uh.
BARAK. *Bay*-ruk or *Bair*-uk.
EHUD. *Ee*-hud.
HAROSHETH. Ha-*ro*-sheth.
HAZOR. *Hay*-zor.
HULDAH. *Hul*-duh.
JABIN. *Jay*-bin.
JAEL. *Jay*-ul.
KEDESH-NAPHTALI. *Kee*-desh-*naf*-tuh-lye.
KENITE. *Ken*-ite.
LAPIDOTH. *Lap*-uh-doth.
RAMAH. *Ray*-muh.
SISERA. Sis-er-uh or *Sis*-uh-ruh.
TABOR. *Tay*-ber.
ZEBULUN. *Zeb*-you-lun.

Deborah assured Barak of her presence on the expedition. It had been revealed to her that the Canaanite general was to be destroyed by *the hand of a woman.* Barak may have believed, and perhaps Deborah may have thought, too, that the woman into whose hand Sisera would be "sold" would be Deborah herself. The unexpected turn events would take was not foretold, as far as we know. God had promised victory over the Canaanites as a whole, and now the personal ill fate of the powerful general of their armies was also predicted. With that, Deborah went with Barak to his hometown, Kedesh, where Barak proceeded to gather his army.

All events are in God's hands, and the things He says will happen in the future will, indeed, "come true." Sometimes, however, fulfillments come about in most unusual and unexpected ways. The coming of Messiah from Bethlehem was prophesied, for example, but who could have ever guessed that the "One who should rule Israel" would be born in a stable and laid in a manger? It was predicted that Elijah would come before the Messiah came (Malachi 4:5, 6), but John the Baptist was the fulfillment, for he went in "the spirit and power of Elijah" (Luke 1:17; Matthew 17:10-13; Mark 9:11-13).

This should teach us to be very modest about claiming insight concerning what God is going to do about various matters in the future. We are assured of such things as rewards for faithfulness and the dangers of falsehood or lack of courage. But we are told by Jesus that many who call Him "Lord, Lord" will not enter the kingdom of Heaven (Matthew 7:21-23). He also said that, "many that are first shall be last; and the last shall be first" (Matthew 19:30).

NOT ALONE

In spite of Jehovah's assurances of divine assistance, Moses was reluctant to lead his people out of Egypt until Aaron was "volunteered" to accompany him (Exodus 4:1-17). Barak expressed similar reluctance when commanded, through Deborah, to wage war with Sisera. Though Barak too had God's promise of victory, he would not accept the challenge without the prophetess/judge at his side. Because of the uniqueness of these situations, the reluctance of these men cannot be commended.

God's servants today are rightly reluctant to trust in their own strength and ability to perform His work. God empowers us, of course, yet the moral support of a righteous partner is invaluable in labors for the kingdom. Jesus had the practical foresight to send out His disciples by twos (Luke 10:1). There is a certain strength in numbers, and the encouragement of a colaborer is of inestimable value.

Moses and Aaron were finally successful in delivering the Israelites; Barak and Deborah were victorious over Sisera's army; and the "seventy returned again with joy" from their mission. We too can fulfill the Great Commission, with the presence of Christ, and with the assistance of Christian partners.   —R. W. B.

III. Superlative Deliverance (Judges 4:14, 15)

The intervening verses indicate that ten thousand men were assembled to fight for Israel and that they had taken their position at Mount Tabor. Having been informed of this, Sisera gathered together his nine hundred chariots of iron and his vast army and brought them to the plain through which the Kishon River flowed.

A. Deborah's Faith (v. 14a)

14a. And Deborah said unto Barak, Up; for this is the day in which the Lord hath delivered Sisera into thine hand: is not the Lord gone out before thee?

It is obvious Deborah gave an inspiring and heartening message to Barak. In essence she said, "*Up* and at them!" or "Go get them!" Encouraging words of vigorous faith can work wonders. Just as a few words of defeatism, negativism, and doubt can dishearten people, so just a few phrases of dauntless hope, cheer, and optimism can fire the imagination and galvanize the will.

It is worthy of note that Deborah mentions *the Lord* twice and *Sisera* only once. *Sisera* stood for all the forces against them—the armies, the chariots, the arrogance of repression long exercised. But *the Lord* stood for the many deliverances and victories in Israel's past history and for the assurance of present help and power that this prophetess of God said would be theirs.

B. Barak's Action (v. 14b)

14b. So Barak went down from mount Tabor, and ten thousand men after him.

Inspiration can do much, and faith can build fortitude, but ultimately the time of action comes. James tells us so vigorously, "Faith without works is dead" (2:20, 26). They could *believe* it was possible to defeat Sisera and liberate their tribes, they could desire to overcome their arrogant foes, but the final test was the actual encounter itself. Barak led ten thousand dedicated and dynamic warriors down from the foothills of *Mount Tabor* to fling themselves in a fierce attack upon the Canaanites. Swords clashed on shields, armor, and helmets. Swarms of arrows flew, and spears were thrust or thrown with deadly effect. Deborah had called them not to a tea party but to bitter conflict. Now it was that faith must give force to each blow and direction to every stratagem.

Our Christian faith must prove itself in the battle with evil and the evil one. It is in the actual combat of life that we find out whether our profession is indeed a possession or a mere posturing. Just as the arms and fighting men of Sisera were real, so are our foes. We face temptation in many forms—the devastation of sorrow, the burdens of illness, the allurements of sensate "delights," the blows of lost jobs, lost friends, or lost opportunities. We are solicited by the siren calls of materialism and popularity. So our faith must gird itself for struggle and legitimize itself in spiritual warfare.

Some of Paul's admonitions urge us to be vigilant and valiant as those going forth by faith in God's army: "Watch ye, stand fast in the faith, quit you like men, be strong" (1 Corinthians 16:13); "Take unto you the whole armor of God, that ye may be able to withstand in the evil day, and having done all, to stand" (Ephesians 6:13); "Fight the good fight of faith" (1 Timothy 6:12).

C. Sisera's Defeat (v. 15)

15. And the Lord discomfited Sisera, and all his chariots, and all his host, with the edge of the sword before Barak; so that Sisera lighted down off his chariot, and fled away on his feet.

Two factors seem to have been involved in the victory over Sisera's forces. First, God gave force and fervor to Israel's army so that their fighting caused their enemies to be disheartened and to flee. Second, *the Lord discomfited Sisera*, that

is, caused him to panic and put him to rout. Judges 5:21 says of Sisera's forces, "The river of Kishon swept them away." From this we presume that God sent a rainstorm, causing the river to overflow its banks and turning the surrounding plain into a morass. The chariots then became bogged down and Sisera's forces became an easy prey for Israel's army. Realizing that the cause was lost, Sisera got down out of his chariot and ran away on foot to save his own life. By making his way into the hills he could get into narrow gorges, or hide among rocks, or travel overland away from roads.

Though not in our printed text, verses 17-22 tell of Sisera's death. He found the tent of Jael, the wife of a member of a Kenite tribe, with whom the Canaanites were not at war. Jael took him in, gave him a pallet on which to sleep, gave him a drink of milk, and "covered him." Feeling secure, he went to sleep. Because of her sympathy with Israel she took a tent peg and a hammer and drove the peg through his temple into the ground as he slept. So perished Sisera, the mighty Canaanite captain.

OPENING DOORS OF OPPORTUNITY

"Electronic-eye" door openers are so common these days, they tend to be taken for granted. Customers and clients almost feel "put upon" if they must open a door for themselves. All units equipped with automatic openers are triggered when someone approaches the door.

Door-opening devices are visual aids that teach an important lesson about accepting God's call to service. The lesson is that *personal initiative* must be added to *spiritual trust* in seeking the will of God for Christian ministry.

Consider Barak. "At Barak's advance, the Lord routed Sisera" (Judges 4:15, *New International Version*). The battle was won by the power of God, of course, but not until Barak obeyed the Lord by launching an attack. Barak "stepped toward the door" of victory, and the door opened according to divine providence.

The Judges of Israel		
Judge	Years As Judge	Major Enemy
Othniel	40	Mesopotamians
Ehud	80	Moabites
Shamgar	?	Philistines
Deborah (Barak)	40	Canaanites
Gideon	40	Midianites
Abimelech	3	(civil war)
Tola	23	
Jair	22	
Jephthah	6	Ammonites
Ibzan	7	
Elon	10	
Abdon	8	
Samson	20	Philistines
Samuel	?	Philistines

visual 6

That is most often the way God leads His children into new avenues of service. When, in faith, we are willing to step toward doors that may seem closed to Christian ministry, such initiative can cause the portals of opportunity to open wide. Isn't it exciting to know that God leads us and empowers us when we venture out in faith to explore new horizons of His will?

—R. W. B.

Conclusion

A. Victory Assured

The fifth chapter of Judges contains an eloquent psalm or paean of praise to God by Deborah, celebrating the victory over the Canaanites. In the course of her song Deborah says, "The stars in their courses fought against Sisera" (v. 20). This does not mean she believed in some astrological arrangement of the heavenly bodies that made it impossible for Sisera to win because he was fighting against some "sign." But it is a recognition of the fact that the God who created the stars and set them in their courses was against Sisera and for the Israelites. The very God who made and sustains all things in this vast and complex universe, was aiding those who trusted Him. It was as possible to change the courses of the stars as it was for Sisera to overthrow the Hebrew army. What an assurance for us when we link our lives with the Lord Jesus Christ! "If God be for us, who can be against us?" Paul asks (Romans 8:31). That is, who can oppose us successfully? Paul answers the question himself: no power nor person can "separate us from the love of God, which is in Christ Jesus our Lord" (v. 39). If "the stars in their courses" were against Sisera, it was because he was opposing God's way and will. So we may rest assured that as we rely on the Son of God He will always cause us "to triumph in Christ" (2 Corinthians 2:14).

B. Victorious Women

It is noteworthy that in the days of the judges, when so much that was dark and sinful was observed among the Hebrew people, several remarkable women shone like stars. We have seen two of them in this lesson. Deborah was a leader in Israel in a time when they were dominated by pagans. Rather than go with the crowd, she not only held fast her own faith but guided and inspired others. She was a God-directed planner of a successful revolt that liberated her people.

We do not know much about Jael, but we do know she was willing to use an opportunity to be an agent in Israel's victory. In slaying Sisera, terrible as the deed was, she truly "struck a blow" for the cause God was aiding—the defeat of the Canaanites. This required courage and a will that was inflexible in its purpose.

Another woman of character and nobility was the Moabitess, Ruth, as later study in this series will reveal. One other unusually devout and dedicated woman during this period was Hannah, who made the tremendous gift of her son, Samuel, to the Lord's work.

Women today can and do serve God, and are blessed and honored in so doing. Such service varies, but, whatever it is, it will have God's blessing and never will be forgotten by Him. It is apparent from Romans 16, where Paul tells of his "helpers in Christ Jesus" (v. 3), that many women were very significant in the life of the church. That today women should be recognized as increasingly significant in God's work is only in keeping with their heritage from Old and New Testament heroines of achievement through faith.

C. Prayer

Our Father, we render special thanks today for the important role women have had in the winning of spiritual battles across the ages. We are grateful that in our own era renewed attention is being given to the contributions women can make to Christ's cause. Help us all to see the need of sincere dedication of our lives to Your service, if Your kingdom is to rule in the hearts of all people. May we all, men and women, be glad partners in Christian enterprises and sharers in the grace of our Lord. In His name, amen.

D. Thought to Remember

Some of the greatest things God has ever accomplished in this world have been done through women.

Home Daily Bible Readings

Monday, July 3—Deborah Judges the People (Judges 4:1-5)

Tuesday, July 4—True Freedom in Christ (Galatians 5:1, 13-26)

Wednesday, July 5—Deborah Relays God's Commands (Judges 4:6-10)

Thursday, July 6—Deborah Inspires the Israelites (Judges 4:12-16)

Friday, July 7—Israel's Foes Are Slain (Judges 4:17-24)

Saturday, July 8—Deborah Recounts Jael's Heroism (Judges 5:24-30)

Sunday, July 9—Deborah Praises God (Judges 5:1-5, 31)

Learning by Doing

*This page contains an alternate lesson plan emphasizing learning activities. Classes
desiring such student involvement will find these suggestions helpful.*

Learning Goals

As a result of this lesson, a student should:

1. Explore ways in which Deborah exercised leadership in Israel's history.

2. Identify areas in which leadership is needed today.

3. Consider taking a leadership role in one of these areas.

Into the Lesson

Before class, prepare several large sheets of newsprint (approximately 18 inches by 30 inches) with the word *leader* printed vertically. Place these papers on the walls around the room. Provide felt tip pens for writing (be sure they do not mark walls). Ask class members to think of qualities of effective leaders that begin with each letter of this word. Have them work in small groups to complete the acrostics. A completed acrostic is given as an example.

L oyal
E nergetic
A ssertive
D iligent
E mpowered
R espected

Allow approximately five minutes for this exercise and then discuss as a class.

Make your transition into the Bible study by saying, "Today we are going to study a very effective leader of God's people, Deborah. As we study, look for ways in which you may be encouraged to be a leader."

Into the Word

Begin with a brief lecture in which you describe the situation in Israel in the time of Deborah. Use the material in the section, "Surpassing Oppression," on page 386. Note also Deborah's brief comment on the desolation in Israel in Judges 52:6-8. Divide your class into thirds for Bible exploration. Assign each group one of the Scripture sections below. After they read the Scripture, they are to write a brief paragraph describing how Deborah exerted leadership in Israel. Sample answers are given.

Group 1: Judges 4:4-9. Deborah was recognized for her wisdom and as being a spokesperson for God (v. 4). People came to her for the settlement of disputes (v. 5). She heeded the

voice of God (v. 6). She gave encouragement through God's word (v. 6, 7).

Group 2: Judges 4:10-17. Deborah went into battle (v. 10). She inspired the Israelites to take action (v. 14). She was assertive in her commands (v. 14).

Group 3: Judges 5:1-3, 9. Deborah gave honor to those who deserved it (v. 2). She led the people back to the Lord (vv. 2, 3). Her heart was with the people (v. 9).

Allow ten minutes for this and then lead the class in a discussion of the text, using their contributions as a starting point. You may want to list their main points on the chalkboard. The following questions may be helpful:

1. What marks of a prophetess are seen in Deborah in our text?

2. What weaknesses did Barak show by agreeing to go into battle only if Deborah went with him?

3. What strength did Barak show by requesting Deborah to accompany him?

4. What did Deborah's going into battle show about her leadership and influence on the army of Israel?

5. What did Deborah's command (v. 14) reveal about her trust in the Lord?

Into Life

Begin the life application by discussing with your students the following questions: What characteristics do most people look for in a leader? From what we have studied about Deborah, how did she show these characteristics?

Next ask, "What are some of the most pressing needs you have observed in our congregation and community?" List these in a brainstorming fashion. After you have listed these on the chalkboard or newsprint, have each person determine what he or she feels to be the most pressing need. Be sure to emphasize that one of the characteristics of a leader is to recognize a need and then seek to meet it. Perhaps God is calling your students to meet this need. Have them write down two ways in which they may meet the need that they regard as important.

Close the session with this challenge: "We have seen needs and written ways to meet them. Now we must decide what our commitment is. The question each must answer is, 'Will I do something to meet the need I feel is pressing?'"

Let's Talk It Over

*The questions on this page are designed to encourage review of the lesson
Scriptures and to promote discussion of the lesson by the class. The answers
provided are only discussion starters. Let your class talk it over from there.*

1. The Israelites appear to have been troubled by the Canaanites' possession of nine hundred chariots of iron. What tremendous resources or weapons do the enemies of our faith possess, and how do we combat them?

The secular humanists control or influence many of the institutions in our society. Their influence is felt in government, education, entertainment, and elsewhere. The Christian who takes a stand for Biblical morals may well feel like a lone warrior surrounded by nine hundred chariots. Another enemy, the advocates of religious cults, seem to make effective use of the printed word. We encounter their literature often enough that we may also feel surrounded by it. Temptation to sin is one more enemy that seems to be constantly assailing us today. Satan uses the media, conversations with neighbors and acquaintances, and various other means to hammer in his philosophy that it is all right to lie, cheat, covet, take revenge, and indulge in unrestricted pleasure. Listen to John's ringing declaration: "Ye are of God, little children, and have overcome them: because greater is he that is in you, than he that is in the world" (1 John 4:4). We need to remember that the greatest power and the richest resources are on our side.

2. How can a woman contribute to the morale of other Christian workers?

Many churches have prayer groups made up of faithful women. Aside from the power generated through their prayers, they bring a psychological boost to the ministers, elders, missionaries, and other workers who are aware that these ladies are praying for them. Also, it often seems that women are more conscientious about expressing a word of appreciation or commendation to those who serve in the church, and this practice is a definite means of boosting morale. Another observation here pertains to the willingness of women to perform many different tasks in the church. Unfortunately in many churches the men are too much occupied with other things and negligent regarding their Christian responsibilities. When this happens, it is an encouragement to the minister and the elders to see the church's women giving of their time and energy to accomplish much of the work that needs to be done.

3. What are some ways of expressing encouraging words to one another in the church, so that we can spur one another to greater accomplishments?

Public words of encouragement can be very helpful. We may tend to avoid singling out members for commendation in public services, because we may fear "missing someone" when the plaudits are handed out. Or we may fear we will give the impression that the purpose of serving in the church is in order to receive the praise of men. In spite of these hazards, public commendation is worthwhile because it makes people feel good about what they are doing in the church, and it motivates them to continue their efforts. Offering private expressions of appreciation accomplishes some of the same purposes. When a fellow member goes out of his way to express personal appreciation, that can be a very warm and uplifting experience. The sending of letters, notes, or cards to one another can be another way of communicating this private kind of encouragement.

4. What do you think of the following statement: "Too many Christians are sitting back and waiting for inspiration, when they should be stepping out initiating action"?

A legitimate balance needs to be achieved here. It is true that there are a few Christians who have so overextended themselves in service that they need to let up somewhat and take the time to be fed, built up anew in their faith, and given a fresh supply of inspiration. However, it appears that far more church members have the opposite problem. They are engaged in a never-ending quest for "mountaintop experiences"; they are still waiting for just the right feelings to develop, and then they will be ready to take on church responsibilities and throw themselves into the work. Sometimes action in the Lord's cause brings its own kind of inspiration. Many times, however, we must plug along in Christian work even when there is little emotional satisfaction is it. Perhaps Paul's promise to the Galatians is applicable to these leaner times: "Let us not become weary in doing good, for at the proper time we will reap a harvest if we do not give up" (Galatians 6:9, *New International Version*).

Gideon: Reluctant Leader

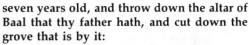

LESSON SCRIPTURE: Judges 6.

PRINTED TEXT: Judges 6:11-16, 25-29, 32.

Judges 6:11-16, 25-29, 32

11 There came an angel of the Lord, and sat under an oak which was in Ophrah, that pertained unto Joash the Abiezrite: and his son Gideon threshed wheat by the winepress, to hide it from the Midianites.

12 And the angel of the Lord appeared unto him, and said unto him, The Lord is with thee, thou mighty man of valor.

13 And Gideon said unto him, O my Lord, if the Lord be with us, why then is all this befallen us? and where be all his miracles which our fathers told us of, saying, Did not the Lord bring us up from Egypt? but now the Lord hath forsaken us, and delivered us into the hands of the Midianites.

14 And the Lord looked upon him, and said, Go in this thy might, and thou shalt save Israel from the hand of the Midianites: have not I sent thee?

15 And he said unto him, O my Lord, wherewith shall I save Israel? behold, my family is poor in Manasseh, and I am the least in my father's house.

16 And the Lord said unto him, Surely I will be with thee, and thou shalt smite the Midianites as one man.

· · · · · · · · · · · · · ·

25 And it came to pass the same night, that the Lord said unto him, Take thy father's young bullock, even the second bullock of seven years old, and throw down the altar of Baal that thy father hath, and cut down the grove that is by it:

26 And build an altar unto the Lord thy God upon the top of this rock, in the ordered place, and take the second bullock, and offer a burnt sacrifice with the wood of the grove which thou shalt cut down.

27 Then Gideon took ten men of his servants, and did as the Lord had said unto him: and so it was, because he feared his father's household, and the men of the city, that he could not do it by day, that he did it by night.

28 And when the men of the city arose early in the morning, behold, the altar of Baal was cast down, and the grove was cut down that was by it, and the second bullock was offered upon the altar that was built.

29 And they said one to another, Who hath done this thing? And when they inquired and asked, they said, Gideon the son of Joash hath done this thing.

· · · · · · · · · · · · · ·

32 Therefore on that day he called him Jerubbaal, saying, Let Baal plead against him, because he hath thrown down his altar.

GOLDEN TEXT: The angel of the Lord appeared unto him, and said unto him, The Lord is with thee, thou mighty man of valor.—Judges 6:12.

Lesson Aims

This lesson should:

1. Help the class understand Gideon's feeling of unworthiness to do great things for God.

2. Lead the class to understand that a sense of our limitations can be a help to God's empowering of us if we are willing to be used by Him.

3. Encourage class members to specify one way they will allow God to work through them this week.

Lesson Outline

Display visual 7 from the visuals/learning resources packet. It expresses an important truth from this lesson text. It is shown on page 396.

Introduction

A. Repetition

Repetition is a fine tool for learning. Does an elementary school child wish to learn the alphabet? He does so by repeating it over and over. Does a Junior girl want to learn the books of the Bible so she can write them from memory? She does so by repeating the listing time and again. The adult choir member learns a new anthem by repetition—line by line, section by section.

Such being the force of repetition, we wonder why Israel did not learn the lesson God was trying to teach them—that faithfulness to Him would bring blessing, and disobedience would bring punishment. The lesson was taught repeatedly. Each time the people turned from God to worship the gods of the Canaanites, punishment came; and when Israel returned to God, the blessings of peace and prosperity followed.

But the attraction of the sensuous and self-pleasing worship of these false gods was strong. In time, a new generation of Israelites would rise up, who either had not learned or chose to forget the lesson imparted to previous generations. They, like their ancestors, began to worship Baal and Ashtoreth and to turn from the way of Jehovah. And so the lesson had to be taught once again.

B. Lesson Background

Forty years of peace had followed the victory of Deborah and Barak, which we studied last week. A new generation had grown up, and of them it is said that they "did evil in the sight of the Lord" (Judges 6:1). At this time the Lord sent the Midianites, Amalekites, and other tough nomads from the desert to punish His people. It seems they persistently brought their flocks and herds into the Israelite areas and pastured them on the fields and crops. Unable to protect themselves, the Israelites took to the hills to hide (vv. 2, 3). Finally they fell under the nomads' domination completely. Their own herds and flocks were destroyed and they themselves were reduced to poverty.

The description of Israel's desperate situation is given in verses 5 and 6: "For [the Midianites] came up with their cattle and their tents, and they came as grasshoppers for multitude; for both they and their camels were without number: and they entered into the land to destroy it. And Israel was greatly impoverished because of the Midianites; and the children of Israel cried unto the Lord." Once again God heard the cry of His people and raised up a deliverer to rescue them from their oppressors. In this lesson and the next, we learn of the exploits of this deliverer—Gideon.

I. Dialogue With an Angel (Judges 6:11-16)

A. A General Objection Answered (vv. 11-14)

11. And there came an angel of the Lord, and sat under an oak which was in Ophrah, that pertained unto Joash the Abiezrite: and his son Gideon threshed wheat by the winepress, to hide it from the Midianites.

The Midianites had come upon the land to exploit and to enslave. The *angel of the Lord* came to deliver and liberate. In times when all seems darkened by force and greed, we must not forget God's reviving and rescuing power. In the very midst of the chains of a Palestinian prison, an angel awakened and freed Peter. In the howling gale and desperate panic of a ship battered in a storm, an angel "stood by" Paul.

The angel found Gideon threshing wheat *by the winepress,* literally, "in the winepress." The *winepress* was a vat cut in the outcropping stone. Here, in season, grapes were trodden so that the juice flowed out into a vat set at a lower level. The vat was not very deep, but in this case it would have provided some "screening" from curious eyes. The normal place to thresh wheat would be on a flat surface on an exposed height where wind could more easily carry away the chaff. To thresh wheat *in* a winepress would be very unsatisfactory, but that Gideon would try to do so was a measure of the fear of the Midianites that lay heavily on all in Israel.

We do not know where *Ophrah* was. Undoubtedly it was Joash's hometown and would have been located in the territory of Manasseh, west of the Jordan River. The *Abiezrites* were a clan of the tribe of Manasseh (v. 15).

12. And the angel of the Lord appeared unto him, and said unto him, The Lord is with thee, thou mighty man of valor.

The Lord is with thee was a common form of greeting among Israelites, but under the circumstances it seems to have been spoken in the nature of an assurance for Gideon. *Thou mighty man of valor* seems a strange salutation to one who was down in a winepress trying to thresh wheat because of his fear of the Midianites. We are given no hint that Gideon's past life provided a basis for this angelic characterization. However, later events would prove the word true. The angel spoke to Gideon of his potential more than of his past. God's presence and power would be made available to him in a special way. His acceptance of leadership would help him become what God saw he *could* be, rather than what he felt himself to be *now.*

God uses us for His service today in similar ways. We may not be given power to work miracles, but nevertheless we can accomplish "miraculous" results as we try to do God's will in obedient surrender to Him. One does not find that Gideon himself worked any supernatural "wonder." But he became willing to follow God's instructions even when those directions were seemingly ridiculous. By doing as directed, tremendous results followed.

13. And Gideon said unto him, O my Lord, if the Lord be with us, why then is all this befallen us? and where be all his miracles which our

How to Say It

ABIEZRITE. *A-by-ez-*rite (strong accent on *ez*).
AMALEKITES. *Am-*uh-leck-ites.
ASHTORETH. *Ash-*toe-reth.
BAAL. *Bay-*ul.
CANAANITES. *Kay-*nan-ites.
GIDEON. *Gid-*e-un.
GOLIATH. Go-*lye-*uth.
JERUBBAAL. Jer-uh-*bay-*ul or Je-*rub-*a-ul.
JEZREEL. *Jez-*re-el.
JOASH. *Jo-*ash.
MIDIANITES. *Mid-*e-un-ites.
OPHRAH. *Ahh-*fruh.

fathers told us of, saying, Did not the Lord bring us up from Egypt? but now the Lord hath forsaken us, and delivered us into the hands of the Midianites.

O my Lord, if the Lord be with us. The first *Lord* in this verse is the Hebrew word for master or owner. Sometimes it means simply the courteous *Sir.* The second *Lord* represents God's personal name, Jehovah.

Gideon found it hard to believe God really was *with* them because they were so unable to escape from their oppressors. He did not recognize that the reason for their difficulties was the persistent failure of the Israelites to be faithful to God's commands. To expect God's help without doing God's will is an exercise in futility.

"WHY DOES THIS HAPPEN TO ME?"

"One of our cars was just repossessed, and our phone has been disconnected. My husband lost his job—they fired him because he was late getting to work a couple of times. I was laid off too. We both have temporary jobs now, but we don't get paid until the end of the week, and we can't get the other car started. *Why does all of this happen to me?*"

The woman did not mention that both cars were running nicely (at least adequately), until her self-styled-mechanic husband attempted to "hop them up." Nor did she acknowledge that the sizeable amounts of cash they spent weekly for pleasure and entertainment could have been applied to car payments or the phone bill. Tardiness at work could have been avoided with some initiative and planning.

Gideon was forgetful of Israel's sin when he asked, "Why has all this happened to us?" Israel could have enjoyed the constant protection and prosperity of divine providence, if only they had remained faithful.

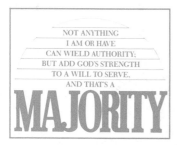

visual 7

Christians are not guaranteed a trouble-free existence. But we can avoid much of the suffering, that comes as a result of our own foolishness and sin. And we can trust that all things will work out for our ultimate good, if our love for God is genuine (Romans 8:28).   —R. W. B.

14. And the Lord looked upon him, and said, Go in this thy might, and thou shalt save Israel from the hand of the Midianites: have not I sent thee?

The Lord . . . said. Because the angel was God's messenger (v. 12), it could be said here that the Lord was speaking. Gideon wondered why God had not acted to save them. God indicated He was acting now through him. Gideon must be willing to lead if God was going to help them. God had liberated the Israelites from Egypt, but not without the leadership of Moses. Now who was to go forth to rally the Hebrews? In effect, God said to Gideon, "You are My man, and I intend to empower you with My might so Israel can be saved."

ON KNOWING YOUR OWN STRENGTH

Have you ever had difficulty loosening lug nuts or the cap on a jar of home-canned vegetables? You probably wondered, "How could I have gotten this so tight? I must not know my own strength!" Underestimating one's strength *can* cause lug nuts and jar rings to be overtightened. At the same time, underestimating one's strength can result in failure to loosen some things that have been previously overtightened.

Gideon was reluctant to answer God's call because he didn't know his own strength. Jehovah said to him, "Go in the strength you have" (Judges 6:14, *New International Version*). Gideon underestimated his power and ability when he considered these only in human terms. When the Lord said, and later proved, "I will be with you," Gideon rightly reckoned the value of divine assistance and was successful in delivering his nation from the Midianites.

Too often, we who are Christian don't even *try* to do what Christ has commissioned us to do, because we underestimate the strength and

power available to us. We truly *can* do whatsoever He has commanded us. We are not *bionic*, but we are "born again," so let us go into all the world with the strength we possess. Jesus has promised to be with us, "even unto the end of the world" (Matthew 28:20).   —R. W. B.

B. A Specific Objection Refuted (vv. 15, 16)

15. And he said unto him, O my Lord, wherewith shall I save Israel? behold, my family is poor in Manasseh, and I am the least in my father's house.

Naturally enough, Gideon was dismayed. Who was he to be able to save Israel, and how could he ever do it? He was *the least* (perhaps the youngest child) in his family, which was very *poor*. He was one of the last persons one would have thought of as a possible leader.

But God may not choose the persons we think are most qualified to be heroes for Him. Joseph was younger than all his brothers, except Benjamin, but he was destined for greatness. David was the youngest of his family, but he became an unexpected champion as he slew the giant Goliath. God can help minor persons accomplish major tasks by the power He gives them.

16. And the Lord said unto him, Surely I will be with thee, and thou shalt smite the Midianites as one man.

The answer God gave Gideon for his feeling of inadequacy was the assurance of His presence. God would not only be *on* his side, but *by* his side as he led Israel against their oppressors. To go into a law court with a famous lawyer by one's side, or be wheeled into an operating room and see a great surgeon prepared to operate on you, or to walk down a dark alley with a powerful expert in martial arts striding with you—all are weak comparisons with the sense of power and security God's promised presence should bring.

II. Demand for Drastic Action (Judges 6:25-29, 32)

In verses 17-24 we read that Gideon prepared meat and unleavened cakes, which he presented to the angel who had spoken to him. The angel touched them with his staff and they evaporated in a flash of fire, after which he disappeared. Gideon then built an altar there to the true God.

A. A Reform Begins at Home (vv. 25-27)

25. And it came to pass the same night, that the Lord said unto him, Take thy father's young bullock, even the second bullock of seven years old, and throw down the altar of Baal that thy

father hath, and cut down the grove that is by it.

That night the Lord commanded Gideon to destroy the *altar of* the god *Baal*, which his *father* had erected on his premises. The *grove*, the wooden idol of the female deity which stood nearby, was to be cut down. The team of oxen would be needed to pull down and remove the altar of Baal and to bring the materials needed for building the altar of the Lord, which is mentioned in the next verse.

26. And build an altar unto the Lord thy God upon the top of this rock, in the ordered place, and take the second bullock, and offer a burnt sacrifice with the wood of the grove which thou shalt cut down.

In the Hebrew *this rock* means the citadel of the city. It was probably a high point of ground visible from all parts of Ophrah. This was an unnerving command Gideon was given. To destroy a worship sanctuary that belonged to his father, to replace it with an altar to Jehovah, and then to sacrifice a choice bull from his father's herd—this was drastic action indeed. There were to be later tests of Gideon's faith, but if he had failed this first one, it is doubtful if there would have been much more to his story. Here he took a stand for God, which was unmistakable and costly. This was where he launched out on his career of leadership, which led to revolt, revival, and the renewal of the fortunes of the Hebrews of his era.

27. Then Gideon took ten men of his servants, and did as the Lord had said unto him: and so it was, because he feared his father's household, and the men of the city, that he could not do it by day, that he did it by night.

Here we have another evidence of that mixture of hesitancy and heroism so characteristic of Gideon. He did indeed do what he had been instructed to do, but *because he feared his father's household, and the men of the city*, he did it *by night*. If he had done this by day he was certain that he would have been confronted by those who did not want Baal's worship center destroyed. God had not said at what time of day this action should be carried out, so Gideon chose that period when he would least likely be noticed. Even so, the task was arduous and fraught with great danger.

Gideon was to call his people back to the worship and the ways of the true and living God. But how could he urge a new way of life upon his fellows as long as the worship of Baal was being carried on at his own home site? If others were to be called to change their ways and to risk their all in the Lord's cause, then Gideon had to be willing to set an example himself.

Any of us who seek for renewal or renovation in the life and work of the church must also be aware of our own need of deeper faith, higher levels of living, and broader sympathies. It is not only charity that "begins at home."

B. Forceful Deeds Are Noticed
(vv. 28, 29)

28. And when the men of the city arose early in the morning, behold, the altar of Baal was cast down, and the grove was cut down that was by it, and the second bullock was offered upon the altar that was built.

Overnight a revolutionary development had occurred. Rude hands had attacked their worship precincts, had thrown down Baal's altar and had destroyed the *grove*, the wooden image of Ashtoreth. On a new altar a sacrifice had been offered to the God of Israel. Now a choice had to be made—whether to defend the honor of the desecrated Baal, or to renew an allegiance to the seemingly forgotten God of Israel. This was not a case where a gradual turning from Baal worship would do. God would brook no rivals. He had said in giving the commandments on Sinai, "Thou shalt have no other gods before me. Thou shalt not make unto thee any graven image.... Thou shalt not bow down ... to them, nor serve them: for I the Lord thy God am a jealous God" (Exodus 20:3-5).

The altar on which the sacrificed bull was placed must have been a very ordinary and elementary one. There surely was no time in one night to erect anything ornate or elaborate. But the plainness of the altar was of no concern to God, the Maker of Heaven and earth. Better it was to sacrifice to God on the most humble altar than to worship a false, debasing deity in a worship center glittering with precious stones. God ever seeks worshipers who will bring Him devotion with sincerity and spirituality (John 4:23). To such worship simplicity is no barrier and luxuriance no aid.

29. And they said one to another, Who hath done this thing? And when they inquired and asked, they said, Gideon the son of Joash hath done this thing.

Since Gideon had taken ten servants with him to help with the work of destruction, many people knew who the leader was. It's likely that one of these men had spoken about it. While Gideon had acted secretly at night, his work was visible and correctly assigned to him by day. Although the next two verses are not in our printed text, they should be considered, for they help explain verse 32.

The indignant devotees of the cult of Baal at once went to the house of Joash and demanded that Gideon be brought out so he could be executed for his deeds. But Joash stood up for his son in a staunch manner. Joash said he would rather seek the death of those who pled for Baal. With persuasive logic he said, "If Baal is a god, he should be able to act for himself. Since his altar has been despised and destroyed, he should be able to defend his own honor." Thus Gideon's own father, who had lost much by Gideon's actions, refused to punish him. Then the angry crowd seemed to dissipate.

C. Gideon's Challenge Accepted (v. 32)

32. Therefore on that day he called him Jerubbaal, saying, Let Baal plead against him, because he hath thrown down his altar.

He called him Jerubbaal. The verb here is equivalent to a passive form, "he was called Jerubbaal," not just by Joash but by the people generally. *Jerubbaal* means "Let Baal plead." This was a recognition of Gideon as a challenger to the authority of Baal. Coupled with Gideon's action in sacrificing a bull to Jehovah, this also was an assertion of God's place as the real diety worshiped by Israel.

A new hero was suddenly made in the broken circles of Israel. The people rallied around Gideon. Even his father, the converted magistrate, took his subordinate place as a follower of the new hero. When, therefore, a new invasion was threatened by the Midianites, the leader, hitherto humble and almost unknown, stepped forward at the head of the army as the recognized general who was to deliver Israel and inflict a crushing blow on the adversaries. This familiar battle is the subject of next week's lesson.

Conclusion

A. Might for the Modest

Gideon did not feel he could become the deliverer of his people. He was very aware of his inadequacy and was most hesitant to think of himself in heroic terms. When the angel greeted him as a "valiant" or "mighty" man, he was quick to remonstrate that he was far from being any such thing. He just couldn't bring himself to believe God was going to use him and empower him. It required repeated proofs and "checkings" by Gideon to be convinced. In such reluctance to accept a position of leadership, Gideon was in good company. When the Lord told Jeremiah he had "ordained" him to be a prophet, he replied, "Ah, Lord God! behold, I cannot speak: for I am a child" (Jeremiah 1:5, 6). Moses himself had made several excuses (Exodus 3, 4).

When we are called to tasks of leadership or responsibility in God's work today, a feeling of

Home Daily Bible Readings

Monday, July 10—The People Cry to God (Judges 6:1-6)

Tuesday, July 11—The Lord Hears the People's Cry (Judges 6:7-10)

Wednesday, July 12—The Lord Calls Gideon (Judges 6:11-18)

Thursday, July 13—Gideon Is Given a Sign (Judges 6:19-24)

Friday, July 14—Gideon Destroys the Altar of Baal (Judges 6:25-32)

Saturday, July 15—Gideon Seeks Another Sign (Judges 6:36-40)

Sunday, July 16—God's Promise of Strength (Isaiah 35)

unworthiness and insufficiency is in no way a disqualification. Those who recognize the significance of the work and the demands for dedication made upon them are the most apt to be pliable in God's hands. We must realize how very much we depend upon God's help and blessing for the accomplishment of His purposes through us. There is a place for self-confidence and assurance, but it must not come from vanity or any sense of superior merit and ability. Rather, it should come from an awareness of our lack overcome by God's fullness, and of our inability ultimately made competent through God's truth, His people's help, and His indwelling presence.

B. Prayer

Our Father, we are insufficient of ourselves to do all the things we are called to do that the church of our Lord may live and grow in our world. We confront false gods that allure us with promises of pleasure, popularity, and material prosperity. Often we do not feel competent to overcome them ourselves, let alone lead others to do so.

Alert us to the shallowness and unreality of the sensual but sterile objects of devotion that would lure us today. May we be willing to accept calls to service and to trust so that our Savior's help and presence will enable us to fill them with forcefulness. Open our eyes to see, our wills to respond, and our lives to be devoted to those opportunities for growth, for service, and for fullness of life that are proffered to us. In Jesus' name, amen.

C. Thought to Remember

Gideon could not defeat a false god until he believed the true One. Neither can we.

Learning by Doing

*This page contains an alternate lesson plan emphasizing learning activities. Classes
desiring such student involvement will find these suggestions helpful.*

Learning Goals

After this lesson, a student should be able to:
1. List the major areas in which Gideon had to take a stand for the Lord.
2. Compare Gideon's call with our call from God.
3. Choose one area in which he will take a stand for the Lord.

Into the Lesson

Bring enough hymnals to class so there will be one for every two students. Have the students work in pairs for this opening activity. Ask them to read through the words of George Duffield's hymn, "Stand Up, Stand Up for Jesus," and then compile a list of activities or issues in which a Christian might stand for Christ today. Allow two minutes for compilation.

Call time and write a list of the students' suggestions on the chalkboard, overhead transparency, or flip chart (be sure to save this list for later in the lesson). Make your transition to Bible study by saying, "We have discovered several areas in which Christians may be called to take a stand for Christ. We recognize too that there may be some reluctance to follow through with that stand. As we study Gideon's life today, we will be looking for ways to overcome our reluctance."

Into the Word

Divide your class into groups of four to six and give each a sheet of paper with the instructions for one of the groups below.

Group 1: Read Judges 6:1-6. Write a brief report stating the problems facing Israel. Identify the oppressors and Israel's response.

Group 2: Read Judges 6:11-15. Report on how God called Gideon and Gideon's response to God's call to lead Israel. Include ideas on Gideon's concept of himself and his concept of God.

Group 3: Read Judges 6:16-24. Identify the actions Gideon took and his purpose for taking them. Identify the signs God used to convince Gideon of His support. Explain Gideon's understanding of God at this point in time.

Group 4: Read Judges 6:25-32. Report on the first task Gideon was to accomplish. Give reasons why this was an important task. Explain how completing it enabled Gideon to become a leader and take a stand for God.

Allow eight to ten minutes for this exercise; then have the groups share their findings. Draw upon the commentary in this book to fill in any gaps in the presentations.

Place the following Scripture references on the chalkboard. Move into the next section of Bible study by saying, "God called Gideon to a task. Today He calls Christians. As we study the Scriptures, we will note some of the calls given to us." Have your students work in their groups again and summarize the Scriptures. (Answers are given for the teacher's convenience.)

1. Matthew 28:18-20 (The call to share the gospel with others)
2. 1 Corinthians 1:9 (The call into fellowship with Christ)
3. 1 Corinthians 1:21-24 (The call to salvation)
4. Colossians 3:15 (The call to peace)
5. 1 Timothy 6:12 (The call to eternal life)
6. 2 Timothy 1:9 (The call to holiness)
7. 1 Peter 2:21 (The call to follow in Christ's steps)

Discuss these questions: "How does God call us today? How should Christians respond to God's call today? What is different about the call of Gideon and the call in the verses we have just searched? What is similar? How does God's promise to be with Gideon help you to be less reluctant in heeding His call today?"

Into Life

Give each student a half sheet of paper and ask each to make a list of individuals with whom he has frequent contact. This list could include spouse, children, brothers, sisters, parents, co-workers, neighbors, friends, and others. Some of these individuals may be people to whom the student does not relate well. Have the student choose an item from the list compiled in the "Into the Lesson" section. Ask, "What must you do to take a stand for Christ before these people? What are you doing now? What do you need to begin to do? How can you best demonstrate your stand to those who do not like you?" Encourage your students to be specific in their answers. When they have done this, ask for volunteers to share their ideas with the class. (Remember to share without using names in order to protect identities.)

Close your session by singing the hymn, "Stand Up, Stand Up for Jesus."

Let's Talk It Over

The questions on this page are designed to encourage review of the lesson Scriptures and to promote discussion of the lesson by the class. The answers provided are only discussion starters. Let your class talk it over from there.

1. How can we help fellow Christians perceive and reach their potential for the Lord?

The lesson writer notes that the angel's addressing of Gideon as a "mighty man of valor" may have been a way of stirring him to a realization of what he *could be* in God's service. Some Bible students see something similar to this in Jesus' assigning the title of "rock" to the apostle we know as Simon Peter (John 1:42). Jesus may well have given him that title to help him become the leader he was capable of being. All of this illustrates what can happen as a result of the way Christians talk to each other. If we emphasize the weaknesses of our fellow believers, that may tend to confirm them in their present undesirable status. But if we emphasize the strength of their faith and commend them for each step they take toward reaching their potential, we will help them to become modern-day counterparts to Gideon and Peter.

2. What are some situations we face in the Lord's service in which it is especially encouraging to know that He is with us?

The Lord's assurance that He would be with Gideon (Judges 6:16) is echoed in Jesus' magnificent promise, "Lo, I am with you always, even unto the end of the world" (Matthew 28:20). This promise is helpful to the person who is engaged in visitation for Christ. It can be rather unsettling to knock on the doors of complete strangers in order to speak to them about the Lord. To know that the Lord is right beside us as we approach that imposing door can help minimize our "butterflies." Another frightening assignment for many Christians is public speaking, whether preaching, teaching, or delivering a Communion meditation. If we can envision Jesus standing beside us as we face the class or congregation, we can speak with greater confidence. A special situation that poses some difficulty for many Christians is visiting a home or a funeral home, trying to bring comfort to the bereaved. We want to say something that will be genuinely helpful, and we want to demonstrate sincere sympathy, rather than to make some empty or pious-sounding remark. How encouraging it is to view ourselves in company with our compassionate Savior as we approach that bereaved person!

3. The lesson writer calls attention to "that mixture of hesitancy and heroism so characteristic of Gideon." Why does this mixture make Gideon an appealing figure for us?

Gideon's human inconsistency makes him a person with whom we can easily identify. When we want to escape for a time into the world of fantasy, we can appreciate the fictional heroes and heroines who have minimal weaknesses and who always succeed. But when we are looking for help in living in the real world, heroes like Gideon are much more valuable. Like him, we are at times bold and at times hesitant. We reason that if Gideon can be labeled a man of faith (Hebrews 11:32), then perhaps that virtue is not out of our reach. In addition to this, we might note that the account of Gideon is such as to confirm our viewpoint of the Bible as accurate history. This man is so human that we feel certain his career must be factual, and not the mere product of human imagination.

4. What should we say to a person who refuses to accept a position of responsibility in the church, claiming to be unworthy?

If the person appears to be qualified for the position in question, then our response may take one of two directions. Since some church members tend to hide behind a facade of false humility when approached about a position of leadership, we may need to deal with that. In this case the person who claims to feel unworthy is really saying he is not willing to shoulder such a responsibility, and that he is not interested in investing the time and effort required. He may not be intentionally lying or trying to deceive us, but avowed unworthiness makes a handy excuse. We need, as tactfully as possible, to point out that his statement of unworthiness is an excuse, that he is clearly fit for the job. On the other hand, if the individual demonstrates a genuine concern over his unworthiness, then our approach should be to show that such an awareness is an asset in accomplishing the task. We can point out from the Bible how God is best able to work through those who are aware of their need of His power and wisdom. Among the appropriate Scriptures that we may refer to are 2 Corinthians 12:7-10 and 1 Timothy 1:12-17.

Delivered by God's Power

LESSON SCRIPTURE: Judges 7.

PRINTED TEXT: Judges 7:2-7, 19-21.

Judges 7:2-7, 19-21

2 And the Lord said unto Gideon, The people that are with thee are too many for me to give the Midianites into their hands, lest Israel vaunt themselves against me, saying, Mine own hand hath saved me.

3 Now therefore go to, proclaim in the ears of the people, saying, Whosoever is fearful and afraid, let him return and depart early from mount Gilead. And there returned of the people twenty and two thousand; and there remained ten thousand.

4 And the Lord said unto Gideon, The people are yet too many; bring them down unto the water, and I will try them for thee there: and it shall be, that of whom I say unto thee, This shall go with thee, the same shall go with thee; and of whomsoever I say unto thee, This shall not go with thee, the same shall not go.

5 So he brought down the people unto the water: and the Lord said unto Gideon, Every one that lappeth of the water with his tongue, as a dog lappeth, him shalt thou set by himself; likewise every one that boweth down upon his knees to drink.

6 And the number of them that lapped, putting their hand to their mouth, were three hundred men: but all the rest of the people bowed down upon their knees to drink water.

7 And the Lord said unto Gideon, By the three hundred men that lapped will I save you, and deliver the Midianites into thine hand: and let all the other people go every man unto his place.

.   .   .   .

19 So Gideon, and the hundred men that were with him, came unto the outside of the camp in the beginning of the middle watch; and they had but newly set the watch: and they blew the trumpets, and brake the pitchers that were in their hands.

20 And the three companies blew the trumpets, and brake the pitchers, and held the lamps in their left hands, and the trumpets in their right hands to blow withal: and they cried, The sword of the Lord, and of Gideon.

21 And they stood every man in his place round about the camp: and all the host ran, and cried, and fled.

GOLDEN TEXT: And it came to pass the same night, that the Lord said unto him, Arise, get thee down unto the host; for I have delivered it into thine hand.—Judges 7:9.

Conquest and Challenge
Unit 2: Judges—A Time of Conflict and Adjustment (Lessons 5-10)

Lesson Aims

After this lesson, students should:

1. Acknowledge that a courageous minority can be used mightily by the Lord.

2. Be able to discuss how God's unexpected ways challenge and comfort us today.

3. Be challenged to take a stand for God regardless of whether it be with few or many.

Lesson Outline

INTRODUCTION
I. AVAILABLE RESOURCES (Judges 7:2-7)
   A. The First Subtraction (vv. 2, 3)
   B. The Second Subtraction (vv. 4-6)
     A Few Good Men
   C. The Promise of Victory (v. 7)
II. AMAZING TRIUMPH (Judges 7:19-21)
   A. The Deployment of Israel (vv. 19, 20)
   B. The Defeat of Midian (v. 21)
     The Sword of the Lord
CONCLUSION
   A. Hold Firm
   B. The Unexpectedness of God
   C. Prayer
   D. Thought to Remember

Display visual 8 from the visuals/learning resources packet. The actions of Gideon's army are the basis for this representation of the Christian's responsibility. It is shown on page 404.

Introduction

Gideon's faith seemed to need constant reassurance and renewal. As we saw in last week's lesson, at first he had difficulty believing God had really called him to be a leader in Israel. The angelic message to him was shown to be from God when fire flared from a rock to consume the offering Gideon had presented (Judges 6:17-24). Now he had summoned the tribes of Manasseh, Asher, Zebulun, and Naphtali to send warriors to meet with him, and thirty-two thousand responded—quite a formidable force. But before leading them against the Midianites and their allies, Gideon asked for another sign from God to reassure him of divine presence and aid.

Gideon put out a portion of fleecy wool on the ground that night and asked God to cause the fleece to become wet with dew while the earth around remained dry. In the morning he wrung a bowlful of water from the fleece, but the ground around it was dry. The next night he asked that the ground be wet and the fleece remain dry. On the next morning he found it as he had requested. Upon this evidence of God's presence, Gideon was ready to proceed with his task of directing his people in the conflict with Midian (Judges 6:34-40).

The hosts of the Midianites, "like grasshoppers for multitude," with camels "without number, as the sand by the sea side" (7:12), were camped "in the valley of Jezreel" (6:33). This is a valley running from the Mediterranean Sea at Mount Carmel down to the Jordan River, about fifteen miles south of the Sea of Galilee. The Israelites had assembled in the hills above and south of the valley.

I. Available Resources (Judges 7:2-7)

A. The First Subtraction (vv. 2, 3)

2. And the Lord said unto Gideon, The people that are with thee are too many for me to give the Midianites into their hands, lest Israel vaunt themselves against me, saying, Mine own hand hath saved me.

The stage seemed all set for the drama of Israel's rescue from the Midianites to unfold. However, at this juncture God told Gideon that the military resources of Israel were too great. Although they numbered thirty-two thousand, they were still greatly outnumbered. But if God should give them victory, they would likely become puffed up with their own success! Gideon himself may have been deciding that because of this great response to his "call to arms" they really might overcome the horde spread out before them. One can imagine his feelings of shock and surprise at God's words.

3. Now therefore go to, proclaim in the ears of the people, saying, Whosoever is fearful and afraid, let him return and depart early from mount Gilead. And there returned of the people twenty and two thousand; and there remained ten thousand.

We can only imagine Gideon's inner questioning as he followed God's command and made the announcement. No questions were to be asked; no penalties assessed. As the prospect of battle loomed, anyone who was afraid was free to leave. It became apparent that the great bulk of the group gathered to do battle with the Midianites had no stomach for conflict, especially when from their height they could see the great expanse of tents and tethered camels filling the valley below for miles on end. About two-thirds—twenty-two thousand of the thirty-two thousand assembled—left the ranks.

It must have been most discouraging to Gideon, but how much more so to the men who remained. At a time when it would have been natural to be cheered by the *addition* of more fighters, it must have been demoralizing to be faced with the sudden loss of thousands of their fellows. Even with their numbers diminished, it is to be questioned whether their actual fighting ability was impaired. How terrible it would have been to have these fearful, timid persons exposed to the shock and storm of battle! They certainly would have fled as soon as arrows flew and swords were drawn. Then their flight could well have led to a general rout.

B. The Second Subtraction (vv. 4-6)

4. And the Lord said unto Gideon, The people are yet too many; bring them down unto the water, and I will try them for thee there: and it shall be, that of whom I say unto thee, This shall go with thee, the same shall go with thee; and of whomsoever I say unto thee, This shall not go with thee, the same shall not go.

No doubt already astonished at the tremendous defection resulting from God's first directive, Gideon must have been really devastated by this second statement. Two-thirds less and *still too many!* The multitude of their enemies carpeting the valley below certainly had not decreased. It would seem the chance of victory became less and less as the Israelite forces were reduced. Now God proposed to "sort out" those who were to be Israel's deliverers. A test would reveal the fighting spirit, that was required if the victory God purposed was to be achieved. At this point God still had not revealed why it was so important to bring the entire group down to a drinking place. *The water* may have been the "well of Harod," flowing near where they were encamped (see verse 1).

5, 6. So he brought down the people unto the water: and the Lord said unto Gideon, Every one that lappeth of the water with his tongue, as a dog lappeth, him shalt thou set by himself; likewise every one that boweth down upon his knees to drink. And the number of them that lapped, putting their hand to their mouth, were three hundred men: but all the rest of the people bowed down upon their knees to drink water.

We are not to think the men who *lapped* their water could do so exactly as does a dog. Rather, the three hundred who lapped scooped up water in their hands and drank from their cupped hands; all the rest knelt down and drank directly from the stream or spring. The former drank with moderation, all the while remaining alert to the near presence of the enemy; the latter, who drank freely, were more intent on the momentary enjoyment of the stream.

Many times simple actions reveal character traits. God's awareness of this should alert us to the significance of seemingly minor acts. So Jesus warned us that "every idle word that men shall speak, they shall give account thereof in the day of judgment" (Matthew 12:36). But it also is true that "whosoever shall give to drink unto one of these little ones a cup of cold water only in the name of a disciple . . . shall in no wise lose his reward" (Matthew 10:42).

A Few Good Men

The United States Marine Corps wants "a few good men." The truth is, they would like to have *more* than just a few good men, but the fact is that truly good men are hard to find. If the standards were not so strict, if the training were not so demanding, if the pay were not so little, the Corps could be *crowded*—with unfit, lazy mercenaries who would compromise our military strength. The point is, Marines emphasize *quality*, rather than quantity.

Similarly, God was selective in reducing Israel's forces from thirty-two thousand men to only three hundred. He, of course, can work miracles with just a few good men.

Christ's church is challenged by the commission of world conquest. "The laborers are few," but if the few are truly *good*, God will give us victory. We must ask "the Lord of the harvest, that he will send forth laborers into his harvest," (Matthew 9:38). At the same time, we "ought to live holy and godly lives" and "grow in the grace and knowledge of our Lord and Savior Jesus Christ" (2 Peter 3:11, 18, *New International Version*).

How to Say It

ASHER. *Ash*-er.

EBED-MELECH. E-bed-*mee*-lek.

GIDEON. *Gid*-e-un.

GILEAD. *Gil*-e-ud.

GOLIATH. Go-*lye*-uth.

HAROD. *Hay*-rod.

JEZREEL. *Jez*-re-el.

MANASSEH. Muh-*nas*-uh.

MIDIANITES. *Mid*-e-un-ites.

NAAMAN. *Nay*-uh-mun.

NAPHTALI. *Naf*-tuh-lye.

ZEBULUN. *Zeb*-you-lun.

visual 8

Jesus never lowered standards of righteousness to recruit disciples. Each of His followers must "deny himself, and take up his cross, and follow" Him (Matthew 16:24).   —R. W. B.

C. The Promise of Victory (v. 7)

7. And the Lord said unto Gideon, By the three hundred men that lapped will I save you, and deliver the Midianites into thine hand: and let all the other people go every man unto his place.

Just imagine the blow God's words must have been to Gideon. There was not so much shock right at first when the three hundred were given special recognition. Perhaps for a fleeting moment Gideon thought, "These three hundred will be the ones to lead the first charge against our enemies. Perhaps they have been selected for some special service, or even as captains over groups of warriors."

But right after the selection of the three hundred for "special mention" came those words of unbelievable direction: *Let all the other people go.* This meant thousands upon thousands, so that only that seemingly insignificant, that totally inadequate, little group of three hundred remained. As yet Gideon had not been shown how it was that the small number remaining would be able to win a victory. God seemed to lead him step by step, unveiling each link in the chain of His purpose little by little.

The next eleven verses are omitted before the concluding section of our lesson Scripture continues with verse 19. Those verses tell of one last bit of encouragement given to Gideon after the final reduction of his forces. God told him to take his servant, Phurah, and go down to the area where the Midianites were camped. This they did, apparently creeping to where they could hear conversations in some of the encampments—probably on the outer perimeter. They overheard one man telling another of a dream of "a cake of barley bread" tumbling into the Midianite camp and overturning a tent. The second man interpreted the dream as a prophecy of Gideon's victory over "Midian, and all the host" (vv. 13, 14).

Overhearing the interpretation of this dream greatly encouraged Gideon, and he returned to his post as the Israelite commander full of confidence. He then divided the three hundred men into three groups and gave each man a trumpet and a torch hidden in a clay jar. There was no hand left for a weapon, but no man would need one as the conflict began. The three groups were strategically placed about the enemy camp, probably on low hills overlooking the valley. Gideon instructed his men to blow the trumpets when he signaled and to break the pitchers so the torches would flash forth. They also were to shout, "The sword of the Lord, and of Gideon" (vv. 16-18).

As this account unfolds we begin to see how much can be accomplished by a determined and resourceful minority. These three hundred were a tiny group in comparison with the hosts of Midian and their allies. They were a decided minority of the thirty-two thousand who had originally enlisted to fight Israel's enemies. But most of the beneficial changes in the history of humanity have been accomplished by minority movements. Individuals and small groups have won righteous victories, even when struggling against overwhelming odds. They have blown trumpets of alarm and arousal until some great social change has occurred: child labor laws, women's right to vote, emancipation of slaves, prison reform, and other human-rights advances. We never should underestimate the influence of committed crusaders, however few.

II. Amazing Triumph
(Judges 7:19-21)

A. The Deployment of Israel (vv. 19, 20)

19. So Gideon, and the hundred men that were with him, came unto the outside of the camp in the beginning of the middle watch; and they had but newly set the watch: and they blew the trumpets, and brake the pitchers that were in their hands.

The night was divided into three watches of four hours each: from sunset to 10 p.m., from 10 p.m. to 2 a.m., and from 2 a.m. to sunrise. The *beginning of the middle watch* would have been soon after 10 p.m. The new groups of guards, still sleepy-eyed, had just taken over guard duties when this sudden action occurred. How the hundreds of torches would illumine the night, showing up in the hills surrounding the camp! How alarming and chilling the blast of so many trumpets, echoing through the hills!

20. And the three companies blew the trumpets, and brake the pitchers, and held the lamps in their left hands, and the trumpets in their right hands to blow withal: and they cried, The sword of the Lord, and of Gideon.

Usually one torch would be enough to light the way for as many as twenty or thirty men. Therefore the three hundred torches gave the impression that from three thousand to nine thousand men were gathered, ready to plunge down upon the Midianites from every side. One trumpet sound could easily rally one hundred men, so three hundred trumpets could mean that thirty thousand foes were in the immediate vicinity. Imagine the confusion—frantic men scrambling to find their swords and their armor, shouts, cries, and camels rearing and plunging in fright. Since many groups had come together from rather independent and seminomadic tribes, there may have been no established, central command or disciplinary structure among the Midianites. To this confusion were added the shouts about *the sword of the Lord and of Gideon.* identifying the forces of Israel now prepared to assault them.

B. The Defeat of Midian (v. 21)

21. And they stood every man in his place round about the camp: and all the host ran, and cried, and fled.

They stood every man in his place. The men of Israel did not attack or run at the camp at all. They simply blew the trumpets and doubtless waved the torches. A panic was set off in the camp of the Midianites as the din of trumpets, the shouts of the Israelites, and then the yelling of frenzied, half-awake warriors threw everything into confusion. Seeing figures running wildly toward them in the dark, the Midianites mistook their own comrades for attacking enemies, and they began to kill one another. Doubtless the light of the three hundred torches accentuated the darkness among the myriad of tents and helped cause the panic. Some started to run away, shouting and screaming, and the stream of fleeing Midianites became a steadily thickening river of frantic, frightened men.

Gideon quickly sent word to the surrounding Israelite tribes to pursue the fleeing Midianites. Men of Ephraim especially were asked to guard the fords of the Jordan River and cut off retreat. This was done, princes and kings of Midian were slain along with their men, and only a remnant of the invaders escaped to the desert. As a result of this engagement, Midian's power over Israel was now broken. Gideon was established as the judge over the Hebrews, and the land had peace for forty years (8:28).

THE SWORD OF THE LORD

A popular self-improvement book of recent years is entitled, *Winning Through Intimidation.* The book does not encourage bullying one's way through life. Rather, it suggests that strength can be communicated with a self-confident spirit, successful appearance, poised presence, and enthusiastic and precise verbalization of convictions. Such attitudes and behavior can be very persuasive, and yes, *intimidating.*

Gideon and his small regiment won their battle through intimidation. Strategic deployment of troops, a burst of light, and the enemy was so startled and confused that they began to fight each other! Only three hundred men created the illusion of a much larger force, and thus did not have to lift a sword to send their foes scurrying into the night, and to their defeat.

It is ironic that Gideon's men, holding a light in one hand and a trumpet in the other, shouted, "The sword of the Lord!" The Lord's "sword" that night was the trust and obedience of Israel. Christians win victories day by day through faithfulness to the Word of God, the "sword of the Spirit" (Ephesians 6:17), not by bloodshed or bullying. Our strength is no illusion, for "The word of God is ... sharper than any two-edged sword" (Hebrews 4:12).   —R. W. B.

Conclusion

A. Hold Firm

The calamity that befell the Midianite hosts can teach us several lessons. One is that it is easy to be stampeded into confusion and defeat. The Midianite army was aware only of flashing lights, loud noises, and shouts. If they had held steady they would have realized no arrows were flying, no foes were charging at them with drawn swords. They were defeated by their own imaginations of disaster. We must not allow ourselves to become cowardly in God's service or panic at the first sign of opposition.

On the other hand, we must realize that determination, faith, and fervor are priceless ingredients. We may not be great in numbers as we face spiritual opposition. But even small groups, obeying God and holding firm for Him, can win great victories.

B. The Unexpectedness of God

Gideon's story accentuates the unusual way God sometimes fulfills His purposes. Gideon appears to be an unusually reluctant "hero" to begin with. One would think his repeated questioning would disqualify him for his important service. But God kept patiently "proving" His

Home Daily Bible Readings

Monday, July 17—The People Warned to Remember (Deuteronomy 8:11-20)

Tuesday, July 18—Gideon Chooses an Army (Judges 7:1-8)

Wednesday, July 19—The People the Lord Delivers (Deuteronomy 7:6-11)

Thursday, July 20—The Army Prepares for Battle (Judges 7:9-18)

Friday, July 21—Power Perfected in Weakness (2 Corinthians 12:7-10)

Saturday, July 22—Gideon's Army Defeats Midian (Judges 7:19-25)

Sunday, July 23—Victory Belongs to the Lord (Psalm 98)

presence and reality to him. God's dismissal of such large segments of the armed forces Gideon had gathered is surprising to us. Finally, to tell Gideon the principal offensive weapons he would have for his three hundred men would be pitchers, torches, and trumpets seems unbelievable. But God's strategy resulted in great success. These unlikely implements became more powerful armaments, with God's blessing, than an equal number of "chariots of iron" would have been without Him.

Again and again, God has acted in unorthodox ways to forward His cause. He used Moses' rod as an instrument of power, David's sling to kill Goliath, and ravens to feed Elijah. It was a slave girl who spoke the words that led Naaman the Syrian to seek God's healing, and it was Ebed-melech the Ethiopian who rescued Jeremiah from the slimy pit. John the Baptist fostered a revival while preaching in a desert wilderness. God's Son was born in a stable, worked as a carpenter, and chose fishermen as some of His apostles. He applied mud to open blind eyes. After one of Jesus' healing and teaching sessions, this general observation was made (an appropriate commentary on many of Jesus' activities): "We have seen strange things today" (Luke 5:26).

Who would have thought that Saul, a Jewish rabbi who persecuted Christians, would become one of the leading apostles of Jesus whose church he had attacked? Who could have imagined that the apostle John—one of two "sons of thunder," as Jesus called them—who asked that fire from heaven be called down to burn up those resisting Jesus, would become known as the "apostle of love"? Paul speaks truly in 1 Corinthians 1:27, 28, "But God chose the foolish things of the world to shame the wise; God

chose the weak things of the world to shame the strong. He chose the lowly things of this world and the despised things—and the things that are not—to nullify the things that are" (*New International Version*).

We are not at the end of God's surprises. Who knows what great Christian leadership may arise from totally unexpected places? May it be that great workers for our Lord will arise from Communist China? Perhaps the church there will become the strongest in the world. It is possible that the Moslem world may become penetrated and profoundly changed by our Lord's presence and power. It may yet be that dedicated missionaries from Asia or Africa will one day work with apostate and indifferent Europeans and Americans to change them and reestablish them in the faith.

New inventions in home video communications may open unexpected avenues for Christian teaching and ministry. Some new archaeological "find" may bring new light upon Biblical passages, clearing up difficulties and opening up new opportunities for the Christian penetration of previously closed scholarly bastions of indifference or opposition to the message of Jesus as Lord.

C. Prayer

O Father, increase our faith. Like Gideon, so often we only half believe. We are engaged in a spiritual struggle. At times it seems that we too are armed only with torches and trumpets. But, through studying Gideon's victory, may we be encouraged to know that "the weapons of our warfare are not carnal, but mighty through [Thee] to the pulling down of strongholds" (2 Corinthians 10:4).

In times when many of our fellows give up and go away, as did thousands of Gideon's troops, help us hold fast and keep on believing. May we find encouragement in knowing it is possible for spiritual victories to be won even though our numbers may be few. Let Gideon's valiant three hundred be a challenge to our determination and an inspiration to faithfulness.

We are grateful for every faithful Christian who is willing to hold steady and to let his light shine. We are thankful for every example of devoted dedication to the cause of our Lord. May we know humility in our achievements, patience in our afflictions, and courage in our confrontation with every form of evil. In Jesus' name, amen.

D. Thought to Remember

God's infinite resourcefulness is our unending assurance.

Learning by Doing

This page contains an alternate lesson plan emphasizing learning activities. Classes desiring such student involvement will find these suggestions helpful.

Learning Goals

This lesson should enable a student to:

1. Determine key character traits in Gideon that God could use to fulfill His purposes.

2. State how, like Gideon, God challenges us and comforts us through His power.

3. Praise God for His working and power in the believer's life.

Into the Lesson

As the class members arrive, give each a copy of the incomplete sentences below. Ask them to complete the sentences before talking to other members of the class.

1. My definition of God's power is—

2. God's power is best expressed by—

3. I could do anything if God would just—

When all have completed the sentences, have them share with one or two others. After a few minutes, ask several to share their response to each question with the entire class.

Make the transition to Bible study by stating that God has given us His power, but it is often demonstrated in ways that we do not expect. Like Gideon, we need to develop wisdom to accept God's working in our lives.

Into the Word

Begin with a brief overview of the "Introduction" section of the commentary material on page 402. Then examine the details of today's text through character studies. Divide your class into groups of five or six, making up at least three groups (use fewer people per group, if your class is smaller). Give each group one of the following assignments:

1. Read Judges 7 and develop a character sketch of Gideon from the passage.

2. Read Judges 7 and develop a character sketch of the Israelite army of three hundred from the passage.

3. Read Judges 7 and develop a character sketch of God from the passage.

Give the groups fifteen to twenty minutes to complete their assignments. Then let the groups share their character sketches with the whole class. Summarize these sketches on the board or overhead transparency. Among the attributes suggested should be these:

1. Gideon was obedient, teachable, cautious, anxious, confident, forceful, hesitant.

2. The three hundred were alert, obedient, precise, responsible, brave.

3. God is wise, powerful, just, a promise keeper, encourager, personal.

Although Gideon was hesitant, emphasize the fact that he was both teachable and obedient. With these key characteristics, God could accomplish much in Gideon's life.

Have several volunteers read the following verses of Scripture: Matthew 28:18; Romans 1:16; 15:13; 2 Corinthians 12:9; Ephesians 1:19-21; 3:20, 21; 6:10-18; 2 Thessalonians 3:9, 10. After each Scripture is read, ask the class, "How does God demonstrate His power in the life of a believer? What kind of power is this verse demonstrating?" Summarize the answers and move on to the "Into Life" section.

Into Life

Ask this question: "In what ways are we like Gideon?" Record the class's answers on the chalkboard or overhead transparency. Possible answers include the following: We believe in safety in numbers; we don't expect God to do the unexpected; we need to be encouraged by the Lord; we need to obey the Lord's commands/instructions.

Next, have your students divide again into their original groups. Ask each group to write a letter to an imaginary friend who has written to them about his difficulty in seeing God work in his life. The groups should use information learned in Judges 7 and the New Testament Scriptures given above to answer the friend. The groups should be aware of both the challenge and comfort that are available through God's power. When their letters are completed, have a spokesperson for each group read their letters to the class.

Give each class member a copy of the following questions. Ask each to answer the question as a means of making application of today's lesson truths to his own life.

1. According to the Scriptures studied today, how has God demonstrated His power in your life?

2. How can you better submit to God's wisdom and power in your life?

3. Write a prayer of thanks to God for His power in your life in the midst of bad times and good times.

Let's Talk It Over

The questions on this page are designed to encourage review of the lesson Scriptures and to promote discussion of the lesson by the class. The answers provided are only discussion starters. Let your class talk it over from there.

1. Gideon's experience illustrates that God sometimes reveals His purposes to man one step at a time. Why does God do this?

"We walk by faith, not by sight" (2 Corinthians 5:7). Paul's statement tends to go against our basic outlook on life. We want to know before hand where we are going and what we shall be doing. But God may put us into positions in which we must trust Him for guidance in taking each step. This faith walk that God requires of us is the key to a more satisfying life. If we always had everything we felt we needed, life would be rather routine. Besides, we would likely grow complacent and begin to take God's blessings for granted. But seeing ourselves as "strangers and pilgrims on the earth" (Hebrews 11:13) we can take delight in experiencing God's adequate provision and strength for every new leg of our Heavenward journey.

2. Gideon's three hundred were a relatively small group through whom God worked a mighty victory for His people. How does God similarly work through small groups in the church?

Of course, our small groups are more likely to consist of a dozen or twenty or perhaps thirty members. But much of the work of the church is accomplished by such groups. Committees, for example, can take care of many details and free the minister and elders for evangelism and shepherding tasks. Perhaps the term *committee* is a problem here. It tends to suggest a group of people "talking a problem to death," but coming up with no solutions. However, if committee members saw their task as one that could make an impact for evangelism, missions, education, etc., God could accomplish great things through them. Sunday-school classes are another kind of small group. They may be seen only in terms of an hour to endure each Sunday morning. But again, if we grasp the possibilities involved when a group of Christians come together to study the Bible, we will see greater victories in and through the church.

3. When it was clear that Israel was defeating the Midianites, many fresh volunteers were available to complete the rout. Are there parallels to this in the church?

Unfortunately, the church often seems to have many "fair-weather friends" or "sunny-time supporters." When the attendance is up, various programs are going well, and members are getting along well with one another, these people are eager to be part of the excitement. And this is understandable in a way, since human nature makes us want to be where there is contentment, victory, and progress. But churches go through times of difficulty, when the attendance, offering, additions, and general spirit are not so bright, and it makes matters worse to have these fickle members vanishing at such times. Another aspect of this situation is the practice of "church-hopping." Some Christians go from church to church in an apparent quest to find one that will be problem-free. How desperately the church needs members who will remain steadfast through the trying times as well as during the times when things are going well!

4. Who are some of the unexpected people through whom God can work wonders in the church?

Paul told Timothy, "Don't let anyone look down on you because you are young" (1 Timothy 4:12, *New International Version*), indicating that some folk underestimated the young man. We may overlook the young people in our church, as far as what they could contribute to the church's growth. But by their example, their enthusiasm, their willingness to work, and their readiness to respond to a challenge, our youth can be effective instruments through whom God can work.

Another group that we sometimes take for granted are the senior citizens. We may expect them to be little more than spectators, that their "service days" are over. But they possess experience, wisdom, patience, and faith that God can use in remarkable ways.

Many churches have handicapped persons among their members. While in recent years we have learned of handicapped individuals who have accomplished feats that seemed nearly impossible for them, we are still slow to see their potential in the church. It is exciting to ponder how God is able to use any person who is committed to Him to magnify Christ and build His church.

Fate of a Self-Appointed Leader

LESSON SCRIPTURE: Judges 8:22—9.

PRINTED TEXT: Judges 9:1-15.

Judges 9:1-15

1 Abimelech the son of Jerubbaal went to Shechem unto his mother's brethren, and communed with them, and with all the family of the house of his mother's father, saying,

2 Speak, I pray you, in the ears of all the men of Shechem, Whether is better for you, either that all the sons of Jerubbaal, which are threescore and ten persons, reign over you, or that one reign over you? remember also that I am your bone and your flesh.

3 And his mother's brethren spake of him in the ears of all the men of Shechem all these words: and their hearts inclined to follow Abimelech; for they said, He is our brother.

4 And they gave him threescore and ten pieces of silver out of the house of Baal-berith, wherewith Abimelech hired vain and light persons, which followed him.

5 And he went unto his father's house at Ophrah, and slew his brethren the sons of Jerubbaal, being threescore and ten persons, upon one stone: notwithstanding, yet Jotham the youngest son of Jerubbaal was left; for he hid himself.

6 And all the men of Shechem gathered together, and all the house of Millo, and went and made Abimelech king, by the plain of the pillar that was in Shechem.

7 And when they told it to Jotham, he went and stood in the top of mount Gerizim, and lifted up his voice, and cried, and said unto them, Hearken unto me, ye men of Shechem, that God may hearken unto you.

8 The trees went forth on a time to anoint a king over them; and they said unto the olive tree, Reign thou over us.

9 But the olive tree said unto them, Should I leave my fatness, wherewith by me they honor God and man, and go to be promoted over the trees?

10 And the trees said to the fig tree, Come thou, and reign over us.

11 But the fig tree said unto them, Should I forsake my sweetness, and my good fruit, and go to be promoted over the trees?

12 Then said the trees unto the vine, Come thou, and reign over us.

13 And the vine said unto them, Should I leave my wine, which cheereth God and man, and go to be promoted over the trees?

14 Then said all the trees unto the bramble, Come thou, and reign over us.

15 And the bramble said unto the trees, If in truth ye anoint me king over you, then come and put your trust in my shadow; and if not, let fire come out of the bramble, and devour the cedars of Lebanon.

Jul
30

GOLDEN TEXT: Pride goeth before destruction, and a haughty spirit before a fall.
—Proverbs 16:18.

Lesson Aims

As a result of this lesson, a student should:
1. Be able to tell the story of Abimelech and his brief reign.
2. Be encouraged to do all they can to spread Christ's truth, knowing that evils such as flourished in the days of the judges may be overcome as men are converted to the Christian way.

Lesson Outline

INTRODUCTION
    A. Politics
    B. Lesson Background
I. ABIMELECH'S AMBITIOUS AGITATION (Judges 9:1-3)
II. ABIMELECH'S DEADLY TREACHERY (Judges 9:4-6)
    Clamor for a King
III. JOTHAM'S SYMBOLIC STORY (Judges 9:7-15)
    Wasted Rhetoric?
CONCLUSION
    A. A Brief and Bloody Career
    B. Disasters Due to Disobedience
    C. Prayer
    D. Thought to Remember

Display visual 9 from the visuals/learning resources packet. It is shown on page 413.

Introduction

A. Politics

There are good people involved in politics, people whose intentions are honorable and whose influence is wholesome, people who try to end corruption and promote the welfare of all who are under their jurisdiction.

But there are also people in politics for what they can get out of it. Sincere concern for the welfare of the people they govern is replaced by concern for their own advancement. The seizure of power takes precedence over services to the populace. These greedy persons go into politics for purely selfish reasons.

This insincerity is not peculiar to the twentieth century. In this week's lesson we see a qualified and worthy man declining the kingship of his people and an unworthy man seeking it— and finding much support.

B. Lesson Background

Gideon's trust in God required several "proofs" to sustain it. Yet once convinced of God's presence and purpose, he complied with the Lord's directives so that a great victory for his people was achieved.

Following their victory over the Midianites, the Israelites wanted to make Gideon their king. But Gideon refused, saying that the Lord was the one who should rule over them. Although he was not their king, Gideon did exert great influence over Israel for forty years. During that period, some of the abuses associated with kingship began to creep in.

First, Gideon made an ephod out of the gold earrings taken from the slain Midianites, and it came to be regarded almost as an idol. An ephod was part of the Jewish high priest's garments. To it was attached the breastplate with the mysterious Urim and Thummim by which the will of God was revealed (Exodus 28:6-30). Some conjecture that Gideon's ephod was used in divination as a means of ascertaining what events might occur in the future. In any case, it was something that led his people astray, for "all Israel went . . . a whoring after it" (Judges 8:27).

Second, following the practice of kings, Gideon had many wives, which was in direct violation of the law (Deuteronomy 17:17). We are not told how many wives he had, but we know that he fathered seventy sons (Judges 8:30). There is no mention of the daughters who may have been born to him. Gideon had also a female slave from Shechem, who became his concubine, a second-class wife. She also bore him a son, named Abimelech.

Although Gideon's spiritual and moral examples were not what they should have been, still Israel did not turn to the worship of Baal until after Gideon's death. It was then that the seeds that had been sown bore their bitter fruit.

I. Abimelech's Ambitious Agitation (Judges 9:1-3)

1. And Abimelech the son of Jerubbaal went to Shechem unto his mother's brethren, and communed with them, and with all the family of the house of his mother's father, saying.

Shechem was a city situated in the southern part of the territory allotted to the tribe of Manasseh, of which *Jerubbaal* (Gideon) had been a member. It was located in a narrow valley between the mountains of Ebal and Gerizim.

Abimelech had seventy brothers from several mothers. But he himself was an outsider—at least he was not the son of a regular marriage as were the other sons of Gideon. He felt closest to his mother and his mother's people, who lived in Shechem. Apparently he had brooded over the situation confronting him from a political point of view. It would seem a son of Gideon would be the natural successor to his judgeship. But which of the seventy sons should have the priority? It seems that none of them had been selected or had come forward to claim preeminence at this time. There was a "power vacuum" in Israel, which Abimelech decided to fill. As his first step he went to Shechem seeking to enlist the cooperation of his mother's family in his quest to seize the reins of power.

2. Speak, I pray you, in the ears of all the men of Shechem, Whether is better for you, either that all the sons of Jerubbaal, which are threescore and ten persons, reign over you, or that one reign over you? remember also that I am your bone and your flesh.

The diffusion of authority among the many sons of Gideon is emphasized here. There was no likelihood that the direction of the life of the Israelites could be unified under seventy rivals, all with an equal claim to the succession to Gideon's leadership. Abimelech urged his relatives to convince the men of Shechem that the need for only one leader was obvious, and that none was better qualified for such a position than he—especially since he was a son of Gideon from their own city and from their own family.

3. And his mother's brethren spake of him in the ears of all the men of Shechem all these words: and their hearts inclined to follow Abimelech; for they said, He is our brother.

Abimelech was supported in his plot to seize power by the citizens of Shechem. They felt an affinity for him since he was from their own city, while all Gideon's other sons seemed to be living in and around Ophrah. There may have been some feeling that Gideon had not treated Abimelech's mother altogether properly, since he had never made her an "official" wife. This, however, is only conjecture. For whatever cause, the men of the city supported Abimelech in his quest for power.

II. Abimelech's Deadly Treachery (Judges 9:4-6)

4. And they gave him threescore and ten pieces of silver out of the house of Baal-berith, wherewith Abimelech hired vain and light persons, which followed him.

The betrayal of Gideon's sons for pieces of silver reminds us of the betrayal of Jesus. Of course, the circumstances and persons involved differ greatly, but in both cases a deed of infamy

How to Say It

ABIMELECH. Uh-*bim*-uh-lek.
BAAL-BERITH. Bay-ul-*bee*-rith.
EBAL. *E*-bul.
GERIZIM. *Gair*-ih-zim or Guh-*rye*-zim.
GIDEON. *Gid*-e-un.
JERUBBAAL. Jer-uh-*bay*-ul or J*e*r*ub*-a-ul.
JOTHAM. *Jo*-tham.
MILLO. *Mill*-o.
OPHRAH. *Ahh*-fruh.
SHECHEM. *Shee*-kem or *Shek*-em.
THUMMIM. *Thum*-im (*th* as in *thin*).
URIM. *You*-rim.
ZEBUL. *Zee*-bul.

was done because of the attraction of money. Surely "the love of money is the root of all evil" (1 Timothy 6:10). In this case the crime was compounded because the money was taken from *the house of Baal-berith*, the false god worshiped at Shechem. The name of this deity means "Lord (or Master) of the covenant." The Hebrews were to be the people of the covenant because God had "covenanted" with them to be their God. Now, they had devoted themselves to a god that led them far from the purity and goodness that the high and holy God of their fathers sought to inspire in them.

Abimelech's relatives did not engage personally in the bloody deeds he instigated. But they did provide the money from the treasury of their god so he could employ others. The description of the people Abimelech *hired* to do these acts of murder tells us they were *vain and light persons*. The *Today's English Version* reads "a bunch of worthless scoundrels."

5. And he went unto his father's house at Ophrah, and slew his brethren the sons of Jerubbaal, being threescore and ten persons, upon one stone: notwithstanding, yet Jotham the youngest son of Jerubbaal was left; for he hid himself.

We do not know the grisly details about how this slaughter was done, but it would seem they were herded together and led forth, one by one, to be killed on "the stone." In the midst of this scene of terror and murder Gideon's *youngest son Jotham* somehow managed to evade those seeking to destroy him.

6. And all the men of Shechem gathered together, and all the house of Millo, and went, and made Abimelech king, by the plain of the pillar that was in Shechem.

Possibly *the house of Millo* was a fortified part of the city or a military post nearby. The soldiers there joined with the citizens of Shechem to proclaim Abimelech king. The ceremony was held *by the plain of the pillar*, apparently a gathering point where important public ceremonies were held. Abimelech was not designated a "judge," a title that had sufficed until this time, but the *royal ruler*. This is a sign of that great longing the Hebrews had at this time to have a king like all the other nations round about. In the later records of Israel, Abimelech is never recognized as a king. He was made a monarch by his own self-will, not by God's will.

All possible sources of opposition to Abimelech's taking power were eliminated, he thought—drowned in a sea of blood. But not quite all was secure. One of Gideon's sons had escaped, and from him a voice against tyranny and terror was lifted in brave opposition to Abimelech's seizure of ruling power.

CLAMOR FOR A KING

Do children still play "Follow the Leader"? If memory serves correctly, youngsters select one from their peers to "lead" them through a maze of risky passages and gymnastic exercises, to test the balance, coordination, and courage of the other players. When a "follower" is unable or unwilling to imitate the leader, he is "out," eliminated from that round of competition. The leader continues the challenges until all followers have been eliminated.

Some people play "Follow the Leader" all of their lives. Like sheep, they simply follow the one in front of them, without exercising individual discernment. Just as sheep need a gentle shepherd, people need a caring leader.

The citizens of Shechem and the house of Millo foolishly chose Abimelech as king. Years later, Israel clamored for a king, too, against God's better judgment. People still seek leadership, some of them in all the wrong places. This instinctive need for a ruler explains the sociological phenomenon of cults. Christians must avoid inordinate love and loyalty to human leaders. We must never allow humans to usurp the throne of God in our hearts or the lordship of Christ in His church.   —R. W. B.

III. Jotham's Symbolic Story (Judges 9:7-15)

7. And when they told it to Jotham, he went and stood in the top of mount Gerizim, and lifted up his voice, and cried, and said unto them, Hearken unto me, ye men of Shechem, that God may hearken unto you.

Mount Gerizim was one of the two mountains between which Shechem was situated. Jotham

seems to have spoken to a group gathered there from the city. It may be that the group was not large but representative, so that Jotham's message could be carried to those who were not present. The substance of his remarks were embodied in what has been called a fable, since plants are represented as speaking and acting as humans.

Hearken unto me. Jotham believed that giving heed to his veiled denunciation of Abimelech, and probably rebelling against his sway, they would have God's help and blessing.

8. The trees went forth on a time to anoint a king over them; and they said unto the olive tree, Reign thou over us.

Anointing was the pouring of oil on a person's head as a means of inducting him into office among the Hebrews. Prophets and kings were anointed (1 Kings 19:15, 16), as well as priests (Leviticus 16:32). *The olive tree* was one of the most useful, widely cultivated plants in ancient Palestine. The oil was used for cooking, fuel, and medicinal purposes. Besides, it was a tall, strong tree.

9. But the olive tree said unto them, Should I leave my fatness, wherewith by me they honor God and man, and go to be promoted over the trees?

The olive tree was producing oil used in sacrifices to God and burned in the lamps of the tabernacle (Leviticus 2:1; Exodus 25:6), and it was filling many of the needs of man. To spend its time ruling over others would interrupt this useful service. It may well be that some of Jotham's slain brothers had been offered an opportunity to rule, but had felt too preoccupied with other tasks to do so.

10. And the trees said to the fig tree, Come thou, and reign over us.

The fig tree also was handsome, and it produced abundant and tasty fruit. Because the fruit could be dried, it made a nutritious item of the diet year round.

11. But the fig tree said unto them, Should I forsake my sweetness, and my good fruit, and go to be promoted over the trees?

The *fig tree* also refused to become a ruler, because it believed it was serving a more important function as a producer of food.

12. Then said the trees unto the vine, Come thou, and reign over us.

Although the grapevine was not so stately as the trees, yet it was graceful and beautiful. The producer of attractive and delicious grapes, it was worthy to be king.

13. And the vine said unto them, Should I leave my wine, which cheereth God and man, and go to be promoted over the trees?

Wine is said to *cheer man* (Psalm 104:14, 15), though its immoderate use was severely condemned (Proverbs 23:29-35). Wine could be pleasing or *cheering* to *God* when men used it as part of those offerings He had prescribed (Exodus 29:40; Leviticus 23:13; Numbers 15:5).

14. Then said all the trees unto the bramble, Come thou, and reign over us.

The *bramble* was a low, thorny bush. It was not strong or graceful, nor did it bear any fruit to delight God or man. It stood in stark contrast to the olive and fig trees and the grapevine.

15. And the bramble said unto the trees, If in truth ye anoint me king over you, then come and put your trust in my shadow; and if not, let fire come out of the bramble, and devour the cedars of Lebanon.

The thorn bush wanted to be sure the trees were serious and that its authority would be absolute. So it demanded that the trees put their trust in its shadow. How absurd, to see tall, beautiful trees bending low to find shelter under a lowly thorn bush! But if the trees refused, then the bramble would proceed to destroy them. Sometimes whole forests were wiped out by fires that began in the scrub bushes of the area. The bramble warned that such would be the fate of the trees if they did not accept its rule.

Of course, the whole aim of Jotham's fable was to point out the poor judgment of the people of Shechem in choosing Abimelech, rather than any of Gideon's legitimate sons, to be their king. Jotham did not leave the men of Shechem in doubt about his parable. He explained exactly what he meant. His father, Gideon (also known as Jerubbaal), had rescued them all from Midian, only half a century before. Had they dealt truly with him when they had supported Abimelech in murdering his sons and then had made Abimelech their king? If they had, then Jotham wished them all happiness with Abimelech. But if not, he said, "let fire come out from Abimelech, and devour the men of Shechem, and the house of Millo; and let fire come out from the men of Shechem, and from the house of Millo, and devour Abimelech." In other words, if Abimelech and the men of Shechem had conspired in a dirty deal, then Jotham prayed that they would destroy each other, for that was what they both deserved (vv. 16-20).

WASTED RHETORIC?

"I talk to the trees, but they won't listen to me." That could have been Jotham's song! Actually, he talked *of* the trees. But for all the good his message accomplished, he might as well have been talking *to* the trees. Jotham preached courageously and eloquently on behalf of God

visual 9

WHEN SELF-SERVING PERSONS HOLD THE REINS OF GOVERNMENT, A NATION IS ON THE ROAD TO RUIN.

and on behalf of his dead father and brothers. Yet his words were wasted on ears that were deaf to truth and on hearts that were hardened against justice. The citizens of Shechem were not listening.

God's prophets of later years met with a similar response. With only a few exceptions, they were largely unsuccessful in persuading people to turn from wickedness back to God.

Jonah, of course, was a most notable exception, when the whole city of Nineveh heard his message and repented. John the Baptist experienced a measure of success when the people of Judah and Jerusalem came out to Jordan to hear him preach, and were baptized. But as a rule, prophets preached to audiences like Ezekiel's, of whom it was said, "They hear thy words, but they do them not" (Ezekiel 33:32).

But this is all history. The question is, are we any different from God's people of those earlier times? Are the words of God's messengers today wasted on us?

—R. W. B.

Conclusion

A. A Brief and Bloody Career

Whether Jotham's fable was inspired or not, it proved to be prophetic. After Abimelech had ruled three years, rebellion was stirred up in Shechem. Probably Abimelech had taken over his father's headquarters in Ophrah, leaving Shechem under the authority of a man named Zebul. Some in Shechem may have thought their king was neglecting them. After all, they were the ones who had made him king. Abimelech brought his troops, crushed the rebellion, and destroyed the city. When one thousand men and women took refuge in a hold of the temple of Baal, Abimelech set the hold on fire, killing everyone in it. Then he went to take over another city, but there he got too close to the citadel while he was attempting to burn it down. A woman threw a heavy stone down from the top of the wall and broke his skull. With a last flash of pride, Abimelech ordered one of his men to kill him so it could never be said that a woman had done him in. Thus, amid tumult, flames, cries, and bloodshed, Abimelech came to his violent end (9:50-55). His life is a vivid illustration of Jesus' statement that those who take the sword shall perish by the sword (Matthew 26:52).

B. Disasters Due to Disobedience

Abimelech's career is one long illustration of how deviations from God's way can bring tragic consequences in many lives. As we have mentioned, the seeds of departure from the holy and uplifting worship of God were sown in Gideon's later days. The ephod Gideon made, which became an object of worship, was instrumental in leading the people to the degrading worship of Baal. Further, his example of multiple wives was far from God's idea of marriage.

The many children resulting from Gideon's conduct led to Abimelech's jealousy and hatred. Abimelech's evil disregard of God's commands caused him to incite men to murder and later to treachery toward his hometown. At point after point, one can see how false worship, pride, ambition, cruelty, ferocity, and lust debased and deranged men. God's way leads mankind to true devotion, humility, service, kindness, gentleness, and purity.

Many Bible teachers in the past century gave this brief summation of the main emphases of the Bible—"The Bible contains facts to be believed, commands to be obeyed, promises to be enjoyed (or embraced), and warnings to be heeded." Certainly the main value of the book of Judges lies in its warnings as we contemplate the events depicted in it. They present many warnings to us about attitudes and actions to be avoided. One may say it is a detour through an area where many explosions are occurring, numerous structures are being torn down, and faithful road signs are obscure or defaced. Red flags of warning confront the thoughtful Christian everywhere in the book of Judges.

Again and again Jesus and the New Testament writers urge us to "beware" of various evils. (For example, see Matthew 7:15; Luke 12:15; Philippians 3:2; Colossians 2:8; 2 Peter 3:17). We are not to "give heed" to fables or to seducing spirits (1 Timothy 1:4; 4:1), but to give "earnest heed" that our Christian standing not "slip" away from us (Hebrews 2:1). In many places we are told what we *should* be, but in many others what we *should not* be or do (Romans 12:16; 1 Corinthians 14:20; 2 Corinthians 6:14; Ephesians 5:17).

The book of Judges gives us several examples of what God can do for and through His people when they really trust Him. But there are many more instances when we are appalled to read of

Home Daily Bible Readings

Monday, July 24—Abimelech Gains Power (Judges 9:1-6)
Tuesday, July 25—Jotham Tells a Parable (Judges 9:7-15)
Wednesday, July 26—Jotham Prophesies the People's Fate (Judges 9:16-21)
Thursday, July 27—Revolt in Shechem (Judges 9:22-29)
Friday, July 28—Abimelech Quells the Revolt (Judges 9:30-41)
Saturday, July 29—Abimelech Captures Shechem (Judges 9:42-49)
Sunday, July 30—God Judges Abimelech (Judges 9:50-57)

broken faith, betrayal of trust, the repudiation of God's way, and the excesses of human passion and pride. The tenth chapter of 1 Corinthians lists many of the failures of the Hebrews during their journey from Egypt to Canaan (vv. 5-10). The words Paul uses concerning these sad instances may well apply to a survey of Judges and its tales of departure from God's ways: "Now these things happened to them as a warning, but they were written down for our instruction, upon whom the end of the ages has come. Therefore let anyone who thinks that he stands take heed lest he fall" (1 Corinthians 10:11, 12, *Revised Standard Version*).

C. Prayer

Our Father, we are shocked and saddened as we see the examples of human frailty and ferocity exhibited in the book of Judges. We still see evidences of these same traits of abandonment to sensate desires and of calloused indifference to human suffering in the conduct of people in our world today. We know this arises from hearts insensitive to Your mercy and kindness and from wills that are not yielded to Yours.

Father, help us see how important our Lord Jesus Christ is to our understanding of life, its purposes and conduct. Help us to yield ourselves to Him, that His grace may conquer our cruelty, His peace overcome our unrest, and His purity cleanse our stains. Help us make Him Lord of our lives and seek to lead others to make Him Lord of theirs. In His name, amen.

D. Thought to Remember

The light of Christ's life, way, and truth helps us see how dark were the days of the judges. It also reveals to us the darkness of our day too, apart from Him.

Learning by Doing

This page contains an alternate lesson plan emphasizing learning activities. Classes desiring such student involvement will find these suggestions helpful.

Learning Goals

As a result of this lesson, a student should:

1. Recognize characteristics of godly leaders and self-appointed leaders.

2. Use his influence in a godly way.

Into the Lesson

Display these two sentences:

"Power corrupts, and absolute power corrupts absolutely."

"When it comes to leadership, people get what they deserve."

Ask, "Do you believe these statements are true or false?" Then have the students give examples to support their view. Discuss briefly.

Suggest that the possession of power affects people in different ways. This lesson brings out the negative effect.

Into the Word

Briefly present the background for today's lesson, using the "Introduction" on page 410.

For today's Scripture search, provide a copy of the crossword puzzle below for every two students. Have the students read Judges 9:1-21, 55-57 silently then close their Bibles and work in pairs to complete the puzzle.

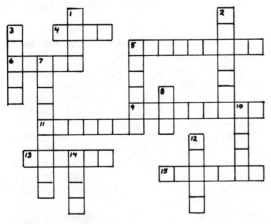

Across

4. The men of Shechem and the house of Millo made Abimelech _____ (v. 6).

5. Another name for Gideon (v. 16).

6. The first tree that was asked to reign over the forest (v. 8).

9. This man wanted to be king (vv. 1, 2).

11. The mountain on which a man stood to deliver a parable about the trees (v. 7).

13. Abimelech was paid in this (v. 4).

15. The city of Abimelech's mother (v. 1).

Down

1. The bramble threatened the cedars of Lebanon with this (v. 15).

2. The plant that accepted an offer to be king (vv. 14, 15).

3. Gideon's sons were slain on this (v. 5).

5. Gideon's son who survived the massacre.

7. To deal "truly and sincerely" is to act with _____ (v. 19).

8. The tree with "good fruit" (v. 11).

10. All the evil of Abimelech and the men of Shechem was paid to them according to "the _____ of Jotham" (vv. 56, 57).

12. These went forth to anoint a king over them (v. 8).

14. The fruit of this plant "cheereth God and man" (13).

Answers. *Across:* 4. king. 5. Jerubbaal. 6. olive. 9. Abimelech. 11. Gerizim. 13. silver. 15. Shechem. *Down:* 1. fire. 2. bramble. 3. stone. 5. Jotham. 7. integrity. 8. fig. 10. curse. 12. trees, 14. vine.

After the puzzle is completed, ask, "What is the point of this Bible account? What are some characteristics of godly leaders? (Knowledge, imagination, sound thinking, initiative, hard work, sensitivity to God's leading, etc.). What are some characteristics of self-appointed leaders? (Self-seeking, devious, pompous, cruel, etc.). How are ordinary people tempted to misuse power and influence?"

Into Life

Divide your class into groups of six. Ask half the groups to develop a list of five or six "how-tos" in choosing a good leader. The other half should list five or six ways that Christians should respond to an ungodly leader. Have groups share their lists. Then discuss this question: "How can a person avoid misusing his power and influence?" Close by having each student complete the following sentences:

1. My biggest temptation to misuse power and influence is—

2. I plan to use my power and influence for the Lord better this week by—

Let's Talk It Over

The questions on this page are designed to encourage review of the lesson Scriptures and to promote discussion of the lesson by the class. The answers provided are only discussion starters. Let your class talk it over from there.

1. The story of Abimelech demonstrates the danger of unbridled ambition for power. What are some signs that an individual has allowed his ambition to get out of hand?

The quest for power can be seen in government, business, the church, and elsewhere in our society. In any of these institutions a person may be tempted to *use* people in order to fulfill his ambition. Jesus warned against such an approach to leadership (Mark 10:41-45). The excessively ambitious individual also tends to bend or break the rules as circumstances seem to dictate. He may congratulate himself on his cleverness in doing this without being caught. Both of these tendencies may be part of the popular thinking that the "end justifies the means." Abimelech held that philosophy, but he carried it to bloody extremes that few people would imitate today. But if we believe that our goal, however worthy, entitles us to utilize questionable methods and tactics to reach it, then we have the same kind of ambition as Abimelech, and it can bring us to ruin.

2. The response of the olive tree in Jotham's parable may have reflected an unwillingness on the part of his brothers to take over the reins of leadership because of business or personal commitments. That left a vacuum, which the wicked Abimelech sought to fill. How do similar situations develop in our society?

One way we Christians can act as "salt of the earth" and "light of the world" (Matthew 5:13, 14) is by accepting positions of leadership in our society. We may feel that Christians should not be involved in government, but when Christians do not occupy the offices of mayors, councilmen, governors, senators, congressmen, etc., the way is open for people with worldly, humanistic values to move into those places of leadership. The same observation could be made regarding leadership in business, labor, service organizations, and other areas of our society. Some of our fellow citizens object to efforts made to impose Christian values on our society. But adherents of other philosophies and viewpoints are not hesitant to try to mold our society according to their beliefs, and it is vital that we also make our influence felt.

3. One wonders if Abimelech felt left out and discriminated against, because he was not the son of a regularized union between Gideon and one of his wives. What can we do to keep children born and reared under similar circumstances from growing up to be Abimelechs?

This question could lead us to recall the original purpose of the Sunday school. While today our Sunday schools are made up largely of the children of adult members of the church, in the beginning this teaching program was designed to provide Biblical instruction for poor, disadvantaged youngsters. It would be well for the church to make a fresh resolve to work out a ministry to such children in their community. From the standpoint of reaching the parents of these children and increasing the church's financial resources, this endeavor may not prove very successful; but if it could rescue some youngsters from a life of ungodliness, immorality, and crime and bring them into friendship with Jesus Christ, it would be well worth it. This program could be a united effort on the part of the church or it could be a project undertaken on an individual basis, with a Christian individual or family opening up their home to neighborhood children for a regular Bible teaching time.

4. How can we best profit from a study of the book of Judges?

From the standpoint of Christian faith and morals, the events described in Judges are quite dismal and depressing. The heroes of God's people lacked consistency in their moral and spiritual character. But it is interesting to note that in Hebrews 11:32 no less than four of these heroes are mentioned as men of faith. So we should be able to read Judges and have our faith strengthened. We do this by noting the difficult conditions of idolatry, immorality, and ignorance of God's ways that prevailed then. These men practiced their faith in a time when "everyone did as he saw fit" (Judges 17:6, *New International Version*). We also live in difficult times, but we possess superior resources for our faith and moral behavior. Viewing it in this way we can benefit from the examples of the judges, recognizing our responsibility to live according to the further revelation of God's will which we have.

Samson: Man of Weakness and Strength

LESSON SCRIPTURE: Judges 16.

PRINTED TEXT: Judges 16:23-31.

Judges 16:23-31

23 Then the lords of the Philistines gathered them together for to offer a great sacrifice unto Dagon their god, and to rejoice: for they said, Our god hath delivered Samson our enemy into our hand.

24 And when the people saw him, they praised their god: for they said, Our god hath delivered into our hands our enemy, and the destroyer of our country, which slew many of us.

25 And it came to pass, when their hearts were merry, that they said, Call for Samson, that he may make us sport. And they called for Samson out of the prison house; and he made them sport: and they set him between the pillars.

26 And Samson said unto the lad that held him by the hand, Suffer me that I may feel the pillars whereupon the house standeth, that I may lean upon them.

27 Now the house was full of men and women; and all the lords of the Philistines were there; and there were upon the roof about three thousand men and women, that beheld while Samson made sport.

28 And Samson called unto the Lord, and said, O Lord God, remember me, I pray thee, and strengthen me, I pray thee, only this once, O God, that I may be at once avenged of the Philistines for my two eyes.

29 And Samson took hold of the two middle pillars upon which the house stood, and on which it was borne up, of the one with his right hand, and of the other with his left.

30 And Samson said, Let me die with the Philistines. And he bowed himself with all his might; and the house fell upon the lords, and upon all the people that were therein. So the dead which he slew at his death were more than they which he slew in his life.

31 Then his brethren and all the house of his father came down, and took him, and brought him up, and buried him between Zorah and Eshtaol in the buryingplace of Manoah his father. And he judged Israel twenty years.

GOLDEN TEXT: Samson called unto the Lord, and said, O Lord God, remember me, I pray thee, and strengthen me, I pray thee, only this once, O God, that I may be at once avenged of the Philistines for my two eyes.—Judges 16:28.

Conquest and Challenge
Unit 2: A Time of Conflict and Adjustment (Lessons 5-10)

Lesson Aims

After this lesson a student should be able to:

1. Explain how Samson used God's gift of great physical strength, and how he lost it.

2. Recognize that our gifts from God should be used for His glory and the good of mankind.

3. Determine to use properly the gifts that God has given to him.

Lesson Outline

INTRODUCTION

I. A PAGAN THANKSGIVING (Judges 16:23, 24)
   Mistaken Identity
II. SAMSON—FLAUNTED AND TAUNTED (Judges 16:25-27)
III. SAMSON'S PRAYER AND PURPOSE (Judges 16:28, 29)
   Vengeance Belongs to God
IV. Triumph and Tragedy (Judges 16:30, 31)
CONCLUSION
   A. Strength and Weakness
   B. God's Gifts
   C. Prayer
   D. Thought to Remember

Display visual 10 from the visuals/learning resources packet and refer to it as you review Samson's life. It is shown on page 422.

Introduction

The account of Samson's life and work occupies four chapters in the book of Judges (13—16). For forty years the Israelites were in subjection to the Philistines, a warlike people who lived along the Mediterranean seacoast. Toward the end of this period "the angel of the Lord" appeared to the wife of a man named Manoah, who lived in Zorah. Though the woman had been barren, the angel told her she was to bear a son, who would "begin to deliver Israel out of the hand of the Philistines" (13:2-5).

Special instructions were given concerning this child. He was to be considered a *Nazarite.* Such a person was separated or dedicated to God, either for a specified period of time or for life. In Samson's case, his separation was to be for life. The details about this practice are found in Numbers 6. No razor was to touch the child's head. He was not to come near any dead body and was to abstain from the use of grapes in any form. This included wine, fresh grapes, raisins, or vinegar made from wine. No other type of fermented beverage was to be used either. Manoah's wife was told she herself was to drink no wine nor "eat any unclean thing" during her pregnancy (13:4, 5).

Manoah could not really believe this until the angel gave him the same information. After finally becoming convinced, Manoah made an offering to the Lord. When the flame rose from off the altar, the angel "ascended in the flame," and Manoah saw him no more (13:8-20).

After this the account of the birth of Samson is terse and beautiful: "And the woman bare a son, and called his name Samson: and the child grew, and the Lord blessed him" (13:24).

The account of Samson's life begins with the story of his marriage to a Philistine girl of the city of Timnah. During the week-long wedding feast, Samson made a wager with thirty young men of Timnah that they could not solve a riddle he would put to them. In danger of losing the wager, these young men threatened violence to the bride-to-be and to her father unless she revealed the secret of the riddle. She finally wheedled the answer from Samson and told the young men. Enraged, Samson went to another Philistine city, where he killed thirty men and took their possessions, with which he paid the debt he owed. During Samson's absence, the woman he was to marry was given to one of his closest companions (14:1-20).

Samson later tried to reestablish contact with his wife, but was rebuffed by her father. Refusing to accept his wife's younger sister as a replacement for her, he burned up large areas of ripe grain among the Philistines by tying firebrands to the tails of three hundred foxes and turning them loose in the fields. In response, the Philistines burned Samson's wife and her father. From this time on there ensued a series of conflicts with the Philistine people, during which Samson destroyed many of them in unusual ways (15:1—16:3).

However, Samson continued to be attracted to Philistine women, and this led to his undoing. Finally he fell in love with a Philistine woman named Delilah. Her countrymen bribed Delilah to find Samson's source of strength and to betray him to them. In spite of several episodes that should have warned him, Samson persisted in his infatuation and ultimately yielded to her coaxing and told her the secret of his strength. It lay in his long hair, never cut, as his condition as a Nazarite required (16:4-17). Knowing that Samson had finally told her the truth, Delilah had his hair cut while he slept. Of course, his ultimate source of strength was God, who finally ceased to help this persistently disobedient man. As the record says very graphically, "He awoke from his sleep and thought, 'I'll go out as before and shake myself free.' But he did not know that the Lord had left him" (16:20, *New International Version*).

Samson's enemies quickly subdued him and put out his eyes. They then brought him to Gaza and bound him with fetters of brass. Fastened to a treadmill, he was used as a workhorse, grinding grain for his captors.

Our lesson begins at this point. A significant note is added, however, and that is that his hair "began to grow again" (16:22).

I. A Pagan Thanksgiving (Judges 16:23, 24)

23. Then the lords of the Philistines gathered them together for to offer a great sacrifice unto Dagon their god, and to rejoice: for they said, Our god hath delivered Samson our enemy into our hand.

Samson's seizure and imprisonment was the cause of national celebration in Philistia. Here was one who had killed hundreds upon hundreds of their fellows, who had devastated their land, and who had encouraged their subject people in Israel to revolt against them. Now they saw him blinded, bound to servile work, and completely neutralized as an enemy agent. Little wonder that they felt a great celebration was appropriate. This took a religious turn, for they believed their god Dagon had shown his power and dominance by enabling them to be so successful against Samson. *Dagon* was the national male idol of the Philistines, so called from Dag, a fish. Both the male and female idols seem to have resembled a human down to the waist, and a fish below the waist (see 1 Samuel 5:1-5). It was natural for a pagan people living on a seacoast to adopt the fish as the emblem of fertility and productiveness.

It is a sobering thought that these devotees of a false god were eager to hold a service of praise and thanksgiving for their god's goodness to them. Of course, they were mistaken in praising a nonexistent deity, but not in their impulse to offer praise for a victory won. We have a true and living God to whom we can and should give thanks every day for our eternal redemption.

24. And when the people saw him, they praised their god: for they said, Our god hath delivered into our hands our enemy, and the destroyer of our country, which slew many of us.

How to Say It

ARTAXERXES. *Are*-tuh-*zerk*-seez.
DAGON. *Day*-gon.
ESHTAOL. *Esh*-tuh-oll.
GAZA. *Gay*-zah.
MANOAH. Mah-*no*-uh.
NAZARITE. *Naz*-uh-rite or *Naz*-ih-rite.
PHILISTIA. Fi-*lis*-ti-a.
PHILISTINES. Fi-*liss*-teens or *Fil*-iss-teens.
ZORAH. *Zo*-ruh.

Dagon was being glorified by the Philistines for having delivered Samson into their hands. This, of course, brought reproach on the name of the Lord. Alexander Maclaren observed, "The worst consequence of the fall of a servant of God is that it gives occasion for God's enemies to blaspheme, and reflects discredit on Him, as if He were vanquished. Samson's capture is Dagon's glory. . . . And is not all this true today? If ever some conspicuous Christian champion falls into sin or inconsistency, how the sky is rent with shouts of malicious pleasure! . . . How much more harm the one flaw does than all the good which a life of service has done!"

As the Philistines sang their mocking song—*Our god hath delivered into our hands our enemy*—how the conscience of Samson must have smitten him! Through his own failure this reproach of God now came.

MISTAKEN IDENTITY

Every Christmas, a great many gifts and surprises are attributed to Santa Claus. Even older children and adults who know better, enjoy perpetuating the myth of "Jolly Old Saint Nicholas," the rotund, red-suited philanthropist who honors holiday wishes and fulfills sugarplum fantasies. It is a mistake, of course, to believe that Santa is any more than the cheery figment of festive imaginations, the pretended personification of the giving spirit.

The Philistines were perpetuating the Dagon myth. They were convinced of his reality, though he was merely the invention of superstitious minds. Dagon was powerless. Yet, the Philistines credited him with delivering the "enemy," Samson, into their hands. They were mistaken, of course.

The "gods" who were truly involved in the arrest and imprisonment of Samson, were the spiritual idols in his heart. Samson forsook his vows to Jehovah and began to exalt lust, pleasure, pride, and selfishness instead. Those were sins of the flesh that contributed to Samson's downfall. Those same sins lurk among us today. Let us recognize them for what they are and avoid the sad ending that befell this once mighty man.   —R. W. B.

II. Samson—Flaunted and Taunted (Judges 16:25-27)

25. And it came to pass, when their hearts were merry, that they said, Call for Samson, that he may make us sport. And they called for Samson out of the prison house; and he made them sport: and they set him between the pillars.

The great assembly, feeling especially jubilant and convivial, had Samson brought up from his work of servitude to be exhibited as a living, tangible trophy of what they had achieved with the help of their god. Before being finally led to the great central *pillars* that supported the building, he was, in all likelihood, paraded around the crowded hall, drawing choruses of cheers, boos, and catcalls. The greatness of their previous fear and apprehension about Samson now contributed to the heightening of their exuberance at his evident powerlessness and helplessness as their captive and victim.

26. And Samson said unto the lad that held him by the hand, Suffer me that I may feel the pillars whereupon the house standeth, that I may lean upon them.

The blinded Samson was led about by a boy assigned to him for this purpose. Samson asked to be taken to the place where two central *pillars* supported the entire structure. The boy may have understood Samson to mean that he wished to rest momentarily against the pillars. If Samson pretended to be tired, then his request would not have seemed strange.

The *King James Version* calls the structure *the house.* Other versions have "building" or "temple." In Old Testament times temples were referred to as *houses* of God, or of the god to whom a structure was dedicated. Thus, in a letter to Ezra, Artaxerxes, king of Persia, referred to the temple of God in Jerusalem as "the house of your God" (Ezra 7:17; also verses 19, 20, 23). In any case, it was a large structure where thousands could be seated for this great patriotic and religious celebration.

27. Now the house was full of men and women; and all the lords of the Philistines were there; and there were upon the roof about three thousand men and women, that beheld while Samson made sport.

The exact design of this building is not clear from the text. It appears that there was a large flat roof, from which the people could look down upon the stage in front. The main floor under this roof was also open to the front toward the stage. The roof seems to have been supported mainly by two pillars at the front. It seems that the lords and principal persons were seated on the main floor, under the roof, while the common people, numbering three thousand, were on the roof. The sudden removal of the two middle pillars would cause the roof to come down at that point, crowded as it undoubtedly was with people. This would create a chain reaction, quickly bringing the entire roof and the people thereon falling amidst stone and timbers upon the people below.

III. Samson's Prayer and Purpose (Judges 16:28, 29)

28. And Samson called unto the Lord, and said, O Lord God, remember me, I pray thee, and strengthen me, I pray thee, only this once, O God, that I may be at once avenged of the Philistines for my two eyes.

Luxuriating in the sinful ardors of his affair with Delilah, Samson forgot God so completely he didn't even know that God was no longer with him. But now, betrayed, beaten, and blind, in his despair he called on the Lord. He now asked for one last bestowal of the mighty power that had enabled him to kill lions, dispatch hundreds of enemies, and even carry off a city gate.

In making this request, it may be that Samson desired to strike one final blow against the false gods of the Philistines. Shamed by the reproach he had caused to be brought on God, Samson may have desired this opportunity to show that God was superior to the Philistines and their pagan deities. But we can only assume that such thoughts came to Samson. It appears that his principal concern was to get revenge on his enemies. If so, this is but another indication of the imperfection of his character and of his limited spiritual development.

VENGEANCE BELONGS TO GOD

The recently published biographies ("unabridged" and "uncensored") of certain celebrities are disillusioning. None of us likes to see our heroes' "feet of clay." One of the reasons we trust the truth of Scripture, however, is that the characters are portrayed with realism. Their failures and transgressions are not disguised. Samson is a case in point.

Samson was no model of righteousness by any means. His story, like all biographies in the Bible, reveals flaws in character and even grievous sins. His prayer for revenge on the Philistines is an example of behavior not meant to be emulated, certainly not by New Testament Christians. Personal vengeance has no place in the agenda of those who follow Jesus.

"Vengeance is mine; I will repay, saith the Lord" (Romans 12:19). Though retribution for wrongdoing may seem to have come more swiftly in past eras, God still pays the wages of sin according to His own timetable. He should not be expected to cater to our selfish desires to "get even." Christians are to pray *for* their enemies, not *against* them.   —R. W. B.

29. And Samson took hold of the two middle pillars upon which the house stood, and on which it was borne up, of the one with his right hand, and of the other with his left.

It is not necessary to suppose that the two pillars Samson took hold of supported all the weight of the roof. Since they were the *middle pillars*, there may have been one on either side of them, between them and the walls. But, as we have already indicated, the removal of these main pillars would cause a chain reaction as the terrific weight of the roof with its three thousand occupants began to crash downward.

IV. Triumph and Tragedy (Judges 16:30, 31)

30. And Samson said, Let me die with the Philistines. And he bowed himself with all his might; and the house fell upon the lords, and upon all the people that were therein. So the dead which he slew at his death were more than they which he slew in his life.

It was only fitting that Samson, who had insisted on linking himself with Philistine women during his life, should have met death in the company of many Philistine men and women. This final event in Samson's life is vividly described by Milton in *Samson Agonistes:*

... straining all his nerves he bow'd;
As with the force of winds and waters pent
When mountains tremble, those two massy pillars
With horrible convulsion to and fro
He tugged, he shook, till down they came, and drew
The whole roof after them with burst of thunder
Upon the heads of all who sat beneath,
Lords, ladies, captains, counsellors, or priests,
Their choice nobility and flower. . . .

31. Then his brethren and all the house of his father came down, and took him, and brought him up, and buried him between Zorah and Eshtaol in the buryingplace of Manoah his father. And he judged Israel twenty years.

Eshtaol was a small village near Zorah, where Samson had been born. After all his stormy life, Samson at last could rest in peace. He ended his life with a great victory over the Philistine ad-

versaries of Israel. He had been famous for feats of strength and for the rescue of his people from complete subjection to Philistia. Now he had effectively destroyed their principal leaders, giving Israel another chance to gain greater freedom, if they would accept it.

As the days of Samson's life had come and gone, he had become less and less sensitive to the presence of God (16:20). But just before his death he prayed earnestly to God for the power to avenge himself on his enemies, on a pagan people who ascribed great power and prominence to the god Dagon. At the very last, God heard him, strengthened him, and enabled him to pull down the building.

God had been active in Samson's life from before his birth. He had given him great strength and the ability to do great work for Him. In many ways Samson had been unwise and unworthy of all God's blessings. God could not remain close to him during his sinful conduct. But after Samson was overcome, blinded, and imprisoned, it seems that his continued rebellion against God's ways ceased. When blinded, he probably saw more clearly than he did when he possessed his sight and his freedom. Now Samson called upon the Lord in a desperate "last chance" appeal for a renewal of strength and victory over the Philistines. Apparently God heard and granted his prayer. We must never underestimate the persistence, forgiveness, and power of God as shown in His treatment of Samson.

Conclusion

A. Strength and Weakness

Samson appeared to be scrupulous about certain aspects of the Nazarite vows to which he was dedicated by his parents. He let his hair grow as required, and we have no record of his indulgence in strong drink, which was also a condition for being a Nazarite. But while faithful in these areas, his great weakness lay in the moral realm. Thus he repeatedly entered into alliances with idolatrous Philistine women, in spite of God's prohibition (see Exodus 34:15, 16) and in the face of opposition and advice from his father and mother (Judges 14:3).

The writer of Judges tells us that Samson's fixation on the first Philistine woman who became his wife was "of the Lord" so that an "occasion" could be found "against the Philistines" (14:4). In His providence God was able to cause ultimate good to come from Samson's unfortunate obsession by increasing the intensity of Samson's opposition to the Philistines, who were keeping God's people in subjection. It is

visual 10

SAMSON'S LIFE
WILLFUL DISOBEDIENCE
WANTON BEHAVIOR
WEAKENING DISCLOSURE
WOEFUL CONDITION
WRATHFUL VENGEANCE
WASTED OPPORTUNITY

not that God deliberately *made* Samson stubbornly desire this Philistine woman, but that God was even able to *use* this fixation to work out His will of opposition to the power and influence of these pagan people.

Samson's connection with a prostitute in Gaza (16:1-3) and his later relationship with Delilah point up his weakness of his when it came to women. His leadership as a judge, his reputation, and his very freedom itself were all ultimately lost because he refused to curb his sexual desires. The story of Samson's failure is duplicated in the lives of other important Biblical characters. Bad actions by David, Solomon, and many others are directly traceable to this cause.

But we need not look only to the Bible for examples of spiritual failures brought on by the force of sensual appeals. Such impulses, once yielded to, have brought many to spiritual disaster. Anyone acquainted with the life and work of the church can remember ministers, organists, elders, deacons, and others whose immoral behavior has disrupted families, divided churches, and curtailed service for Christ.

Our age with its constant stress on attractiveness and relaxed standards, with the many work situations in which men and women are closely associated outside the home, makes such temptations frequent and pervasive. Samson knew success, fame, and power, but lost it all because of his reckless indulgence in sensual pursuits. He thus serves as a warning and helps bring home to us the force of Paul's testimony concerning his need of physical discipline: "I am my body's sternest master, for fear that when I have preached to others I should myself be disqualified" (1 Corinthians 9:27, *Phillips*).

B. God's Gifts

God's gift to Samson was great strength. Used for God, it could have accomplished much good. But even Samson must have realized that reliance on brute force alone may well be self-defeating. We must not suppose that God ap-

proved of all that Samson did. The gift of strength was from the Lord. The responsibility for its use rested firmly on him.

God's gifts to His people today are many. Whatever the ability that is given, each of us should receive it as a sacred trust. But the mere possession of some great endowment from God is no evidence of His approval. The approval depends on the use we make of the gift. It is possible that we may neglect it or waste it on trifles. We may even prostitute it to evil purposes. Or, and surely this is the will of God, we can use our gift in such a way as to fulfill His purposes and bring good to humankind.

C. Prayer

Dear Father, we offer our thanks for the many truths we learn from the story of Samson. We can see that we need not only Your blessing on our childhood and our parents' support, but must ourselves be yielded to Your will. We see also that great gifts are not enough apart from our wise use of them. We learn how easily some special weakness, given in to, can cause us to lose all our influence for our Lord. We are also reminded that it is never too late to turn to You for forgiveness, help, and renewal of strength.

Forgive us, O God, if, because of our unfaithfulness, the power of Christian witness has gone from our lives. Renew a right spirit within us, so that our lives may once again bear testimony to the world that we are Your children, channels of Your love and blessing to others. In Jesus' name we pray. Amen.

D. Thought to Remember

Spiritual failure is certain if we do not stay close to God; spiritual success is certain if we do.

Home Daily Bible Readings

Monday, July 31—An Angel Visits Manoah's Wife (Judges 13:1-7)
Tuesday, Aug. 1—Manoah Visits the Lord (Judges 13:8-20)
Wednesday, Aug. 2—Samson Is Born (Judges 13:21-25)
Thursday, Aug. 3—Samson Takes a Wife (Judges 14:1-7)
Friday, Aug. 4—Samson Loses a Bet (Judges 14:10-19)
Saturday, Aug. 5—The Secret Is Out (Judges 16:13-17)
Sunday, Aug. 6—The Final Curtain (Judges 16:28-31)

Learning by Doing

This page contains an alternate lesson plan emphasizing learning activities. Classes desiring such student involvement will find these suggestions helpful.

Learning Goals

After participating in this lesson a student should be able to:

1. Identify the areas of strength in Samson's life.

2. Determine his own strengths.

3. Develop a plan to improve the use of his strengths for the Lord.

Into the Lesson

As the students arrive, distribute sheets of paper with *Samson* written at the top. Ask your participants to list all that they can remember about Samson. After two minutes, have them divide into groups of three. Have each group share their recollections and compile a group listing. After three minutes, share their compilations with the entire class. Write these on the board and save them for the "Into the Word" activity.

Make your transition into the Bible study by saying, "Today we will consider one of the strongest men who ever lived. He was able to accomplish much for Israel when the Lord was with him. When he misused his strength, however, tragedy struck."

Into the Word

In the week prior to class time, assign one member of the class the task of preparing a three-minute report on the Nazarite vow. Following the report, present a brief background of the lesson by using the "Introduction" section of this commentary on page 418.

Next, have the students work in the same small groups to prepare a one-minute sermon from Judges 16. Assign Judges 16:1-22 to one-half of the groups, and Judges 16:23-31 to the other half. Prepare index cards (one per group) with these instructions: "Prepare a simple outline and application for your sermon from your assigned text. Select one person from your group to present your sermon to the entire class."

Allot the groups ten to twelve minutes to complete this task. Then call the class back together and have the spokesperson for each group present the sermon. Be sure that all relevant material is covered in the explanations of the text. Fill in anything missed by the groups. Refer to your "Into the Lesson" exercise by asking these questions: "What was Samson's strength? How did he use it or misuse it?"

Give copies of the following case studies to your groups, one per group.

Case 1: Sherrie is exceptionally good with children. She has had several classes on child development and leads some classes for children at a local "Y." She really wants to be involved in the church's children's ministry and has volunteered to do so. She doesn't want to attend teachers' meetings or use the curriculum the church is providing. She wants to be creative and feels the curriculum ties her down. What is Sherrie's strength? What keeps her from using it fully? What advice would you give to her?

Case 2: Stan is good looking, empathetic, and an exciting communicator. He owns his own business, which he built from scratch. He has a wife and three daughters. Many of the men and women in his congregation look up to him. Recently he has been having trouble at home with one of his children. She doesn't want to mind him, so he has told his wife to talk about this issue with the daughter. What is Stan's strength? What keeps him from using it effectively? What advice would you give to him?

Allow the groups five minutes to work on their case studies; then have each group report to the class. Let the class discuss the reports fully.

Into Life

The object in this section is to make specific application to your students' lives. Use the following questions as the basis for discussion and application:

1. How are we like Samson?

2. What situations could we face in which we would be tempted to misuse our God-given abilities?

3. How can we avoid some of the problems Samson experienced?

4. How can Christians better use their strengths for God's purposes?

Give each student a copy of the following statements and ask them to complete them.

My strengths are—

I will use my strengths for the Lord this week by—

Close with a prayer of commitment.

Let's Talk It Over

The questions on this page are designed to encourage review of the lesson Scriptures and to promote discussion of the lesson by the class. The answers provided are only discussion starters. Let your class talk it over from there.

1. Samson appears to have been a man of violent temper. How can Christians with temper problems best deal with them?

"Better a patient man than a warrior, a man who controls his temper than one who takes a city" (Proverbs 16:32, *New International Version*). This shows us that it is possible to gain control over one's temper, but it also indicates that heroic effort is required. We can find a significant challenge in this verse. Instead of imagining ourselves as conquerors of an evil enemy or vicariously sharing in the glories of the athletic star we have cheered on, we can be real heroes in bringing discipline to our wayward emotions. Jesus, in the Sermon on the Mount (Matthew 5:38-48), and Paul, in Romans 12:17-21, illustrate part of what may be involved in dealing with an unruly temper. We are not merely to "grin and bear it" when we are provoked, but we are to channel that energy we feel into positive, gracious words and actions. God was able to use Samson in spite of the man's temper, but He can surely best use us when we demonstrate His power and wisdom in overcoming the temptation to react violently.

2. Like the worshipers of Dagon, many pagans display an intensity of devotion to their gods that often puts Christian worship to shame. What should our reaction be to such an observation?

We could answer that many heathen are intense in their worship because their religion is based on fear and on the desire to placate an angry god through works of worship, sacrifice, and devotion. On the other hand, we worship our God who has revealed himself to us as a loving and merciful Father, and we obtain our salvation through His grace and not by our works. However, it is still a sad circumstance that the worship in many churches is lacking in enthusiasm, and that individual worshipers show little devotion in their efforts for God's kingdom. We should meditate often on the superior promises and blessings that are ours as Christians: cleansing from our sins, the indwelling presence of the Holy Spirit, the assurance that God hears and answers our prayers, the expectation of eternal life, and many others.

Surely these blessings should lead us to a constant, sacrificial devotion to our God that is in no way inferior to that which heathen worshipers demonstrate.

3. The Philistines gloated over Samson's downfall, and we see a similar gloating today when a Christian experiences a downfall. How should we respond to this?

It is disgusting to us when the media or unbelievers overlook the numerous acts of righteousness and benevolence done by the vast majority of Christians and focus on the moral lapses or spiritual confusion of a few professors of faith. We recognize that this reaction is a device unbelievers use to justify their rejection of Christ. They appear ready to regard the failings of an isolated few Christians as proof that "there's nothing to it." If we fall prey to the temptation to be angry or hateful toward those who hold such an unbalanced viewpoint, we will merely give them more of the evidence they are seeking. It is better for us to respond to such unhappy situations with a quiet, determined resolve that, through God's power in us, we will live a blameless life. Such an example will demonstrate the glorious realities of the Christian faith and frustrate those who would seek some glaring inconsistency in us.

4. Did God approve of Samson's desire for revenge? Does He ever approve of our seeking revenge? Why, or why not?

In contrast to Samson's longing for revenge over the loss of his two eyes, we have Paul's admonition, "Do not take revenge, my friends, but leave room for God's wrath, for it is written: 'It is mine to avenge; I will repay,' says the Lord" (Romans 12:19, *New International Version*). It may appear that God granted Samson's request for revenge, but in light of principles taught by the greater Biblical context, we know a vengeful spirit is not approved by God. It is obvious that Samson's life fell far short of what God wanted it to be. It could be said that God used Samson and his hunger for vengeance to punish the Philistines, even as He later used the Assyrians and the Babylonians to chasten Israel.

The Commitment of Ruth

LESSON SCRIPTURE: Ruth 1.

PRINTED TEXT: Ruth 1:1-8, 16-18.

Ruth 1:1-8, 16-18

1 Now it came to pass in the days when the judges ruled, that there was a famine in the land. And a certain man of Bethlehem-judah went to sojourn in the country of Moab, he, and his wife, and his two sons.

2 And the name of the man was Elimelech, and the name of his wife Naomi, and the name of his two sons Mahlon and Chilion, Ephrathites of Bethlehem-judah. And they came into the country of Moab, and continued there.

3 And Elimelech Naomi's husband died; and she was left, and her two sons.

4 And they took them wives of the women of Moab; the name of the one was Orpah, and the name of the other Ruth: and they dwelt there about ten years.

5 And Mahlon and Chilion died also both of them; and the woman was left of her two sons and her husband.

6 Then she arose with her daughters-in-law, that she might return from the country of Moab: for she had heard in the country of Moab how that the Lord had visited his people in giving them bread.

7 Wherefore she went forth out of the place where she was, and her two daughters-in-law with her; and they went on the way to return unto the land of Judah.

8 And Naomi said unto her two daughters-in-law, Go, return each to her mother's house: the Lord deal kindly with you, as ye have dealt with the dead, and with me.

. . . .

16 And Ruth said, Entreat me not to leave thee, or to return from following after thee: for whither thou goest, I will go; and where thou lodgest, I will lodge: thy people shall be my people, and thy God my God:

17 Where thou diest, will I die, and there will I be buried: the Lord do so to me, and more also, if aught but death part thee and me.

18 When she saw that she was steadfastly minded to go with her, then she left speaking unto her.

GOLDEN TEXT: And Ruth said, Entreat me not to leave thee, or to return from following after thee: for whither thou goest, I will go; and where thou lodgest, I will lodge: thy people shall be my people, and thy God my God.—Ruth 1:16.

Lesson Aims

After this lesson, a student should:
1. Understand the nature and importance of Ruth's commitment to Naomi.
2. Realize that some of the decisions we make have long-lasting and life-changing impact.
3. Commit himself without reservation to the love and service of Jesus.

Lesson Outline

INTRODUCTION
  I. GOD'S PEOPLE IN A FOREIGN LAND (Ruth 1:1-4)
     A. The Promised Land Unpromising (vv. 1, 2)
     B. "Separate People" Unseparated (vv. 3, 4)
 II. NAOMI—DECISION AND DISSUASION (Ruth 1:5-8)
     Roots Run Deep
III. RUTH'S HEROIC COMMITMENT (Ruth 1:16-18)
     In-laws and Outlaws
CONCLUSION
     A. Dimensions of Ruth's Decision
     B. Prayer
     C. Thought to Remember

Visual 11 from the visuals/learning resources packet illustrates the main thought of this lesson. Display it throughout this session. It is shown on page 428.

Introduction

In the midst of the dark and often depressing accounts of the events during "the days when the judges ruled," we find the beautiful story of Ruth. Many of the incidents narrated in the book of Judges are of betrayal, murder, idolatry, immorality, and apostasy. In the book of Ruth the emphasis is on love, loyalty, trust, faithfulness, and devotion. Amid many tales of battles, of great civic occasions, and the leadership of whole tribes or groups of diverse people, we have this simple, pastoral idyll. The persons involved are ordinary people. Their lives include personal tragedies and decisions, hopes and disappointments. The scenes are of country life. This narration is heartwarming, giving us a great feeling of satisfaction and fulfillment when it "comes out right" in the end.

Only two Bible books are named after women—Ruth and Esther. One finds a great contrast between these two stories. Ruth was a foreign woman who became important among the Hebrews, while Esther was a Jewish woman who became important among an alien people. Both had to confront great decisions that involved their lives, and both made choices that evidenced love and trust and adventurous faith. Ruth made her decision in a simple, rural setting, while Esther's was made in a palace amid marble and majestic surroundings. Both women became honored in Israel—one as the ancestress of David and the other as a savior of her people from disaster.

We turn with relief and anticipation to the lovely story of Ruth. Here we shall be thrilled with the blessings that came to a heroic, devoted, and earnest girl.

I. God's People in a Foreign Land (Ruth 1:1-4)

A. The Promised Land Unpromising (vv. 1, 2)

1. Now it came to pass in the days when the judges ruled, that there was a famine in the land. And a certain man of Bethlehem-judah went to sojourn in the country of Moab, he, and his wife, and his two sons.

A famine in the land. Though God blessed His people and cared for them, natural difficulties arose. Jesus told us that God sends rain on the just and unjust (Matthew 5:45). It is also true that drought, hail, and other unfavorable natural phenomena occur without respect of victims. And special difficulties sometimes confronted the Israelites during this period because they so persistently ignored God and even rebelled against Him. In any case, the situation was very unfavorable in Israel. *A certain man* named Elimelech (v. 2) decided to leave his own land and live in Moab. He was from Bethlehem, a town later made famous as the birthplace of David, and, of much greater interest, the "little town" where Jesus was born. *Bethlehem* was about six miles south and a little west of Jerusalem.

Moab was an area on the east side of the Dead Sea, occupying about half the distance along the eastern shore—the southern half. The territory was about sixty miles long and thirty miles wide. The Moabites were descended from Lot, a nephew of Abraham (Genesis 19:37).

The fact that Elimelech went from Judah to Moab may be thought of by some to demonstrate that he was not willing to trust God to care for His people in the land He had given them for their inheritance. On the other hand, we know that Isaac was considering going to Egypt during famine conditions among the Hebrews, but was deterred by a specific command from God (Genesis 26:1-4). Years later Jacob sent his sons into Egypt to purchase grain when there was another famine in Canaan (Genesis 42:1-3).

2. And the name of the man was Elimelech, and the name of his wife Naomi, and the name of his two sons Mahlon and Chilion, Ephrathites of Bethlehem-judah. And they came into the country of Moab, and continued there.

Many considerations could have caused Elimelech to be concerned about this move to Moab. He would be living among a people with customs and practices different from those of the Hebrews. Hostilities often arose between Israel and Moab, so he was apt to find himself among those warring against his own people. He would be among people who worshiped heathen gods instead of the true God of Israel. His sons were almost certain to marry Moabite women, as indeed we know they did after their father's death. But in spite of these considerations, Elimelech thought it prudent to move his family to that land.

B. "Separate People" Unseparated (vv. 3, 4)

3. And Elimelech Naomi's husband died; and she was left, and her two sons.

Even though Elimelech sought refuge in Moab, the physical benefits he secured did not keep him from death. In our time many Americans seek more favorable living conditions in areas with milder climates. While there may be temporary benefits, we need to recognize the inescapable frailty of our lives. It is God who is our true dwelling place, and the only ultimate security for our lives lies in Him. One aged and whimsical native of upstate New York returned after living for a time in a "sun belt" state. He said, "I went there with the hope of living much longer, but I found they had undertakers and cemeteries there, too."

4. And they took them wives of the women of Moab; the name of the one was Orpah, and the name of the other Ruth: and they dwelt there about ten years.

A strong current of teaching in Israel was against the marriage of Hebrews with people of other nations. Moses warned against intermarriage with the tribes they would conquer as they occupied Canaan (Deuteronomy 7:1-4). The Moabites worshiped the god Chemosh. To what extent Ruth and Orpah participated in this worship, we do not know. We know that Ruth came to put her trust in the Lord (1:16). It is possible that Orpah did likewise, but we cannot be sure.

II. Naomi—Decision and Dissuasion (Ruth 1:5-8)

5. And Mahlon and Chilion died also both of them; and the woman was left of her two sons and her husband.

The *New International Version* translates the last phrase in this verse into more modern English: "Naomi was left without her two sons and her husband." The passing of a decade in Moab had now left Naomi in a truly tragic situation. Widows in that era were in a notoriously disadvantaged position. It was customary for a widow to depend on her family, especially on any sons she might have. In Naomi's case, with her sons dead, she was left with only her two daughters-in-law. These were Moabite girls who might be expected to feel more at home with their own parents and relatives. This was especially true since both were now widows themselves. Naomi had no relatives to whom to turn.

6. Then she arose with her daughters-in-law, that she might return from the country of Moab: for she had heard in the country of Moab how that the Lord had visited his people in giving them bread.

It is no wonder that Naomi's thoughts turned toward home. This yearning was accentuated by the news that came to her informing her that the famine in Israel had ended. It seems she was in close touch with her daughters-in-law, and the impression is given us that they were all living together. When it is said that *she arose with her daughters-in-law, that she might return*, we are led to believe that all three of them would go to Judah together. This is, of course, made more apparent in the next verse.

7. Wherefore she went forth out of the place where she was, and her two daughters-in-law with her; and they went on the way to return unto the land of Judah.

The company of the two younger girls would strengthen Naomi on her journey home. Further,

---

How to Say It

CHEMOSH. *Kee*-mosh.
CHILION. *Kil*-ih-on.
ELIMELECH. E-*lim*-eh-leck.
EPHRATHITES. *Ef*-ruh-thites.
MAHLON. *Mah*-lon.
MOAB. *Mo*-ab.
MOABITES. *Mo*-uh-bites.
NAOMI. Nay-*o*-me, Nay-*o*-my, or *Nay*-o-my.
OBED. *O*-bed.
ORPAH. *Or*-pah.

it would be very helpful to have their assistance in reestablishing a home in Israel. All the household duties could be done more easily by younger women. Besides, women could make and sell things, and various employment opportunities would be open to them. Of course, they would be leaving their own country and all their kinfolk. But they would have Naomi's guidance in mastering a new language and in adjusting to their new environment.

ROOTS RUN DEEP

Kenny Rogers' song, "Twenty Years Ago," tells of a nostalgic visit to a hometown where "life was so much easier" for a youngster growing up in those proverbial "good old days of yesteryear." Such "back home" visits can be disillusioning, even painful. But still there is that curious longing to return to the place where we formed our first fond memories.

Naomi's spirit thus was called back to Bethlehem in Judah. Life for her was much easier ten years before, when she had a husband and two sons to provide for her and protect her. Though circumstances could never be exactly the same again, she sought the comfort and security of that familiar locale and culture. She wanted to renew friendships, to return to the exercise of traditional religious expression.

"Going home" can mean remembering with great affection one's parents, siblings, and friends. For some it may mean a return to old paths of righteousness, integrity, and faith. Of such persons was the song written that says, "I've wandered far away from God; now I'm coming home." —R. W. B.

8. And Naomi said unto her two daughters-in-law, Go, return each to her mother's house: the Lord deal kindly with you, as ye have dealt with the dead, and with me.

We do not know why Naomi's remonstrances were not uttered before they started on the way

to Judah. Perhaps she *had* tried to discourage them from accompanying her before they ever started out. In any case, she now began to seriously oppose their intention of going with her. Perhaps she had thought at first that their companionship with her as far as they had gone was just to "see her off" or to get her comfortably started on her journey.

Naomi went on to more specific arguments following her general suggestion that they return to live with their own mothers. These arguments are not in our printed text, but are important to notice. She pointed out that she could not furnish more sons for them to marry.

She concluded by saying she was distressed because it seemed to her she was out of favor with God. It appeared to her that the disasters she had known—losing her husband and *both* of her sons—were enough to be considered not just ordinary, but judgmental, calamities. It was too bad that God's dealings with her had caused tragedy in the lives of these two girls.

Bitter as Naomi may have been about all the heartbreaking losses her family had suffered, she could not and did not want to deny that her daughters-in-law had been good wives to her sons. They had also been unusually kind and helpful to her. For this she was thankful to God and hoped He would deal with them kindly and graciously. We must also note how unselfish Naomi was as far as her daughters-in-law were concerned. Undoubtedly it would have been easier for her to have the company and help of these two younger women. As has been suggested, they could have assisted her on her journey and in setting up new living quarters in Bethlehem. But Naomi felt it would be better for these girls to be in their own country among their own people. It was especially difficult to part with them because they were genuinely fond of one another. Their kisses and tears expressed the deep affection they felt for each other. But, having kissed her mother-in-law, one of the girls, Orpah, turned back toward her mother's house.

III. Ruth's Heroic Commitment (Ruth 1:16-18)

16. And Ruth said, Entreat me not to leave thee, or to return from following after thee: for whither thou goest, I will go; and where thou lodgest, I will lodge: thy people shall be my people, and thy God my God.

Verses 16 and 17 contain the only words of Ruth recorded in the entire first chapter, but they are expressions of affirmation and dedication that have lived for centuries. Many couples

The Commitment of Ruth   visual 11

have used these words as part of the pledges made to one another at their wedding. Ruth here affirmed her determination to go with Naomi. One can see she had thought long and hard about what she ought to do. Her decision was complete, unqualified, unwavering. Wherever Naomi went or stayed, she would share her lot. She was willing to give up her Moabite heritage and identify herself with the Israelite people to whom Naomi belonged. The God of the Hebrews would be her God.

Ruth did not need to be coaxed to leave her people, nor did she seem concerned about parting from her family and friends. Surely Ruth loved her country and her kinfolk as much as anyone else. But she felt compelling loyalty to Naomi. Neither Naomi nor Ruth knew just what their future situation might be in Judah. For Naomi, it was a return to a familiar area. For Ruth it was a prospective entrance into an entirely strange land with conditions, customs, and religious practices unknown to her except as explained or illustrated by Naomi.

Many missionaries make commitments to go to areas of the world where they encounter customs, languages, attitudes, and religious disciplines different from their own. Such evangelism is called "cross-cultural ministry," and it involves many of the problems Ruth encountered when she went from Moab to Judah.

In our time quite a number of servicemen have married Oriental, Asian, and European women. All these marriages bring young girls to our culture, many of whom are just as much in need of friendship, understanding, patient concern, and loving support as was Ruth. In "Ode to a Nightingale" Keats pictures Ruth hearing a bird song that touched her as an exile in Israel:

... the self-same song that found a path
Through the sad heart of Ruth, when, sick for home,
She stood in tears amid the alien corn.

17. Where thou diest, will I die, and there will I be buried: the Lord do so to me, and more also, if aught but death part thee and me.

Ruth indicated that she was making an irrevocable pledge to unite herself with Naomi's people and her God. It was not just "until Naomi got settled." It was not "till my mother needs me," or "if things seem to work out all right." No, this commitment was meant to be lifelong and beyond. It was until she died and, even then, she did not request to be buried in her home soil, or to be "returned home to be buried in her family plot." Ruth's words to her mother-in-law emphasize her utter determination, the inflexibility of her purpose. One can just feel the strength and stability of Ruth's character in these courageous words.

18. When she saw that she was steadfastly minded to go with her, then she left speaking unto her.

This comment is only what we should expect, for it tells us Naomi stopped trying to keep Ruth from accompanying her when she saw *she was steadfastly minded to go with her*.

IN-LAWS AND OUTLAWS

Mother-in-law jokes are stock in trade for comics, and such humor is based upon a type of family conflict that is as old as the human race. A great many folk have difficulty getting along with in-laws. (At least some of that difficulty may be due to the fact that such conflict is *anticipated*, and afterward is *precipitated* by defensive behavior.) If in-law trouble is typical, however, notable exceptions also abound.

The relationship between Naomi and her daughters-in-law is a prime example of the latter: Love and respect bound those three souls together as if they were blood relatives. When Naomi decided to return to Judah, Orpah and Ruth apparently did not even consider letting her go alone, until their mother-in-law urged them to stay in Moab. Even then, Orpah stayed behind reluctantly, while Ruth insisted on accompanying Naomi.

Family relationships can be exceptional; you don't have to conform to what the world regards as the norm. Goodwill and harmony *can* prevail, even between relatives-by-marriage from different backgrounds. Unselfish love can minimize the differences of background and culture. Paul states the ideal: "If it is possible . . . live at peace with everyone" (Romans 12:18, *New International Version*).   —R. W. B.

Conclusion

A. Dimensions of Ruth's Decision

1. *It was a difficult decision.*—Ruth's commitment to return to the land of Israel with Naomi was difficult because of *what she had seen happen to God's people.* The very reason Elimelech's family had come to Moab was an indication that Israelites were not always blessed materially as a reward for their faith. There had been a severe famine in Israel. There was more to eat in Moab, which is why these Hebrews had left Judah.

Further, Ruth had seen Elimelech become ill and die. Then she had seen the death of her brother-in-law, and finally of her own husband. Certainly it didn't seem that long years of good health was a blessing with which God favored His worshipers.

She was discouraged by an Israelite from going to that land. Naomi seems to have been very negative about Ruth and Orpah's returning to Judah with her. Further, Naomi felt very bitter as she herself admitted. (See 1:20, 21. *Naomi* means "pleasant," and *Mara* means "bitter.")

Ruth saw someone who had been through a similar experience make a different choice. Orpah had known both Elimelech and Naomi, and had lost a husband, just as Ruth had. And when Naomi urged her to return to her people and her gods, she kissed Naomi good-bye and left.

Similar facts must be faced by someone deciding to become a Christian, or by someone determining to be a more faithful church member. Becoming a Christian is not a sure way to freedom from sickness, poverty, or problems. Rather we find that many followers of Christ have physical handicaps, deaths in their families, financial reversals, etc. Becoming a Christian does not guarantee an easy life.

2. *It was a definite decision.*—As noted, the decision was firm, unqualified, and unmistakable. Ruth was going with Naomi and she was going to stay with her. It was not a "trial run." So our decisions for Christ should be. We should yield to Him all that we are, all that we have, and all that we hope to be. The mystery of Christian dedication is that the more we give over to Him, the more grace and goodness flow into our lives. Instead of becoming conscious of increasing poverty, we experience abundant riches of the soul. This is true even in the midst of circumstances that seem to be unfair, most difficult, and even disastrous. Paul discovered, "When I am weak, then am I strong" (2 Corinthians 12:10).

3. *It was a determinative decision.* —When Ruth made her decision, it shaped her future and determined her destiny. It meant she had new responsibilities: to look after and care for Naomi. It meant she now would live in a new country with different customs and laws. It determined her loyalties, which were now to be with Israel and Israel's God. Though she did not know it, it determined future blessings for her—her marriage to Boaz, her childbearing, and a fulfilled life. It also determined her place in posterity. Her child Obed became the father of Jesse, who was the father of David (Ruth 4:13-22). We find her name in the earthly genealogy of Jesus (Matthew 1:5). She could scarcely have believed that all of these depended on this one great decision she declared on the road to Judah.

When Pizarro and his men landed on the beach at Peru and faced the lofty mountains and the Inca empire, he drew a line on the beach with his sword. He asked all those determined to go forward with him, to conquest or perhaps death, to cross over the line and stand with him. All others could get into one of his ships and go back to Spain. Everyone stepped over the line. Then Pizarro said, "All right, burn all the ships!" So they burned their only way of escape and faced forward toward conquest or disaster. This all-out decision was the kind of step Ruth took. It is the sort of commitment, when applied to Christian discipleship, that truly makes "all things new" for us.

4. *It was a durable decision.*—We read, "So they two went until they came to Bethlehem" (1:19). Ruth went with Naomi until they reached their destination, and then stayed with her and continued to help and bless her. So our decision to commit ourselves to the Lord must be enduring. Paul's words to the Colossians echo down to us yet today: "Continue in the faith . . . and be not moved away from the hope of the gospel" (Colossians 1:23).

B. Prayer

O Lord, help us to make decisions that will honor our Redeemer and express true dedication to His will. Make us aware of the vital nature of decisions that we face at every turn. Help us as we choose our work, our life partners, our places of living, our areas of activity in the church, and our entertainment. Help us to make wise decisions for the use of our spare time. May we be as committed, dedicated, and wholehearted, as Ruth was in her day. In Jesus' name, amen.

C. Thought to Remember

Our decisions are inward, but their results are seen in outward life. Our decisions are free, but they may bind us to various actions and situations for years to come. Our decisions may take only moments, but their effects may last forever.

Learning by Doing

This page contains an alternate lesson plan emphasizing learning activities. Classes desiring such student involvement will find these suggestions helpful.

Learning Goals

This lesson should enable a student to:

1. List the values of making specific commitments to others.

2. Explore the circumstances of Ruth's commitment to Naomi.

3. Determine to make a commitment to God or another person for something specific this week.

Into the Lesson

Write the word *commitment* vertically on the chalkboard. Distribute paper and pencils to the students as they arrive. Ask them to use each letter of the word *commitment* in another word that relates to its meaning. After five or six minutes, have volunteers share their words. Below is one possible solution.

> **C** ourage
> b **O** ldness
> **M** ission
> **M** ind-set
> aff **I** rm
> **T** estimony
> i **M** portant
> **E** xpress
> co **N** fidence
> s **T** and

Make your transition to Bible study by saying, "Commitment is something we come in contact with each day. Paying bills and preparing meals are commitments. We recognize that not all commitments are easy. Today we are going to consider a familiar account: Ruth's decision to go with her mother-in-law, who was returning to her homeland. As we do so, let's look for areas where we need to make commitments."

Into the Word

Briefly present the background of today's text by explaining the significance of Ruth 1:1, 2. Use the commentary material in this lesson to prepare your remarks. This is to help your students see the setting for today's text. Have a student prepared who will then read Ruth 1:3-22.

Divide your class into three groups and assign to each group the development of a monologue based on today's text. One group should prepare a monologue that Naomi might have spoken, another Orpah, and another Ruth. Each should include feelings, discoveries, decisions, and other aspects revealed in the text. Some inferences may be drawn. Each group should tell their character's story in the first person, as their character saw the events.

Provide writing materials for each group and allow fifteen minutes for the students to develop their monologues. Then have each group give their monologue. You may wish to discuss some of the points made by the groups.

Into Life

Give each student a copy of this letter.

Dear Ruth,

Each time I read the account of your loyalty to Naomi, I think that's just what our church needs! It seems many of our people are less than dedicated. How do I help them to see the value of making and keeping promises?

Ruth, if you had one thing to tell us about faithfulness, what would it be? What kind of things have you noticed that keep us from fulfilling promises, both to others and to God? I look forward to your answer.

Allow your class time to read the letter and to consider their answers. As they give their suggestions write them on the chalkboard and then lead a class discussion of "commitment." Especially note difficulties in carrying out intentions. Then ask, "What are some commitments that we need to make, both individually and as a congregation?" You may have some students who are not yet Christians. If no one mentions "surrendering your life to Christ," be sure the subject is brought up.

To close the session, give each student a small index card on which the following is written:

I _____ , commit to God _____
 (name of student)

_____
        (action, word, or thought)
 beginning _____ .
                      (Date)

_____
Signature

Ask each student to consider a commitment he or she needs to make to God and then complete the card. Have them put the card in a place in their homes where they will see it each day as a reminder.

Let's Talk It Over

The questions on this page are designed to encourage review of the lesson Scriptures and to promote discussion of the lesson by the class. The answers provided are only discussion starters. Let your class talk it over from there.

1. Many people today move from one community to another or from one church to another in an effort to get away from difficult circumstances. What do you think of this approach to handling problems?

During a severe famine, Elimelech and his family moved from Judah to Moab to find relief. Although that may have been the wisest choice they could have made at the time, they had no guarantee of a trouble-free existence in the new land. Indeed, after a few years, Elimelech and his sons died there.

In our times people may move from a community beset by crime and vandalism and then find themselves in another where drugs and alcohol are major threats. Or Christians may withdraw from one church because they feel the leadership is too dogmatic and strict; then they learn that their new church suffers from a glaring lack of leadership. There are times when moving away from a bad situation is the only course of action to take, but at other times the wisest decision may be to stay put and seek solutions to the problems around us.

2. The story of Ruth serves as a reminder of the difficulties that accompany widowhood. How can the church best minister to the widows among its membership and encourage them to serve?

The church's responsibility to widows is a matter of some emphasis in the New Testament. The ministry to their needs in the church at Jerusalem gave rise to the selection and ordination of the men we call the seven deacons (Acts 6). James insists that "religion that God our Father accepts as pure and faultless is this: to look after orphans and widows in their distress" (James 1:27, *New International Version*). A good portion of 1 Timothy 5 discusses various aspects of ministering to widows. That ministry must have both spiritual and practical aspects. The church needs to provide the kind of fellowship and teaching that can help to fill the awful void produced by the death of a mate. And it is vital that members who have expertise in such areas as taxes, insurance, home repairs, and automobile maintenance be available to offer counsel and help to widows who have no one else to turn to about these matters. As far as service in the church is concerned, widows could be of immense help in areas such as secretarial work, letter-writing, telephoning, home visitation, assisting with missionary and benevolent projects, etc.

3. One appealing aspect of the story of Ruth is the glimpse that it gives us of a beautiful relationship between a mother-in-law and her daughter-in-law. How can we cultivate similar positive relationships with in-laws?

There are so many unflattering jokes told about mothers-in-law and so many unpleasant accounts described of conflicts among in-laws that couples contemplating marriage may be led to assume that such things are an inevitable part of family relationships. But the mutual love and trust that Ruth and Naomi shared can surely be an attainable goal in Christian families. Working out a harmonious relationship with in-laws is a challenge that begins before marriage. It is well to remind prospective brides and grooms that they are in a sense marrying each other's families and that they need to give some consideration to what that will involve. Once a couple is married, one of the keys to maintaining a healthy relationship with one another is the communication of feelings, hopes, disappointments, concerns, etc. This kind of rapport with in-laws could also contribute understanding, respect, and trust to that relationship.

4. What are some examples of "small" decisions that may prove to be determinative in altering the course of our lives?

A negative example is that of the temptation to lie or deceive. A person may conclude that "a little white lie" or an occasional "harmless" deception will prove insignificant. But many people have found that small lies can lead to larger ones, and from there to habitual lying.

On the positive side a Christian may not consider it a momentous decision when he commits himself to a daily period of personal Bible study and prayer. But this hiding of God's Word in our hearts (Psalm 119:11), this continual seeking to know and keep God's Word (Psalm 119:44), this regular use of the Word as a source of light and guidance (Psalm 119:105), is certain to influence the direction and quality of our lives.

The Compassion of Boaz

LESSON SCRIPTURE: Ruth 2, 3; Deuteronomy 24:19-21.

PRINTED TEXT: Ruth 2:5-12, 19, 20.

Ruth 2:5-12, 19, 20

5 Then said Boaz unto his servant that was set over the reapers, Whose damsel is this?

6 And the servant that was set over the reapers answered and said, It is the Moabitish damsel that came back with Naomi out of the country of Moab:

7 And she said, I pray you, let me glean and gather after the reapers among the sheaves: so she came, and hath continued even from the morning until now, that she tarried a little in the house.

8 Then said Boaz unto Ruth, Hearest thou not, my daughter? Go not to glean in another field, neither go from hence, but abide here fast by my maidens:

9 Let thine eyes be on the field that they do reap, and go thou after them: have I not charged the young men that they shall not touch thee? and when thou art athirst, go unto the vessels, and drink of that which the young men have drawn.

10 Then she fell on her face, and bowed herself to the ground, and said unto him, Why have I found grace in thine eyes, that thou shouldest take knowledge of me, seeing I am a stranger?

11 And Boaz answered and said unto her, It hath fully been showed me, all that thou hast done unto thy mother-in-law since the death of thine husband; and how thou hast left thy father and thy mother, and the land of thy nativity, and art come unto a people which thou knewest not heretofore.

12 The Lord recompense thy work, and a full reward be given thee of the Lord God of Israel, under whose wings thou art come to trust.

. . . .

19 And her mother-in-law said unto her, Where hast thou gleaned today? and where wroughtest thou? blessed be he that did take knowledge of thee. And she showed her mother-in-law with whom she had wrought, and said, The man's name with whom I wrought today is Boaz.

20 And Naomi said unto her daughter-in-law, Blessed be he of the Lord, who hath not left off his kindness to the living and to the dead. And Naomi said unto her, The man is near of kin unto us, one of our next kinsmen.

Aug
20

GOLDEN TEXT: Why have I found grace in thine eyes, that thou shouldest take knowledge of me, seeing I am a stranger?—Ruth 2:10.

Lesson Aims

After studying this lesson a student should:

1. Be able to discern God's hand in Ruth's life as she trusted that life to Him.

2. Understand that we are called to have faith in God in untried ways today.

3. See that Boaz' spirit was such that his kindness and generosity were extended to a person who was a foreigner in Israel.

4. Show greater compassion to the stranger and the needy.

Lesson Outline

INTRODUCTION
   A. Harvest Practices
   B. Lesson Background
  I. RUTH IDENTIFIED (Ruth 2:5-7)
    Finding a Job
 II. RUTH ADVISED (Ruth 2:8, 9)
III. RUTH APPRAISED (Ruth 2:10-12)
    Under His Wings
IV. RUTH INFORMED (Ruth 2:19, 20)
CONCLUSION
   A. In God's Care
   B. Prayer
   C. Thought to Remember

Display visual 12 from the visual/learning resources packet and refer to it when appropriate. It is shown on page 437.

Introduction

A. Harvest Practices

Our lesson has as its backdrop the harvesting scenes of Israel in the time of Ruth and Boaz. In Judah the grain harvesting period was in the spring. Flax was usually reaped in March and April. Then in the months of April, May, and June came the barley and wheat harvests. The reaping was done with sickles. Handfuls of grain stalks were bound together into bunches, which were then gathered together and carried on the backs of donkeys or camels to the place where the threshing was done.

When the fields were being harvested, poor or disadvantaged people followed behind the reapers, picking up any sheaves of grain that were dropped and cutting any that were missed. This was called gleaning. Special instructions were given in the Hebrew legal codes to allow this practice of providing for the needy. The regulations regarding gleaning involved the harvest of fruit, as well as grapes, and also that of grain. The directions relating to grain were as follows: "When you are harvesting in your field and you overlook a sheaf, do not go back to get it. Leave it for the alien, the fatherless and the widow, so that the Lord your God may bless you" (Deuteronomy 24:19, *New International Version*). In today's lesson we see one who was both an alien and a widow benefiting from this gracious provision of God's law.

B. Lesson Background

In last week's lesson, we noted that when Naomi decided to return to her homeland in Judah, Ruth, her daughter-in-law, could not be talked out of coming with her. Ruth was willing to leave Moab, the land of her birth, to go to a land strange to her and share the life of her widowed mother-in-law. So the two of them set out for Bethlehem, and they arrived there "in the beginning of barley harvest" (Ruth 1:22). Their arrival at this time was indeed fortunate, for hunger was imminent. The Biblical record suggests that without delay Ruth asked permission of her mother-in-law to join those who were gleaning in the fields, following after those who were reaping the barley harvest. The work was humbling, but honest. Because of their need, Naomi granted permission.

Ruth's willingness to labor as a gleaner demonstrated her sense of responsibility for helping out in the situation in which she and Naomi found themselves. We don't know what Ruth's status would have been as a widow in her own land of Moab. However, here in Israel she was ready to take her place among those who were "meek and lowly in heart."

Making her way out of the city to the surrounding fields that were ripe with golden grain and alive with reapers, binders, and gleaners, Ruth asked the overseer of the reapers in a certain part of the field if she might glean there. We are told "her hap was" to attach herself to a group gleaning in a field owned by Boaz. The *New International Version* reads, "As it turned out, she found herself working in a field belonging to Boaz" (2:3), who was "a mighty man of wealth, of the family of Elimelech" (2:1). If Ruth picked out the field by chance, as verse 3 seems to suggest, we may say that the choice of her place of labor was providential. Later, Boaz himself came from town to see how the harvesting was progressing. It is at this point that the text for this lesson begins.

I. Ruth Identified
(Ruth 2:5-7)

5. Then said Boaz unto his servant that was set over the reapers, Whose damsel is this?

It is very likely that Ruth's dress and carriage were enough to distinguish her from the other women who were engaged in gleaning. It seems, to have been a task done mostly by women. Boaz was at once interested in the foreign girl gleaning in his field. We know he had already heard of Ruth and her relationship with Naomi (v. 11). It may be that not very many foreign girls were found at gleaning tasks in this area of Israel. Boaz may well have guessed Ruth's identity, but he wanted some more definite information.

6. And the servant that was set over the reapers answered and said, It is the Moabitish damsel that came back with Naomi out of the country of Moab.

This answer confirmed conjectures Boaz probably had made about the identity of this stranger gleaning after his reapers.

7. And she said, I pray you, let me glean and gather after the reapers among the sheaves: so she came, and hath continued even from the morning until now, that she tarried a little in the house.

It seems the custom was for reapers in ancient Palestine to begin work at daybreak and continue working through the coolest hours of the day. After three or four hours of labor, a breakfast of modest proportions would be eaten out in the fields. Then work would continue until perhaps two-thirty or three o'clock. A fortifying meal would then be eaten in *the house*, a temporary shed or booth that provided shelter from the sun in the heat of the day. A siesta might follow. Then from four-thirty or five o'clock, work would continue until dusk. In all probability it was after the first "break" that Ruth spent but a brief time in *the house* or shelter. Boaz determined from this answer that Naomi had not requested a job for her daughter-in-law, but Ruth had applied for it in person. This indicated self-reliance, just as her work habits demonstrated diligence.

FINDING A JOB

What Color Is Your Parachute? is a popular manual published annually for job hunters and career changers. The book features helpful counsel and practical ideas that promise to guide readers to employment that is well suited for them, adequately gainful, and most fulfilling. Many folk have found the material to be highly beneficial and especially encouraging as they have sought positions in the work places of the world.

Ruth had no books to help her find a job. She had only her mother-in-law's advice and moral support, and one more essential: *the will to work*. That was the real secret of Ruth's success. She was willing to take a lowly job, and she worked steadily with only a short rest. She won privileges and "fringe benefits" due to her character and attitude.

Regardless of what books one reads for finding and keeping jobs, there is no substitute for the qualities of industry and dependability demonstrated by Ruth. Certainly every Christian worker would do well to follow the spirit of her example. As Paul advised the Christians in Colossae: "Whatsoever ye do, do it heartily, as to the Lord" (Colossians 3:23).   —R. W. B.

II. Ruth Advised
(Ruth 2:8, 9)

8. Then said Boaz unto Ruth, Hearest thou not, my daughter? Go not to glean in another field, neither go from hence, but abide here fast by my maidens.

The first phrase in this verse sounds awkward to us today. It is simply one way of saying, "Please pay attention to this, young lady." Boaz urged Ruth not to go to another field, but to remain among the servant girls and others who were gleaning after his workers. As we have mentioned, the law gave poor people the right to glean after the reapers. But Boaz' invitation to glean only in his field gave a special authorization and legitimacy to Ruth's work.

9. Let thine eyes be on the field that they do reap, and go thou after them: have I not charged the young men that they shall not touch thee? and when thou art athirst, go unto the vessels, and drink of that which the young men have drawn.

Boaz underscored his wish that Ruth confine her gleaning to his fields. But he also realized that if Ruth gleaned after his workers each day, she would become a familiar figure who might

---

How to Say It

BOAZ. *Bo-*az.
COLOSSAE. Ko-*loss*-ee.
ELIMELECH. E-*lim*-eh-leck.
GOLIATH. Go-*lye*-uth.
MOAB. *Mo*-ab.
MOABITISH. *Mo*-uh-*bite*-ish.
NAOMI. Nay-*o*-me, Nay-*o*-my, or *Nay*-o-my.

also become vulnerable to sexual harassment. As she followed their reaping and drank from their water supply, they might attempt to become more and more unrestrained in their behavior toward her. Boaz sought to allay any fears Ruth might have about this by telling her he had already warned his young men to leave her alone. Boaz not only extended to Ruth a special invitation to work in his fields, but also offered her his protection.

As this story develops, we see more and more clearly that Boaz became what the Hebrew law considered a "kinsman-redeemer" to Ruth. Because he was a relative of her husband's family, he fulfilled certain obligations and accorded to her certain privileges. This was one reason, he so readily allowed her to glean in his fields. In addition to pointing out rewarding work she could do, he promised to protect and care for her. Our Redeemer Jesus, our Lord, gives us areas of service in His harvest fields today. We are told laborers are needed and are invited to work for Him. We also are assured of His care and help, for He says, "Go into all the world . . . and, lo, I am with you, *always.*"

III. Ruth Appraised
(Ruth 2:10-12)

10. Then she fell on her face, and bowed herself to the ground, and said unto him, Why have I found grace in thine eyes, that thou shouldest take knowledge of me, seeing I am a stranger?

If Ruth's obeisance before Boaz seems extreme, we must remember the vast difference between their social, economic, and national status. Boaz was a "mighty man" (v. 2), that is, one of the upper-class persons, a member of what would be called the power structure of that society. Ruth was trying to eke out an existence from the wisps and bits of grain that could be salvaged from what was left over or missed in the harvest. Boaz was a man "of wealth" who owned the field and the grain that was harvested, who employed the workers, and whose goodwill made possible what little Ruth could glean. He was a leading citizen of Israel; she was a poor widow. He was an Israelite, one of the chosen people of God. She was a foreign girl, a Moabitess, one of a tribal group that frequently had warred with the Hebrews.

The special consideration she was being shown puzzled Ruth, for as yet she apparently did not know of the fact that Boaz was a kinsman of her husband's family.

11. And Boaz answered and said unto her, It hath fully been showed me, all that thou hast done unto thy mother-in-law since the death of thine husband; and how thou hast left thy father and thy mother, and the land of thy nativity, and art come unto a people which thou knewest not heretofore.

What Ruth had done and was doing because of her love for and loyalty to Naomi had become well known to Boaz and, one may be sure, to the Bethlehem community. One would have thought her relationship with her own father and mother or her own people would have dictated that she remain in Moab when her mother-in-law left. But no! She had voluntarily left the land of her birth and had come to live in Judah. Amid a strange people in a strange land, she now was working as a lower class worker to help support her mother-in-law. This moving demonstration of self-denial, devotion, and determination had deeply impressed the wealthy employer, Boaz. He let Ruth know he was not insensitive to her situation.

12. The Lord recompense thy work, and a full reward be given thee of the Lord God of Israel, under whose wings thou art come to trust.

This wish that God's blessing might come to Ruth came naturally to the lips of Boaz. Not only was he a wealthy and powerful figure, but one who expressed a sincere faith in God in all his activities. When he came out from Bethlehem to spend time in the fields with the harvesters, his greetings to them were in God's name, as were their responses to him (2:4). In his relations with his employees, in his treatment of Ruth, and in his later actions as a kinsman, he manifested a spirit of compassion, integrity, and consideration.

A child had received quite satisfactory grades in most subjects on her report card, except for one category listed as "Conduct." On being questioned about this, she said, "Conduct is my most difficult subject." This is all too true in life. It is one thing to perform the rituals of religion and to repeat the acceptable phrases of religious commitment, but it is quite another to really live as one who loves God and people. Boaz was one whose genuine piety was attested to by his conduct in everyday life. In his poem "They Who Tread the Path of Labor," Henry Van Dyke writes of Christ, saying,

> Where the many toil together,
>   There am I among My own;
> Where the tired workman sleepeth,
>   There am I with him alone.
> . . . .
> Every task, however simple,
>   Sets the soul that does it free;
> Every deed of love and mercy,
>   Done to man, is done to Me.

UNDER HIS WINGS

visual 12

Under His wings, what a refuge in sorrow!
How the heart yearningly turns to His rest!
Often when earth has no balm for my healing,
There I find comfort, and there I am blest.

Ruth and Boaz certainly were acquainted with the sense of divine security that inspired William Cushing to write this lyric. Ruth, along with Naomi, needed refuge in her bereavement and loneliness. Leaving her idolatrous homeland of Moab, Ruth embraced the God of Israel and came to live among His people. There she found comfort and healing. Divine providence supplied her physical and emotional needs. Jehovah sheltered her just as He protected all of faithful Israel, much like a hen who gathers her chicks beneath her wings.

In time Ruth married into the Jewish family. She became the grandmother of David. Centuries later, the most famous descendant of Ruth and Boaz, Jesus Christ, was born in Bethlehem. Near the close of His earthly ministry, Jesus wept over Jerusalem, because they would not seek spiritual refuge under His wings (Matthew 23:37). Much of the world still rejects the rest, comfort, and blessing to be found in the Lord. Have you found refuge in Him?   —R. W. B.

IV. Ruth Informed

(Ruth 2:19, 20)

Before turning from Ruth to attend to his duties, Boaz invited her to have lunch with the reapers, and he himself ate with them under the shelter out in the field. During the meal he made sure she had sufficient to eat. It is most likely that they had some conversation during this period, but nothing of it is recorded. After she left, Boaz told his workers to let her glean wherever she wanted to, even if it were to be very close to the harvesting process. They were also to let drop several handfuls of harvested barley purposely to add to her gleaning. The result was that when Ruth was finished for the day and she had beaten out the grain (pounded and shook it to separate the grain from the stalks) she had an "ephah" of barley. This was about one bushel, an unusually large amount for one person to gather in one day. When she took the results of her day's labor home, plus the bread and parched corn she had saved from her lunch, it at once aroused Naomi's curiosity (vv. 14-18).

19. And her mother-in-law said unto her, Where hast thou gleaned today? and where wroughtest thou? blessed be he that did take knowledge of thee. And she showed her mother-in-law with whom she had wrought, and said, The man's name with whom I wrought today is Boaz.

Naomi knew that someone had been unusually helpful to Ruth or she could not have been so successful. Ruth was a foreign girl, working in unfamiliar fields among maidens who doubtless were more experienced gleaners. For her to secure such a large gleaning of barley signified something most unusual. The mention of the name of Boaz brought an immediate explanation to Naomi's mind and a thrill to her heart.

20. And Naomi said unto her daughter-in-law, Blessed be he of the Lord, who hath not left off his kindness to the living and to the dead. And Naomi said unto her, The man is near of kin unto us, one of our next kinsmen.

In ancient Israel near *kinsmen* possessed certain duties and rights. One duty had to do with the treatment of the widow of a brother (see Deuteronomy 25:5-10). In such cases a man was to marry his brother's widow so that the first son who might be born could bear his brother's name, "that his name be not put out of Israel" (v. 6). The near kinsman also had the right to redeem or buy back previously sold property, so it would not be lost to the family (see Leviticus 25:25). He also had the first right to purchase property yet in the family's possession. Seeing the evidence of Boaz' great kindness shown to Ruth, Naomi had reason to believe that this godly man would in some way fulfill the role of near kinsman to Ruth.

It may seem strange that Naomi had not told Ruth about their kinsman Boaz before she happened to glean in his fields. It may be she had been back in Bethlehem such a short time that the position of Boaz had not become clear to her. We must remember that Naomi had been away from Judah for more than a decade. Getting settled in a new home, and reestablishing associations must have required all of her attention.

In her excitement at the good fortune of Ruth's meeting with Boaz, Naomi did not forget to offer a quick expression of thanks to God. Earlier Naomi felt that God had dealt with her in a very bitter way (1:19, 20). Now, however, she could see that God had not forgotten her after all.

Naomi and Elimelech had left Judah in *doubt* concerning God's care of them during the famine. She had lived in *despair* because of the deaths of her husband and her two sons. She had returned to Judah in *desperation*, her only support the hope of some brighter future and the presence of her foreign daughter-in-law. Soon now she would know *deliverance* and *delight* as gloom gave way to gladness.

Conclusion

A. In God's Care

The future must have seemed bleak for Ruth as she made her decision to go to Bethlehem with Naomi. We have already considered the difficulties that confronted her as she made up her mind. Naomi herself did not seem to be a person who could help assure her of any stable future. Naomi had left Judah because of bad times. Some of her former acquaintances might have said, "Here is Naomi, returned once more. When things were dark here, she 'ran away' to Moab. Now that times are better here she comes back wanting those of us who have endured the hard days to welcome her with open arms." Furthermore, several may have resented Naomi's bringing "that strange foreign girl" among them.

It truly was providential that Boaz was harvesting his fields near Bethlehem, that it was possible for Ruth to join gleaners, that she unwittingly chose to work in one of Boaz' fields, that he noticed her, and that he was a kinsman of Naomi. It was fortunate that he was unmarried and that their age difference was not a hindrance to thoughts of marriage. (Boaz' commendation of Ruth that she had not chased after the young men indicates that there was an age difference—see Ruth 3:10.) That Ruth's faithful-

ness and fortitude had come to Boaz's attention could perhaps be expected. But that he should have been in the area where she was gleaning and had a chance to see and talk with her was unusual. His later desire to exercise his kinsman's right that every impediment could be cleared away so they could be married, was most remarkable.

Thomas Hood pictures Ruth as Boaz might have seen her:

> Round her eyes her tresses fell,
> Which were blackest none could tell,
> But long lashes veiled a light,
> That had else been all too bright.
>
> And her hat, with shady brim,
> Made her tressy forehead dim;—
> Thus she stood amid the stooks,
> Praising God with sweetest looks:—
>
> Sure, he said, Heaven did not mean,
> Where I reap thou shouldst but glean,
> Lay thy sheaf adown and come,
> Share my harvest and my home.

So it was that Ruth, loyal to Naomi, diligent in service, nonassertive in behavior, but alert and self-respecting, progressed from dependent gleaner to wife of the "mighty man of wealth." From being a stranger and foreigner, she became "a mother in Israel."

B. Prayer

Our Father God, how difficult some decisions are! But often the problem is not that we do not see what we ought to do. The real difficulty is that we find it hard to go courageously into a clouded future trusting You. The reason is that we just can't see how things can come out well, but we *can* see many ways they could come out in a bad way. Forgive us our lack of faith, especially when a glance back across the roads we have already traveled shows us how our burdens have been lifted, our hurts eased, and our lives given power for work that seemed too difficult. Help us, dear God, to remember Ruth's blessings because of her devoted commitment and unqualified trust.

May we also remember the compassion Boaz showed to the foreign woman, Ruth. May we too be sensitive to the emotional, economic, and spiritual needs of the strangers who are in our midst. We pray in Jesus' name. Amen.

C. Thought to Remember

If Ruth, the widowed Moabite girl, could decide bravely and trust God truly, so can we. In some way we will be blessed in our day as Ruth was in hers. When God's way is *respected*, His blessings and benefits often will be *unexpected*.

Learning by Doing

This page contains an alternate lesson plan emphasizing learning activities. Classes desiring such student involvement will find these suggestions helpful.

Learning Goals

This lesson should enable the student to:

1. Describe the compassion of Boaz shown to Ruth and Naomi.

2. Identify the results of Boaz' compassion on Ruth and Naomi.

3. Express thanks to God for His compassion upon himself.

Into the Lesson

Before your students arrive in the classroom, write the following words on the chalkboard as shown:

JUSTICE

COMPASSION

REDEEMER

When you are ready to begin the class session, distribute pencil and paper to each student. (If your class uses the student book, space is provided there for this activity.) Draw your students' attention to the words you have written on the chalkboard and ask them to list at least five words that are brought to mind when they think of each word. Allot three minutes for them to write their word lists. Ask for volunteers to share their words with the class. As they do so, record the words on the chalkboard.

Make the transition to Bible study by saying, "God used Boaz in today's passage to communicate these three ideas to Ruth. The Old Testament law called for justice toward the poor. Boaz showed compassion as he invited Ruth to glean exclusively in his field and as he made provision for extra gleanings for her. He became a redeemer to her as he fulfilled the duty of a near relative."

Into the Word

Begin this section with a brief lecture on the practice of harvesting in the Hebrew community. Use the material in the Introduction section of the lesson commentary. Be sure to explain the provisions for gleaning in the Hebrew law. Then read aloud Ruth 2:1-23. For variety, you may divide this Scripture into three parts—2:1-7; 2:8-16; 2:17-23—and recruit three students, each to read one of the sections.

Next, divide your class into four groups. You should have four to six members in each group. If you have more class members, create more groups and allow more than one group to work on an assignment.

Three groups will prepare diary entries for the day that is described in the second chapter of Ruth. One group should write a diary entry for Naomi, one group for Ruth, and one group for Boaz. Each diary entry should review the events of the day, explore the possible feelings of the person they are writing for, reflect on God's involvement.

The fourth group will be involved in a Scripture search determining what our response should be to God's compassion for us. They should explore the following Scripture passages and summarize their findings:

Compassion for Today

Psalm 146:5-9; Luke 6:36, 38; 12:29-34; 2 Corinthians 8:9; Philippians 4:11-13; 1 Timothy 6:17, 18; Hebrews 13:5, 6; James 2:14-17; 1 John 3:16-18.

Allow your groups to work for twenty minutes to prepare their reports. When the time is up, ask the groups who prepared diary entries to share their reports with the entire class. Save the report from Group Four until the "Into Life" section. Lead a brief discussion of the diary entries in order to clarify and/or expand them.

Into Life

Begin the application section of your lesson by asking, "What were some of the results of the compassion that Boaz showed to Ruth and Naomi?" Of course, several benefits to Ruth and Naomi will be evident; but ask also of the benefits to Boaz.

At this time allow group four to share their findings. Remind the class that Group Four was studying what our response should be to God's compassion toward us. Allow a short discussion following the report.

Read aloud Ruth 2:12 and Ruth 2:20. Point out that these two verses reflect a worshipful attitude to the Lord for His compassion. Allow two minutes for the students to think of a time when God showed His compassion to them through another person. Ask them to write down that event and then compose a brief statement of thanksgiving and worship to Him. Close with prayer, thanking God for His undeserved compassion. Then sing the Doxology.

Let's Talk It Over

The questions on this page are designed to encourage review of the lesson Scriptures and to promote discussion of the lesson by the class. The answers provided are only discussion starters. Let your class talk it over from there.

1. Instead of waiting on God to supply their needs, Ruth and Naomi determined that Ruth would go out and glean in the harvest fields. When they followed through with that, God's providence took over to bless them in a remarkable way. How does God's providence work in similar fashion in our lives?

It is possible to get in God's way by trying too hard to solve our own problems and supply our own needs. The popular counsel, "Let go, and let God," is legitimate if we find that in relying on our own cleverness and power we have failed to trust God for the supply of all our needs. But we do need to put ourselves into position to receive God's help. If we need financial help, we may need to seek a better job; if we have personal problems we are unable to solve, we may need to talk to a counselor; if we want to have new friends, we may have to take the initiative in forming friendships. As we step boldly in the direction of self-help, God may then meet our faith and courage with His providential care, as He did with Naomi and Ruth.

2. In speaking with Ruth, Boaz referred to "the Lord God of Israel, under whose wings thou art come to trust." Why is this a particularly appealing description? How can this be practical for Christians?

This expression appears several times in the Psalms. David pleads to God, "Hide me in the shadow of your wings from the wicked who assail me, from my mortal enemies who surround me" (Psalm 17:8, 9, *New International Version*). The psalmist assures his readers in Psalm 91:4 that God "will cover you with his feathers, and under his wings you will find refuge" *(New International Version)*. Whatever bird we may picture here, the symbolism of the protecting wings speaks of a warmth and security that is very appealing. And if we think especially of an eagle, with its fearsome talons warding off an enemy, the sense of protection is heightened. Hymn writer William O. Cushing gives us picturesque guidance in applying this description personally when he leads us to sing,

Under His wings, O what precious enjoyment!
  There will I hide till life's trials are o'er;
Sheltered, protected, no evil can harm me;
  Resting in Jesus I'm safe evermore.

3. Even persons who hold a general dislike for foreigners are usually touched by the sight of a hungry or suffering child of another race. Why is it so much easier to feel compassion for a child? How can we develop the same kind of compassion for adults?

Even Jesus demonstrated a special regard for children (Matthew 18:1-6, 10; 19:13-15). However, He seemed to view the struggling, spiritually hungry masses of adults as being like children, and He was filled with compassion for them (Mark 6:34). There are many adults whose ignorance and poverty render them as helpless as children.

4. How should we respond to a situation in which we seem to have no chance of succeeding?

God's working in the life of Ruth to bring blessings out of improbable circumstances has its parallel in other Biblical accounts. The odds appeared to be overwhelmingly against David when he headed for his showdown with the Philistine Goliath. In a den crowded with hungry lions, Daniel's chances for survival seemed nonexistent. Paul's chances of getting out of Jerusalem alive after being rescued from a Jewish mob (Acts 22, 23) may have seemed extremely slim. But God appears to take delight in delivering His servants from what may seem impossible situations. So, if we feel that what we are doing or planning is in harmony with God's will, we have good reason to be confident and persistent in following through with it. It is easy to become pessimistic and to give up, because other people are likely to remind us of the apparent hopelessness of the situation. But when God chooses to show His mighty power for us, what would seem the obvious outcome may not materialize (see Romans 8:28).

5. What should our attitude be toward those who cling to heathen religions after coming into our country?

While we can never compromise the unique quality of our Christian faith (Acts 4:12), we must be patient with these new neighbors. Our love and our patience may accomplish much more than our theological arguments in leading them to see the beauty of Jesus.

The Fulfillment of Hope

LESSON SCRIPTURE: Ruth 4.

PRINTED TEXT: Ruth 4:9-17.

Ruth 4:9-17

9 And Boaz said unto the elders, and unto all the people, Ye are witnesses this day, that I have bought all that was Elimelech's, and all that was Chilion's and Mahlon's, of the hand of Naomi.

10 Moreover Ruth the Moabitess, the wife of Mahlon, have I purchased to be my wife, to raise up the name of the dead upon his inheritance, that the name of the dead be not cut off from among his brethren, and from the gate of his place: ye are witnesses this day.

11 And all the people that were in the gate, and the elders, said, We are witnesses. The Lord make the woman that is come into thine house like Rachel and like Leah, which two did build the house of Israel: and do thou worthily in Ephratah, and be famous in Bethlehem:

12 And let thy house be like the house of Pharez, whom Tamar bare unto Judah, of the seed which the Lord shall give thee of this young woman.

13 So Boaz took Ruth, and she was his wife: and when he went in unto her, the Lord gave her conception, and she bare a son.

14 And the women said unto Naomi, Blessed be the Lord, which hath not left thee this day without a kinsman, that his name may be famous in Israel.

15 And he shall be unto thee a restorer of thy life, and a nourisher of thine old age: for thy daughter-in-law, which loveth thee,

which is better to thee than seven sons, hath borne him.

16 And Naomi took the child, and laid it in her bosom, and became nurse unto it.

17 And the women her neighbors gave it a name, saying, There is a son born to Naomi; and they called his name Obed: he is the father of Jesse, the father of David.

GOLDEN TEXT: The women said unto Naomi, Blessed be the Lord, which hath not left thee this day without a kinsman, that his name may be famous in Israel.—Ruth 4:14.

Lesson Aims

After this lesson students should:

1. See that God is able to bring happiness where previously heartbreak was known.

2. Be able to tell what part Ruth played in God's redemptive plan.

3. Be challenged to follow Ruth's example of unselfish love.

Lesson Outline

INTRODUCTION

I. RUTH BETROTHED (Ruth 4:9-12)

II. RUTH—BRIDE AND MOTHER (Ruth 4:13)
   Where Do Babies Come From?

III. NAOMI—BLESSED AND BENEFITED (Ruth 4:14-16)
   Grand Relatives

IV. THE BABY NAMED AND IDENTIFIED (Ruth 4:17)

CONCLUSION

   A. The Radiance of Ruth

   B. Prayer

   C. Thought to Remember

Display visual 13 from the visuals/learning resources packet and refer to it when appropriate in your lesson presentation. It is shown on page 444.

Introduction

In last week's lesson we studied Ruth's first encounter with Boaz. We saw also that Naomi, Ruth's mother-in-law, informed her that Boaz was a relative of her deceased husband. She urged Ruth to accept Boaz' invitation to glean in his fields exclusively. Ruth did so through the remainder of the barley harvest and throughout the wheat harvest (2:22, 23).

During those weeks of harvest, Boaz' kindness to Ruth continued, a fact that did not escape Naomi's notice. Doubtless Boaz often was a visitor in Naomi's home. Out of loving concern for her daughter-in-law who was such a blessing and comfort to her, Naomi devised a plan whereby Ruth could know the love, happiness, and security of a home of her own. It involved invoking the law that provided for a widow to be wed to a kinsman of her deceased husband. Naomi's plan arranged Ruth's marriage to Boaz.

Naomi instructed Ruth to approach Boaz as he slept in the field on the threshing floor, supervising and guarding his harvest. Those sleeping in the fields would be fully clothed, and covered with a single shawl or blanket. Ruth was to uncover his feet and lie down. Doubtless this was according to the custom of that era. Ruth followed Naomi's directions exactly; however, it must have been with considerable hesitancy that she approached the sleeping Boaz.

Boaz awakened at midnight and found Ruth there at his feet. She spoke to him, asking him to fulfill his duty as a kinsman. He spread the "skirt" of his garment over her. That is, part of his flowing robe, as well as the outer covering, was placed over Ruth as a symbol that he was willing to marry her and protect her. However, Boaz indicated that there was one man who was a closer relative than he, and he would find out if this person desired to fulfill the duties of a kinsman. If not, Boaz would do so himself. No doubt several matters were discussed as the night wore on. Before dawn Ruth arose, took six "measures" of barley Boaz gave her, and returned to Naomi. The gift was for Naomi's benefit. It indicated to Naomi the sincerity and integrity of Boaz' intentions in this matter. Probably Ruth had told Boaz during the night that the whole idea of her approaching him as he slept was Naomi's.

The very next day Boaz went to the city gate to secure the right to fulfill the kinsman's duty toward Ruth. The city gate was the place of meeting for business and of legal matters in those days. Boaz' negotiations are recorded in Ruth 4:1-8. The closing part of this ritual is where our printed text for today begins. A very interesting human touch is given us concerning Ruth's anxious tension as she awaited the outcome of these transactions. She had made many decisions and had taken direct action in several matters in the past that had affected her life and Naomi's. She had chosen to return to Bethlehem with Naomi and to share her fate. She had acted forthrightly in going into the fields as a harvest gleaner. She had honored Boaz' request to work only in his fields. She had done as Naomi urged her and had gone to Boaz at night willing to trust herself to his care and keeping. Now, however, she had to wait and see what the other kinsman would do. Nothing she could do would make any difference in decisions and actions that were in the control of others. No wonder, therefore, we find Naomi saying to her, "Sit still, my daughter, until thou know how the matter will fall" (3:18). We can imagine the tension of the situation agitating Ruth with its uncertainty, coupled with her inability to do anything to resolve it.

I. Ruth Betrothed
(Ruth 4:9-12)

9. And Boaz said unto the elders, and unto all the people, Ye are witnesses this day, that I have bought all that was Elimelech's, and all that was Chilion's and Mahlon's, of the hand of Naomi.

Ten "elders of the city," selected by Boaz, sat with him at "the gate" or main entrance to the town (4:2). He then had the kinsman, who was a closer relative to Naomi than he, come sit with them while he explained his wishes concerning Naomi's inheritance and respecting her daughter-in-law Ruth. The kinsman said he would not be able to act as a "redeemer" in this case, so he removed his shoe and gave it to Boaz, indicating that he was giving up his rights in the matter. Boaz then stated publicly, for the record, that he had met the legal requirements for the transfer of kinship rights.

10. Moreover Ruth the Moabitess, the wife of Mahlon, have I purchased to be my wife, to raise up the name of the dead upon his inheritance, that the name of the dead be not cut off from among his brethren, and from the gate of his place: ye are witnesses this day.

To read that Boaz said he had *purchased* Ruth to be his wife is offensive to us at first. Something as personal as marriage should not be thought of in commercial terms. Boaz' statement was more a reference to his fulfillment of the legal requirements regarding the inheritance of property rights, than to his intention to marry Ruth. His meaning was, "Today I have fulfilled the part of the near kinsman by purchasing the estate of Elimelech. As an extension of that legal transfer, I have secured the right to take Ruth the Moabitess as my wife."

We presume Boaz and Ruth talked over their future relationship, not only during the one night in the harvest field, but at other times. So Boaz' statement here is not to be construed as suggesting that there was no emotional involvement between them. Affection and romance were simply not appropriate considerations in a legal transaction.

11. And all the people that were in the gate, and the elders, said, We are witnesses. The Lord make the woman that is come into thine house like Rachel and like Leah, which two did build the house of Israel: and do thou worthily in Ephratah, and be famous in Bethlehem.

The *people* and *elders* affirmed the fact that they had witnessed the transfer of kinship rights to Boaz. They added their good wishes that the wife Boaz had taken might be like *Rachel* and *Leah.* These were the two wives of Jacob, whose union with them and with their handmaids produced the twelve sons who were the founders of the tribes of Israel. Thus the prayer was that Ruth too would bear many children.

Ephratah was either the ancient name of the city of Bethlehem or the name of the district that surrounded it. The wish of the elders and the people for Boaz himself was that he would enjoy good standing in the community.

12. And let thy house be like the house of Pharez, whom Tamar bare unto Judah, of the seed which the Lord shall give thee of this young woman.

The house of Pharez. Pharez was a son of Judah by Tamar (Genesis 38). Judah had two other sons who were the heads of houses in Israel, but Pharez' house was more numerous (see Numbers 26:20, 21). Boaz himself was a descendant of Judah through Pharez. The wish of the people and the elders for Boaz was as their wish for Ruth—that his descendants would be many. Their use of the phrase *this young woman* seems to be another indication that Boaz was considerably older than Ruth.

II. Ruth—Bride and Mother
(Ruth 4:13)

13. So Boaz took Ruth, and she was his wife: and when he went in unto her, the Lord gave her conception, and she bare a son.

Ruth had married a foreign young man when she was living in her native country of Moab. But after several years of childless marriage, her husband died, leaving her a widow. When Ruth went to Israel with Naomi she seemed to be in a depressing and hopeless situation—a widowed stranger in a foreign country. There she found it necessary to work as a gleaner in fields owned

---

How to Say It

BOAZ. *Bo*-az.

CHILION. *Kil*-ih-on.

ELIMELECH. E-*lim*-eh-leck.

EPHRATAH. *Ef*-rah-tah.

MAHLON. *Mah*-lon.

MARA. *May*-rah.

MOAB. *Mo*-ab.

MOABITESS. *Mo*-ub-*ite*-ess (strong accent on *Mo*).

NAOMI. Nay-*o*-me, Nay-*o*-my, or *Nay*-o-my.

OBED. *O*-bed.

PHAREZ. *Fay*-reez or *Fay*-rez.

TAMAR. *Tay*-mer.

by other surrounded by other women who were secure in happy homes with husbands and children.

Yet now, in God's providence, her days of lonely toil were ended. Now she was a radiant wife with a loving, respected husband, and blessed with a child of her own. The birth of a child was looked upon by Hebrew women as evidence of God's favor, and the bearing of a *son* was counted a great honor.

Earlier on the road to Bethlehem, when her mother-in-law urged her to return to her people, Ruth announced a valiant and fixed decision. She committed her life to God's way and to Naomi's care and companionship. What blessings resulted for her, for Naomi, for Boaz, for Israel, and for the world! Even she never could have guessed what amazing results would flow from her steadfast commitment to Naomi and to Naomi's God. So often we stand at places of decision. Are we ready to place our futures in God's keeping?

WHERE DO BABIES COME FROM?

An amusing story is told about the youngster who asked his mother where babies come from. She answered him with the classical stork myth.

"You mean I was brought by a stork?" he asked.

"Yes," she lovingly lied.

"Was Daddy brought by a stork?"

"Yes," she replied.

"And was Grandpa brought by a stork, too?"

"Yes, Grandpa, too."

The child thought for a moment, then exclaimed, "Good grief! There hasn't been a normal birth in our family for three generations!"

Modern society has become far too sexually sophisticated to believe the stork story anymore. And it is right that adults and adolescents know the truth about human reproduction. Conception and childbirth should be explained in terms, not of storks and cabbage patches, but of God's plan and providence.

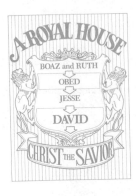

visual 13

The Lord enabled Ruth to conceive, for He is the source of all life. He designed and created the human reproductive system, "male and female created he them" (Genesis 1:27). Procreation is nothing short of a miracle, and even experienced obstetricians still marvel at the advent of human life.

Where do babies come from? The truest answer is, Babies come from God.   —R. W. B.

III. Naomi—Blessed and Benefited (Ruth 4:14-16)

14. And the women said unto Naomi, Blessed be the Lord, which hath not left thee this day without a kinsman, that his name may be famous in Israel.

The *women* of Bethlehem who knew Naomi rejoiced with her that new life had now been given to sustain her family line. They expressed the hope and belief that this new baby might be one who would become *famous in Israel*, at least that his name would be held in enduring honor. Of course, this came true when this child, Obed, became the father of Jesse and thus the grandfather of David. David was the most famous and beloved of all the kings of Israel. It was David who extended Israel's borders, subdued enemies, and laid the foundation for Solomon's unparalleled splendor and success.

In our days of Social Security and women's independent business activity and success, we may find it difficult to understand how important it was in ancient times for older women to have close male heirs or relatives. It was the recognized responsibility of the younger married people to provide for older relatives and in-laws. With husband and both sons dead, Naomi seemed to have been left with no such prospects. When Ruth married Boaz, however, Naomi was freed from fear for the future.

15. And he shall be unto thee a restorer of thy life, and a nourisher of thine old age: for thy daughter-in-law, which loveth thee, which is better to thee than seven sons, hath borne him.

Joy was occasioned by the birth of the child, who was considered as much Naomi's as Ruth's. Now Naomi would have someone to look after her in her old age. Naturally, this was cause for great rejoicing by Naomi, and all of her women friends rejoiced with her. These women were especially perceptive, for they noted that Naomi's joy and brighter prospects for the future were the result of Ruth's love for her. Ruth's love prompted her to help support Naomi and to undertake strenuous work to do so. Her love had moved her to follow Naomi's advice about her relationship with Boaz. Now, safely married and a happy mother, Ruth's love for Naomi developed a new dimension as the baby, Obed, was placed in his "grandmother's" arms.

When love prevails in human relationships, happiness, peace, and harmony result. Love solves problems, smooths relationships, sweetens bitterness, and calms unrest. In contrast, a spirit of hatred brings uneasiness, sadness, tension, and apprehension. The lives of both Ruth and Naomi were greatly enhanced, due to their mutual respect and affection.

Sir Walter Scott wrote,

True love's the gift which God hath given
To man alone beneath the heaven:
. . . .
The silver link, the silken tie,
Which heart to heart and mind to mind
In body and in soul can bind.

Ruth's example is a reminder to us that love is expressed not only in *words* but also in *actions*. This certainly is true of Christian love. In his "love chapter," 1 Corinthians 13, Paul tells us, "Love is patient and kind; love is not jealous or boastful. . . . Love does not insist on its own way; it is not irritable or resentful. . . . Love bears all things, believes all things, hopes all things, endures all things: (vv. 4-7, *Revised Standard Version*). Whatever emphasis we may prefer in describing the nature of love—whether it is mostly an emotional attachment, or a "meeting of minds," or a willingness to do well toward the loved one—it is certain that loving declarations apart from loving actions are meaningless.

Jesus said, "If a man love me, he will keep my words," and also, "If ye love me, keep my commandments" (John 14:23, 15). The love we have for our Lord is demonstrated by our conformity to what we believe to be His will for us. This, of course, is based on His revelation of His will in His words and ways.

Ruth had no way of knowing in advance what the outcome of her loving commitment to Naomi would be. She knew only that she was making a lifelong declaration of devotion and loyalty. The results were servanthood and labor, then fulfillment and great joy.

16. And Naomi took the child, and laid it in her bosom, and became nurse unto it.

The *New International Version* translates the last phrase of this verse "cared for him." Through her daughter-in-law's love and God's providential blessing, the widowed and childless Naomi now could take care of this baby as lovingly as if he were indeed the son of her son. Now she is assured of being surrounded with helpful and loving people as she lives out her days on earth.

What a contrast this is with Naomi's estimate of God's dealings with her up until the time she returned to Bethlehem! At that time she felt that her name really should be *Mara*, or "bitter," because, as she said, "the Almighty hath dealt very bitterly with me" (1:20). What should have been Naomi's name as she held the infant Obed in her arms, feeling joy and serenity? Perhaps she might have been called "Fulfilled" or "Blessed" or "Peaceful."

We should take courage and instruction from this story. Sometimes it seems that we are dealt one blow after another, with disappointment piled on disaster, and with our lives teetering on the brink of despair. But God has unusual ways of blessing us and of giving us "songs in the night." We need to hold on to our trust in God; and to hold out rather than to give out. If we can do so, we may be sure God will demonstrate His ability to do "exceeding abundantly above all that we ask or think" (Ephesians 3:20).

GRAND RELATIVES

With one child married, and our other two in college, our "nest" is relatively empty. We look forward to the day when we will be grandparents, if the Lord is willing. We are already planning to spoil our grandchildren a bit, and we expect that they will "renew our life and sustain us in our old age." Little children *can* keep one's thinking young, and one's life-style active.

Naomi's friends knew that little Obed would be "just what the doctor ordered" for her. Ruth's baby was going to be a truly *grand* son, a child who would bring joy and hope back into Naomi's heart, and light back into her eyes. She would possess again the qualities of life necessary for happiness: meaningful work, reciprocal love, and optimistic expectancy.

Home Daily Bible Readings

Monday, Aug. 21—Boaz Gains the Right of Redemption (Ruth 4:1-6)
Tuesday, Aug. 22—Boaz Claims Ruth as His Wife (Ruth 4:7-12)
Wednesday, Aug. 23—Ruth and Boaz Have a Child (Ruth 4:13-22)
Thursday, Aug. 24—David and Jesus Are of Ruth's Line (Matthew 1:1-6)
Friday, Aug. 25—Hope for the Nation Israel (Jeremiah 31:27-34)
Saturday, Aug. 26—Hope for All Peoples (Isaiah 55)
Sunday, Aug. 27—Hope for All Time (Revelation 21:1-7)

Just as Obed was a real blessing to Naomi, she likewise became a *grand* mother to him. She "laid him in her lap and cared for him" (Ruth 4:16, *New International Version*). It was a mutually rewarding relationship. Grandmothers can be such special people, and no one knows that better than the grandchildren who are loved by their grandparents. Thank God if your children are close to caring grandparents, or if you cherish fond memories of good times with your own grandparents, or if you have the privilege of showering love and affection upon your grandchildren.   —R. W. B.

IV. The Baby Named and Identified (Ruth 4:17)

17. And the women her neighbors gave it a name, saying, There is a son born to Naomi; and they called his name Obed: he is the father of Jesse, the father of David.

The women . . . gave it a name. It seems strange that a baby born to an important resident of Bethlehem like Boaz would not be named by his father. However, Ruth was very close to several of the women of the town. She had come as an outsider and a foreigner, and apparently she had been received by them without rancor or ridicule. Ruth's relationship to Naomi and her loyalty to her had been noted and appreciated by these women. Boaz had heard only favorable reports about Ruth before he met her in his harvest fields. The attitudes of her neighbors must have contributed to his good feeling about Ruth. Now their suggestion of a name for her child was accepted. *There is a son born to Naomi.* The women referred to the child as a *son* of Naomi. This was true in the sense that he would be the heir of Elimelech (and also would receive the devoted attention of Naomi).

The name *Obed* means "worshiper" or "server." It seems to be a reference to Ruth's adoption of the God of Israel as her God. Now the new child would be reared to respect and reverence the true and living God—to be His worshiper.

He is the father of Jesse, the father of David. We have seen how the lovingkindness of God was shown toward Ruth and Naomi. For the first time we are introduced to David, and this is a reminder to us of the far greater dimension of God's goodness and faithfulness, which extend to all mankind. In His covenant with Abraham, the Lord promised blessing for all families of the earth. Later, that covenant was confirmed through David, as God's Messiah descended from him. In the story of Ruth, with its famine and heartache, yet with steadfast love and loyalty, we see the mercy of God at work in history in His larger purpose of providing for the salvation of humankind. Truly, God's mercy is everlasting.

Conclusion

A. The Radiance of Ruth

As we think of Ruth, her character and career, the term *radiance* comes to mind. In her we see *the radiance of renewal.* She did not just mourn after her husband's death, but decided to go with Naomi to help her start her life again in Israel. Her work and openness in relation to Boaz renewed his life. Her bearing of Obed renewed the hope and happiness of Naomi.

Ruth's life shines with *the radiance of discipline.* She refused to go back to her country, people, and gods, but so ordered her life that she could adopt new ways and a new God. She disciplined herself to work, to appeal to Boaz, and to trust both him and Naomi.

Ruth demonstrates *the radiance of selfless love.* She thought of Naomi's needs, not just her own. She was willing to cast herself on Boaz' mercy. She was perceptive about Naomi's need to tend her baby, and let her do so.

There is about Ruth's life *a radiance of blessing.* Her decisions blessed Naomi, benefited Bethlehem, gave new life to Boaz, and helped bring the Messiah to our world.

In all of this, Ruth shows us *the radiance of God's recognition and reward.* Naomi was rewarded for trusting her. Ruth was rewarded for her commitments. Boaz was rewarded by receiving a loving wife and son, and the Bethlehem community was rewarded by becoming the "little town" where our Savior was born.

B. Prayer

Father, our lives are refreshed and stimulated by this ever-new story of Ruth and her faithfulness. We are put to shame when we think how easily we are tempted to give up when we face difficult and tragic times. Worse than this, we give in when tempted to blame You for them.

May Ruth's example of courageous commitment lead us to yield ourselves more completely to Your way. May we see what our nearest duty is and do it gladly and graciously. Bless us by making us blessings to others. In Jesus' name, amen.

C. Thought to Remember

The experience of Ruth and Naomi reminds us that our loving Heavenly Father is able to bring blessing out of the unhappiest of circumstances.

Learning by Doing

This page contains an alternate lesson plan emphasizing learning activities. Classes desiring such student involvement will find these suggestions helpful.

Learning Goals

This lesson should enable a student to:

1. Describe how Ruth and Naomi demonstrated hope.

2. Determine the uniqueness of Christian hope.

3. List areas where he has hope in Christ.

4. Express joy at the hope he has in Christ.

Into the Lesson

Write this question on your chalkboard or overhead screen: "What events or situations may cause us to temporarily doubt that God is in control?" As students arrive, have them form groups of four. Provide each group with magazines, newspapers, poster board, glue, felt pens, and scissors. Ask them to cut out pictures, headlines, etc. and form a montage in answer to the question you have displayed.

After eight minutes, have each group display its poster and review the content. Then state, "Today's lesson concludes our study of Ruth. We have seen the difficult times she went through, and today we will see fulfillment for her and Naomi. We will see that even in the darkest times God is still in control."

Into the Word

Present a brief lecture on the events that transpired in the story of Ruth between the texts of last week's lesson and this. The "Introduction" section of this lesson contains helpful materials for your lecture. See page 442.

Next, read aloud Ruth 4:9-17. Then divide your class into three groups of six or eight students for the following activities. Give these written instructions to the groups.

Group 1. Survey the book of Ruth and prepare a Jeremiah graph for Ruth. A Jeremiah graph shows the up-and-down emotional fluctuations a person may have in response to the events recorded. List each event and give an emotional "read out" for each of them on a scale of one to ten. *One* signifies extreme depression and *ten* emotional exhilaration.

Group 2. Survey the book of Ruth and prepare a Jeremiah graph for Naomi. A Jeremiah graph shows the up-and-down emotional fluctuations a person may have in response to the events recorded. List each event and give an emotional "read out" for each on a scale of one to ten. *One*

signifies extreme depression and *ten*, emotional exhilaration.

Group 3. Survey the book of Ruth and develop a character sketch of Ruth. Present her apparent motivations, values, and attitudes.

Allow each group ten minutes to complete its assignment. Develop a brief discussion of their findings by using the following questions:

1. How would you have responded to Naomi or Ruth in their darkest moments?

2. How did Ruth demonstrate hope? How did Naomi?

3. How did the character traits of Ruth help her to develop hope?

4. Why was the birth of a son to Ruth and Boaz so important?

Into Life

One of our greatest needs is hope. In this section, we will explore our Christian hope. Let the students work in the same three groups as in the previous study activity. Give each group a copy of the form below:

Christian Hope

How we receive it

Why it is a reality

Have the groups read 1 Peter 1:3-9 and fill out the form. Give them three minutes to finish this exercise. Call the groups together and ask them to share their findings. In this sharing time ask, "In what areas do you have hope in Christ?" Their answers could include: in the certainty of salvation, in facing trials with joy, in facing the future with confidence, in seeking to live an obedient life. Ask, "Why is Christian hope unique?"

State that the fulfillment of hope brings much joy; then read these two expressions of joy from the book of Ruth: 2:20 and 4:14.

In closing, give each student a small index card and ask them to write a memo to themselves. In the memo each should answer the following questions:

1. What does the message of hope mean to me personally?

2. What can I do to better express joy in my Christian hope this week?

Close the class session with prayer and ask for God's grace on folk who are struggling with a feeling of hopelessness.

Let's Talk It Over

The questions on this page are designed to encourage review of the lesson
Scriptures and to promote discussion of the lesson by the class. The answers
provided are only discussion starters. Let your class talk it over from there.

1. The marital customs reflected in our text seem rather cold and formal compared with what is done in our society. Do we tend to over-emphasize romantic love? If so, why?

The story of Ruth as we have it gives little hint of any romantic feelings between Boaz and Ruth, but that does not mean that such feelings were absent from their relationship. However, it is clear that neither was "swept off his or her feet," so that they formed only a fleeting emotional attachment. The emotional aspect of love between a man and a woman is continually popularized in books, movies, and television shows. And the influence of these presentations leads many young people into marriage on the basis of a mere romantic infatuation. When their emotional high diminishes, couples discover that they have little left to keep them together. Christian parents and church leaders must not relax their efforts to remind young people that marriage involves responsibility, resourcefulness, and resoluteness as well as romance.

2. Elderly people gain great satisfaction from their children and grandchildren. How can this benefit be enhanced?

Elderly persons can derive greater satisfaction from their children and grandchildren by giving priority to intergenerational contacts in the family schedule. Parents can seek the counsel and assistance of their own parents in rearing the latter's grandchildren. Grandparents will feel more needed and appreciated. The wisdom of age and the experience give the grandparents some valuable insights that can be beneficial. Grandchildren themselves should be encouraged to seek information and guidance from their grandparents as well.

3. What are some ways in which we can cultivate more love in action in the church and the home?

We usually express our love by saying, "I love you," or by handshakes, hugs, and kisses when appropriate. But if our love is demonstrated only in these ways, it is lacking in depth. One very practical way to express love more carefully is by taking time to listen. The listening required is not passive, for the loving listener will actively ask questions and demonstrate interest in what is being said. Another way of putting our love into action is through involvement with the lives of others. Paul urges us to "rejoice with them that do rejoice, and weep with them that weep" (Romans 12:15). We can show our love by sharing in times of rejoicing, such as weddings, graduations, births, and anniversaries. We can also demonstrate our love by being close by in time of illnesses, accidents, and funerals.

4. Many of the citizens of Bethlehem took an interest in the birth of Ruth's son. Some of the women even had a voice in naming the child. What are some ways in which we may share the blessings of a Christian home with our neighbors?

While we often treasure the relative peace and privacy of home, it is a good thing if we can practice an "open-door" policy toward our neighbors. We can let them know that if they have some burden they need to share, they can do that in our home. Or if they have good news to communicate, they should know we will be glad to hear it. It hardly needs to be said that this policy of openness will provide opportunities to share our faith in Christ.

5. The Scriptures do not give us information about Ruth's physical appearance, but the beauty of her character impresses us. Why do we need to emphasize this particular kind of beauty today?

Peter's instructions in regard to feminine beauty may seem old-fashioned. But there is divine wisdom in his counsel: "Your beauty should not come from outward adornment, such as braided hair and the wearing of gold jewelry and fine·clothes. Instead, it should be that of your inner self, the unfading beauty of a gentle and quiet spirit, which is of great worth in God's sight" (1 Peter 3:3, 4, *New International Version*). The entertainment world and media advertising give us the opposite viewpoint. According to them the right clothing, cosmetics, jewelry, and hairstyle are the popular ways to achieve beauty. There is nothing wrong with a desire to look one's best, but Peter's words are a reminder that the inner person is the key to real beauty.